# A Southern Life

The

Fred W. Morrison

Series in

Southern

Studies

Letters of Paul Green, 1916–1981

Edited by

Laurence G. Avery

The University of North Carolina Press *Chapel Hill & London*

The publication of this volume
was aided by the generous support of
Walter R. Davis and The Paul Green
Foundation, Inc.

The paper in this book meets the
guidelines for permanence and
durability of the Committee on
Production Guidelines for Book
Longevity of the Council on Library
Resources.

Library of Congress Cataloging-in-
Publication Data
Green, Paul, 1894–1981.
A southern life : letters of Paul Green,
1916–1981 / edited by Laurence G.
Avery.
p. cm. — (The Fred W. Morrison
series in Southern studies)
Includes bibliographical references (p.)
and index.
ISBN 9781469613734 (pbk.: alk. paper)
1. Green, Paul, 1894–1981—
Correspondence. 2. Dramatists,
American—Southern States—
Correspondence. 3. Dramatists,
American—20th century—
Correspondence. 4. Southern States—
Social life and customs. I. Avery,
Laurence G. II. Title. III. Series.
PS3513.R452Z48 1994
812′.52—dc20
[B] 93-24738
CIP

*For Rachel*

# Contents

# Acknowledgments

An editor of letters depends on the help and goodwill of many people, and any edition that is over a decade in the making accumulates a debt that is, like the national debt, unimaginable. But a few people have been so instrumental in the completion of the Green edition that I welcome an opportunity to express my thanks.

In the Introduction I go into detail about Paul Green's commitment to the project, which of course was an indispensable condition for the work. Knowing and working with him was among the great pleasures of my life, while the sharpest disappointment of the project was not finishing it in time for him to have a look.

Also in the Introduction I suggest Elizabeth Green's relation to the project. My admiration for her grew in proportion to our acquaintance. One afternoon following Paul's death, she and I found ourselves reminiscing. A memory from her college days in the 1920s came to mind, and she said rather sharply, "When I was in school on the Hill we sometimes walked to Durham for lunch. And you know what, it was just as far then as it is now [about eight miles]. Have you ever walked that far to eat, or any of your students?" A capacity for accomplishment beyond the expected was a hallmark of her life. No one did more to facilitate my work on the edition, and I make clear in the Introduction that her remarkable life awaits the biographer, social historian, and poet.

Paul and Elizabeth's children supplied letters for the edition, read and commented on an early draft, and filled in blanks in my knowledge of family history. They are Paul, Jr., Byrd Cornwell, Betsy Moyer, and Janet Green. For their support throughout the project—and their continuing friendship—I am grateful.

Two other family members also contributed substantially to the project: Paul's older sister, Mary Green Johnson, and his youngest sister, Erma Green Gold. Three times I visited Mary, the family historian, in her lovely home on a farm outside Lillington, North Carolina, to talk about their lives as children and take notes (my tape recorder made her nervous). On one visit we drove all over the countryside to see the house where they grew up, the churches and schools they attended, the cemeteries where their parents and relatives are buried, and other places of interest. She supplied letters and was always ready to answer questions about family history. Erma lived in Chapel Hill during the years I worked on the edition, and I only had to pick up the phone to get needed information. Since she had attended the University of North Carolina (UNC) and been involved in Carolina Playmakers activities (in 1923 she collaborated on the play "Fixin's" with her brother), she was a mine of information about the lives of the Greens. The factual base of the edition reflects the help of many people, but none were more helpful than Erma and Mary and none more gracious.

Rhoda Wynn, Green's last administrative assistant and first director of the Paul Green Foundation (established by his estate following Green's death to promote work in the arts and human rights), guided me to books and papers in Green's large personal library, helped with difficult readings and other matters, and cleared away what could have been numerous problems of access and copyright. Marsha Warren, current director of the foundation, commented on a draft of the Introduction and, in the final stages of my work, provided crucial guidance tactfully. To both of them I am grateful.

Colleagues in and around Chapel Hill rendered assistance in the spirit of the place, and I am grateful. They are Daphne Athas, Jonathan Avery, Robert Bratcher, Edwin Brown, Alice Cotten, George Daniels, John Ehle, Christine Flora, William Friday, Werner Friederich, Stirling Haig, William Harmon, Lois Ann Hobbs, Fred Hobson, Matthew Hodgson, Edith Keene, Erika Lindemann, Townsend Ludington, Patty McIntyre, James MacKenzie, Michael Martin, Jerry Mills, Barry Nakell, Daniel Patterson, Jack Raper, Kenneth Reckford, Ida Reid, Jack Roper, Richard Rust, John Sanders, Frances W. Saunders, Carlyle Sitterson, Richard Shrader, Tom Stumpf, George Taylor, Judy Via, Carolyn Wallace, Deborah Webster, John White, and Joseph Wittig.

A real pleasure of the project was watching graduate students discover that research is exciting and that to succeed you must be as much detective and diplomat as scholar. The talent and dedication of the research assistants who worked with me bode well for their future and that of the profession. They are Michael Cornett, Patricia Gantt, Marina Harris, Brenda Kolb, Amy Koritz, Terry Medalen, Karen Moranski, Angela O'Donnell, Taimi Olsen, and Curtis Scott. In addition to the assistants, generations of students encountered Green's letters in English 298, the research course required of all graduate students in the UNC English department. They will recall the weeks devoted to "the scholarly editing of personal papers," which used Green's letters as examples, and I recall the enthusiasm they developed for Green. Their reactions always renewed my faith in the edition and lifted my spirits about the future.

# Introduction

Books were Paul Green's favorite gift. He gave them for birthdays and anniversaries, at Christmas or graduation, and often just as greeting cards. At Christmas in 1955 he sent his son *The Dark Eye in Africa* (1955) by Laurens van der Post. Discussing an early era in African history, van der Post describes a perennial problem: "One of the most common errors in contemporary judgments is our knack of wrenching people and events out of their proper time context and assessing them as if they were part of the contemporary sequence of things."

If it is hard to maintain historical perspective on the distant past, it may be even harder when the past is recent. The world of long ago is obviously different and has the fascination, sometimes even the charm, of the antique. About recent decades, however, we are easily fooled. They are not at first glance strikingly different from our own, and since they are still a part of living memory, we tend not to think of them as "the past" at all.

But nothing reveals a life in its own time more vividly than letters—that is their attraction. By particularizing the past without the coloring of later states of mind, they allow us to meet a person and visit an era otherwise closed to us. And Green's era, the first eight decades of this century, was not long ago.

Green's letters make it easy to understand why he was a force in his day. Letters were necessary for conducting business and maintaining relationships, but he would not have written so many, and so many that are zestful, if they had been only a chore. Carl Sandburg called him "one of the best talkers in the U. S. A.,"[1] and the sentiment was echoed by many who knew him. A vigorous and delightful conversationalist, he looked on letters as but another form of conversation.

With their easy flow of thought and language, the letters often seem spontaneous, and compared to his plays, fiction, and essays, they are. But no one, certainly no writer as accomplished as Green, fails to take into account the person he or she is writing to and the impression he or she wants to make. What Green says, and doesn't say, as well as the way he says it—those things

1. Carl Sandburg to Paul Green, 12 April 1961, Paul Green Papers, Southern Historical Collection, Wilson Library, University of North Carolina, Chapel Hill.

accumulating over a lifetime produce the many-sided image of him that emerges in the letters.

Determined to make a difference on behalf of his social and artistic ideals, he sometimes wrote in a swirl of controversy. About his plays he was passionate, as he was about questions of social justice and education. Passion, we tend to think, hinders clearheadedness. It is a mark of Green's mind and character that people not part of the turmoil are apt to find *his* views the sane ones. To a remarkable degree, time has confirmed his moral vision.

More often he wrote in a congenial atmosphere to push forward a project, react to a request or suggestion, outline a view, inform a relative or colleague of his doings, extend a word of comfort, thanks, or advice—the myriad things people write letters about. Great mental and physical energy is clear in the letters, as is an astounding memory. The letters also reveal a natural generosity toward others. Able to put himself in their place and imagine their outlook, he reached out instinctively to help. And clearly he enjoyed dealing with people through letters. The challenge was to get down words that were both honest and appropriate, a challenge requiring perception, sensitivity, and tact. I imagine readers of the edition, seeing the letters in the circumstances that gave rise to them, frequently will finish a letter thinking, "Nice! Just what was needed! That's well done!"

Readers won't be surprised that the letters cluster in the areas of the arts, education, and human rights, because those are the areas where Green's activities clustered. The only surprise from the letters may well be a sense of how swiftly the past recedes yet how stubbornly it lingers.

## GREEN'S LIFE

Paul Green was born on 17 March 1894 on his family's farm in Harnett County, North Carolina, the second child and older boy in a family that came to include six children: two sons and four daughters. The farm lay along the Cape Fear River, and Paul's father, William Archibald Green, was a progressive farmer who increased his landholdings from 150 to about 500 acres by the time of his death at the age of seventy-four in 1926. Paul's mother, Bettie (her spelling) Byrd Green, taught music before her marriage in 1889 as William's second wife and throughout life published poems in newspapers and church journals. When anyone of consequence visited the neighborhood, she invited the person for dinner and reminded her children that the visitor had started life with no more advantages than their own. To amount to anything, she let them know frequently, they must have ambition, education, and a large capacity for work. She died at the age of forty-six in 1908 when Paul was fourteen, leaving the management of the house to Paul's older sister, Mary, then sixteen.[2]

Both parents were religious, and his mother's hope that Paul would become a preacher is shown by his given name.[3] William Green usually had three or four tenant families to help with the farm but also counted on his sons, Paul and Hugh (two years younger than Paul). Cotton was the principal crop in the Cape Fear River valley, as elsewhere in the South, but William also had tobacco acreage, raised hogs commercially, and grew corn for feed. In addition to working the farm, Paul and Hugh hunted together and played semiprofessional baseball in towns up and down the river. Paul became such a fine ambidextrous pitcher that he supported himself a couple of summers with his baseball earnings. To his teammates, however, he seemed withdrawn, even solemn, as if lost in thought—except during the game itself.[4]

After graduating from nearby Buies Creek Academy in 1914, Paul taught school for two years and saved his money for college. Archibald Campbell, the Baptist minister who founded and presided over Buies Creek Academy (now Campbell University), encouraged Paul's interest in college but argued passionately against the state university at Chapel Hill, where some of the professors were atheists. He urged Paul to attend the Baptist college at Wake Forest and got him a scholarship. But pressure from Campbell only made Paul more determined to test the open water at Chapel Hill, where people must have "some deep reason for disagreeing with the theology in which I had been

2. Interview with Mary Green Johnson, 5 April 1985. Unless otherwise noted, the interview is the source of details from Green's childhood.

3. William was Methodist, Bettie, Presbyterian. Local churches had preaching only once a month, however, and Bettie took the family where the preaching was—Methodist, Presbyterian, even Baptist.

4. Interview with Daniel Stewart, 23 April 1988. Stewart played baseball several summers with Green and thought him the only one of his acquaintances with major-league potential. Green could pitch with either arm because when he was ten he had an operation on his right shoulder that forced him to use his left hand for about a year. According to Stewart, Green usually pitched right-handed to right-handed batters and left-handed to lefties but occasionally changed hands while pitching to the same batter.

reared."[5] In September 1916 he went there and enrolled in the University of North Carolina (UNC) as a twenty-two-year-old freshman.

The next summer, swept along by Woodrow Wilson's call to help make the world safe for democracy, he enlisted in Company B of the 105th Engineers. The company trained for a year at bases in North and South Carolina then landed at Calais in July 1918, their task to lay mines, set other explosives, build bridges and barbed-wire defenses, and string up communication lines. Green was in heavy fighting through September, when the Hindenburg Line of the Germans was smashed, then was withdrawn for Officers Candidate School. In December (following the armistice of 11 November) he was commissioned a second lieutenant and given a job as clerk in the U.S. Army Purchasing Office in Paris, a job he held until discharged in June 1919.

Before embarking for France, he had begun to write poems and keep a diary.[6] The war itself left him with a deep sense of waste and the conviction that President Wilson was right: a just and peaceful world order required a world government. But he found the winter, spring, and summer of 1918–19 a heady time in Paris. He played baseball, studied French, explored museums, courted a Red Cross nurse and a Parisian mademoiselle, and kept up with the news as Allied leaders negotiated the Treaty of Versailles. He was part of the tumultuous throng in the streets on 14 December 1918 welcoming Wilson to Paris as the hero of humanity, and the following May he went to the American military cemetery on the outskirts of Paris for the president's Memorial Day Address. As he told one of his sisters, during the months in Paris he felt "as if his ear were leaning to the heart of the world."[7]

Returning to UNC in September 1919, Green doubled up on course work and graduated in two years, receiving his bachelor of arts degree at the June commencement in 1921, shortly after his twenty-seventh birthday. He majored in philosophy, which means he majored in Horace Williams, sole member of the university's philosophy department and chief atheist Archibald Campbell had previously cried out against as Green considered which college

5. Autobiographical memorandum, in Paul Green to Henry Grady Owens, 9 October 1941, Paul Green Papers, Southern Historical Collection, Wilson Library, University of North Carolina, Chapel Hill.

6. Just before shipping out in May 1918, he published *Trifles of Thought*, a little book of his poems brought out at his own expense to let the world know, in case he did not return, that he intended to be a poet (see letter 323). He continued writing poems throughout his stay in France.

7. Letter 6; see also letter 293.

to attend. A nominal Hegelian, Williams was in fact a cantankerous Socrates bent on stimulating honest thought in his students by pushing them to question received opinion. His "philosophy" was the application of critical intelligence to contemporary life. Before Green graduated, Williams began grooming him to become the second member of the department.

In addition to academic work, Green continued to write. While Green was away at the war, Frederick Koch joined the UNC faculty. Koch had studied playwrighting with George Pierce Baker at Harvard and was inspired by J. M. Synge, W. B. Yeats, and others of the Abbey Theatre group in Dublin who were exploring the folklife of Ireland. To foster an exploration of the folklife of North Carolina and the South, Koch established the Carolina Playmakers, a producing organization for student plays. The Playmakers quickly became a vital enterprise on campus and eventually a force in the development of the drama throughout the country and the world. Green took Koch's playwrighting course during his first quarter back at school and over the winter saw two of his plays produced. The experience of people in the subcultures of the region—notably tenant farmers, Indians, and blacks—remained at the heart of his concerns throughout his life.

Following graduation in 1921, he stayed in Chapel Hill for a year of playwrighting and graduate work in philosophy, got married in the summer of 1922, then went with his bride to Cornell for a second year of writing and study.

Elizabeth Atkinson Lay, born in Concord, New Hampshire, on 6 April 1897, was the daughter of an Episcopal minister and educator. In 1907 her father moved the family to Raleigh, North Carolina, where he became rector of St. Mary's School, a high school and junior college for women. Elizabeth finished the college program at St. Mary's in 1916, taught a year, then enrolled at UNC in the fall of 1917 as one of fifteen women in a student body of about one thousand. Talented, confident, and energetic, she took Koch's first playwrighting class in the fall of 1918, and her "When Witches Ride" was the first play produced by the Playmakers. (The second play on the bill that night—14 March 1919—was by Thomas Wolfe.) She graduated in the spring of 1919, then remained at the university as Koch's chief assistant. Her job was to organize the hefty schedule of Playmakers productions and regional tours, but she found time to take graduate courses in English and continue her own writing.

She and Paul met as he involved himself in theater activities. At first her parents weren't elated at the idea of their daughter marrying a farm boy (her father had a Th.D. and her extended family included several admirals and Episcopal bishops). A visit by Paul put to rest their worst fears, however, and the young people were married by Elizabeth's father at his church in Beaufort, North Carolina. (Dr. Lay had retired from St. Mary's and become pastor of St. Paul's Episcopal Church in that historical coastal town.) The wedding took place on 6 July 1922, and the next day the couple caught a train for Ithaca. Elizabeth was twenty-five, Paul twenty-eight.

The next summer they returned to Chapel Hill—where they lived the rest of their lives—and in the fall of 1923 Paul joined Horace Williams in the philosophy department at UNC. Conscientious as a teacher, he threw himself into his career as a writer and by 1927 had become a presence in the state, the region, and even the country. In the minds of people, his name had come to stand for things.

The Pulitzer Prize for *In Abraham's Bosom*, announced in May 1927, boosted his national reputation but was only the latest in a series of developments. He had already published two collections of plays, and the plays were being produced widely. In 1925 "The No 'Count Boy," in a production by the Dallas Little Theatre—among the most prominent regional companies of the day—won the Belasco Prize in a national competition in New York City for the best one-act play of the year. Also in 1925 he became editor of *The Reviewer* and brought that literary magazine from Richmond to Chapel Hill. The magazine survived for only four issues because Green could get no financial backing without a willingness to move to New York City,[8] but during the year it was a lively presence for emerging southern writers. A Richmond founder of *The Reviewer* caught the spirit of Green's operation. After visiting Chapel Hill, she told H. L. Mencken she found there "an atmosphere of plain living and high thinking that I never experienced before. . . . [Green and his friends] rather thrilled me . . . like unkempt young prophets out of the wilderness."[9] In the first number under his editorship, Green called for a new literature in the region, stressing the rich material for art in the experience of the South and the dawning critical intelligence among southern writers.[10] The zeal with which he went about his job of drumming up submissions, proposing revi-

8. See letter 48.

9. Emily Clark to H. L. Mencken, 29 November 1925, Mencken Collection, New York Public Library, quoted in Fred C. Hobson, *Serpent in Eden: H. L. Mencken and the South* (Chapel Hill: University of North Carolina Press, 1974), p. 86.

10. Paul Green, "A Plain Statement about Southern Literature," *Reviewer* 5 (January 1925): 71–76.

sions, and handling other business of the magazine confirms the seriousness of his intention to help along the development of southern literature beyond his own writing. Through his plays and *The Reviewer* Green was already known to people associated with the arts before the Provincetown Players produced *In Abraham's Bosom* and brought his name to a larger public.

While his achievements were real, his standing in the public mind owed something as well to the historical moment. In the decades between the world wars, North Carolina and the rest of the South were considered the backwater of the nation. As late as 1938 Franklin Roosevelt could refer to the South as the nation's economic problem number one, and a few years earlier his secretary of labor particularized the point with unintended humor when she called the South "an untapped market for shoes." You would create a social revolution, she added, getting in deeper, "if you put shoes on the people of the South," to which a North Carolina senator retorted that in the South, Madam Secretary, even the mules wear shoes.[11] Economically deprived, lagging behind other sections in health and education, saddled with segregation, the South probably deserved the epithet "benighted."

Not only were conditions actually bad, but also southerners were becoming sensitive to how bad they were. An attitude of defeat lingering from the Civil War had dampened expectations for decades, but now such things as Mencken's "The Sahara of the Bozart" (1920) and the Scopes trial (1925) sharpened southern awareness that the South had contributed little to the artistic and intellectual life of the country and to other sections often looked ludicrous or grotesque. By the late 1920s embarrassment over conditions in the region was high, as was resentment against baiters of the South. Southerners needed a champion, one of their own whose achievements were not ignored or laughed at in the world beyond but applauded. The Pulitzer Prize made Green such a person.

Another foundation of his public presence—although more important over the long run than at first—was his relation to life. A great deal of his time went to activities he considered responsibilities of citizenship. In that respect at least, he resembles Bernard Shaw or Paul Claudel more closely than any American writer among his contemporaries. Unlike his friend Thomas Wolfe, he stayed at home. Unlike another friend, William Faulkner, he involved himself deeply in the affairs of his state and region.

11. The story is told in George B. Tindall, *The Emergence of the New South, 1913–1945* (Baton Rouge: Louisiana State University Press, 1967), p. 575.

As a playwright he was an innovator, and his earliest experiments were with subject matter, in particular, with bringing authentic black experience into the drama. *Lonesome Road,* one of his early collections of short plays, is subtitled *Six Plays for the Negro Theatre. In Abraham's Bosom,* his first Broadway play, is the moving tragedy of a black man with Moses-like aspirations who fails to lead his people out of bondage because of their inertia, racism in the larger society, and flaws in his own character. The 1920s saw an awakening of the need to rid the drama and literature generally of stereotypical depictions of blacks. But among the playwrights interested in black experience at the time—Ridgely Torrence, Eugene O'Neill, and Marc Connelly were others—Green was by far the best acquainted with the daily life of any real black people and the best able to imagine the experience of a black person sympathetically.

In 1926, even before *In Abraham's Bosom* went into production, Green began work on a play that pioneered another kind of subject matter. *The House of Connelly* is among the early works of imaginative literature to forge the picture of the South later used in one version or another by Faulkner, Lillian Hellman, Margaret Mitchell, and Tennessee Williams: a South whose aristocrats go back in memory to a time when social power and enlightened values coincided in their families but who in the present lack the will or character to act and find themselves threatened with extinction.[12] Green wrote different endings for the play—one hopeful, the other not—and in 1931 in its hopeful version, *The House of Connelly* became the first production of the Group Theatre, the most vital organization in the American theater of the 1930s until the arrival of the Federal Theatre.

From the late 1930s on, much of Green's effort went into the historical plays he called symphonic dramas. By the time of his death in 1981, he had seen sixteen of these plays produced in ten states and in Washington, D.C. During several summers, seven or eight of them ran simultaneously. Five were still running a decade after his death.[13] Like early Greek drama and the Corpus

12. European playwrights, notably August Strindberg and Anton Chekhov, had dealt with similar transitions in their own societies since before the turn of the century.

13. These were *The Lost Colony,* which opened on Roanoke Island in North Carolina in 1937; *The Stephen Foster Story,* which opened at Bardstown, Kentucky, in 1959; *Cross and Sword,* which opened at St. Augustine, Florida, in 1965; *Texas,* which opened at Palo Duro Canyon, Texas, in 1966; and *Trumpet in the Land,* which opened at New Philadelphia, Ohio, in 1970.

Christi cycle plays of medieval England, Green's symphonic dramas were designed for production outdoors before large audiences, which has serious implications for their form, and were intended to dramatize themes central to their culture with the aim of revivifying communal beliefs. For instance, *The Lost Colony*, earliest of the outdoor plays, shows the origin of a democratic society founded on the principles of equality of condition and individual social responsibility.[14]

The symphonic dramas are experimental in technique rather than subject matter, however. Always restive under the constraints imposed by the aim of creating an illusion of lifelikeness on stage (dominant artistic goal in the theater during his formative years), Green in the early 1930s began to explore ways of opening up the drama to all presentational arts. *Roll Sweet Chariot* (1934) has characters projecting thoughts over a speaker system and group movement choreographed with dancelike precision. *Johnny Johnson* (1936), a poignant antiwar musical written with Kurt Weill, has a full complement of songs, one of them performed by a battery of cannons. But it is the outdoor historical plays that gave his imagination full scope. He called them "symphonic" from the Greek root meaning "sound together," and it was the presentational arts he had in mind.[15] Beginning with *The Lost Colony*, the plays are filled with music (sound), dance (movement), and special lighting effects, all of them "sounding together" with the action and dialogue of the plot.

Green's life was of a piece, and the concerns of his plays were his social concerns as well. In the 1920s his racial views were, to say the least, uncommon. Having accepted the humanity of blacks as a child, a perception not prevalent in his locale or even his family,[16] he was one of the few white southerners in the 1920s who could envision integration. When he voiced his outlook, of course, he precipitated a storm. In 1927 he wrote an introduction for *Congaree Sketches: Scenes from Negro Life in the Swamps of the Congaree*, a collection of black folk tales by E. C. L. Adams, and in it he called for an American social order in which race doesn't count. He supported W. E. B. Du Bois's crusade for full equality for blacks and concluded by saying he could

14. For a discussion of its theme, see Laurence G. Avery, "Paul Green, *The Lost Colony*, and *Native Son*," *Journal of American Drama and Theatre* 3 (Spring 1991): 5–13.

15. Paul Green, "Symphonic Drama," in *Dramatic Heritage* (New York: Samuel French, 1953), pp. 14–26.

16. Paul Green, "Rassie," *Pembroke Magazine* 10 (1978): 3–11; see also letter 220.

"see no sense in the talk of segregation, back to Africa, and the like. . . . It all seems beside the point."[17] The University of North Carolina Press was in the process of publishing the book when its board of directors discovered the introduction. Fearing it would incite demonstrations in the state and cause the legislature to cut university appropriations, they did their best to squash the project but were thwarted by a courageous and wily assistant director.[18] For his part, James Weldon Johnson, black writer and official of the National Association for the Advancement of Colored People, thought the introduction "one of the finest approaches by the written word to interracial understanding and good will ever made."[19]

From the 1920s on, Green put time, energy, and money into efforts to secure basic human rights for blacks and Native Americans, particularly fair treatment in courts of law and access to education, jobs, and public institutions. His concern for the poor and uneducated in prison led him to advocate abolition of chain gangs and capital punishment—causes that became crusades at times. At the university, where science and research seemed to attract more and more attention, he was a force for the arts and humanities and for the importance of teaching. He was a fierce opponent of the gag laws and loyalty oaths inflicted on the university in the aftermath of the hysterical McCarthy era. From the 1950s on, he became increasingly active and outspoken in opposition to the Cold War between the United States and Soviet Union and the resultant arms race (his correspondence with North Carolina senator Jesse Helms on this point is lively), and he was among the early opponents of American involvement in Vietnam.

Green dealt with problems at all levels. While he helped raise money to support a handful of Lumbee Indian children denied access to the high school in their county, he also served as a presidential appointee to the U.S. National Commission for the United Nations Educational, Scientific, and Cultural

17. Paul Green, "Introduction," in E. C. L. Adams, *Congaree Sketches: Scenes from Negro Life in the Swamps of the Congaree* (Chapel Hill: University of North Carolina Press, 1927), p. xi.

18. The assistant director was William T. Couch. The story is given in Daniel Joseph Singal, *The War Within: From Victorian to Modernist Thought in the South, 1919–1945* (Chapel Hill: University of North Carolina Press, 1982), pp. 265–301.

19. James Weldon Johnson to Henry R. Fuller, 13 July 1927, in "Adams, *Congaree Sketches*" file, University of North Carolina Press Papers, Southern Historical Collection, Wilson Library, University of North Carolina, Chapel Hill.

Organization (UNESCO), where he worked with educational leaders from around the world. And social issues inspired several of his imaginative works. "Hymn to the Rising Sun" (1936) came about as part of his campaign to abolish the chain gang system, and *Wilderness Road* (produced 1955) was in part an attempt to prepare public opinion in the South to accept integration of schools. A felt need to deepen understanding between the races moved him to dramatize Richard Wright's *Native Son* (produced 1941) and write the film script of John Howard Griffin's *Black Like Me* (produced 1963).

Green died at his home just outside of Chapel Hill on 4 May 1981 at the age of eighty-seven. Two days later a memorial service was held in the theater named for him on the UNC campus, and he was buried not a hundred yards away in the old town cemetery. He had come into prominence in the 1920s just as the South was emerging from Reconstruction and North Carolina was beginning to acquire a reputation as the most progressive of southern states. His life is a reason for the changes. A member of the generation that launched the southern literary renaissance and the first playwright from the South to attract national and international attention, he also played a part in the broader social developments we now associate with the emergence of the New South during the first half of the century.

## EDITING THE LETTERS

I met Green in 1976 while editing Maxwell Anderson's letters. Green and Anderson were friends. Both had been students of Frederick Koch (Anderson, while Koch was at the University of North Dakota before coming to Chapel Hill), and they met in 1931 at a camp in Connecticut where the Group Theatre spent the summer rehearsing the play that launched its auspicious career, Green's *The House of Connelly.* Thereafter they saw one another in Hollywood over the years and corresponded occasionally. Green helped me with information for the notes to Anderson's letters and, when the edition was published, reviewed it favorably. He even bought a dozen copies to give to friends. When I raised the possibility of editing his own letters, he told me, "There are thousands and thousands of them and most of them are of no importance I'm sure. But I say go bravely ahead, and I will be glad to cooperate in any way I can."[20]

My first substantial talk with Green about his letters came in March 1979. It

20. Paul Green to Laurence Avery, 11 July 1978.

was a dark, cold afternoon with snow on the ground, and we sat before a fire in his large study in the old farmhouse a few miles outside of Chapel Hill that he had fixed up and christened Windy Oaks in the middle 1960s. He would turn eighty-five that month, but there was nothing feeble about him. As we drank coffee and talked, he was alert, poised, and energetic. Mainly we talked about Anderson, how much Green enjoyed being reminded of his friend through his letters, and the theater in the 1920s and 1930s. He did call my attention, however, to several large filing cabinets scattered around the room and said there were others, he forgot how many, elsewhere in the house. In them, it turned out, was the foundation of this edition—copies of his own letters plus the letters he had received from the 1920s onward. For a personal file, the record was remarkably full, with matching correspondence filed together in chronological sequence. A diary note in which he likens the letters to a "thread" shows how Green thought of this huge collection of correspondence: "Life is an ever forward excursion into limbo and the thread we unroll after us is tradition—only by it do we know how far we have come; but never do we know how far we shall go."[21]

He said he wanted me to have complete freedom in the use of his letters, except those he wrote to Elizabeth before their marriage in 1922. Nobody wants to make public what he wrote his girl before they were married, he said. There was no telling what those letters had in them, and he didn't want to embarrass himself and Elizabeth at this late date. Everything else was an open book, but not those love letters. He seemed apologetic. Before I left, his assistant, Rhoda Wynn, showed me through some of the filing cabinets. Altogether there were about two dozen.

Green was better than his word about helping. To work in, he gave me a room with a large table—a spare bedroom, where he went for a nap that afternoon in May 1981 and never woke up. I had free access to the house and Green's books, manuscripts, and diaries as well as the letter files. Green himself took the lead in rounding up family letters not in the files, particularly those he wrote to his father and sisters from France during World War I. Frequently on arriving I would find a stack of material on my table with a note from him saying I might find "this" interesting. It would be a volume of his diary or a play manuscript or something else relating to a question we had talked about recently. Since I tried not to interrupt the routine of the house,

21. Green diary, [September 1934], Paul Green Papers, Southern Historical Collection, Wilson Library, University of North Carolina, Chapel Hill.

however, I was glad to find this note in his diary: "Rhoda and I on the word book. Laurence Avery out carrying on (to himself and with no bother to us) his P. G. researches" (3 October 1980).

One morning I arrived while Paul and Elizabeth were still at the dining table with their coffee, and they invited me to join them. Elizabeth, the hostess, raised her hazel eyes and asked, "What kind of person are you, mug or cup-and-saucer? In this family we're sharply divided." Erect in her chair, a cup and saucer held elegantly before her, she watched me and waited. Paul, coddling a mug, seemed to be studying something out the window. My answer couldn't have been worse. I said it didn't matter to me, that I drank coffee only to keep from smoking and hardly noticed what it was in but guessed I usually took a mug as being more convenient while I worked. Of course the answer showed I hadn't thought deeply about life's finer points (and also was lacking in presence of mind), and my stock went way down in the eyes of some at the table, at least temporarily.

Another morning the session around the table had a different outcome. When I arrived, Paul insisted that I join them, and I could tell I was coming into the middle of a discussion. He asked how I was getting along with the letters. "Slowly," I said, "since you wrote so many," and we all laughed. He was at a large window looking out over the patio into the woods behind the house, and, careful to avoid Elizabeth's eyes, he started talking as if delivering a speech. He began by referring to the edition of Anderson's letters, how open and honest it was, how carefully done. It would defy time, he said, because little would ever come to light to amplify or contradict it. He was glad I was doing his letters in the same way. He had said the things he had said, done the things he had done, and even if they weren't always things to be proud of, they were nevertheless his. He had made his tracks, and pretty or not, he didn't want them wiped out or hidden.

Elizabeth shifted in her chair, and he glanced at her. "But Paul," she said, "nobody wants to see our love letters." That's when I realized what the discussion was about.

"But we made those tracks," he said, his voice a pitch or two higher. "We walked that way. Why hide it? I don't want anything hidden."

Elizabeth didn't say anything, Paul came from the window, and we all got busy with the coffee. It was a bright May morning, and the conversation turned to Elizabeth's roses in the garden by the patio. Paul said she always grew the most beautiful flowers. She said she did love the beautiful things in nature, and loved them for their beauty. So she was different from Paul. When he looked at a sunset, what he saw was a reflection of the moral order of the universe, and she didn't understand that at all.

Marina Harris was my research assistant during the early years on Green's letters, and she did a beautiful job of the diplomatic as well as scholarly aspects of working in the Greens' home. One day in the fall following the discussion of tracks, she told me Elizabeth had some folders in her own filing cabinet that she wanted Marina to help her go through. Thinking we might get some letters from the "gap" years in the early 1920s, I asked Marina to take off from our work in Paul's files and do it. A month later she handed me the love letters—about forty that Paul wrote to Elizabeth between the fall of 1919, when he came back to Chapel Hill from France, and July 1922, when they were married.

With all the fuss about those letters, I was almost afraid to look in the folder. What if they were erotic? *That* would tax my diplomatic skills! Of course, what I found was nothing of the kind. There was much about his activities at school and at home, much about family members and acquaintances, much about his own writing and Elizabeth's. Basically, however, the letters were a record of his mental and emotional life at a time when he was struggling to find out who he was. The story has its "downs" as well as "ups." A lack of money, his growing need for Elizabeth, uncertainty about what he would do in life—such pressures could depress as well as challenge. There is even a climax of sorts, a letter refreshingly free of introspection with a new clarity about the future and a new tone of assurance (letter 25; the handwritten original is twenty-two pages long). While nobody's life follows a neat pattern, those "love letters" are a moving record of Green's search for identity.[22]

## SELECTION

Green's concern for his tracks suggests my aim in selecting letters for this volume. In addition to the letters in his own files (which are carbon or

22. Later on Elizabeth opened all her files to me. What they revealed, in addition to much that was helpful to this edition, was her own remarkable person. Her booklet *The Paul Green I Know* (Chapel Hill: North Caroliniana Society, 1978) makes clear their long and loving relationship. It also suggests something of her tough-minded independence. At the end of a litany of the many crusades for social justice they participated in, she adds as an afterthought: "As I remember, though, he never got really wrought up about the injustice in the way we women were treated by society" (p. 19). Her papers are preserved in abundance, and her life awaits study.

photographic copies, sometimes with typed or handwritten preliminary drafts), I got his letters from numerous individuals who saved them and from the libraries that collect his papers or those of his correspondents. Probably I have access to most of his letters that survive. Between nine and ten thousand have come to hand.

Omitted letters tend to lack a recoverable context, to be routine ("Sorry, I can't speak to your group." "Yes, I will attend that meeting." "Thank you for the good word about the play"—that kind of thing), or to duplicate the substance of included letters. Such letters help establish the chronology of Green's life but add little to the picture of him created by the edition.[23] The only sustained activity not thoroughly reflected in the edition is Green's attention year after year to production details in every one of his outdoor plays. Included letters show that *kind* of activity (and trait of mind) in connection with *The Lost Colony*, first and best known of the outdoor plays, and I document the origin of each play along with interesting episodes in its development. But from the late 1940s onward, Green had at least two or three outdoor plays running each summer, and usually six, seven, or eight. The mountain of correspondence about the production of each one would be of interest to a student of that play, but to include it here would make the edition too large. More importantly, it would blur the outline of Green's life. Even when eight plays were going, he didn't spend every waking minute thinking about them.

During a few brief periods he also sent out flurries of letters in connection with some project or other, and the activity gets little attention in the edition because the letters are uninteresting. In 1925 while editing *The Reviewer* he wrote dozens of letters soliciting, accepting, or rejecting submissions. It is interesting that he consistently turned down poems by the "Fugitives" in Nashville (Donald Davidson and Allen Tate were the two who sent him poems), but the letters for the most part are perfunctory. Again in 1941–42 he wrote dozens of letters as a founding member and first president of the National Theatre Conference. It is revealing but not surprising that he devoted time to this organization designed to stimulate serious theater beyond the commercial centers, especially New York City. But letters about the project do little more than refer to conversations or meetings without giving their substance. The edition loses little by omitting such letters.

23. If an omitted letter adds anything substantive, it is apt to be quoted or paraphrased in a footnote. The substance of dozens of omitted letters thus appears in the edition.

With the aim of preserving his tracks, "pretty or not," I have selected letters showing the main lines of Green's activity and the facets of his personality. The first and last letters in the edition illustrate the point.

The first letter was written in 1916 shortly after he arrived in Chapel Hill to attend UNC. He was twenty-two but had never been away from home for any length of time and probably had not written many letters. In any case, this letter is the earliest that survives. It is to his sister Mary and asks her to send along some things he needs at school. It also says he is looking for ways to double up on course work so he can graduate early. In other words, it sounds a theme readers will get used to in the letters to come: the drive to get things done. The last letter in the edition, written in 1981, sounds the same theme. Not the last letter Green wrote, but among the final handful, it is to his friend, the novelist John Ehle, and pushes two projects: a novel by Ehle and Green's own folklore collection, later published as *Paul Green's Wordbook: An Alphabet of Reminiscence* (1990) with a foreword by Ehle. Written sixty-five years apart, the two letters show a fundamental trait, Green's habit of looking to the future and pushing impatiently to get on with the work at hand.

The aim of revealing Green's mind gives rise to two elements of the edition that deserve comment. One is the inclusion of three letters he didn't mail: letters 217, 236, and 315.

The first two are similar in situation. In each case Green started by writing a letter that goes into his thinking on a subject he cared deeply about. The first (letter 217) gives his reasons for feeling it important to dramatize historical material. The second (letter 236) explains why he believes UNESCO should play a more active role in national and world affairs. After writing each one, however, he decided to send a brief perfunctory note in its place—which itself is revealing in ways that will be clear when readers confront those letters. With the third letter, neither the unmailed nor the mailed version is perfunctory, and the edition gives both. The unmailed version (letter 315) shows Green's reaction—you could say eruption—against the depiction of violence in advertisements for one of his plays. In tone it is angry and bleak. In tone the mailed letter (316) is encouraging and supportive, yet still makes the point against violence. Together, the two letters show Green's sense of tact and the care he took with correspondence—insights neither letter alone would stimulate.

Across the top of letters 217, 236, and 315 Green wrote "not sent," and in a note to each one, I remind the reader of its status as an unmailed letter.

The other matter needing comment is the almost unbroken run of letters to Elizabeth in 1920, 1921, and 1922. While few letters to others survive from those years, the ones to Elizabeth are from the "love letters" group, which came at a crucial time in Green's development and are among the most revealing he wrote. In order to represent the development, the edition sacrifices diversity in those years for depth. Throughout their lives, in fact, whenever the two were apart Paul wrote to Elizabeth, and what he wrote to her is apt to be more revealing and interesting than anything he wrote to anybody else.

The letters divide themselves into ten chronological sections, and at the beginning of each section I list significant dates during the period. A three-generation family tree precedes the first letter, and the edition ends with a list of Green's works. These basic facts, collected at convenient places, should help readers stay on track as they move through Green's life. In the letters themselves, Green tells the story of his life. And the telling is always in the kaleidoscopic present, without the distortions that knowledge of the outcome and the ordering tendency of the mind invariably bring to formal autobiography or biography. I think of the edition as an autobiography in the rough.

## TRANSCRIPTION

A list of letters at the end of the frontmatter shows the kind of document each text in the edition is based on: a mailed letter or a copy, a handwritten letter or a typed one, a preliminary draft or the final version. Texts are based on a copy from Green's files only when the mailed letter was not available. It is always possible that he altered a letter in ways not reflected on the copy (by revising its language or adding a postscript without noting it on the copy), but he did that rarely, to judge by the numerous cases where I have both copies. The basic reason was a concern for the accuracy of his files. Sometimes he even signed copies before filing them (thus some letters in the edition transcribed from file copies show a complimentary close, while others do not).

In the edition I follow a set form for the headings of letters. Each heading gives the number of the letter in the chronological sequence and the usual full name of the recipient. The place and date of composition follow, with information supplied in square brackets if missing in the original. For clarity, in the headings I abbreviate state names, standardize capitalization, and use the form *7 December 1934* for dates.

Green's handwriting, once I got used to it, wasn't hard to read, and in any case help was always near at hand. All of the letters were transcribed after Green's death, but to check a reading I could turn to his wife Elizabeth, his assistant Rhoda Wynn, or his sister Erma Gold. For the words or phrases that remained unreadable, I inserted "[word illegible]" or "[phrase illegible]" as the case may be. But those are few. To enhance accuracy, all transcriptions were read at a later date against the originals at least twice, once by me, once by one or more research assistants with experience in Green's papers.

Like most people in the rush of writing, Green gave titles of works one way today, another way tomorrow. To forestall confusion about the work he means, I give titles in their generally accepted form. Titles of book-length works are italicized (full-length plays, novels, etc.), titles of shorter works enclosed in quotation marks (one-act plays, short stories, etc.). Anything of interest about Green's rendition of a title I point out in a note.

Green was a careful writer. Typographical errors in the letters or slips of the pen—unintended deviations from standard usage—are infrequent and usually clear-cut (but occasionally amusing: concerning Andy Griffith, who graduated from UNC and acted in *The Lost Colony*, a producer asked if there were any more actors like him in Green's fold, and Green replied, "no such joyous duplication or even sililarity is available"). Since such things are unintentional, the momentary confusion they cause a reader is pointless, and I have silently corrected the few that occur.

He was also a good speller, and usually I have retained his erroneous spellings and provided a footnote about the word. In the few cases where he unknowingly misspelled a person's name, however, I have silently corrected the spelling to prevent confusion for the reader and to insure that the name shows up correctly in the index. If there is any significance to the misspelling, I retain it in the letter and use the correct spelling in a note. (For instance, if he misspells a name in a long historical disquisition, it suggests that he is writing from memory rather than looking things up.) If he deliberately misspells a name—for humor, for instance—of course I retain that spelling.

The spelling of Green's own name needs a word. Until 1922 he usually spelled it "Greene" (others in the family spelled the family name sometimes with a final "e" and sometimes without it). Elizabeth, however, was thrifty with the alphabet, and when she devised the announcement of their wedding that year, she dropped the final "e." She also reduced the doubled letters in his middle name. The announcement therefore said she was marrying, not Paul Elliott Greene, but Paul Eliot Green. He liked the new look and stayed with her spelling the rest of his life, as did his sisters. In letters in the edition, I spell the family name the way it is spelled in the original letter, which means that until July 1922 it has a final "e" and afterward it doesn't. (The middle name doesn't appear in the letters.) In notes to the letters, however, I use the shorter form consistently throughout.

While in general Green remained within the bounds of conventional usage, he did enjoy playing with language for effect. Especially in the early letters to Elizabeth, dialect spellings abound ("We sho' got to git us a job rat now"), and the practice never wholly disappears. In the same vein he liked to show off his languages—the Greek and Latin he learned at school and the French he picked up in France in 1918–19. Occasionally there are even such reverberating combinations as "*Mon heure* ain't come yit." He also liked to make up words ("divisioning," "fictionized," "mergins") and occasionally to tinker with usage ("Thanks for your kindly attention. We are turmoiling over the problem"). And sometimes he used ellipses points for emphasis. The edition gives letters in their entirety, with no words or phrases omitted, and all ellipses points in the text of letters included in the edition are Green's. Also, especially during the 1930s, after returning from a Guggenheim year (actually eighteen months) in Berlin and London, he affected a few British spellings ("defence," "prophecy," "behaviour"). Moreover, to soften the expression when giving an opinion or a direction, he sometimes used the word order of a question but ended the sentence with a period rather than a question mark ("Will you send along the books."). A reader should be alert to Green's free use of language because the edition tries to render what he intended exactly.

Anything of interest about a revision by Green in a letter is covered in a note. Most of the letters show little revision—a word or two scratched out, a new word or phrase added between the lines or in a margin. In such cases, the edition gives a fair-copy reading. Deleted words are omitted, added words inserted at their proper place—both silently. Especially in handwritten letters, however, Green used margins for all sorts of things, among them comments on adjacent paragraphs ("Mum's the word on this matter, of course. Would you believe such a thing possible?"). In the edition that kind of marginalia is always quoted in a note at the point of interest. He also used margins for what amount to postscripts, and that's how the edition gives them—as remarks following the complimentary close.

## ANNOTATION

Annotation plays a special role in editions of letters. Letters are written to individuals. Frequently the individuals are well known to the writer, and the letters depend acutely on the writer's assumptions about the knowledge, experience, and outlook of the recipient. To someone else the letter is apt to appear elliptical, as if things had been left out. To anyone other than the recipient—to readers of an edition of letters, for instance—a letter without annotation can be in a real sense unintelligible. The following brief letter illustrates the point:

October 28, 1955

Dear Dr. Peck—

Many thanks for sending me the copy of John G. Hanson's letter. How the man must have suffered, and really how needlessly! I count it one of the mistakes of mankind that we fail to realize the finality of our acts. Most of us live in a queer sentimentality of second and third chance possibilities. There are no such possibilities. Cruelty is finally and irrevocably cruel when it occurs. Oppression the same, blindness the same, ignorance likewise. The new deed and the new trial are just that—new. The past error and the past sin are forever that—old and done. St. Paul with all his good works could never bring back to life one of the martyrs he had cheated of life. But then good deeds in turn also are eternal in their reality. We the living can gain strength and confidence in this latter truth too. Right now we in North Carolina and most of the South are turmoiling over an evil fiction, namely, that deeply sunburnt men (Negroes) are not of the same soul's worth as bleached-out men (Whites) and do not deserve the same rights of opportunity and personal dignity. The governor of my state and I have had some public argument. It will continue. I will never yield to his prejudice. Do we count in the scheme of things? I maintain we all do, whatever color, calling or kind we may be. Question—do we count for good? We should, we must. Thus the program of work and striving is obvious and imperative. It is always good to hear from you.

Elizabeth and I send our love,

Paul Green

Forgive my preaching. I've got into the lamentable habit lately, maybe because time seems to be running out.

Clearly the letter concerns cruelty and injustice in race relations and is deeply felt. But that is only a hazy understanding of the letter. The details that bring it into focus in its world are missing. Who is Peck? Who is Hanson? What was the nature of his suffering? What does his letter say, and why did Peck send it to Green? Then the public argument with the governor—what is that about? Until such questions are answered, the letter is not fully intelligible.

Questions frustrate. Understanding satisfies. To see the role of notes in the experience of reading letters, look at the annotated version of the letter to Elisabeth Peck in the edition (letter 256).

In the notes I try to anticipate a reader's questions, answer them at the point where they arise, and do it in a way that takes the reader's mind back into the letter. Since they are an integral part of the letter, notes should enhance the reading experience rather than interrupt it.

The first note to many of the letters provides necessary background information: identification of the recipient and his or her relationship to Green, circumstances out of which the letter arose, particular matters to which Green is responding, and any other information needed to make the beginning of the letter clear. While these background notes need to clarify the context of letters, I try not to repeat details from previous letters, especially ones near at hand. Detailed identifications of recipients are given only with the first letter to the person.

Notes through the body of a letter clarify matters as they arise. They identify people and events, cite the source of allusions (allusions to the Bible abound; others are frequent), and provide textual details. They also quote relevant passages from Green's play manuscripts and diaries, other letters by Green, and letters of recipients. Nothing equals quotation from original documents for conveying tone as well as content, and frequently Green echoes phrases from the letter he is responding to. Quotation not only enriches a reader's sense of the past but also allows readers to appreciate an element of Green's response that paraphrase would hide.

Many of the letters are like episodes in a story. They show the beginning of some project or development, or its middle or end. If a letter leaves the outcome of something up in the air and it isn't concluded within the next few letters, then I describe the outcome in a note. Typically it is the last note to the letter.

While the aim of the edition is the traditional one of presenting a life in letters, the role of the annotation is a little out of the ordinary. Rich archival resources allowed me to think of placing the letters in the whirl and sweep of their own day. When the annotation succeeds, letters should unfold for the reader like buds opening into roses.

# Abbreviations

The following abbreviations are used throughout to indicate the location of letters and other unpublished documents or to describe the letters.

| | |
|---|---|
| AL | Autograph letter, draft, usually with revisions |
| ALs | Autograph letter, signed; the mailed copy |
| AL[s] | Autograph letter, incomplete, presumed signed; the mailed copy |
| BGM | Betsy Green Moyer, Wayland, Massachusetts |
| Br | Papers of the recipient, Hutchins Library, Berea College, Berea, Kentucky |
| BS-NCC | Betty Smith Papers, North Carolina Collection, Wilson Library, University of North Carolina, Chapel Hill |
| C | Spanish Refugee Manuscript Collection, Butler Library, Columbia University, New York City |
| Ca | Carbon of mailed letter from Green's files (typed or autograph) |
| *COAP* | Percival Wilde, ed., *Contemporary One-Act Plays from Nine Countries* (Boston: Little, Brown, 1936) |
| EG-SHC | Elizabeth Lay Green Papers, Southern Historical Collection, Wilson Library, University of North Carolina, Chapel Hill |
| Gr | Papers of the recipient, Special Collections, Walter Clinton Jackson Library, University of North Carolina, Greensboro |
| I | Manuscript Collections, University of Iowa Libraries, Iowa City |
| JDP-V | John Dos Passos Papers, Manuscript Department, University of Virginia Library, Charlottesville |
| JG | Janet Green, Ashtabula, Ohio |
| MGJ | Mary Green Johnson, Lillington, North Carolina |
| NCC | North Carolina Collection, Wilson Library, University of North Carolina, Chapel Hill |
| *NO* | *News and Observer*, Raleigh, N.C. |

| | |
|---|---|
| PG-SHC | Paul Green Papers, Southern Historical Collection, Wilson Library, University of North Carolina, Chapel Hill |
| PGJr | Paul Green, Jr., Mt. Kisco, New York |
| R | Roanoke Island Historical Association, Manteo, North Carolina |
| SHC | Southern Historical Collection, Wilson Library, University of North Carolina, Chapel Hill |
| SHCr | Papers of the recipient, Southern Historical Collection, Wilson Library, University of North Carolina, Chapel Hill |
| T | Telegram, the sent copy |
| TC | Typed copy of lost ALs (ALs not examined for edition) |
| Tel | Telegram, draft, usually with revisions |
| TL | Typed letter, draft, usually with revisions |
| TLs | Typed letter, signed; the mailed copy |
| TL[s] | Typed letter, incomplete, presumed signed; the mailed copy |
| Tr | Papers of the recipient, Harry Ransom Research Center, University of Texas, Austin |
| TWT-NCC | Thomas Wolfe Papers (Terry Series), North Carolina Collection, Wilson Library, University of North Carolina, Chapel Hill |
| TWW-NCC | Thomas Wolfe Papers (Fred Wolfe Series), North Carolina Collection, Wilson Library, University of North Carolina, Chapel Hill |
| Yr | Papers of the recipient, Beinecke Rare Book and Manuscript Library, Yale University, New Haven, Connecticut |

# List of Letters

| Recipient | Date and Place of Composition | Type and Location of Original |
|---|---|---|
| I. EDUCATION, 1916–1922 | | |
| 1916 | | |
| 1. Mary Greene | 3 Sept.; Chapel Hill | TC; PG-SHC |
| 1917 | | |
| 2. William A. Greene | 22 Nov.; Camp Sevier, S.C. | TC; PG-SHC |
| 1918 | | |
| 3. Erma Greene | 25 Aug.; Proven, Belgium | TC; PG-SHC |
| 4. Mary Greene | 20 Oct.; Langres, France | ALS; MGJ |
| 1919 | | |
| 5. Erma Greene | 30 Mar.; Paris | TC; PG-SHC |
| 6. Gladys Greene | 9 May; Paris | TC; PG-SHC |
| 7. William A. Greene | 16 May; Paris | AL[s]; MGJ |
| 8. Gladys Greene | 7 June; Paris | TC; PG-SHC |
| 1920 | | |
| 9. Elizabeth Lay | Spring; Chapel Hill | ALS; EG-SHC |
| 10. Elizabeth Lay | 30 June; Lillington, N.C. | ALS; EG-SHC |
| 11. Elizabeth Lay | July; Lillington, N.C. | ALS; EG-SHC |
| 12. Elizabeth Lay | Aug.; Lillington, N.C. | ALS; EG-SHC |
| 13. Elizabeth Lay | 22 Aug.; Lillington, N.C. | ALS; EG-SHC |
| 14. Elizabeth Lay | Fall; Chapel Hill | ALS; EG-SHC |
| 15. Elizabeth Lay | Early Oct.; Chapel Hill | ALS; EG-SHC |
| 16. Elizabeth Lay | 28 Dec.; Lillington, N.C. | ALS; EG-SHC |
| 1921 | | |
| 17. Elizabeth Lay | Feb.; Chapel Hill | ALS; EG-SHC |
| 18. Elizabeth Lay | 19 June; Lillington, N.C. | ALS; EG-SHC |

## II. WRITING AND RACE IN THE SOUTH, 1923–1929

| | | |
|---|---|---|
| 167. Mary G. Johnson | 19 Apr.; Chapel Hill | TLS; PG-SHC |
| 168. George R. Coffman | 8 Oct.; Chapel Hill | Ca; PG-SHC |
| 169. E. M. Land | 18 Nov.; Chapel Hill | Ca; PG-SHC |
| 1943 | | |
| 170. Betty Smith | 11 June; Beverly Hills, Calif. | ALS; BS-NCC |
| 171. Norman Förster | 27 July; Pacific Palisades, Calif. | Ca; PG-SHC |
| 172. James Boyd | 16 Aug.; Pacific Palisades, Calif. | ALS; SHCr |
| 173. Elizabeth L. Green | 10 Sept.; Beverly Hills, Calif. | ALS; EG-SHC |
| 174. Elizabeth L. Green | 1 Oct.; Beverly Hills, Calif. | ALS; EG-SHC |
| 175. Elizabeth L. Green | 16 Oct.; New York City | ALS; EG-SHC |
| 176. James Boyd | 29 Nov.; Chapel Hill | ALS; SHCr |
| 177. Bela W. Norton | 29 Dec.; Chapel Hill | Ca; PG-SHC |
| 1944 | | |
| 178. Louis Untermeyer | 19 Jan.; Chapel Hill | Ca; PG-SHC |
| 179. Robert Lynn Gault | 1 Feb.; Chapel Hill | Ca; PG-SHC |
| 180. Frank J. Sheil | 15 Feb.; Chapel Hill | Ca; PG-SHC |
| 181. M. M. Marberry | 11 Mar.; Chapel Hill | Ca; PG-SHC |
| 182. Katharine Boyd | 27 May; Pacific Palisades, Calif. | Ca; PG-SHC |
| 183. Robert B. House | 24 Aug.; Pacific Palisades, Calif. | Ca; PG-SHC |
| 1945 | | |
| 184. Henry Grady Owens | 1 May; Chapel Hill | Ca; PG-SHC |
| 185. John Harden | 4 May; Chapel Hill | Ca; PG-SHC |
| 186. R. Gregg Cherry | 17 May; Pacific Palisades, Calif. | Ca; PG-SHC |
| 187. William T. Couch | 17 May; Pacific Palisades, Calif. | TLS; SHCr |
| 188. Katharine Boyd | 22 May; Pacific Palisades, Calif. | Ca; PG-SHC |
| 189. Harry K. Russell | 23 July; Santa Monica, Calif. | Ca; PG-SHC |
| 190. Samuel Cornwell | 30 July; Santa Monica, Calif. | Ca; PG-SHC |
| 191. William T. Couch | 23 Aug.; Santa Monica, Calif. | T; SHCr |
| 192. Harry S. Truman | 18 Oct.; Santa Monica, Calif. | Tel; PG-SHC |

VII. SYMPHONIC DRAMA AND INTEGRATION, 1952–1955

IX. SYMPHONIC DRAMA, THE SOVIET UNION, AND INTEGRATION, 1962–1967

# A Southern Life

William Archibald Green
(1852–1926) m.
Elizabeth Spence (d. 1879)

William
John
Alda

m. 27 Mar. 1889
Bettie (Avery) Byrd (1862–1908)

Mary (1892–1988)
Paul (17 Mar. 1894–4 May 1981)
Hugh (1896–1959)
Gladys (1898–1990)
Caro Mae (1901–1988)
Erma (1902–1993)

George W. Lay (1860–1932)
m. 1893
Anna (Atkinson) Balch (1870–1956)

George (1895–1948)
Elizabeth (6 Apr. 1897–21 May 1989)
Ellen (1899–1978)
Nancy (b. 1901)
Lucy (1903–1956)
Henry (1905–1974)
Virginia (1907–1972)
Thomas (1910–1915)

Paul Eliot Green
m. 6 July 1922
Elizabeth Atkinson Lay

Paul, Jr. (14 Jan. 1924)
m. 20 Oct. 1948 Dorrit Gegan
Byrd (25 Feb. 1926)
m. 25 Dec. 1945 Samuel Cornwell
Betsy (14 July 1930)
m. 4 Apr. 1952 William Moyer
Janet (18 Dec. 1931)
m. 6 Nov. 1955 Herbert Lauritzen
m. 15 Aug. 1964 John Catlin

# I

## Education, 1916–1922

17 March 1894
Born at home on farm in Harnett County, North Carolina.

1914
Graduates from Buies Creek Academy in Buies Creek, North Carolina. Begins two years of teaching at Olive Branch School nearby.

September 1916
Enrolls at the University of North Carolina at Chapel Hill. Earliest surviving letter.

16 July 1917
Enlists in 105th Engineers. Trains for a year at bases in North and South Carolina. Begins writing poems.

June 1918
105th Engineers land at Calais, soon in heavy fighting.

October 1918
Sent to Officers Candidate School at Langres, France.

14 December 1918
With throng in streets welcoming President Woodrow Wilson to Paris.

30 May 1919
Hears President Wilson's Memorial Day Address at the American military cemetery in Suresnes, France.

25 June 1919
Discharged in Paris.

9 July 1919
Sails for home.

September 1919
Returns to UNC. Begins writing plays for Carolina Playmakers.

15 June 1921

Receives B.A. with major in philosophy.

17 September 1921

Begins eight-day trip to visit fiancée Elizabeth Lay and her family in Beaufort, North Carolina, then to Roanoke Island for filming of reenactment of Sir Walter Raleigh's 1587 colonization attempt.

1921–22

At UNC for graduate work in philosophy and writing plays.

6 July 1922

Marries Elizabeth Lay in her father's church, St. Paul's Episcopal, in Beaufort.

1922–23

At Cornell University for graduate work in philosophy. Elizabeth works in Cornell community drama program.

## 1. To Mary Greene[1]

[Smith Building, UNC Campus] Chapel Hill, N.C.
3 September 1916

Dear Mary:

Perhaps you have received my short note asking for sheets, etc. Please ship two quilts. You can put them all in a small box and express them prepaid or not. I had to buy a couple of blankets, but they are not much good.

I have just come from having an interview with the professors about taking the full amt. of Freshman work and part of the Sophomore. They are undecided yet, as this is something they never have done. All I want is just a chance to try it! I know I can make it. I shall find out for certain this P.M.[2]

You people will have to excuse me if I do not write often, for when I get settled to work I will not think of writing.

Tell Hugh[3] to keep my cotton straight. I shall need every bit of it next summer.

This is a very fine place. The people believe in society—that is the members of the fraternities do. I am rooming in Smith Building and there are about a dozen fraternity halls around it. The boys had a big dance across the street from here last night. The music was grand. I was not there because the college authorities won't let a freshman join a fraternity. Possibly it's best for me that they don't.

Tell Caro and Erma[4] my pocketbook was too weak to remember them in Raleigh—by the way, I had a big time over there; and also met Mr. Connelly—Mattie's one. Pretty nice fellow I guess.[5]

Please send the quilts and sheets as early as possible.

Paul

1. Mary Green (1892–1988), twenty-four and oldest of the Green children, became mistress of the family home in Harnett County near Lillington, North Carolina, at the death of their mother, Bettie Lorine Byrd Green, in 1908. On 1 or 2 September Paul had come to Chapel Hill to enroll at UNC for the term beginning 6 September.

2. Probably he got the chance since he was able to graduate after three years in school.

3. Their brother, two years younger than Paul.

4. Their sisters, fifteen and thirteen at the time.

5. Green had come to Chapel Hill by way of Raleigh to attend the wedding of their cousin Martha Green (Mattie) and Willard Moss Connelly.

## 2. To William A. Greene[1]

Camp Sevier, S.C.
22 November 1917

Dear Papa:

Mary's good letter came today, and under the spell of it I'm writing home. I should write oftener, and really I wish I could, but the chances for writing often are slim enough here. During the day one has no time for writing, and in the night there always is a crowd of boys talking and standing around the stove in my tent. Even tonight there are a half-dozen in here telling jokes, etc. Despite this, I should write you once or twice a week, but for the fact that I'm writing for the Greenville *Daily News*—writing verses of little value, but they ease me inside. That takes nearly all my spare time. The verses are written under the title of "Songs of a Soldier," and consist of some half-dozen poems, printed weekly. I'm going to try to keep this column up as long as I stay here. It will help me no little in mastering the English language, which thing I expect to do at some faroff time.[2] There are *only* two reasons that I especially wish to come safely through this war. One is for the sake of the homefolks; the other is that I may write something worthwhile. I don't love life enough to dread the shells and gases of Europe. The two reasons I spoke of are all that makes me anxious about the outcome so far as I am concerned. But perhaps that point of view writers call the fatalistic (what's to be will be), which most of the soldiers believe in, is the best way for a fellow to believe after all. But somehow I can't believe such a way now.

As I mentioned, I am writing some, but doing very little reading. Nevertheless a few weeks ago I read a book by Mr. H. G. Wells of England, called *Mr. Britling Sees It Through.*[3] I'm going to mail it to you. Perhaps you already have

1. William A. Green (1852–1926), Paul's father and a farmer in Harnett County, North Carolina, did not share the patriotic fervor that swept the Chapel Hill campus during the spring of 1917 after President Woodrow Wilson carried the United States into World War I. Paul did, however, and in Chapel Hill on 16 July 1917 he enlisted in Company B of the 105th Engineers. In September, after short stays in two camps in North Carolina, the unit went to Camp Sevier near Greenville, South Carolina, for basic training.

2. Green continued to write poems, then gathered them into a small book, *Trifles of Thought,* which he had printed in Greenville in May 1918 as his company left for France.

3. Published in 1916, Wells's novel was a huge success in the United States as well as in Great Britain. He had already issued the pamphlet "The War That Will End War"

heard of the book as it is world famous. After you've read it, doubtless your idea about sacrifice in this war will be changed considerably, although there are few men in Harnett County paying the price for this conflict that you are paying.[4] To be sure, you are proud of it. I am. As much as I should like to see Hugh back at home. Somehow I don't mind going through it for my part, but I don't like to see Hugh in it, although he is faring as well as I. You know how I feel, and you feel the same way about it. He always will seem young and dependent to me.

Hugh passed here this afternoon, coming from the rifle range on the mountains. The infantry has been there at rifle practice for the last week or two, and all day long we could hear a steady roar of fire. I'm getting a good idea of what a battle means. The sound of rifle fire is enough to deafen one, not taking into consideration the heavy artillery. I haven't heard any of that yet, but I shall soon as a heavy artillery range is being built beyond the rifle range back in the mountains.

And another touch of real war I am getting is the gas—gas exactly like that the armies are using in Europe. A doctor from Europe is here teaching the use of the gas mask. Last week Captain Boesch[5] appointed Sgt. Cureton and myself to attend the gas school. Of course I was pleased with the honor, small tho' it was. Well, before the first lesson was over I was heartily sick of the whole thing. We had real gas masks like those among the allies. Here is a crude drawing of the thing taken from the satchel.[6] Now think of having to wear that thing hour after hour. The most disagreeable thing about it is that the saliva gets all over one's face and clothes. My, I sometimes felt as if I'd vomit, but there was no taking it off. They drilled us hour by hour with that thing on. Yesterday we took a test of chlorine gas. With the mask on you are safe. But the minute it is taken off, the gas almost suffocates you. When one is in a gas attack, at the word "gas!" he stops stock still holding his breath while he puts the mask on. The required time to take it from the satchel and place it over the face, with the mouthpiece and nose clip adjusted perfectly, is 6 seconds. Very

(1914), and in the novel he couples disillusionment over the war with a deep faith that the waste of young lives will awaken mankind to the necessity of a league of nation-states, or World Republic.

4. In September Paul's brother, Hugh, also enlisted, so William Green had two sons in the army. Hugh was in an infantry division also stationed at Camp Sevier.

5. Commander of Green's company.

6. The handwritten original of this letter, with its drawing, is lost.

few have been able to put it on in that time. The ability to do it comes with practice. Of course, I've done it only twice so far in the required time. I shall be glad when I get out teaching the other fellows how to do it.

Now for a few jerky paragraphs:

We are quarantined for an indefinite time on account of measles, pneumonia, and meningitis. Many poor boys have died, as many as six in one night. But I think I am safe from any attack.[7] I'm trying to see after Hugh, too.

I've taken out $10,000 insurance for Caro and Erma, $5,000 each.[8] You see there's no telling what may happen to me. This with the bond takes nearly all my salary, but I'm wanting them to be sure of an education either way.[9] Tell Erma and Caro I'm proud of them both.[10] Wish I could write; too busy now.

Tell Mary I'm writing to the beautiful Miss Byrd in Greenville. Can't say how I like her tho she writes a splendid letter.[11]

Will send you some copies of the *Daily News* with my stuff in them. I'm going to try to get away Xmas. Don't know. Tell Mary to leave off the turkey for Tkg. Send other things.

Am working to get into officer's training school. Slim chance. Too many old men ahead of me.

Love, Paul

7. Because as supply sergeant he spent most of his time in the supply tent away from others, compiling records and readying supplies. He even slept there frequently (Green diary, PG-SHC).

8. The limit on life insurance for a soldier was $10,000 (Green diary, 13 November 1917, PG-SHC).

9. His salary at the time was $33 per month, of which $20 went toward insurance and a $200 bond that Paul assigned to his older half-brother John, William's second son by his first marriage, who remained on the farm with their father (Paul Green to Mary Green, 23 December 1917, PG-SHC).

10. They were in school at Buies Creek Academy.

11. Mabel Byrd was the foremost of several girls Green wrote to, perhaps because she was the closest (Camp Sevier was four and a half miles from Greenville) and he could visit her on weekends. Their relationship continued, with ups and downs (she was appalled at his cigar smoking and nontraditional religious views), until his unit left for France in May 1918. His sister Mary was Paul's special confidant in affairs of the heart.

## 3. To Erma Greene[1]

[Proven,] Belgium
25 August 1918

Dearest Erma:

Your letter of July 28 has just reached me. Like all the letters from home—and I've received several lately; keep writing—it was the most enjoyable feature of the day's existence.[2] From what I gathered from your letter, the folks at home don't hear from me very often, and yet I write to them a great deal. Perhaps the censor stops them. Anyway I get a pleasure from knowing I have written, but the pleasure would be greatly increased if I were certain of your receiving them. Here's hoping you get this short note, scribbled in haste while business is dull; that is to say, while everybody is at dinner. You understand that there is no such thing as a day off, or a Saturday afternoon at the ball game here. There are a plenty of ball games, to be sure, but the balls are never caught; they just go thru and on.

You asked a few questions—and certainly you deserve to know the answers to them. Your first question was concerning the sort of work I'm doing. Honey, it's hard to tell you exactly what I am doing. At the present I'm a sort of bookkeeper for the whole regiment of engineers. I am what is called a Regimental Sergeant Major. Quite a long title, but full of empty sound. Yes, I look after all secret papers for the "105," fighting orders, reports, etc., write the regimental diary every day; draw rations (we say "rations" in the army) for Hdqrs. troops, look after 50 or 60 men, etc., etc., etc., etc. The most unpleasant thing of all is the casualty list. Reporting the killed and wounded is

1. Erma Green (1903–1993), Green's youngest sister and a high school senior at Buies Creek Academy, wrote him frequently while he was in the army. His division left Camp Sevier by train on 18 May 1918, traveled to New York City then Quebec City, sailed to Liverpool, took a train through London to Dover, and sailed for Calais, landing on 14 June. On 28 June, following two weeks of training, they began to march toward Ypres (present-day Ieper) in Belgium, where a major battle was in progress. After working a few days to repair reserve trenches, they reached Ypres on 16 July, where they remained into September. On 30 July Green was promoted to regimental sergeant major and moved to regimental headquarters at Proven, a few kilometers behind the line at Ypres.

2. On 4 August Green got "five or six letters from home" and that they "were worth more than a drink of heavenly ambrosia. Also in one letter was a rose from the arboretum at Chapel Hill. What can one say when such things as old memories, dead love, and fond regret begin to pull at his heart? Nothing" (Green diary, PG-SHC).

my job also. And alas! I've marked up several friends whose mothers today are speaking to God about the eternal *Why*?[3] But withal our losses are extremely light, it appears to me, compared to those of Germany. I must not talk tho, for there is the censor; and even the leaves have ears these days.

Now as to the hours I work—when and how long, I may answer all by saying that I never keep track of time. Scarcely ever can I give the name of the present day. It may be Monday; it may be Sunday, I don't know. All I'm concerned with is the day of the month, 21, 22 or 23. Foreign service already has taught me one thing—that 8 hours of sleep are not essential to good health. Yes, and I've learned another thing I was forgetting: the poor tired earth has drunk enough blood within the last four years as to be offensive in the sight of God. Not long ago I was on an old battlefield. We were digging trenches. One could hardly push his spade into the ground without striking a bone of somebody's boy.[4] Yes, horrible; but war. And a few days ago I was at another place where 54,000 men "went west" in one day. Awful! Yes, but war. Oh, I tell you the people in America never dreamed of what our brave allies endured for three long years. They were content to slide around in noiseless automobiles, absent and high in hope, while thousands of boys who loved the fields of England or the skies of France went down into the Valley, and went without a rod or staff to comfort them.

Yes, Woodrow Wilson is a great man, a king among men, but he didn't enter the war soon enough.[5] Decide that for yourself; I have decided for myself.

Now that I have erred by speaking of the dark side, let me retrieve myself by speaking of the bright. Germany is lost! Irrevocably lost! She realizes it! Slowly but steadily the sands of her political and economical life are running down. A short while and the last golden grain will be gone. By using slang let me show you the difference between the allied and German armies. Our men are just "rarin' to go," while the enemy fights sullenly as if driven to it. And I have a

3. "Reports of casualties are sickening," he noted in his diary; "every day we lose 6 or 7 men from our regiment" (24 August 1918, PG-SHC).

4. On 18 July Green and his squad were out at night repairing trenches in an area where a Canadian battalion had been gassed in 1915. "Remains of long dead soldiers found in grass. Found many exposed from too shallow graves" (Green diary, PG-SHC).

5. Fighting began in Europe in the summer of 1914, and President Wilson delivered his war message to Congress on 2 April 1917.

strong suspicion that many a poor German boy has been shot in the back by his silver-spurred Prussian officers. Anyway, every German soldier captured appears as much pleased as if he were going home on a furlough.

Honey, I don't want you to be cold and cynical towards people, but you will please me by hating with your whole soul the cruel masters of Germany. Any people that will deliberately kill mothers and babies as *I have seen* the Germans do deserves not one thought of forgiveness at the great judgment seat of human justice.[6] I wish I could compose a "Song of Hate" in answer to the brutal insolence of Lissauer.[7] But whether I write it or not, *I feel it*! If I get time to write, I shall send you a hurriedly written piece of free verse showing some of Germany's acts in the past.[8]

But there were other questions in your letter were there not? Yes, you wanted to know about the gas. We have had gas to endure two or three times. But our losses have been slight thru that alone, our masks proving a sure protection if adjusted correctly and in time.

You asked about my having seen old friends. No. I have seen only Hugh since I came over—saw him once a few weeks ago.[9] *But remember he is on the line with all his Greene blood crying for a German to come and face him.* If the worst should happen to him, which God forbid!—you will agree with me in saying, "He was a man. He could not have died more gloriously. It is well." The day he and I met, we had just returned from the front, and naturally had to tell each other our experiences up there. And when we separated I said to him, "Hugh, be careful. You know how they love you back home."

He looked at me with that funny smile of his and answered, "Well, it don't

6. Several times Green heard such stories: "A pretty Belgian girl told me something of German atrocities, babys' hands amputated, girls' breasts disfigured. Horrible!" (Green diary, 30 July 1918, PG-SHC).

7. Ernst Lissauer, writer of patriotic German poetry, recently had been awarded the Order of the Red Eagle by Kaiser Wilhelm for his "Hassgesang gegen England," which attracted attention to the poem in the British press. The song, or hymn of hate, cites atrocities committed against Germans and, in translation, ends: "You will we hate with a lasting hate, / We will never forgo our hate. / . . . We have one foe and one alone—England!"

8. Although Green's poetry notebooks contain several lists of material for such a poem, he apparently did not write one.

9. Hugh's infantry division was in the thick of the fighting around Ypres. On 27 July, as they withdrew from a battle on Kemmel Hill, he visited Paul and described how his company had lost about half of its men (Green diary, PG-SHC).

make much difference either way. I'm no better to be knocked off than anybody else's boy."

Since then I've thought a great deal about that statement. He was right. But let's cheer up. There are heavy odds in favour of all the boys around home returning.

Let whatever will betide, there is but one course. Forgetting all successes we have had or may have, there is but one course. The premier of England hit it when he said, "Well done—but—Carry on."[10] We are doing well now, but we must keep hammering. There is no peace. There can be no peace until the end.

Yesterday I stood beside the grave of a daring young aviator "dead in battle." The propellor blade of the plane he loved so well marked his resting place, and on the ground was laid a small cross with its sacred burden. He was such a youthful captain! "Age 22." How many churchyards with their innumerable crosses—too many of them newly made—have I seen.

Now in closing this hurried letter let me enjoin you at home to realize the sacredness of our duty. All that we ask of you is unity of purpose and moral support. We ask that there be no more a tone of complaint anywhere. Let those who complain walk once among the ruins of Ypres, what then![11] . . . Let all letters to the boys be cheery and full of fighting spirit. Every mother who has a boy in France should feel as that boy will feel when the General pins the Croix-de-Guerre upon his blouse. Let her wear that fact as a bride wears her orange blossoms. I've seen boys get a blue spell after receiving a letter from mother that lasted thru a week. Now when a boy falls into that condition, he is useless as a soldier as long as it lasts. We must get most of our fighting stimulus from home. We . . . must . . . have . . . your . . . support.[12]

As for me I'm going to give my best as all the boys are. The thought of those

10. The British prime minister was David Lloyd George, but perhaps Green meant King George V, who "came to visit us today . . . [and] shook hands with several of our boys. Ah, Aristocracy, ye shall bend and worship reviled Democracy" (Green diary, 6 August 1918, PG-SHC).

11. Ypres was the site of three major battles during the war, and Green's company, arriving at 2:00 A.M. during the final battle, found the town "lighted by flaming shells and flares. Awful sight. Big moon looks sadly at it all" (Green diary, 16 July 1918, PG-SHC). Two days later on reconnaissance he "visited all demolition posts in and around Ypres. Explored the ruin of Ypres closely. Devastation appalling. Not a building standing" (18 July 1918).

12. Ellipsis points throughout the edition are Green's, for emphasis.

who fought three years for us unaided makes me consecrate anew what little strength I have for the grand cause. I'd like for you girls to write all the boys from and around Lillington over here. Make them feel that they are the pride of their State. You understand. And if you do this, I venture to say that many a Boche[13] will receive a knockout blow that otherwise would not.

I'm sending you something Clara sent me from Mrs. P.—Let nobody see it.[14] *Save* it for me and

> If deep within the earth I lay
> And learned, old friends, that you had lost
> Or quit the game for which we paid
>   Such bitter cost,
> I feel that death would fail to hold
> Me there in slumber with the dead,
> Tho' drowsy poppies held their cups
>   Above my bed.[15]

Love to papa, John[16] and the rest.

Your foolish brother, Paul

## 4. To Mary Greene

[Langres], France[1]
20 October 1918

Dear Mary—

Doubtless you feel that I have forgotten everything back home or have happened upon some misfortune that prevents me writing. But neither is the

13. Slang term for a German.

14. Clara is Green's cousin Clara Byrd in Greensboro, North Carolina, but what she sent and the identity of Mrs. P. are unknown.

15. Poem by Green entitled "Carry On!" and dated "Ypres 1918," in his poetry notebook (PG-SHC).

16. Their older half-brother.

---

1. Green remained in the area of Ypres until 4 September, then moved about forty kilometers south as his unit prepared to attack the Hindenburg Line at Bellicourt. The attack began on 28 September. On 30 September German defenses began to collapse, and by 2 October the fighting was over, casualties in Green's regiment being ten killed and ninety-eight wounded. On 4 October he left for Officers Candidate School at Langres, above Dijon (Green diary, PG-SHC).

case. I am well and enjoying my present surroundings to the fullest extent. And never for a moment think that I can forget all that home means and will mean to me and thousands of others when we get back where life can smile with one who has been where smiles—deep smiles—are rare. As I have mentioned before, the censorship hedges one in so, that a great amount of the pleasure in writing home is curtailed. There is satisfaction to me and to you, however, in the simple statement that I am well and pretty much alive.

And as for Hugh, I can say that he was well and hearty the last time I saw him. That was 3 weeks or more ago.[2] Since then I have moved several hundred miles from him, and up to the present, I haven't heard from him. But I'm sure he's safe wherever he is. Just before I left, I had a five minute's talk with him. He had just come out of one of the fiercest battles of the war. As to the narrow escapes he has had, the number of Germans he has killed, and the part he has played in several fights—and as to the part I have played on the front—I cannot tell you now, of course. But both of us shall have more to tell back there, to be sure.

I am enclosing a Christmas Package Coupon for you to use in sending me a package for Xmas. Please use your discretion in choosing a gift. Pray do not send anything costly—cigars, candy, or the like will do.

How is papa, John and the rest? And how are the girls[3] enjoying their year at school? As yet, I haven't heard from Gladys. Does she like the conservatory?[4]

Write me all the news of home. Are you teaching at Barclaysville?[5] And let me know whether Mrs. Johnson has heard from Irving. The last news I had from him was to the effect that he was progressing finely enough.[6]

Love and best wishes to all. Paul

2. Hugh was gassed in late August but returned to duty in late September. Paul saw him just before Hugh's regiment went over the top at Bellicourt, and they visited briefly after the fighting ceased (Green diary, PG-SHC).

3. Caro Mae and Erma.

4. Their other sister was studying music at the Durham Conservatory of Music in North Carolina.

5. Community in Harnett County.

6. Irving Johnson, Harnett County boy who was catcher on several baseball teams for which Paul pitched, had lost a leg in a battle during the summer.

## 5. To Erma Greene

Paris, France[1]
30 March 1919

Dearest Erma,

Last week I received a letter from you. Really I had begun to think that you had done with writing. But I know how busy you are, preparatory to finishing high school. Honey, I can't realize that my baby sister is a senior at Buie's Creek. Indeed, I can't. You remain in my memory as a little slip of a thing. And, oh, I wish that you always might remain that, yet you cannot—even as I write I realize that you are almost grown. When I was a boy I often wondered why the old mockingbirds made such a racket over their young ones when they were beginning to leave the old nest. Now I know exactly how and why. Even today Papa, Mary, John or I can hardly think of you as you used to stand in a chair and sing "Oh, lo-ey, he-hoey, and hush-a-by, baby" without the tears coming, you know. You know. This growing up must be endured; and may you and Caro in your womanhood make us as proud and fond of you as you did in your babyhood. Yes, it's strange that you and Caro are growing wise in books—study, study, and read and read—and then, when you have time write me a letter, just as you and Caro did this last week.

In truth I have been getting *beaucoup* mail during the last few days. Besides the letters, I received a book from Mary entitled *The New Poetry*.[2] I have been reading this book much of late—especially is it my companion on the subway—but I'm hardly in a position yet to criticise it. Although I like its freshness, I fear there is little of worth in it. All this swarm of *Vers librists*, this motley crowd of discordant street musicians, are poor ragged illegitimate children of the powerful Walt Whitman—nothing else. Still, I enjoy reading

1. After the war ended on 11 November 1918, Green finished Officers Candidate School in Langres on 2 December, then spent a few days in Paris, where on 14 December he was among the crowd welcoming President Woodrow Wilson into the city for the peace conference. Reassigned to his old unit, Company B of the 105th Engineers, as an acting second lieutenant, he spent a month with them, then on 18 January 1919 was assigned to the Disbursing Section of the Engineers in Paris, with offices in the Elysées Palace Hotel. His job—not strenuous—was to pay the French government for goods and services supplied to American troops and bill the French for goods and services provided by the United States.

2. An anthology of contemporary American and British poetry first published in 1917 and compiled by Harriet Monroe, editor of *Poetry*, a leading magazine for modernist verse. Mary had sent Paul a copy of the expanded second edition of 1919.

these verses; their jaggedness makes them hang in your mind. There are a few spring poems (Let me change pens!) that are very good,[3] and whenever I read them, I want to be home for the spring. Mary's letters telling about the flowers, sunny days and all that also make me want to go home worse than anybody knows.

Yes, I know that everything in the Old North State is waking to life now. I can smell the new grounds burning and see the smoke settling in the hollows. And it will not be long before the trees will be green and then the dogwoods will be blooming—and on and on. After a long time, I've learned that our farm is the prettiest place in the world. Even the Champs Elysées here in Paris with its budding acacia trees and rhododendron shrubs cannot compare with our dogwoods and grape-vined farm. The beautiful gardens all remind me of home, and I hope by the will of God to set my foot back there before many months. Do you want to see me? Do you feel my absence? Well, know this, that you don't *know* what it is to miss people as I miss everybody at home. Then you wonder why I came to Paris. Child, I came to learn something, to get a taste of beauty at first sight. And I have got it—am still getting it. I've climbed to places that made me dizzy with their terrible height.

Volumes could not hold all I've learned in these last two months. I've walked at least a thousand miles and ridden many more. Today I stand where kings lost their heads; tomorrow where saints were massacred. One hour I see the most marvelous creations of art; the next I see the most abject misery on earth crawling along the streets. And read! I read all the time. Day in, day out, I carry a book with me. Erma, I'm just beginning to wake up to see what there is to be learned—and I realize that my alphabet isn't learned yet. Oh, I wish I had nothing to do but read, study, read, study, and think—and think, and go to the grave with a book in my hand.[4]

3. Perhaps Sherwood Anderson's "American Spring Song," Robert Frost's "Mending Wall," Edna St. Vincent Millay's "Spring," Harriet Monroe's "On the Porch," Sara Teasdale's "Morning," or John Hall Wheelock's "Spring."

4. Usually Green's diary does not specify which works he read. ("Did nothing tonight but read and write" is a typical entry for the period.) In addition to *The New Poetry*, however, there are references to *The Adventures of Tom Sawyer* (Mark Twain), *The Blue Bird* and *The Betrothal* (Maurice Maeterlinck), *The Twilight of the Gods* (Richard Garnett), *Olympian Nights* (John Kendrick Bangs), *She Stoops to Conquer* (Oliver Goldsmith), *Hamlet* (which he vows to reread every month), *Peer Gynt* (Henrik Ibsen), several O. Henry stories, *The Rubáiyát of Omar Khayyám* (Edward FitzGerald), *The Golden Treasury of the Best Songs and Lyrical Poems in the English*

Along with learning things, I've met some of the keenest, most wide-awake minds in the world. Particularly am I thinking of a Mademoiselle Boislet who took me with her to see some treasures in the Louvre.[5] She is only 25 years old, slender, young-looking, dainty, like all Parisians, and yet she has the most marvelous mind of any woman I've ever met. She knows Grecian and Roman mythology from A to Z. In the Louvre we saw *Venus de Milo, Diana of the Chase,*[6] *Apollo,*[7] Michael Angelo's *Captives*[8] (all originals), *The Winged Victory of Samothrace,* and hundreds of other things by such men as Rodin, Barye, Barrias, Dubois, Bartholomé,[9] and others whom I forget just now. And the paintings! Later I shall tell you all about them. And this woman! She sees every beauty, she knows every fault. Before long I think I shall be a pretty fair art critic, if I keep reading, studying, and talking with her.

This afternoon I took my first tea among the intellectuals as they style themselves. And what a time I had! Such talk. For once in my life I felt happy. Every person present was gifted in some way—The brilliant conversation now in English, now in French went to my head like wine and never have I talked as I did with those eight persons. From the deepest bass note to the keenest treble I ran like the fool I was. Now it was Victor Hugo, now it was Molière; now it was Verlaine, the estaminet poet,[10] now Richepin,[11] and on and on.

Let me see if I remember who was present? First there were three elegant Frenchmen, one a member of the Russian Mission, another a sort of literary critic, and lastly a youth who is in charge of the Russian Library. Then there were the girls: Mademoiselle Boislet, her sister Cecile, her friends Jacqueline—and an Alsatian girl; Sgt. Pettit an old Latin teacher and long friend of Miss B's, and myself.

---

*Language* (Francis Palgrave), *Les Misérables* (Victor Hugo), several William James essays, and a few books on mythology and sculpture borrowed from friends.

5. For weeks Green had been visiting museums and galleries with an army buddy, Sergeant Pettit, and Pettit arranged for him to go to the Louvre with Voilet Boislet on 23 March. "Well, of all women she proved to be the most wonderful. Only 25 and lacks 2 months of having a Ph.D." (Green diary, PG-SHC).

6. Several possibilities.

7. Several possibilities.

8. Probably Michelangelo's *Two Slaves,* carved about 1513.

9. Current or recent French sculptors.

10. Barroom poet.

11. Poet and dramatist best known for his work in the 1890s, when his *Le Chemineau* rivaled Rostand's *Cyrano de Bergerac* in popularity.

Yes, we had a wonderful time talking of the gods and drinking chocolate. There is no danger of my forgetting this first *soirée* with the intellectuals, and there will be others. But I must close.

Oh, I hope I shall be home by June. Write me, honey, tell Papa and John to write. There's nothing like getting a letter from home.

Love to all, Paul

## 6. To Gladys Greene

Paris, France
9 May 1919

Dearest Gladys—

Honey, why don't you write to me? Just once now and then? This is the third letter I've written since I received a word from you. But I should think you are too busy to write to anyone. Now I understand; and if you must, why wait until your school is over. Whether you write or whether you don't, I'll understand, tho', to be sure, I want to know how you are faring.

Received a long letter from old Hugh today.[1] At the time of writing he had just returned from Monaco. Gladys, that boy's a bird, and like me, he is having the most profitable experience of his life, so I believe. If travelling can broaden one, he ought to have a good sound sense of the world when he returns. His letter of today has so many personal things in it that I cannot send it. I am, however, enclosing one which I received a short while ago.

Yes, 'tis true. I am having one of the most wonderful—well, in short, I am gathering knowledge which, I hope, will someday be worth the absence which is required. In no letter could I give you an idea of all I've seen, all I've learned, and all I've enjoyed. Wait until we meet. Can you imagine it—can you believe that soon two years will have passed since I saw you? But if all goes well, I shall be with you before September 1. Often I think that it will be too good to be true—But I must think of other things now.

Tomorrow I am going to Verdun.[2] And after getting back, I shall send you a few Kodak pictures of things of interest there.[3]

1. Following the armistice in November 1918, Hugh volunteered for extended service as an M.P. and spent most of his time in eastern France.

2. Area of the longest and costliest battle of the war (February to November 1916; German, French, and British casualties combined: 1.5 million).

3. On 10 May (Saturday) Green and an army buddy left the office at noon and took a train eastward. At Chateau Thierry they began seeing shell holes and American

Next week I shall go to Rheims, Chateau Thierry, and Bar-le-Duc; then to Amiens, Péronne, and Arras.[4] Possibly after that I shall be ready to go home. But will the C.O. be ready for me to go?

Oh, I wish you could be in Paris now. So much beauty, so much freshness, and so much laughter are here. No other city is like it—none. Now as I write, the flashy cars are humming on the Champs Elysées below me. Yes, it's all beautiful. And then, such momentous things are being done here. One feels as if his ear were leaning to the heart of the world.[5]

Am enclosing also a letter from Hugh's friends, Mon. et Mme. Simon.

Love and a thousand best wishes.

Hurriedly, Paul

---

graves, with a little American flag atop each grave. At 4:30 P.M. they got to Bar-le-Duc, where in a driving rain they walked about, admiring public statues and visiting the American military cemetery, then found lodging at the YMCA. Sunday morning they overslept, missed the train to Verdun, and took the noon train back to Paris. Hugh's unit was in the vicinity of Verdun, so Paul was doubly frustrated by his failure to get there (Green diary, PG-SHC).

4. Green did not make the northern trip (to Amiens, Péronne, and Arras, which marked the farthermost advance of the German army above Paris) until late June 1919, shortly before sailing for home (Green diary, PG-SHC).

5. Green admired President Wilson and his vision of a League of Nations (after a French acquaintance told Green, " 'I love the States but I hate their leader,' " Green noted, "Man, I bawled him out" [Green diary, 28 May 1919, PG-SHC]), and he followed the peace conference closely. When the leader of the Italian delegation threatened to withdraw, Green noted in his diary that there was "great excitement in town over Signor Orlando's withdrawal from the Peace Conference. But majority of the people are with Wilson, I think" (24 April 1919). One evening, unable to get into a crowded performance by Sarah Bernhardt for American troops, he "spent the night in reading and studying the Covenant of the League of Nations" (29 April 1919). The day before the present letter he "bought a map of Europe with which to follow Peace Conference" (8 May 1919).

## 7. To William A. Greene

Engineer Purchasing Office, Paris, France
16 May 1919

Dear Papa—

To-night I've been thinking of home, and so I must write a note. Whenever I feel the desire strongly to see everybody back there, I usually write, and then I'm reconciled to "Gay Paree" and everything she means.

As I've told you before, my work consists of helping to pay French Government bills. During these last days, business has been slowing up, and from the outlook now it appears that we shall have finished everything before the fall. Now don't worry; Hugh and I will be there before the old China tree turns yellow in September. Anyway, aren't you just a little pleased with us that we had grit enough to play the game through; that though we both wanted to go home, we realized that this was an opportunity of learning and experiencing things that would never come again? Really after every A.E.F.[1] man has left France you can say, "Well, my boys went into it, and they stayed (*of their own free will*) and saw the last inning played. One helped settle the thousand and one accounts; the other helped keep the peace of the country. Yes, they saw the whole thing through, and the pain of a few months of separation was overbalanced by the knowledge of the world they gained. Yes, as the Greenes ought, they played to the last hole." Can't you say that? Thank God, neither of us is so babyish that he dreams nightly of his bottle and nipple on the mantelshelf back home. We wanted to see something of the world, and we're seeing it, believe me. No. I'm not praising ourselves, I hope, but I want you to let bother pass when you see the boys coming home. Of course we want to go home, Hugh and I, but we can stick it out a little longer.

I'm having a pretty good time now—working at the office, playing ball, and studying. And how I enjoy the ball games in the Bois de Boulogne.[2] We have a league here, and the team that wins the pennant is to tour the A.E.F. Now our team is going to win that pennant—sure. The captain already has made arrangements concerning our traveling. My, what a time I'm going to have—from the Mediterranean to the bridgeheads of the Rhine. Oh, boy! But I shall write you about that more fully—later.[3]

1. American Expeditionary Force.

2. Large wooded park with open recreational areas on the western edge of Paris.

3. The Signal Corps won the pennant. The Engineers—Green's team, for which he pitched (with either hand) and played first base—won most of its games, but only one

Perhaps I've never mentioned in my letters of the time I've spent studying engineering since I came into the army. But how many hours I've pored over maps and tables no one knows. Since I knew nothing of engineering when I enlisted, I realized that I ought to know something about it, and at last I became a pretty good surveyor and, I believe, construction man. Anyway I know how to survey land and build any sort of military bridge needed, and a few other things.

And so, at last they sent me to a training camp, at Langres, but, as you know, I failed to capture a Sam Browne.[4] Well, on May 9 I—*at last*—was commissioned.[5] Yes, Sam Browne, bars, salutes, "sirs" and 'tenchuns, are mine now. Really I don't know how to take it—funny feeling. One day, an enlisted man; the next an officer.[6] Papa, for your sake I'm proud of this belated honor. If I had been a doughboy,[7]

## 8. To Gladys Greene

Paris, France
7 June 1919

Dearest Gladys—

In a letter from Mary yesterday, she told me that you were home again, that you were as happy as a lark, that you had made a wonderful record in school, and that your playing was wonderful. All of which made me wild with longing to be there. Though I cannot tell you face to face, let me tell you in this letter that I am proud to call you my sister. I am proud that you did not let the name of Greene fall, as some have done. And, child, keep dreaming your high dreams. All of them cannot come true, but some of them will, and therein lies our success. Height does not mean happiness, but it means usefulness, and

---

of the several played against the Signal Corps. Games and practice occupied two or three afternoons a week (Green diary, PG-SHC).

4. Leather belt and shoulder strap worn by officers, named for the British general who invented it.

5. Since leaving Langres in December 1918, Green had been an *acting* second lieutenant, which meant little. His pay did not increase, and in Paris he had to live at the barracks for enlisted men at Clignancourt.

6. On Sunday, 19 May, he walked about town for the first time in his new uniform and noted in his diary: "Ouch! What a funny thing to be reaping salutes where for 20 months I have been giving them" (Green diary, PG-SHC).

7. Surviving letter breaks off here.

usefulness is excuse enough for living; so I've found after two years in the army.

Further in her letter, Mary mentioned that everything was beautiful over there, and that the farm work was going along well enough. I'm very homesick for the beauty—tho' there is a world of beauty here—and I'm hungering for a chance to help in the farm work. Yes, I'd gladly give over my bars and Sam Browne for a pair of plow lines and a pair of overalls. And by honkey, it will not be long before the exchange will be made. On June 30—yes! yes!—I'm leaving for home. Now some hot day in July you're going to see me come blowing up the lane. And in three jerks of a sheep's tail I'm going to have my arms full of girls. Hugh will be there, too, before or soon after. Wonder how fodder-pulling will be after these months, these years, these centuries!

Mary also told me that Willie had *got married.*[1] I am still in a state of surprise, but further than that I have nothing to say.

Now come to Paris. Everything is beautiful here—at least it is to me. My work is heavy, but in the afternoons and nights I have marvelous pleasures. Now the word *marvelous* isn't one bit too strong. The parks, theatres, my books, and my friend Mlle. Renée Bourseiller make life a pleasure, never a burden.

May I tell you about Mlle. Bourseiller? Just a sentence or two.[2] She is one of the most refined, intelligent, and charming girls I've ever met—yes, the most. Educated in Paris, Berlin, and London. You may know that her conversation is interesting to me. Since she is a perfect lady, and different from most girls I've met, I cannot but enjoy every minute spent with her. 'Twould surprise you to know how much time we spend together. Every afternoon I dress up, eat supper and go to her home. Then we take our books and go to the Bois de Boulogne. What a time we have reading English and French poetry. Tomorrow, Sunday, we are going to take lunch to the *Lantern of Diogenes* in the

1. Their cousin and neighbor Willie Cutts had married a local boy, Vernon Stacy.

2. During Green's first months in Paris, he spent time with a Red Cross nurse from Nebraska, Miss Cummings, but by late March their relationship began to cool. On receiving his commission in early May, he moved from the barracks for enlisted men at Clignancourt to a room in the home of Mme. Cassord in Boulogne. Renée Bourseiller, who lived with her mother and worked in Paris, was a neighbor and friend of Mme. Cassord. On 26 May she visited Mme. Cassord, met Green, and the two talked the evening away (Green diary, PG-SHC).

woods outside of Paris and stay all day—just we two.[3] By the way, tell Caro and Erma they will find in *Les Misérables* something about the *Lantern of Diogenes.*[4] Among the Kodak pictures I'm sending you are three of Mlle. Bourseiller. But more of this subject when I get home.

I wish you could have been here on Memorial Day. My letter would be too long to tell of the exercises there, but you can read it in my diary some day.[5] Mr. Wilson made a beautiful speech.[6] Among the notables were a dozen or more peers, Marshal Foch,[7] M. André Tardieu,[8] Mr. Wallace,[9] and of course Mrs. Wilson. One time Mr. Wilson was moved to tears. If there ever was a man sincere in what he proposes, that man is our President. As I came away from the cemetery, I heard one doughboy say to another, "I'd follow that man clean to hell and back." And we would, all of us.[10] The other day one boy from our office met Mr. Wilson on the Champs Elysées. Of course he pulled off his best salute. But you could have killed him with a feather when Mr. Wilson, instead of passing by, stopped and said, "Good evening, son," asked him how

3. At St. Cloud, just across the Seine from Boulogne, Napoleon I had a palace and atop an adjacent hill built a light tower, the Lantern of Demosthenes. The light burned whenever he was in residence there, and in popular parlance the tower took the more appropriate name, the Lantern of Diogenes (*Baedeker's Paris and its Environs* [1888], p. 298). Paul and Renée found a secluded spot beyond the tower "where running ivy made a thick carpet [and] made our home. Read and talked all day long, took pictures of each other, and came home in the evening. Took dinner with her and her mother" (Green diary, 8 June 1919, PG-SHC).

4. In part 1, book 3, chapter 3, Fantine is in a group that also visits the Lantern of Diogenes.

5. Green devoted eleven pages of his diary to the ceremony on 30 May 1919 in the American Army Cemetery at Suresnes, where 1,500 U.S. soldiers were buried (Green diary, PG-SHC).

6. Which Green found "tender, noble, warlike and yet hopeful and trusting," and which reminded him of the "Gettysburg Address."

7. Commander in chief of the French, British, and American armies at the end of the war.

8. Prominent member of the French delegation to the Versailles Peace Conference.

9. Hugh Campbell Wallace, U.S. ambassador to France.

10. Following the speech came Chopin's "Funeral March" and taps, then "Mr. Wilson descended from the stand and laid a wreath of flowers on a private's grave, and drove away to shoulder again, like Atlas, his burden of the world."

he liked the army, where he lived in the states, and a few other things. Of course Mr. Wilson could not speak to every soldier he meets, but then, he rarely walks out. Now I'm convinced that in such actions, our President is not playing the Kronprinz's game of kindness. No.[11]

Next week I'm going to visit the Somme region. Some of my friends sleep up there, Rass Matthews, Charlie Speas, Lt. Marrian, and others. I hope to get a photograph of their graves.[12]

But it's time for supper. I must close.

Has papa ever heard from my liberty bonds? Months ago I wrote to the bank in N.Y. to send them to the Bank of Lillington.

I'm not saving much money now. Board, room, and laundry cost me $80 per month.

Love—love, Paul[13]

11. Edward, prince of Wales (later Edward VIII, then duke of Windsor), was with his father George V when he visited Green's unit at Ypres (letter 3, n. 10) and since the armistice had received much attention for his efforts to associate with common soldiers—British, Commonwealth, and American. In February he came to Paris, where his activities were reported in newspapers daily.

12. Matthews, from Harnett County and with Green since the days at Camp Sevier, was the only one whose grave Green found. Matthews had been killed at Busigney near the end of the war, but when Green got a pass on 25 June and took a train to Reims, then to Lille, he could make connections for Busigney at neither place. Frustrated, he returned to Paris on the afternoon of 27 June, saw a Charlie Chaplin movie, and spent the evening with Renée. On 2 July he and Hugh decided to make one more attempt. They got a train to Busigney, hiked all night into the country, and next morning a farmer "took us thro' his deserted barnyard out into his orchard and there we found several English and American soldiers. Rass was among them." Green sketched the cemetery. They paid the farmer 150 francs to tend Rass's grave and returned to Paris, arriving at 10:30 P.M. (Green diary, PG-SHC).

13. On 4 July, the day after finding Rass's grave, Green took the train to Brest, on 7 July boarded the transport ship *Victoria*, and sailed on 9 July. The restful crossing was disturbed for him only by the fact that black officers and men were segregated from whites. On 18 July the *Victoria* docked at New York harbor, and Green took an overnight train for North Carolina. Hugh did not return until September, when Paul was back in school at Chapel Hill (Green diary, PG-SHC).

## 9. To Elizabeth Lay[1]

[Chapel Hill, N.C.]
Sunday morning [Spring 1920]

Dear Elizabeth—

Last night was a mess, wasn't it? I'm sorry if I was so blokish-like the evening through—I was just lost in everybody else, tho' my actions didn't show it—That was it. But I was tired and blue and whipped—by something the meaning of which I don't understand. And, too, I'm sorry about the way I acted toward Prof. Koch—[2] After I had gone to bed last night I thought and thought about him, trying to get a line on him—by imagining, for one thing, all sorts of professors in his place. And he himself was the only man I could imagine trying such a daring thing. And I know—me with my changing moods—[I] must try to overlook his indefiniteness, for after all this indefiniteness permeated by an everlasting childish enthusiasm and trust is what makes the "she-bang" go—if it is going—I hardly know why I am taking time to scratch this bundle of words to you. They don't mean nothing. But I woke up this morning so down in the dumps that things ain't right. And I reckon one reason for my blueness is that last night was thrown away. Of course I'm the one who did the throwing, and so I condemn myself for it. I did a little work on the poem last night after I came back, but I wasn't interested and I'm not now. It will be a dead number, for I'm writing it because I'm forced to. I don't feel it—Don't work too hard on those plays. I'm afeerd on it!

Paul

1. Elizabeth Lay (6 April 1897–21 May 1989), who had graduated from UNC in 1919, directed the Bureau of Community Drama founded by Frederick Koch to assist drama groups throughout the state and traveled with the tours of Carolina Playmakers productions. At the time of the present letter she had just gone on tour with the fourth series of productions (to be staged 30 April and 1 May 1920 in Chapel Hill), which included Green's first play with the Playmakers, "The Last of the Lowries."

2. Frederick H. Koch (1877–1944) came to UNC from the University of North Dakota in the fall of 1918 and immediately set about developing the Carolina Playmakers to encourage the writing and production of original plays. Many of the plays are published in the series of books Koch edited entitled *Carolina Folk-Plays* (including two by Elizabeth, "When Witches Ride" and "Trista," in the 1941 volume). In Green's view, Koch lacked the ability to analyze.

## 10. To Elizabeth Lay

Lillington, [N.C.]
30 June [1920]

Dear Elizabeth—

Do you remember how you used to open a package of long-expected books, and how that night you read and read? It was just like that with me when your poem, letter, and other things came. I dived right in and read them all. Since then I've re-read them; but even yet I am not prepared to criticise. The rhyme-scheme and meter are delightful in your poem. As for the imagery and theme (if it has one) I'm not just prepared to say. And that impressive study "que vous avez"—etc. is beautiful, considering it is the work of an eighteen-year-old girl.[1] As for the philosophy thesis, I am weak there. Next Sunday I shall try to understand and criticise. Now I come to your letter. It was, of course, best of all—(oh, I hear a whippoorwill down the lane. He sings every night—never changing his song—but—). Everything is quite clear in it. And I'm glad you explained. It's best to be blunt even if the bluntness hurts? Don't you think so?

To-night I'm tired—(I almost quoted Henry Berry)—dog-tired.[2] It has been a hard day on the farm.—(Why, yes, I work on the farm, hard like a nigger. Everybody works around papa.) I shan't try to write a decent letter to-night. I shall devote the whole of next Sunday to you and your writings. Of course this devotion is to include the preparation of some of my poems—junk, for you. I'm still writing something every night. My program doesn't allow for much poetical musings though. I get up at five, take two hours for noon and quit at seven-thirty P.M., finish supper at 8:30, play the violin perhaps an hour, and then read and write an hour. So you see that Sunday is the only time I can do any real thinking.

I have just received a letter from Dr. Greenlaw[3] concerning the scholarship—fellowship, rather—which you mention. It's grand of him to be so kind, but really I doubt that I shall be able to take it when the time comes. There will have to be something better attached to it if I do, at least I think so now.[4]

1. Elizabeth was eighteen in 1915 and going into her final year at St. Mary's. The study was one she did then, or was by someone else, or Green's remark is a joke.

2. Henry Berry Lowrie, in Green's "The Last of the Lowries" (in rehearsal for performances in Chapel Hill on 22 and 23 July), says "I'm tired, damned tired."

3. Edwin A. Greenlaw (1874–1931), chairman of the Department of English at UNC.

4. Green returned to UNC in the fall with a teaching assistantship (one section of freshman English each quarter).

Oh, I should like to see "Riders to the Sea" but I think I shall be busy when it is given.[5]

I'm hungry for that course you're taking under Dr. Royster.[6] Learn enough for two, please.

Best wishes, Paul

By the way, last night I read your study of the shrines and after that I read some stories in the O. T. and I came across a momentous piece of writing, unapproachable simplicity and right choice of words. Please read II Kings IV, 18–21. You know the story. I think the word "grown" in verse 18 is translated wrong.[7]

## 11. To Elizabeth Lay

[Lillington, N.C.]
Tuesday night [July 1920]

Dear Elizabeth—

Just a note to let you know that I received your letter after yesterday's mail had taken mine away. Now I feel that there was little use in writing what I did yesterday or the day before. Please understand what I said just as you see fit. Your letter with its assurance that I in no way exert an enervating influence—if you want to call it that—over you has cancelled all those words. They mean nothing now. And so we can go on writing with perfect frankness and good-will and forget this bursting bubble of foolishness in an ocean of frank, clean friendship, can't we?

I'm sorry about the operation.[1] But I'm sure you're brave enough to stand it

5. On 19 July a troupe from the Abbey Theatre in Dublin headed by Frank McEntee was to present two of John Synge's plays in Chapel Hill, "Riders to the Sea" (which inspired "The Last of the Lowries") and "In the Shadow of the Glen."

6. James F. Royster (1880–1930), visiting UNC from the University of Texas, gave a course that summer entitled "Tendencies in Recent English and American Poetry." Royster would join the UNC Department of English in 1921.

7. The Hebrew verb translated "grown" in the King James Version means "to become big." The story, about a son who dies in his mother's lap, suggests a child rather than a man, and recent translations, taking advantage of the indefiniteness of the verb, make his age at the time of his death consistent with the rest of the story. In the *Good News Bible*, for instance, he dies "some years" after his birth.

---

1. A tonsillectomy forthcoming for Elizabeth.

with a smile. After all ether isn't so bad. I speak from experience, since I once had a long grind at Johns-Hopkins.[2] And the novelty of ether-land is worth all the pain, if there is any, and discomfort.

The programs[3] are quite interesting. But more interesting is what you have to say about the modern poetry course. I'm glad you like it. For years I've been wrapped up in Masefield, Millay, Teasdale, Lindsay, and a host of others. It seems to me that they have a better grasp of man's place in nature than all the Shelleys, Keatses, and Byrons that time has afforded, and then their verse is not lacking in freshness and imagery. Teasdale or Millay literally "wallows" in sights, sounds, and perfumes of a luxuriant flower world. Really I like all these poets. It's fine that you are using *The New Poetry* as a textbook. You and I can talk with more knowledge since we each have a copy. When the book first came out I bought it[4] and you may be sure that I haven't regretted it. Some of my favorite lyrics, crushed rose leaves, I call them, are "The Old Woman"—p. 38; "Spanish Johnny," p. 44; the battle lyrics of Gibson; "Watching by a Sick-bed," p. 203; "God's World," p. 225; "The Flight," p. 335; "Songs in a Hospital," and others, and others.[5]

I'm anxious to get your notes on the poetry course. I know of nothing I should enjoy reading more. Please send them and a copy of your paper on tragedy in Masefield.

I've just re-read Brooke's sonnet, "The Dead," and if you listen I'm sure you will know that I echo all you said about "proudly friended."[6]

Goodnight—Paul

2. Where a metal pin was inserted in his right arm for osteomyelitis when he was ten.

3. For the Playmakers production of "The Last of the Lowries" and two other plays in Chapel Hill on 22 and 23 July.

4. Green's sister Mary sent it to him while he was in Paris.

5. Page references are to Harriet Monroe and Alice Corbin Henderson, eds., *The New Poetry*, 2d ed. (New York: Macmillan, 1919), which Royster assigned in his course on modern British and American poetry. The poems, in order, are by Joseph Campbell, Willa Cather, Wilfrid Wilson Gibson, John Masefield, Edna St. Vincent Millay, and Sara Teasdale (the last two).

6. From Rupert Brooke's "The Dead" (*New Poetry*, p. 31), part 4 of his "Nineteen-Fourteen."

## 12. To Elizabeth Lay

Lillington, [N.C.]
Wednesday P.M. [August 1920]

Dear Elizabeth—

I guess you're out of the hospital by this time. Hospital life, the life of a patient, must agree with you, if I am to judge your feeling from what your letter says. Your few paragraphs gave me the hospital atmosphere, all right. And the bit about the woman and her snuff was Maupassantian, to be sure, in its mirror-like qualities. In this connection you make the remark, "Life is funny after all," and I want to launch out into a tirade—no panegyric, remember—upon the funniness of life. Since you already have topped me home there, I shall go no further, however. And it would be easy for me to say a great deal, for a few minutes ago I finished a book on birds, flowers, and bees, their characteristics, habits, etc. But what impressed me more than anything in the whole book was the unmistakable evidence that some power above and outside moved these creatures of an hour, a day; or else they have an intelligence far superior to ours, which, of course, we shall never acknowledge. Once I saw a "Venus-flytrap." The thing was uncanny in its actions, a sort of half-animal and half-plant. Yes, life is funny, funny. I can't understand one thing, nothing. Each particle of matter is so tangled up in its relations with every other particle of matter in existence that only a divine mind can in any way begin to grasp the significance of it. How absolutely ignorant is man. He knows nothing and can never know anything. He might as well take his tin cup of ignorance, with a sign-board of despair around his neck, and travel the ways of the world, crying to the gods that ain't, "Blind! blind! Help the blind!" In reality, judged by the eternity of time, that's about all that he does. God's talk to Job out of the whirlwind could be applied to man of to-day. All of His "where wast thou?"-s would receive no answer now.[1]—But I must stop this, for you will think I'm narrow to talk so. After all it won't do to stand off too far and judge everything so objectively, will it? One grows so awry, so blue, so funny. But "life is so funny," isn't it?

I'm anxious to get your notes on the poetry course. Can't you send them soon? And what about some verses? But I'm terribly slow there too. Perhaps I shall be able to work up something during the next few days. At the present I'm laid up with a wrenched back—got it in a baseball game, too much pitching, two games in succession. To-morrow I shall try to get up something.

1. Job 38.

Right now I'm too inert to think or do anything but read something enjoyable. And truly *The New Poetry* comes in for its share. I once told Dr. Hanford[2] that I enjoyed modern poets far more than Shelley, Keats, Byron, and the others, and that I feared there must be something wrong with my make-up. But now I don't feel so badly lost since I find that you and others have liked Masefield, Frost, Teasdale, and the rest in the book. Don't you like the poem on page 335?[3] There's something poets call "poignant" in it. The refrain, "But what if I heard my first love calling me again?," is like "a sob in the midst of cheering."[4]

Elizabeth, your letter, as they all are, was an inspiration. Somehow after hearing from you I feel as if I might accomplish something in this world. You help a great deal, and if I weren't so all-fired despondent or what not your help would be worth more. I must be lazy. Here's the whole summer gone and I haven't written more than twenty poems (not poems but fragments). Tomorrow I shall begin getting up a bundle for you.

Best wishes, Paul

## 13. To Elizabeth Lay

Lillington, [N.C.]
22 August 1920

My dear Elizabeth—

I've just finished several letters that I dreaded writing and now it's certainly a relief to talk to you. I wanted to write you as soon as I got the notes,[1] but so many baseball games were on deck I had to shelve it. And, too, there was the matter of poems. I felt I couldn't write without sending something! And now the ball games are past [and] I've written a few things, I'm writing this. As soon as I secure a large envelope I shall mail you some stuff.[2] Most of this

2. James Holly Hanford (1882–1969), professor of English at UNC, who taught English romantic poetry.

3. "The Flight" by Sara Teasdale.

4. From another Teasdale poem, "Morning" (*New Poetry*, pp. 334–35).

---

1. From Royster's course in modern poetry.

2. It was over a week before Green sent her his poems, which he was pretty sure were "trash" and knew were unfinished. "If I ever get time to revise anything I'll do it for your sake," he said, "though to be honest with you, I've never taken writing poetry

afternoon I spent in studying your notes and reading *The New Poetry*. I don't know how to thank you enough for taking the course for me. I know what the word *proxy* means now. I've got a concept of it. Heffner writes me that Seeger was his favorite poet.[3] But I can't see how he can prefer such a boyish verse writer to a man like Masefield or one like Gibran. Anyway he liked Alan well enough to write a paper on him.

And this reminds me of your Masefield paper. Just now I can't give judgment upon it. Your sentences in it *whop* me into a labyrinth often with the minotaur after me seeing red. By this I just mean you've got a mighty deep min(e)d—often too deep for me.

Do you know I've got a thousand questions to ask you about the poetry course, and if I ever meet up with you again it will be a reproduction of the Ancient Mariner and wedding-guest drama.[4] I'll hold you with my "glittering eye" and I shall have my "will."

What do you suppose? I've been teaching a Bible class this summer. Once I was a regular Sunday School worker but I outgrew it. Now I'm into it again—one who hasn't a shred of faith in anything or anybody as far as "religiosity" goes. Our lesson to-day was a puzzler to me.[5] Old David puts up a swell prayer, is forgiven by God, mends his ways, and everything goes along well enough. But what about old Uriah? He sleeps beneath an already matted tombstone. How settle his side of the question? Really I'm not much on this "to every man perfect justice" sort of doctrine. All don't receive equity at the hands of the Gods, or non-gods, if you wish. There is a god of Chance (see

---

as anything more than a pastime. . . . One who loves baseball and such things better than poetry will never be a poet" (Paul Green to Elizabeth Lay, 31 August 1920, EG-SHC). Not much of Green's early poetry was published, but an example is "Song of the Dead ('America First')," *New Carolina Magazine*, n.s., 38, no. 3 (December 1920): 41. The poem, forty-seven lines long, laments the suffering and destruction of war and is written from the point of view of soldiers who died in World War I.

3. Hubert C. Heffner (b. 1901), who would have a distinguished career in three university theater programs (UNC, Stanford, and Indiana), was at the time a fellow undergraduate at UNC (B.A., 1921; M.A. in English, 1922) and a member of the Playmakers. He also took the summer course in modern poetry and wrote his paper on Alan Seeger (1888–1916), American poet killed in the war in France, whose *Poems* (New York: Charles Scribner's Sons, 1916) shows his devotion to "my three idols—Love and Arms and Song" (p. 145).

4. In Samuel Taylor Coleridge's poem.

5. From 2 Samuel 11 and 12, the story of David, Bathsheba, and her husband Uriah.

Haeckel)[6] stronger than any Moloch of iron or Buddha of spirit, it seems to me. *Requiescat.*[7]

Now your letter! And what a letter. Quite an effort for a cur pup. If you can write such jolly, "lackadaisical" (your word) letters in that puppish mood, then I cry out, "Long live the pup!" Indeed it was one of the most enjoyable letters I've ever read—due no doubt to the fact that when I received it I was in a "blue Monday" trance. It was just what I needed.

How is the weather in Beaufort?[8] (Lovely name, Beaufort.) It's awful here. Hot, hot, hot, and rain, rain, rain. Right now a cloud is making in the west; and the poor moon, pale sad lady of the sky, is shivering and preparing to put on her rain-coat. She has always reminded me, especially on stormy nights, of the banshee wandering across a lonely moor in Ireland, wringing her hands and wailing over the death about to happen.

But I've got to stop—two poems to write to-night, and it's late now. Are you going back on the 15th?[9] You mention it.

Best wishes, Paul

I've fed the hogs over this letter. Such a pue! *Excusez-moi*!

## 14. To Elizabeth Lay

[Chapel Hill, N.C.][1]
[Fall 1920] Sunday night—7:30

Dear Elizabeth—

I've just received your letter—the one mailed to Lillington. And reading it, I've decided that a good kicking is what I need most in this world. How could

6. Ernst Haeckel (1834–1919), German zoologist whose *The Riddle of the Universe* (trans. 1900), particularly chapter 14, describes a universe devoid of any moral or divine order and subject only to the blind chance of Darwinian natural selection.

7. *Requiescat in pace*—rest in peace.

8. Where Elizabeth's parents had recently moved. She was there recovering from her operation.

9. To Chapel Hill.

---

1. Green had just returned to school after dropping out and spending about two weeks on his father's farm. Many years later he said he quit school in a fit of despair. He remembered "how discouraged I got with everything. I seemed to lose my faith in the righteousness of the universe, and especially my trust in the humanity of man." Also he was "broke." Then one "hot afternoon while I was following the mule up and

I cause you so much wearying uncertainty! It was shameful to act in such a way. I will not ask your pardon. Sins are never pardoned, though often they are fondly overlooked. What an opinion you must have of me! Did you really think I could go away so easily? Goodness, it's worse than a "Just for a handful of silver he left us" sort of going.[2] Indeed, I had to go home because of my father and the—panic.[3] He's lost a great deal on account of the low prices and I wanted to be sure he could afford to help me through college, for it happens I've gone flat busted in the scramble. I invested a lot of time and money (all I had) last summer,[4] hoping to get rich this fall, and bang! down I went. Now the doctor part was spoken of in earnest, but all else jokingly. I thought you understood. If I had known how it was, I should have written you at once or come back in a hurry. You see I realise how you felt, I think, for I can imagine you running off like that, leaving me with nothing to do but conjecture as to everything. Give me a mental kick, shrug your shoulders, and say *tant pis* (s'no matter), and let it go at that. And let me plead "first offense" as an excuse.

My dear, your letter touched me deeply. I guess you'll never say anything that will touch me more deeply than the passage beginning, "I'm sitting over the fire just as we did the other night" and ending "But even if I must always sit over the ashes of our dreams, I'll try to make my life," etc. God is good, but the mystery of life is still before me. Oh, I wish I could be swept away on the wings of an ideal love, nothing physical in it. Why can't one drown himself in the shining sea! You know how I feel and it's good to know you sympathize with me there. But why can't "that which drew from out the boundless deep" turn "again home" in this physical world?[5] Is it because the home doesn't exist here on earth, or is it that a remembrance of "trailing clouds of glory"[6] makes

---

down the row I suddenly seemed to come to myself. 'What am I doing here,' I asked the air around me. This is not my life. I should be back at the university studying and trying to find my way forward" (Paul Green to Janet Green, 6 March 1952).

2. Opening line of "The Lost Leader" (1843), Robert Browning's poem about William Wordsworth's betrayal (as it seemed to Browning) of liberal political ideals when he accepted a pension and the office of poet laureate from the conservative government.

3. In the fall of 1920 farm prices plunged: cotton from thirty-five cents per pound in 1919 to fifteen cents; tobacco, from thirty-one to seventeen cents.

4. In a tobacco crop.

5. Alfred Tennyson, "Crossing the Bar," lines 7–8.

6. William Wordsworth, "Intimations of Immortality," line 64.

him dissatisfied with all that tends to bind one to earth? I risk a guess that you and I shall never know. Excuse me for quoting so much, but the poets help one out when he is philosophical and sentimental.

I think that after our talk out on the hill this afternoon, we understand each other a little better. Remember, too, that if I fail to be dipped in the Jordan seven times, it's not that anything's wrong with the Jordan,[7] but that the trouble's in me. If my God answered prayers, I should ask him first to give me a responsive soul (a regular sea in itself), a soul responsive to what I love. Is there a contradiction here? Christ said, however, that he who thirsts "after righteousness shall be filled."[8] Teach me this righteousness. Help me if you can, so that life will not cheat me of the one supreme gift—an all absorbing love. You know that's what I pray for.

Always—Paul

## 15. To Elizabeth Lay

[Chapel Hill, N.C.]
Sunday night [Early October 1920]

Dear Child—

Excuse me for addressing you thus, but your letter has just come and it's so full of jumping, kiddish *abandon* that I see the face of a child staring from its pages. And too, I'm so far removed to-night from that mood that I can only touch you with the gloved fingertips of imbecile old age. Rather strange. But the blue devils have been in my room all day. They sit on my bookshelf and jeer at me, they blow their tiny wisps of poisonous breath in my face, crowd around my pen point, pit-pat they walk on my shoulder and touch my cheek with their hot little tongues, they prick my hands with their sharp tridents, and now and then I shiver when one of them touches my neck with his tiny clammy webbed hand. Indeed, they're a fearful lot. Most of the afternoon one has been sitting on my violin box looking at me. And looking up a few minutes ago, I saw him, and saw him as he was. For an instant, a queer shock ran through me. I saw in that tiny imp myself, myself as I would look in a distant concave mirror. Oh, there is no study so profitless and so interesting as the study of one's self. One is apt to discover—so little!

7. In 2 Kings 5, Elisha tells Naaman to bathe in the Jordan River seven times if he would be cured, and the haughty general at first refuses, thinking it too easy a cure.

8. Matthew 5:6.

There are times when I am a stranger to this world. All that I generally love and admire seems to fall far behind me like the lone trees in a field to one passing on a train. I don't know what makes it. There are times I love something with all my strength, later it doesn't strike a sympathetic chord in me. To-day, tears will come to my eyes because of a rush of emotion. To-morrow I will wonder at it, really doubt that it was I who was so strangely moved. To-night I will shudder at some sin committed in the past, and to-morrow night I will wonder at it, and not care a snap for all the sins in the world. Often I fall to musing on the insignificance of *it all*—you know—and then it is that I, like a miserly jeweler, look upon my stock of jewelry. I find many, many pretty rings—save for the settings. They're always empty—little cruel holes for eyes. And I know that I'm the man who stole them, sold them and spent the money. To-night I've been counting my stock. You see?

Oh, you must see, Elizabeth. I am hurting something real. You have already found it. Can't you teach me that all things are good.[1] No, I'm not asking for your love. But won't you help me to find in you the proof that "God's in his heaven"?[2] It's not pleasant to live with little faith in anybody and none in yourself. You're right in saying that I have more faith in the future, more faith in you than I did at first. But I want something more, something to anchor to. As you hinted in your letter, I don't want to be

> Lost as a sob in the midst of cheering,
> Swept as a sea-bird out to sea.[3]

And you have helped me wonderfully. The fire in me was almost dead, but you have fanned it—almost—into a flame. It is burning now. I do want to do something *worthwhile*. But what is it! And if I ever accomplish anything, I shall owe most of it to you. For you can never know just how much I've crippled my own life, yes, hobbled myself for the race, when the victory was to go to the swiftest-footed. And since I was so self-crippled, I found in you something that has helped me along wonderfully.

When I came to the Hill last fall, I was pretty near down and out. There's no slipping around there. It's the truth. No one but myself will ever know just how near I was to quitting the game. True that I began my studies and made pretty good marks. It was nearly mechanical—even to most of the play-

1. Green's punctuation. Frequently in this letter he ends questions with periods.
2. Robert Browning, *Pippa Passes.*
3. Sara Teasdale, "Morning."

writing. Back of it all there was a blackness, a void, a place of dust-choked voices. And then something began to change, a tiny beam of light struggled to pierce the darkness. The light grew. It warmed. It was you. And because of you I am nearer what I think a man ought to be.

And yet there remains one cavern into which no light can come. I digged it! I know! My sisters don't think I've ever been wicked, that I ever helped the devil with his traps. They tell me that it's not like me to be low. It's not. But *me* used to be *me* only a day at a time. To-morrow *me* might be *he.* And so because of this, I shall never let myself love you, nor let you love me. That is the law of the Medes and Persians. I know that I said a few days ago that I loved you. But it was done impulsively. I regret it. It wasn't true. I never shall. This isn't what most men would say to you. But sharp brick-bat words of truth are better, I've learned, than lie-glazed palliations. I'm sure they will be better now in our case.

Now you may smile at some of the things I've said, but I think we are just a little nearer to understanding each other in that we know that we can go so far and no farther. By that, I mean that we can be good friends, comrades, but nothing more. I mustn't keep on talking about "so far and no farther," but I can say finally that if I should find someday that I loved you, I would kill that love—dead. No matter how strong it might be I'd kill it! And there might be a sort of savage delight in doing it, since the primitive and civilized aren't so very far apart, as we learned at the Pickwick[4] last night.

Along with this letter, I'm mailing one I wrote last Friday night, immediately after getting the one you wrote Thursday night. It's been lying here on my table, sealed, addressed, and stamped, but somehow I've hesitated about letting it go. Whatever's in it—I've forgot—is an expression of what I felt at that time, no matter how much it may differ from what's in this.[5]

Doesn't it make you feel worthless to plan to do a great deal, and in the end do nothing. Often I say I shall never make another resolution. But I always do, and straightway break it. Last Friday evening I made out a list of things to do by Monday morning. Here they are. The X denotes those I've completed.

4. Motion picture theater in Chapel Hill.

5. The Friday night letter elaborates the point of the two previous paragraphs here, that his declaration of love on Thursday night was done on impulse, that his emotions are frighteningly strong and he is fighting to control them, and that henceforth "I *won't* give you anything but my friendship, I *won't*, and you *shant* give me anything more. Do you hear!" (undated, EG-SHC).

1. Write negro meeting poem (300 lines).
2. Study Greek 3 hrs.

X 3. Read French.

4. Write notes on Comparative Literature.

X 5. Write letters—to—etc.

6. Write scenario for 3-act play.
7. Read literature of Charlemagne's Reign.

X 8. Write speech for Prof. Koch and revise "Caper play."[6]

Now you see I've completed only the easiest ones. Another failure registered. What makes it so easy to say "I will" and so easy to do "I won't"? Everyone is greedy, more or less, usually more, and naturally bites off more than he can chew.

This frailty is apparent in our saying we are going to work up a pageant for *Souvenir de Virginia Dare.* Of course we say we will. And of course we—won't. And yet I'm a little *enthused* over the pageant idea too.

Yes, Mr. Heffner has consulted with me about the Caper. In fact he consulted with me all last night until 4:30 this morning. It's a mess.

Please, my lady, don't start "a voice in the cheering crowd" sort of stuff. If I didn't have such a high opinion of your seriousness I'd laugh at you, laugh long, too. I think so much of your friendship that a few words from you mean enough. Never put many to work. That's not you. When you feel deepest you say least. You say you wish *everyone else* would criticise. Well here goes just a few strokes. Take "When Witches Ride," for instance.[7] It's a great play. I like it, but there are a few places where I think you could improve it. One is where Jake goes outside to dig Phoebe's grave. Measured by his "sensible" conversation, he is not down enough to make such a foolish proposal. And I'm sure that in real life he would not go out to dig Phoebe's grave. Isn't this a device to get Jake outside so he may see the devil. A better device could be used.

The second weak place is where Ed, Jake, and Uncle Benny make such a to-do about the frog's having moved. Are frogs supposed to sit still forever.

6. On 15 October 1920 the Playmakers presented a Carolina Playmakers Caper, which spoofed Koch with a performance of "Kochomania," described on the program as by Henry Berry Green, Phoebe Ward Lay, and Dodgast Ye Heffner. (Berry is the central character in Green's "Last of the Lowries," as is Ward in Lay's "When Witches Ride." Heffner's most recent play was a comedy, "Dod Gast Ye Both!")

7. Elizabeth's play depicting an evening spent by the witch Phoebe Ward with three men, one of whom, Jake, does not at first believe she has supernatural powers.

Another device to get the audience to wonder how the frog did move and when. Isn't it? Why not change these places before you send the play off.[8]

Now I've already mentioned some criticisms I had to make on "Peggy."

1. Cotton at 30 c. and labor $1.25 day? No. Out of proportion.[9]

2. Shouldn't Jed address May as "Miss May." A young farm hand who hopes to marry a girl like Peggy would hardly address her mother flatly—"May."

3. Page 8. Peggy should say "go off ter school." She has been to school.[10] Modern times, cotton 30 c.

4. Page 16–17. Not enough time elapses between Herman's going for the McDonalds and their return.

5. P. 9. Peggy says "Did he say it were dangerous?" Plainly used to gain suspense etc.

6. P. 11. The bread hasn't had time to cook.

7. P. 22. McDonald is entirely too hard. Not possible that he should speak so carelessly of Warren's body. Overdrawn here.

All of these observations are made from my viewpoint of the tenant people, as I know them in my County. And Williamson's home (Carthage, N.C.) isn't many hundreds of miles from mine.[11] Why not ease up on poor North Carolina landlords just a little bit?

Well, cold weather is coming as you say, and there's danger that our poetry (?) will suffer frost bite or something as bad. We ought not to mind that. If we turn the Greene-Lay textbook—which certainly could be nothing but our lives—loose upon the world, it will have to be able to stand more than cold weather, you know! Suppose the world weren't so officious, we could sit by my fire at night and write, and I could walk home with you and shiver with the stars. No, we won't encroach upon the inhabitants of *La petite maison.*[12] They

8. She did not revise "When Witches Ride" for publication in Koch, *Carolina Folk-Plays* (1922 and 1941). The same volumes show that "Peggy," another Playmakers play that Green now turns to, by fellow student Harold Williamson, also was not revised before publication. "Peggy" is about a girl's inability to escape from the harsh life of a sharecropper, her failure finally assured by the death of her father and the insensitivity of their landlord McDonald.

9. The wage is low.

10. Her remark is: "(*looking out of the window, wistfully*) I reckon it'd be nice to go to school" (Koch, *Carolina Folk-Plays* [1941], p. 26).

11. In fact, it is about forty.

12. Where Elizabeth lived, at the corner of Franklin and Hillsborough streets in Chapel Hill.

would tie a can to poetry's tail, and Chapel Hill would be awakened some night like the Turks when Bozzaris fell upon them.[13]

Please forgive this long letter. I got started and couldn't stop. After this you will know what's meant by "pouring out one's soul."

Yes, I shall be glad to serve on the committee. And you needn't blow me up about publicity. Doubt as you may, I was in earnest last spring.

Life would be strange if you should go away and never come back. I've missed you, missed you these few days.

Good night—Paul

## 16. To Elizabeth Lay

Lillington, [N.C.]
Tuesday A.M. [28 December 1920]

Dear Elizabeth—

I have decided not to make the trip among the Croatans this Xmas.[1] There are many reasons, one of them being that it would cost more than I at first anticipated. Another, and the main reason now, is that there is an element of danger in it that makes it prohibitory. Not that I'm afraid, but that it would be rather uncomfortable trying to deal with folk lore, folk music, and the like, and all the time expecting to be killed or robbed. Father doesn't want me to go now. Times are *hard*, and even here in Harnett County robberies are beginning to happen real often on account of these hard times. Last week—Friday, I think it was—three young boys from near here had started to Raleigh one night when they were stopped, robbed, and one of the boys was shot and killed. So because of such possibilities as I have mentioned and some others, I shall not attempt the trip now. Therefore if you write to me, address me at

13. In 1823, at the battle of Karpenizi during the Greek War of Independence, Marco Bozzaris (1788–1823), with a band of 300, routed a Turkish army of 4,000 in a surprise night attack.

---

1. A small band of Croatan Indians (the Coharis) lived in Harnett County near his father's farm, and the main tribe (the Lumbees) lived in Robeson County near Lumberton, about ninety miles to the south. "The Last of the Lowries," first produced by the Playmakers on 30 April and 1 May 1920, is based on Croatan history, and its introduction includes a note on unusual pronunciations in Croatan speech (Koch, *Carolina Folk-Plays* [1941], p. 71).

C.H. I'm going back to-morrow. Somehow I can't get down to work here, and I have so much to do I can't afford to waste these spare hours.[2]

Somehow this *yuletide* has been rather dismal. I wanted to go to Beaufort as your friend. Yes, I had wanted to meet your mother, your father—all of them, but—well—but! When we get back on the job, I want us to do some work and not so much theorising and *I-wonder-if* kind of talk. Neither of us knows what will become of us but we are certain that there is work that can be done. Now whether this work is worthwhile no one knows. There is no way of knowing—no standards—I mean real standards—by which we can measure it. Yet after all, there is nothing worthwhile but work. And too we could say equally true—There (let me change pens) is nothing worthwhile but love. Since I poured all my mind into that paper for Doctor Williams last Tuesday night, I have been all upset. I seem to have dissolved my mind in a universal mind, essence, or something.[3]

It's raining here, dark and gloomy all day. And to-night—black, unearthly black and not a star. Saturday Gladys and I tried to straighten up some rose bushes that had fallen away from their arbors, but a languorous feeling got hold of me and I quit all effort. To-day I've done nothing more than read a few of Keats' letters and play cards. I feel as one might feel in the "lonesome later years."

Tell "Sis"[4] I send her my love—whatever that is—Tell her that if the piano keys are trembling to be a-playing—say that I'm a-dying to be there but I gotta git whar I'm a-gwine—that is to say, "the Hill."

Well, I hope you have your fill of cooking, and feel for once that your life is good for something. After all what is playmaking worth compared to bread-making, dress-making and the like? The one is such stuff as dreams are made of and the other is reality made real, that makes all our days go rounded with a sleep—that is, the bread-making.

2. Winter quarter began on 5 January 1921.

3. Horace Williams (1858–1940), professor of philosophy at UNC. Born in Gates County, North Carolina, Williams graduated from UNC in 1883, receiving a B.A. and an M.A. in English at the same time. In 1888 he earned a B.D. at Yale and in 1890 joined the faculty at UNC as professor of mental and moral science. In 1895 he founded the Department of Philosophy. The course Green took under him during fall quarter 1920 was Philosophy 16, "a study of the forces that shape life" (UNC Catalogue, 1920–21).

4. Elizabeth's sister Ellen (1899–1978).

When are you coming back to C.H.? I'm sure you'll need to stay the full Xmas time at home. Your mother must be quite overwhelmed with all her daughters—home again from the wars.[5]

Child o' mine, I hope you and your mother have meant more to each other these few days than ever before. What you told me long ago about the *aloofness* between you, has always seemed [word illegible]. It ought not to be. I'm sure you're done of such an attitude, aren't you?

Look out with longing eyes from Beaufort towards the sea, and know, dear, that I'm with you there. Whatever beauty you see, remember that I'm there too—because I wish to be.

"O whar you gwine, my torch?
I's a-gwine on down de road."[6]

Paul

## 17. To Elizabeth Lay

[Chapel Hill, N.C.]
Monday evening [February 1921]

My Dear—

I've made my resolution at last and do or die I'm going to keep true to it. Part of it goes like this in my mind: Hereafter we *will* be only friends outwardly no matter what we are inwardly—with each other.

I have made this resolution because deep down in me there is something as dead as the root of an age-old stump—something that has never thrilled into life with all the waves of feeling that have flowed from me to you and from you to me. In the most sacred and happiest moments of our companionship something has been lacking—And because that is true, and because it is borne in upon me that I can never change there, *I* am determined to be true to that dim shadowy "thing" I call my ideal.

Never for one instant blame yourself—There is nothing to be blamed for. If

5. Elizabeth, oldest of the Lay daughters, had four sisters. In addition to Ellen, they were Nancy (b. 1901), Lucy (1903–1956), and Virginia (1907–1972). Virginia still lived at home, but the others were all students at UNC.

6. Which for Paul led to Beaufort. The next morning he sent Elizabeth a telegram, "WILL ARRIVE BEAUFORT WEDNESDAY EVENING DEC 29" (EG-SHC), and set out by train to see her.

flowers will not bloom in the polar region there is no need of wasting the flowers. To-night I was reading your article on the pageant in THEATRE,[1] and I was overwhelmed with the genius of you. You are wonderful to me, dearest, but somewhere far off in a dim recess of "me heart" is a little white casket of someone dead who was dear to me. I've never known that dead one nor will I ever know her. And perhaps the casket is empty, but the *casket is there.* You will do much in this world, and I could walk by a hedge all a winter's day weeping thinking on the old times.

Paul

## 18. To Elizabeth Lay

[Lillington, N.C.]
Sunday afternoon [19 June 1921]

Dear Elizabeth—

Here I am down in the woods sitting on a log writing to you after these days of rushing around.[1] A cool north wind is sighing through the pines, several thrushes singing up through the hollow, and now and then I hear the high whining of a mosquito. But everything considered, I guess it's a fitting place to be writing in.—A fitting place to gather up the events of the last four days, thinking over the question of *this here* thing called living. I hardly know what to think now about anything. My mind is all astray, dreaming of nothing.

After leaving Raleigh the other afternoon, I went back to Duke,[2] arriving there in time to see the *finish* of a rather exciting ball game. I rode home with my brother Hugh and two other boys. And the whole conversation was of—baseball! baseball! They lived the game over and over, talking of this play and that, etc. That seemed enough for them. Life was full because of that—for one afternoon at least. It was funny that I found myself tiring of that, for I remember how I used to dream and talk of the ball game that was to be next Saturday. (Then we didn't have them so often.) Well, I must be getting very,

1. Elizabeth Lay, "*Raleigh, the Shepherd of the Ocean*: The Tercentenary Pageant Recently Produced at Raleigh, N.C.," *Theatre Magazine* 33 (February 1921): 118, 142.

---

1. He had received his B.A. at commencement exercises in Chapel Hill the previous Wednesday, 15 June.

2. Now Erwin, a mill town near Lillington, as are Benson and Coats mentioned below, which also had baseball teams.

very old. Methuselah's consciousness traded for mine of the days gone by. While I was in Duke the manager of the team tried to get me to try out with them for the next day preparatory to taking the job. But somehow the situation, those howling mill people, dirty, careworn, sickly, hopeless people, hurt me to the bone, and I no longer had the desire or will-power to live in Duke this summer. And so I refused point blank. Then he asked me to come Monday, but I put him off again. Now I know that if I made three-hundred a month I couldn't exist in that miserable town during the hot sickening days to come.

Yesterday I received an offer from Benson—to play with the team there. I haven't replied yet. I know now that I don't want to play any more baseball—not for money, under which circumstances I'd have to put my whole time into it. Friday I pitched for Lillington, and yesterday for Coats—and last night, after going to bed, I tried to think about writing poetry and plays. But I was artistically dead. Every thought would be shot through with the zizzing white ball. Figures racing around the diamond, slapping of gloves, people yelling in the grand stand—all kept me awake, and when I did sleep, it was only to play it all over through the night, and to get up this morning tired and haggard. You know how it affects me. But I've told you all this rigamarole in order to let you know why this letter is so dead. I don't believe any thing of beauty would thrill me to-day. More than ever I see how imperative it is that one woo beauty as an elfin-spirited creature—or at any rate realize that the love for it must be nurtured, cherished as a tiny flame in a freezing wind.

Child, I need you now to keep me—no not to keep me but to help me—retain the uplifting vision of the ideal. Over me the lazy clouds float, float idly, aimlessly—blowing as the wind blows—purposeless forever. And right now as the sun goes down behind the woods over there I feel just as helpless, just as aimless—and you might say of me

> He's somewhere in the
> straying clouds,
> or lost along the sighing
> wind.—[3]

for all I am. 'Cause *I'se seed a heap, seed a heap* lately that has told me of the thousands in this country that have forgot their childhood. Driven home in

3. Excerpt from an unpublished Green poem, as are the lines given later.

*mon âme* is this fact, that only now and then is there one left to interpret life in the fullest way.

To-day we have had a string of visitors, kins people, most of them. Always they talked of making money, of the failures here and there—of this person and that—now and then talking of the Bible, religion—condemning to the gallows here, condoning there, and on and on. Aunt Emma came up from Dunn in her car, and her loquaciousness added to the conversation. For an hour she and two or three others debated whether the Catholics would be saved after death, she stoutly denying it, her son affirming it. Once or twice she turned on me and rather pityingly said she was afraid that I with all my "knowledge" was farther from the true life than when I started to college. Oh, I'm sick of a world where everybody is waiting for his dream to be fulfilled beyond the grave—and I want to say "fools! fools!" but since I have a sickly sympathetic love for every living thing, I can't do it. When Aunt Emma left, she asked me to visit her, urging me to come while "Mr. Blalock" (her husband) "is away," for when her husband is at home she feels his lordly will. He is at Asheville now, just staying off and having a good time, not having much interest in his wife any longer. And once they strolled in the moonlight, and once they tasted their first kiss, and a million after. But now they're both too old for kissing and life's gone dry. I suppose for twenty years neither of them has felt the beauty of a sunset or sweetness of a bird's song. Is life just main street? Tell me.

Somehow there seems to be something of a crisis with me now. If I go in for playing ball and working in a bank or store, I fear that by next fall I shall be as empty as a rusty pail in a garbage heap. I can't do it. If it does mean hardship on others, I must write this summer and try to bring toward a full harvest the only thing in me that makes me want to live. I must move into that little tenant house with its lonely hours, and ugly walls, and there try to save my soul. People won't understand but you know I don't care for conventions, it's not liking to hurt people that makes me hesitate. (How funny! Everything I'm saying seems empty. Can't I get to the absolute sincerity of life! Let me start again.)

My half-sister, the one who has all my sympathy. You know her.[4]—She came over this afternoon. Unconsciously I caught myself looking at her as she sat beside papa and comparing them. She might have been his wife so far as age in looks goes. Wrinkles and a tired useless expression on her face. She has

4. Alda, daughter of William Green by his first marriage.

one daughter about 16, and has adopted a little girl about 5, and in truth she isn't very much interested in either. She has no longer a good figure or any beauty. Her hands are those of a scrubwoman. All these I can forgive. But what I can't overlook is the withering up of her woman's soul in a round of hard conditions, petty duties, and the like. She has one main topic of conversation, and that is the extravagance and irreligiousness of the young people. Every Sunday she goes to the country church, sitting silent through Sunday School and returning to her pitiful home "down the road" to begin another week's existence with a man she doesn't love—a man who jes' tinkers through life, one who is satisfied with enough roof to keep the rain from his head and a rocking chair to sit in. I am not exaggerating, although I know there are joys in any life, no matter how bleak it is or may appear. But I am crying out for the vision of—well, truth, goodness, and beauty—for a being bigger than circumstance. Who wants to own that high thinking is no more and plain living and hard dying is all there is? Is farm life a failure? Is it false when Tim[5] says, "I like fresh air, green things, and the like"? No! No! No! But they's something wrong, chile, something wrong. Either I'm viewing everything morbidly or there are millions of farm people (and it's even truer of mill people) who are born to wilt in the sun before it is noon even in this life. What can we do about it? *Rien! rien! rien!* Words—words—words. But I think these lines are true—too horribly true—

> Beneath the hammer's beat that builds
>     towards institutions,
> Beneath the whirr and roar of the
>     singing loom
> Efficiency and industry, the sweep
>     of power—
> I hear the ancient gods talking of
>     doom.

By this time perhaps you'll want to say "durn" once more. This is an awful letter, but I can do no better. After these few days of so much action, words are nothing more than words. I am thinking of the time when I only shall write to let you know that I am alive—not trying to catch any of the depths of life in such sieve-like vessels. Every day the limitations of language, its frailty and insignificance compared with the infinity out of which it arose are more

5. Unidentified.

apparent, and every day the less I try to wrap words around the living beauty's soul. You and I have expended about a million words between us, and of the five-hundred thousand that I have spoken to you I ask myself whether a single one has come from the very I. Can the real self express itself in any way? I doubt it. The only way one can express the *ego* is through his child. And even then he can't express that alone. That child is an individual. Voila! Every person dwells in a neighborless house—man and wife, sweethearts, friend and befriended—all alike. We are as lonely beings as a single inhabitant on some dark star. Could we not say that everything built by man is the product of the effort—futile effort!—to express his inner self? Here I am trying to write to you, but I'm not saying what I want to say. *I simply can't!* If I should say "I love you" a million times, still deep down in my heart would be my real self, untroubled, untouched by the storm of emotion passing above. Can I ever break through this ice, this darkness even and dip my pen into the current of life and write of *things* as they are? Always over me hangs that suffocating cloud—a presentiment of lonely death with the ice and darkness unpierced.

Doubtless it's superfluous to state here that I'm plumb wore out with the way people are living their lives. Can't they wake up and work the *carpe diem* stuff on it? Qui sait? Qui sait? Or am I crazy to understand them and since I can't am growing disappointed? I guess a hundred people have told me that I take life too seriously. Lord, what else have I to take? Horace[6] would say that I need a new view of religion. Maybe so. I need something.

I spent Friday night at Mary's[7] and she and I sat on her little vine-clad porch and talked till two o'clock. She is happy happy. But the evil days have not yet come. She still has the fresh green vision that young motherhood always has. She is perfectly happy to pour her whole existence into Billy-boy. Someday she'll wake up with empty arms and nothing but memories, and if the gods prove unkind they will be bitter memories. And who knows the thoughts of the little wizened gods that play behind the veil?

Just now I hear a whippoorwill, all the ages of life behind him finding expression in his liquid notes. He sings because he must. Is that good, is it true, is it beautiful? Or is it worthless and might as well never have been? I don't know. And I'm afraid I never shall know. But if my bones are licked clean

6. Williams.

7. His sister Mary Johnson, who lived half a mile down the road from their father. Her son William was born 1 September 1920.

by the lean-flanked wolves of doubts errors and despairs, I'm going to find out.

Goodnight, Paul

## 19. To Elizabeth Lay

Lillington, [N.C.]
Saturday P.M. [25 June 1921]

Dear Elizabeth—

The girls tell me the stationery is out, and so I'm writing on this fished-up tablet.[1] Pardon, please.

I'm just back from Norfolk—arrived here this afternoon.[2] Now what do you think? After Caro left for Chapel Hill, or rather just before she left, I learned from Mary that she was willing to see about giving Caro the summer at the hill. I hadn't known before that she and her husband[3] were willing to shoulder the duty and pleasure. This decision left me free to write, as I thought. But papa in a silent way, I knew, wanted me to get out and make something to help lighten his heavy expenses. About this time Heffner wrote me that he was sailing[4]—everything o.k. and the like. The thought of playing ball was distasteful, you know, and so I decided to go to Norfolk.

The afternoon I decided to go, I pitched ball for Lillington against Sanford and beat them. Before, they had tried to hire me, but I couldn't stand the idea of clerking—a store or bank and playing ball three or four times a week. Well, after the game I drove over to Dunn to catch the train. There I was again assailed by a crowd of baseball cranks, but I hung on to my sea-desire and went on to Norfolk. There I found the strike[5] over and men literally begging for a job. When I got down to the shipping office, a regular mob of dagoes, wops, and everything else was lined up waiting for a chance to get back their old jobs on the sea. Things looked glum for me. However I decided to *get a job*, and so I went up town to the president of the co., walked in and told him

1. Of small, lined sheets.

2. Green took a train to Norfolk, Virginia, on Thursday evening, 23 June, spent Friday in Norfolk, and left for home that night.

3. Alton Johnson, hardware store owner in Lillington.

4. As a merchant seaman.

5. Of seamen and dock workers.

what I wanted. After half an hour I convinced him that I was a man he needed, and so he said he'd fix me up. He gave me a letter to the head of the hiring department, and back I went to see him. My letter got me through the hungry crowd, and the policeman let me in. I was about the only pure American in that vicinity, and I thought how interesting it would be to spend a few weeks with this pitiful motley crew on the ocean. The boss told me, when I handed him my letter—said he'd fix me up, and then he handed me a telegram from Lillington, which asked me to call up the mgr. of the ball team. I did so, and he made me another offer, begging me to come back. Not begging either—but requesting me to. The offer was so splendid that I had to accept it and I answered that I would return at once. I didn't want to give up my trip to sea, but I had already realized that I couldn't get a chance to write there, and too, I wanted to take the course with Mr. Hinckley in playwriting this summer.[6] The Lillington job gives me a chance to do that. I shall have a quiet room in the hotel, play ball twice or three afternoons a week, and have all the other time to myself.—Really, I hope you won't blame me for turning back. The money had a lot to do with my decision, I know, but the spare time had more. Yet even now I see those big ships sailing out of Norfolk in the grey of the morning, their noses scenting adventure, ploughing towards the rising sun, and I not there to go wid 'em. I wanted to go, but there was no money in it, and little spare time. And so to-night here I am back at home ready to start on the *job* Monday.

I got back to Raleigh this morning and hung around there several hours. I missed connection with the Lillington train and for awhile I was on the point of going over to see you and "ma"[7] and Caro—and all the family. Finally I compromised by trying to call you up on the phone, but the line from Durham to Chapel Hill was out of whack and I failed. A friend brought me home on his car. I wish now I had gone over to the Hill and stayed until Monday. But I didn't, and *voila*!

Your letter was waiting here—rather your note. You must be worked to

6. Theodore B. Hinckley, editor of *The Drama*, offered a correspondence course in playwrighting, one year of training for $60.

7. Elizabeth's sister Ellen, who got the nickname from playing Ma Dixon in "In Dixon's Kitchen," a play she wrote in collaboration with Wilbur Stout. The Playmakers first did the play on 29 and 30 April 1921 and now had it in rehearsal for performances on 18 and 19 July.

death. Write me all about your class—your—everything.[8] Maybe now I shall be able to get to see the play in July, or whenever it is. Erma and I both are planning to go.[9]

By the way, I'm going to send you the data on this playwriting course. Let Prof. Koch look over it, and if he wants to know why I'm such a fool as to take it, tell him I want to be a playwriter and not a piddler. The course may not be worth a hurrah, but I'm going to risk it. It's the best thing available now.

Caro, in her letter, says she thinks you are "real nice."—I'm glad she likes you.

Tell *ma* I'll write 'er or bust. My son paul's been running round so much lately that I ain't had time to do nothing but keep 'im from breaking the family and his neck too. He tuck it in his haid to go to Norfick, and in two days he's back saying he's goin' play ball. A week ago he was goin' write old book mess—well, I 'on't know what he'll do next. Something must *Lay* near his heart or in his mind that makes him act that quair nobody knows what to think of him.

It's bed-time now—

Goodnight Paul

## 20. To Elizabeth Lay

Lillington, [N.C.]
Monday night [27 June 1921]

Dear Girl—

I'm mailing two letters to-morrow. One I've carried around in my pocket all day.[1] Read it before you do this.

Well, here I am perched on the third floor of this dingy bug-eaten hotel in Lillington. Below me on the street is the roar of cars full of young people riding, talking of to-morrow's ball game, happy, indolent, aimless, dreaming

8. Elizabeth, director of the Bureau of Community Drama in UNC's Extension Division, also taught two courses at UNC that summer, English 5 (Dramatization for Children) and English 14 (Dramatic Interpretation and Play Production).

9. On 13 July the Playmakers were to present a double bill, Shakespeare's *Merchant of Venice* in the afternoon and Eugene O'Neill's *Beyond the Horizon* that night.

---

1. Unlocated.

in a dim way of doing something, of living in the days to come. None of them seem to realize that one day they will wake up in the morning oh so early and say "the summer is ended, the harvest is past, and I am not saved."

Last night I talked with Mary and Erma, and there in the darkness sitting on our porch, hearing the June bugs and whippoorwills calling—there in that wonderful mixing of day and night I preached a sermon. For all day I had sat and watched people go by, had listened to people talk about this and that, seeing in their faces the ebb and flow of suspicion of neighbor, fear of hard times and this and that, knowing that here again was the problem Christ had died in solving—namely, teaching people to live, to grow, to turn the other cheek, to "go with him twain."[2] Yeh, I preached. Maybe most of my sermon smacked of Horace,[3] but it came from my heart. Why are people not growing? Why can't they be like the flowers they plant to beautify their home?

I know someone would say that I am young and feel the world's weight like young dreamers, and that after all this old world is all right. But, honey, it isn't all right. There is pain and sickness, despair and sorrow—failure—all. On my return from Norfolk two bodies of soldier boys were taken from the train at Norlina.[4] There in the darkness of the mid-night their flag-draped boxes were left upon the platform—and to me came the picture of them as babies clutching at their mother's breast, of the time when they first smiled and she was happy. And there was a great rebellious cry in my heart. Why should such a thing happen? Oh, poor, poor misguided world. It is the same old sob of, "O Jerusalem! Jerusalem! how often would I . . . !"[5]

And last night talking to Mary and Erma I felt as if I couldn't stand it much longer. I must get to see through this tangle. People are not living. They are existing. You know that nine out of ten count success in life making money, "doing well" as they say. They are as aimless as the automobile they drive. Nothing beyond making money, getting married, living a few years, and dying without going over into Canaan. I'm sure you have never had this *fact* driven into you perhaps as fiercely as I have. Your father more or less lives in the Promised Land, but he is an exception, and he has helped train you. But we shall see! We shall see, and in some far hour I'm going to know what a man

2. Matthew 5:39–41.

3. Williams.

4. Small town near Henderson, North Carolina, a few miles south of the Virginia state line.

5. Luke 13:34.

must do to be saved, or in other words, what he must be. Honey, I thank God that he gave you to me to listen to me play the eternal *dead march.* But how shall I get by "My boys wuz good boys" and "what's any of us worth on account of him"? How shall I make the world see that the Negro whose flesh burns as he writhes out his last few seconds of "life" in the electric chair—once made frog houses in the sand and made his mammy laugh with joy? How shall you and I teach them that he was a good boy? Tell me, honey? You can't, kin you?

Yes, here I am with nothing to do but play ball four or five hours a week—that outwardly—while inwardly there is always the wrench of things that won't let me be. A few minutes ago Mr. Baggett came into my room and asked me to take the principal's place here in the high school next year, finally offering me a price the people are maybe not just able to pay. I should like to take it, and for one year tell these children about the true Christ as I know him, but I cannot. *Mon heure* ain't come yit. Do you know I feel somewhat flattered because of the number of jobs I've had offered me. Here in these hard times, it seems that everywhere I turn, something pops up. Papa can't understand it. For he's told me time and time again that people would lose confidence in me because of my infidelity, atheism, and the like. Somehow though, it's the other way. But they don't know me down to the bottom of my heart. Now and then I want to tell them that it's all a lie! lie! lie! They wouldn't believe it. They'd say, "why you've never been a mean boy. Everybody *knows* Paul Greene," and so the days go by, and the evil days draw nigh, when I shall say I have no pleasure in them—mebbe so they do.

Your letter came to-day, and all the *material,* and my mind won't get down to work. I'm proud of you and all your accomplishments. I knew you'd be besieged with folks for your course[6] and I wish I could come up there and help you teach them. But here I'm stranded to make a baseball team for the indolent business men to stake their money on. Child, you'd be surprised at the amount of money bet around here on games. Somebody take me off this subject!

I'm glad you like Caro Mae.[7] There's a great deal to her, as there is to all my sisters, "praise be!" They must have their chance—and that's sure.

I wish I could let Mary read your letter. It is so you-ish. May I?

6. On either children's theater or play production, both of which Elizabeth taught that summer at UNC.

7. Who was living with Elizabeth in Chapel Hill for the summer.

If you don't write, what is going to happen to you? You are so busy *doing* that *being* will wail its infant voice into heartsick silence if you don't watch out. See, I preach your own doctrine back at you.

Can't you write me just what you are doing in your course? You spoke of preparing a lecture. What do you lecture on?

You also said Caro didn't have any idea what I was. Often I think that she knows me a great deal better than you. But the other day Erma said, "Paul, you've changed a great deal since you met Miss Lay," and I let her go in her truth—or delusion. Which?

Write me. Paul

Excuse the pencil. I left my pen over home. Tell "Ma" he said he'd write as shore's sin. I'll see ye both afore long.

## 21. To Elizabeth Lay

[Lillington, N.C.]
Thursday night [Late July 1921]

Dear Sweetheart:

I am back from the sing, 11 P.M.—a hectic time.[1] Prof. Leslie Campbell[2] away on a vacation—and I had charge of the practicing. And I put 'em through a lot of hard work. Miss Camp[3] is busy too. I went to L—to see her this morning while the dew was heavy on the fodder. Have another engagement tomorrow and next day. Surely is a busy time. Pulled fodder all day—Tired, tired, lawd how tired! Your sweet letter came today. Please keep driving on and make the poetry come! This afternoon, working late in the fields, I was at peace. The clouds were piled up in the grey sky, trees standing and some alert off to the north, in the west more clouds and smears of red. Somewhere a dog was barking. I was alone and yet the silence and the beauty of it all eased me like I don't know what.

Life is harsh here in many ways. There has been some hard-feelings between papa and his neighbors—tenants. And the whole matter seems so

1. Rehearsing at Buies Creek Academy (now Campbell University) for a county-wide singing competition to be held later in the summer.

2. Leslie Campbell (1892–1970), later president of Buies Creek Academy (1934–70), taught English there beginning in 1911.

3. Organizer of community musical and dramatic programs in Lillington and Harnett County.

useless. A straight, honest, heart to heart talk would straighten it all out. I wish Henry might come.[4] But everything seems inadvisable. Tell them all how I love them. And whisper a lot of things to Ellen. Above all write your poetry honey and take care of yourself. Stay in Beaufort. Nothing you can do here.

I love you—Paul

## 22. To Elizabeth Lay

[Lillington, N.C.]
Monday night [Early August 1921]

My dear Girl—

Please bear with me for awhile. I cannot write anymore until I feel that I must. Everything is in such a whirl with me now.

Your letter came and it was just as I expected it to be. You seemed a little hurt at my conception of your love. Child, do you not know when I am writing on the surface? Life is so deep, so deep. When I say childish things as I did about Renée's letter,[1] please remember that back of it all is *me* who stands lost in the wonder of everything. Something queer has taken possession of me. I talk philosophy and religion all the time. I've just come from the courthouse where a crowd of us loafers were gathered, and for about a half hour I preached or did something that amazed everyone.

I am reading Everett's *Science of Thought* during every spare moment.[2] I can't write any poetry. You spoke of *Prometheus Bound* as containing *food for thought.* You like myself, dear child, speak trivially sometimes, don't you?

While I was talking to this crowd of fellows at the courthouse, I happened

4. Elizabeth's brother, Henry C. Lay (1905–1974).

---

1. With an undated letter to Elizabeth on the previous "Tuesday Night," Green included a letter from Renée Bourseiller, with whom he spent much time during his last month in Paris (see letter 8). "From the tone of [Renée's letter] she is trying to forget," he guessed in the letter to Elizabeth, but he was sure "she never will." He went on to imagine, in what must have seemed to Elizabeth excessive detail, how Renée would recall their "hot, hurried, heartbreaking months" together for the rest of her life and ended by declaring that he felt honor-bound to write to Renée regularly through the years. He hoped Elizabeth would not mind (EG-SHC).

2. A Hegelian exposition of its subject by Charles Carroll Everett and one of the texts in Horace Williams's philosophy class (rev. ed., 1890). (The other text was also Hegelian: F. H. Bradley's *Appearance and Reality* [1893].)

to glance out toward the jail, and there in the lighted window were two hands clenching the bars. They were woman's hands. The window sill was so high that no head could be seen—only those two protesting hands. The sight of them took my breath away. I asked some of the fellows what it meant. They told me that it was nothing but "an old hussy" locked up because of her improper relations with a man—And then I fell on them like a bolt—Why should we have jails? Suppose she loved the man. They called her an "old bitch" that had been in trouble times before. Oh, my Lord! I think I'll go crazy if I don't see through this tangle about me. I must. Somebody's got to see it. Horace says we must have a new view of God. Why doesn't he give it? Often in a thrilling moment I feel that I must get this view of God—world! world! Oh, Jerusalem![3] Don't expect to hear from me any more until I think a few things out.

I love you, dear, you and everything that is. I can't tell much difference between my love for you and everybody else—Katharine, Ellen, Adeline—everybody—[4]Forgive me, it's like that. Maybe I'm crazy, I don't know. But it's hell to me—this whirl of things. I must see—the sun.[5] Goodbye—Paul

## 23. To Elizabeth Lay

[Lillington, N.C.]
Wednesday night [Mid-August 1921]

Dear Girl—

Your note and telegram came this afternoon,[1] and I am anxious to take the trip to Manteo and the other places of life's autumnal melancholy, but, Lord,

3. Luke 13:34–35.

4. All three were involved in Playmakers activities: Katharine Batts (b. 1900) as actress (she played Trista in Elizabeth's play of that title) and, after graduating in 1922, as Koch's secretary; Ellen Lay (B.A., 1922) as actress and playwright; and Adeline Denham (1900–1988; B.A., 1922,), Koch's niece, as musician and stagehand.

5. Henrik Ibsen, *Ghosts*, act 3.

1. Telling Green that the North Carolina Department of Public Instruction would fund a project to reenact and film the first English settlements in the New World, those at Roanoke Island beginning in 1585, including the one in 1587 that came to be known as the "lost colony" because of its mysterious disappearance. The filming would take place in late September at the site of the fort near Manteo on Roanoke Island, and Elizabeth knew Paul would be interested in the project for its historical

how can I do it! I don't know. Work is piling up every day and expenses piling with it. It appears now as if I can't get off until I start back to school.[2] *Je ne suis pas content,* but must endure it. However if there's a chance that looks like wisdom offering it, I shall jerk loose and go. You know. It would be wonderful to be down there with the moon and skyey glory to thrill one from a clod into a god, but—*mais, il faut être plein de raison dans ce monde où le peuple crient*[3] *"d'argent, d'argent"*[4] *tous les jours, et où ils n'ont que, la crie.*[5] *J'espère que vous songiez*[6] *à moi un peu, mais pas trop*—Well, English is better—tho' I should like to write in French for a change.

I've wanted to write your father a long letter, but the rush and go have been awful for the last week. And I'm due to write your mother. Maybe tho' she understands that I have nothing to write, yet a million things to talk with her about. And again I must say that I'm going down to Beaufort if there is a chance.—Please write me all about the family. And what has become of Ellen? A few days ago I received a letter from Katharine Batts—full of praise about something indefinite and shadowy—my having opened a new vision to her in viewing the expressionless life of the poor whites and tuneful darkies. She seems to think it a great boon, but I am still questioning whether it's the best thing for one to view life's workings objectively. After one has caught the habit, there is no more peace in this life except the peace of the throbbing ocean that rests in little creeks and bays—here and there—that is to say, eternal motion in the great open, and to the outward gaze there is peace among little duties and cares but back of them the wonder and surprise that went with Christ up to the rough-hewn cross. He expressed it when he exclaimed in astonishment—asking God why he had deserted him.[7]

The Community Sing[8] was a great success—not in that we had a huge crowd, not in that my class (for it was my class) won the loving cup, but in that

---

and artistic dimensions. A trip to Manteo could also take Green through Beaufort, home of Elizabeth's parents.

2. On 27 September 1921. In addition to playing baseball that summer, Green had taken a job in July auditing the Harnett County financial records.

3. That is, *crie.*

4. That is, "*de l'argent, de l'argent.*"

5. That is, *le cri.*

6. That is, *songez.*

7. Mark 14:34

8. At Buies Creek Academy.

a few people caught the vision splendid of riches laid up where nothing corrupts and no thieves break in and steal.[9] Dr. Horton[10] was one of our judges and he was just overjoyed with the meaning of the day. And Hoffmeister was grand through it all, and yet he is not grown up, not up to the work he is doing; for once here he spoke harshly to his wife. I don't think he loves her—and all he does runs counter to that. What must he do to be saved? Suppose he can't love his wife. Then should they keep on staying to-gether because they both like the same work? Christ couldn't answer it, how can I? or you? Court is in session here and all day *they* have been trying a case—dealing with a disastrous love affair. A sixteen-year-old girl, her baby, a boy hardly twenty, and no marriage vows tell the story. How will sending him to the roads right anything? The earth cannot answer, nor the seas that mourn. Things like this burn me through all my love for you, for everything that includes you centers in finding the answer. And if I don't find it, then, I have failed. *Beyond the Horizon* only touches on it with horrible discords. How shall the glorious strains arise, the heavenly words be sung, the flash of changeless prophecies—and—it's so easy to get lost in words, isn't it? Last night I had the realest dream of Renée and it kept me awake—hearing her words across three thousand miles. Maybe I ought not to speak of it to you but it is a part of my life and everybody ought to know it. Someday I feel that I shall tell the world about it. The growth of one's self is a queer thing, and my desire to be absolutely open with the world grows stronger every day. Where will it lead us? Nobody knows. If I could lose myself in the joy of loving you, it wouldn't be so hard, but I can't. I don't know whether it brings me pleasure, a deepening of—well, I don't know. Driving over to Buie's Creek to a ball game this afternoon, I thought of you, and somehow I wanted to run away, to go where I might never see you again.—It's true. You know that. There is something in me that calls me away from a home, children, and all that—to a losing myself in searching for the riddle's answer. It seems that being with you, with everybody drags me away from that queer something that calls forever. Perhaps this isn't in keeping with the plan of life. Qui sait? But it's like that. And we've hurt each other so terribly that often I feel we have no right to each other's love. We have not harmonized with what we believed in, or said we believed in, have we?

9. Matthew 6:19–20.

10. W. C. Horton, a physician from Raleigh, who would also act in the film made about the early English settlements at Roanoke.

There are a thousand things we might write about, but words can't express them. Please don't write any more as you did in to-day's letter—praise and longing. It hurts and doesn't sound right. I can't tell you such things, for I don't feel as you and just write of anything, please, but that.

Have you received your hat? The girls here in the office[11] had a lot of fun fixing it up for you—winks, grins, and whispers—at me. Miss Camp says she is going to write you—thanking you for—I don't know what. The spiritual life accepts of no thanks, does it?[12]

Love to all, Paul

Excuse this paper. I came down to the office to work and decided to write you—[13]

I've read this over and it sounds awful. I wonder just how much truth there is in it. Can one tell the truth?

## 24. To George W. Lay[1]

Lillington, N.C.
10 September 1921

My dear Dr. Lay:

It's entirely impossible for me to talk to you through a letter as I should like. I've delayed writing an explanation of many things that now and then you necessarily must have wondered at—hoping all the time to go down to Beaufort and have a conversation with you not beholden to a fountain pen and a few sheets of paper. What with the community sing and auditing the tax-books, I've been put to it for good. And in addition to that I was under contract to play ball until Sept. 7. However from this last I hoped to be released—but wasn't. Now that the sing is over and baseball done, I can get

11. Of the Harnett County auditor in Lillington.

12. Elizabeth had sent Camp music and other material for use in the community sing.

13. On stationery with the letterhead: "Harnett County, D. P. McDonald, Auditor, Lillington, N.C."

---

1. Elizabeth and Paul had decided to get married, and the wedding would take place the following July in Elizabeth's hometown of Beaufort, North Carolina, at the church pastored by her father, George W. Lay (1860–1932), St. Paul's Episcopal Church.

away with a clear conscience; and so you may look for me soon. In the meantime, please won't you prepare against a parlour session almost *sine die*?[2]

Don't think that I have failed to value your goodness and strength in letting certain silly conventionalities go snap, and coming forward without questioning to give Elizabeth and myself a father's blessing, and a bigger hope towards success. Someday I think I shall be worthy of this, Elizabeth already is. You don't know how glad I am that I have found someone who believes that rules were made for men and not men for rules.

I'm not going to attempt to tell you how wonderful it is to have won the love of one so deep, so true as Elizabeth. Words are useless there. Part of our lives lies in a shadowland so dim and thrilling that words are not there, doesn't it? You understand what I'm trying to say. The years of spiritual growth that belong to so many as man and wife attest the truth of this, I believe.

But let us talk it over at Beaufort where we can understand each other better.

Love to all and a hug for Virginny.[3]

Paul Greene

## 25. To Elizabeth Lay

Hatteras, [N.C.]
Tuesday night [20 September 1921]

Dearest—[1]

Well, here I am at Hatteras—desolate of desolates. It is about dark now and I'm in the tiniest room imaginable staying at Mrs. Rollinson's waiting for

2. Paul finished auditing the county tax books on 15 September and on Saturday, 17 September, went by train to Beaufort (telegram, Paul Green to Elizabeth Lay, 14 September 1921).

3. Virginia, Elizabeth's younger sister still at home.

---

1. This letter describes a trip of several days to Roanoke Island. In 1918 Frederick Koch wrote his only dramatic script, the pageant *Raleigh: The Shepherd of the Ocean*. Involving over 500 people in cast and crew, the pageant was to be presented on an athletic field in Raleigh on 29 October 1918 to commemorate the tercentenary of Sir Walter Raleigh's death, but had to be postponed because of a flu epidemic. Two years later it was performed at the same place, on 19, 20, 21 September 1920. Elizabeth took part in the production and wrote an account of it that was widely circulated in state

supper. But let me bring my trip up to date by retracing, if I can, every lap of the journey from Beaufort here. I don't know whether I can or not, since so many scenes have passed across my senses that everything's in a medley of pictures.

Your father got to the dock after seeing you off[2] in time to chat with us for ten or fifteen minutes before our little boat showed up from Morehead. They loaded me on. Virginia and I kissed. We others shook hands—and so it was good-bye. Chug-chug-rat-tat-spr—r-r-Boom! and we started sailing into the sun—everything fresh and dewy. The marsh grass waving in yellow grainy hypocrisy, grackles flying above the fluffs of wind, and boattail darters—as a negro told me they were called—shooting here and there. Far to the southeast like a giant polyphemus staring through the morning mist rose the lighthouse at Cape Lookout. After we had got out from Beaufort, I began to examine our passengers. We had about eight negroes aboard who sprawled fore and aft like lizards and soon lost themselves in the weak mind's friend—peaceful sleep. There were two or three women and two men aboard also. Only one of the whole number attracted my attention. She was a queer creature—blind, one eye was gone. She kept her lip full of snuff and every few minutes would feel for the window, open it and spit carefully into the sea. Oh, she was pitiful!—

---

and national newspapers and journals (e.g., *Christian Science Monitor*, 7 January 1921, and *Theatre Magazine* 33 [February 1921]: 118, 142). The pageant celebrated Raleigh as the first Englishman to envision a colony in the New World, and it met with a response so enthusiastic that the state legislature, during the summer of 1921, appropriated several thousand dollars for a film about the settlement and destruction of Raleigh's colony on Roanoke Island, which would be shown in schools and communities in the state. The filming was to take place at a reconstructed fort on the historical site near the village of Manteo for about two weeks beginning on Tuesday, 20 September 1921. It was to watch work on the film that Green made the trip described in the present letter. By boat from Beaufort, where he visited Elizabeth and her family, it took three days to get to Manteo. He left early Monday morning, 19 September. Traveling just inside the Outer Banks, he reached the village of Ocracoke that evening. On Tuesday about noon he reached Hatteras, and, unable to find a boat going farther, he began the letter there. Sailing early in the morning on Wednesday, he reached Manteo in the afternoon. That night he finished the letter.

2. Elizabeth, who had gone to Beaufort for Paul's visit, returned by train to Chapel Hill, where she was in charge of the statewide Bureau of Community Drama in UNC's Extension Division.

Nearly all the time she hummed a song to herself—something about the love of Jesus and the like. She surely believed in what you quoted to me a few days ago—"Though he slay me, yet will I trust him."[3] At Sealevel she got off, and as she was passing by me, she begged me to give her some money towards getting her little girl a few books "fer schull"—Of course I did—all the time wondering whether she were putting one over on me.

The trip to Ocracoke was long and tiresome—a fierce wind beating in our faces, rough water all the way. One thing that relieved the tediousness was bits of conversation with Capt. Gorrish, Bo'sun at Ocracoke Life Saving Station. But even he had little new to add to my store—I read *Gioconda* on the way,[4] slept awhile, watched the waves—smoked, dreamed of you and all that is to be—and along in the afternoon nearly starved, but going "furrard" I got some bread and molasses from Capt. Piner—By the way, I got on the trail of Prof. Koch and Hibbard[5] when I met up with Capt. Gorrish. He told me about two strange fellows who had come to their station a few days before, almost dead—as he put it, and from what he said, the laugh is on those two profs. They almost had to work "recess'tation" on them—to get them straight. "Why," he said, "the sun had completely et holes in 'em"—and so on!

About five o'clock we got to Ocracoke—with its great white lighthouse a hundred years old. (See poem called "The Greater Light," written by Frank Fulture.)[6] I got off at the landing and walked ashore immediately in the hope

3. Job 13:15.

4. On the trip, Green carried the recent anthology *Chief Contemporary Dramatists*, 2d ser. (1921), edited by Thomas H. Dickinson. Gabriele D'Annunzio's *La Gioconda* (trans. Arthur Symons) is in the anthology, as are the other plays mentioned in this and the next letter.

5. Who were also on their way to Manteo to watch the film making. Addison Hibbard (1887–1945) had come to the Department of English at UNC in 1919, following graduate work at the University of Wisconsin, and would remain until 1929, when he moved to Northwestern University. His particular field was southern literature (*The South in Contemporary Literature* [1930]), but he is best known for the work he coauthored with W. F. Thrall, *A Handbook to Literature*, continuously revised and republished since its first appearance in 1936.

6. Fulture, formerly a preacher, at present a sailor and a bit of a poet, took Green by boat from Ocracoke to Hatteras on Tuesday morning. His poems have not been published, but Green wrote down one of them and three of Fulture's sea chanties (along with Fulture's tune for one of them, "The Merman's Song") and included the batch with the present letter. The poem, "The Greater Light," in five stanzas, draws a

of getting someone to take me up to Hatteras—a distance of 22 miles and not 15 as I had thought—A crowd of townspeople was hanging around the P.O. waiting for the mail, barefooted men and boys, and slender, shy girls, who gathered together as soon as they saw me—the girls—and giggled, all the while casting sly glances at me. Maybe they were flirting, poor marooned creatures! I wanted to kiss everyone of them and bring a glow into their cheek and a sparkle of life into their sleeping downy eyes. We have a certain code in this life that says such carryings on would have been wrong. But I don't know. While talking to the Methodist minister, Mr. Stephenson, a big bearded man with a twisted neck—I learned later that he had fallen from a cart a few years before and broken his neck—I caught sight of a sign that read "Sunday, come to the Methodist Church and hear Col. Fred A. Olds, noted author, educator, and historian of the North Carolina Historical Society, Sunday at 2 P.M. Everybody wanted." I felt like a lost man seeing a friend. They told me that Col. Olds had left for Washington that morning.[7]

Try as I might I could get nobody to make the trip to Hatteras that afternoon, and so I went down to Mr. Gaskill's boarding house to wait until to-day. There I ran into a fishing party from Raleigh—Maj. Myers—my old army major,—his daughter, Mr. Ashe, Mr. Thompson, and Mr. McLannighan. The last man informed me during a conversation about the Roanoke Island proposition that Miss Grimball was his cousin and that he had acted as secretary and treasurer of the Raleigh pageant affair—I felt at home[8]—They all

---

parallel between improvements in the lighthouse at Ocracoke that have made it much brighter and the crucifixion of Christ.

> There's another light that dimly shone,
> Which the people could not see,
> Until the Father sent His Son
> To the cross of Calvary.
>
> And now the lighthouse shines all round
> The earth from sea to sea,
> In the darkest parts its rays are found—
> The light of immortality.

7. Fred A. Olds (1853–1935), who had been a newspaperman in Raleigh, founded the State Hall of History in 1887 and for the rest of his life investigated and lectured on North Carolina history.

8. Elizabeth B. Grimball, president of the Woman's Club in Raleigh, had directed

were preparing for a fishing trip in the surf. I got permission to go with them, and after a snatch of supper off we went down Ocracoke Sound towards the sea—through the twilight, and, honey, I wish I could describe the beauty of that scene—The sky was a wonderful orange, deepening to a purple near the horizon, with long shimmering streamers of glory shooting from the hidden sun. Far to the west near Beacon Island a group of fishing boats hovered on the water, white, still—like pure souls in the great harbor of light—as I imagine them—It was too wonderful to try to describe.—At good dark we came to the surf, rounding the point of land stretching south, disturbing a flock of sea mews, gulls, and shearwaters. We unloaded, and the fishing for drum began, while I lay on the sand and watched them, thinking of you, hearing the roar and pound of the waves, with the shearwaters flying in the dusk around our heads, grey ghostly creatures flitting past, uttering now and then sharp plaintive cries like a new born babe—I longed for a voice to speak of all this beauty—the terrible beauty of it all—And as a climax the moon came up near 9 o'clock—strewing a silver mist over the sea, earth and sky—It was so beautiful that it hurt—The great great stretches of beauty—I almost broke into poetry "feeling of it so"

"I am all drunk with seeing
endless spaces—
Stretches of windy earth and sea and sky"[9]

About 10 o'clock we came back and went to bed—having two drum fish to pay for our trouble.

This morning I got up early and made a tour of the town. It is the dearest place imaginable—no streets, little white houses here and there half-hid like pearls in a setting of greenery—live oak, wild hawthorn, bay, crepe myrtle, white myrtle, oak, pine, cedar—a dozen other trees—all grow in tangled masses in the living sand.

About 9 o'clock I found a man to bring me to Hatteras for $8. And going back to Mr. Gaskill's I got my grip, and we started. As I left I told Mr. Gaskill I would come again, thinking of you at the time. Dearie, it would be a lovely place to spend our honeymoon. (I must stop now. In order to get off in the morning to Manteo I must get up at 4 o'clock—The boat leaves at 4:30. I am

---

the pageant there in 1920, then had been one of the main movers in getting a state appropriation for the film being made at Manteo, which she also directed.

9. His own verse.

spending the night where Mr. Koch and Hibbard stopped. But all of that tomorrow on the boat. I'll mail this at Manteo. Money is running short. Wonder if I shall be able to cash a check in Manteo. If not, look for me to hike into the Hill about Nov. 1. Good night. I think of you all the time. A few minutes ago I noticed a hair pin on the floor in this little room. When I saw it, a sharp flooding thrill went through me—dreaming that this was our room—and you and I—I wonder if I am getting too much like that—electrified—You know dear—how I am there!)

Wednesday Night—at Manteo

I had thought to finish this letter on the boat but several things prevented—rough weather and a splitting headache. But let me go back—(Your letter has just come in. Miss Thomas gave it to me. I love you, dear!)

As I said, I got a man about 9 o'clock Tuesday morning to take me to Hatteras.[10] In a fair head wind we started just he and I on a small gasoline boat. For the first few miles neither of us spoke much—I was a-thinking on ye and feeling the pitiful yearning of beauty—But when the sun got hot he opened up and began to talk while I drove the boat. I asked him at least a thousand questions, and to my delight found that he had been all over the world on tramp steamers—and everything. He told me wonderful things about his sailing from Hamburg to Sidney,[11] Australia, rounding the Horn—(Miss Claire Thomas and Dr. Horton are singing at the piano downstairs.—But I must resist the temptation to go down.[12]) After a while this man informed me that he had written some poetry—quoting the inclosed "Greater Light." Then our talk fell on sea songs and he gave me the inclosed chanties—He was a wonderful fellow—barefooted, bearded—a true seaman. Once he had been a preacher, but the call of the sea dragged him back to it. He loves it with his whole being—Oh, we had a great time to-gether—When we parted at Hatteras I shook his enormous paw with the respect I should give the president of these here United States—Thank God, that's the truth.

I got off at Hatteras about noon, went up through the sleepy town and found a place to stay—at a Mrs. Rollinson's. It happened they had a piano

10. Frank Fulture.

11. Sydney.

12. Claire Thomas, with the State Department of Education, assisted in the direction of the film. W. C. Horton, a Raleigh physician, had portrayed Sir Walter Raleigh in the pageant and now had the part of John White in the film.

there, and after I had got settled I wrote down the music to "The Merman's Song" as best I could.

Mrs. Rollinson gave me a tiny room about 10′ × 10′—a desolate little place, almost as desolate as she was. Of all the women that I've ever seen she had the most tragic face—She was scrubbing clothes all the afternoon—while her daughter, a girl 13 or 14, played with dolls—Poor child, she had nothing else to keep her company. I think Mrs. Rollinson had once known finer things. Her husband appeared to be a ne'er do well—sitting around never saying anything and doing less—Who can tell what that woman has suffered there in that windswept village? By the by, Mrs. Rollinson tried to hire me to teach school for $115 a month. How would you like to teach with me a year in such a place?

In the afternoon I took a nap. I was awakened by the slow tolling of the church bell. It must have rung two hours in all. I got up and walked out to the surf. As I passed the church I asked a boy what the ringing meant, and he said "Old Frank Wallis is dead." "Where did he live?" I asked. "Down the banks thar," he replied. "He warn't nothing much, lived on his kin, never didn't marry 'n nothing." I wanted to go to the "settin' up" but it was too far away. I went on out to the sea and watched it for most an hour with the Cape Hatteras lighthouse watching me from far away. As I sat there looking at the green and white roaring waves, I had a queer desire to jump into the water and be swept away. The shore was very steep and the waves like sisters as they made a strident music grinding the gravel on the sand. I went to bed early and got up at four this morning. When I left Hatteras the moon was shining bright and Orion was up about 40 degrees in the Southeast. A little in the Northeast rose Venus about as high and as brilliant among stars as that goddess was among women. The sunrise by the lighthouse was beautiful, beautiful. I read and slept much of the trip. At a little place called Salvo—not a tree to be seen; houses perched here and there; wild wind forever blowing; danger and death for friend to those sturdy souls—I changed boats, a sailor boy and myself. Our last boat was long and narrow, and it wasn't long before we struck rough weather blowing from portside. I've never seen a boat cut up so. Water would wash across the stern in great slushes, and she would turn and turn. I can feel the motion of it now. It was so terrible that I had to go inside and lie down. I fell into a heavy sleep, and when I awoke with paralyzed bones we were coming into Manteo.

However, on the trip I did read Ervine's *Mixed Marriage* and the character of Mrs. Rainey is a dear. How true it is when she says to Nora "Ye know, they're quare oul' humbugs (men) when ye know them. They think they're that clivir, an' they make us think it too, at first; but sure, ye soon find them out. Och, dear, they're jus' like big childher."—"Ye jus' feel that men are not near as clivir as they think they are, an' ye're not sarry fur it." And Nora says, "Ye wud think mebbe ye'd be disappointed at fin'in' them out; but ye're not."[13]

All of us are like that, dear, and I've got my father's portion all right. Bear with me.

As soon as I got a room in Manteo this afternoon, I put out for Fort Raleigh, but before going far met the Indians and colonists coming in.[14] However, I kept on and tramped out the 3 and a half miles. Just as I got near the fort I met Dr. Horton, Miss Grimball, and Mrs. Crisp coming out. The Dr. and I knew each other, and he introduced me around—and so on. Then I went out to the place where the Spirit of the Renaissance first built its altar in the New World. Nothing much to be seen. On one side of the fort they've put up a log palisade (fence). Tomorrow they stage the Indians attacking the fort. I'm going out to write it up "fer" the papers.[15]

While out there I measured off the ground of the ancient site of sorrow, hope and despair. And there alone for one tiny minute I felt a passing breath of the dreadful story. Oh, if I only could give it expression—the thoughts that lay anchored in the depths of Virginia Dare's eyes, the emotions, the thrills, bravery, sunny laughter changed to the curdling cry for Death—Well we are finite—and it's best. The fort is somewhat like this—the raised part of ground—[16]

Walked back to town. Found that Prof. Koch and Hibbard would be here to-morrow—After supper talked with the pageant crew, or rather heard them talk. Sorry for Miss G—— She needs a tiny baby and other things—you know.

Will stay here to-morrow—Pencil giving out.

"Good night, love" Paul

Don't say anything to Adeline about us. Let me tell her—please.

13. Act 2 (*Chief Contemporary Dramatists*, ed. Dickinson, p. 138).

14. Most of the parts in the film were taken by people of the area. The bank and several other businesses in Manteo closed for the week so their employees could act in the film.

15. The making of the Fort Raleigh film was well covered in state newspapers (e.g., *NO*, 21 September 1921, p. 5; 23 September 1921, p. 7; 26 September 1921, p. 3; and 30 September 1921, p. 5), but none of the articles can be identified as Green's.

16. Sketch given on page 66.

Oh, if I only could give it expression — the thoughts that lay awakened in the depths of Virginia Dare's eye. The creation, the thrill, bravery, piercing laughter changed to the curdling cry for Death — well we are finite — and its best. The fort is somewhat like this — the raised part of ground —

N

40 yds

Monument

Trees, — etc

log fence for pictured attack.

Direction of attack

## 26. To Elizabeth Lay

Lillington, [N.C.]
Sunday P.M. [25 September 1921]

Dearest Girl—

I arrived in town yesterday afternoon,[1] and at once made a bee-line for the post office where I found two letters from you with *The Drama*, and several other letters, one being from a lady teacher in Columbia—Dorothy Scarborough—congratulating me on "Granny Boling" and wanting me to aid her in her book of folk-songs by sending her all the negro songs I could. Offered to give me due credit and the like, talk that traps the human race allus, and I wonder if I'll ever get where I can do for the joy of doing and "let the credit go."[2]

It was real nice seeing oneself in print and reading a tiny editorial note about "me."[3] Oh, that we may get above praise, get away from being a fool. I know well enough that I am a great booby often, often—you and I both. Do you remember how much weaker we make ourselves at times? Mon âme est maudite.

I'm sorry that Miss Monroe failed to accept any of your poetry,[4] but just the same it was nice of her to acknowledge that you've got talent. And, dearie, I wouldn't send my poetry traveling again. I'd lay all I'd written away and start anew. You haven't written any poetry yet—I mean in amount. Why don't you write and write and then send your poems off? But I have no right to preach. However that's the way I feel about it. You can write poetry and I wouldn't be

1. Paul left Manteo, and the filming of the Fort Raleigh story, Friday afternoon, 23 September, crossed Albemarle Sound to Elizabeth City, took the train to Raleigh, where he spent the night, then continued by train to Lillington on Saturday.

2. Scarborough (1878–1935) had seen Green's folk play "Granny Boling" in the current issue of *The Drama* (11 [August–September 1921]: 389–94). A poet and novelist on the faculty of Columbia University, she also collected material from the folk tradition such as legends and songs. The book she seems to have written Green about, *On the Trail of Negro Folk Songs* (Cambridge: Harvard University Press, 1925), mentions no assistance from him.

3. The page of notes on contributors in *The Drama* included the following: "You have never heard of Paul Green? Well, after listening to him when he tells his story of 'Granny Boling' and her family, you will book your seats ahead of time for his next performance" (p. 385).

4. Harriet Monroe (1860–1936), founder and editor of *Poetry*, the leading poetry magazine of the era.

so awfully disappointed in not getting my first efforts in the most exclusive magazine around. My, you air ambitious, ain't you, dear?

Child, I surely was disappointed the other night. As soon as I got to the hotel in Raleigh I tried to call you. Called Dr. Chase,[5] then Mrs. Klutz,[6] then Library, and finally Prof. Koch's. Nobody and nothing knew a thing about you. Where in the world were you hid? And all the time my bill mounting up, until I had to pay $1.20 for hunting after you. Shame, shame and me broke. But let 'er go. Perhaps you'd be interested in knowing how much I did spend on my trip. $97.80 exactly. Wasn't it awful? You see I got where I had to cash checks and the people here and there didn't mind doing it.—But I don't regret a cent of it. I learned a life and already have a play planned out—and a place near Rhodanthe,[7] treeless, bare, desolate place for two souls to try to snatch the secret of the universe from the sea gulls' cries and the moon. But for the life of me I can't decide how it should end—whether they should win the secret or die with the secret before them. There are a thousand facets to this subject.

I've read *John Ferguson*—read it to-day.[8] In my mind it is a wholesome play—something patriarchal in John himself. On the whole it is uplifting, the kind we need more of. But good as it is, it isn't by any means a great play. As Ervine himself says, his plays are not those of a genius—merely talent, which is saying a heap. Now to contrast this play with *Beyond the Horizon* I think it is a far better piece of workmanship, but it hasn't one tenth of the "collisive" force. It lacks power, the power of the storm, the mountains—fate, you know. And what's the use of my spilling hot air to you when you already are acquainted with what I'd say.

However, in regard to *The Easiest Way*,[9] I think you're completely off the track when you say it is punk. I'll acknowledge that about the first half is rather amateurish, but then it begins to gain power and the end is something

5. Harry Woodburn Chase, president of UNC.

6. In whose boardinghouse in Chapel Hill Elizabeth frequently ate.

7. On the Outer Banks, a stop on his trip from Beaufort to Manteo, now spelled Rodanthe.

8. By St. John Ervine (1883–1971), Irish writer and for a time manager of the Abbey Theatre in Dublin.

9. Early (1908) realistic problem play, by Eugene Walter, about a young woman, Laura, destroyed by life in New York City.

terribly beautiful. I read the play on my way from Manteo to ELIZABETH[10] City and after I had finished I sat for a long time aching all over. It was awful. Yes-sir-ee, it is as powerful as Ibsen—in places. I have been wondering how in the world you could call it "punk." Talk about the "God behind the veil," He is surely the officiator through and through poor Laura's life—Fate! anything you want to call it is there—It's great. I think, really, it's the best play in the book—although *Milestones*,[11] and *Mixed Marriage*,[12] not to say anything of our old friend *Abe Lincoln*[13] are good. Several plays in this volume could well have been left out—such as *Pasteur*, *Living Hours*, *The Concert*, and yes, *Gioconda*.[14] This last certainly hasn't enough of the intellect in it to make it a play that will last. But let this pass.

Miss Camp has been talking with me about getting you down here for this week (Sept 26–Oct 3). She is anxious for you to do some dramatization with the kids and get rehearsals for two or three one-act plays under way. She wrote you yesterday, I think. Maybe you'd better wire her as soon as you get her letter. I wish you might come, and stay over until Monday and we could go back to the *Hill* together.[15] But let the biggest vision control in your decision about coming—(I don't say duty).

By the way Mary has borrowed the copy of *The Drama*. I asked her to return it to you direct—

Wish I could write a play this week but can't; got to work.

Love—goodnight Paul

10. Green used a triple underline for this word.

11. By Arnold Bennett and Edward Knoblock.

12. By St. John Ervine.

13. By John Drinkwater.

14. By Sacha Guitry, Arthur Schnitzler, Hermann Bahr, and Gabriele D'Annunzio, respectively.

15. Registration for the fall quarter at UNC was set for Tuesday and Wednesday, 27 and 28 September, with classes to begin the next day, so Green would miss the opening of the quarter in which he began graduate work in philosophy.

## 27. To Elizabeth Lay

[Chapel Hill, N.C.]
[December 1921]

Dear Elizabeth—[1]

Of all the things I possess, I count this the most precious, and that is the reason I wish you to have it. Not that its material value is so great, for it could have cost only a few dollars, perhaps, years ago, but that it is something around which one can build a myriad of golden or pathetic dreams.

I got it from a wrecked house in Poperinghe, Belgium.[2] A shell had struck a piano in one of the rooms and torn everything to pieces. This little statuette was lying on the floor chipped and disfigured by the explosion as you now see it.

The symmetry of it is beautiful, especially from behind, and even in front the broken parts possess a sort of terrible beauty, emblematic (to me) of what the war did to our winged ideals. And there is the look of age about it, a worn look as if it had been washed with woman's tears, as if it had suffered with the mother who once held her baby on her breast and now knew him as a muddy corpse somewhere in Flanders.

Looking at it from a distance of several steps all its scars melt into beauty, and the trustful pose of the little baby's head wrings my silly heart in two. You understand. Because you understand, I give you this rather than a book or picture or the like.

I should have sent this to you but that I couldn't trust it in the mails.

Paul[3]

1. This letter accompanied a Christmas present Paul hand-delivered to Elizabeth. In *The Paul Green I Know* (Chapel Hill: North Caroliniana Society, 1978), she describes the present: "a little madonna, not an artistic art museum piece, but the sort of good statuary one would find in a French provincial store where the general run of country people would buy their gifts" (p. 4).

2. During the fighting around Ypres in the summer of 1918.

3. In *The Paul Green I Know*, Elizabeth adds that "the madonna has been on our mantelpiece since then, protected, tied sometimes with a string to a nail at the back of the mantel so it couldn't be knocked off or injured" (p. 4).

## 28. To Elizabeth Lay

Lillington, [N.C.]
Sunday night [25 December 1921]

My Dear Girl,

Yesterday went by without my writing you, and I felt as if part of the twenty-four hours was gone astray—or lost, or something. I did, however, send some Christmas cards to the others.

I got here Friday night all petered out surely. But at last I'm finding a little rest in the end of all. More than I can tell you I wish I might see you. Faith, and I'm already anxious to go back to the Hill. As much as I want to, I think I shall not be able to do any writing here. Child, child, it hurts me to think of the good you and I might do down here in Harnett. Oh, it is selfish—the way things are around Chapel Hill, men working day and night over the dry roots of things long dead, when they might be working in the depths of life, helping many and many a one into a glimpse of what you and I see now and then—"The light that never was on sea and land."[1] Even through this harsh expression, I hope you'll see what I'm driving at. My mind is all like a cat in a gale of wind. People here in the room talking about this and that—subjects right in the soil, near the heart, homely,—and true. Beneath all the worry at low prices, sickness, bad luck and everything else around here there is a note of eternal freshness and life bubbling at the brim that one never finds in places where the god of English grammar and servants of rhetoric live and move and have their being. Sometimes I hate the thought of teaching philosophy—or anything—and drying up in a merciless atmosphere of learning. Well, I could go on indefinitely contrasting the academic with the farm life. They both, of course, have their place. The only thing that will suit me, and I hope you too, is a combination of the two. (Excuse so much assonance.) Something has been said again by a few friends about my trying for the place of County Superintendent of Schools here. If there were a chance of my getting it, I don't see how I could do it. But think of the good you and I might do. All the schools in the county, etc. etc.—pageant work, county sings, spelling matches, athletic contests. Oh, my—and a thousand other things. But though our minds are infinite our actions always will be finite for they are exclusive, limiting in their

1. William Wordsworth, "Elegiac Stanzas Suggested by a Picture of Peele Castle," line 15.

nature. Isn't it awful to try talking to each other in a letter when we have become so heart to heart that looks, touches, a whisper now and then are enough for us to understand each other? I shall be glad when I see you again. Maybe there'll come a letter from you to-morrow. Write me all about what you're doing. Perhaps you'd like to know what all the homefolks are doing here and so on. Let me retrace.

Friday night John[2] met me at the station in Angier. We drove on out, and when we got home papa was sitting by the fire, his leg all bound up in a plaster *cast.* And, dear, he certainly is down *cast.* There's no denying it. (Such punning!) I don't know what to do to him.

Monday Night

I was interrupted and haven't been able to finish. Saturday I worked on a barn John is building at his place and in the afternoon Erma and I cleaned up, building fences, planting rose bushes, sweeping yards, etc. Sunday was a dull rainy day, with a wet wind moaning ceaselessly, you know. We had lots of fun exchanging presents. All mine—those you did up so nicely—were left at Chapel Hill. I came off like a crank and forgot them. But I wrote for them from Durham. Perhaps they'll come to-morrow.—This night is a blue one surely. The girls—Caro, Erma, and Gladys—have gone to a dance in Lillington and figuratively I'm biting my nails. To-day we tried to talk about the matter seriously. And I tried my best to show them the logic in the matter, plain common sense of the thing. And they said they saw it, but just because they wanted to go they DECLARED they were going. The long and short of it is this: I don't approve of the boys who go to the public dances in Lillington—most of them drug store loafers and gamblers and drinkers when they can get whiskey—without ambition or the will to do anything. And the girls know it and yet they persist in keeping company with them, arguing they must have somebody to go with. Maybe I'm cranky, but I feel this strongly. And their going flippantly off when I had shown them how the matter stood with me made me feel blue.—Say, I wish you would not try to come by here. I just can't stay. I'm going back to the Hill in a few days. Will write to-morrow.

Paul

2. Paul's older half-brother, who had a farm near their father's farm.

## 29. To Elizabeth Lay

[Chapel Hill, N.C.]
Tuesday night [17 January 1922]

Dearest One—[1]

By the time you receive this you already will have read my incoherent note of last night. Please do not worry about it too much. Let me do that for you, if it be possible. The tiny ray of light in the letter was the knowledge that she wasn't being entirely fair to me—as I see it.[2] The rivers run into the sea and the sea is not full. The wind whirleth about continually—from the east to the west and from the north to the south. And the wind is never still. The sun riseth in the east and setteth in the west and hasteth unto the place from whence he arose. All things are full of labor. The tongue cannot utter it nor the heart of man understand it. The eye is not satisfied with seeing nor the ear filled with hearing. Vanity of Vanities saith the preacher. All is Vanity.[3]

I have been feeling like this, but I'm trying hard to get out of it all day. At noon I went to the P. O. and in my box I saw a letter from Paris not written in her hand. My knees almost gave way beneath me. All at once it ran over me "She's dead! They've written to let me know." Honey, it was foolish, but real enough. In a second I thought of the letters about going to the Sorbonne, and I knew then nothing was to be feared. I'm sending you the letter from Mlle. Bourseiller.

My work is going to be splendid this quarter.[4] I feel that I am dressing off my heretofore ragged year. I'm taking Greek 43 (New Testament. It's fine) at 8:30. At 9:25 I have German I (Enlightening to say the least), at 10:15 Music (Harmony), at 12:30 Philosophy, and at 2:00 Architecture under Dr. Bernard.[5]

1. Elizabeth, who left Chapel Hill the previous Sunday (15 January), was touring in the northern part of the state with three Playmakers plays: "The Miser" by Green, "In Dixon's Kitchen" by Wilbur Stout and Ellen Lay, and "Trista," her own play. The group would return on Wednesday, 25 January.

2. Green had just received another letter from Renée Bourseiller, in which she accused him of deserting her. She was physically ill, she said, and had little interest in living because of his treatment of her (Green diary, PG-SHC).

3. Opening verses of Ecclesiastes in paraphrase.

4. Winter quarter classes began on 5 January 1922.

5. William Stanly Bernard's architecture course dealt with the "history and principles of Greek and Roman architecture, sculpture, painting, with some account of the minor arts" (UNC Catalogue, 1921–22). Bernard (1867–1938), in the classics department, also taught Green's class in New Testament Greek and biblical translation. The

All these courses are *plumb* good, and I'm going to be sorter happy at it all. I want to be able to see the logic in building and now I have a good chance in the last-named course. It'll come in fine for next year.[6] And of course the German and New Testament are even more essential to my philosophy. And music certainly has a place in philosophy. It is so close to the ideal and scientific worlds.—Yes, I'm free from the teaching.[7] But I'm not wholly pleased there. More or less the dept. has taken the attitude of being a little raw. But I did right, I know, and so there is little to trouble here.[8]

All day I've been head over heels in work. Prof.[9] wants to get the plays off to Holt to-morrow,[10] and so I must write forewords to "Witches Ride,"[11] "The Lowrie Gang"[12] and "Blackbeard,"[13] besides revising the last two. I think they will leave out the "Lowries" yet. Possibly put in "Trista,"[14] and replace "The

---

philosophy course (Philosophy 17, taught by Horace Williams) studied "the forces that shape life." In a letter written to Elizabeth the next day, Green says: "I'm getting into my philosophy work somewhat—reading now Hegel's Philosophy of History. It is great. He shows the history of the world as the history of the individual—moving, aiming, trusting, failing, achieving humanity—an enormous individual—And more or less, H—— suggests the rare kinship of all things" ([18 January 1922], EG-SHC).

6. When Green expected to teach philosophy at UNC.

7. In English.

8. The nature of this problem is unknown. The catalog for 1921–22 lists Green as a teaching fellow in the English department and shows that he was scheduled to teach a class of English 1 each quarter. Over the Christmas holidays, however, Horace Williams awarded Green a $500 fellowship for the remainder of the school year (Paul Green to Elizabeth Lay, 29 December 1921, EG-SHC), and that may have caused the loss of his English department job. Or the fellowship may have provided enough money for him to resign the job.

9. Koch.

10. For publication in Koch, *Carolina Folk-Plays*, first series (1922).

11. By Elizabeth.

12. That is, "The Last of the Lowries."

13. A collaboration between Elizabeth and Paul.

14. Paul's favorite among Elizabeth's plays. In a letter two days earlier to Elizabeth, he wrote: "I took supper with Mr. and Mrs. Koch at the cafeteria. We talked of 'Trista' all the time nearly. Dear, they ain't no denying that you have writ the greatest play of us all if you will just carry it to completion. The more I think about it, the better I like it. It has spirituality. But you've *got to let it loose* for me. . . . I want to feel it to my toes!" ([15 January 1922], EG-SHC).

Bellbuoy" with B.B.[15] My! You'll own the volume then, won't you? But I'll be proud on ye in my feeble way gist the same.[16] I told prof to let's leave out the "Lowries" if there was any likelihood of the public's linking it up with "Riders to the Sea." Tom Peete mentioned it, and you know F. H. K.[17]

Adeline D.[18] and I had a long talk to-day, and she got nearer to my heart than ever before. She's all blue. And this morning when we met she was just tickled and said "I've longed for you more than"—well, I didn't know what to say. She was plumb discouraged. We came up into your office and began to talk—rather she to listen and I to talk. All I said was that come what might, I was going to go on and try, try, try to see the light—and so on. It was very real to me. As I was talking, she suddenly sprang up, looked at me hard and with a mistiness in her eyes said, "Paul, I don't see how I could do without you. I've missed you so." And with that she ran out the room slamming the door behind her. It was queer. And I couldn't help letting the silly tears come to my eyes when I thought of what she'd said. Really she has meant a lot to me and I hope I've helped her some. And it was sweet to know that she missed me a

15. "Blackbeard."

16. Koch, *Carolina Folk-Plays* (1922), includes "When Witches Ride," "Peggy" by Harold Williamson, "Dod Gast Ye Both!" by Hubert Heffner, "Off Nags Head (Bell Buoy)" by Dougald MacMillan, and "The Last of the Lowries." "Trista" is included in the 1941 edition and later editions of *Carolina Folk-Plays.* "Blackbeard" (Paul Green, *The Lord's Will and Other Carolina Plays* [New York: Holt, 1925], 47–96) is the only play Elizabeth and Paul wrote together. With characteristic modesty, she says she "finished a version and handed it to Paul for him to make certain minor changes (I thought), and the play that came out was so completely his that I didn't feel really I should put my name on it" (*The Paul Green I Know*, pp. 5–6).

17. Tom Peete Cross (1879–1951), Celticist and folklorist since 1913 at the University of Chicago, taught at UNC for a year (1912–13), and his folklore studies focused on the Southeast (several of his articles provided background for Playmakers plays, for instance "When Witches Ride"). Frequently he advised Koch about regional dialects (see Koch, *Carolina Folk-Plays* [1941], pp. 483–91). Koch retained "The Last of the Lowries," but to cover the obvious structural similarity between it and John Synge's "Riders to the Sea," he inserted a note at the end of it: "It is interesting to note that the actual story . . . of the old Lowrie mother somewhat parallels that of Maurya in Synge's 'Riders to the Sea.' In the one case the mother sees her sons sacrificed before the power of the law. In the other she sees them claimed by the terribleness of the sea. So far as the suffering is concerned, the forces in both cases might be the same" (*Carolina Folk-Plays* [1922], p. 148).

18. Denham, Koch's niece and fellow Playmaker.

little as a sister and brother might miss each other. This afternoon we talked a little bit and I think she and I both lost some of our blueness, though we only talked a few minutes on books and like things. One trouble with her, and the big trouble, I believe, is that she's in love with someone and she isn't sure that he loves her. She won't tell me who, more than that he likes music, is a frat man and takes her at times to dances. Poor child, I hope he's a good man.[19]

Now, honey, the plagued scenery is in a fix for several reasons. Your telegram came this noon. After dinner I took it to George[20] and Prof. K. to get their authorization for sending it. They both were a bit upset. They want to help you out and yet are loth to adopt the policy of sending Playmaker scenery about. But just for your sake I think they'll do it this once. It's fine to see how much they both think of you—and Ellen and KB.[21] George figured it out and the express on the scenery and postage etc. will be over $11.00. Now I'm [word illegible] you as to whether you think the people there can afford to pay these expenses. FHK suggests that perhaps they would rather make their own scenery. They could do it cheaper—with your master arm to help.

To-day I got *Midsummer Night's Dream* illustrated by Arthur Rackham. It is wonderful. I showed it to Ellen and Mither.[22] Will send the ballads to-morrow. Mary T was to send your coat. Have you got it? Trip is [word illegible]. Dr. Greenlaw came back Thursday. How about your play? Heard nothing of Eng. 126 or 127.[23] Not given I guess.

I love you[,] love
your Paul
a thousand *kisses*, not "thanks"

Honey, take care on yourself and don't work too hard—"Oh, Lindy Lu, Lindy Lu, I misses you."

19. Denham graduated in 1922, remained in Chapel Hill, married Fred B. McCall of the UNC Law School faculty, and had a lengthy career as a musician and music teacher. She helped Green find and arrange music for *The Lost Colony* and other plays, and in 1981 she received a UNC Distinguished Alumna Award.

20. Denny (1899–1959), business manager of the Playmakers, who later came to national prominence as creator and moderator of the radio program, "America's Town Meeting of the Air" (1935–52).

21. Katharine Batts.

22. Mary Thornton, Elizabeth's roommate.

23. Koch's courses in playwrighting.

## 30. To Elizabeth Lay

[Chapel Hill, N.C.]
Thursday—12:30 [P.M.] [19 January 1922]

Dearest—[1]

Last night I intended writing you, but at supper I was persuaded by Tyre Taylor[2] and my own self to go to *Wake Up Jonathan.*[3] After the show we were delayed in Durham nearly an hour and consequently when I got back to my cold room it was past mid-night and no time for writing. As for the play, I can't say very much. It was raggedly done,—I mean the technique of the composition—and ended rather unsatisfactorily to me. When you get back we'll talk it over.

On the way back from Durham last night I went into the P.O., hoping "mebbe thar'd be a letter" from you, but they wuz nothing. Peut-être ce sera un aujourd'hui, qui sais?[4] There is so much around me here.

A few minutes ago I finished O'Neill's new play *Gold*, the last act of which is a rewriting of the one-act play, "Where the Cross Is Made." It is powerful but so full of human errors, sufferings, despairs, hopes, loves, joys and the like that it hurt me more than a little. The theme is the power of deeds—the haunting action they have, even when they are committed in times of undue stress, moral blindness even—or physical weakness. The moral consciousness has its own *Erynnes* (sp?),[5] its avenging spirits. I want you to read it. There is little poetry there, but plenty of the warp and woof of troubled being.

A time this morning I was in your office,[6] and everything within was speaking of you. And there came to me a shy little pain of longing for you. Since you left, more and more have I begun to live in retrospect and I don't want to do that surely.

Yesterday I read an abbreviated version of *Anna Christie* in *Current Opin-*

1. Elizabeth was still on the Playmakers tour of the state.

2. Fellow graduate student (1898–1970), later a lawyer and prominent in state politics.

3. Comedy (1921) by Elmer Rice and Hatcher Hughes that ends with the wife tricking her husband into a reconciliation in order to save their marriage.

4. That is, "Peut-être que ce sera une aujourd'hui, qui sait?"

5. Greek term for the furies, usually transliterated "erinyes."

6. The office of the Bureau of Community Drama in Hill Hall on the UNC campus.

*ion.*[7] You will like it. The Irishman has some of the *playboy* characteristics[8]—though how nearly these characteristics are of the type I cannot say. But it is like all of O'Neill's plays—weirdly fatalistic and lacking in sublimity. But faulty as he is, we must be proud of him—he's interpretating[9] the parchments of life—joining sea and land—rediscovering beauty and goodness in sorrow—twisting and turning, putting currents of pure water into our American tarns of Auber and the shallow sea sickened pools of Wright and a hundred others.[10] We *must* do something like this—something greater than this.

I should like a bit to hear what you are doing. As yet I haven't seen a single notice of the Playmakers in any paper. Are you having the success of last year? I'm afeard on it.

Wilbur[11] said he'd received a letter from Ellen telling a few things—of the performance in Henderson—clearance of $86, etc. Say 'Ello to Hellen for me—and give Kate B.[12] my love—all that's left from Hellen. I haven't writ your mother yet. Nor have I made any clearly defined plans about you know what.[13] Are you going to stop in Raleigh about that matter?

Love fer ye, me darlint, Paul

I haven't an envelope up here and so I'm going to your office and borrow one.

7. "*Anna Christie*: A Play Both Above and Below the Dramatic Sea-level," *Current Opinion* 72 (January 1922): 57–66.

8. That is, characteristics of Christy Mahon in John Synge's *Playboy of the Western World* (1907).

9. Green's spelling.

10. The setting of Edgar Allan Poe's "Ulalume" is near the "dank tarn of Auber, / In the ghoul-haunted woodland of Weir." Harold Bell Wright (1872–1944) was a popular moralistic novelist during the early decades of the century.

11. Wilbur Stout, fellow graduate student in philosophy (Ph.D., 1926), Playmaker, and coauthor with Ellen Lay of "In Dixon's Kitchen," one of the plays performed on the tour.

12. Katharine Batts, who played Trista in Elizabeth's play on the tour.

13. Perhaps an engagement ring.

## 31. To Elizabeth Lay

[Chapel Hill, N.C.]
Wednesday night [25 January 1922]

Dearest—dearest—love—[1]

Your two letters came to-day at noon, and if I only could tell you how they lifted me out of myself and set my heart singing for the wonder of you. I think I realized more clearly than ever before how all these many years I have been waiting for you, and in my blindness, dear, I came so near losing you and all that you have and may mean to me and me to you. A sort of great peace came over me with your words, a regeneration of spirit—a cleansing. It seems that now I can never do a crooked unclean thing again. Somehow I feel more and more lifted towards the light. Oh, dear heart, soul of my soul and body of mine, what have we to face together in years before—dancing flames of joy—colors of pleasure—tears and sighs—grey days and fair—and through it all the pure, unconquerable—the everlasting spirit of ourselves—freed—freed from bondage of narrowness—envy, hate, jealousy—all littleness—friend of Jew and gentile—no longer listening to flattery—all ways, always striving to remember the hidden snowbitten violet as well as the molten lava furnace of industry. I almost see white streaming figures of luminousness go by me in the night—angels, comforters by me saying "follow! follow! follow!" There is a far away voice crying in the watches "There was a light come from god."—Darling, I want you here to kiss the tears from my silly eyes and. . . . Oh, honey, it seems as if a voice were calling me to live, live and go high and be humble. Even I am one of these—the beggar, the convict, the fool, the wise man. Where shall we find grace amd mercy to help them all. I hardly can write. There is so much I feel.—Dear love, there is an unutterably tender feeling in me for everything. Your love has helped me so. Stay wid me dear. And in sunshine and rain, bad appearance, shabby forms of us two, let us live knowing that "Consider the lilies of the fields" dwells in us too.[2] I almost feel the thoughts of people I am so tuned to all that is to-night. And that dear girl[3]—I love her so that she should suffer. You know, sweet—and I accuse myself.

But let me try to tell you a few bits of news. Wait. It was too terrible about Gladys.[4] She is physically weak somewhere, and being a woman, I think you

1. Elizabeth would return from the Playmakers tour within a few days.

2. Luke 12:27–28.

3. Renée Bourseiller.

4. Before Christmas Gladys became seriously ill with the flu and had to leave the

can guess what I mean. She has had those fainting spells since she was about 16. No one, I suppose, ever told her about the secrets of life, and maybe she overstrained herself or did a thousand and one things that are now responsible for her suffering. I wish you had not let her go away so early. Write me as soon as you hear from her.

I'm mailing your wigs in the morning. They're already tied up. What about the scenery? Do you wish it at the price of the express?—please wire or write.

I've just finished the foreword to "When Witches Ride," the revising of "BB," and reworking "The Lowries."[5] It is now 10:30 P.M. K. B.[6] is typing for me, we both being in K's office. To-morrow the plays go to Holt.

To-day I saw Horace. He was grand—and told me he knew exactly where I was and that he knew I'd get through O.K. "You are on the wide ocean now, and your anchor won't reach to the bottom. But it'll all come right. I know you'll make it. I've been there too"—This he said.

My courses are good. I've prepared my Greek lesson. There is something queer and thrilling about reading the original of such expressions ἐν ἀρχῇ ἦν ὁ λόγος—in the beginning was the word.[7] I am right up against the heartbeat of those who strove and suffered and overcame—poor Peter, John and the rest. And the music to-day (my first lesson) was a revelation. The wonderful way in which chords grow in and out of each other. The philosophy, the mystery of it all—the certainty, too—hold me to them. I've got my German to prepare. Honey, I miss! miss you! May the time soon come when we can be one—Thou in me and I in thee that we both may be one. Pray for me—not for my sake but for the sake of him that sent me.

Oh, that I could love you so that the whole wide world put away old low desires and be born of the spirit—one with that which is high.

Good night, Paul

---

Durham Conservatory of Music and return home. Her recovery was slow and she did not return to the conservatory (interview with Erma Green Gold, 16 June 1990).

5. Her "When Witches Ride" and his "The Last of the Lowries" were to be in Koch, *Carolina Folk-Plays*, published later that year. Each play in the volume has a brief foreword giving its historical source and information about production. "Blackbeard," written by Elizabeth and revised by Paul, was first published in his collection of plays, *The Lord's Will.*

6. Katharine Batts.

7. John 1:1.

## 32. To Elizabeth Lay

[Chapel Hill, N.C.]
Sunday night [16 April 1922]

My darling;[1]

Now I come to you, after writing a long letter to your pa, one to [name illegible], and one to Frank Fulture at Ocracoke, asking him to see about renting us a shack[2]—etc., etc. Writing those letters has made a sort of luminousness and warmth spread over me, thinking of you. Honey, I want you so. It is on a desolate, cloudy time like this that I seem to need you so—even in sunshine and rain I wants you. And yet, though it sends a sharp thrill through me to think of lying beside you, of having you near me for years and years, still I know that these are of the essence of change, and we must build deeper. But we are so young and strong that this side must yearn with a thousand pulsings—Our first night at Ocracoke! Something rises up in me and almost suffocates me at the thought. I must not think of it anymore.

The world is beautiful and mysterious here—all the spring is out. Wouldn't it have been wonderful to have been married in the spring?

Your letter came this afternoon. I was askeered you wouldn't write me today. It is so sweet to get these little notes from you—just telling me that you love me. Will, love, oh will it be someday, that we shall not care much for that magic word. Even if I become distilled intellect, maybe the wonder and mystery will still exist—

Miller[3] and I played tennis to-day—Easter Sunday—a fitting way to commemorate the risen Lord. But I think he would have done some such thing himself—to express the boundless youth within him. Honey, it's amazing to me how tough I am—what animal spirits exist under my melancholy, half-saturnine appearance. I played and played and played—from 9 until 12:30 and poor Miller was dead, but I couldn't tell any fatigue except of brain, for when I'd close my eyes, I'd see balls here and there—you know—I can't help being like a little boy—sorter proud of the muscles that slide noiselessly under my skin, the vigor and bubbling joy. *I do love to play.* I can't get enough of it. What can we play together when "we uns gits merried"—

1. As part of her job in the Bureau of Community Drama, Elizabeth was traveling around the state assisting with play productions.

2. For their honeymoon.

3. Fellow graduate student James Bennett Miller (b. 1892).

I don't see how you can work on *Tristram Shandy* up there, with all your other work.[4] To-morrow I begin on my plays[5]—we ought to be able to write some at Ocracoke—what a magic name!

Have you written to Mr. Riddle about the scenery and pictures? I've heard nothing from them.

I am still thinking of the safety and rewards of Cornell, but also of the risk and wonder of Europe.

When you sleep to-night think on selfish me—and remember that I am your own Paul.

A day or two ago I was talking to Horace about next year, and told him that of course you and I were going to Europe together. He said he knew that and thought it was fine.[6] Then he said "She is a splendid woman," and I said "Yes, yes, and no one knows her as I do." With a merry eye he said, "No one is supposed to." He's a sharp un—See ye.

## 33. To Elizabeth Lay

[Lillington, N.C.]
Tuesday morning [27 June 1922]

Dear Girl—[1]

The wedding here draws nigh and nigher. Everything whirls and turns as if a young cyclone were about. Out of the rush and storm it is hard to find a

4. In her spare time Elizabeth was studying—among other things, Sterne's novel—for an M.A. in English.

5. Among them, "Wrack P'int," first done by the Playmakers on 26–27 January 1923 but not published. It is set on Cape Hatteras, known as the "graveyard of the Atlantic" because of the numerous shipwrecks that have occurred off its point.

6. Plans were fuzzy, but Paul hoped to get a Ph.D. in philosophy from Cornell University on the basis of his present graduate work at UNC along with some time at Cornell and Oxford. He said Williams had told him "there was a distinct feeling (at UNC) that I (anyone [on the faculty], for that matter) ought to have a Ph.D." (Paul Green to Elizabeth Lay, [22 May 1922], EG-SHC).

---

1. On 14 June Green had an operation on his nose (submucous membrane) at Macpherson's Hospital in Durham. He tried recuperating at his father's farm, but after a few days infection and severe pain forced him to go back to Durham for treatment. He was not well enough to return to the farm until 24 June. Elizabeth was at her home in Beaufort planning their wedding, which was to take place on Thursday, 6 July. At the farm Paul found himself in the midst of preparations for the wedding of his sister Gladys and Louis Sylvester on Thursday, 29 June.

quiet place and time to write to you. I am out on the front porch now. The girls are moving hither thither, with mops, brooms, and clothes chasing away distances before beauty of vision. And maybe after all the shebang will be pretty. Gladys is so anxious that the gods be merciful to her in regard to the weather that all of us are sure it will rain and be a mess.

Really I think of her wedding more than I do of our own. In fact it is impossible for me to believe truly that in a bit over a week I'll be a married man with all that that means. Whenever I do let myself think on it all it takes my breath away and also fills me full of sorrow and wonder about a million things. Honey, I'm just so worthless and contemptible that I oughtn't to be allowed to marry ye. Somehow up here in all this quietness and simplicity, rather than becoming wrapped up in it and lifted into exaltation I have just become a man with the hoe spirit.[2] The beauty of these happy fields and the patience of people's lives have not meant to me what they should. Whether it's because I am not yet fully well, I don't know. I have a 'spicion that I need you more than anything to make me feel—(Gladys wants me to beat the foot-mat.)

Please don't worry about me any more. I'm getting along fine. My nose is still a little sore, but is getting better fast.

I've just been helping the girls shell beans and gab. They gave me a great deal of advice as to how to treat you. For one thing they bawled me out about my clothes, saying that I didn't try to go dressed decently. I agreed and promised to buy nicer clothes and keep them nicer. They are fine sisters, but honestly they don't even seem to glimpse the borderland of our country—they don't even suspect the real bonds between thee and me, love. And somehow I can't talk seriously about it all. I joke the whole matter far too much, I'm afraid. Oh, it won't be long before we shall know each other more fully, and we have so much to learn. Last night I lay awake just wondering about you and asking myself whether I had really known you. You seemed so far away.

A few minutes ago I itemized a bill of expenditures necessary before we leave,[3] and the amount staggered me. Caro and Erma's way to be paid to B—,[4] insurance, hospital and doctor's bill, and I'm trying to pay papa back some-

2. That is, numb, as is the man in Edwin Markham's "The Man with the Hoe," who is made "dead to rapture and despair" by incessant labor (*The Man with the Hoe and Other Poems* [London: Gay and Bird, 1902], p. 15).

3. For school at Cornell.

4. Beaufort, where they were to be bridesmaids in Paul and Elizabeth's wedding.

thing of what I owe him. Child, child, we sho' got to git us a job rat now when we get to Cornell—They ain't no disputing it—How we'll ever make it through to Oxford I don't know. But we'll make it somehow, if our health keeps right and other things go the same.

Your letter came yesterday with the invitation.[5] I wanted to answer last night, but such a crowd was here that there was nothing to do but listen to the jaw. I think the invitations are nice. Maybe it's better that the *e* was left off my name. I wish we might spell it that way. It seems less affected.[6]

Yesterday I received a copy of the plays from Chas Scribners'.[7] I'm sending it to you. Perhaps you'd like to read the introduction sometime. None of them here have appeared interested in it. Of course I've asked no one to read any of them. I don't expect you to find time to read any now, but maybe later you will. Take it as a little gift.

Say, what flowers am I to have—what other things whatever am I to bring. Please write me full directions for myself—kind of suit to be married in, shoes, etc., time to come to Beaufort—what to bring—bed linen, and so on—you know—Take a long breath and send me my papers.

Have you got your certificate yet? I'll get mine as soon as I feel better. When is your father coming back?

I wish you could see Earl.[8] He is cute, a sight. He and I play marbles and baseball more than a little. Mary's Billy is a terrible little man too. Oh honey, honey, my heart is running out of me thinking on ye. Please take care of yourself—please—It is so easy for us to cheat ourselves now. *Take care of yourself.* Don't let the times run you to death. Oh, darling I love ye, I love ye—Soon you will rest in my arms!

Your Paul

5. A sample of their wedding invitation.

6. Up to that time, Paul and others spelled his family name "Greene" (and his middle name "Elliott"), but on the wedding announcement Elizabeth gave her fiancé's name as "Paul Eliot Green," spellings Green used thereafter. According to her, she made the changes deliberately but broke the news to him by calling them accidents.

7. B. Roland Lewis, ed., *Contemporary One-Act Plays* (New York: Scribner, 1922), an anthology including Green's "White Dresses" (pp. 215–37) and an introduction by Lewis on the nature of the one-act play (pp. 3–15).

8. Son of the woman who kept house for Paul's father, about eight years old (interview with Erma Green Gold, 21 October 1982).

## 34. To Mary G. Johnson

[416 Eddy Street] Ithaca, N.Y.
11 November 1922

Dearest Mary,[1]

The box has come, and a thousand thanks to you for sending it. It was a great surprise and a welcome comer. I am saving it nice until Elizabeth comes back. She is somewhere out in the State, giving dramatic institutes. I've just received a letter from her, telling me all the ups and downs she is going through. Well, she's a brave one. Naturally she isn't gifted at talking and appearing in public, but just the same she makes herself go ahead. I've changed from the box to a subject that is inexhaustible. I want you and Elizabeth to know each other to the bottom, if that's possible. In our farm talk, "She's the beatingest thing in all the world." She's the purest person I've ever known, and the only human being that could save my poor soul like a brand from the burning. Of course, selfishly if for no other reason, I ought to love her. I don't suppose we will ever have a quarrel. We just don't seem to have any reason to. Our basic principle is that each one is trying to do the best he can, and since this is true there is no reason to be unkind. Perhaps I'd better not get started too headlong here. It will be enough to say that anyone who can get along with me ain't in the ordinary run of humans. Let it rest there. And she loves everybody at home as much as me. She thinks Hugh is about the finest boy she has ever seen. As Mis' Callie Jones would say, "She jest puore loves him." I have a feeling that I am telling secrets, and therefore must stop.

We wish we could go home Christmas, but just now we fear it would be a little unwise. It would cost us at least two-hundred dollars. We think we shall go to New York for a week or more, not just for pleasure but to try and raise some money. E. wants to get a publisher to take a book she is working at on play production. Already she has it about half-done.[2] And I am trying to get a

1. Following their wedding in Beaufort on 6 July, Paul and Elizabeth went to Morehead City for the night, then took a train north for Ithaca, New York—for lack of money skipping Ocracoke and the honeymoon they hoped to spend on the Outer Banks. In Ithaca they rented a house at 416 Eddy Street, near the railroad tracks. Elizabeth took a job at Cornell, with the Department of Rural Social Organization, doing much the same work she had done with the Bureau of Community Drama in North Carolina: traveling throughout the state to assist in play productions and hold workshops on drama. Paul entered the graduate program in philosophy.

2. Expanded version of a booklet she was primarily responsible for: *Play Production*

play on in the great city, also a book of negro plays published.[3] Maybe we can get enough money to go to Europe. But unless I can borrow at least eight-hundred dollars, I'm afraid we'll never see it, that is, this next year. But we are going someday, and I'd like to take Caro and Erma along. Of course there might be, speaking frankly, other drawbacks. By that time we might have a whole army of dirty-eared little Greens. We'd have to charter a whole boat then. Elizabeth says she isn't going to be satisfied with less than twenty or twenty-five. But I think fifteen will do me for quite a while. Mr. Bill Deal[4] will be pushed off the map numerically, I'm afraid.

Well, it seems that we ought to be very happy, but for myself I've never been more unhappy—in a sense. I'm all up in the air about what I ought to do in this great world and wide. Day and night I think about it. I'm not just satisfied with the idea of settling down as a teacher of philosophy and finally become president of the University and die respected and full of years and rest with my fathers. Excuse grammar. Well, that's where the trouble is. Dr. Williams and Pres. Chase[5] are depending on me—especially Dr. Williams, to start a great school of study in the Southland. And I could do it if my whole heart was in it. Who in the world could wish for a more brilliant beginning? But somehow I am not certain. I am always planning books, and plays, and stories. And the truth is I can't do both and be of most value. It is getting near to an either or proposition. Before starting this philosophical career, I told Dr. Williams and Pres. Chase just where I stood. They told me to go ahead and work at it a year or two, and then if I didn't like it, I could change. Very true. But just the same I know that they are depending on me. They feel that I will decide their way. And too it keeps Dr. Williams from finding a successor while I am making up my mind. And the worst part is that I don't know which I want to do. Several

---

*for Amateurs*, by Frederick H. Koch, Elizabeth A. Lay, John E. Lear, and Norman M. Paull (Chapel Hill: University of North Carolina Press, 1922). She had already published *A Study Course in Modern Drama* (Chapel Hill: University of North Carolina Press, 1921).

3. Such as "Sam Tucker" (revised as "Your Fiery Furnace"), "Granny Boling" (revised as "The Prayer-Meeting"), and "White Dresses," all eventually included in *Lonesome Road: Six Plays for the Negro Theatre* (New York: McBride, 1926).

4. Harnett County man with a large family.

5. Harry Woodburn Chase (1883–1955), president of UNC, one of whose chief interests was developing a faculty that met national standards of achievement.

of the big dogs here say that I am wasting my time, adding that I am cut out for writing. Do something for American art, they say. Yes, but I must have something to say, and learning of the world movements in politics, economics, art, everything will make it possible for me to say something. And so it goes, around and around. Elizabeth says she'll do whatever I want to do. And often I'm tempted to go back to Harnett County, buy a mule (on time), rent some land, and enjoy myself. But Dr. Lay, to whom I mentioned this plan before he ever married me to his red-haired gal, said I could do that but that one never got anywhere by shirking his duty. I had a duty to society, he said, and that duty could never be fulfilled by hiding in the bushes. So it is. I know that I could go over to New York and get rich writing for the theatre. But I want to have words with people about the way of life, and that would come with teaching.

Maybe I take everything too seriously, too sadly. Man is a shadow. Today he is, tomorrow he is not. Yes, there is that side of it. But we mustn't give up. Hogs do that. To be human is to fight it out even to the crack of doom. And to be heroic is[6]

## 35. To George W. Lay

416 Eddy Street, Ithaca, N.Y.
6 December 1922

My dear Father—

Excuse the sudden crack of the ice in my making such an address.[1] Let it stand for what it formally and internally means. For a good while, in fact, ever since we got to Ithaca, I have been repeating to Elizabeth, "Really, I must write to Dr. Lay. He has taken me into the family, me a stranger and maybe a fellow likely to turn out an impostor, and it is a fitting thing that I make to him a sort of confession of faith, a statement of what I am, as nearly as I can do so." But the days have gone by and I have been wrapped up in studying Kant and Hegel and Aristotle. The thing that has determined me is our Mither's little letter that came this morning and in a gentle way spoke of my silence that made her speechless. And so tonight, while the snow pours down and the wind taps on the window and while Elizabeth is away in Morrisville leaving

6. The surviving letter breaks off here, tantalizingly.

1. Always before, Green had addressed Elizabeth's father as "Dr. Lay."

me lonely as a sparrow, I will sit into the late hours giving you an account of myself.

I grew up, as you already know, on the farm among Negroes and tenants. There is no sort of work I haven't done and can't do. I've ditched, rolled logs at a saw-mill, ploughed, hoed, dug stumps, everything. Whatever work was to be done, I must be the champion. I could pull more fodder than any man in the neighborhood. This I demonstrated one day by beating the title claimer. I could pick more cotton than the other fellow. And this I proved by picking 403 lbs. in ten hours, a record then. My father is a hard-working, what is called a "stirring" man. And he made us work, until the habit was fixed. Ever since I can remember I have been poor, not an unusual thing under the sun. My grandfather[2] was well to-do, thousands of acres of land and oodles of slaves.[3] But the war broke him financially and spiritually. And so in 1866, if I remember correctly, he died worn out, a comparatively young man, and left several sons and a widow with their proud Scotch blood and a tall house set in a grove of oaks as their greatest inheritance. The land was divided among the boys. And then an existence began on a plane that has lasted until this day. There has been little change. My father married and went to work as a farmer. He will die a farmer. My mother was intelligent and musical and my inspirer.[4] She was the daughter of William Byrd the ninth or tenth who came from Virginia when he was a boy and who claimed to be a direct descendant of the famous Col. William Byrd.[5] He was known as the smartest man in Harnett County, a preacher, a musician, and a great disputant on theological problems. Your son-in-law is said to be a replica of this gentleman. I hope, however, my will is stronger than his is said to have been, though I fear I have little to make me think so.

2. John Green.

3. Prior to the Civil War John expanded his farm in Harnett County from 100 to 1,500 acres but owned no slaves, according to Green's sister Mary, the family historian (interview with Mary Green Johnson, 5 April 1985).

4. Bettie Lorine Byrd was born in 1862, into a well-to-do Harnett County family, and had a good education in the arts and literature. According to Paul's sister Mary, their mother wrote poetry, exposed the children to any cultured visitor to the community, and had an organ and a piano, which she played beautifully (ibid.). She died in 1908, when Paul was fourteen.

5. Of Westover (1674–1744), prominent in colonial affairs and author of *The History of the Dividing Line*, based on a journal he kept while surveying the boundary between Virginia and North Carolina in 1729.

The earliest remembrance I have of my mother was her singing. She knew poem after poem, ballad after ballad, and it was her delight to recite to us kids at night or sing or play for us. She was tall with big grey eyes and good to look at. She always would tell me that I must go to college and be a great man, that was why she had named me after Paul. I must be a preacher. And I have heard her pray at night that I might come to some great use as a servant of the Lord. Under her influence I became a little saint of God, and at ten years of age had read the Bible through. Then she died. She had always been lonesome on the farm and had worked too hard. She was too ambitious for us all.

After she died, I drifted about intellectually, knowing the long deadly days of farm work. When I was sixteen I woke up again and entered Buie's Creek Academy.[6] There I graduated in two years and a half. I wanted to go to college but had no money. Father said for me to teach a year and then maybe he would be able to send me. I did.[7] Then he was as poor as ever. He said teach another year. I did, at fifty or sixty dollars a month. Of course I saved little. Then he said teach a third year. I didn't, I went to Chapel Hill anyway. Seeing I was going, he agreed to furnish me the money.

At C.H. I was a sight, green as grass, but rearing[8] to go. I won the freshman prize in English, wrote a successful(?) play in a contest,[9] and at the end of the session joined the army.[10] I was terribly patriotic then. I might say that my study of English was a terrible task, for after mother died, I had saturated myself with *Diamond Dick*, *Wife in Name Only*, *The Broken Wedding Ring*, *Orange Blossoms*, etc.[11] Shakespeare was dull reading compared to Bertha M. Clay. I hope I've outgrown her now.

6. In 1912, shortly before his eighteenth birthday.

7. At Olive Branch School in Harnett County, 1914–15.

8. Green's spelling.

9. "A Surrender to the Enemy," based on a romantic incident in Chapel Hill during the Civil War and written at the urging of Norman Förster, a professor in the English department. The play was judged best play by the senior class and performed in an outdoor theater on campus one afternoon in May 1917. Later Green destroyed the script.

10. The 105th Engineers, on 16 July 1917.

11. Dime novels that proliferated between the Civil War and World War I. *Orange Blossoms, Fresh and Faded* (1871) is by T. S. Arthur (1809–1885), better known for *Ten Nights in a Barroom and What I Saw There* (1854). *A Broken Wedding Ring* (n.d.) and *Wife in Name Only* (1883) are by Charlotte M. Braeme (1836–1884), prolific British writer whose pseudonym was Bertha M. Clay.

The war was such an unspeakable thing to me that I'll pass it over. It weighed on me so heavily that several times in France I thought of killing myself. Outwardly I made a success of it from buck to corporal, to sergeant, to sergeant-major, to lieutenant in the engineers. Once I thought of running away to Africa, there was a chance with some other officers. The roar on the front, a little too much of death, no sleep, remembering things, the uselessness of living nearly sent me west, as they said. But something too much of that. Elizabeth knows all the bitter story, and in a thousand ways she has lifted me out of it. I perhaps took it too seriously, but—the rest there is silence.

After the war I drifted back to C.H.[12] I had managed to save eleven hundred dollars from the cataclysm. I gradually got on my feet again. But I was an old man compared to the freshman of three years before, in many ways. I refused to join any organization. Such things were childish.[13] I got in with the playmakers and finally met Elizabeth. And so forth.

Of course during these years there were religious trials. Everybody has them. When I was a student at Buie's Creek, I met up with *The Origin of Species.* Naturally I became a scoffer at religion. Formerly I had been a teacher of the men's Bible class and even superintendent of the Sunday School in a little country church nearby. Soon it was rumored about that Paul Green was "a athe'st." In a way I was proud of the term. And to this day the people around home think of me so, although it perplexes them that they have no remembrance of any misdeeds of mine. They have no idea why one should be moral if no reward is forthcoming.

I joined the church (Christian) when I was ten years old. It was revival time. A fiery preacher had come from Texas to do the preaching. And how he could roar! His sermon on Judgment Day sent the shivers up my spine. And with tears streaming down my face, I trotted barefoot to the mourner's bench. He told me to squat down and pray, which I did. Soon I quit praying and began to watch the crowd through my fingers. There was shouting a sight. Old Miss Kate Howington screamed once or twice and old Mrs. McLeod went up and down the aisle shouting and clapping her hands. After about an hour the tumult died down. By this time I was cramped, and my bare knees on the floor were nearly blistered, and worse than everything else was the fact that my

12. Reentering UNC in the fall of 1919 as a twenty-five-year-old sophomore.

13. But in *Thomas Wolfe, Undergraduate* (Durham: Duke University Press, 1977), Richard Walser describes Green's initiation into the Sigma Upsilon literary society (p. 102).

waist kept slipping up over my suspenders showing my bare back. Finally the preacher came and asked me if I felt better. I told him I did. Thereupon he lifted up his voice and said praise God. And so I became a member of the church.[14]

There have been many, many changes since then. And I suppose it behooves me now to try to express to you just how I feel about the pageant of this world. By that I mean try to let you see what I hold worthwhile and what useless.

But before I start on the taking of my spiritual inventory, let me say a word or two about that St. Mary's advertising business.[15] I didn't mean to be rude or unfair to anyone in saying what I did. And I'm glad you did not think so. Maybe I was a little too strenuous in my condemnation. I don't know. But just the same, I cannot refrain from saying that I think such methods are pernicious. I abhor drives and movements in which you must wear some sort of button to show that you've done so and so. Nine-tenths, yea more, of these campaigns are the expression, to my mind, of a diseased social consciousness. Freedom and real thinking are—almost—no more. Perhaps I shall outgrow it, but—well, if I get started here I shall say something not just nice. Tell our Mither that Elizabeth has laid before me the story of St. Mary's and the rest. It burns me all over. May I make a young promise or prophecy here to the effect that in a few years I shall have a great deal to say just there? But right now I best keep my mouth closed.

And so I come to the statement of the present days of this man. To-morrow I may not believe what I shall say here, but as I see it now, this is somewhat my view of religion and the world in general. Perhaps it will bore you. But please remember Bertha M. Clay and be patient. Now let us mount a wingless Pegasus and be off. Here goes. (Should we entitle it, "Words from a Student to His Father-in-law"?)

All the dreams of man have dealt with two worlds—the world of cause and effect and the world of freedom. These stories have differed in their pattern

14. The experience is narrated in "Age of Accountability," *Words and Ways*, special issue of *North Carolina Folklore* 16 (December 1968): 8–12. For a fictionalized account, see "Salvation on a String," in *Salvation on a String and Other Tales of the South* (New York: Harper and Brothers, 1946), pp. 1–17.

15. Business (unidentified) pertaining to the Episcopal high school and two-year college for women in Raleigh, of which Lay was rector in 1907–18 and from which Elizabeth graduated in 1916.

and language, centuries have elapsed between many of their variations, but essentially they have been of three classes: one has run that God is the only reality, another that man is the true finality, and the third that both are real. All history is the record of man's consciousness of these two worlds and his efforts to pass from restlessness to peace. Change and oblivion have been the predominations for hosts in the past. An ideal land to be obtained by the miraculous intervention of the Lord there has brooded in the minds of millions more, and still others—a chosen few—have known themselves as children of the light, and the poem of their days has been a record of deepened living and freedom of the true and good and perfect. And too there has been a single motif in the melody of these songs that rise from the fields of strife and contentment. All have sounded of man's effort to attain to certainty for uncertainty, changelessness for change, ideality for a harsh reality, and freedom for slavery. It all is and has been a recounting of the passage into Canaan,[16] whether spatially, temporally, or ideally. And the chantings of triumph and overcoming have sprung from the lips of those who have reached their abiding place, those who have reached the land of milk and honey, those who have been transfigured and have seen the weird handwriting on Mount Sinai.[17] They are those that have overcome and found an abiding place in the spirit. And how few these supreme men have been in proportion history affords us an account—Buddha, Confucius, Abraham, Moses, Daniel, Jesus, St. Paul, and a few others. But what of the questioning, searching multitudes? we ask. They too have tried and overcome. But contention and disorder have been among them. Their lives have been spent consciously in one of two worlds, an existence on the plane of fact—in the world of separatingness and not in two worlds in a completingness. And by surveying these phases of man's endeavor given by thinkers we shall find that every expression of their consciousness denotes an effort towards the supreme in life. And further we shall find that the supreme life is the spiritual life, some attributes of which the most casual mind may uncover.

Before history was we know that the first sparks of intelligence lighted up questions to be solved. And coexistent with solutions was the feeling for finality—as religious consciousness. The first form of man's action was religious, and so will be his last—an effort at relating the finite and infinite. The

16. Promised Land of the Hebrews when they fled from slavery in Egypt (Exodus 12–19).

17. Where Moses received the Ten Commandments (Exodus 20).

questions that were asked by Adam remain to be answered by his youngest son. Religion then as the most perfect of all relations, in a sense includes whatever others may exist.

Long ago a man in authority not satisfied with the sweep of power came to a humble teacher to inquire the way of life and to learn the likeness thereof. The teacher said: "The wind bloweth where it listeth and thou hearest the sound thereof but canst not tell whence it cometh and whither it goeth; so is everyone born of the spirit." And the wise man of laws said: "How can these things be?" And we can imagine the teacher answering in sympathetic irony: "Art thou a man of affairs and a great power in Judea and knowest not what I say? If I have told you of earthly things and ye believe not, how shall ye believe if I tell you of heavenly things?" And Nicodemus went away amazed, repeating to himself, "How can these things be?" There is no record that he ever grew into that world of which Jesus taught.[18] This exemplary Jew has been representative of a number like to the sands of the seashore. In divers voices they have not only said how can these things be but have also said they do not exist or if they do they are beyond the ken of Abraham's sons. Zophar the Naamathite in his zealous anxiety to crush Job into this latter belief unrolled before him the unknowableness of the mighty one.

"Canst thou by searching find out God? Canst thou find out the Almighty to perfection?

"It is as high as heaven; what canst thou do? Deeper than hell; what canst thou know? The measure thereof is longer than the earth and broader than the sea. If he cut off and shut up or gather, then who can hinder him?"[19]

And another has exclaimed, "O the depth of the riches of the wisdom and knowledge of God! How unsearchable are his judgments, and his ways past finding out."[20] And so the story has run—now denying, now affirming the possibility of man's union with God—and sometimes with Jesus declaring the God in man and man in God, the unity of life, the spirituality of man. But whatever the variation, the theme has been the same—the conscious effort of intelligence to attain to absoluteness. Witness it in the Brahman's feeling for the pervading essence; the Hindu's figure of the dewdrop on the lotus leaf and its sliding descent into the shining sea; the Parsee, the Chaldean and Assyrian with their listenings for the voice of the lawgiver; the founder of the Jewish

18. John 3:1–13.
19. Job 11:7–14.
20. Romans 11:33.

race[21] with his vision of God and man cooperating in life; the long crystalizing process of Moses's dreaming by the burning bush into full-grown Judaism; the Greek humanistic lookout on the changing world; the Roman shackled before his taskmaster state; the expression of Jesus burgeoning through the debris of lifeless systems; the toss and stress of Luther's prophecies; and finally the world-wide movement towards the apparent narrow view of an apriori existence in this twentieth century. There has been change but not of essence. For in the light of common day we are "Haunted forever by the eternal mind," and humanity is always conscious of "A presence which is not to be put by."[22]

As in religion so with its foster-child art there is the unending quest for the ultimate treasure-trove. Its narrower form literature has had value to man only in so far as it has dealt with the relation of temporal to eternal. Great art in whatever form is the spontaneous expression of this relatedness,[23] and its message and effect do not depend on race and environment as has been claimed by a most versatile French critic.[24] The Bible, the sacred Hindu writings, and the great epics of the world show man, the particular, fighting his way into the general, the free. Likewise the novel and the drama have their places in this growth to new levels and expansions. All literature whatsoever, be it philosophical, religious, or secular, only has value in proportion as it is grounded in that which exists from generation to generation. There is a fundamental in the statement that great books can never go out of fashion.

The same is true of painting, architecture, and music. The artist experiences a rapprochement with the spiritual, and he creates living works of beauty, veiled in loveliness of the divine. The effect upon the spectator or auditor is often indescribable, only an approximation of its unearthliness being snared in words. An artist looks into the slumbrous eyes of Mona Lisa and feels a single electric shock as if he had met a living dream in the noon of the marketplace. Or before Raphael's madonnas encircled with the laughter

21. Abraham.

22. William Wordsworth, "Ode: Intimations of Immortality."

23. For an example of that idea using Green himself, see Jane Ross Hammer, ed., *Logic for Living: Dialogues from the Classroom of H. H. Williams* (New York: Philosophical Library, 1951), pp. 262–63. Here and elsewhere in the letter Green is indebted to the logical idealism and technical vocabulary of Williams.

24. Hippolyte Taine (1828–1893), whose "Introduction" to his *History of English Literature* (1863) is the *locus classicus* of the idea that literature depends on race and environment (and epoch).

and light of the heavenly city, he knows the spell of consecrated and all-comprehensive motherhood. The masters are spiritual and forever great. And a proof of our spirituality is that we hail them so. The Parthenon and Erecthium[25] are witnesses to the fierce, unyielding search for beauty and self-expression within us. And so the cathedrals of Europe's gloomy and idea-ridden years. All testify to the unconquerable spirit of man and his union with that which is infinite. For example, Amiens with its devil-fashioned gargoyles and spires at heaven's gate, rose-windowed and golden in the evening light. The hopes and aspirations not of time and place fashioned it into being. And so of Rheims, Chartres, Notre Dame and Saint Chapelle.[26] The last almost pendulous in air and the supreme embodiment of the Gothic soul. And no one can foreswear the masters of music whose harmonies have sprung from the depths of wonder. From Beethoven's stormy symphonies to Chopin's lazy poignant preludes there is expressed a universal yearning that no one denies. Wagner, Bach, and all the rest have touched the chords fundamental in the human breast.

History's chroniclings are the same. Not the unwieldy masses are of absorbing interest to the student of records—although they have played their part too, of course,—but the great men who have captained them, the Alexanders, the Caesars, and Napoleons. And these men have invariably been great personages seeking absoluteness in authority, freedom for themselves. The law we are arriving at holds here also. And the historian soon or late must evolve a philosophy of history that will be conversant with the movements of men and nations, foretelling much of the future for an eager world from the past. Already the historian with the philosopher is realizing that man's efforts towards freedom and a complete life are not to be made real through tyranny and any form of power.[27] The tombs of the mighty and the oblivion that forever creeps upon them are proofs enough of this. History proper is an account of men's strivings to liberty; but almost invariably it has been a striving actuated by a partial view of life's intricacies.

And just so it seems that the enormous scientific endeavor of these days is in the main an expenditure of effort that in the end will only illuminate a half

25. Temples to Athena from the fifth century B.C. on the Acropolis in Athens.

26. The palace chapel in Paris built by St. Louis in 1248, a beautiful example of pointed architecture.

27. "This I most firmly believe," Green wrote here in the margin after I returned the original to him on 30 May 1980.

truth at the most, the materialistic side of man, while it leaves all that gives existence sanity and clearness to the province of quacks and dream specialists. The thou shalt not live by bread alone is an expressed fundamental, and lasting nonchalance towards it will bring disaster. Science has taken all learning for its province. And from the standpoint of quantity it appears to be the final interpreter for the king. But it is only appearance and cannot last. Humanity, the individual, as a recent critic said,[28] at bottom is not a scientist. Things are judged in terms of value, and value hypothesizes ultimate standards. The work of the understanding will never bring wholeness to life. Physics with its resolution of all things into motion, and chemistry with its search for the ultimate element will some day arrive at nothing. The only finality to analysis is nothing to be analysed. Yet every bespectacled laboratory man from hither to yon is accumulating facts with the hope that at some future time a master mind will catch sight of the goal towards which they are, as he believes, pointing. This betrays the philosopher back of the man of acids and tests—looking to the absolutely reliable in a universe of flux and flow. Psychology is determined to bring mind to the level of matter, a thing for the senses to perceive, thereby erasing all relation as to subject and object. And our university philosophers are going over to the garage and dynamo men, preparing hammers and wrenches as it were for handling a mechanistic order of things. Biology offers little hope to the home-seeking ideal.[29] As for mathematics, once a calling and election sure for the world of unchanging form, it is lost with Bertrand Russell,[30] so it seems to me, on a wide moor.[31] Science rules supreme. It is the age of iron and the clang of dollars buying youth and ambition. Principle has covered her head and walks silently through the streets. To the casual looker-on honor and high thinking are going from the earth. This on the face of things.

But on closer examination conditions are not so irremediable as they seem at first sight, for the mechanic becomes tired of his machine, and the man of industry of his power. The overwhelming bustle and rummaging among facts are signs rather of health than of anemia. Even with more gusto than ever before we are searching for Eldorado and the fountain of youth, and the fact is

28. Norman Förster (Green marginal note, after 30 May 1980).

29. "You may dispute this but isn't it true?" (Green marginal note, after 30 May 1980).

30. In Russell's *Introduction to Mathematical Philosophy* (1919).

31. "Not sure of this" (Green marginal note, after 30 May 1980).

that our search only has taken on a different appearance. There must be a reasonableness back of all that we might term abandon of principle. The purpose as I see it of all material advancement is that the immaterial, the pure reality may thrive because of it, in a sense as it were be built upon it. Of what lasting good are electric lights, cars, radio, home conveniences, and the thousand and one things that economize time and labor if they are not to contribute to the deepening and enriching of one's life? A minute saved in cooking dinner is not a minute saved unless it be transferred to the consummation of ideal living. The short-cuts of modern improvements are of no avail if they do not help towards self-development. And it must be confessed by the shabbiest student of affairs that the present harnessing of nature's forces into obedient engines of speed is not serving to put us safely into a promised land of ever-broadening living. We are so busy with the game of action and reaction that the inner meaning of the word progress is not written in our books.

Yet there is no reason to believe that this will not right itself and all the play of force and matter in the end show itself in and of the spiritual life. Prejudice, ignorance, a moulding of minds by laboratory methods, lack of an apropos interpretation of Christianity, the self-centeredness and abstraction of our innumerable philosophical systems have all played their part in befogging the true light. But there are heard far and near the murmurs of awakening ones. The sweep of the democratic theory, the downfall of kings and orders of oppression, the multitudinous stirrings in the fields of thought, suggestive but as yet lacking in achievement, bespeak a great movement towards individual and race freedom. The theory and the practice of the spiritual life will come into its own.

From what has gone before, perhaps a conclusion as to the nature of this life already has been formed. It exists neither in time nor space, and yet it is the realest of realities. It is the absolutely free life, self-contained, self-formulated, and self-imposed, the life that is in and by and for itself. It is spontaneous and in no way a product. In it a complete expression of the trinity in which it lives and moves and has its being is brought to pass. There mind and will and feeling are one. It is all-inclusive and self-negating. And it is law-abiding but superior to law. It has no rules and regulations but keeps them all to the tittles. It is not found in any action of the ego but is both the act and the ego. The spiritually-minded man, to put it in academic words, sees life steadily and whole. He finds a place for all antagonisms that rend the lives of lesser men to shreds by viewing contradictions in a higher synthesis. He is the final whole of the complete individual. For all the greatness, the elusive yet satisfying conceptions of life reside in the spirit. And he who would the more quickly and ultimately grow into it must make the life of such as Jesus of Nazareth part of his own. Out of him came the first comprehensive sorrow-riven message of the life that passeth understanding.

> Blessed are the poor in spirit, for theirs is the kingdom of heaven.
> Blessed are they that mourn, for they shall be comforted.
> Blessed are the meek, for they shall inherit the earth.
> Blessed are they which do hunger and thirst after righteousness, for they shall be filled.
> Blessed are the merciful, for they shall obtain mercy.
> Blessed are the pure in heart, for they shall see God.[32]

and also,

> I in them and thou in me, that they may be made perfect in one.[33]

And in later years one who had followed him gave utterance to the way of the principled life.

> For they that are after the flesh do mind the things of the flesh; but they that are after the Spirit the things of the Spirit.
> For to be carnally minded is death; but to be spiritually minded is life and peace. . . .
> Therefore, brethren, we are debtors, not to the flesh, to live after the flesh.
> For if ye live after the flesh, ye shall die; but if ye through the spirit do mortify the deeds of the body, ye shall live.
> For as many as are led by the Spirit of God, they are the sons of God.[34]

And so in the end I should say that he who would be free in a world of confusion must with all his mind and soul and strength enter into the supreme life of right-mindness and illuminating thought, into the life that holds within itself the balm of Gilead for the ills that flesh is heir to.[35]

32. Matthew 5:3–8.
33. John 17:23.
34. Romans 8:5–6, 12–14.
35. Hamlet mentions the ills that flesh is heir to (act 3, scene 1). A cure for the ills derives from Jeremiah 8:22 by way of the Negro spiritual "There Is a Balm in Gilead."

Well it's time to get off Pegasus and let him rest. And as it grows on towards the morning hours, I should stop. And perhaps you have grown wearied at this poetizing and extended race. But as I see it now, most of this is what I believe. My head is swimming. Good-night to you all, and my love always.

I've sent the letters on to Elizabeth. She comes back Sat. As for Oxford, who can say? Our expenses have been high—some fifteen hundred dollars since we came here, will be that by Xmas. But don't worry about us. She shall have her trip to Europe and other things to her heart's joy and content if I can give them. We are happy and beggarly, but we live deeply, I believe.

Paul

P.S. The little pictures of E—— are sweet and priceless in a way. Thanks a thousand times. I'm glad you've invited Wilbur down Xmas.[36]

I'm enclosing a letter from Dr. W. His remark about taking care of Elizabeth is interesting. I think I have found another man for us next year.[37] If Ellen is getting poor I am getting fat. 186 without overcoat. E—— weighs 138. We are both well.

After reading this letter over it doesn't sound so good. But please excuse weaknesses in it.

36. Wilbur Stout, suitor of Elizabeth's sister Ellen.

37. That is, someone else to join Horace Williams in the Department of Philosophy at UNC if the Greens go to Oxford. But the Greens returned to Chapel Hill, where Paul became assistant professor of philosophy.

# II

## Writing and Race in the South, 1923–1929

Summer 1923
Paul and Elizabeth return to Chapel Hill.

September 1923
Joins Horace Williams as second member of UNC philosophy department.

14 January 1924
First child, Paul, Jr., born.

Summer 1924
Works on *In Abraham's Bosom.*

1925
Edits *The Reviewer* (moved from Richmond, Virginia, November 1924). First number (January) carries his editorial, "A Plain Statement about Southern Literature."

Summer 1925
Begins *The Field God.*

25 February 1926
Second child, Nancy Byrd, born.

Summer 1926
At MacDowell Colony, Peterboro, New Hampshire, drafts *The House of Connelly,* works on other plays.

April 1927
Writes controversial "Introduction" for E. C. L. Adams's *Congaree Sketches: Scenes from Negro Life in the Swamps of the Congaree.*

2 May 1927
Receives Pulitzer Prize in drama for *In Abraham's Bosom.*

Summer 1927
Drafts *Tread the Green Grass.*

Summer 1928

Drafts *Potter's Field.*

11 August 1928

With family leaves Chapel Hill to study European theater on Guggenheim fellowship.

September 1928

Reaches Berlin, where family stays over the winter. Sees productions of Moscow State Jewish Theatre, meets its director Alexis Granowsky, is excited by possibility of folk musical plays. Revises *Potter's Field.*

May 1929

With family moves to London. Revises *The House of Connelly* for Theatre Guild and begins first novel, *The Laughing Pioneer.*

17–19 August 1929

Visits Thomas Hardy country in Dorchester.

Mid-October 1929

Spends evening with Bernard Shaw at Shaw's home.

November 1929

With family returns to Chapel Hill.

## 36. To Ruth Suckow[1]

[Davie Circle] Chapel Hill, N.C.
4 December 1923

My dear Miss Suckow;

Here in my study a few moments ago I was plundering in a pile of magazines to find something to read before retiring for the night. I picked up *The Century* for August and casually turned through it. The title of your story—"Renters"—interested me, and I read it. Although I didn't like the beginning very much, I found the body of it one of the most compelling pieces of work I've read in many days. I know something about this class of people—tenants we call them usually in N.C.—and have written some articles and short plays on them.[2] Your study strikes through muscle and bone. Apart from Beth[3] (you see so much through her eyes), the characters are very striking and sure. I congratulate you.

Truly yours, Paul Green
Dept. of Philosophy
University of North Carolina

## 37. To Elizabeth L. Green

[Davie Circle, Chapel Hill, N.C.]
Sunday night [27 July 1924]

Dear Honey Child;[1]

Here I am in the house by myself. The July bugs are chitter-chattering outside like mad. The girls[2] are off somewhere with their everlasting escorts—

1. Ruth Suckow (1892–1960), Iowa writer whose stories and novels deal with farm and small-town life in the region. At the time of the present letter, she had not yet published her first novel, *Country People* (1924). In 1926 Knopf brought out a collection of her stories, *Iowa Interiors*, which includes "Renters" (pp. 108–31), a story Green had just read in *The Century Magazine*, 23 August 1923.

2. Most of Green's plays and stories to that time dealt with people in the farming communities of the Cape Fear River valley, and "The Lord's Will," "Old Wash Lucas," and "White Dresses" deal specifically with tenant families.

3. Long-suffering and resentful wife of Fred Multcher, the "renter."

---

1. Elizabeth, with Paul, Jr. (born on 14 January 1924), was visiting her parents in Beaufort.

2. Green's sisters, Caro Mae and Erma.

Bill Couch and J. O. Bailey.[3] Lucy[4] is with them. She doesn't seem to make much of a hit with the boys or at least doesn't want to—with this sort. "They're crude," she says.

I went up to the p.o. before sunset hoping there would be a note (I can't hope for a letter) from you, but nothing doing. You're resting, I hope, and I won't blame you. Honey, I'll try to send you some money soon. Better not cash a check, for we're thin, thin.

There is no news worth telling. I've talked with Luther Hargrove, and he says he thinks he can construct the house in six weeks easy. I doubt it though.[5] Also talked with Mrs. Pratt.[6] She is leaving for Asheville tomorrow—six weeks' stay. The deeds are all fixed up—I mean ours—and I'll bring them to Beaufort Friday for you to sign. Then we can arrange everything with your Pa and Ma—that is, if they're still in the notion to take the land.[7] I think we'd better sell them all but a tiny lot for ourselves so we can get enough to build a respectable shack. Above all things, we must secure them against any loss—agree to buy the land back if they get dissatisfied—anything to suit them.

B. C. Brown[8] was up here today. He says he'll go to Beaufort from New Bern with me next Friday.

I want to see you two bad already. I dreamed last night you were with me. Really I don't see how I am going on with the house-building and you in Beaufort. Please write me any plans about the pesky thing you may have.

Caro and Erma are going tomorrow. Poor children, they're enough to worry the saints—haven't cleaned up a thing—rooms strewed. But don't worry, for we'll get everything straight.

I'm plumb wore out trying to write. I run away from it, hesitate, put off, try again, worry, worry, worry—Jonah and Nineveh all over again.[9] I've worked

3. William T. Couch, undergraduate at UNC (B.A., 1926), later director of the University of North Carolina Press. Bailey, also an undergraduate, later a member of the UNC English department.

4. Elizabeth's sister.

5. The Greens were buying several acres (called the Glen) on the northeastern edge of the UNC campus. Their idea was to build a home there (which they did in 1925) and finance it through the sale of building lots in the Glen.

6. From whom they bought the land.

7. As a building site for their retirement home.

8. Attending Harvard Law School, had been an undergraduate at UNC (B.A., 1922) and a teaching assistant with Green in the English department.

9. It was while trying to evade God's command to preach in Nineveh that Jonah

ten hours on this Sam Tucker[10] and got just five pages written and what's to come seems a mess. But I've just made a resolution to finish it before I go to Beaufort. It's trying to resolve itself into nine scenes, and I'll have to do at least two scenes a day to get through with it by Friday.[11] Besides, I'm going to try to work over all the finished stuff for Holt.[12] I've vacillated, a lick here and there, run around the house to do this and that until my mind is all wishy-washy.

Please write whether my coming Friday and returning Sunday or Monday will be satisfactory. I can't remain away longer than Monday. School time is lowering down, and this play business must be finished.[13] It would be fine for us to be back here together and everybody gone.

Love—Paul

## 38. To Elizabeth L. Green

Hotel Marwood, 242 West 49th Street, New York City
Wednesday night [10 September 1924]

Dearest Honey—[1]

I am in my little old room 8′ × 8′—$1.50 a day—This hotel is pretty nice and cheap. I have water in my room. Got in this morning at 9:30. Got

---

was swallowed by the whale (Jonah 1). A few days earlier Green told Elizabeth he was "trying to get along with this writing business but without much success in any way, it seems. I'm so discouraged—day after day—wanting to break loose and pour out what's in me. . . . It would be a thousand times easier to give it all up, become a calm teacher of philosophy or English and ride on the rim of the world. But I can't do it. I'm going to starve or write!" ([July 1924], EG-SHC).

10. Which became *In Abraham's Bosom.*

11. *In Abraham's Bosom*, produced in 1926 (Pulitzer Prize), and published in 1927, resolved itself into seven scenes, the first and last based on separately published one-act plays: "In Abraham's Bosom" and "Your Fiery Furnace," both included in *Lonesome Road: Six Plays for the Negro Theatre* (1926). "Your Fiery Furnace" is the only scene not conceived and written during the summer of 1924. It is based on an earlier one-act play, "Sam Tucker," written in 1923 and published in *Poet Lore* 34 (June 1923): 220–46.

12. Six one-act plays collected as *The Lord's Will and Other Carolina Plays* (1925).

13. Registration for fall quarter that year began on 16 September, classes on 18 September.

---

1. Green was in New York City to find a publisher for his one-act plays about

something to eat and called up Mr. Home of Scribner's at once. He was just leaving to go out of town for the day. I am to see him Friday A.M. He suggested that I bring the plays over and leave them so that he could look them over. I did so, but he had already gone. I left them in his office. I have had a full day. Spent two hours at the public library. Then went down to Greenwich Village to take a look over the Provincetown Theatre. They were rehearsing a new play. From what I gathered from the man who let me in, *All God's Chillun* is doing mighty poor with the public. They don't even give the first part—read it—where the children come in.[2] They told me at the Drama Book Shop that it was pretty poor, others have told me so. But I'm going down to matinee there tomorrow if I can get away from dinner with R. Holt in time. This afternoon I saw *The Show Off.*[3] Pretty good—Bartels seems just made for the part. House filled up now. I have just come back from *Rain*,[4] and that thing sure got me again. Same cast and everything, with the exception of the doctor.[5] House packed. Tomorrow night I'm going to try to get to *The Miracle*.[6] I'll try to get in touch with Nancy[7] tomorrow A.M. Think I'll go back

---

blacks. On the trip he saw editors at Scribner's and at Holt (Roland Holt). In 1926 McBride published the plays as *Lonesome Road: Six Plays for the Negro Theatre* ("In Abraham's Bosom," "White Dresses," "The Hot Iron," "The Prayer-Meeting," "The End of the Row," and "Your Fiery Furnace").

2. Eugene O'Neill's play had opened on 15 May 1924 amid controversy because it chronicled the relationship of a black man and a white woman. The city of New York attempted to prohibit the production but succeeded only in preventing the use of child actors in the opening scene, where the principals are children. One of the adults in the company, usually director James Light, read scene 1 from the stage to begin each performance.

3. George Kelly's play, which opened on 5 February 1924 and starred Louis John Bartels as the main character, Aubrey Piper.

4. Dramatization by John Colton and Clemence Randolph of Somerset Maugham's short story "Miss Thompson."

5. The play opened 7 November 1922, and the Greens saw it on their Christmas trip from Ithaca that year. Fritz Williams played the part of Dr. McPhail in that production and also in the present revival, so Green must have seen a performance using an understudy.

6. Max Reinhardt's staging of a medieval legend had opened 16 January 1924.

7. Elizabeth's sister.

Sat.—getting home Sunday—not sure just yet. I want to see Miss Grimball[8] and Liz Taylor[9]—There aren't very many good plays going.

Love to ya and the boy—I wish you were here to enjoy yourself!

I love you, Paul

## 39. To Edith J. R. Isaacs[1]

[Chapel Hill, N.C.]
9 January 1925

My dear Mrs. Isaacs:

I am enclosing a check for a year's renewal to *Theatre Arts*. I should like to secure for review some of your recent dramatic publications.[2] At the present time I am working on a negro play in six or seven scenes, entitled *In Abraham's Bosom*. In it I am trying to embody a concrete illustration of the negro struggle towards freedom, real freedom. It will run around a hundred type-written pages, shorter than *The Colonnade*, I think.[3] Would you be interested in looking at a play of this length?[4]

Sincerely yours,

8. Elizabeth Grimball, who ran a drama school in New York City, had directed the filming of the Fort Raleigh story at Manteo in 1921.

9. Actress in a number of Playmakers productions.

---

1. Edith J. R. Isaacs (1878–1956), one of the founders and longtime editor of *Theatre Arts* (1922–50), had a particular interest in black culture. Long a collector of African art, much of which she donated to the Schomburg Center for Research in Black Culture and to Howard University, she would devote the August 1942 issue of her magazine to blacks in the theater, then expand it into the book, *The Negro in the American Theatre* (1947). She had published one of Green's plays, "The No 'Count Boy," in *Theatre Arts* 8 (November 1924): 773–84.

2. For *The Reviewer*, of which Green had just become editor.

3. Stark Young's play, published in *Theatre Arts* 8 (August 1924): 521–60.

4. Green sent her *In Abraham's Bosom*, but she replied that it still needed work (Edith Isaacs to Paul Green, 28 July 1925, PG-SHC).

## 40. To Sarah Haardt[1]

[Chapel Hill, N.C.]
10 January 1925

My dear Miss Haardt:

I think Mr. Mencken is wrong. " 'Lasses" so far as I can see is not so good as "Miss Rebecca" which appeared in the July *Reviewer.* It is good though, and I have debated with myself up and down as to whether to return it. I am doing it, however, in the hope that you will shorten and intensify the really remarkable story too long drawn out. For to my mind there is a very powerful tale here, but I don't think the most has been made of your opportunity. Isn't there a constant unartistic moving from 'Lasses to the General, to Mrs. Haviland, back and forth among the Greek chorus, i.e. Aunt Kiziah and other onlookers? Rather than following too closely the pedestrian activities, pathetic and yet somewhat uninteresting, of 'Lasses, can't you draw the whole thing to a dramatic climax by having more stress upon the unconscious and sardonic revenge of the foolish boy?

I can imagine in my own mind the story of an impeccable leading citizen, admired and respected especially for his moral integrity. Such a character as 'Lasses is present among the people of the town in which this citizen resides. The relation between him and his real father is not suspected. Then on the burial day of this citizen, such a one as you have described, 'Lasses appears, wearing innocently enough some cast off clothes belonging to the dead man.

1. In November 1924 Green had taken over as editor of *The Reviewer,* a little magazine founded in Richmond, Virginia, in 1920 by Emily Clark and others, under the auspices of H. L. Mencken and James Branch Cabell, to help develop literary talent in the South. Clark had published Green's play, "In Aunt Mahaly's Cabin," in *The Reviewer* 4 (April 1924): 190–218. After Clark resigned in October 1924, Green, with an editorial board of Gerald Johnson, Addison Hibbard, and Nell Battle Lewis, proposed moving the magazine to Chapel Hill, and the Richmond group accepted. In his first issue as editor, Green announced his standards in "A Plain Statement about Southern Literature," *The Reviewer* 5 (January 1925): 71–76, in which he rejected sentimentality and escape into the past and demanded a true interpretation of the present. Sarah Haardt (1898–1935) of Montgomery, Alabama, who had published the story "Miss Rebecca" in *The Reviewer* 4 (July 1924): 276–84, and would marry Mencken in 1930, sent Green another story, "'Lasses," with the comment that Mencken thought it better than "Miss Rebecca" (Sarah Haardt to Paul Green, 13 December 1924, PG-SHC).

Now the resemblance between them, recognized for the first time, brings the disastrous fact into acknowledged truth.

Of course this is a new tale, and will not allow for such loving and prolix picturization perhaps. You may not think anything of it and I may be wrong. If you don't take to this suggestion, try to shorten the present story somewhat and return it at once. I think we can use it.[2]

Sincerely yours,

## 41. To Director, Studio Players[1]

[Chapel Hill, N.C.]
12 January 1925

Dear Sir:

It has been called to my attention that you are producing or have produced a play of mine entitled "The No 'Count Boy." This play is protected by copyright and a royalty of five dollars is charged for each performance, though *Theatre Arts Monthly* for November made no mention of the fact.

I am preparing a volume of negro plays for publication. It is to include "The No 'Count Boy." I am anxious to list in the volume the performances of each play, and especially the first one. In this case yours happened to be the first performance of "The No 'Count Boy." Could you please send me a program of that performance, with special care to have the names of the actors?[2]

Sincerely yours,

2. Haardt replied that she had no time to rewrite "'Lasses" and sent another story, "Paradox" (Sarah Haardt to Paul Green, 14 January 1925, PG-SHC), which Green used in his first issue (*The Reviewer* 5 [January 1925]: 64–70). Haardt sent several other stories to Green, one of which, "A Southern Lady Says Grace," he used in his last issue (*The Reviewer* 5 [October 1925]: 57–63). In 1931 Haardt published her autobiographical novel, *The Making of a Lady.*

---

1. "The No 'Count Boy," published in *Theatre Arts* 8 (November 1924): 773–84, was first performed by the Studio Players at the Little Theatre in Chicago on 6, 7, 13, and 14 December 1924.

2. The Studio Players sent a program, which Green reproduced at the beginning of the play in *The Lord's Will and Other Carolina Plays* (New York: Holt, 1925), p. 144.

## 42. To Emily Clark[1]

[Chapel Hill, N.C.]
18 February 1925

My dear Miss Clark:

I hope you received your issue of *The Reviewer* and have not been overcome by our immature efforts. We hope to make the April issue much better and therefore are anxious to get your "Dismal Swamp" sketch or anything else you wish to offer.[2] And too we would like to have your reviews of the books we sent, or of any other more recent books you may prefer. Please send me a letter of criticism of this issue and tell us how we can improve it.[3] I certainly hope you will be as persevering as the Ancient Mariner in stopping people and telling them of our needs. We are depending upon the continued activity of your genius for getting contributions. I appreciate your letter and the references you gave in it and the accompanying postal. I have written to all those mentioned. We hope that all the directors can get together some time during the year and formulate a more definite policy for the continuance of the magazine. We are certainly looking forward to your first visit to Chapel Hill.[4]

Sincerely yours,

1. Emily Clark (1892–1953), one of the founders of *The Reviewer* in 1920, had resigned as editor in October 1924, married Joseph S. Balch, and moved from Richmond to Philadelphia, where she continued to move in literary circles and to write. Recently she had written to Green, explaining that her marriage kept her from reviewing several books for him, offering to send a short essay on the Dismal Swamp, and mentioning several people who in recent conversations had expressed interest in contributing to *The Reviewer*: H. L. Mencken, Carl Van Vechten, Joseph Hergesheimer, Ellen Glasgow, Irita (Mrs. Carl) Van Doren, and Stuart Sherman. She also asked him to send her several copies of the January 1925 *Reviewer*, the first under his editorship (Emily Clark to Paul Green, 8 February 1925, PG-SHC).

2. Clark did not do a piece on the Dismal Swamp but sent a story, "Fast Color," which Green ran in *The Reviewer* 5 (July 1925): 83–85.

3. Clark replied that she liked the January number tremendously, praising most of the pieces, especially his editorial, "A Plain Statement about Southern Literature" (Emily Clark to Paul Green, 20 March 1925, PG-SHC).

4. Clark did not visit Chapel Hill until Thanksgiving, 1925, when the editorial board met and decided, for lack of financial support, to discontinue *The Reviewer*. But her letters frequently mention a desire to come to Chapel Hill, where her father had been Episcopal rector before moving to Richmond.

## 43. To Julia Peterkin[1]

[Chapel Hill, N.C.]
18 February 1925

My dear Mrs. Peterkin:

You mention in your letter recently received, that you have plenty of stories of the gruesome sort on hand. Could you let us look at something for the April issue of *The Reviewer*? I should prefer it to be somewhat shorter than "Maum Lou." I am not particularly interested in the gruesome for itself, but I certainly should like to have a story as strong and direct as your "Foreman" was.

Thank you for your good words concerning *The Reviewer*.[2] I hope you will not judge our first issue, sent to you some days since, too harshly. We hope to [do] better next time.[3]

Sincerely yours,

1. Julia Peterkin (1880–1961), mistress of Lang Syne Plantation near Fort Motte, South Carolina (which she depicts in *Roll, Jordan, Roll* [1933]), had published a collection of short stories, *Green Thursday* (1924), and soon would begin a succession of three fine novels: *Black April* (1927), *Scarlet Sister Mary* (1928), and *Bright Skin* (1932). She published numerous stories in *The Reviewer*, among them "The Foreman" (4 [July 1924]: 286–94) and in Green's first number "Maum Lou" (5 [January 1925]: 17–32).

2. Peterkin had written that it thrilled her to get a check from *The Reviewer*. "I almost am returning it to you," she added, "thinking maybe you are not quite in a position to pay for things yet; and still, to pay is somehow a definite step on for you. I congratulate you. I feel that the *Reviewer* has become a thing that is permanent. I rejoice for myself since it is curiously a part of me and what I have thought" (Julia Peterkin to Paul Green, undated, PG-SHC).

3. Peterkin replied that "Maum Lou" was the poorest thing in the January *Reviewer* and enclosed another story, "Manners" (Julia Peterkin to Paul Green, 24 February 1925, PG-SHC), which Green also published (5 [July 1925]: 71–80).

## 44. To Benjamin Brawley[1]

[Chapel Hill, N.C.]
24 February 1925

My dear Mr. Brawley;

I am sorry that I have let so much time slip by before answering your letter of the 17th. I certainly want to see the article On Re-Reading Browning, and I hope you still have time to finish it for our April issue which goes to press early in March. Probably you are right in wanting to leave a biographical contribution until later. Please send the Browning article as soon as you can.

Sincerely yours,[2]

1. Benjamin Brawley (1882–1939), educator and poet, was a prolific literary and social historian best known for *The Negro in Literature and Art in the United States* (1918), *A Social History of the American Negro* (1921), *Paul Laurence Dunbar, Poet of His People* (1936), and *The Negro Genius: A New Appraisal of the Achievement of the American Negro in Literature and the Fine Arts* (1937). Educated at Atlanta Baptist College (now Morehouse College) (B.A., 1901), the University of Chicago (B.A., 1906), and Harvard University (M.A. in English, 1908), Brawley taught at Morehouse and Howard University before moving to Shaw University in Raleigh as professor of English in 1923. He contributed sayings and stories to Green's folklore collection (*Paul Green's Wordbook: An Alphabet of Reminiscence* [1990]), and for a few years beginning in 1924–25 Green put up the $25 prize for a writing competition Brawley conducted at Shaw. As soon as Green took over *The Reviewer*, he invited Brawley to contribute. Brawley wondered what kind of subject Green wanted him to treat—something from the broad field of literature or something focused on black writers in America (Benjamin Brawley to Paul Green, 18 December 1924, PG-SHC)? In a letter that took Brawley's breath away but is now lost, Green said, no, he hoped Brawley would do a piece on himself, on his own experience growing up in the South around the turn of the century (paraphrased in Benjamin Brawley to Paul Green, 17 February 1925). Brawley hesitated. The son of a Baptist minister, he had lived throughout the Southeast, but his life had not been filled with racial strife or excitement of any kind, only with hard work, and he failed to see how it could interest anyone. Anyway, he didn't want to be represented first by an autobiographical piece. For his first article in *The Reviewer*, he wanted to treat a subject "strictly in my field." He had "in mind some radical things to say about Browning" and proposed a piece entitled "On Re-Reading Browning" (Benjamin Brawley to Paul Green, 17 February 1925).

2. Brawley sent the piece in time for the April issue ("On Re-Reading Browning," *The Reviewer* 5 [April 1925]: 60–63). He also went to work on an autobiographical article and sent along the first installment in May, saying he hoped it was "reasonably satisfactory. I could not write a harrowing story when my life had been one of fair

## 45. To Frances Newman[1]

[Chapel Hill, N.C.]
25 February 1925

My dear Miss Newman:

I am very sorry to hear that you are sick and I hope you will soon be well again. We don't want to seem too persistent, but couldn't you have some article ready by the middle of March? The April number will not go to press before that time.[2]

*Mutations* seems to be going very well indeed. Congratulations![3] And a thousand congratulations too on the O'Henry prize. You are increasing light in Southern letters.

Sincerely yours,

---

advantages" (Benjamin Brawley to Paul Green, 27 May 1925, PG-SHC). Green used "A Southern Boyhood" as the lead article in the July *Reviewer* (5 [July 1925]: 1–8). Because it was by a black person, it offended some readers, who canceled subscriptions (see "About Contributors," *The Reviewer* 5 [October 1925]: 125), but Green ran the remaining installment in the October issue ("The Lower Rungs of the Ladder," *The Reviewer* 5 [October 1925]: 78–86). With pieces in three of the four issues Green edited, Brawley appeared in *The Reviewer* that year more often than any other contributor.

---

1. Frances Newman (1883–1928), librarian at Georgia Institute of Technology in Atlanta, came into prominence as a writer in 1924 with the publication of her book on the development of the short story, *The Short Story's Mutations*, and the award of the O. Henry Prize for her story, "Rachel and Her Children" (*American Mercury* 2 (May 1924): 92–96). Despite failing eyesight, she would publish two novels: *The Hard-Boiled Virgin* (1926) and *Dead Lovers Are Faithful Lovers* (1928). Shortly before the present letter she promised a contribution to *The Reviewer* but had been delayed by illness (Frances Newman to Paul Green, 8 and 14 January 1925, PG-SHC).

2. Newman sent a witty article on censorship and public libraries entitled "Immorality in a Library" (Frances Newman to Paul Green, 12 March 1925, PG-SHC), which Green used in the April issue (5 [April 1925]: 55–58).

3. Hansell Baugh reviewed *The Short Story's Mutations* in *The Reviewer* 5 (July 1925): 105–9. Later Baugh edited *Frances Newman's Letters* (1929).

## 46. To Charles Bayly, Jr.[1]

[Chapel Hill, N.C.]
6 March 1925

My dear Mr. Bailey;

I am today sending you by registered mail the Carolina Negro Folk Plays in MSS. Out of the eight plays I think a volume could be chosen worth enough in a literary way and financially to warrant publication. Still, I speak from inexperience perhaps. But I do know that as a casual buyer of books the Negro plays could attract me first in preference to the other folk plays from here. And too, I think a small volume put out in advance of the other book you are to publish for me, which I understand is to be in the fall, would stimulate interest in that. And behind all is the Carolina Playmakers organization which would advertise and help sell both books. Well, you know all the twists and turns of the game better than I.

Professor Koch or Dr. Archibald Henderson[2] will be glad to write an introduction to the book;[3] George Denny, business manager of the Playmakers, has said he'd do all he could to sell it; and I shall be glad to add an article (if desired) on the Negro dialect of the Cape Fear River section.[4] And in addition, my work as editor of *The Reviewer* will help carry the book to the personal attention of every newspaper book-review page in the South. All this on the level of Babbitt,[5] I'm sorry to say, and yet a necessary level.

As I told Mr. Katzenbach,[6] Mr. Roland Holt[7] had a look at most of these

1. Henry Holt and Company had already scheduled *The Lord's Will* for publication in the fall, and Green wrote to Bayly (without knowing how to spell his name), editor at Holt, about the plays that eventually went into *Lonesome Road: Six Plays for the Negro Theatre* (New York: McBride, 1926).

2. Professor of mathematics at UNC, best known for his work on Bernard Shaw (culminating in *George Bernard Shaw: Man of the Century* [1956]).

3. Koch wrote the foreword for *The Lord's Will* ("Paul Green," pp. xi-xiii). When *Lonesome Road* appeared, it had an introduction by Green's friend, theater worker Barrett H. Clark (pp. vii–xviii).

4. *Lonesome Road* has a brief "Author's Note," in which Green says his aim in the plays is "to say something of what [blacks in the Cape Fear River valley] . . . have suffered and thought and done" (p. xx).

5. Title character and stereotypical booster satirized in Sinclair Lewis's novel (1922).

6. Another editor at Holt.

7. Vice president of the company and quite interested in the theater (*A List of Music for Plays and Pageants* [1925]).

plays in their first form and found them a bit too raw and perhaps lacking in appeal to little theatre groups. As an aid to judgment here, I am enclosing two letters (in answer to letters I wrote asking for programs to use in the possible book) from two groups.[8] They may or may not mean anything.

I thank you for your interest in the plays and for your suggestion as to the Theatre Arts company. I believe, though, that if you find them unavailable, I'd rather not have Mrs. Isaacs do them. Of course she's welcome to put out one or two or three of them, but her company doesn't publish full volumes, does it? And isn't the advertising method of that company pretty well limited?

Well, after all, do anything you see fit, and it's very kind of you to have an interest in them at all.[9]

Sincerely yours, Paul Green

P.S. Could you let me know the latest date by which I must have the MSS. for the other book of plays in the hands of your company? I think Mr. Elliot Holt[10] has agreed on early September 1925 for bringing it out, but no set date for the delivery of the manuscripts has been agreed upon. I ask this because I need as much time as possible to revise and get two other plays worked out.

## 47. To Donald Davidson[1]

[Chapel Hill, N.C.]
21 March 1925

My dear Mr. Davidson,

Pardon me for holding your poems so long, but they had to go the rounds and be read by Mr. Hibbard and one or two others. Out of them all I think we

8. The Studio Players in Chicago (who had produced "The No 'Count Boy") and the Fireside Players in White Plains, New York (who had presented "White Dresses").

9. Holt rejected the plays, and *Lonesome Road* was published in 1926 by Robert M. McBride and Company.

10. A director of the company.

1. Donald Davidson (1893–1968), poet and member of the Department of English at Vanderbilt University, was a leading spokesman for the group associated with the literary magazine *The Fugitive* (1922–25). As the group developed its agrarian agenda, he helped organize and contributed to the three symposia: *I'll Take My Stand* (1930), *Culture in the South* (1934), and *Who Owns America?* (1936). His own work includes several volumes of poetry and essays and a historical study of the Tennessee River valley. At the time of the present letter he was working on his first book of poetry, *The*

possibly can use the one entitled "The Bryony," although Mr. Hibbard likes "All Fools' Calendar." But I for one have never cared much for any sort of roll-call. Still, I think it is a very good poem.[2] Now, there is one thing that worries me about "Bryony." Does it really belong too closely to the "Miniver Cheevy" "Richard Cory" class?[3] I am returning all but this one, which I am using in the April issue of *The Reviewer.* I am not decided as to whether we shall have to put it in the "at random" column or not. I'll let you know in a few days.[4]

Many thanks for your kindness in letting us have a look at these poems.

Sincerely yours,

## 48. To Elizabeth L. Green

Hotel Times Square, 43rd Street West, New York City
Friday [6 November 1925]

Dear Honey Chile;[1]

I got here yesterday after a fairly easy trip. Sat up nearly all the way up here reading *The Idiot.*[2] I couldn't sleep. Now don't blame [me]. My head was in such a whirl! Had lunch with Mr. Clark yesterday at the place we did. Mr. Shields of French's was there too.[3] Couldn't get to see any publishers in the

---

*Tall Men* (1927), and struggling to keep *The Fugitive,* which he edited, alive. When he sent a few poems for consideration by *The Reviewer* board, he asked Green to make his selections quickly (Donald Davidson to Paul Green, 2 March 1925, PG-SHC).

2. "All Fools' Calendar" has not been published.

3. Character studies of dissatisfied men by Edwin Arlington Robinson. Davidson replied that his poem reminded no one in Nashville of the Robinson poems (Donald Davidson to Paul Green, 25 March 1925, PG-SHC).

4. *The Reviewer* paid for poetry at the rate of five cents a word, except for poems in the "At Random" column, which were not paid for at all. "The Bryony" appeared in the "At Random" column of the April issue (5 [April 1925]: 100).

---

1. Green went to New York City to talk with publishers about his own work but primarily to seek financial backing for *The Reviewer.*

2. Dostoyevski's novel.

3. Green soon learned to spell the surname of Frank J. Sheil, president of Samuel French, Incorporated, which became Green's primary publisher, for his name was on the checks for royalties and advances that Green began to receive from the company in 1926. Green's long association with French was due largely to the presence there as

afternoon and so I went to the Garrick Gaieties.[4] Clever and beautiful bare ladies' limbs, but hardly rich enough to move me to tears or lamentations of joy. The take off on Michael Arlen[5] and the attendant foibles of the great hulk—the public—were subtle and full of the sting of reality. There were other good things in the show, especially the finale where Shaw, the old father of The Guild is lying in his bed summoning before him characters from his plays.[6]

Last night I went to *Outside Looking In*.[7] Pretty poor. Portner was with me.[8] Found him in the public library. He's crazy still about writing plays and is starving doing odd jobs, and everything. Poor boy! He deserves to succeed. Spent the whole morning with the Viking Press people.[9] Mr. Huebsch and the others were nice as they could be and were immediately taken with the *Reviewer* idea. The two younger men who have the money in the firm were inclined to some sort of action, but Mr. Huebsch, who lost $300,000 before

---

editor of Barrett H. Clark (1890–1953), who had a varied career around the theater. Green refers to Clark frequently before the first letter to him (letter 65). Born in Toronto, Clark joined French in 1918 and remained as literary editor until 1936, when he organized and became president of the Dramatist Play Service. During his years with French he translated numerous European plays, compiled the influential *European Theories of the Drama* (1918), inaugurated the twenty-volume edition of *America's Lost Plays* (1929), and wrote *Eugene O'Neill* (1926) and *Maxwell Anderson, the Man and His Plays* (1933). Green came to look on Clark as a friend and adviser as well as a literary agent. Frequently he stayed with the Clarks on trips to New York City, and the Clarks visited him and Elizabeth in Chapel Hill. Clark published several short pieces on Green and *Paul Green* (New York: McBride, 1928).

4. Annual fund-raising revue for the Theatre Guild.

5. Naturalized British novelist whose *Green Hat* (1924) was a current best-seller.

6. The Theatre Guild gave the world premiere of *Heartbreak House* in 1920 and thereafter produced a Shaw play nearly every season.

7. By Maxwell Anderson, which opened 7 September 1925.

8. Mayer Portner, aspiring writer who met the Greens in 1923 at Cornell (Mayer Portner to Paul Green, 16 January 1954, PG-SHC). One of his plays, *Soil*, is included in French's Standard Library of American Plays, vol. 70.

9. Harold K. Guinzburg (1899–1961) and George Oppenheimer (1900–1977) incorporated Viking Press on 13 March 1925 and over the summer brought into the firm as editor-in-chief the veteran publisher B. W. Huebsch (1876–1964), whose influential magazine of opinion, *The Freeman*, founded in 1920, had failed in 1924.

he failed in the other business, so he said, is older and cautious. Finally he advised against going into it now with the press so young. Guinzburg, who seems to have most of the money, said frankly he liked the idea of backing *The Reviewer*, even taking it over completely, but it would require at least $50,000, hiring new office space, and so on, and it was too big a thing to decide hurriedly, quite naturally so. So we left everything unsettled. I believe though that Mr. Huebsch will not agree to it. If it meant our moving to New York, I should hesitate. I believe though that if I offered to move the whole thing here, they would be more inclined to take it over. And after poking around, it does appear the only thing to do—come here and work awhile and get into the swim. Portner says I'm crazy not to do it. He declares with religious fervor that I could come here and be the great American playwright in two or three years. And so on. I don't know. It is so much fun to be where you can hear and see what you want, *ain't* it? And then the teaching and staying in the hollow![10] But "safe is best."

Tomorrow I'm going to see Minton-Balch,[11] Boni and Liveright, and Simon and Schuster, then home—Sunday P.M.

I love you! Paul

To have lunch with Barrett Clark tomorrow. We're going to straighten out the French business.[12] Mr. C—— says the editor of a big magazine wants to find imaginative comedy. I want to hurry back and fix over "Doctor Manuel."[13] Maybe that will give us another $100. Tonight to *Lucky Sam McCarver.*[14] Portner furnishes seats. I miss you!

10. The Glen, a narrow valley on the northeastern edge of the UNC campus where the Greens moved earlier in the year. The restricted view there always frustrated Green (Elizabeth Lay Green, *The Paul Green I Know* [Chapel Hill: North Caroliniana Society, 1978], p. 21).

11. Publishing house, founded in 1924, merged with G. P. Putnam's Sons in 1930.

12. Perhaps concerning "In Aunt Mahaly's Cabin," "The Man Who Died at Twelve O'Clock," and several other one-act plays by Green that French copyrighted in 1925 and issued in acting scripts.

13. Alternate title of "Quare Medicine," a one-act comedy presently in rehearsal by the Playmakers for performances beginning 23 November 1925. It was not published until 1928, when Green included it in *In the Valley and Other Carolina Plays* (New York: Samuel French, 1928), pp. 49–79.

14. By Sidney Howard, which opened on 21 October 1925.

## 49. To Elizabeth L. Green

Hotel Times Square, 43rd Street West, New York City
Thursday, 10 June 1926

Dear old gal:[1]

I am back in the mezzanine of this Times Sq. Hotel,[2] after spending the night out with the Clarks at Briarcliff Manor.[3] I had a lovely time there. They have a very simple little place, everything informal, Barrett jumping up from the table to make coffee, etc. Mrs. Clark is *charming*. I like her a great deal. Nancy, the little 3 year old, is of course spoiled and yet pleasant. She looked at me and said, "I like 'at man." We sat up until quite late talking and hearing Cecile (Mrs. Clark) play the piano. She is sending you a bit of her "real maple sugar cream." They both deplored your absence. We must have them down to Chapel Hill. You'd like her and their way of living. It's like ours.

Yesterday I met Portner on the street!!!! Failed to get to *The Big Parade*.[4]

I've just called up McBride and marvelous!—they say they'll let me have some money.[5] I'll wire it to you as soon as I draw it. You perhaps will get it before this letter comes.

On the way in this morning we sat with Sheldon Cheney.[6] He's a very sensible and open-minded fellow so far as I could gather from an hour's

1. On 8 June Green took the overnight train from Durham to New York City on his way to the MacDowell Colony near Peterboro, New Hampshire. The colony, established by the widow of composer Edward Alexander MacDowell (1861–1908) at their former farm, provided quiet working conditions for writers, artists, and composers. Green planned to stay there and write until the end of July.

2. Whose letterhead stationery he used for the letter.

3. Town up the Hudson River from New York City where the Clarks lived.

4. Motion picture adapted by Laurence Stallings from one of his stories. Green wanted to see the movie because Stallings had a North Carolina connection (he graduated from Wake Forest College before serving in the U.S. Marines during World War I) and because his film (released in November 1925), a product of postwar disillusionment, was acclaimed for its depiction of battlefield horrors.

5. As advance payment of royalties on *Lonesome Road*; probably $150 or $200, the range of a second advance in July (Paul Green to Elizabeth Green, 5 July 1926, EG-SHC).

6. A founding editor of *Theatre Arts* (1916), member of the advisory board of the Theatre Guild, and author of several influential books on the theater: *The New Movement in the Theatre* (1914), *The Art Theatre* (1917), and *The Theatre: Three Thousand Years of Drama, Acting, and Stagecraft* (1929; rev. ed. 1952).

association. O'Neill is in the Bermudas and won't be back until June 21 so he says in a letter to Clark. Barrett and I went over the proofs of the O'Neill book last night,[7] reading his (O'Neill's) corrections, letters, etc., and I was terribly disappointed in the man's attitude. He is careful, contrary, sore-tailed and a lot of things. He certainly is very anxious not to have people think bad of him. He had Clark to cut out a lot of his punk poetry, etc. Why in the devil didn't he say, "go ahead and write what you think of me. It'll all come out anyhow. It's your judgment"? He ought to have kept out of his biography, I think. For instance this will give you a touch of the way he's acted about the book. Barrett said that last year O'Neill dropped into the theatre at a performance of *Desire Under the Elms.* Two opulent and puritan ladies were sitting in front of him. Number one said to number two, "Ah, that O'Neill! They say he's a terrible drunkard." "And more than all he takes dope," answered number two.

Thereupon O'Neill in a rage sailed into them, vociferating that he *did not* dope, that he wasn't a rake and scapegrace. He was so vehement that the poor women backed out of the theatre in weeping confusion. Sensitive plant![8] In the Clark proof one of O'Neill's insertions in pencil is that he's never had anything to do with dope, going out of his way to say it.[9] Well, I don't like his recent external reformation. I thought he knew too much about this living business to bother about what certainly was he in the days gone by. I hope to see him when I come back through here from the Colony. Of course I'm not keen about bothering him.

Lord, I already think about my boy and hone for all three of you.[10]

I love ye, Paul

7. Clark's *Eugene O'Neill,* which McBride would publish later in 1926.

8. Clark acknowledges that O'Neill corrected the notes for and drafts of the book (Clark, *Eugene O'Neill* [New York: McBride, 1926], pp. 3, 26) and adds that O'Neill said "most of my picturesque anecdotes were apocryphal" (p. 3). The one recounted by Green is not in the published book.

9. Perhaps one of O'Neill's remarks quoted by Clark: " 'I never attempt to write a line when I'm not strictly on the wagon. I don't think anything worth reading was ever written by any one who was drunk when he wrote it. This is not morality. It's physiology. Dope I know nothing about, but I suspect even De Quincey was boasting what a devil he was!' " (Clark, *Eugene O'Neill,* pp. 29–30).

10. The Greens' second child, Nancy Byrd, was born on 25 February 1926.

## 50. To Elizabeth L. Green

[MacDowell Colony, Peterboro, N.H.]
Monday night, 21 June 1926

Dear Honey Chile,[1]

I'm in bed at the MacDowell lodge ready for sleeping. As I told you in a card mailed from N.Y.C., I spent the night—Sunday—out at Barrett's. After supper we went to the Scarborough-on-the-Hudson Theatre to *Prunella*[2] given by the Theatre Guild school, coached by Winthrop Ames.[3] There met Barry for a second,[4] nice, insurance agent type, but with no telling what in him, of course. Came into town this morning and found that there was no possible way to get from Keene to Peterboro without a day's lie-over. So I got a check cashed at French's ($10) and came around by Worcester and finally after the awfullest ride on jerky trains got here at 7:30. Got a taxi to bring me on up to the Colony. Emil the do-it-all gardener showed me here to the lodge where I sleep. Then I washed and went back to supper. Everybody had eaten and gone. After supper I drifted into the livingroom of the Colony Hall and behold there sat Frances Newman talking away. She introduced herself at once. E. A. Robinson was sitting by the fire also.[5] He got up in a moment and went to his room upstairs. Gosh, I am surprised that they were tickled to find I was *the* Paul Green, as one woman put it. A Miss Richardson—don't know her from beans—said we have two distinguished people now, Mr. Robinson and

1. On 10 June, after he mailed the letter of that date, Elizabeth wired Green that his father had died. Instead of going on to Peterboro, he returned home for the funeral. On 19 or 20 June he again took the train to New York City, then on the day of the present letter continued to Peterboro, still planning to stay at the MacDowell Colony through July.

2. Verse play with music by Laurence Housman and Harley Granville-Barker, first produced in 1904 and frequently done thereafter.

3. Managing director of the prestigious New Theatre in 1908, who remained active in New York City theater circles until shortly before his death in 1937.

4. Philip Barry (1896–1949), an advertising agent during the early days of his playwriting career. His next play, *White Wings*, would be produced by Ames in October 1926.

5. From 1911 onward Robinson (1869–1935) spent his summers at the MacDowell Colony. He had already received two Pulitzer prizes for poetry, in 1922 for his *Collected Poems* and in 1925 for *The Man Who Died Twice*. In 1928 he would receive a third, for

Mr. Green—ahem! I ain't fooled though. Wait till I do something right. Most of the Colonists were down town when I came, and so I didn't meet many. Only fourteen are here now. More coming the first of July.

The place isn't so much architecturally, but it is wonderfully quiet. The air is fine and bracing, frost last night, they say.

Oh, me, I miss my gal! It'll be so hard to stay up here without you three. But I'm going to try to make it count financially. Haven't decided whether to start on a novel or plays.—Plays, I think, since I'm to be here such a short time. And then when I get one or two on in N.Y. (if), I want to have plenty to shoot to them. Clark says the Provincetown is seriously considering *The Field God*—Funny, it wouldn't thrill me to have them do it! I've felt both sides of the coin lately. He saw O'Neill last week and he (O'Neill) has taken *Abraham* home to read. He led Clark to believe that if he said for the G.V. theatre to do it, they'd do it.[6] He's finished his *Lazarus Laughed* play—all to be done in masks. Now planning a series of nine plays all of one man's life, to be given on nine successive evenings and repeated, etc.[7]

I'm worried about how you'll make out there with everything in a mess. Get that town manager to fix up the road part of the way if necessary so that the delivery wagons can come in.[8] The dirt can be leveled up at the turn and cinders put on it. Maybe George[9] could help you out. I was awfully sorry about hitting the negro's car going into Durham. Henry[10] paid it—$5—we must pay him back sometime.

I got here with $3. I won't need to cash a check, I think, until I go back. I've

6. The Provincetown Players postponed the production of *The Field God*, opening it at the Greenwich Village Theatre on 21 April 1927, and first did *In Abraham's Bosom*, beginning the run on 30 December 1926.

7. Reference unclear. Probably too early for the O'Neill cycle entitled *A Tale of the Possessors Self-Dispossessed*, from which only *A Touch of the Poet* and *More Stately Mansions* escaped burning by O'Neill in his last years. Still ahead of O'Neill in 1926 were the extralong plays *Strange Interlude* (produced in 1928 in nine acts) and *Mourning Becomes Electra* (produced in 1931 as a trilogy in thirteen acts).

8. The unpaved road from Franklin Street down to the Greens' home in the Glen was steep, winding, and narrow. Throughout the ten years they lived there, the road was difficult to travel.

9. Denny.

10. Elizabeth's brother.

got to buy a comb and brush, some stamps and cigarettes. $3 will do it. Pore Gal, I wish you were here with me. F. Newman asked very kindly after you.

More tomorrow night.

I love you, Paul

Sending this in *Reviewer* envelope. No stationery tonight.

## 51. To Elizabeth L. Green

[MacDowell Colony, Peterboro, N.H.]
Monday morning, [28] June 1926

Dear Child,

Here I am down at the studio ready to begin on something, I'm not able to say what, not having decided on a plot for my next play.[1] Yesterday Uncle Beirne and Aunt Marian[2] came over from Concord and called on me at the studio here. We decided to have lunch together down town, visitors not being allowed to dine with the colonists. I had fifty cents in my pocket. So I went by Colony Hall and borrowed five dollars from Emil the steward. Lo and behold, a very poor lunch cost three-seventy-five. I hated to see it happen. They went back about two o'clock. I plan to go over this week-end. Uncle Beirne says one can get a farmhouse up in that section pretty cheap for the summer and I'll look around. I hope we can arrange to do that next year.

Honey, your letter came this morning at breakfast, telling about taking the children to Dr. Brooks.[3] I am worried about little Paul. To have lost a pound and gained nothing through all that period—since we took him over last—looks bad. Please do be careful, poor child. I know you are worn to death.

Frances Newman and I went for a walk last night down town—after the

1. In a letter the previous Saturday Green described the play he wrote that week, which became *Shroud My Body Down*, calling it his "wild blood" play: "The idea [incest] cannot be illustrated in the round, and I'm afraid I've been too rough, but anyway I've created a sort of lyrico-dramatic spectacle, and the characters are wonderful, if I can but do them" (Paul Green to Elizabeth Green, 26 June 1926, PG-SHC). Green arrived at the colony with the hope of getting down the draft of a long play each week.

2. Beirne and Marian Lay, Elizabeth's uncle and aunt.

3. Baird V. Brooks, pediatrician in Durham. Paul, Jr., had had the flu for a week, with fever and diarrhea (Elizabeth Green to Paul Green, 22 June 1926, EG-SHC).

colonists had been dinnered at Mrs. MacDowell's. I bought some cigarettes. She is terribly disappointed in the place here—nobody to talk to with much in his head. She is the frankest person about things of sex I've ever met, and apparently hypped on matters of lost virginity. She is all the time talking about her Virgin book—you remember the three episodes from the hard-boiled virgin that came out in *The Reviewer*.[4] It is clearly autobiographical, and she has as good as told me that after many love affairs she through curiosity gave up her innocence to some man—might be Mencken, might be a common X. She has told me too about some of these love affairs, especially how deeply in love she was with the Mercury Bull,[5] but I suppose it was all on her side. As an example of her frankness, let me give this. Last night we were walking along and she got off somehow on the subject of love in Greek literature and naturally she pushed it over into the boy-love business, and then on to phallicism. Her laugh—perfectly spontaneous—broke out in the night as we passed Edward MacDowell's grave and she said, "That reminds me. Not long ago I was up to see Mr. Cabell[6] and he and Mrs. Cabell had moved into a new house, a house that comes to a point in the funniest way. As soon as I met Mr. Cabell I said, 'How funny! Now you're living in a house that represents a phallic symbol.' " She said Mr. Cabell told her that nobody else had thought of it but that it was perfectly true, and seemed very much tickled at it. She is sending him parts of her Virgin book to criticise and no doubt worrying him, unless, and I can believe it, he likes her salted, silly complex.

I had the most awful dream last night about Hugh and all the rest at home. I woke up in a sweat, it was so terrible. Like a hidden spectator I saw him and Caro and Erm at the table after supper. He was abusing them in a white heat of fury, Erm was crying and Caro sitting smiling at him with a devilish malignancy. He cried out that he was going to kill Caro because of the way she had acted about papa's death, her laughing and giggling and not being hurt.

4. "Three Episodes from the Hard-Boiled Virgin," *The Reviewer* 4 (October 1924): 341–43. Newman finished the novel during her stay at the colony and published it late in 1926.

5. H. L. Mencken, who founded *The American Mercury* in 1924 and edited it until 1934.

6. James Branch Cabell (1879–1958), writer who lived in Richmond, Virginia. In 1919 his novel *Jurgen* was banned for violating New York's pornography law, and through the 1920s he remained one of the United States' more celebrated writers. A strong supporter of *The Reviewer*, he edited three issues in 1921.

Then suddenly all of us heard a most forlorn voice up at the barn. It was papa calling his hogs. The sound of it froze us with horror. Then as we listened we heard him coming down the road talking to himself. Hugh and I ran out and met him before the house and tried to persuade him to go back into his grave, but he pushed us away from him and said he wanted to sit at the table as he did before, he wanted to go around and see the crops for it had rained on them. So he pushed his way by us and went clumping into the house. Then a loud scream burst from the kitchen. Hugh and I ran around the house and met Erm coming out into the yard, tall and swaying like a reed. Her face was sightless, burned into a wad of awful roasted flesh. And beyond the house I heard Caro Mae giggling as she went out into the fields. Papa came on down the porch and went into the dining-room. Hugh fled to me and hugged me tight screaming and beating himself in terror. . . . Then I woke up terrified and reaching out to find you . . . Lord, it was awful. . . . I can't begin to relive the feeling of it. . . .

I must stop now and get to work. . . .

I love you, Paul

## 52. To Elizabeth L. Green

[MacDowell Colony, Peterboro, N.H.]
Wednesday afternoon, 30 June 1926

Dear Honey Chile,

I am stopping work for the day to go down town to get a hair-cut and some little odds and ends. Your letter came this morning with the Heffners' epistle and other things. Poor Ruth and Heffner, it's terrible to have to write when one doesn't want to.[1] The news about Ellen is encouraging. Maybe she'll make a go of the marriage business this time.[2] Aunt Marian asked in a rather suggestive tone the other day, "Have you met the man Ellen is going to marry?" I told her no, and she said no more, but I inferred that she's against

1. Hubert Heffner and Ruth Penny (also active with the Playmakers) married on 8 April 1922, shortly before he received an M.A. in English from UNC. During the summer of 1926 the couple moved back to Chapel Hill, after holding teaching positions in the West, and in the fall Heffner became associate director of the Playmakers.

2. Ellen, who for a time in 1922–23 was engaged to Wilbur Stout, recently told Elizabeth she and Harold Hodgkinson planned to marry.

him. By this time perhaps the Reverend is with you.[3] Poor child, you are having a time. I'll come home as soon as I can to help you out. Really I'm not able to get on here as I had hoped. I've worked like a dog and sweated, but things don't come out right. One reason is that I'm not able to refer to books of folklore, look up facts and things about North Carolina places. I never before realized how necessary such hints were to me. So far I haven't done a thing that will mean any money. I've never worked so hard before, but I can't get anything to grip me, no vision, no penetration. The thing I should have done, I believe, was write stories or do the little book starting with "The Beginning." But I left all my unfinished short sketches back there, most of which I planned to rewrite and put in that book—e.g. "Bare Fields."[4] Your suggestion for a comedy is right, of course, but I have nothing in mind. If I were back there where I could look up about country dances, parties, etc., I should try to build "Quare Medicine" into something. But I need the hints, etc. I doubt very much that I'll get over to Concord at all. I'll be busy right up till I leave here and somehow I have a feeling Aunt M. and Uncle B. didn't take to me very much. I was terribly wild and woolly when they came down to the studio, having blood on one side of my face from a razor cut to top things off, a fact I didn't discover till after they had gone in the afternoon. Oh, me, I must get something big done! Pray for me. You'd be completely shamed if you could see what I've written. I've done more than a hundred pages of stuff and it's every bit worthless. I went over some of it last night and it made me shout with chagrin. That four-volume novel on Carolina life stirs in me all the time. I could just run away writing that, but I can't get to it in this short time. I may decide tomorrow to write short stories and give up plays for the time I'm here. Oh, I don't know. I'm so glad the little fellow is better.[5] I know you'll take care of him as best you can, but do be careful, careful. Use your own judgment in paying the bills, but save enough money to carry you through. And can't you take about fifty dollars and go to Durham and buy yourself some clothes. Of course you'll need some if Ellen gets married.

3. On 29 June Dr. Lay arrived in Chapel Hill for a short visit (Elizabeth Green to Paul Green, [30 June 1926], EG-SHC).

4. "The Beginning" appeared in *The Reviewer* 4 (October 1925): 99–102. Green included it, "Bare Fields," and twenty-six other stories in *Wide Fields* (New York: McBride, 1928).

5. Paul, Jr.

You did right in keeping H.[6] and others off the Ford. It's old and won't last forever anyway.

Must stop, I love ye, Paul

No word from the Provincetown or McBride.[7]

## 53. To Elizabeth L. Green

[MacDowell Colony] Peterboro, N.H.
1 July 1926

Dear Old Gal;

Your letters certainly are skimpy, but I understand your imbroglio in the conservatory.[1] And I'm so glad that the Doctor and Ellen are there. They will be company to you in "that lonesome place, company." You certainly must have your hands full, and I wish I could be there with you. To think of you all sitting down together and my eating down here in the woods alone, all, all alone worries me. But then I've got to grit my teeth and go to it. If only that gnawing pain in the side of my stomach would leave me alone. I'm taking every precaution possible—except leaving off smoking, and I've begun to suspect that maybe a certain amount of nicotine gets into my stomach and that may be causing the trouble, though Dr. Stanford[2] said smoking moderately wouldn't hurt me. If it keeps up, I'll drop the tobacco entirely. For I've got too much on me—them young'uns, etc., and the etc. is a big part—to start

6. Henry, Elizabeth's brother.

7. The Provincetown Theatre was considering productions of *The Field God* and *In Abraham's Bosom*, and McBride was considering publication of the two plays.

---

1. Elizabeth, in Chapel Hill with an infant and a sick two-year-old, had just told Paul in a letter that she expected her father and sister Ellen to arrive for a visit by "tomorrow" and that in the meantime "I have just been cleaning up some of *The Reviewer* mail and feel as if I were destroying the unhatched eggs of a mother hen. The study has hardly been touched since you left. To finish the Negro bulletin outline [for a study guide published in 1928 as *The Negro in Contemporary American Literature*] I merely sat down on top of the mess and worked, for I knew if I began to clean up and sort out there would be no end to the job" (Elizabeth Green to Paul Green, [28 or 29 June 1926], EG-SHC).

2. William Raney Stanford (1892–1979), a physician in Durham.

any coil shuffling in this mortal vale.[3] The h. w. bottle hasn't come yet, nor the laundry.[4] I need the laundry, having had none done since coming here. I'm waiting for a laundry bag, not able to get one down town. I suppose some of the things will be in tonight's mail. It certainly is nice for Cornelia to include *Lonesome Road* in her bulletin. Does that mean a reference, or was it chosen for a study meeting?[5] I'll know before you can answer, if the bulletin comes. Have we got E. A. Robinson's collected works in one volume? If not, I want to get it for you here and have Mr. Robinson write something in it for you. I've got to know him very well indeed.[6] Frances Newman talks him to death. We had a talk together yesterday afternoon at dinner down at the tea-barn where they entertain all the colonists on Thursday evening. The barn is built on the edge of the Nubanusit River and a balcony looks out over the falls. I haven't made many friends, too busy. A young composer—Roy Harris—is my best.[7] He is a demon at the piano and is composing some wonderful music. They say here that he is very gifted. His first symphony is to be played at the Lewisohn Stadium by the Philharmonic on July the fifteenth. He is copying parts now night and day. He'll be through tomorrow night. His wife[8]—secretary to the editor of *The Forum*—is coming up tomorrow night. They are going back to New York together to be at the stadium. She is a playwright. People up here have shown quite a bit of interest in *Lonesome Road.* Miss Newman says she's

3. *Hamlet,* act 3, scene 1.

4. In an earlier letter he asked Elizabeth to send him a hot water bottle and a laundry bag, neither of which he could find in Peterboro.

5. Cornelia Spencer Love (1892–1981), head of the Acquisitions Department in the UNC Library 1917–48, did several bulletins, or study guides, for the UNC Extension Division, one of them on "Current Books" (1926). In it she devoted the fifth of fifteen meeting outlines to *Lonesome Road.*

6. Elizabeth replied that of Robinson's books they had only *Dionysus in Doubt* (1925) and that she hoped Paul would get an inscribed copy of Robinson's *Collected Poems* (Elizabeth Green to Paul Green, 5 July 1926, EG-SHC).

7. Reared in Oklahoma and California, Roy Harris (1898–1979) became a leading Americanist composer. His *First Symphony* (1933) celebrated the pioneering spirit of the West, and his music fell more and more into the folk tradition, culminating in the melodic *Seventh Symphony* (1952). Before going to Paris in the fall of 1926 on a Guggenheim fellowship, he spent the summer of 1926 at the colony arranging and copying parts for the andante section of a symphony he did not finish, a piece performed in New York City in July.

8. Unidentified. Harris is not known to have married until 1936.

terribly afraid that Harris and I are geniuses, and she is so afraid of geniuses. Harris says—being very frank—that he "likes that fellow Green. I think there's something in him." He's a funny fellow. But oh, if they could only see how terrible I am now, bowed down in the doldrums of imagination. A Mrs. Kenneth Brown here started reading *Porgy*[9] the other night and threw it down in terrible disgust, saying it was a horrible book, indecent, etc.

Miss Newman is going to slip *Lonesome Road* into her hands to see what will happen. She is a Greek woman and has written lots of novels, I understand, on that part of the world.[10]

I am on my second play now,[11] wrote twenty pages today, hope to do more than thirty tomorrow, getting off to a late start this morning. It is not much, a good idea, but my poor head is slow to dig up plots. What I have in mind is a Southern family—the Connellys, related to the Connellys in Virginia, one of whom has been a supreme court justice—worn down and out, two prim and dried up old maids, a younger brother, about 35, living in the old Connelly country home, going to ruins, the brother trying to farm and making no success, the tenants taking everything to run them, gradually going down and down. This brother falls in love with a tenant farm girl, the very vital blood his effete strain needs. But his pride and the pride of his sisters keeps his better impulses down. The girl loves him. A liaison is established. The father of the girl, a very devout patriarchical man, drives her from home when he finds she is going to have a baby. She has begged the Connelly man to marry her. He has wanted to, hesitated, sunk his best nature below his pride and let matters go on. The girl terrified and distraught over her condition—having been raised up on the Bible and the law of Moses—staggers off and makes her way to town and in a boarding house gives birth to her child and tries to kill herself. The news is brought to the Connelly home, the young man in a passion of

9. Novel (1925) of black life along Catfish Row in Charleston, South Carolina, by DuBose Heyward (dramatized and produced, 1927; basis of opera *Porgy and Bess* [1935]).

10. Demetra Vaka Brown (1877–1946), who came to the United States from Greece when she was seventeen, published numerous novels, several in collaboration with her husband Kenneth Brown, most recently *The Unveiled Ladies of Stamboul* (1923). Elizabeth replied that "I have read one of Mrs. Brown's books, a study of harem life, rather well written as I remember" (Elizabeth Green to Paul Green, 5 July 1926, EG-SHC).

11. *The House of Connelly.*

contrition stands up before his family and curses himself and them, owns up that the little baby boy is his and he has loved her all the time and rushes away to see her. To his surprise the old maids want the girl brought in, having concluded that their way of living is empty. He marries the girl, and the whole family has something to live for in the child. I am not sure that is the way I shall end it. I'll know Sunday night. Oh, me, I'm no good![12]

Paul

## 54. To Elizabeth L. Green

[Chapel Hill, N.C.]
Monday night, 6 September 1926

Dear Old Gal—[1]

There is nothing to write about tonight—no news. Little Paul has been just as angelic as usual and refuses to show any emotion at your being away. We

12. The conclusion of *The House of Connelly* has a detailed history. In the comic version outlined here a tenant girl (later named Patsy Tate) marries into the aristocratic southern family and saves it from extinction. The script Green sent the Theatre Guild in 1928 was the tragic version, however, in which Patsy is murdered by two old black women who see themselves as guardians of the southern past. When the Guild turned over the script to its offspring, the Group Theatre, Harold Clurman and other leaders of the Group argued that a hopeful ending was better suited to the play, and Green returned to the version suggested in the letter (Clurman, *The Fervent Years: The Story of the Group Theatre and the Thirties*, 2d ed. (New York: Hill and Wang, 1957), p. 44). That version became the inaugural production of the Group, opening in New York City on 28 September 1931, then it was published in *The House of Connelly and Other Plays* (New York: Samuel French, 1931) and *Out of the South: The Life of a People in Dramatic Form* (New York: Harper and Brothers, 1939). Later Green discussed the play and its ending in "Tragedy—Playwright to Professor," in *Dramatic Heritage* (New York: Samuel French, 1953), pp. 81–91, then in *Five Plays of the South*, ed. John Gassner (New York: Hill and Wang, 1963), he published *The House of Connelly* in its tragic version.

1. On 3 July at the MacDowell Colony Green got a wire from Barrett Clark asking him to come to New York City to talk with directors of the Provincetown Theatre about a production of *In Abraham's Bosom*. On the evening of 4 July he took an overnight train and arrived in the city the next morning. After three or four days there, during which he arranged for the production with Eleanor Fitzgerald, James

talk with him about you and he receives it all with the mask of the sphinx. We say, "Where is mother?" and he answers as gaily as a sparrow—"Her in Beaufort," and goes on with his work. Today I had three tons of coal brought, and since then he's been hauling it to the kitchen for me in his "t'uck"—meaning his wagon. He pulled some rather heavy loads and dumped them with wild shouts. And you ought to hear him g-r-r-r-rrr-ing as he cranks up. He goes around now cranking chairs before he climbs in them, and the guttural noises he accompanies it with are deafening, his lips stuck out like two semicircles of sausages.

Tell Henry[2] I thank him for his invitation to come to Beaufort and bring you back, but it's impossible. I'm going to keep on trying at this play even if I don't get a line written. Today went by and I'm no nearer the goal, the thing just won't come out. Horace[3] is back, came in yesterday just as I had started up to his house to work. So I cleaned up everything a bit, moved my stuff out, and I'm here working in the study. I get along just as well. Last night I had him to supper with me at the cafeteria, thinking he'd be terribly lonely here with nobody in the house with him, etc. He is.[4] A note from Wind yesterday.[5] Ruth and Radoff[6] were here to dinner—seems we just can't help having a crowd all the time, and the way the poor milkman and market man and Pickard[7] look at me. Oh me. Radoff is here tonight. Caro and Ginger[8] are making curtains for the dining-room. Tonight I waxed the floors again, trying to get a good foundation built up for mud, etc. They shine like a mirror. But the front

---

Light, and others of the Provincetown management, he went on to Chapel Hill rather than returning to Peterboro for the remaining three weeks of his projected stay at the colony. In Chapel Hill Green worked on *The House of Connelly*, and on 31 August Elizabeth took their daughter, Nancy Byrd, to Beaufort for a visit with her parents, leaving Paul, Jr., in Chapel Hill with his father.

2. Elizabeth's brother.

3. Williams, in whose house Green had written since returning from New York City.

4. Williams's wife, Bertha, had died, but not recently (18 October 1922).

5. Edgar Wind, whom the Greens met at Cornell, was in the process of moving to Chapel Hill, where he would be instructor in philosophy, 1926–27.

6. Morris Leon Radoff, who received a B.A. from UNC in the spring and would earn an M.A. in French at UNC, 1926–27, then remain as instructor in French, 1928–29.

7. Unidentified.

8. Elizabeth's sister, Virginia.

porch is terrible. That boy keeps it like a hog pen—back again to him. This morning at six he woke me up talking with the cat, and he was tickled to death. I looked out and the Black Annie was walking up and down the porch railing looking at him and apparently showing off for his benefit. He would say to her, "Turn awound, Black Annie—hee—lee—lee—lee—lee. Gray Annie in the cage, Black Annie on the choo-coo track," etc. I went out, and his clothes were stuck to him, drownded rat, but he was happy. Again today he's been singing, "De blind man stood on de woad and cwied."[9] He doesn't know it, but he's singing about his father, poor fellow (Paulie).

Of course we (I) miss you, but stay a long time and enjoy yourself. You deserve it if anyone ever did. I'm worried also about Nancy.[10] Things sound mighty dark. Try to cheer your mother up, for Nancy is somehow her pet, I think. I feel mean when you talk about the tempo of your natural home life. Lord, I ain't nothing but a bag of erraticisms, and I don't see how anybody stands me.

I don't know whether it will be better for you to come on the train or not. It might be, for a long drive like that would be a bit dangerous unless you had a very experienced driver. And by the way, tell Henry he'd better buy a cheap lock and with a chain fasten the spare tire on well. It would be easily stolen.

Love to all, Paul

## 55. To Nell Battle Lewis[1]

Chapel Hill, N.C.
16 March 1927

Dear Nell;

From you I learned first that Madry was sending out a story on me for the

9. Line from a black folk song, later used by Green as an epigram to *Five Plays of the South.*

10. One of Elizabeth's sisters, who was sick.

---

1. Nell Battle Lewis (1893–1956), friend and associate, grew up in Raleigh, went to school at Smith College in Northampton, Massachusetts (B.A., 1917), then worked in a YMCA canteen with the American Expeditionary Force in France (1918–19) during World War I. In 1920 she returned to Raleigh and began her career as reporter and feature writer with the *News and Observer* (1920–48), during which time she participated in numerous political, historical, and artistic endeavors. While Green edited

Sunday papers, although he told me sometime ago that he planned to do so.[2] I passed by his office a few minutes ago and one of the boys there (Bob was out) gave me a mimeographed copy of the tale. And now after glancing over it I cry out for salvation from my friends. The thing made me weak. The story he sent to the A.P. was shorter and therefore more restrained. This thing out-journals journalese. As soon as he comes in I'm going to try to get him to tone it down. My shyness is puffed to heaven, my ambidexterity at baseball pitching rivals the powers of the Bambino, and in every way I am a hell of a violet heretofore unnoticed by the jaundiced public's cowlike eye.[3] Great God! When I say salvation from my friends, I don't mean you, for I do trust in you to say what you think and not what will fit an immediate and spontaneously silly need. So treat me white, that is put in the warts and odors along with the rest. Of course the whole thing appears more important to me, I guess, than to anyone else. But I do think that an adequate statement of the facts is the first and maybe final necessity. It is for me at least. (I mean in criticism.) So voilà.[4]

My opinions on the drama may not be worth anything, but since you've asked I'll say what I think at this present moment, as near as I can. Most of the American drama seems to be bosh to me. Of some two-hundred plays produced annually in New York there usually [are] not more than half a dozen worth much. And among the half dozen not more than one or two are likely to last many years. Such farceurs as Avery Hopwood, George Abbott—the well-known playfixer of *Broadway* and other million-dollar successes—are not at all to my liking.[5] They do their juggling act and amuse and pass along. And

---

*The Reviewer*, she served on the editorial board. Recently she told Green she wanted to do an article on his work for her paper.

2. Robert W. Madry, in the Department of Journalism at UNC, also served as director of the University News Bureau. *In Abraham's Bosom* was causing the flurry of interest in Green. The play opened at the Provincetown Playhouse in New York City on 30 December 1926, and by mid-January 1927 rumors circulated in New York and North Carolina that it was a strong contender for the Pulitzer Prize in drama (Barrett Clark to Paul Green, 14 January 1927, PG-SHC).

3. Madry's article appeared as "Obscure Harnett County Farm Boy Wins Fame As Dramatist," *Greensboro Daily News*, 20 March 1927, sec. A, p. 3, cols. 1–2.

4. Lewis's article ("Paul Green Is Native North Carolina Dramatist Who Found His Inspiration and Achieved Success at Home," *NO*, 20 March 1927, sec. 1, p. 10, cols. 1–8) quotes much of the remainder of the present letter.

5. *Broadway* (1926), written in collaboration with Philip Dunning, was the first of a long line of popular comedies and musicals that George Abbott (b. 1887) was involved

all real art, so far as I can see, must do more than simply amuse. It must demand from the audience or spectators a creative and active enjoyment. That means work for all concerned, work in the sense that William James used the word.[6] Otherwise there will be no vindication and salvation for whatever feeling for the fine and beautiful we may possess. It will atrophy. Among the modern dramatists who make such demands on me—and I'm speaking only of those whose work I know—are Chekov, Werfel of Germany,[7] Eugene O'Neill, and Benavente of Spain.[8] This of course means that I not only find for myself a difference in kind but a difference in value in the work of such theatrical masters as Arthur Schnitzler, Pirandello and Galsworthy. They do seem to me to lack the breath of life which asks for energetic enjoyment. (I'm not speaking here of Galsworthy the novelist and short story writer, but of Galsworthy the dramatist.)[9] By this same crude test the accepted great—Aeschylus, Sophocles, Shakespeare and the rest—are great, great for me, and often tiring in their intense demands.

As for what I think of North Carolina and her materials for drama, I can answer that apropos of a word about the plays I am now working on. At the present I have three plays which I hope to finish before the fall. Two of them will be offered for New York production. The first of these two is called *The Connellys* and deals with an aristocratic old Southern family in North Carolina who are gradually drying up in their old run-down mansion, remembering their blue-blood and their days at the University and St. Mary's and their kinsfolk in Virginia. Their sandy land is washing away under them, the plaster

---

with as writer and actor, and sometimes also as director and producer. Avery Hopwood (1882–1928) had numerous Broadway successes, the biggest one his collaboration with Mary Roberts Rinehart, *The Bat* (1920).

6. If James stressed a particular sense of the word, it was the verb meaning to organize a collection of data, as in "the truest scientific hypothesis is that which, as we say, 'works' best" (*The Will to Believe* [Cambridge: Harvard University Press, 1979], p. 8).

7. Actually of Austria, a novelist and expressionistic playwright best known at the time for *Goat Song*, produced by the Theatre Guild in 1922.

8. Best known for *The Bonds of Interest* (1907), a comedy that launched the Theatre Guild's first season in 1919, and the tragedy *The Passion Flower* (1913).

9. Long established as a novelist (the first volume of *The Forsyte Saga* was published in 1906), Galsworthy (1867–1933) also wrote numerous plays, the best of which are plays of social protest: *Strife* (1909), *Justice* (1910), *The Skin Game* (1920), and *Loyalties* (1922).

peels from the walls, the stock is mangy and poor, and decay and rot are in them body and soul. Salvation comes to the single male survivor when he breaks through the fence of foolish conventions and loyalties and marries an earthy fruitful tenant farm gal—if I may use your feminine word. But my what a wail goes up from the relatives who count behind them a state supreme court judge, a governor, a lawyer, and Uncle Robert whose courtly figure and empty head graced the state senate for twenty years. And so on.[10] The second play deals with a young North Carolina lawbreaker and outlaw. I idealize this *Andy Jones* somewhat Robin Hood-like, being interested in getting at a statement of freedom having now and then the necessity of running counter to what most gentlefolk call sanity and law.[11] The third play is to deal with Jesus of Nazareth.[12] I suppose everybody has to try his hand at this subject soon or late. In this case my preoccupation is with the blasphemy of showing a figure, neither religious nor irreligious, a man who got hold of a truth that humanity is bigger than any creed or purpose or ideal; that humanity is really the source, and should be understood so, of all statements about it; that all religions and institutions and practices have value only in so far as they recognize that they are for the service of man and not man for them. "The Sabbath was made for man."[13] So for me Jesus was a pagan soul and not a Christian or ologist in any specific way. There have been others like him, of course—Buddha, Confucius, Shakespeare. They were all great human beings and belonged—in spite of scientific and scholarly research—to no nation, sect or time. For them there was neither black nor white, Jew nor Gentile—but people, people, everywhere people. As poor old blundering Abraham McCranie tries to say in *In Abraham's Bosom*—"It's the man, the man that counts. There ain't no difference at the bottom."[14] And even when he staggers out to make a futile last gesture of human supplication to the white mob he stammers forth something about a light, "a light and it will be."[15] If it only might! Jesus was like Abraham McCranie to me—Abraham McCranie a North Carolina Negro. And Jesus would have broken through all restraints and stretched a hand out to meet

10. Thus, at the time of the present letter, the play, produced and published as *The House of Connelly,* still had a hopeful ending.

11. Play not located; probably not finished.

12. *Tread the Green Grass.*

13. Mark 2:27.

14. *The Field God and In Abraham's Bosom* (New York: McBride, 1927), p. 112.

15. Ibid., p. 139.

him and lift him towards the light. But we don't do it, do we? We get in session assembled at the Capitol and bend our ears into the political wind and consider profit and loss most carefully and edge forth a puny hesitant bill about some damnable senseless prejudice. And the poor Negro and the ignorant child have to be like another Lazarus with "Thankee suh," for the crumb.[16] The show put on by this recent legislature was one of the most obsequious and inane performances I have ever had the sorrow of witnessing. And then a look abroad in this old North State gives us little hope. Leaders of institutions playing, forever playing their little solo of opportunism and expedience. "Let us go slow, be careful, soft pedal. Heigh there you're reckless, you'll ruin everything!" And so far as I can see Jesus was a most reckless person. He wasted himself and thereby saved himself. He said something about that too.[17] Well, I'm going to try to write about this man who a long time ago lived a most buoyant and reckless life. He was in love, he committed deeds which were known of as sin, but were not sin. For there can be no sin except the sin of denying the spirit of man. And that is not a thing to pass laws about or modify with legislation or to build churches on. It rather seems to me to be the source of all that. And so—to be dogmatic and cattily specific—the Jesus I know would have, if he had been here provided with a good whip, he would have adjourned some recent gatherings *sine die.* And so I have answered, it seems to me, your question as to dramatic materials in North Carolina. There is drama and potentially every form of art where there are human beings alive. North Carolina is no more provident in this than other states so far as I can see. I say that even though I have heard of its Anglo-Saxon purity and *The Observer*'s protégé Reuben Bland. (By the way didn't I read in *The News and Observer* some months back that what this state needed was

16. The story of Lazarus, who before dying and going to heaven had to eat the crumbs from the rich man's table, is given in Luke 16:19–31. The North Carolina legislature had adjourned the previous week, and two prominent issues during the session had been the public schools (whether the tax base in the state would permit the legislature to require all public schools to increase the length of the school year to eight months) and the Ku Klux Klan (several anti-Klan bills were introduced). The legislature passed none of the anti-Klan bills but did mandate a uniform eight-month school year (*NO*, 13 March 1927, sec. M).

17. Perhaps in the lecture to his disciples on the theme: "For whoever wants to save his own life will lose it; but whoever loses his life for my sake will find it" (Matthew 16:25).

more Reuben Blands? I should like to hear from Reuben's wives, both the dead and the living, but more especially the one now dead.)[18]

But then these are words and I guess I might as well stop and think of the sentence awaiting me five years hence.

With all good wishes,

P.S. I think our native state came in for some good discussion recently among the Yankees. The Negro magazine *Opportunity* bought the house out one night and invited an audience of well-known people to see Abraham.[19] There were some spittings and ear-burnings. I'm sorry in a way but actually glad.

## 56. To George W. Lay

Chapel Hill, N.C.
16 August 1927

Dear Dr. Lay:

Many thanks for the nice letter of several days ago. Elizabeth and I have talked matters over, and we have decided that maybe you are right in your decision about putting off the C.H. business another year.[1] *We* are terribly

18. On 25 December 1926 the *News and Observer* began a series of articles on Reuben Bland, seventy-two-year-old farmer from Robersonville, North Carolina, who claimed to have the largest family in the United States. He had thirty-four children, fifteen by his first wife, who then died, and nineteen by his second, with whom he still lived.

19. The date of that occurrence is unknown, but the magazine carried laudatory references to Green and *In Abraham's Bosom* throughout 1927. *Opportunity: A Journal of Negro Life*, published in New York City by the National Urban League, was edited by Charles S. Johnson, with Countee Cullen as assistant editor. Among its activities was an annual literary contest, and in 1927 Green served as a judge in the playwriting section and went to New York to speak at the awards dinner on 7 May (*New York Times*, 8 May 1927, p. 19, col. 5; *Opportunity*, June 1927, p. 159).

1. The Lays, retired now, considered moving to Chapel Hill, and the Greens offered financial help in buying a house and lot. In a recent letter, however, Lay said he and his wife had decided to remain in Beaufort at least another year, when they should be in better financial shape. He added that it would be unfair to accept help from Paul and Elizabeth, who were already in debt. "You are both of you so incurably generous by disposition and so prodigal with any money on which you can get your hands, that

reckless about many things and right now it might not be best to try this particular thing. Still I have hopes that our good fairy will not entirely desert us and that in a few years the road will straighten and smooth out. The theatrical year is opening up auspiciously. *Abraham* begins a new run in September[2] and I've just received word that *The Field God* begins in London during September with the "famous Jean Forbes-Robertson" in the leading role. My agent in N.Y. has written that this is a good thing all around. The contracts will be here for signing tomorrow or Thursday.[3] Then I'm writing two new plays[4] and other things. A new book will be out this fall—the material will go off this week[5]—So maybe I'll get ahead of the game in money sometime, though, alas, I don't have any sense about that commodity and my dear wife agrees in spirit and practice.

I've read the Millikan book[6] and am sorry to say that I've trod on the same lonely ground and he told me nothing new. His conclusions are not scientific but rather artistic and religious. So the gap remains. Friday I was down in Harnett where they dig sustenance from the soil and along with it a simple and most durable metaphysic. But it's not satisfactory to me, alas. I'm sorry Va. found me harassed.[7] But so I was and I'm afraid she got no pleasure from

---

we feel we would be ourselves responsible, if you got into a tight place on our account" (George Lay to Paul Green, 27 July 1927, EG-SHC).

2. *In Abraham's Bosom* had closed shortly before receiving the Pulitzer Prize on 2 May 1927, then reopened for a run of two weeks at the Provincetown Playhouse beginning on 8 May. In the fall the Provincetown group revived the production for a run of three weeks beginning on 6 September, then took it on tour through the Midwest to the West Coast, with runs of two weeks in Chicago and San Francisco.

3. Jean Forbes-Robertson (1905–1962), rising star of the London stage and member of a famous acting family, did not perform in *The Field God* when it opened in London in late September 1927. The part of Rhoda was played instead by Gillian Lind.

4. *The House of Connelly* and *Tread the Green Grass.*

5. For *In the Valley and Other Carolina Plays,* publication of which was delayed until the week of 21 January 1928.

6. *Evolution in Science and Religion* (New Haven: Yale University Press, 1927) by Robert Andrews Millikan, physicist at California Institute of Technology, who won a Nobel Prize in physics in 1923. In the book, sent to Green by Dr. Lay, Millikan maintained that science was not hostile to religion and that the scientific spirit and religious faith were quite compatible.

7. Virginia, Elizabeth's sister, had visited the Greens recently.

my section of the environment. In the old days a man's soul got out of order, now it's his stomach. I side with the ancient churchmen.

With love to all and a pleasing remembrance of your visit,

Paul

P.S. Congratulations on the continued intensification of the state of grandfatherhood. I hope to continue my part of the practice.

## 57. To Mary G. Johnson

[Chapel Hill, N.C.]
Wednesday night, 8 August 1928

Dear Mary:

Just a note to tell you how glad I was that you all came up last Sunday.[1] We both regret that we shan't see the children for so long, but we appreciate the glimpse we had of you. I hardly knew how to say goodbye, so I just said nothing. Some days everything seems unreal and like a dream, and last Sunday was one of the days. I couldn't keep my mind off our childhood and the mystery of our growing old. There sat Allie[2] across the room from me, and it came sharper to me than ever before that I didn't know her. She was a stranger to me, and it seemed that that ought not to be. Something was wrong. She will never talk. Has she anything to say? What is happening in her head? Anything? I can just remember her as a young lady. She was different then, and I remember a little curl on the back of her neck I used to think was so pretty. It's all gone now, of course, but something else far more rare is gone—that spirit that flashes in you. May the world never put that out! It won't, I know. And we can always understand each other! I've always felt that.

Paulie was taken with Mabel.[3] When I was giving him a bath Sunday night, he looked up suddenly and said:

"Do you like Mabel?"

"Yes. Do you?"

"Yes."

1. Green had a Guggenheim fellowship to study the theater in Europe and, with Elizabeth and their two children, was to leave Chapel Hill for Germany on 11 August. Mary, her children, and other family members and friends from Harnett County came to Chapel Hill for a send-off visit.

2. Alda, older half-sister of Mary and Paul, who had come with Mary.

3. Wife of Hugh Green, younger brother of Mary and Paul.

"Why?"

"I like her."

Other than that he's given no reason. I guess that is sufficient. He's so sensitive and independent that maybe her apartness struck him right. I rather surmise, though, that he liked her eyes. She really has lovely ones.

By the way I don't doubt that a certain kind of Christianity has kept more people miserable in this world than liquor, debauchery, or anything else—miserable in not seeing the wonder of, say, dew and flowers and babies and the like.

Was Gilbert disappointed in his trip?[4] I'm afraid so. He's a remarkable fellow. In talking about his wife, he crossed the line of religion and I heard him say, "when the mind and the body—they is separate, they ain't nothing else to do about it."

Just a word to say fare you well through all the coming year. And when the fall comes on and the November sunsets flame strangely up the sky think of me. And ask Billy[5] to look closely at the streaks of light spreading wide and high from the cartwheel of the sun.

—— X —— Paul[6]

4. Perhaps the man who worked the farm owned by Mary and her husband Alton Johnson.

5. Mary's son, nearly eight.

6. The Greens would stay in Germany, then in England, until November 1929. They left Chapel Hill by train on 11 August: "Off babies, baggage, books and all to N.Y. Nancy Byrd with fever 104, vomiting. We two forlorn parents live like fools. But the train carries us on. Stop at Hotel Thorndyke" (Green diary, PG-SHC). They remained in New York City through 15 August, discussing publishing prospects with Barrett Clark and production prospects with James Light of the Provincetown Players. They also spent an evening with Paul's sister Caro Mae. On 16 August they boarded the *Westphalia*, on 29 August docked at Hamburg, on 30 August took a train to Berlin, and by 5 September had found a house to rent in "a shabby district" at Kreuzbergstrasse 9 (ibid.).

## 58. To Mary G. Johnson

Kreuzbergstrasse 9, Berlin S. W., Germany
25 December 1928

Dearest Mary:

A thousand thanks to you and the others for the $25 Christmas gift. It came at exactly the right time, for my money from New York[1] only reached here today as a (German) check, and the banks won't open again until day after tomorrow. So if your gift hadn't come when it did the kids would have had a thin visit from Saint Nick—really it was fine! You do such right things! We had a tree—it is still up—Paulie[2] got a train, bus, some animal toys, books, etc. Byrd[3] got a doll, menagerie, books, etc. The old folks sat around and enjoyed by proxy. Paulie is now in bed with his train singing "Stille Nacht" in German at the top of his voice—it's our "Silent night, holy night"—he's burning up with a fever—103—and as red as a beet, all suddenly developed this evening. I'm writing now and waiting for the doctor—something to occupy my mind with. Have Bill and Billy[4] ever got the many cards and bits of news I've sent them? I hope they have. Today a letter came from Gladys, giving news of the kids, your visit to her and other things.[5] She didn't say anything about Edward Green.[6] Please write me all about it. Caro Mae just mentioned the poor boy's tragic act in one of her letters. I wanted to sit right down and write him a long letter out of my heart and then the more I thought of it the more I wondered if there wasn't some mistake and misunderstanding about it and perhaps I'd better get the facts. This is all Caro Mae said in a recent letter which I answered the same hour—"Edward Green tried to kill himself the other day. Got the gun and went into the bathroom and"—(I can hardly write the word—it is so terrible on him, Miss Myrtle[7] and the little girls)—"and shot himself. Miss Myrtle and Doctor Joe[8] saved him though against his will, but the doctor says he'll do it again as soon as he gets a chance." And that's all she

1. From the Guggenheim Foundation.

2. Almost five.

3. Almost three.

4. Mary's son and the son of a helper on her farm.

5. Gladys lived in Richlands, North Carolina, toward the coast from Mary's home near Lillington.

6. First cousin of Paul and Mary (1882–1942), who farmed in Harnett County.

7. Edward's wife (married 1912), sister of Mary's husband.

8. Joseph McKay, the family physician.

said. The thing made me sick. Write me the truth. What is bothering the poor fellow?[9] Gladys says Alton[10] has done well this year, and I'm so glad. Tell Hugh[11] not to get discouraged. It's so easy to get saddled with discouragement. Everybody has a bad year now and then, and he'll come through another year all right. I hear the doctor coming in. (Few hours later). The doctor has been and found Paulie with a sort of bronchitis, not serious, for which we are thankful! We've bathed him, sweated him, given him medicine, and now his fever's gone down. He's playing he's a lion now, and such braggadocio roars! The doctor comes again tomorrow, assuring us everything's all right. Fine! And you know what I mean.

(a week or more later)

This is certainly a hectic letter. Since the foregoing we've been through some mess. Paulie grew worse after the doctor left. The next day the doctor came again. He's been every day since—and said we must get out of this section or all of us would be sick. So I set out again hunting a place. Nothing in Berlin! I went to Vienna in Austria, Salzburg, and then over into Czecho-Slovakia at Prague—At last after four days and nights of weary travelling I came home worn out, having been some 12 or 1,500 miles—and then I found not only Paulie in bed but Elizabeth and Byrd also stretched out. It was so bad I had to laugh at it. And in all my trip I got no house. Well yesterday by chance I heard of a place just vacated by the Egyptian ambassador in the suburbs.[12] I drove there in a taxi and in an hour rented it. Tomorrow we move, since the doctor says the children won't suffer any ill effects if wrapped up and taken in a closed car.—They're all better now, thank goodness! We have a fine governess for them now[13]—only $15 a month and keep.—She does their sewing etc.—Well to be brief we're practically all right now—after having had the worst time in my experience.[14] So don't worry over us! We're all right for

9. He suffered from deep depression, brought on, as far as Mary could tell, by financial problems and failure to have a son. Although he lost his farm in the early 1930s, Edward gradually overcame his depression and died of a heart attack in 1942 (interview with Mary Green Johnson, 5 April 1985).

10. Mary's husband, who owned a hardware and farm implement business in Lillington.

11. Who also farmed in Harnett County.

12. At Friedbergstrasse 5 in Berlin-Dahlem.

13. Erna Lamprecht.

14. Worried about his family's health, frustrated over his own writing career, which

money too. I have $1,000 in hand and will get more soon. I'm wondering though about next summer when we start paying our way back. But we'll manage.

Two nights here, Mary, when I walked the floor and saw my little boy lying with glazed eyes and raging-fevered body I came as near praying and crying as I have in a long time. And I thought of you and Mamma and took courage! Deep down in me I talked with my own will power, and found it held up. I said if everything in the world said no I'd still say yes that Paulie must get well! Such is love! Yet he wasn't deathly sick at all. But he seemed so sick and weak and pitiful and his everlasting rattling breathing was about as pleasant as coffin clods. You know of course. But now he's on the way to sunshine. Byrd is practically well; so is Elizabeth—the most patient of the world. In a few months when she and I are travelling and having a good time and learning a lot—the children being taken care of back here—we'll have a better time because of these days. Enough of our sickness!

Has the flu struck among you yet? I've watched the accounts of its spread in the U.S. and hoped it missed you all.

Again, tell Hugh not to worry and to plan for a big crop next year—and so on.

Give our love to Alton and the kids. Tell Alton[15] I'll write him how everything looks in Paris when I go down there next month. I'll ride out to Clignancourt[16] and see that, Elysée Palace hotel,[17] etc. I must stop—Paulie wants his train fixed.

This is the awfullest pen![18]

Love always, Paul

I've just jotted down these few things on the run to let you hear from us.

---

seemed at a standstill, much concerned about having enough money to get through the winter, disturbed by the drunkenness, homosexuality, suicides, and general despair in Berlin, and feeling isolated in a country whose language he hardly knew, Green himself suffered extreme depression into the spring of 1929 (Green diary, PG-SHC; Elizabeth Green to Barrett H. Clark, 10 March 1929, Yr; conversations with Elizabeth Lay Green, 1982).

15. Who was stationed in Paris with Green at the end of World War I.

16. Site of their barracks.

17. Where Green's office was.

18. The letter shows signs throughout of uneven inking, sometimes too little, frequently too much, so that a few words are faint and many are blotched.

## 59. To Joseph Chapiro[1]

Friedbergstrasse 5, Berlin-Dahlem
13 April 1929

My dear Doctor Chapiro—

Some months ago I called on Herr Granowsky relative to writing an article on his work which I so much admired.[2] It was my hope that I might get some photographs to illustrate with, and indeed he promised me as much. But I know something of the difficulties that soon came his way and I have not pursued the matter further.[3] It happens now that at the request of the New

1. Joseph Chapiro (1893–1962), Berlin drama critic (*Für Alfred Kerr: ein Buch der Freundschaft* [1928] and *Gesprache mit Gerhart Hauptmann* [1932]), active in the affairs of Jewish theater groups in Germany before immigrating to the United States in 1933. Green met Chapiro shortly after arriving in Berlin, and probably it was Chapiro who introduced him to Alexis Granowsky (1890–1937), Russian director then in Berlin with his company, the State Jewish Theatre based in Moscow. Green was attracted to Granowsky's work because he used music as the basic element to control mood and tempo in his productions, a technique Green was exploring in his own plays.

2. During October 1928 Green saw several Granowsky productions, including *Die Reise Benjamins des Dritten,* which he described as "a grotesque and sentimental operetta, played in Yiddish and thoroughly delightful. With the aid of music the grotesque of mask, gesture, movement, passes rightly before you. Again [I] returned to ideas of folk musical plays" (Green diary, 4 October 1928, PG-SHC). He also saw *Die Nacht auf dem Alten Markt,* at which he sat "up in the third gallery (money getting low) and could see little. . . . See more and more my way towards some folk operatic pieces, adequate use of balladry and drama" (25 October 1928). On 1 November Green visited Granowsky in his room at the Hotel Au Zoo and found him "very agreeable." Granowsky talked mainly about his plans, which included tours to other European countries and the United States, some motion picture directing, and new productions with his own company. Green noted that "Granowsky is much like an American business man forty-five or more, somewhat stout, bald-headed and on this occasion tired about the eyes."

3. Granowsky and his State Jewish Theatre troop left the Soviet Union ostensibly as representatives of the government, but (like the Habima, another important Jewish theater company that left the Soviet Union for Berlin in 1926) they actually saw their tour as a chance to escape anti-Semitism by going to Germany. Shortly after Green's visit with Granowsky, the Soviet government ordered the State Jewish Theatre to return to Moscow. After Granowsky and most of the company refused to leave Berlin, the Soviet government withdrew its financial support and effectively dissolved the company.

York *Times* I am doing an article on the Berlin season, and since to my mind Herr Granowsky's Jewish Theatre was outstanding I wish especially to emphasize what his performances meant to me. Could you I wonder help me secure a few photographs of his productions? I should be more than glad to have your help. If by chançe Herr Granowsky is averse to having a stranger try his hand at an appreciative statement, then I won't bother with it more. But I should be glad to submit what I write to him for approval.[4]

Excuse the above business matter first. The real point of this note is to ask whether you and Mrs. Chapiro would join Mrs. Green and me at lunch or tea some day within the next week or so. I know you are very busy and therefore we could meet together at some place along Kurfurstendamm. Perhaps Roberts'[5] would not be so bad. Any place that is most convenient for you would suit us. I am sure that with a mixture of English and most broken German we could manage a short session. We hope so.

With kindest regards, Paul Green

4. Chapiro replied by inviting Green to a meeting with Granowsky on the evening of 23 April 1929 (Joseph Chapiro to Paul Green, 22 April 1929, PG-SHC). Attending also were Otto Kahn, American financier who proposed to sponsor Granowsky's American tour, Alfred Kerr, prominent Berlin theater critic, Erwin Piscator, German director, and Chapiro. At the meeting Granowsky announced the collapse of his company and "said quite openly," according to Green, "that he looks towards America or Mexico for founding again a real folk theatre. I begged him to come to America and start a Negro theater. With his sense of pattern and, as Mr. Koch would say, of the dramatic he could do something wonderful" (Paul Green to Barrett Clark, 3 May 1929). Granowsky remained in Berlin through 1930, when he directed Karl Gutzkow's *Uriel Acosta* for the Habima, then moved to Paris, where he died in 1937. Green did not write a newspaper article on Granowsky but in several essays recorded Granowsky's important role in the development of his own conception of the drama (e.g., "Music in the Theatre," in Paul Green, *Dramatic Heritage* [New York: Samuel French, 1953], pp. 38–41; and "Symphonic Outdoor Drama: A Search for New Theatre Forms," in Paul Green, *Drama and the Weather: Some Notes and Papers on Life and the Theatre* [New York: Samuel French, 1958], pp. 1–44).

5. An American café.

## 60. To Eleanor Fitzgerald[1]

Friedbergstrasse 5, Berlin-Dahlem, Germany
23 April 1929

My dear Miss Fitzgerald—

It is more than fine news that you at last seem to be getting the good things coming to you in the way of help. At least I like to read between the lines of your letter and believe that such is the case. I hope it means that somebody has seen the light and is really helping with a bag of shekels. It pleases me as much as you—if that is possible. I'm hastening to return a word in answer to your stated opportunity to do so. I'm sending it off in a hurry, for you mention that you go to press within two weeks. Alas that time is gone with the coming of your letter, but anyhow I'll send this short statement along so if you have opportunity you can get it in. Please pardon its insufficiency. Stating the truth without metaphors is unbelievably hard for me, it is so much better to describe objects and beings in action, leaving the matter of their significance to be read by the prophets or mumbled over by excavators.[2]

Naturally I hope the "help" means you can do *Tread the Green Grass* in the Garrick or somewhere.[3] I hope too the matter of the contract is fixed with

1. Eleanor Fitzgerald (1877–1955) had been business manager of the Experimental Theatre (Provincetown organization in the third phase of its history) when it produced *In Abraham's Bosom.* Born in Hancock, Wisconsin, she joined the Provincetown Playhouse as a secretary in 1918, following editorial work on Emma Goldman's magazine, *Mother Earth*, and quickly became the driving force on the business end of the operation. At the time of the present letter she was executive director of the Experimental Theatre and was planning its move from the cramped quarters at the Greenwich Village Theatre on Macdougal Street to the large and comfortable Garrick Theatre for the season of 1929–30. Since expenses at the Garrick would be greater than on Macdougal Street, she and her staff spent much time raising money during the spring and summer of 1929, and one of their projects was a promotional booklet, "The Past Present and Future of 'The Theatre of Opportunity,' " which they began to distribute in May. To Green and other artists associated with the theater she had sent a letter asking for statements she could use in the booklet about the importance of the Provincetown Playhouse in their own development.

2. Apparently Green's statement arrived too late for inclusion in the booklet, and no copy has come to light.

3. One of the reasons frequently given by Fitzgerald and others for the move to the Garrick Theatre was the impossibility of doing plays such as *Tread the Green Grass*, which made unusual demands on the stage, at the Greenwich Village Theatre (see her

French's. I was sorry to have to write Jimmy Light[4] that I'd have to leave it up to him and French, but the truth is I have to let them settle such things. And it seems that they're always pretty fair. Mr. Clark just writes that the contract is extended. Good.[5] I plan to be back in the late fall or early winter. If I can be of any help with the play then I hope you'll call on me.[6] I've written Jimmy Light congrats on the Guggenheim. Will he come to Europe?

With [illegible]

## 61. To Virginia Vernon[1]

72 Temple Fortune Lane [Hempstead Garden Suburb, London, N.W. 11]

14 June 1929

My dear Mrs. Vernon—

Do you remember certain of Edgar Poe's short story solemnics, beginning,

---

"Valedictory of an Art Theatre," *New York Times*, 22 December 1929, sec. 8, p. 1, col. 8; p. 4, cols. 3–6).

4. Artistic director of the Experimental Theatre.

5. In April 1928 the Experimental Theatre took a one-year option on *Tread the Green Grass* (then entitled *Tina*). Unable to produce the play during the 1928–29 season but planning to present it in 1929–30, they had just taken a second one-year option. For the first option the Experimental Theatre paid Green $500; for the second, $600 (William W. Vilhauer, "A History and Evaluation of the Provincetown Players" [Ph.D. dissertation, University of Iowa, 1965], p. 626).

6. The Experimental Theatre did not produce *Tread the Green Grass*. In part because of the poor economy and fearful public mood following the stock market crash in October 1929, Fitzgerald was unable to raise enough money to complete the 1929–30 season, and in mid-December the company disbanded.

---

1. Virginia Vernon (b. 1894), actress, singer, translator, and producer, was an accomplished woman of the theater. Raised in an American theater family, in 1920 she married the British actor and producer Frank Vernon. At the time of the present letter she had just completed her own translation into French of *Journey's End*, R. C. Sherriff's play that was the hit of the 1928–29 season in London in Maurice Browne's production, and in the fall she and her husband would produce the translation in Paris. While the Greens were still in Berlin, she wrote to Paul about her wish to translate some of his plays into French (she had already translated "In Aunt Mahaly's Cabin" and had secured the rights through Samuel French to translate others) (Virginia Vernon to Paul Green, 11 February 1929, PG-SHC). Now, following the

say, "I am by nature a nervous man"?[2] If you do you'll the better understand when I say my hand trembles as I read your list over.[3] Notwithstanding I think it's all very nice and you and Major Vernon are very gracious indeed. I promise to do my best not to fall down in a swound. Mrs. Green and I can think of no one we should like to add to the group you propose. We will be on hand a little early as you suggest—about four o'clock. Until Monday afternoon then.[4]

Cordially yours, Paul Green

We heartily thank Major Vernon for the theatre tickets.[5]

## 62. To Hugh Green[1]

72 Temple Fortune Lane, Hampstead Garden Suburb, London, England

18 June 1929

Dear Hugh—

Your letter with the clippings and news[2] came just before we left Berlin, and we all thank you for the first and send you congratulations and love about the latter. I for one hope to see you and the heart's desire the first thing when we hit North Carolina. I expect you'll have him out breaking land when spring comes, and it won't be long before he'll be toting a watch. It's good news and we are all happy as doodles over it.[3] I've heard nothing about John's expectations but rumors.[4] But I shake my own hands over them. He's not much given

---

arrival of the Greens in London on 28 May, she was giving a reception to introduce them to London theater society.

2. "The Tell-Tale Heart" begins: "True!—nervous—very, very dreadfully nervous I had been and am."

3. Names of a few of the guests appear in other letters written around this time: Arnold Bennett, John Drinkwater, the American Phillip Moeller, and Sir Nigel and Lady Playfair.

4. 17 June.

5. Perhaps to the Vernons' production of *Red Rust*, their translation of Vladimir Kirshon's play then running in London.

---

1. After the war Hugh (1896–1959) returned to Harnett County and at the death of their father in 1926 took over the family farm.

2. That his wife, Mabel, was pregnant.

3. On 1 August 1929, shortly after the present letter, Hugh and Mabel's first child, Anne, was born.

4. Older half-brother of Paul and Hugh, who farmed near Hugh.

to writing letters. I keep up now and then with what's being done in the National and American leagues, but I never see the Observer,[5] and your clippings were the first baseball news I'd had from N.C. I [am] pulling for old Connie Mack and his Athletics this time and I believe he'll win out.[6] I would have answered your letter sooner, but we've been having a hectic time for several weeks. By the way what's happened to Mary?[7] We haven't heard from her in ages, although I've written several times. I also have written to Billy[8] three times since I got his letter months ago, but so far I haven't heard from him. I think some of my letters go astray. I've had two important letters go astray. In one case I sent a check to the Federal Land Bank in Columbia for interest and insurance[9] and the check never reached them, for a month or two later they sent me a letter saying that the loan was standing for immediate foreclosure or something to that effect. I had to send a second hurried Express check to them. In the second case I paid my taxes last December and lo and behold here a month ago the sheriff writes me that my county taxes have not been paid. Again I have to send a cable and straighten it out. Another case is where Mary's box never reached us and we've never heard a word about it. These are the only certain cases I know of, for plenty of other business dealings have gone through all right, but it must be that Mary hasn't been getting my letters few as they were during the winter months. I've written oftener since we all got on our feet again.[10] I hope there's nothing wrong more than that she is very busy. And we hope to hear from her soon.

We began packing up our stuff in Berlin on the 20th of May, replacing broken dishes, paying for torn counterpanes, broken rockers, etc. (Paulie and Byrd know how to tear up wherever they go, and I don't blame them much, for most of the German furniture must be several hundred years old and will hardly stand on its legs.) Then we went around and paid up the last cent of

5. *News and Observer*, Raleigh, leading regional newspaper.

6. In 1929 the Philadelphia Athletics, under manager and majority-owner Connie Mack (1862–1956), ran away with the American League pennant race and on the date of the present letter were leading the second-place New York Yankees by seven and a half games. In the World Series that fall, they also demolished the Chicago Cubs, winning four games to one.

7. Their sister, who lived near Hugh.

8. Mary's son, eight years old.

9. On his loan for the land in the Glen.

10. After the bad winter in Berlin.

our doctor's bills, which without exaggeration had in all amounted to nearly $1,500. It was sore parting with good money, but we were thankful that Paulie was still in the land of the living no matter how much it took, and what was spent on the rest of us had to be thought of in the same way. Then I went down and bought tickets for Elizabeth and me, the German girl,[11] and half ticket for Paulie. Byrd cost nothing, although she had to have a ticket to carry, so I fixed her one out of pasteboard and she felt as grown up as anybody. I also paid for our baggage. They don't allow you to ship it on your ticket, and that with the tickets made my little pile look weaker and weaker. But with few dollars and a lot of foolhardy grit we set out from Berlin on an express train May the 27th. All day we travelled across Germany and in the evening reached Holland. About dark we were nearly across Holland, reaching Rotterdam after eleven and it still a little light in the west. From about eight o'clock on Paulie and Byrd slept most of the time. We had a compartment to ourselves and laid them down on the long cushions and they seemed quite at home. By this time they're used to travelling and don't mind it a bit. About twelve o'clock we got off the train at the Hook of Holland. Fraulein Lamprecht carried Byrd in her arms still sleeping, and Paulie walked along half asleep holding to my hand. I must say that at that hour of the night he looked somewhat pitiful. It took us a long time to get through the customs people, there was such a crowd. But about one o'clock all was finished, passports examined, baggage checked, and berths on the ship arranged. Then we got on board. We had a cabin with three berths for Fraulein L. and the kids and in two minutes they were dressed in their nighties and fast asleep, although Paulie had already asked to inspect the engine and things that made it go. E. and I had a little old cabin—the last one available—with a huge standpipe running down through it, and all night—what was left of it—the thing squeaked and rumbled most terribly. The ship started off and believe me it was a rough trip. The wind was blowing a gale and the waves hammered as if they'd tear everything up. But before long it was six o'clock and we were up and dressed and out on deck. The ship had anchored and we were at England. Soon we went down the gangplank into the customs house again where a doctor examined us all to see that we brought no contagious diseases into their

11. Erna Lamprecht, nurse for the children in Berlin, who stayed with the Greens through their time in London. Later she visited them in Chapel Hill, then settled her family there.

fair country. And I imagine we all looked as if we needed examinations and other things. Then we got on a train that was waiting and in a few minutes were on our way to London. We got into London about 8:30, and after searching around decided on a hotel, bundled ourselves into a taxi and went there. We tried to get the cheapest thing we could near a park and I suppose we did, but the best the hotel-keeper would come to was $10 a day for the five of us, which included meals. After inquiry we decided that was about as good as we could do and so we took it. Then after washing up, E. and I left the Fraulein with the kids and set forth to look for a house. Already we had had plenty of sinking feelings about the cost of things, for England is every bit as expensive as America. We wanted a place near the country where the children could have good air and where we would be convenient to London. So we set forth, going to real estate offices, calling on people we knew here. For five mortal days we searched and at last we found this place, address above, which rented for about $80 a month. It was as cheap as anything we could find but we just couldn't pay that much. At last we offered seventy and after much doing about the lady who owns it said she'd take it, and so we moved in. In a few days our baggage arrived and lo and behold we owed $12 more on that for some unearthly reason, though I had paid and had a receipt for its delivery in London before we left Berlin. Rather than agonize over the question I paid it. By that time shekels were getting mighty low, but we were glad to have a roof over our heads. We have a nice quiet place, garden at the back where we've already planted and set vegetables and where I've put up swings for the kids. We have a study, a reception room, four bedrooms, kitchen, etc. Enough to get along in fine. Tennis courts are near, also a park. The children have plenty of room to run around in and watch the airplanes. I expect Paulie will grow crooked backwards if he doesn't quit watching them, but then he's mechanics crazy. He's got the whole garden a network of strings and boxes—electric lines to him and he travels all over the world on them every day. Byrd puffs along with him without much interest in it. She misses her doll but we've told her when she quits sucking her thumb she shall have one. She's about stopped. The house is not much to look at inside—the furnishings are not so much and the walls are pecked up a bit, but on the whole we don't mind that. They can't say when we leave it that we have done it. The weather here is a mess, it rains practically every day. Today we had sunshine for a rarity. The days are long, long. It is now ten minutes past ten at night and I'm writing this by daylight. But we are a great deal better off than we were in Berlin. People here have been nice to us, too nice. We've been to dinners and all sorts of things. Last night some people[12]—a Major who had been in India and his wife who comes from Richmond, Va.—gave a dinner in our honor and I thought we'd never get done meeting people. We were introduced and reintroduced until I hardly knew one from another. Among the gang we met a Sir and Lady Playfair who came bowing and scraping in,[13] authors, producers, poets, what not. We had enough. We had a grand time and felt flattered, but while it was going on I thought of being down in the juniper or somewhere siding corn or pulling fodder. That's more my style, and when I set my feet back home there's going to be glue on the bottom of them. Elizabeth is really seeing the world and she'll have enough to talk of to last a generation. The only fly in her ointment is her old sinus trouble which has begun to bother her again. We are making moves to find a good nose, throat and ear specialist. We both hope no other operation is coming, but we have our doubts.[14]

Our most surprising news came this afternoon in a telegram from Caro Mae.[15] She is in Paris and says she will be over to see us next week. I didn't know she was coming. The first we heard of it was last week when Radoff[16] wrote us from Paris and said we ought to "come over about the 20th and meet Caro Mae and the gang." We were completely mystified and thought perhaps he was fooling. But today we had it straight from Caro herself. E. went up in the air over it and we both are tickled right. The question is, where is Erm?[17] I wrote to them weeks and weeks ago but neither of them answered. Why didn't Erm come? Maybe she has and Caro didn't mention it in her telegram. Of course we'll get it all straight when C. does come.[18] But it will be a sight for sore eyes to meet some of the homefolks. I feel—no matter how good a time we've had and how much we've seen—as if I'd been away from N.C. two or

12. Frank and Virginia Vernon.

13. Nigel Playfair (1874–1934), actor and director, best known as manager of the Lyric Theatre in Hammersmith (1918–32), and knighted in 1928 for his work at the Lyric.

14. Elizabeth had a sinus operation in February in Berlin (Green diary, PG-SHC).

15. Younger sister of Hugh and Paul, then living in New York City.

16. Morris Leon Radoff, instructor in French at UNC, 1928–29.

17. Erma, youngest sister of Hugh and Paul.

18. Erma did not go with Caro Mae to Paris but joined her at Paul and Elizabeth's in Hampstead in mid-September. The two sisters took jobs transcribing Elizabethan documents and stayed in London for several months after Paul and Elizabeth went home (Erma Green Gold to Laurence Avery, 21 October 1982).

three years. I've seen foreign faces until I'd about decided there were no more homefolks.

By the way, you reckon you'll be able to help me out a little in the early fall. I'm sure going to need it. I mention it now so you'll understand sorter how I'm fixed. I'm not suffering or anything like that, but I'll be able to use a little kale in getting my gang back home. My young'uns seem to eat as much as two horses—never saw the like—and as the food goes so does most all the rest. Don't bother yourself in any way about money, but in case you find yourself with right much coming in in the fall then you can slip me a little.

I must stop now. Write us again when you have time and let us know how things are going. I hope the juniper will pay you this year,[19] the rest of the crops too of course.

With love to you and Mabel and all the rest.

## 63. To Theresa Helburn[1]

72 Temple Fortune Lane, Hampstead Garden Suburb, London, N.W. 11
4 August 1929

My dear Miss Helburn—

I have recently been working at the Connelly play again, trying, as you suggested, to cut it to the theatre idea more.[2] It is finished and I am mailing it by today's registered post. I hope it strikes you as being as much improved as I

19. Also known as Atlantic white cedar and much prized for its rot-resistant lumber in such trades as boat building. A large stand of the trees grew on Hugh's farm.

---

1. Theresa Helburn (ca. 1888–1959), a director of the Theatre Guild, to whom Green sent *The House of Connelly* shortly before leaving for Germany in August 1928. The Guild accepted the play for production during the 1929–30 season (Paul Green to Theresa Helburn, 18 April [1929], PG-SHC). Helburn had been in London recently (Paul Green to Barrett Clark, 21 June 1929) and during the visit discussed the play and its production with Green.

2. Helburn's suggestions seem not to have concerned the ending of the play. By the time Green submitted *The House of Connelly* to the Guild, it had the tragic ending in which Patsy is killed by two old servants (Green diary, 17 June 1928, PG-SHC). It still had that ending when the play went into rehearsal in the summer of 1931 (Paul Green, *Plough and Furrow: Some Essays and Papers on Life and the Theatre* [New York: Samuel French, 1963], pp. 48–49).

think it is. I do not know Mr. Mamoulian's address,[3] but I should like him to have a copy of this draft before he considers production.

It was a great pleasure to meet you at the Rubensteins,[4] and I wish I might have such a pleasure some other day in this dispensation.

Sincerely yours,

## 64. To Philip Ridgeway[1]

72 Temple Fortune Lane, London, N.W. 11
7 August 1929

My dear Mr. Ridgeway—

For a long time I have, like everybody else, been a great admirer of Thomas Hardy's work and have read everything he has written. Naturally I have been interested in your production of *Tess of the D'Urbervilles* and also I've wanted if possible to get a copy [of][2] the text of the play. A few days ago I called by the theatre and the box keeper there said that if I wrote to you you might be able to help me. I'm an American writer of plays and am to be in London only for a short while. Could I possibly procure a copy of the script from you? I'd gladly

3. Rouben Mamoulian, scheduled to direct *The House of Connelly* in the Guild production.

4. Harold Rubenstein, London theatrical producer.

---

1. Philip Ridgeway, London producer, twice staged *Tess of the D'Urbervilles*, first in 1925 and again in 1929. Thomas Hardy himself dramatized the novel in 1894–95, but that version was not performed professionally until 1925, when Ridgeway produced it in London. Ridgeway's attention had been drawn to the play by an amateur production in Dorchester in 1924 by the Hardy Players, a group of Hardy's neighbors who, nearly every year since 1908, performed dramatizations of his novels. Their productions were acted, staged, and costumed by people of the community, and Hardy sometimes assisted with the dramatizations or demonstrated music and dances at rehearsals. Ridgeway saw the folk quality of the Hardy Players and, following the success of his 1925 production, decided to incorporate elements of their production in a second professional production, which opened at the Duke of York's Theatre in London on 23 July 1929. A few nights before the present letter, Green saw one of the performances.

2. The surviving draft of the letter is on a sheet torn along most of its right-hand edge. The word here noted seems to be the only one lost, but several remain only partially or are faint.

pay for it, of course. Or failing that, could you possibly tell me where I might read the script. I understand it has never yet been published.[3]

Sincerely yours, Paul Green

## 65. To Barrett H. Clark

72 Temple Fortune Lane, London, N.W. 11
4 October 1929

Dear Barrett—

First to acknowledge receipt of $250 from French which saved my face, and for which I return the proper appreciation of thanks.[1] I must do something in return to the "boss" someday,[2] though what I don't now know.

You were quite right not to waste money in a reply cable to mine. I would not have sent it but for the fact that the tradesmen were at the door. The money has come all O.K.

I have reread the *Potter's Field* play after letting it cool and find there are a

3. It was not published until 1950, in Marguerite Roberts, *Tess in the Theatre* (Toronto: University of Toronto Press, 1950), pp. 131–203. Ridgeway sent Green a script and arranged a trip for him to Dorchester. A member of Ridgeway's staff drove Green to Dorchester on Saturday morning, 17 August, then picked him up for the return to London on Monday afternoon, 19 August. During the stay Green talked with Hardy's widow, Florence (Hardy had died on 11 January 1928), but spent most of his time talking with people active in the Hardy Players and walking through town and the outlying district viewing buildings and other places where Hardy laid scenes in his novels. On Sunday morning he walked out to the cemetery by Stinsford Church and sketched several of the Hardy family graves, including the one in which Hardy's heart is entombed. Then on Monday just before leaving, according to a notebook he kept at the time, he went "down to the Post Office where a tablet designed by Hardy was put up to the P. O. men who lost their lives in the war. It is very simple with the real Hardy touch in the inscription—'None dubious of the cause none murmuring' " ("Notes on a Trip to Hardy Country," Paul Green Collection, NCC, p. 15). The notebook is the basis of Green's essay, "A Visit to Hardy's Dorchester," in Green, *Drama and the Weather*, pp. 185–220.

---

1. In 1928 before leaving for Germany Green arranged a line of credit with Samuel French whereby he could borrow small amounts from the company against future royalties, the company taking a larger percentage of his royalties after any loan until it was paid back. The arrangement continued with modifications throughout his life.

2. Frank J. Sheil, president of Samuel French.

few things to smooth up, but on the whole I think it could be produced and "flowed" across the stage quite effectively as it stands.[3] I'd like to help produce it and bring out the subtle tones and intonations that show the unbelievable mystery of so-called folk conversation. Quite commonplace statements when spoken true to life and situation are quite otherwise. Take at random, for instance, a statement of the character Seeny to Ed Uzzell—"I bet you know heaps the ladies told you."[4] There are nine words in the statement and accordingly nine apparent ways of saying it not counting the possible rhythmic modifications. And out of the nine ways there is one rightest way. The more I think of the "folk" the more I know that their lack of book knowledge does not affect their subtlety. Their characters are not less complex than Hamlet. It happens that those who have tried to record their lives have been more or less of the Hamlet environment.

No doubt you have received Sobienowski's contract for *The House of Connelly*.[5] And he will hear from you soon. Somebody wrote me—not of the Guild corporation—that scenery is being painted for this buffeted play. I hope so. If you hear any news thereon let me know please. And what's happened to Lynn's last? I hope they'll do it this year at the Guild.[6]

I have just sent off *The Field God* to Stevens[7] and am sending a copy to you.

3. Green completed a draft of *Potter's Field* before leaving the United States and sold production rights to the independent American producer Sidney Ross. Probably during the few days in New York City in August 1928 before sailing, Green met with Ross and Jasper Deeter, director of the Hedgerow Theater in Philadelphia, to plan a production to be directed by Deeter (Paul Green to Sidney Ross, 26 March 1929, PG-SHC), but so far nothing had come of their plans.

4. *Potter's Field*, in *The House of Connelly and Other Plays* (New York: Samuel French, 1931), p. 130. "I bet" is not in the published text.

5. Floryan Sobienowski, Polish translator living in London (his translation of Shaw's *The Apple Cart* was produced in Warsaw in the spring of 1929), who wished to translate *The House of Connelly*.

6. Lynn Riggs (1899–1954), folk dramatist from Oklahoma, had written to Green that "*Green Grow the Lilacs*, my first poem for the theatre has attracted some attention. Three of the Guild Board are in Europe, but the other three are enthusiastic, and have taken a $100. option until the others see it in September" (Lynn Riggs to Paul Green, 27 July 1929, PG-SHC). The Theatre Guild produced the play in 1931, and in 1943 Oscar Hammerstein II and Richard Rodgers adapted it as the musical, *Oklahoma!*

7. Thomas Wood Stevens, head of the School of Drama at Carnegie Institute of Technology, who had told Clark he was interested in producing the play.

The play has cost me two or three weeks hard work. It's a better play now, but I fear a far from perfect one. I succeeded in clearing out many things and continued to save Gilchrist's life, though it would have been so aesthetically easy to let him kill himself and repeat the Job story with a different ending only.[8]

I am taking a couple of days' rest before starting something else. I hope to have the most of another play done before I leave here, but can't promise. I have half a dozen schemes buzzing around. I'd like to do, as I said before, the real tale of this younger and disillusioned Freudian generation, but fear I'll have to wait till I can get back to America and read a lot of books by the hardboiled critics. Then a farce on the American millionaire—I see him waking in his bed, his monologue, his going about, schemes, vanities, romanticisms, fads, etc., etc. How would a scene on his lawn [do] and he smiling amid a gang of theosophic neophytes—a long-robed fakir out of India fattening on him, spiritualism, or a scene in his home with a phrenologist measuring his skull with a pair of callipers and chanting—"This organ is situated at the inferior and posterior or mastoid angle of the parietal bone, upwards and backwards from the external opening of the ear.—It marks a considerable endowment, such endowment being indispensable to all great and magnanimous characters," etc.? I mean a real Molière farce with pageantry, music, and show. Well, there is plenty of fun to be had.[9]

I am passing a copy of *The Field God* on to Curtis-Brown for use,[10] also sending a copy to Oesterheld as per contract.[11]

8. In the original version of *The Field God*, produced and published in 1927, Hardy Gilchrist survives great pressure from religious fanatics in his community. In 1933, however, Green would revise the ending so that Gilchrist succumbs to the pressure and commits suicide. For the revised version, see A. G. Halline, ed., *American Plays* (New York: American Book Company, 1935) or Samuel M. Tucker and Alan Downer, eds., *Twenty-Five Modern Plays* (New York: Harper and Brothers, 1948). In "Tragedy—Playwright to Professor," Green discusses the ending (Green, *Dramatic Heritage*, p. 82).

9. Neither idea became a play.

10. Spencer Curtis-Brown, literary agent in Samuel French's London office.

11. Berlin publisher who had the right of first refusal on Green's plays in German translation (Paul Green to Oesterheld, 26 March 1929, PG-SHC). While the Greens were in Berlin, Elizabeth Loos-Bab translated *In Abraham's Bosom*, which Oesterheld brought out later in 1929 as *In Abrahams Schoss, die lebensgeschichte eines negers in sieben scenen*. Although Oesterheld published no more of Green's plays, Bab translated

And now to think that we'll see you all about November 12!—if the bailiffs don't get me beforehand. The Vernons have made a great success in Paris with their production of *Journey's End.* Mrs. V. translated it. We surely appreciate our meeting them through you.

## 66. To Frederick H. Koch

72 Temple Fortune Lane, London, N.W. 11
27 October 1929

Dear Proff—

Thanks for your two letters—one from Los Angeles and a later one from Chapel Hill. I should have answered them sooner, but I've been head over heels in writing and theatre-going—and people.[1] You'll forgive me for my laugh when I heard you'd been robbed in Aimee McPherson's temple of God.[2] I hope your loss wasn't large enough to change the comedy to tragedy—for that's one of the main differences between those, as the philosophers say, essential forms, isn't it—a seeming of the seriously real and the seriously real itself? or again tritely—appearance and reality. So perhaps without all the truth of the matter, I think it's very funny, and we've repeated it to the great amusement of several English friends—for the evangel of the golden hair is well known over here, and consequently the joke is appreciated.[3]

---

several of the one-acters: "The Hot Iron," "In the Valley," "Supper for the Dead," "White Dresses," "The No 'Count Boy," and "The Prayer-Meeting" (Paul Green to Elizabeth Loos-Bab, 24 October 1929).

---

1. Koch had spent the summer teaching drama at the University of California in Los Angeles. From Los Angeles, and from Chapel Hill after returning in late August, he wrote Green asking for news of the family and London theater world to publish in the *Carolina Play-Book*, monthly magazine of the Playmakers. In the second letter he also said that "sometime I want to tell you some of the 'horrible details' of my dramatic doings [in Los Angeles]—having my pocket picked in Aimee's Angelus Temple, bringing suit in the Small Claims Court against a Jew woman to recover a lost pair of pants, riding two hundred miles over the Arizona desert to the Hopi reservation, experiences in the Sound Studios of Hollywood" (Frederick Koch to Paul Green, 26 September 1929, PG-SHC).

2. Aimee Semple McPherson (1890–1944), faith healer and revivalist based at the spectacular Angelus Temple in Los Angeles, built for her by admiring followers.

3. Throughout 1929 Aimee McPherson was in the news. That year she was accused

The theatre is as usual—rather tame. No combining of forces, every manager on his own—clubs, subscription theatres, halls carrying on individually and with little inspiration or comprehension so far as I can see. A good commentary on how the theatre is going here is to be found not only in a list of the plays that are being done and the manner of production but also in such an incident or movement even as the following: This summer when several members of the Theatre Guild were over here there got started a lot of talk about creating an English Theatre Guild. Evidently the idea grew as well as the talk, for I've read during the last few weeks of half a dozen different theatre managers and producers who (separately) are planning to start an English Guild. Already one has started a campaign for subscriptions. A week ago it came out in the papers that some person unknown had already patented or registered the name Theatre Guild and so there's been a lot of jaw-dropping. These producers won't organize—won't combine, and so they'll go on feeding rough recognizable pigs soft dove food. For the English theatre public is about like that of America—lively, healthy as a pig and anxious for good trough-feed as well as walking in the parlor, and like all publics easily fooled by those they think superior. To carry the figure on—they will come running time without end to the rattle of an empty basket, hoping for corn and never getting it, and what they need of course is not sound and wind but corn. Maybe it will be provided. Maurice Browne who is now firmly on top of financial security—so I hear and don't see why he shouldn't be after the overwhelming *Journey's End* success—seems to me to be about the best bet for growth in right producing and the evoking of good plays.[4] Such men as C. B. Cochran, Sir Barry Jackson,[5] Sir Nigel Playfair do good things, but they strike me as being too

of staging her own abduction in 1926 to gain publicity, investigated for bribing a judge, sued for misappropriation of funds donated to the Angelus Temple, and sued also by her lawyer for breach of contract.

4. Maurice Browne (1881–1955), British producer, had been prominent in the noncommercial theater movement in the United States, where he established and directed the Chicago Little Theatre (1912–18); later, in 1939, he would be the first producer of T. S. Eliot's *Murder in the Cathedral* in London. He had returned to England in the mid-1920s, and with his production of R. C. Sherriff's *Journey's End*, which opened in London on 22 January 1929 and had the success in 1928–29 that Green describes, established himself as a producer in the British theater.

5. C. B. Cochran (1872–1951), prolific British producer, concentrated on musicals, revues, and other light entertainment, but his current production was Sean O'Casey's *The Silver Tassie*, which opened in September. Sir Barry Jackson (1879–1961), founder

safely ensconced in tradition to ever catch the spirit of true experiment. I may be wrong of course and hope I am. A few small theatres are trying experiments—notably the Gate Theatre. But they all are too small and circumscribed to break through into leading a movement or affecting public consciousness at large. Again of course, one can never tell. Anyhow, I would say a good organization somewhat like the American Theatre Guild is the only thing that will pull the present English drama out of its riveted coffin. And I believe Maurice Browne will be the engineer of it. I hope so—again. I shouldn't forget to mention one organization which has done a great deal over here—that is the Arts League of Service run by Miss Judith Wogan and a Miss Elder. You might have read about it in a recent number of *Theatre Arts.*[6] It is mainly a travelling theatre—has a van, a group of actors who are stagehands as well, plays towns all over Scotland and England on a small guarantee basis, like the Playmakers, and in short is something of a counterpart to our group, but without the concentration on Folk Plays. This is really something alive and full of, well—corn. The other night when I was down to see Shaw he said it was one of the finest things they have over here. Recently Miss Wogan has secured a small building in London which will serve as a sort of experimental place. But it's rather small to play much part in the public's likes and dislikes. It may grow to a larger thing, of course. Several people have backed the scheme. (But not Shaw among them, by the way. He gives his same old answer when requested to help on such enterprises, "I take money out of the theatre, not put it in." He is not mad in that particular direction, or his answer would be quite different.)

Well, despite the dullness of the present London stage, one can find a play now and then worth seeing, but only one out of dozens. There are three good ones now running—*The Three Sisters, The Silver Tassie,* a Sean O'Casey work with the usual puzzling mixtry of the expected and unexpected,—*The Apple Cart*—a different and not so good Shaw play (to me). Otherwise the real stuff is in the Talkies to which all the people flock while the higher and more lifted

of the Birmingham Repertory Theatre in 1913, was the first producer of such plays as John Drinkwater's *Abraham Lincoln* (1918) and George Bernard Shaw's *Back to Methuselah* (1922). In the summer of 1929 he inaugurated the Malvern Festival for the production of Shaw's plays, beginning with *The Apple Cart.*

6. In "Theatre On Wheels," *Theatre Arts* 13 (August 1929): 583–86, Gordon Bottomley described the Arts League of Service, a traveling theater founded in 1919 by actresses Judith Wogan and Eleanor Elder.

brows see nothing in them. As in all the European countries the American Movies and Talkies have inundated London, and the English critics and producers continue to curse them to no avail.[7] They interest the peepul (à la Art Ward[8]) and the peepul go to see and hear them. I have seen nothing thrilling here like Granowsky's Jewish group from Russia and I don't hope to, not even if we stayed on a year or so. I was about to forget Diaghilev's Ballet which was very good this summer, but that has played and long ago gone. There are rumors of the Habima's[9] as well as the Moscow Art Theatre's coming here within the next year. Well, it is a good place to come to for missionary and pioneer work. For, to repeat, if we dismiss those not quite senescent and hunt for the full theatre-vigored [ones], we shall hunt a long time. Take the dramatists—Shaw, Galsworthy, O'Casey, and who else? "Who else should there be?" someone replies. "Well, plenty," is the answer of course. For of the three mentioned Shaw is the real one. We don't know yet exactly what O'Casey may do.[10] (It seems to me that all the Noel Cowards, Lonsdales[11] and their kind don't matter at the bottom. Do you think so?) There are Barrie the *playwright* and Maugham too, but again that is not the point—the point of the *new* theatre. Galsworthy we know and can prophecy about, as well as about all the rest except Shaw and O'Casey, and I would venture a guess about O'Casey. That leaves Shaw, and he is—is he old? What I'm trying to say is that there are no new, energetic visionaries writing plays in England,

7. An article entitled "Prospects of the Talkies" in the London *Times* of 18 September 1929 began: "The one question which is giving concern to the film industry more than any other at the moment is whether the talkie has come to stay or whether it is merely a passing phase which either has already reached, or is fast approaching, its zenith. Many of the shrewdest leaders of the American industry have suggested that the talkie 'boom' will not last more than five years" (p. 12, col. 2).

8. Nineteenth-century American humorist noted for colloquial spellings.

9. Hebrew language theater founded in Moscow in 1917. It left the Soviet Union in 1926, toured Europe and the United States until 1931, then settled in Palestine, where it became the National Theatre of Israel in 1953. Granowsky directed Karl Gutzkow's *Uriel Acosta* with the Habima in Berlin in 1930.

10. In 1926, following riots caused by the Abbey Theatre production of his *The Plough and the Stars,* O'Casey left Dublin and settled in London, where his next play, *The Silver Tassie,* having been rejected by William Butler Yeats in part because of its experimental nature, was running at present.

11. Frederick Lonsdale (1881–1954), author of several witty comedies, including the then-current *Canaries Sometimes Sing.*

just as there are no new and strong producers in sight here. So [there] is no new dramatic writer except Shaw, and I shouldn't have said that about him if I had not had a long talk with him the other night and caught from him something of the youthful spirit and startling ideas that still energize that man of seventy. So although the pulse beat of the English drama is weaker each succeeding day—I am willing to bet that out of Shaw will come the newest and most poetical play of modern times, and that's why I say for myself that in England there remains Shaw the youngest, strongest for the future and the best.

"Well," as the old revivalist down home used to say, "I reckon I've preached long enough," and shot my mouth off into the air, but I should like to tell you a bit about my visit with Shaw, even if it is late. If I put down all he said it would make a book, and I imagine I could do it, for I remember very vividly almost everything he said, and believe me he said a lot.

Some months ago a friend of mine[12] mentioned to St. John Ervine[13] that I would like to meet Shaw. Ervine was very nice and said he would try to arrange it, though it was difficult. Sometime later[14] Shaw's secretary wrote he'd be glad to see me after the Malvern Festival. So the other night I went down[15]—It was one of those terrible Dickens nights to be experienced only through a book and by the fire. But finally I got down to 4 Whitehall Court ten minutes late and wet to the skin.—Taxis were scarce and I had stood out half an hour or more trying to catch one. The maid put me by a nice fire and said Mr. Shaw was out in the storm also. I had time to dry myself before he came. At last he entered profuse in apologies for his delay in a traffic jam just as if I had been the King of the Jews or say—a post. Do you remember in Stanislavsky's remarkable book—it is remarkable I think and every drama student ought to read it—*My Life in Art*—where he is talking of Anton

12. P. Beaumont Wadsworth, a friend from undergraduate days at UNC now living in London (Paul Green to P. Beaumont Wadsworth, 28 June 1929, PG-SHC).

13. Playwright, later a biographer of Shaw.

14. In early August (Paul Green to St. John Ervine, 8 August 1929, PG-SHC).

15. On Thursday, 24 October (Blanch Patch to Paul Green, undated, PG-SHC). About the visit with Shaw, Green told his sister Mary: "I'm looking forward to talking with that—as people say—great man. We've met quite oodles of people, but I suppose of them all Shaw will be the best known. I'll have nothing to say, for he already knows all I could tell him, but he's a human kind of a man, and I'll try not to be scared of him" (17 October 1929, EG-SHC).

Rubinstein the musician and says, "Unlike us earthly beings, he was not ashamed to look at people as if they were things. I noticed the same habit in other great men whom I met, for instance in Leo Tolstoy."[16] I thought of that at the beginning of my conversation with Shaw—I should say his conversation for he did about 99 percent of the talking. But after a few minutes I was no longer the post but a human being to whom he was expressing himself as well as one at whom he was preaching.

He first took me out on the balcony of his study and pointed out different sights of London. The rain was falling heavily and the Thames half reflected the lights of the city in the raindrops spattering on it. Shaw murmured something about the night being rough and we turned back into the warmth of his study.

"Yes, a certain kind of Dickens night," I said.

"No. Dickens didn't know the modern London."

I didn't quite catch the point of his reply, but it was no matter. For already he had sat down, stretched out his long legs, begun squirming in his chair, twisting his hands, and shooting a dozen questions at me at once. His physical appearance is strangely curious—legs long as a pole, small hips, smallish shoulders, long arms and a massive domed head—the beard that everybody knows. His eyes are small, bright and now full of fun, now deadly serious—but always alive and direct. From his shoulders down he gives one an inexplicable suggestion of a light boyish body or a sexless lithesome girl. His head with its dome, white beard and gentle mouth—around the corners of which still lurks a trace of the saturnine that used to be prominent in his whole face but is so no more—looks like that of a saint or a sage you read about in the old days. But in every way he is full of spring, pep, and go! He asked me several questions almost simultaneously—about Chapel Hill, his friend Archibald Henderson,[17] life in the South, O'Neill, and so on. When he found out I was interested in philosophy he tore loose and talked for half an hour by the clock without my saying a word or wanting to, for that matter. He reviewed the old dispensation—as he called it—before Darwin, the coming of the natural science outlook, ending with the advent of Einstein on the scene. Then he talked about Einstein whom he admires greatly, told me one or two

16. Konstantin Stanislavsky, *My Life in Art*, trans. J. J. Robbins (Boston: Little, Brown, 1927), p. 110.

17. Shaw's chief biographer, with whom he had worked since 1905, in the Department of Mathematics at UNC.

anecdotes of their acquaintance which you may be sure I remember and will tell you later, and then swung around to the present-day scene of thought in England—J. B. S. Haldane,[18] Bertrand Russell, and others. Half the time he was jollying and half the time working at his words—but always with a terrific flow of words—never hesitating, never too involved. For instance he said once he was walking by the Thames on a moonlit night, and met a very famous scientist who was attending an astronomical meeting in England. He said he knew the scientist though that gentleman didn't recognize him. (I didn't ask him how that could be.) The scientist said,

"My good friend, I see you looking at the moon."

"Yes," said Shaw, "I like looking at it."

"You find it beautiful?"

"Yes," Shaw replied—"interesting."

"How far away do you suppose it is, for instance," the scientist went on.

"I was just thinking of that myself," Shaw answered. "Well, it can't be more than forty miles."

"How remarkable," the scientist exclaimed—perhaps he had begun to suspect the nature of his customer—"The actual distance is 37 miles."

And so he streamed on with such nonsense, half in earnest, half joking. But finally he was quite vehement in discussing standards of measurement, the sense findings and those of scientific instruments. "Don't you know," he declared, his eyes dancing, "that the sun is not 93 millions of miles away—that light doesn't travel 186 thousand miles something a second. You know that from common sense!"

Finally I asked some questions that led around to the drama—by way of the modern religious feeling for science, especially in physics and astronomy, which so many dramatists and theatre artists are trying to use on the stage,—and we had quite a session of it. He is keenly alive to all sorts of possibilities and thinks—unlike most Englishmen I've met—that the Talkies have a tremendous future. Then followed lots of incidents about his speaking for the Talkies, experience in writing plays, etc., etc. From his talk at this point I had a feeling that he had in mind some grandiose, startling new dramatic work which would make use of some modern religio-scientific idea calling for the most modern stage devices in production of it. I didn't ask him, for it was none of my business of course, and he didn't tell me outright, but such was my

18. Biologist then at Cambridge University (later at the University of London) and vigorous Marxist controversialist on social and philosophical issues.

feeling about it, my impression. Finally I rose to go, but he waved his hand and said he'd spare 5 more minutes. He began again and talked for another 15 minutes with hardly a pause. Well I'll tell you in detail when I get back about our conversation—the many, many things he said or suggested. And I believe then you'll agree with me that he is the *youngest man in Europe* and about the only surviving hope for the English drama—still the Shaw drama of course.

I must stop now. Best wishes to you all. I'll see you sometime in November, the Lord willing.[19]

As ever Paul

19. Koch published portions of the present letter in the December 1929 issue of the *Carolina Play-Book.* Green used the account of the visit with Shaw as the basis of an article, first published as "G. B. S. the Mystic," *Tomorrow* 8 (August 1949): 29–35, then as "The Mystical Bernard Shaw," in Green, *Dramatic Heritage*, pp. 112–31.

# III

## New York, Hollywood, and Capital Punishment, 1930–1936

January 1930
Resumes teaching philosophy at UNC.

Summer 1930
Completes draft of novel, *The Laughing Pioneer.*

14 July 1930
Third child, Elizabeth (Betsy), born.

August 1930
In Iowa City for drama festival at the University of Iowa.

June–July 1931
At Brookfield Center, Connecticut, with newly formed Group Theatre as company rehearses *The House of Connelly.*

September 1931
Takes leave from UNC (until fall 1938). In New York City for rehearsals of *Connelly,* which opens 28 September.

19–20 November 1931
Sponsors talks by Langston Hughes at UNC.

18 December 1931
Fourth child, Janet MacNeill, born.

February 1932
At University of Iowa to confer about production of *Tread the Green Grass,* then to Los Angeles to write film scripts. First film script, *Cabin in the Cotton,* released later in the year starring Richard Barthelmess and Bette Davis.

July–Mid-August 1932
In Chapel Hill.

Fall 1932

With family to Los Angeles. Writes film script for *State Fair* (released 1933) starring Will Rogers.

Winter 1932

Writes film script for *Voltaire* (released 1933) starring British actor George Arliss.

Early 1933

Writes film script for *Dr. Bull* (released 1933) starring Will Rogers.

Summer 1933

In Chapel Hill. Joins effort to establish National Folk Festival. Begins second novel, *This Body the Earth.* Buys 200 acres just east of Chapel Hill.

October 1933

To Los Angeles. Writes film script for *David Harum* (released 1934) starring Will Rogers. Revises script for *Carolina,* motion picture based on *The House of Connelly.*

Early 1934

In Chapel Hill begins to work for abolition of capital punishment.

April 1934

In Boston for production of *Potter's Field.*

May–September 1934

In Los Angeles revises *Potter's Field,* changing title to *Roll Sweet Chariot.* Writes film script for *Work of Art* (released 1934).

October 1934

In New York City for production of *Roll Sweet Chariot.*

December 1934

*Shroud My Body Down* produced by Playmakers.

January 1935

In New York City plans *The Enchanted Maze* with Group Theatre.

Winter–Summer 1935

In Chapel Hill finishes second novel, *This Body the Earth.*

Summer–Fall 1935

Writes "Hymn to the Rising Sun," drafts *The Enchanted Maze.*

Fall–Winter 1935

In Los Angeles writes film script for *Green Light* (released 1937). Sends copies of "Hymn to the Rising Sun" to North Carolina legislators, judges, and newspaper editors.

December 1935

*The Enchanted Maze* produced by Playmakers.

Spring 1936

In Chapel Hill collaborates with composer Kurt Weill on *Johnny Johnson.*

Summer 1936

With Weill joins Group Theatre in Connecticut for rehearsals of *Johnny Johnson.* Builds home on land east of Chapel Hill, area later known as Greenwood.

Fall 1936

In New York City for rehearsals and production of *Johnny Johnson.*

## 67. To Barrett H. Clark

[Chapel Hill, N.C.]
9 January 1930

Dear Barrett—[1]

I hope my many suggestions about plans for publication were not too confusing. The original plan was to publish a large volume in which *The House of Connelly* was to be included. From events I understood that the Guild preferred to publish their play on production. The second plan was to publish the revised versions of *Abraham* and *The Field God* with *Potter's Field*.[2] Then on my last visit to N.Y. it seemed that no production is sure yet for this season, and I wished to break the gap of long silence in some form or another, and it appeared better to bring out something relatively new. Bulgakov[3] who seemed to be so anxious about getting *Potter's Field* was in favor of publishing the play, though we did not discuss the question of whether it was to be singly or otherwise published. He said he thought he could use the published version to good advantage in working up critical interest in it. I do not know what is best, but a few days ago in N.Y. I talked it over hurriedly with Mr. Sheil and he said O.K. But of course whatever is best for all concerned[,] that I want.

Is this idea worth anything? To publish now the revised versions of *Abraham* and *The Field God* in a volume—I imagine McBride would give the rights if you asked them or if I did[—]and then a few months later publish *Potter's Field* and *Tread the Green Grass* in a volume and then follow that scheme of publication in the future—two plays to the volume or vary as occasion suited. Be as it may, I feel that I must keep things somewhat before the public. I await your (French's) suggestions. One reason I did not send you *The Honeycomb*

1. The Greens sailed from England on 6 November 1929, docked at New York City around 12 November, stayed there several days while Green negotiated for production and publication of the plays he had written or revised in Europe, then returned to Chapel Hill around 20 November. Some time in December, before his schedule would become restricted by the beginning of winter quarter classes at UNC on 3 January, Green went back to New York City to continue negotiations.

2. For revision of *The Field God*, see letter 65, n. 8. The version of *In Abraham's Bosom* current at the time of the present letter is in Thomas H. Dickinson, ed., *Chief Contemporary Dramatists*, 3d ser. (Boston: Houghton Mifflin, 1930), pp. 21–63.

3. Leo Bulgakov, Russian director trained at the Moscow Arts Theatre, who had worked with the Provincetown Players and others in the New York theater since 1923.

along with P.F. and T.G.G. was that its romanticism and imagination are somewhat toned like T.G.G., and it might be better to publish that later in another volume.[4]

My suggestions about format were suggestions only. In your letter tonight you say you will follow the general plan of *In the Valley*.[5] That suits me, though I should like a bit warmer page and the binding I sent a sample of—a sort of gray-streaked olive green. Aber ce n'est rien if it costs more.

In view of the fact that production seems still in the future I sent Mr. Sheil a letter offering to sell French's a still further slice of two plays. I have no idea as to what is a good gamble, but it seemed to me fairly one. I hope to hear from him soon. Here work is very heavy and interesting and I see not far off the possibility of heading the Philosophy department here and becoming more and more important.[6] It causes no happiness in me. Every day or two I get MSS. from people wanting to write and asking for advice about following their dream or sticking to their bread and butter job. Sometimes the authors come themselves as yesterday and today and talk over it all—as they no doubt do with you so often and as I so often have. Invariably I tell them it might be better to work along slowly and see, and I know quite well what it means too.

Lynn talked twice of coming down for a visit and rest.[7] Please convey to him in passing our standing invitation. Mabie is coming to visit us this month from Iowa.[8] I wish you were here a night or two. And what long talks and world talkings at that.

We all send love. Elizabeth has had book-presents for your children tied up

4. *In Abraham's Bosom* and *The Field God* were not published together again in a single volume, as McBride originally published them in 1927. *Potter's Field* and *Tread the Green Grass* are in *The House of Connelly and Other Plays* (1931). *The Honeycomb*, completed in 1934 (then entitled *Shroud My Body Down*) and produced that year in Chapel Hill by the Carolina Playmakers, was not published until 1972, when Samuel French issued a revised acting script of the play.

5. Green's most recent book, a collection of one-act plays published by Samuel French in 1928.

6. Horace Williams, head of the Department of Philosophy, was seventy-one on 16 August 1929.

7. Lynn Riggs, then living in New York City.

8. Edward C. Mabie, director of an extensive theater program at the University of Iowa, was coming for a conference on drama sponsored by Koch and the Carolina Playmakers.

ever since a week before Christmas and the Lantern[9] and household have kept her from getting them off. They go immediately. By this mail I return the contracts (new) with the Lab.[10]

Ever, Paul

## 68. To Elizabeth L. Green

Hotel Jefferson, Iowa City, Iowa
16 August 1930

Dear Honey Gal—[1]

This is the first minute I've had since I've been here, and I'll take it to scratch you a note. I've been going hard—drama, drama, drama. Mabie is doing more here in a week than Proff[2] does in a month. It seems that while we spend a lot of time at C.H. talking about what we're doing, Mabie is doing. I have attended rehearsals of five long plays written by students and being produced by students, and they're good, very good. I've seen some fine acting too, fine as you care to see among amateurs.

But Iowa isn't like Chapel Hill. What a difference. I know what the crude Middle W. means now. And that's why their work here in the drama strikes me as remarkable. Yet on second thought there may be a relation there.

I am enclosing my wire from Ross,[3] so you see the chances are I shant go to N.Y., but shall return to C.H. straight. Before I received Ross' wire Mabie had made arrangements for me to get off to N.Y. on the night of the 18th. So we

9. "The Literary Lantern," a weekly newspaper book review column appearing in numerous newspapers in the Southeast that Elizabeth had written since 1926.

10. Contract dated 3 January 1930 giving the American Laboratory Theater an option to produce *Tread the Green Grass* within the year (PG-SHC).

---

1. Probably on Saturday, 9 August, Green left Chapel Hill by train for Iowa City and arrived on 11 August to participate in a week-long drama festival at the University of Iowa conducted by Edward C. Mabie, director of the theater at the university and a leader in the noncommercial theater in the United States during the first half of the century.

2. Koch.

3. Sidney Ross, New York producer, who held an option on *Potter's Field.* Green left Chapel Hill intending to meet Ross in New York City on 20 August to discuss directors and revisions in the script (Paul Green to Sidney Ross, 9 August 1930, PG-SHC).

won't change that. I expect then to leave here evening of 18th, arrive Chicago next morning—it's a long way—then catch the next train, getting back about the 20th. I'll wire you later.

Kiss the younguns and take care of yourself.[4]

Tell Lamar to have the bulletin done, or partly so.[5]

Love Paul

## 69. To Vassili Kouchita[1]

Chapel Hill; N.C.
17 October 1930

My dear Mr. Kouchita—

Thanks for your letter which has just come. I gather from it that the Shuberts are not so enthusiastic, not even Mr. Gaites, who I thought had been

4. Elizabeth (Betsy), the Greens' third child, had been born 14 July 1930.

5. Lamar Stringfield (1897–1959), musician and friend of the Greens in Chapel Hill, was to have a distinguished career as composer and first conductor of the North Carolina Symphony. At the time of the present letter he was writing a study guide, *America and Her Music* (Chapel Hill: University of North Carolina Press, 1931), for which Green wrote the foreword.

---

1. Vassili Kouchita, who left his native Russia in 1919, was the American Laboratory Theater director currently trying to stage *Tread the Green Grass.* On 8 March Francis Fergusson, associate director of the theater, came to Chapel Hill to tell Green the company lacked funds for a spring production but hoped to raise money for a production in the fall (telegrams, Francis Fergusson to Paul Green, 3 and 4 March 1930; Green to Fergusson, 20 June 1930, PG-SHC). While plans for a commercial production were thus up in the air, Green began arrangements for an amateur production by describing the play to E. C. Mabie during the trip to Iowa in August, then sending Mabie a script (Paul Green to American Laboratory Theater, 22 August 1930; Green to E. C. Mabie, 4 September 1930). In September the Lab renewed its efforts, and Kouchita hoped to get financial backing from the Shuberts (largest producing organization in the commercial theater, headed at the time by Lee Shubert). A few nights before the present letter, however, Kouchita read the play to Joe Gaites, administrative assistant to the Shuberts, and Gaites said, " 'I can't see putting forty thousand dollars in this!' What really makes them hesitate," Kouchita went on, "is the unusual quality of the production and they are afraid to take the risk upon something which is so utterly beyond their comprehension and out of their line as a

trying to buy the play time without end—he being so enthusiastic in former days. But of course one has a right to change his interests. So it seems to me that the Shubert organization is not likely to back *Tread the Green Grass.* I hope I am mistaken, but I think not. Thank you for suggesting that I might communicate with Mr. Lee Shubert as to my desiring him to do the play with the Am. Lab. Since you mention also that I might not care to do it, I needn't refer to it any more. So that much is closed.

I shall certainly not present the acting version of the play to any producer until the Laboratory's control expires. I have no right to nor inclination, for if you can find a way to direct it I think with my present knowledge that is best of all. In reference to Mr. Clark's statement which I quote from your letter that "Brooks Atkinson had approached you"—that is, me—"on the play for Jed Harris" I must add that Mr. Atkinson[2] did not approach me on the play at all but wrote me saying he and Harris[3] had had some conversation and that Harris had some talk about the low state of the American drama, and that he Atkinson spoke of my plays to Harris, after which Atkinson wrote to me suggesting that it might be worth while to send some of my things to Harris for his consideration. There was no reference to *Tread the Green Grass,* and I doubt that Harris has ever heard of the play. After getting Atkinson's letter I thought the matter over and got in touch with French saying that if the Laboratory people had not renewed their contract (which I mistakenly thought expired on October 3—I had failed to take note of the fact that the contract excepted three summer months from the time covered therein), that I would confer with them French and they with me before renewing. This was with the idea that perhaps if the Lab had had to drop the matter—I had not heard, nor had you the Lab time to settle everything with Shubert as I see now—I could be free to approach Harris. French promptly informed me that I was mistaken as to date and that the Lab contract would not expire until around Jan. 3, 1931. I looked up my copies of the same and found French was correct, so that matter too is closed. I simply add that I wish you an early production and a good one. Anything I can do while the play is yours to help

producing office" (Vassili Kouchita to Paul Green, undated). Nevertheless, Kouchita added, he still hoped to get financial backing from the Shuberts.

2. Drama critic of the *New York Times.*

3. Broadway producer.

along I shall be more than glad to. It is of course to my interest and that of everybody else to do so.

You doubtless have my letter by this time in which I approve your production plans. Also, yesterday I sent a telegram to Miss Crowne[4] for Mr. Stringfield in which he wishes to know whether he shall go ahead with the music per his terms. He has to make a living and if he stops his small but remunerative jobs of scoring, doing bits here and there for the little but living wage he gets, he will be somewhat handicapped, for the complete music to *Tread the Green Grass* is a long job and an intense one. This of course you already know, but perhaps not the others in your organization.[5]

A concluding comment if you will pardon me which you and I know quite well; namely, that the noble art of the American theatre has much to free itself from.

Ever and with all good wishes,
A copy to Mr. Clark for his information.

## 70. To Sidney Ross[1]

Chapel Hill, N.C.
23 October 1930

My dear Mr. Ross—

As yet I have seen no reference to Meyerhold's coming to the U.S. in the daily press, and I presume that the matter has been dropped or that he has

4. Marion Crowne, business manager of the American Laboratory Theater.

5. Crowne wired Green that the Lab could make no advance payment to Stringfield until they found a backer for the production (18 October 1930, PG-SHC). Stringfield did a score for *Tread the Green Grass*, but not until the summer of 1931.

1. Before the Greens left for Germany in 1928, Sidney Ross, protégé of producer and director Kenneth Macgowan, took an option to produce *Potter's Field* and met with Green and Jasper Deeter, founder of the Hedgerow Theater in Philadelphia, to plan a production. Green left the meeting thinking they had decided to do the play during the 1928–29 season with Deeter as director, trying it out at the Hedgerow, then moving it to New York City. During Green's stay in Germany and England, however, Ross did nothing to carry out that plan (Paul Green to Sidney Ross, 26 March 1929, PG SHC). After returning to the United States in November 1929, Green had several meetings with Ross and by May 1930 had a commitment from him to produce *Potter's*

been delayed for no short time.[2] Of course I am interested in an early *Potter's Field* production. Have you talked any more with Mr. Gering, now that apparently the Meyerhold connection with the play is off? I understand that Bulgakov is at work on something already[3] and so I speak of Mr. Gering who I think is going to be, if he already isn't, a very fine director.

Now, Mr. Ross, may I suggest this—that [since][4] Meyerhold is definitely out of mind as director or co-director of *Potter's Field* due to his absence[,] we go ahead immediately with Mr. Gering or somebody else as director. I have been studying the script and have made quite a few changes in linking up the road intimately with the lives of the people so that the intermittent blasting far off, gradually coming nearer, in a way suggests the fate of the road and [the] iron-snouted steam shovel which will plough through them and scatter them willy-nilly. But humanity ever has a defence and voice in and against the power of iron or whatever heavy matter that would crush them, and therefore at the moment the steam shovel and the road uproot their lives the wisdom

---

*Field* during 1930–31 (George Auerbach to Paul Green, 15 May and 24 June 1930). Then on 4 August 1930 Green got a telegram from Ross canceling the tryout, rejecting Deeter as director, and telling Green to revise the script. Green's reply was testy, but he did ask if Ross had any particular suggestions about revisions (9 August 1930). Ross answered that there was not enough action early in the play to catch audience interest. He added grandly, "I am bringing to America Mr. Meyerhold, the outstanding Russian director of whom you have undoubtedly heard. Mr. Granowsky, whom you met in Berlin, is regarded as a disciple of Meyerhold. Mr. Meyerhold is expected in New York in October. There is a pupil of his, Marion Gering, here in New York, who has directed several plays successfully in the last two seasons and who is tremendously interested in *Potter's Field.* It is possible that Meyerhold, with the assistance of Gering, would direct *Potter's Field*, and both of them may visit you in Chapel Hill to acquaint themselves with the locale" (Sidney Ross to Paul Green, 4 September 1930).

2. Meyerhold did not come to the United States in 1930 or 1931.

3. Bulgakov, given a script of *Potter's Field* by Shepherd Strudwick, actor trained in the Carolina Playmakers, wanted to direct the play until he learned that Ross was its producer (Leo Bulgakov to Paul Green, 26 August and 17 September 1930, PG-SHC). Then he turned to *The Life Line* by Gretchen Damrosch, which opened on 27 December 1930.

4. The text of this letter comes from a carbon copy of the mailed original that is narrower than the mailed sheets. A few words along the right-hand margin, and final letters of a few others, are thus lost. Conjectured words are given here within square brackets, predictable letters added silently.

voice of John Henry which speaks beyond blood and iron in the truth rises on the road, and that wisdom voice gradually centers the mind and being of the convicts, representatives of those over whom the road has run, centers their minds on the infinite goal—a goal which is not there but is objectified in the setting sun which will rise again. I do [not] mean to defend the play but to explain it somewhat[,] for I feel that your hesitancy in producing it has been your uncertainty as to its form and clarity. One English critic who read the script, if I may speak a bit further on this, said the play stood still for an hour and then ended with the speed of a rocket. Of course the play does not stand quite still. Rather a meteorological analogy seems to me better, say a humid summer sky, slow thickening up of the atmosphere, presently a bit of cloud, more cloud, finally *a* cloud, a low rumble of thunder, presently another, a wind springs up fanning dry trees and grass, the cloud now stretches across the heavens and down [word illegible] far below the horizon, it would seem to swallow up the world with its onrushing jaws, now a jagged flash of lightning, the wind roars, the trees are bent far over, the grass is swept flat against the earth as if pressed down by a powerful and invisible broom, then like the drumming of feet on a floor the rush of rain against the ground, for awhile nothing but the sky and earth full of rain, then a gradual slackening, the wide shadow moves towards the east, then the clean red of the sun again shows in the west. Somewhat like this is *Potter's Field* to be produced[;] it was so written. I don't believe the effect of the play will be tiresome or confusing at all if it is produced with the right sort of integrated impressionism—if I make myself clear.

Now I strongly suggest, even urge, that we at once engage Mr. Gering—if he is available—or whomever you wish (as I said before Mr. Deeter suits me, but then if you prefer someone else, all right), and have him come down here and work with me on the script and locality[5] in building up a mental production in every way that is necessary. I believe the play can be put across in an impressive way, and the sooner the better for both you and me. If since I saw you two months ago you have got your own plans underway then mine are qualified, and I await the next decision.

If you have no more definite plans and are not satisfied with what I suggest above and do not see your way clear to producing the play at all, would you mind my suggesting again that you release it to me so that I can try to get it produced elsewhere. You have an option on it until January I think, and even

5. *Potter's Field* was set in the black section of Chapel Hill on the northwest of town.

if you began definite work now towards a production you could hardly get it on before the new year. Believe me I prefer that you get it produced, but if you *know* now that you will not I should be glad for you to tell me so and let me start other negotiations.

Sincerely yours,

## 71. To Barrett H. Clark

Chapel Hill, N.C.
8 December 1930[1]

Dear Barrett—

This is the status of the plays when I left New York Friday (I was to remain over Saturday for a conference with Kahn and Bulgakov,[2] but Kahn was called out of town and so I was able to get my other matters off Friday night):

The American Lab people gave me to understand that they intended to renew the option on *Tread the Green Grass* if they had not secured production before first option expires. They say, however, that they are sure they will be able to produce it and that with the Shuberts. Miss Bell of the Shuberts, so Miss Marion Crowne of the Lab says, told her that as soon as this present Pirandello is out of the way[3] that she is sure she will be able to persuade Mr. Lee[4] to do the play, and that already he is half-inclined to throw unpaying caution to the winds and go ahead with it. In the meantime the Lab people are trying everybody under the sun in the hope of getting hold of the money. Albert Johnson (the designer for *The Criminal Code, Half-Gods, Three's A Crowd,* etc.)[5] is much interested in its experimental possibilities and is at work making drawings for it. I should like to have them reproduced in the book if they are as good as they appear they will be. Johnson says if the Lab loses the play he wants to buy it and do it himself and he will promise New York

1. Monday.

2. Concerning *Potter's Field,* which Bulgakov hoped to produce with financial backing from Otto Kahn.

3. *As You Desire Me,* produced by the Shuberts, opened out of town on 24 November 1930 and would come to New York City on 28 January 1931.

4. Lee Shubert, head of the Shubert producing organization.

5. Later a motion picture director and producer, Albert Johnson (b. 1910) designed the first two plays in 1929, the third in 1930.

something to look at and hear. He says he's already invented a fourth dimension in light for the play and is enthusiastic with youth. He's just twenty I hear, and Erskine,[6] Saks and others say he's one of those real geniuses. "And money, Mr. Johnson?" says I. "I know some oil men," he replies with fire in his eye.[7] Ross says he's interested in the play, but I asked did he think it would be snowing before Christmas; to myself I meant to commune that he was an uncertain weather man in the theatre and that without instruments at all. Still I like him, he's a rather nice fellow, as you find him, you say.

*Potter's Field* is waiting Erskine's decision to continue or not continue with the Frohmans. If he steps out he says he will buy the play at once. I told him he had first choice. Bulgakov was anxious to close the deal before I left but agreed with me that if Erskine could do a production and that at once it would be best. Erskine promised to let me know as soon as possible—within the next few days.[8] In the event he carries on his movie connections and cannot buy the play I agreed to let Bulgakov have it with the understanding that we get to work rehearsing at once. He agreed, and I am in that case to come back during the holidays and help him cast. He is to arrange all money matters with Kahn and others himself, and my name (in the event we go halves) is to appear only as author, which I insisted upon. Macgowan[9] perhaps by this time has a script and he might make some sort of offer but it would all depend on acceptance upon what goes before with Erskine and Bulgakov.

Miss Crawford[10] says the Guild plans to do *House of C.* this spring and says it would no doubt be done sooner if the board felt agreed upon the nature of the play. I'm going through the script again with a certain feeling of symbolism in mind with the hope of welding or fusing it somewhat more.

I'm going to try to get my two big plays done this winter and spring[11] and I

6. Chester Erskine, in the producing organization of Charles Frohman.

7. Johnson did not design or produce *Tread the Green Grass.*

8. The next day Erskine telegraphed: "AFRAID CANNOT GIVE YOU ANYTHING DEFINITE ON PLAY THIS SEASON STOP HOWEVER AWFULLY ANXIOUS TO DO ONE OF YOUR PLAYS AND WORK WITH YOU" (Chester Erskine to Paul Green, 9 December 1930, PG-SHC).

9. Kenneth Macgowan, Broadway producer and critic.

10. Cheryl Crawford, on the board of the Theatre Guild, had been selected to direct *The House of Connelly.*

11. Probably *The House of Connelly* and *Potter's Field.*

do hope Harris will like the one he said he'd like, that of the white man, the machine god.[12]

It may be that I'll take the coming year off just to devote to the theatre and writing. The division is rather telling, but it was a pleasure to get back to the boys and move towards the blackboard. In the case I get off we might rent our house here and come near N.Y. or in case we can see our way clear to holding the house here I might come up to the town and live a few weeks or months at the time. I'll be clearer about it all Christmas.

It was nice to see you looking so well and Mr. Sheil [and] the crowd happy and going ahead. Give them my regards and love.

Yours,

## 72. To Elizabeth L. Green

Hotel Bristol, 129 West 48th Street, New York City
Sunday morning [14 December 1930]

Dear Girl—

I am here at the Bristol waiting to have breakfast with Caro Mae and Erma.[1] Kouchita and I have had a long early morning talk over the condition of *Tread the Green Grass*, and I don't see any hope myself—and told him so—of such a bankrupt organization as The Am. Lab ever getting anybody reputable and with money going in with them. It is of course the old old story. I've learned my lesson. Never again will I let French sell a play of mine to a shoestring organization without guarantees far greater than I've had—guarantees in fact that will prove *ipso* that the organization is not shoestring. (I sent through French $80 to Fraulein Lamprecht[2] with this cablegram—25 words for $1—"Cabled money today. Expect you New York by steamer Ballin December nineteen. Will meet you. Love, Elizabeth Green.")[3] I had lunch

12. At the suggestion of *New York Times* drama critic Brooks Atkinson (Brooks Atkinson to Paul Green, 17 October 1930, PG-SHC), Green sent a play, perhaps *Tread the Green Grass*, to the Broadway producer Jed Harris.

1. Green's sisters, who worked in New York City and shared an apartment.

2. Governess for the Green children during their stay in Berlin and London.

3. Erna Lamprecht arrived on 19 December but because of high unemployment was classified an "excluded alien" by New York immigration authorities and held on Ellis Island for deportation. To the secretary of labor Green appealed the classification on the grounds that Lamprecht would deprive no American of a job. She had come to

yesterday with Mr. Sheil and Ross[4] and with the hearty concurrence of Sheil spoke quite definitely to Ross and found he was still talking air and vague plans. I asked him to release the play suggesting that there would be no renewal. He was slow at first and then agreed and so tomorrow I start forth to peddle the play. Chester Erskine is my first bet. Barrett had already sent him the new script of P[otter's] F[ield]. R. E. Jones[5] has just read it and says it's "a remarkable play, maybe a great play." I'll see Jones tomorrow. Gently and persuasively I'm going to try to ease the Lab people from Tread Green G.—At one o'clock today I have a meeting with them. At Barrett's suggestion I sent Miss Helburn a note yesterday and said I'd be glad to talk over House of Connelly with her while I'm here. Monday night Brooks Atkinson and I are going to the opening of Susan Glaspell's play—*Alison's House* at Eva La Gallienne's place.[6]

Deep down let our hearts beat together always, for that is our reality and without it we both live confused. I know it. The rest will always follow if that leads us.

I love you, Paul

## 73. To the Mayor of Memphis[1]

[Chapel Hill, N.C.]
27 February 1931

AS A CITIZEN AND LOYAL DEMOCRAT I WISH TO ENTER A PROTEST AGAINST THE UNJUSTIFIED IMPRISONMENT OF MY FRIEND HENRY R. FULLER IN THE MEMPHIS JAIL ON SATURDAY, FEBRUARY 21.[2] IN EXPRESSING THIS PROTEST, I AM

---

visit, not work for, the Greens (night letter, Paul Green to members of North Carolina congressional delegation, 22 December 1930, EG-SHC). On 24 December the secretary reversed the New York decision and granted Lamprecht a six-month visa.

4. Whose option to produce *Potter's Field* would expire at the end of the month.

5. Robert Edmond Jones, who came into prominence as a designer with the Provincetown Players and now designed productions for the Theatre Guild and others.

6. Civic Repertory Theatre.

---

1. Watkins Overton, mayor, 1928–40.

2. Fuller (B.A., UNC, 1926), southeastern textbook representative of Houghton Mifflin, went to the Memphis police station on Saturday evening, asked about local

GIVING VOICE NOT ONLY TO MY OWN FEELINGS IN THE CASE, BUT TO THAT OF SOME TWENTY-FIVE OR THIRTY OTHER CITIZENS OF NORTH CAROLINA WHOM IN THE LAST DAY OR TWO I HAVE HEARD DECLARE THEMSELVES AS UNALTERABLY OPPOSED TO THE ACTION OF YOUR POLICE COMMISSIONER, MR. CLIFFORD DAVIS. WE FEEL THAT IN YOUR RIGHT AS THE HONORABLE MAYOR OF THE CITY OF MEMPHIS YOU OWE IT IN YOUR OFFICIAL PREROGATIVE TO REQUIRE MR. DAVIS TO ISSUE A PUBLIC APOLOGY TO MR. FULLER[3] (WHO, BY THE WAY, IS THE GREAT GRAND-SON OF TENNESSEE'S JOHN SEVIER).[4] I AM FORWARDING A COPY OF THIS TELEGRAM TO THE GOVERNOR OF TENNESSEE[5] AND ALSO A COPY TO THE EDITOR OF THE MEMPHIS PRESS-SCIMITAR.[6]

PAUL GREEN
ASSOCIATE PROFESSOR OF PHILOSOPHY
THE UNIVERSITY OF NORTH CAROLINA

## 74. To Barrett H. Clark

Chapel Hill, N.C.
1 April 1931

Dear Barrett:

The books and *Under the Gaslight*[1] have just come. Thanks ever so much. No news, everybody hard at work, and quiet is pretty much over everything. It was good to have you with us; and come again![2]

---

Communist party activities, and was promptly jailed without charge and held until the following Monday morning (23 February).

3. The mayor, like the commissioner a member of the Crump machine that controlled Memphis politics, did not require an apology by Davis (George F. Milton to Frank Porter Graham, 9 March 1931, Graham Papers, SHC).

4. Sevier (1745–1815), one of the founders of Tennessee, its first governor, and later a congressman.

5. Henry Hooton, governor, 1927–32.

6. On 24 February 1931 the Memphis *Press-Scimitar* carried an editorial condemning the police for violating Fuller's civil liberties. In the same issue the paper ran Fuller's own account of his thirty-six hours in jail.

---

1. Popular nineteenth-century melodrama written by Augustin Daly in 1867, revived by Elmer Rice in April 1929.

2. Clark stayed with the Greens when he visited Chapel Hill for a few days in March to acquaint himself with Playmakers activities.

I've been thinking over the plan Elmer Rice has for allowing the amateur theatres to do his *Left Bank* before it has had a New York run, that is, contemporaneous with the N.Y. production if so wished.[3] So far as advance toward the freedom of the theatre goes, I don't see anything in the idea and I'm writing you because I strongly feel that if definite progress is to be made in the true way, nothing should be done to blur the issues. As I understand it, the facts are these: Rice is to produce, direct and manage his play in N.Y. next season. He will make this play available to amateurs the night it opens. It can be played in C.H. the same night if we wish. He requests some sort of guarantee. Frankly I see nothing in this except that Rice has all to gain and the little theatres have the privilege of making up their own mind and choosing something before New York has said this or that. Suppose Rice's play is a flop; then the amateurs are perhaps already committed to do it here and there. Suppose it is a great success, they will do it more anyway. Rice wins both heads and tails, and wherein does he yield so much in his plan? If Gilbert Miller,[4] say, were doing the play and Rice yielded something in his contract with Miller so that the amateurs could have the play at the same time Miller had it, then he might have something of a selling point, though not so much. But Rice is the *author* and producer. No, I see nothing to it, and I for one should not like to see the relation of the future between Broadway and Oshkosh (it will come) begin this way. Please understand that I'm not criticizing Rice's play. I haven't read it, and as you know I admire his work very much. But apart from other things I think the scheme above referred to would not help Rice with the Little Theatres any either.

Hurriedly as my class is assembling. Paul

3. Rice would produce and direct *The Left Bank*, which he wrote, when it opened in New York for a long run on 5 October 1931. His scheme, outlined by Green, was one of many during the 1920s, 1930s, and 1940s for increasing cooperation between amateur and professional theaters.

4. Prominent Broadway producer.

## 75. To Frank Porter Graham[1]

Chapel Hill, N.C.
5 May 1931

Dear Frank,

Relative to my conversation with you some time ago concerning the possibility of Lamar Stringfield's association with the University for the coming year in some sort of musical capacity,[2] and relative further to that part of our conversation connected with the raising of money for such a possibility, I am outlining here a rough scheme of work which, after having talked it over with Lamar, we both feel would be a more or less satisfactory outline to follow:

First, in co-operation with the Carolina Playmakers and the University Music Department to solicit compositions by music students and young native composers with the view of performing them in public and giving the works constructive criticism both as musical material and examples of technique.

Second, to give public performances of new music originally composed by students and others, and where feasible to offer these compositions for publication by reliable music houses.

Third, to give chamber music concerts featuring music based on native folklore.

Fourth, to hold when feasible fiddlers' contests (including players of guitars, banjos and other so called folk instruments) to encourage the perpetuation of our folk music.

Fifth, to help when necessary those students in Playmaker productions who wish incidental or integral music for their plays.

1. Frank Porter Graham (1886–1972) had a long association with the University of North Carolina. He graduated from UNC in 1909, earned an M.A. in history at Columbia University in 1916, and after military service in France during World War I returned to UNC in 1919 as a member of the Department of History. In 1930 he became president of the school, a position he held until his appointment to fill an unexpired U.S. Senate term in 1949. During the 1930s he came to be known as a champion of civil liberties and a president bent on strengthening ties between UNC and the life of the state.

2. Stringfield and Green had been friends since serving together in the 105th Engineers in France during World War I. Stringfield had won a Pulitzer Prize in 1928 for his suite, "From the Southern Mountains," and at present was composing the score for *Tread the Green Grass*, but Green had been unable to secure him an advance from a publisher or producer.

Sixth, to give possibly a course in the Music Department which shall be for the purpose of helping towards original compositions:—To be specific, to do in this course musically what is being done dramatically in some of the English composition courses.[3]

Seventh, to establish at the University of North Carolina a headquarters for all effort in the field of amateur composition and arrangement of native music, and to use this headquarters for the encouragement of festivals, concerts, programs, and all things musical whatsoever.

Eighth, to establish here at the University a place for the collecting and preservation of original compositions, that is, a library of original music.

This is roughly and hurriedly put, but in general I think it offers something very advantageous for us all. And, of course, before I begin asking certain people to give money for this endeavor, I should like—and I'm sure you would—to talk it over with all concerned.

Sincerely yours,[4]

## 76. To Theresa Helburn

Chapel Hill, N.C.
10 May 1931

My dear Miss Helburn,[1]

I shall be very glad for Miss Crawford to come down here in connection with *The House of Connelly*. I can see, of course, both advantages and

3. Playwriting courses, where student plays were tried out before audiences, who then discussed them with the authors.

4. This letter led Graham to create the Institute for Folk-Music with Harold S. Dyer, chairman of the Department of Music, as its head. Stringfield was taken on as research associate in the institute (Harold Dyer to Frank Porter Graham, 23 May 1931, Graham Papers, SHC). During the academic year 1931–32 Stringfield offered classes in American folk music in the fall quarter, practical composition and orchestration in the winter, and chamber music in the spring (Lamar Stringfield to Paul Green, 13 September 1931, PG-SHC).

---

1. The Theatre Guild had planned to launch its 1931–32 season with a production of *The House of Connelly* (Theresa Helburn to Paul Green, 17 March 1931, PG-SHC), but recently Helburn told Green about a special interest in the play among younger members of the Guild who added an impassioned social conscience to their passion

disadvantages in such a tryout as is outlined in your letter. Since I am not able to comprehend, perhaps, the disadvantages as well as I am the advantages, and accordingly I say let's go ahead.[2] If the company is good and the production means adequate—and I have no doubt they will be—then it seems to me that a preview such as this will make it possible to eradicate certain faults which everybody seems to feel are present in the play. As a first step in whatever direction I strongly suggest that Miss Crawford come down for a few days where we can talk and look things over.

I don't know about my being able to go to Danbury for rehearsals, but if my affairs are in order so that I can, I certainly will want to.[3]

Cordially yours,

## 77. To Elizabeth L. Green

144 West 16th St., New York City
[Early September 1931]

Dear Honey—[1]

Your sweet letter came today, so did Paulie's catalog and the curls and all. You are a sweet family, and make me try to be better and fuller of this world,

---

for the theater, particularly Cheryl Crawford, Harold Clurman, and Lee Strasberg. They wanted to work on the play over the summer, she said, and, if the Guild board thought the work went well, do it in the fall as the first production of their Group Theatre. Crawford, a ring leader of the Group, also wanted to visit Green in Chapel Hill and go over the script with him (Theresa Helburn to Paul Green, 8 May 1931).

2. As given.

3. In early June Crawford, Clurman, Strasberg, and their actors from the Theatre Guild assembled at Brookfield Center near Danbury, Connecticut, and began a summer of rehearsing *The House of Connelly.* Green spent several weeks with them in June and July and, at the urging of Clurman and others, revised the last scene of the play so that Patsy Tate, symbol of new life in the South, can live rather than die. Clurman recounts the summer, the formative period of the Group Theatre, in *The Fervent Years: The Story of the Group Theatre and the Thirties,* 2d ed. (New York: Hill and Wang, 1957), pp. 36–50. Green describes his stay with the Group in "With the Group Theatre—a Remembrance," in Green, *Plough and Furrow: Some Essays and Papers on Life in the Theatre* (New York: Samuel French, 1963), pp. 42–56.

---

1. Following his stay with the Group Theatre as they rehearsed *The House of Connelly* in Connecticut, Green went home briefly, then returned to New York City

and thereby it goes back to you again. I have just this minute finished after twenty hours work a new last scene for H. of C. I have prayed and struggled with myself, and after yesterday's rehearsal came home and shut myself up. I think I have it at last. In this Will tears his father's portrait from the wall and figuratively tramps on it, and he and Patsy remain in "Our house, not yours."[2] Tonight we rehearse the whole play with the old ending.[3] Kahn,[4] Stark Young,[5] the Moses,[6] Paul Osborn,[7] Barrett and Mr. Sheil, O'Neill, and several other celebrities are expected to be by and see it.[8] Today I got poor French to send fifty dollars to the bank, for I had to cash $25 for Erna's trip home,[9] and something for myself to live on. Please lay off it if possible, for I must cash another check tomorrow. I have forty cents left. Don't worry about my health. I've already lost twelve pounds and am getting down to about the right weight. Tomorrow I see some folks at the Paramount building. Mr. Hart[10] called up yesterday and said he was ready to do something active about *Potter's Field* and wanted to talk with me before he started. What that means I don't know. Anyway I count nothing—as you know—until I see it, not in this business anyway. If I can I may get off this week and go home for a few days real sleep. I've about forgot how—but really it doesn't bother me. The only reason I wouldn't come would be the cost. If something happens about *Potter's F.* immediately I should of course have to stay here until that's settled. Erma is

---

in late August for final rehearsals before the play opened on 28 September. Thematic implications of the new ending did not satisfy him ("The more I study the H. of C.," he wrote Elizabeth a few days before the present letter, "the more I am convinced that my original idea of an unhappy ending was correct" [28 August 1931, EG-SHC]), but he did want to insure at least the tonal and structural appropriateness of the revision.

2. The point is preserved in the first edition but details differ (*The House of Connelly and Other Plays* [New York: Samuel French, 1931], p. 119).

3. That is, earlier version of the optimistic ending.

4. Otto Kahn, financier and patron of the arts.

5. Drama critic for *The New Republic*, from Mississippi.

6. Theatrical producer Harry Moses and his wife.

7. Playwright and screenwriter.

8. Clurman says the Theatre Guild board also attended a rehearsal, then offered to produce *The House of Connelly* if its tragic ending were restored. The Group refused to comply and produced the play themselves, with financial assistance from the Guild, Eugene O'Neill, and Maxwell Anderson (*Fervent Years*, pp. 51–52).

9. Erna Lamprecht, visiting relatives on Long Island.

10. Producer Walter Hart.

coming next Monday, she writes. Mrs. Harrington the landlady has been over and kindly asked after the girls. She was very nice and seemed to be quite willing to make whatever arrangement was necessary about the rent. I told her Erm would see her next week.

Tell Paulie I'll send in an order pretty soon. I guess Erna has arrived by this time. Poor child she hated to leave this city the worst I've ever seen one. She's a sweet high-flying angel, woman to the heart, and I wish she could be happy. But,

Say my gal laid her head down,
Laid her head down and cried.
Tears fell on the cold ground,
Can't be satisfied.

I saw very little of her while she was here—she spent most of her time on Long Island with her cousins and down at Lucy's.[11] I was so sorry she had no money and had her style cramped.

I love you, Paul

## 78. To Tyre Taylor[1]

Chapel Hill, N.C.
28 November 1931

Dear Tyre—

Since the meeting in Raleigh I have been studying the plan you have drawn up, and I hope you won't mind if I tell you frankly what I think of it—something I'm sure all your friends and well-wishers won't do, though for the

11. Elizabeth's sister.

---

1. Tyre Taylor (1900–1970), classmate of Green at UNC and now a lawyer serving as executive secretary to North Carolina governor O. Max Gardner (1929–33), had proposed a "Ten Year Plan for Tar Heelia" to help stimulate the depressed economy (*NO*, 19 July 1931, p. 3, cols. 1–7). Major aims of the plan were to attract tourists and industry to the state by such means as highway beautification, development of a state symphony and historical attractions, and construction of outdoor sports and recreation facilities. On 17 November Green attended a meeting in Raleigh to form the corporation that would administer Taylor's plan. Green was also appointed to the Committee on Country Life (Tyre Taylor to Paul Green, 23 November 1931, PG-SHC).

good of all concerned I believe they should. As you already know, I am wholeheartedly for anything that will brighten up the countryside, get people more interested in where they live, and make for a general quickening of vitality and imagination throughout the state. There are ways of working towards this, but one of them is not necessarily the effort of making money; nor is another necessarily plans and purposes of politics. That, Tyre, seems to me to be—after no little consideration—the trouble with your scheme. It is too much concerned with bringing financial profit to some and political pulling to others. Of course these are not bad things in themselves, but in this case they are bad so far as what I have at heart is concerned; namely, an effort to tell the people—no, show them—that there are other things to live for in the world around them than matters ever beholden to dollars and position. I don't mean to say you or anybody else ought to get out and begin stumping for aesthetics and Moore County sunsets,[2] but I do mean that in a practical way we could do a lot of smaller things to help bring other and realer values into the lives of the people of North Carolina—and these realer values are not economic nor political. There are government departments and social technologies already of long standing that are functioning in these fields, and I believe an organization such as yours now appears to be won't be of any particular help therein. Even if it could, I for one don't give a hang about flooding the state with tourists. You evoke the shade of Virginia, and I say look at Virginia. We don't want to be like her, saying to the hurrying motorist—see what we did, or what was done to us.[3] North Carolina's life is the future, and the surest way to hurt her strength and forward drive is to tease into her borders a restless, unappreciative gang of transients who with their money you folks talk so much about will help to develop a lackey and yes-man spirit in thousands of our people whose time and abilities could well be put to something better. And it was because I thought you had in mind some fine way of acquainting the people with how to use these abilities that I have been so much interested in

2. County in south-central part of the state.

3. In "Ten Year Plan for Tar Heelia," Taylor noted that in North Carolina little had been done to mark the sites of historically important events, whereas "Virginia has found it desirable to make a state appropriation for this purpose." He added that "from a modest beginning, the movement for the preservation of Virginia antiquities has grown until at the present time Mr. Rockefeller is spending $1,000,000 on a single project" (col. 4), that is, the Colonial Williamsburg Restoration, which John D. Rockefeller, Jr., began to fund in 1926.

what you're trying to do. The city of Asheville is a standing rebuke to us all, and surely we can experience beforehand some kind of lesson from her Babbittry.[4] The truth of this whole thing as I see it is that you and your group have a chance to do something through Harrelson[5] or Allen[6] or some other heads of departments and have no business at all of trying to become a super state government or state chamber of commerce. And again to be frank, I must confess that that's what you don't seem to be doing—not concentrating upon or lending your influence to channels already established for the real betterment of the people. It seems you are planning to use them to help you. And it's not going to work that way—not in the end. If you try it, you'll find that sectional representation and personal aggrandizement will wreck the whole thing soon or late, for you can't weld a body together the way the different functioning departments are welded under the one head as a state government. So that would seem to give your organization an anomalous and gratuitous position, whereas the whole necessity for its meaning is an integral one. I'll try to make myself a little clearer:

1. Your organization claims to be interested in doing something in art, music, and landscaping for the people of North Carolina. (And so on.)

2. You want to give North Carolina a sounder business system—more money, more profits.

3. You want to make North Carolina more conscious of her possibilities and her actual and potential greatness.

4. You wish to sell North Carolina to the Nation—to make the country interested in North Carolina and pay dollars for that interest.

5. Etc.

To do this you found an organization of leading citizens, hoping to enlist bodies, institutions, individuals and manifold means of every shape and fashion. What can such an organization do in itself? I'll tell you—nothing but stand up and tell you they'll cooperate in every way and that they're all for the plan proposed. Naturally they would be. And the reason they can't do anything but talk and help you form committees is that right off the bat you

4. For decades Asheville had been a resort for the wealthy, and for people suffering with tuberculosis, because of its cool mountain climate; and during the prosperous 1920s tourism in Asheville boomed.

5. J. W. Harrelson, chief of the North Carolina Department of Conservation and Development (1929–33).

6. A. T. Allen, state superintendent of public instruction (1925–37).

involve them in two fronts—the economic and the political. The former is individual or corporational (which at bottom is individual), the second is governmental; and they are both already taken care of under our capitalism system and our democracy form of government. Complete organization has taken place in both fields. And any group that forms itself on a basis involving both must be reduced to talk and advertisement. Of course you might say that talk and advertisement would be something gained if no more, but the waste of time and effort and confusion of ideals would be too great to make it worth while. But there remains that one phase of our life which has not received its proper encouragement, neither from the business offices, the pulpit, nor the executive chambers—and that is (I'll use the word)—the aesthetic. And the mention of that attracted me to your program. People are hungry for something besides money, money, and business, business. The women's clubs, garden clubs, and all kinds of clubs and individual school teachers have been doing something for this side of our life, but they have been so handicapped both in funds and personal encouragement that they haven't done enough. They need help, and help of an authoritative kind. And when your program came out with a call for concerted action in such an endeavor I know that many of them thought, "Well, thank God, we've heard something from Raleigh besides the same wrabgle[7] of the dollar." And now it seems that you've turned back, and have formed another chamber of commerce. Politics and other things have got control of you[r] plan, and unless you get them out[,] it seems the best part of your program will be lost and sunk.[8]

## 79. To Barrett H. Clark

Chapel Hill, N.C.
8 December 1931

Dear Barrett—[1]

No, I don't mind autographing books a bit. The more the better, for it's a sign of business.

7. Made-up word.

8. Green continued to serve on the Committee on Country Life into March 1932, after which time the plan faded from view.

---

1. Several times recently Samuel French, Incorporated, had passed along requests for Green to autograph copies of *The House of Connelly*, and on the latest one Clark

I've heard no more from Hart. I hope things are going ahead.[2] Munsell[3] writes of a tour of Connelly in the spring. That sounds very hopeful.[4] Will you get to see the Group production on the tenth? I'd appreciate a word as to what you think. My boys—as I presume to call them—the *Contempo* two seem bent on stirring up a little fun.[5] I try to guard them as much as possible, but I expect a showdown before long. If the worst comes to the worst I'm going to stand with them in a way more outspoken than I have. They are doing a bright intelligent, snappy paper, and it'll be too bad if they go under. Local advertisers have already boycotted them. Elizabeth gave them a long boost in her Lantern column which helped with quite a few subscriptions.[6] Sinclair Lewis has subscribed, with a long praising letter—which has been made

---

appended the note: "Do you mind this sort of thing?" (Charles Brustman to Paul Green, 2 December 1931, PG-SHC).

2. In November Walter Hart, former student of Jasper Deeter now with the producers Ray-Minor in New York, had taken an option to produce *Potter's Field* (Charles Brustman to Paul Green, 14 November 1931, PG-SHC) but now was in the process of assigning his rights to Margaret Hewes (Barrett Clark to Paul Green, 25 November 1931).

3. Warren Munsell, business manager of the Theatre Guild, parent organization of the Group Theatre.

4. *The House of Connelly* opened in New York City on 28 September 1931 and ran into December. Its tour opened in Philadelphia on 4 January, in Washington on 25 January, and in Boston on 1 February 1932.

5. Anthony Buttitta and Milton Abernethy, owners of the Intimate Bookshop in Chapel Hill, launched *Contempo: A Review of Books and Personalities* in May 1931. In July they began extensive coverage of the Scottsboro Case, in which nine black men were convicted in April of raping two white women on a freight train in northern Alabama. Death sentences for eight of the men, originally scheduled for July, were suspended during the summer and fall of 1931 as the case was appealed through higher courts. Between July and the time of the present letter *Contempo* carried articles by Carol Weiss King, attorney for the men, and a host of writers (among them Theodore Dreiser, John Dos Passos, Lincoln Steffens, and Langston Hughes) protesting racism in the trial and in the South.

6. Elizabeth said *Contempo*'s "editors have an uncanny ability for extracting unpaid contributions from well-known writers whose names spell interest as well as money. And in addition they are rash but wily showmen. . . . For such a young review, *Contempo* has received remarkable press notices, though we regret to add that none of them seem to be from the southern press" ("Literary Lantern," *Greensboro Daily News*, 29 November 1931, sec. B, p. 5, cols. 1–2).

public.[7] It's my hope that they'll get dug in so well with the leading literary people that they won't be ousted from here. But they are a tactless two. They even took Langston Hughes into a cafeteria (students' eating place) for supper. But no disturbance occurred. I also had Hughes out to my house for the evening, reading and talking. But then there are a few things I can do, but these boys can't see why they can't step right in and do what they wish too.[8] All being proof that they don't yet comprehend the local mores. Your name will give them strength here, and if it all comes to mayhem I'll ask you for a word in their behalf. If all remains quiet hereafter you'll know the Potomac is still emptying into the sea.[9]

7. A remark by Lewis appears in an advertisement for *Contempo* in its issue of 1 January 1932: "If nothing else would make me subscribe, the charming praise of *Contempo* from the Gastonia *Daily Gazette* would make me." The *Daily Gazette* "praise" appeared in an advertisement for *Contempo* in its issue of 15 December 1931: "*Contempo* is nasty. It is common, filthy, obnoxious, putrid, rancid, nauseating, rotten, vile, and stinking. If you should happen to run across a copy of *Contempo* read it, by all means, and then burn it, by all means."

8. In October Hughes had written to Green about a lecture tour that would bring him to North Carolina in late November (Langston Hughes to Paul Green, 13 October 1931, PG-SHC), and Green, with Guy Johnson, professor of sociology at UNC, arranged an open lecture for Hughes in Gerrard Hall on campus for the evening of 19 November. The lecture was well attended and the visit uneventful (*Daily Tar Heel* [UNC student newspaper], 21 November 1931, p. 1, col. 2; p. 4, col. 5), even when Buttitta and Abernethy dined with Hughes in the Cavalier Cafeteria below their bookstore. Following the lecture, Hughes spent the night at Green's house, then continued his tour (conversation with Paul Green, fall 1980). But the 1 December 1931 issue of *Contempo*, available at the time of Hughes's visit, carried his poem "Christ in Alabama" and his article "Southern Gentlemen, White Prostitutes, Mill-Owners, and Negroes" (p. 1). These pieces antagonized several newspaper editors and business people in the state, who by late November had begun to protest Hughes's visit to UNC (Tatum Petition, Graham Papers, SHC). During the civil rights demonstrations of the 1950s Hughes wrote an account of the visit ("Color at Chapel Hill," in *The Langston Hughes Reader* [New York: George Braziller, 1958], pp. 404–6) that imposes onto the events of 1931 the atmosphere of confrontation typical of the late 1950s.

9. Clark replied by saying he knew nothing about the Scottsboro Case but giving Buttitta permission to quote the following: "I welcome and support any statement of the truth or what appears to be the truth, particularly when it is addressed to those who are likely to oppose it. Only thus has the world been able to muddle along" (Barrett Clark to Anthony Buttitta, 10 December 1931, PG-SHC).

Now for something of business which I wish you would pass to Mr. Sheil. French owns 25 percent of Connelly. On Dec. 13—unlucky day—I have to meet my last big payment on my belongings.[10] My account is rather overdrawn with you and since Connelly has a chance to go on the road and will no doubt as time goes on do business with little theatre groups, I'd rather sell another part to French than ask them for credit. I've tried to get these notes renewed further, but nothing doing here. I need $1,200 on the 13th of December and will sell French an additional 15 percent of the play for that amount—which will bring their holdings to 40 percent. I don't believe there's any chance of its not paying French for the investment and as for me—it'll pay me to get this load off so I can go ahead with my work. If it's satisfactory have a bill of sale made out and I will sign it at once.[11]

Ever to you,

## 80. To Elizabeth L. Green

On a train    Near New Mexico
21 February 1932

Dear Honey—[1]

Left Des Moines last night at 12:*30*. Tolerably decent night on the train. Am certainly having the hermit's life now and plenty of thought of my own.

The conference at Iowa was a success, with everybody there. I made four speeches and ended as usual feeling like a fool. Underneath all talk I know my business is first to write and then talk. I've had it backward the last three or four years. Well—

Coming from you the other day on the train to Lynchburg I had a feeling that that was a momentous time for me—as if my life were coming upon a moment of complete meaning good or bad so far as I was concerned. In fact I

10. Home and property in the Glen.

11. Sheil accepted the offer and on 12 December sent Green a check for $1,200 (Frank Sheil to Paul Green, 12 December 1931, PG-SHC).

---

1. In the week of 15 February Green went to the University of Iowa for a drama conference organized by E. C. Mabie, director of the theater there, and to confer with Mabie about a production of *Tread the Green Grass* planned at the university for July. On Saturday, 20 February, he took a train for Los Angeles and his first screenwriting job.

doubt I'll ever go back into the school room again except maybe to give a single lecture. As soon as I am clear in my mind and see further ahead about it all I'll say more. I do not know where *these roads* are leading us, but I have faith—faith.

Love, Paul

## 81. To Elizabeth L. Green

[3460 Bennett Drive, Hollywood, Calif.]
29 February 1932

Dear Honey—[1]

I've just got back to my room after the first day's work at the studio. My hours are from 9:*00* to 5:*30*, eating lunch on the lot. I have an office next to Elliott Nugent[2] and have spent the afternoon blocking out the scenes in *Cabin in the Cotton.*[3]

Alas, my child, I don't get paid till a week from next Wednesday, and having to pay my room rent in advance, laundry, etc. I have had to cash a check for $25. If there's a deficiency in the bank to cover it you'll just have to wire French I wish him to send $50, but don't do it unless you absolutely have to. I'll make this $25 last me somehow till March 9. As soon as I am paid, I'll wire you two or three hundred dollars. I have to pay back the $145 sent to you for me by Lovelace.[4]

1. Green's new West Coast agent, Hunter Lovelace, arranged for Green to write a motion picture script for Warner Brothers based on H. H. Kroll's novel, *The Cabin in the Cotton* (1932). On the train from Iowa to Los Angeles Green revised and wrote the introduction to his own novel, *The Laughing Pioneer*, which McBride would publish in September. After a stop in Tucson, where on Tuesday and Wednesday he lectured at the University of Arizona, he got to Los Angeles on Friday morning, 26 February, with $20.50 in his pockets (Paul Green to Elizabeth Green, 22 and 26 February 1932, PG-SHC).

2. Actor and writer whose *The Poor Nut* (1925) would be the basis of his collaboration with James Thurber on *The Male Animal* (1940).

3. Noted along the left margin: "I spent the morning in the projection room (see how professional I talk) having Barthelmess' former pictures run off for me." Richard Barthelmess (1895–1963), who would have the leading role in *The Cabin in the Cotton*, began his acting career in D. W. Griffith films and most recently starred in *The Dawn Patrol* (1930).

4. Noted along the left margin: "On March 9 I draw one week's salary, $625. Think

Here's a suggestion: why not plan to come out with Janet,[5] leaving March 10, bringing a list of our bills, and the following week we can send checks to pay them up. I'll have a second week's salary available by the time you get here and we could sit right down and make out checks and send them back. If you do, you'd better turn in the car, because another payment will be due on it March 5—I think it is—which will have to wait in any case until I collect here. Also you would have to arrange for somebody (besides Buie)[6] to chaperone the house. These are only suggestions. Please call up young Fowler at the Model Market—the one who comes around collecting[7]—and tell him the check I left with him for $50 to the Durham Industrial Bank will have to wait till I get some money to you about the 10th of March. The check was dated for March 4 or 5. Explain to him my first salary will come in on the 9th. I hate to bother you with these details, but I don't know what else to do. If you decide to keep the car, you'll have to call up Bruce Strowd[8] and tell him the $40 payment for March will be delayed for five or six days. If you don't decide to come out, then I suggest you keep the car.[9]

I have a room—as I wrote you—here in Mrs. Smith's little house, and I'm having plenty of solitude.

Keep knocking through is now me motto.

Love, Paul[10]

---

of making over a hundred dollars a day. That's a lot for me. I used to teach school 2 months for that."

5. Daughter, born 18 December 1931.

6. Daughter of Green's half-sister, Alda Long, who frequently stayed with the Greens and helped with household chores during the depression.

7. James Fowler, younger of two brothers whose grocery business later became Fowler's Food Store, which for many years offered credit and home delivery of food in Chapel Hill.

8. Owner of Strowd (Ford) Motor Company in Chapel Hill.

9. Noted along the left margin: "Say! Get your duds together and come on. Don't buy any clothes till you get here. And at night I can come home like any office man to supper and my wife."

10. Noted below signature: "I saw George Arliss today on the lot—nice old man." Arliss (1868–1946), who played the title roles in *Disraeli* (1929) and *Alexander Hamilton* (1931), would have the leading role in a later motion picture by Green, *Voltaire* (1933).

## 82. To Louis Graves[1]

First National Studios, Warner Brothers, Hollywood, Calif.
19 March 1932

Dear Louie—

Thanks for the paper and for the invitation to write a bit of Hollywood news for the same. I can't write anything on this place for the papers other than to say that I like my work and find working in the movies most interesting—you know.

But as to back behind scenes: I have kept rather much to myself and my job, though I've been out a few nights and times playing tennis on the marvelous courts of these fabulous stars. And on the few times I've been out with the crowd I've stepped along a bit high and a bit wide—the way Rome-stirred yokels have been wont to do since the first ages. This week-end I was invited to go up to Hearst's ranch some three-hundred miles away—where the old man of the wood-pulp sea keeps his dominion.[2] I decided not to go until Elizabeth comes, and if I get another chance we'll both go up and see what's to be seen.[3] The tales I hear of the place are—in the words of Lawrence Stallings[4]—incredible—such as a string of tinted swimming-pools of different

1. Louis Graves (1883–1965) founded *The Chapel Hill Weekly* in 1923 and remained its owner and editor until his death. Raised in Chapel Hill (his father was professor of mathematics at UNC), Graves graduated from UNC in 1902, went to New York City to work on *The New York Times*, enlisted in 1916 and served as a captain with the American Expeditionary Force in France, then returned to Chapel Hill in 1921 to join the Department of Journalism at UNC. On 1 March 1923 he brought out the first issue of the *Weekly*, and in the summer of 1924 resigned from UNC to devote full time to the paper. Shortly before the present letter he sent Green a copy of the paper and asked if he would contribute an article on life in Hollywood.

2. His estate at San Simeon was headquarters for the journalistic empire built by William Randolph Hearst (1863–1951), an empire consisting of up to thirty U.S. newspapers, numerous radio and motion picture companies, and several popular magazines.

3. Elizabeth was to arrive shortly with their infant daughter, Janet, leaving the older children in Chapel Hill under the care of Erna Lamprecht (on 29 March 1932 Green wrote to Barrett Clark: "Elizabeth and Janet are with me, and I am once more a married man and safe from the snares of the high glamorous hills" [PG-SHC]).

4. Fellow resident of North Carolina who burst into prominence as a writer with the production of *What Price Glory* (coauthored with Maxwell Anderson) in 1924,

temperatures—take your choice, John Gilbert, or Norma Talmadge,[5] or cute Marion Davies,[6] or anybody who wants to swim. They tell me too the old fellow is sinister and has several enslaved—several meaning I don't know what, and that he keeps agents in all lands buying trinkets to put on his ranch and in his house. He has just moved a large tree twenty-five feet across his patio—one of his patios—and signed with the contractor for $50,000 for the job—and he stood around sighting by the sun and the stars so much trying to get it right to his taste—all the while the hydraulic jacks and laborers waited on his fancy—that the poor contractor lost $50,000 on the job and was ready to make away with himself and W. R. said in his high quavery voice go ahead and do it—and so on.

I have designated Hollywood to myself as a land of the fur-coat disease. You know how it is in some places; one woman is under the weather if her neighbor has a fur coat and she has none—envy, desires for what the other one has if that what seems better than what you have. The same old story of the cow who keeps wandering on thinking the grass over there is better than it is here, not knowing that it's because the light lies on it different or some such little fact that has nothing to do with the grass—and this poor cow goes on and on until she starves to death while under her feet is all that she needs. Well, it's much that way here. This spurious urge or desire has caused the hills to be all cut up by thousands of roads—one person's palace overtopping another person's, higher and higher until someone more powerful with dollars or trickery gets his house right on the top. And love—love is everywhere—these actors drink their highball and discourse on love and say—not "I wonder who's kissing her now" as the old song went but "I wonder who's sleeping with her now" and all such biological gravy which they think is deep stuff and tragic as the woes of Dante. And polo—every other day I am invited by some fellow who plays to come out and see him do his stuff. So far I haven't been. I don't like to see [a] horse rid to death trying to catch a little ball—I'd rather run after it myself and call it tennis. Waste—plenty of it. Last night I was at a party high up in the hills—wealth like the days of Nero—and being a little full I kept asking did they hear somebody knocking at the door, and they

---

then went to Hollywood for varied motion picture work. He spelled his given name "Laurence."

5. Motion picture stars.

6. Hearst's mistress since about 1917. He had formed a motion picture company (Cosmopolitan Pictures) to give her a career.

said no—did I hear it? and I said yes I did and I believed it was the Niggers of eastern North Carolina hungry and cold trying to get in. For a moment we had the tramp's shadow in the room and we sat a bit quiet, and then we hoch'd our glasses again and had fun—all true according to the ways of history and Brother Spengler.[7] Not that I wanted to be priggish but that since I come of preacher stock and being thereby inclined both to foolishness and wisdom I every now and then have to speak a word for wisdom so I can be foolish again. All of which too fits in with Hollywood. I am of course speaking a few mouthfuls here descriptive of one phase of the place which I think most people believe is the reality of Hollywood. But it's not the whole truth. There are plenty of fine people—hard workers, honest, interested in the art of the moving-picture and determined to do something with it. In fact I'd say that is more typical of the place as I've seen it so far than the other. The other—with its lavishness, divorces, what I'd call again, the Hearsty side of life—is more spectacular and intriguingly shocking, and therefore is heard of more. But it's the minor part. For instance I come to my office at nine-thirty every day—except Sunday—eat a snack of lunch on the lot—and stay at my desk till five-thirty—Saturday afternoon included. That's the routine for writers, though they can break it if they wish. And the other departments work much harder, often all night, catching their rest God knows how. The reason I put so much emphasis on the Hearst phase above was that I too was first looking for that and first found it because that's what I was led to expect before I came.

Really though I like it here—I like writing for the camera—everything in pictures, one growing out of the other strung on a string of plot or rather the pictures spindling off the thread of story as they go. I've just finished the first draft of a story for Richard Barthelmess, and the director and supervisor say they like it very much.[8] They've let me write it the way I want it—haven't tried to tack on a happy ending or anything, though I don't know what they'll do to it when we come to making the film. It is much easier than writing plays, because your range is wider—you aren't confined by the difficulty of changing scenes as on the stage and you can get all sizes of relationships, comparison,

7. Oswald Spengler's *The Decline of the West* (trans. 1926–28) represented Western civilization as exhausted, without the emotional vitality to deal with the problems of life.

8. *Cabin in the Cotton*, released by Warner Brothers later in the year, depicted the hard lot of southern tenant farmers and an attempt by one of them to improve life for his family and friends. It starred Barthelmess and Bette Davis.

perspective, etc. In a way it is much like the Shakespearean stage—change your scene whenever you wish. And of course I like to make the money and be able to pay all my debts and have something ahead—something that's getting hard for me to do with the kind of plays I write for New York and the everlasting difficulty of getting them on there. I may go back to C.H. as soon as this short contract is up, though if they offer me more money for a few weeks I'll stay on till fall[9]—that is offer me enough so I can put away a good sum to protect Elizabeth and the kids if I fell off one of these high hills some night and broke my neck.—Well I've let my tongue run on two ways for Sunday. And the gossip is confidential. We'll get together when I come back.

## 83. To Theodore Dreiser

THE SCOTTSBORO CASE

An Open Letter to Theodore Dreiser[1]

Chapel Hill, N.C.[2]
11 April 1932

My dear Mr. Dreiser:

I am in receipt of another broadcast letter from the National Committee for the Defense of Political Prisoners, signed by you, Messrs Hyde, Heiman,

9. Green and his family would be in Hollywood much of the time through 1935, with several visits to Chapel Hill and some other travel. His first motion picture contract, referred to here, he signed with Warner Brothers on 7 January 1932 (Paul Green to Barrett Clark, 7 January 1932, PG-SHC). It was for eight weeks beginning on 29 February, at $625 per week, for work on *Cabin in the Cotton* (Paul Green to Jacob Wilk, 1 July 1932), and he extended it for five additional weeks to be present during the filming of the picture (Paul Green to Hal Wallis, 25 May 1932).

---

1. The International Labor Defense (ILD), a Communist organization based in New York City, had from the start protested the sentences of the black men in the Scottsboro Case as an example of class injustice. In the spring of 1933 the ILD would begin to provide legal counsel for the defendants in their trials and appeals, which continued throughout the decade (Clarence Norris and Sybil Washington, *The Last of the Scottsboro Boys* [New York: Putnam, 1979], pp. 249–55). To raise money the ILD created a "National Committee for the Defense of Political Prisoners," a paper organization consisting in the main of prominent writers and scholars. Sherwood Anderson, Franz Boas, Malcolm Cowley, and Lewis Mumford typify the sixty-two "members" listed on ILD stationery used when appealing for funds. Green received

and M. P. Levy, in which further aid is requested for the seven[3] condemned Negro boys at Scottsboro. I can answer by saying that even if I were able, I should not enclose any contribution to your organization, for I know it would do no good.

Mr. Dreiser, I also have written, agonized, talked and prayed over the Scottsboro case just as you have, and each day I have seen these boys twenty-four hours nearer death. And did you know that one of the reasons why they are so set and bound for the electric chair is that you and your ignorant but well-wishing friends continue to hang your political theories around their necks. It would seem by this time that you would see where your activities are leading and would try to apply your efforts solely and singly towards preventing this deep damnation and their taking-off. But you don't. You keep on stirring up trouble by linking your half-baked Marxism and social therapies to the race question, and thereby prepare seven blind and dumb but suffering victims for more certain sacrifice. And why?

Do you think that such an offering up of helpless blood and woe will aid in changing our system of government and bring about a social regeneration for a hundred and twenty million people, less these seven doomed to die? If you do you are more confused than I thought you were. Forms of government are still debatable matters, as are the might and rights appertaining thereto. But there is no debate over the need of saving these Negro children. Then why in the name of high heaven are you so bent upon their destruction?

You ask for contributions. Ten thousand dollars are needed at once you say. Well, let me tell you that ten times ten thousand and ten times that won't pull these boys loose from the communistic symbolism in which you and your friends have sought to "frame" them. You and they seem determined to make it appear that they are political prisoners. They are not such and never have been. They are prisoners to a Southern—yes, a local attitude of ignorance, prejudice, hate and fear if you will. And anything in God's world that incites to making that attitude more powerful and uncompromising is that much

---

an appeal dated 31 March 1932 and signed by Dreiser, Melvin P. Levy, secretary of the committee, and two members of ILD, Maxwell Hyde and Julius Heiman (PG-SHC). Green was moved to reply to the appeal in an *open* letter because in the list of members on the stationery, between C. Hartley Grattan and Horace Gregory, he found his own name.

2. Green, in Los Angeles, wanted it understood that he spoke as a southerner.

3. That is, eight.

more certain to bring all seven to death. You have lived in this country long enough to know that, and yet you go on sending out your letters and your statements which at every turn lug in your theories and mouthings about capital and labor and oppression of the worker. The judgment levied against these boys has nothing to do with capital or labor or with any workers' government or system of politics and economics whatsoever. They are condemned to die because as Negroes they attacked Southern white women, or were supposed to. And it is blindness and perversity in the face of facts for you to write to me saying "The majority opinion of the court, if it is not overthrown, establishes a precedent by which workers, especially Negroes, will finally be excluded from American juries. The State of Alabama, it reads, may exclude 'Negroes from the venire' without depriving 'defendants of their constitutional rights.' The decision also attempts to establish the 'right' to 'fix the qualifications of jurors' in such an arbitrary way that workers shall in the future be tried only by representatives of the class opposed to the establishment of their rights. Probably not since the Dred Scott decision[4] has there been a court decision which is so openly and vitally aimed, not only at the American black worker, but at the American working class."

Bosh—Mr. Dreiser—Bosh! And even if you believed this you ought to think twice before you said it.

So in behalf of thousands of Southern men and women who are hoping and believing that Alabama will somehow restrain herself from wholesale murder, I write to assure you again that while you and your friends call for help you also at the same time are helping to send to certain death those whom you say you'd like to save. Please, Mr. Dreiser, throw away your politics and your theories this once and pray and work with us that mercy be done! For it would be an everlasting sin for you to use the bones of seven Negro boys to hammer the drums of a social revolution. Nothing that Alabama is likely to do could ever equal the shame of that.

Yours, Paul Green

4. U.S. Supreme Court decision in 1857 that a slave had no legal rights under the Constitution.

## 84. To Laurence Stallings[1]

Warner Brothers, Inc., Burbank, Calif.
22 April 1932

Dear Laurence—

Thanks for all the news you have given me about North Carolina. It makes me smell, taste, and live what I have temporarily left. I wish I had a lot of news and local color to send you which might in turn fill you with what you have left here—but I'm afraid your subject matter there puts it all over mine—so that you and Helen might decide to set forth in this direction. I have no news. We've been up to Eleanor's[2] once or twice, down to Kiss Bird of Paradeyes (see how I can Movie Gag),[3] and round and about a few times to shows, etc. My first script[4] is finished, turned in, and tests are being made. Zanuck[5] has complimented me, and asked me to stay on awhile, which I've agreed to do, not having to be back in New York until about the first of September. I have just come from the test room or stage, and one of the fellows (the once Little Colonel of *Birth of a Nation*) brought forth my unmanly tears by saying two or three lines about "I want Marvin to be something—I—I ain't never been nothing"—standing there in his old broken shoes, his hands hung down—hung down so low, Lord—with the raspy cotton-stalks about him and the light dying in his eyes.[6] I am on the verge of signing a fanfare sheet with

1. Laurence Stallings (1894–1968), raised in Macon, Georgia, attended Wake Forest College and after service with the U.S. Marines in France during World War I joined the *New York World* in 1921 as book review editor. In 1924 he published a novel, *Plumes*, and collaborated with Maxwell Anderson on the play, *What Price Glory*. In 1925 he went to Hollywood for the filming of *The Big Parade*, a successful motion picture based on his story of the same title. He had married Helen Poteat, daughter of the president of Wake Forest College, and after 1925 the couple spent most of their time in Hollywood but maintained a summer home in Caswell County, North Carolina. Shortly before the present letter they had left Hollywood for Caswell County.

2. Eleanor Boardman, actress and estranged wife of director King Vidor.

3. Vidor was currently at work on the motion picture *Bird of Paradise*, which starred Dolores Del Rio, his current companion.

4. *Cabin in the Cotton*.

5. Darryl Zanuck, chief production executive at Warner Brothers.

6. Henry B. Walthall, the Little Colonel in *The Birth of a Nation* (1915), played Blake, Marvin's father, in *Cabin in the Cotton*. His lines, in response to the landowner's order to put Marvin back to work in the fields, are: "(*Standing up, quivering*)

Dreiser, Dos Passos, and other reds for May Day, calling on all the helpless and poor to rise up. If I had less sense—or Scotch canniness or something bad, I'd do it.[7] Anyhow I'm sending an open letter to Mr. Dreiser in answer to his, begging him and his ignorant friends to help save the boys in Scottsboro. (I'll tell you about my quarrel—though this poor tenant farmer a few minutes ago was about to make me forget it—with Dreiser and the fool ILD crowd.)

Jim has ruined my eyes with his letter.[8] He is such an artist that he makes me want to read what he says, and he's such a master of foxhounds that he makes the trail to find it out eye-blinding. I did decipher the news that you bore my ungallant remarks about the red tiles of Hollywood with manly fortitude. Now Jim's wrong, and it hurts my heart to say that Jim is wrong in anything. He's wrong here however, for my remarks were not ungallant. They were complimentary, and the reason I begged your pardon to Jim was for the style, not for the subject I was telling about. So they must have been gallant—anyhow so-so gallant.[9]

My typewriter gal just tells me (she is not here now, and I'm writing this alone) that Max A.[10] called up while I was out. I called him two weeks ago. He was out, and I've heard nothing till now as to where he is or what state his soul is in. I think I'll have to look around, for he's one of the brethren and may

---

Marvin—Marvin will be something—I ain't—I ain't never been—nothing—nothing—I want him to go to school. (*He falls to coughing and grips his forehead in his two hands*)" (*Cabin in the Cotton*, unpublished screenplay, scene 21, Paul Green Collection, NCC).

7. The "fanfare sheet," unlocated, was written by Edmund Wilson, Lewis Mumford, and Waldo Frank and sent to eight others for endorsement: Dreiser, Sherwood Anderson, Robert Frost, John Dos Passos, Van Wyck Brooks, Evelyn Scott, Edna Millay, and Green (Edmund Wilson to Paul Green, 14 April 1932, PG-SHC).

8. James Boyd, novelist living in Southern Pines, North Carolina, in whose handwriting each letter of the alphabet resembles a tiny dash.

9. In a recent letter Boyd said the Stallings were visiting when a letter arrived from Green and that Stallings "bore your ungallant inferences to his favorite tiles with manly fortitude, convinced that you're a great man (this is true) and therefore not to be taken seriously" (James Boyd to Paul Green, 10 April 1932, PG-SHC). Green's remark, perhaps at the expense of Southern California architecture, is not given.

10. Following production of his *Night Over Taos* by the Group Theatre in March, Maxwell Anderson went to Hollywood for work on several motion picture scripts. During the spring and summer there he also wrote the play *Both Your Houses* (Laurence G. Avery, ed., *Dramatist in America: Letters of Maxwell Anderson, 1912–1958* [Chapel Hill: University of North Carolina Press, 1977], p. xliv).

need to consult a preacher being as how he's where he is and seeing as how Collier Cobb[11] says we're largely what we are because we're where we are, the which I read reversed so far as writers are concerned, including myself to begin with, and therefore feeling it necessary to see Max, for it was said before Aesop preached that in safety there is numbers.

Elizabeth likes it here. We still live in the mill-shack. Every morning at dawn she glides from the bed and feeds her young, and I look with sleepy eyes through the patch of window pane and[12]

## 85. To Hal Wallis[1]

[Warner Brothers, Inc., Burbank, Calif.]
24 May 1932

To Mr. Wallis
From Mr. Paul Green

I've read the synopsis of the Match King story, and think it a first-class piece of work—of its kind. The opening is direct and pictorially fine, and the course of the tale thereafter straight and to the point. Only one or two things I'd mention contrariwise; namely, a reference might be made among the dancers near the opening that Kroll (Krueger) is not always above-board in his dealings—so that his arrangements with the Italian crook on the seashore won't come as a sudden shock to the audience. Again, the use of a certain Scandinavian movie star to seduce a New York banker for Kroll's purposes is a little bit surprising. But all in all, I think the story is good. However I'm sure you have writers here who could do a more satisfactory screen play out of it than I could, for it's not exactly down my alley.

And since my suggestions concerning a negro original don't quite fit in with your plans at this time, I suppose my services for the present are at an end. I

11. Professor of geology at UNC.

12. Surviving portion of the letter breaks off here.

1. Hal Wallis (1899–1986), who in 1944 would form his own motion picture company, Hal Wallis Productions, Incorporated, was at the time of the present letter chief studio manager at Warner Brothers. For him Green had looked over the outline for a gangster movie, *The Match King*, based on a novel of the same title by Einar Thorvaldson and released as a motion picture in December 1932, with screenplay by Houston Branch and Sidney Sutherland.

have enjoyed my work here—specially my association with you and others in the production of *Cabin in the Cotton.* And if you, in the future, should have a job dealing with mine workers, farmers, negroes, or underdogs in general, I should be glad to come and do it for you—to the best of my ability.

I would regret very much if my going at this time should in any way affect Miss Ridgeway's[2] position here in the studio. She has been of great service to me, and I'm sure her abilities would mean much to any other writer with whom she might be associated. I believe she could do very satisfactory continuity, for she evidently knows the development of a screen play from every angle.

## 86. To Darryl Zanuck[1]

[Chapel Hill, N.C.]
22 July 1932

My dear Mr. Zanuck:

Herewith is the Prologue to *Cabin in the Cotton.* You will see that it is not exactly in the terms you requested, the reasons being as I see them—

First, that a prologue spoken by a third person will be a bit extraneous and not in the mood and character of the picture.

Second, that a two-minute explanation of the intricacies of cotton tenantry, book-keeping, marketing, etc. will tend to confuse the audience with matters more or less unimportant to the true meaning of the story—such meaning being the effort of Marvin Blake to find his place among the antagonisms of his enslaving environment.[2] And, too, I think these aforesaid particulars are

2. She had been his secretary.

---

1. Darryl Zanuck (1902–1979), who in 1933 would form his own motion picture company, Twentieth Century Pictures, was at the time of the present letter chief production executive at Warner Brothers. With the script of *Cabin in the Cotton* finished and most of the shooting done, the Greens returned to Chapel Hill at the end of May. Zanuck then asked Green to write a prologue for the film, the point of which, Green said facetiously, was that "neither the writer, nor director, nor producer has any quarrel to pick with either labor or capital" (Paul Green to Laurence Stallings, 22 July 1932, PG-SHC).

2. In the film Marvin Blake, son of a Mississippi tenant farmer, gains a little education, is employed by a landowner, then is caught up in a bloody feud between

made clear enough in the picture itself without having to repeat them in a prologue.

However, I do feel that the sort of prologue I am sending you is not amiss, for—

First, it gives a general introduction of the subject to the audience—the historical placing of the story, a few of the facts surrounding the present situation as to class struggle, etc.

Second, it gives the author and producers a chance to make clear to the audience that their concern is not with pleading the virtues or evils of either side but their sole concern is the presenting of the story with its attendant truthful facts.

May I suggest that this prologue appear on the screen in simply designed words to be read by the audience rather than heard from a spokesman. Also, I think it would be well not to have the atmospheric shots which you mention nor the soft singing of a negro chorus. If an orchestration accompanies the prologue as it appears on the screen, I think the effect would be more in keeping with the total effect desired. If you decide upon having an orchestra, I suggest that the mingled music of "Go Down Moses," "Way Up On the Mountain," and "Willie the Weeper" be played. In case the prologue as written is too long to be lettered on the screen, parts of it could be cut out, as you will see in reading it.

If I were not so anxious that *Cabin in the Cotton* get over and say its say I would not be so full of suggestions. Therefore please charge my extreme care to my exceeding interest.[3]

Sincerely yours

encl.

---

owner and tenants. He resolves the feud by showing both sides that it is in their interests to cooperate with one another.

3. The film as released follows Green's ideas about the prologue and uses "Go Down, Moses" as accompaniment.

## 87. To Sherwood Anderson[1]

Chapel Hill, N.C.
5 August 1932

My dear Mr. Anderson—

Your letter is a follow-up of Theodore Dreiser's and I wish I had time to answer at length what I answered him. The Scottsboro case in the beginning was not a political matter—politics and social theories were injected into it as you know. I have been suspicious of the I. L. D. activities from the beginning, for, in general, I am inclined to believe that one has to take this world piecemeal, and the I. L. D. crowd, with their social therapy would go whole hog or not a hair. The murder of the Scottsboro boys would like as not foster their ends more than hinder them, for the cross, symbol of martyrdom, is one of the most powerful tokens for rallying the mass. But my interest is in the particular saving of these particular boys. And now that the I. L. D. has got control of the matter, there's nothing for me to do but hope that their hearts will be touched at the crucial moment by the pity of the case rather than by the abstract significance of a sacrifice.[2] Therefore I am once more contributing what I am able to. But frankly—but frankly—

Sincerely yours, Paul Green

1. In June 1932 the U.S. Supreme Court agreed to review the Alabama court's convictions in the Scottsboro Case, and the review was set for October. Green spent most of July at the University of Iowa, where E. C. Mabie produced *Tread the Green Grass*, and on his return to Chapel Hill he found another request from the International Labor Defense for money to be used in the Scottsboro appeal, this request signed by Sherwood Anderson and similar to the recent one signed by Dreiser (see letter 83).

2. Green wrote, "by the abstract significance of a sacrifice—yes, a blood sacrifice," then marked out the concluding phrase.

## 88. To W. O. Saunders[1]

7647 Mulholland Highway, Los Angeles, Calif.
24 September 1932

Dear Mr. Saunders:

I am very glad to know that the Roanoke Island Historical Association is still going strong, and I regret my absence from the working. Won't you please keep me informed as to what goes on, for I am still dedicated to the job of writing the story of Virginia Dare and England's first settlement in America. I can be reached here at the [above] address.

With best wishes always.

## 89. To John Dos Passos[1]

7647 Mulholland Highway, Los Angeles, Calif.
26 October 1932

Dear Dos Passos—

Day and night it comes to me that the Scottsboro human sham can be endured no more and that a march of the righteous is demanded. But I tell myself we must be patient—the arms we bear are brittle and on the day and hour of waiting grace we must expend our strength—and not till then. Will

1. W. O. Saunders (1884–1940), crusading editor of the Elizabeth City, North Carolina, *Independent*, was chairman of the Roanoke Island Historical Association, founded in November 1931 to "celebrate . . . the birth of English-speaking civilization on Roanoke Island, Dare County, N. C., by Sir Walter Raleigh and his Colonists in the years 1584 and 1587 . . . and to commemorate the three hundred and fiftieth anniversary thereof" (association charter of 8 January 1932, in William S. Powell, *Paradise Preserved: A History of the Roanoke Island Historical Association and Related Organizations* [Chapel Hill: University of North Carolina Press, 1965], p. 135). Green, whose interest centered on the play proposed for the occasion, was a member of the association, and Saunders wrote that the association would meet on 10 September to plan a fund-raising drive for financing the play (W. O. Saunders to Paul Green, 5 September 1932, PG-SHC).

1. John Dos Passos (1896–1970), novelist and student of American life, now served as treasurer of the ILD's Committee for the Defense of Political Prisoners and had sent yet another request for funds to support the appeals of the death sentences handed down by the Alabama court in the Scottsboro Case. The appeals were now before the U.S. Supreme Court.

Cohen[2] let me know by collect wire if the U.S. Supreme Court's verdict is against the boys—when it comes through[?] Here is $25, all I can spare at this moment, and I wish it were many times that. I have spoken to several people here but received only sympathy, so far no funds. But there are other ways they will help in time. I'm sure of it.

Irrespective of creed, profession or politics, there is one duty ahead of us all—the freeing of the Scottsboro boys; or else we stand accursed at the bar of justice, and our children, our children's children, will live their lives under the degradation and futility of our failure.

Think of it—Roy Wright 15, Eugene Williams 14[3] still behind the bars—after 18 months! And no hope in sight! As I write these words they might be out playing cat with other boys in the alley, or tag, or helping in the fields, or fishing down at the old swimming hole—breathing the fresh air—happy—boys.[4] But all this while, the sovereign state of Alabama, the "pride" and prejudice of an erring system keeps them shackled in the shade of death.

My God what are we—men or brutes! Is this the doing of the South of our fathers—the land that gave us Lee, Washington, Jefferson and a vision of justice to all—yes, even kindness to children. I am doing what I can, so please let me hear as matters go on.[5]

Yours, Paul Green

## 90. To Frederick H. Koch

[7647 Mulholland Highway, Los Angeles, Calif.]
14 December 1932

Dear Proff—[1]

Thanks for the programs and the two articles of your own which you sent me. Reading them brought a lump into my throat—and you'd never guess

2. Elliot E. Cohen, secretary of the Committee for the Defense of Political Prisoners.

3. Youngest two of the defendants.

4. Green wrote "happy—just boys," then crossed out "just."

5. On 7 November 1932 the Supreme Court overturned the convictions on the grounds that the defendants had not received adequate counsel and ordered new trials.

---

1. Koch had sent Green programs from recent Playmakers productions, among them *Uncle Tom's Cabin,* and also copies of two Koch articles, "Making a Regional

why. But I'll tell you when I come back to Chapel Hill. I enjoyed every bit of them. The picture of the old lady, and "the fish she calls 'little red fins' "—was right, for we live by pictures, you know; and the gourd, and the old rifle above the door.[2] Before I leave here I hope to persuade some of these blind behemoths of talkie industry to let me write a real folk movie—with plenty of silence and pantomime, and plenty of concurrent music, something that flows on like the days and nights of the softly breathing and deep-breasted earth—if I do say so. There are such wonderful things to be done here that I view with more and more astonishment the waste over trash and the perversion of the spirit. Like the imaginative word the camera is absolute in its power and as yet only in rare instances has anyone in Hollywood exhibited any use of that power. I hope to do so before I leave. Since the red-letter day back in 1906 or 7 when I stood under a tent with my moist hand in my father's hard dry one and saw a man on a little screen tumble from a board into a pool and back again I have been hypnotized by the movie camera. I have always wanted to get my finger on the thing and see what could be done. Now I am pretty close by it, but as yet haven't been able to project my intentions on the screen—only in the faintest way. I struggled hard for a certain beauty and rhythmic flow in *Cabin in the Cotton*, with the blind chorus of the old Negro weaving in and out and singing "In the darkess night, Lawd, wid haid hung down so low," but could not persuade these folks that I was right.[3] And so in the compromise I kept the picture pretty much free of hokum and they kept it jerky, wooden and too often dull. But sometime I shall do a sort of dark Lear of the Fields if I have to hire my own company and do it independently—that is if I ever have the money to do it. And the trees, the flowers that stand in the hedgerow lifting up their little throats in a hymn to the rising sun, the dark form of the

---

Drama," (*Bulletin of the American Library Association*, August 1932, pp. 1–8) and "A Log-Cabin Theatre" (*Carolina Play-Book*, September 1932).

2. "A Log-Cabin Theatre" told of Koch's visit to a rural community near Chapel Hill where the local schoolteacher, Genevieve Woodson, had inspired the building of a theater. After the evening bill of folk plays, local ballad singer Mammy Jones sang "Barbara Allen" and the next day showed Koch her farm, including the creek where she caught " 'cats' (catfish), perch, and little fish that she calls 'red-fins.' " When he admired it, she also gave him the gourd she had made into a bait bucket. In the margin of the letter next to this passage Green noted, "Blessed are the folk!"

3. Green's film script calls for much music: spirituals, folk songs, even some jazz. The blind black man, a brooding spirit outside the action, appears several times, playing the guitar and singing.

ploughman and his mule going down the fat slope, the cattle—and then that great square house and the volcanic soul that lives therein at war with man and God; how in his old age he sets out on the road in search of the victory vision, to find it in a young girl drawing water at a well; how he stops there to renew his life and warm his hands again at the fire of youth; and how of course nature and biology laugh him down; and finally amid the cold night squeaks of the fence rat and mouse he meets himself face to face and in that deep and mystic communion glimpses a truth strong enough to lean his weary heart on in death. It sounds a little far-fetched perhaps, but if I ever do it (and how many others I know could be done) it will speak for itself. After all man—everyman—is born a searcher, and the parable of man's days is: born with a hunger, then the unconscious reaching out for that which will satisfy that hunger, follows the entanglement in the vines and underbrush of the world, then the struggle to be free, at last freedom, and the first state of life reaffirmed and made conscious and complete in the last. This being the pattern, there are an infinite number of permutations and combinations of characters, manners, time, places, etc. in which the pattern can be worked out, and each new and refreshing in turn. Or in other words, representation (rhythmic representation) is art, and like the sea of deepest deeps, like the space of widest space, like love of essential love, like the hope of eternal hope, is eternal and everlasting and offers the privilege of abnegation and therefore the finding of the self in its service. By this I simply mean that old sermon thesis that we have in our reach that which can sustain us to the end. If we can only believe that, serve that, and hold firm. But so often that dull matter of our bodies which Plato knew so well would darken our counsel and trip us into the slough.[4] Be strong, my soul, the arms you bear are brittle. Now and then walking along, or reading a good book, or remembering a friend, or hoping for something, or writing a little scene as I did in Will Rogers' and Janet Gaynor's next picture[5] where the summer cloud-shaped light ripples along over the alfalfa and a bird slips downward racing along its edge[6]—most anywhere in fact one can glimpse that other world of the—well, spirit with which he is surrounded. The manifest

4. Noted in the margin: "And Freud of course has not helped us with his dire 'unconscious.' "

5. *State Fair*, based on Phil Strong's novel and released by Fox Film Corporation in 1933.

6. Noted in the margin: "And watch, it will be left out for lack of time."

calling is to see more and more the visions of that world, to hear more and more the voices that are talking there. It's hard to do it, isn't it, when one has to bother with taxes, the senseless upboiling facts of present-day history, the hunger and injustice and evil that we do to ourselves, and the too human urge to climb materially over our fellows? But a theory I spoke to myself long ago is that difficulties are opportunities, so shoulder to the collar and keep the wheel turning! Or else the dust that shall cover our mute lips is the only truth those lips shall speak.

I have just finished a long pulling in the collar—a picture on the life of one of the greatest and weakest men that ever lived, Monsieur François-Marie Arouet, nicknamed Voltaire. And now that it is finished the New York office is saying that in these hard times it will make no money, and it better be deferred. Arliss was or is to play the part, and it's a good script if I did write it. I have put more of the camera and less of the blatant sound track in it than usual with pictures of late. And always there is to be music accompanying the action. One scene I especially like is a dream scene at the King's court in Versailles—Voltaire a little Jeremiah figure lost there in the great idle and sensual crowds, his appealing to Louis XV to awake to the needs of his people, how the people and the king's chamber orchestra titter at him, how he flees from the scenes of debauchery, out through the great gardens lighted by hobgoblin and Japanese lanterns, now by the Temple of love and the delicate cold lips of Psyche in the arms of Eros saying in elfin voice—"Hee-hee-hee," then by the colonnade and the stone rapist holding a woman aloft in his arms, looking down at him while from his heavy lips we hear "Ho—ho—ho!," and on by the fountain where the great dragon with wide dark wings lifted as if in flight, his head struck downward to seize his prey, and up from his deep belly the iron tones belched—"Huh-huh-huh!," and so on. But I bet you even if the picture is made that this purely camera and musical scene will be left out.[7] Well, since I came here I have read everything I can on the movies, studied the subject from every angle even to acquainting myself with sound track and reproduction devices, and I feel that I'm beginning to know a little something about this one of the greatest art mediums in the world—if not the greatest, if we except the poetical and imaginative *word.* At this moment I am sure that only two really worthwhile things have come out of American movies—the

7. *Voltaire,* with George Arliss in the title role, was released by Warner Brothers in 1933—without the scene described.

one Charlie Chaplin, the other Walt Disney's cartoons of Mickey Mouse and Silly Symphonies.[8] In fact the two greatest actors in the American screen world are Charlie Chaplin and Mickey Mouse. This simple fact if closely studied will give light on the meaning and method of the camera as an art medium.

I have been asked by different magazines to write something on the movies, but as yet I haven't done so for the reason that I had not formulated my findings. But now I think I am beginning to see what it's all about, and so your invitation to do a short article for The Play-Book suits me to a T. I will sit down at once and write out a short statement hoping you won't mind if I become philosophical and mathematical in places.[9]

By the way, Proff, I have just had lunch with the president of the University of Hawaii. He is looking for a man to come out to his University this summer for six weeks as a sort of visiting scholar, beginning the last of June, ending the first week in August—someone who will lecture on drama, give a course in playwriting. The work is not heavy, about four or five hours' lecturing a week. The pay is $1,000.00 (one thousand) and no transportation. Would you be interested? As yet the matter has only been spoken of in general terms, and the exact offer would not be certain one way or the other until January 1, or later. It would make a fine vacation for you and Mrs. Koch wouldn't it? I told him about you since he seemed ignorant on American dramatic matters. And if you are interested—I have no idea what will come of it—I will ask him to write to you.[10] But what about this pageant at Roanoke? Is anything to be done this summer?[11] Excuse my hasty way of writing,[12] but I know you understand what I've tried to say. And thanks for the programs. The students seem to be doing things. Ever to you, my love to the class.

8. Animated cartoons begun in 1928 and based on fables or other folk motifs such as "The Three Little Pigs" (1935) and "The Ugly Duckling" (1938).

9. See "Apropos Questions Concerning the Cinema," *Carolina Play-Book*, September 1933, pp. 65–67.

10. Koch was already scheduled to spend the summer of 1933 at the University of Colorado (Frederick Koch to Paul Green, 13 January 1933, PG-SHC).

11. Koch, like Green, was a member of the Roanoke Island Historical Association, which was beginning to plan the celebration of the 350th anniversary of English colonization in America.

12. Actually the letter exists in two drafts, the second a careful revision of the first.

## 91. To Elizabeth Bab[1]

[15205 De Pauw St., Los Angeles, Calif.]
29 April 1933

My dear Frau Bab—

Your letter has been forwarded to me here, and as you know it fills me with great sadness. To think that such kindly, generous and talented people as you and your husband should have to endure these foolish woes of politics. It is shameful. Your bravery and calmness far surpass mine, for I should, by this time, be languishing in some iron cell—because of my outbreaks. (Elizabeth shares this feeling, naturally, and the children of course still remember the benign god—as they thought Herr Bab to be.) I can only hope that this situation is as brief as it is irrational.

Now as for something to be done here: The situation in this country is as you know acutely troublous. We have millions of people out of work, and I do not see how any position suitable to yours or Herr Bab's capabilities could be obtained. However, I am speaking to Samuel French with the hope that Barrett Clark—who has more possibilities at his finger tips than any man I know—can do something. Also I have given as much publicity to the matter as I can.

In the meantime our love and affection always.[2]

Sincerely yours,

1. Green met the Babs during his stay in Berlin in 1928–29. Both Elizabeth and her husband Julius were much involved with the drama. Julius (1880–1955) helped establish the Volks Bühne in Berlin early in the century and wrote prolifically on the drama, the five volumes of his *Die Chronik des deutschen dramas* appearing between 1921 and 1926. Elizabeth, formerly an actress, translated several of Green's plays and through Osterheld in Berlin published her translation of *In Abraham's Bosom* in 1929. Recently she wrote Green about the repression of Jews in Germany, especially one thing not often in the papers "because it is less outrageously springing into the eyes than the other things. That is the way in which people like my husband are cut off from any possibility of using their gifts in writing, speaking, and saying their opinion. No paper dares talking anything critical, the firms (publishers etc.) are obliged to dismiss Jews. . . . Things are so dreadful in this respect that it is impossible to outsay it" (28 March 1933, PG-SHC). She closed by asking if Green knew of any job for her husband in the United States.

2. Green maintained contact with the Babs through their son, who lived on Long Island. In 1938 the Babs escaped from Germany and spent the next two years in Paris,

## 92. To Frank J. Sheil

[15205 De Pauw St., Los Angeles, Calif.]
27 June 1933

My dear Mr. Sheil:[1]

I am more than glad to follow your suggestion in your letter of June 20th, for as you know, I have always deeply appreciated your kindness and generosity in helping me out when I happened to need help. Some weeks, almost months ago, I planned to take care of my account with you, and then came along the sale of *The House of Connelly.* But those matters drag on day after day, as I have found out, and the amount due from that was slow and still is slow in coming in.[2] However, I had expected that my part of the sale would be paid directly to you, and if there is any way of arranging that the remaining payments come directly to you, please let me know, for that will save sending the checks for endorsement here and back again. Of course, I make no particular point of this.[3]

---

before getting to the United States on the last day of 1940 (Elizabeth Bab to Paul Green, 13 January 1941). Julius Bab became drama critic for the New York *Staats Zeitung.*

---

1. Over the years, when Green needed sums of several hundred dollars, Samuel French advanced the money in exchange for a percentage of the future earnings of one of his plays. When he needed smaller amounts, French loaned him the money at no interest. Such loans now totaled $1,857.44. In May Fox Films bought motion picture rights to *The House of Connelly* for $15,000, to be paid half down and half in three installments. Sheil recently sent Green a check for $599.98 ($600 less $.02 check tax), author's share of one installment, and asked if Green could apply it to his debt at Samuel French, saying "this is the time of year when capital is very much needed in this business, since we are entering the dead part of the season" (20 June 1933, PG-SHC).

2. The sale was complicated and had to be handled by an arbiter, who resolved it as follows: 45 percent ($6,750) to Theatre Guild; 24 percent ($3,600) to Green; 21 percent ($2,400) to Samuel French (purchased interest in the play); 6.5 percent ($1,725) commission divided between French and Green's new West Coast agent Hunter Lovelace; and 3.5 percent ($525) to arbiter (Samuel French records, 1933, PG-SHC).

3. By September 1933, when the last of his three installments of $599.98 was applied to it, Green's debt at Samuel French was $57.50 (Frank Sheil to Paul Green, 12 September 1933, PG-SHC).

As I wrote Mr. Clark some time ago, I have entered in upon an agreement with Mr. Lovelace with the understanding that a half or five percent, of his commission from my movie earnings, future or past, are to go to you. (May I suggest the possibility of French's authors and French's manuscripts finding a very direct and efficient worker for movie contacts in Mr. Lovelace?) He informs me that he is somewhat behind in payments to you and will bring matters up to date as soon as possible. I have nothing to do with that, of course, and I merely mention for your information that your five percent of my earnings so far out here amounts to around two thousand dollars.[4]

We hope to be back east the latter part of July and my further hope is to bring a new play up to you folks early in the Fall.[5]

With warmest regards,

As always, Paul Green

## 93. To Sarah Gertrude Knott[1]

Chapel Hill, N.C.
17 July 1933

My dear Miss Knott:

As the frog said to the tick, you got hold of something big. Really I think the folk festival idea a grand thing, and I heartily endorse it with every high hope. While reading your letter I began to think of the World's Fair and Norman Bel Geddes' plans for a great dramatic get-together there.[2] It is old

4. Green had been in Hollywood since mid-August, 1932, and the $40,000 implied here was for writing *Voltaire* and working on scripts of several other movies for Warner Brothers and Fox.

5. A dramatization of his novel, *The Laughing Pioneer.*

---

1. Sarah Gertrude Knott grew up in eastern North Carolina, taught drama at Chowan College (1922–27), came to Chapel Hill as state representative of the Carolina Dramatic Association (1927–28), then joined the Missouri Board of Education in St. Louis, where she established the Dramatic League of the city and directed a number of historical pageants. Recently she wrote to Green about her plans for a National Folk Festival in St. Louis in the spring of 1934, at the opening of the new Municipal Auditorium, and asked for his suggestions (25 June [1933], PG-SHC).

2. Hoping to organize an elaborate drama festival as part of the 1933 Chicago World's Fair, Bel Geddes sent a letter outlining his plans to twenty-nine of "the world's leaders in the arts," including Green (2 August 1929, PG-SHC). (Among other

history now that the Geddes idea failed to come through, but his plans were sound just as yours are sound, for they are based upon a vital curiosity and a vital self-expressive need in all of us—Negro, Indian, Polak, Gentile, Jew. I prophesy that if you work this festival up, St. Louis will have such a good time that it will be weeks before it will stop dancing and cutting capers. The country at large has reached a stage of interest in folk art where a national folk festival now and then would be a great thing. In a small way the same idea was tried here at the University of North Carolina this spring in what they called the Dogwood Festival.[3] Folk dances were given, exhibits of folk art were held, there were music, singing, and all the rest. A good time was had by all, and people opened their eyes at the products of the still but indefatigable artistic urge that keeps working (and how often so blindly) in each of us. I imagine your national folk festival would have the same success in manifold as this Dogwood Festival had here.

The only draw-back as I see it to your idea as a whole is the fact that the festival is to be held on occasion of the New Municipal Auditorium opening. There seems to be a little smacking of over-civic pride and gratulation. I mean that the dress looks finer than the wearer, for the generation of a national thing around a local building suggests something of the cart before the horse. But if much were made of the festival and little of the Auditorium, perhaps a proper balance would be kept. After all the main purpose and meaning of the Auditorium would be that it offers a place (I imagine it is large enough, convenient enough and so on) for the festival.

If I can be of any help to you whatever, please call upon me.[4]

Sincerely yours,

---

recipients were Granville Barker, Josef Capek, Jean Cocteau, Robert Edmond Jones, Eugene O'Neill, Pablo Picasso, Luigi Pirandello, Max Reinhardt, Constantin Stanislavsky, and Igor Stravinsky.) On the fairgrounds Bel Geddes planned to have six or eight theaters. Well before the start of the fair he would assemble a group of directors and a larger group of actors who would begin to rehearse plays selected from those submitted by promising young playwrights from all over the world. He hoped Green and the other recipients of his letter would send him the names of appropriate playwrights, directors, and actors.

3. Held in Chapel Hill on Saturday, 29 April 1933 (*Chapel Hill Weekly*, 28 April 1933, p. 1, col. 1).

4. Green became chairman of the National Advisory Committee for the festival, which developed into an annual event, with Knott as executive director (Paul Green to Sarah Gertrude Knott, 2 August and 15 September 1933, PG-SHC).

P.S. One of the problems will be to keep local merchant commerce out of your plan but it can be done.

## 94. To Mrs. O. L. Dossett[1]

[Chapel Hill, N.C.]
26 July 1933

My dear Lady:

My first impulse was to give you a very stern lecture, but the mother of a beautiful daughter deserves better consideration—in spite of her wish to get such a daughter into the movies. The place for your little child is at home and in school. Why you should be selfish enough to wish to exhibit her up and down the land and especially in Hollywood is beyond me. I have had the privilege of dealing with a few mothers and their babies who were Hollywood crazy, and the only hope for them I felt was to get back to their normal life as quickly as possible. Later when your child grows up and has some will and life of her own then if she is still beautiful she can make a choice for herself. As for the present moment I will take no part in your considerations of methods to maim her future.

After all it seems I have lectured you. Please forgive me, for I assure you I mean you no harm—nothing but good. Please take my advice and forget all about Hollywood and see that your baby learns to read Mother Goose, play games and has a natural life.

Sincerely yours,

1. Green came home in early July, and Mrs. O. L. Dossett (name unclear; may be Dussen), who lived on a rural route near Durham, North Carolina, wrote to him: "I was reading in the paper about your return from Hollywood. . . . As I have a beautiful and talented daughter age six, who has won several beauty prizes, among them she won first prize in N.Y. Brooklyn and Long Island, I would like to know what the possibilities are in Hollywood, as every one that sees her comments on her beauty and tells me to take her to Hollywood" (21 July 1933, PG-SHC).

## 95. To Whom It May Concern[1]

Chapel Hill, N.C.
16 September 1933

From personal association with Robert Griffin, I have become very much interested in him and his plans for finishing his education. So far as I have been able to learn from people with whom he has dealt, he is an exceptional young colored man and will prove worthy of any trust reposed in him. The immediate problem facing him is the securing of enough money to return to Lincoln University for this, his senior year. As an interested party, I have agreed to lend him a hundred dollars, in installments, towards this end. But this is not enough, and if a few kind friends could help further, it would be the means of giving this boy his chance. The Reverend Eugene Henderson has also taken great interest in Robert Griffin, going so far as to give him a home and whatever support he has been able to offer. I am sure that any service and courtesy rendered the Reverend Henderson will be helpful.[2]

Sincerely,

## 96. To Barrett H. Clark

[Chapel Hill, N.C.]
25 September 1933

Dear Barrett:[1]

Of course I didn't take your paragraph in Goldberg's paper as personal criticism, for in so far as the personal part goes we all more or less are guilty—

1. Written on behalf of Robert Griffin, a young black man who grew up in Chapel Hill. During the summer Griffin lived with the Reverend Eugene H. Henderson, pastor of St. Paul's African Methodist Episcopal Church in Chapel Hill, and worked at Duke University hospital. Now he wished to return to Lincoln University outside of Philadelphia for his senior year of college.

2. Green sent his last installment of twenty-five dollars in May 1934, as Griffin completed his senior year at Lincoln (Paul Green to Eugene H. Henderson, 15 and 26 May 1934, PG-SHC).

---

1. In *Panorama*, a new magazine edited by Isaac Goldberg, Clark had an article complaining that too many playwrights, in order to pay the bills, were working in Hollywood instead of writing plays. "Paul Green," he noted, "has given us [no new play] for two [years]" ("Success and Failure on Broadway," *Panorama: A Monthly Survey of People and Ideas*, no. 1 [October 1933]: 7). Then in a letter to Green he wrote:

guilty in that we have not properly understood nor properly developed the change of the era that is upon us. All around there is now an effort on the part of a great many theatre-minded people (see Hopkins' effort to say something in a recent issue of the *Times*),[2] and what sort of living conclusions we will derive, I for one cannot tell. I have just this morning received another wire from Fox in Hollywood, asking me to come out and help put the finishing touches on *The House of Connelly.*[3] I have here in my study two or three plays almost ready to offer for "production" in New York[4]—a production which I'd prefer to all the movies, movies now being what they are. But, God wot, it is not what we are but what we shall be, as was well set forth in more ancient times.[5] I think I am going to accede to the Fox request and go to Hollywood for a few weeks, though I don't want to. Now in the statement "I don't want to" lies the only solace I can offer you as regards me and our mutual weeping over the conditions of the theatre.[6] I expect to go on writing plays and novels and some movies—even if the plays are never produced. But in spite of sequences and selahs I maintain that the movies will also some of these days provide the writer with one of his most historical and glorious opportunities.[7] Well, there are a thousand things I am most anxious to talk over with you, and

---

"I hope you didn't take my little paragraph in Goldberg's paper as a *personal* criticism of what you and the other boys are doing. I could answer that by saying that in the circumstances I would do the same thing. I was only weeping" (18 September 1933, PG-SHC).

2. Arthur Hopkins said he left the theater and went into motion picture production because the theater "can speak only to hundreds, while pictures . . . speak to millions" (*New York Times*, 10 September 1933, sec. 10, p. 1, cols. 3–6; p. 2, cols. 4–5).

3. As a motion picture, entitled *Carolina.*

4. A dramatization of his novel *Laughing Pioneer* entitled *The Southern Cross* (one-act version published by Samuel French in 1938) and two original plays, *Shroud My Body Down* and *The Enchanted Maze.*

5. Perhaps by Ophelia: "Lord, we know what we are, but know not what we may be" (*Hamlet*, act 4, scene 2).

6. Green went to Hollywood early in October and stayed until mid-December, finishing his own film script of Edward Noyes Westcott's novel *David Harum*, released in 1934, starring Will Rogers, and revising *Carolina.*

7. A point he developed in "A Playwright's Notes on Drama and the Screen," *New York Times*, 4 February 1934, sec. 9, p. 3, cols. 1–8, an article collected as "The Theatre and the Screen" in Green, *Drama and the Weather: Some Notes and Papers on Life and the Theatre* (New York: Samuel French, 1958), pp. 84–95.

I'd like nothing better than to get in my car today and come on up to New York and see what the land looks like. Give my best to George,[8] and where is Lynn?[9]

Ever to you and the rest, Paul

Did I ever thank you for the *World Drama* books?[10] They are a grand piece of book making and the contents are of the same.

Do you remember, and of course you do since you are the co-translator, that fine paragraph on page four of Gorki's introduction to his play, *The Judge*, beginning, "The characters of a drama should all act independently of the volition of the dramatist, in accordance with the law of their individual natures and social environment"—etc.?[11] I mention this in passing as another one of those pasturage matters which you have given us. Regards to Mr. Sheil and the boys.

## 97. To Elizabeth L. Green

Fox Film Corporation, Hollywood, Calif.
3 October 1933

Dear Honey—[1]

My plans are somewhat settled but not entirely. I am to finish up Harum which will take me another week at least, and then I'll polish up Connelly—which from the script I read last night will take at least another week—these two jobs I should say will last three weeks minimum as a guess.[2] Then

8. Poet and playwright George O'Neil, whose most recent play, *American Dream*, had a short run early in 1933.

9. Riggs.

10. Two-volume anthology of plays (published 1933) from Eastern as well as Western cultures, ancient to nineteenth century, published in 1933 and edited by Clark, who recently sent a set to Green.

11. *The Judge*, trans. Marie Zakrevsky and Barrett H. Clark, (New York: Robert McBride, 1924), p. iv. Gorki adds that among modern playwrights, only Synge has approached this ideal of objectivity.

---

1. Green took a train in Durham on 28 September and got to Los Angeles on 2 October.

2. Revisions to *Carolina*, motion picture based on *The House of Connelly*, occupied Green into November. Some were in the interest of verisimilitude. "Tobacco is topped," he advised, "and only for seed purposes is it allowed to bloom. So in this shot

Paramount wants me to polish off a story they already have written for the screen but which some of the big bugs think ought to be worked over—$1,750 a week. Haven't decided yet what I'll do about that. If I do it that means six weeks in this lonely place. I've stopped at the Beverly Wilshire because it's close and in a pinch I can walk over here. Saw Helen[3]—looks tired and harassed, Laurence on his way back now by Panama.[4] Then I went on over to Pacific Palisades.[5] Saw Rich's mother, the boys were away on a hike—all schools being vacationing because of the earthquake yesterday just before I got here (little damage done because the streets were deserted, but a terrible quake according to Helen, sorrowful Maria, Mrs. Meade, and others who stayed up all night after it happened), and so I didn't get to see them. They miss Paul and Byrd a lot, their mother said. The reason I went to Pac. P. among other things was to look around and get me a little cheap house for my stay here. I even had visions of Mr. Moore[6] letting me occupy the Taylor place at little cost. But as I drove up to our old Home two cars were parked there. Mrs. Reichert told me the dreadful news—the Taylor house is in the hands of Aimee's people,[7] and prayer meetings go on there morning noon and night. She said that they had

---

there should be only one or two plants blooming. The whole field in bloom would be entirely wrong" (Paul Green to Julian Johnson, 26 October [1933], PG-SHC). Others were in the interest of unity. The last scene "ought to be cut out entirely," he urged. "The signs—'Tate's Cigarettes'—'Joanna's Mixture'—'Connelly's Plug Cut'—however specific and practical their justification of Joanna's dream may be [Joanna is the play's Patsy Tate], they mar the beauty of that dream. They are a false and too-Babbitt note in an otherwise beautiful ending. Also they suggest that the family has gone into tobacco manufacturing, whereas the burden of the story is the regeneration of the farm itself" (ibid.). He also did not like the change of title, thinking it "a great mistake to take the word 'house' out of the title, for the civilization and philosophy which the *House of Connelly* typifies are built around a family—that is, a house. . . . After all though," he concluded ruefully, "it is the star's name that matters most, doesn't it?" (ibid.). *Carolina*, starring Janet Gaynor, Lionel Barrymore, and Robert Young, was released by Fox in January 1934.

3. Stallings.

4. From a trip filming newsreels.

5. Where the Greens lived the previous winter and spring in a house rented from a family named Taylor.

6. W. J. Moore, real estate agent.

7. Followers of the revivalist Aimee Semple McPherson, whose Angelus Temple was in Los Angeles.

healing ceremonies and holy-rolling, and that Grace's room[8] was a sort of inner sanctum where difficult cases were healed. Mr. Moore was the agent, and do you know, she says, he is an ordained preacher himself in that church. She was full of news and exclamations. One night when the spirit was on the gathering at the Taylor house stronger than usual the clamors of the preachers and witnesses unto the Lord aroused the neighborhood from sleep and at last brought the police who enquired what about this drunken debauch. And then when they realized it was a church gathering they dropped their tails between their legs and slunk off. Oh, says Mrs. Reichert, if only the Greens were back in that house! Next I called upon sweet Mrs. Robinson.[9] She was astounded and begged for news of her children. Captain Woolridge[10] was there and looked very well. Mrs. Robinson was so disappointed to find that only I came back—Oh, where is Mrs. Green? she said. I finally decided to remain at the Beverly Wilshire—$28 a week for room.

Now this is only a suggestion—I need a car dreadfully but am not going to rent (which is the same as buying) one. If Henry[11] would like to view this country and wouldn't mind driving mine out, I'd be glad to pay his expenses this way, and then he could explore around here and we'd go back together—that is, if I only stay three weeks and not six. Of course if I stay six, he could come out later under the same conditions. It'd be nice if you could come with him—of course, again, if things are all right there and Erm[12] or somebody reliable left in charge. Hunter Lovelace is very anxious for me to stay until time to just get home for Christmas. There'd be $16,000 in it for us. But you know how that money business creeps up on you, and I have no intention of staying unless I find I can do some work at night and carry on my novel[13]—which is not likely, is it? Anyhow it'd be fine, fine if you could be here with me.

Lynn has gone to New Mexico, George[14] as you know is in New York, King Vidor is somewhere around, Eleanor[15] is still in Europe and is going to marry

8. Upstairs bedroom occupied by the Greens' cook, Grace.

9. Piano teacher for the Green children.

10. Mrs. Robinson's husband.

11. Elizabeth's brother.

12. Green's sister.

13. *This Body the Earth.*

14. O'Neil, who had been in Hollywood revising film scripts during the Greens' previous stay.

15. Boardman, former wife of motion picture director King Vidor.

or already is married to Harry D'Arrast.[16] Vernon says the gold mine is coming along fine, though no money has been made from it yet. He is hoping for news of a great strike any day.[17] When I bellyached about *Dr. Bull*,[18] the Fox folks were astounded. They are highly pleased with it and according to the business manager it is making much more money than any Rogers picture has ever made. Next to *Paddy, the Next Best Thing*[19] (which is a phenomenal success—Now how can anyone stay here?) Bull is making more money than any other Fox picture on the road at the present time. And *Voltaire* is a clean-up, they say. So there's a reason for Paramount's wanting me. Hunter told me yesterday he had four or five offers waiting whenever I was ready. I said I wasn't ready and wouldn't be until maybe next summer. I would though somewhat like to do that polishing off job at Paramount to establish a salary basis for future necessity—if it comes. Three summer months at that price would build our house whenever we wanted it to.[20]

Well, my intention at present is to hurry through with Harum and Connelly and come back, and I'd much rather drive than try that train again. So as soon as I let you know my absolute definite plans, it'd be nice for you and Henry to come out and we all drive back together. Better save what money you have (except pay-roll) for I don't know how long it'll take Fox to pay me for Harum.

Kiss the chillun, and all my love. Paul

Tell Henry and your mother I was too sorry not to see them before I left.

I know Henry would like to see Howard Jones' Southern California team in action.[21]

16. Another director.

17. Vernon Stacy, married to Green's cousin Willie Cutts Stacy and living in Los Angeles, had invested in a Mexican gold mine. Before Green left Chapel Hill, Vernon wrote to him saying they were very near a large vein of gold and asking if Green were still willing, as he had been "several weeks ago," "to see us thru on the Mexican mines to the extent of 'Five hundred dollars' " (23 August 1933, PG-SHC). There is no record of Green's response.

18. Motion picture based on James Gould Cozzens's *The Last Adam*, released by Fox in 1933 and starring Will Rogers, for which Green had done the script.

19. Current remake of a D. W. Griffith film of the same title (1923).

20. On a 200-acre farm east of Chapel Hill (later Greenwood) that the Greens bought during the summer.

21. University of Southern California football team, which won the two previous Rose Bowl games.

## 98. To Langston Hughes[1]

Montecito Apartments, 6650 Franklin Ave., Hollywood, Calif.
13 November 1933

Dear Langston Hughes:

Like you I have agonized a great deal over the Scottsboro boys and have contributed what I could both in money and words to their cause, and like you I know that there will never be enough contributions of any kind until these boys are freed. Accordingly I am herewith enclosing a check and the following statement which you, as you request, may release to the press:

—For three years now these helpless negro boys have lived in the shadow of death. For three years now the state of Alabama, the South and the nation have failed to discharge their duty to these victims and give them the merciful justice their case demands. If these Scottsboro boys are allowed to be offered up as a sacrifice to bigotry and perverted racial feeling, then we as a Southern people[2] have no right to boast of either democracy or liberty. We shall have participated in a shameful deed and the cry of outraged innocence will be heard beyond the day of the last orator and demagogue and somewhere far off in the future we shall stand adjudged by our children's children in merciless truth.—

As you well know, Langston, one could go on for reams and reams pouring out imprecations, pleadings and threatenings, wondering whether they would do much good by the time they seep down into Alabama. But we must keep on trying, and then keep on, and always hope for the best.[3] Thank you for writing to me. I shall be back in North Carolina in December and shall then, as now, be ready to do what I can.[4]

Sincerely yours,

1. Langston Hughes (1902–1967), a leader among those protesting the convictions of the nine blacks (eight of whom received death sentences) in the Scottsboro Case (see his *Scottsboro Limited* [1932]), recently sent out an appeal for funds to finance the new trials ordered by the U.S. Supreme Court in November 1932.

2. Green typed "then we as a people" and later added "Southern" by hand.

3. Although none of the nine was executed, each spent most of his life in prison or on parole. Clarence Norris, last of the men to be freed, was pardoned by Alabama governor George Wallace in October 1976.

4. From Carmel, California, Hughes replied: "Your prompt and generous response to our appeal for Scottsboro funds has just reached me. Allow me to express my own personal (and racial) gratitude to you for your letter and check, and for the excellent statement. . . . When a thing drags on so long, it is difficult to keep aid and interest

## 99. To Barrett H. Clark

Montecito Apartments, 6650 Franklin Avenue, Hollywood, Calif.
21 November 1933

Dear Barrett:[1]

You no doubt have received my wire which I sent immediately on hearing from you about the revived state of Madame Hewes. I hope for heaven's sake and mine and anybody else's who is affected that she at last means what she says. Please convey to her as strongly as you can that I shall be glad to do anything possible in cooperating for the production. It is pretty certain that I shall be finished here around the first of December, and I can then hurry straight on to New York via Chapel Hill—if my presence will facilitate things. I am sure that the musical side of the performance would need my help, and the other side too. In rehearsal we might together hit upon several things to improve the show. Let me know any developments.[2]

With best to you and yours,

As always, Paul

---

from waning. Your help is probably worth more than you realize." Then in a postscript he added: "Last spring in Moscow the picture *Cabin in the Cotton* for which (I believe—I didn't see it) you did the scenario, received most favorable comments at a private showing for movie people and artists. When I heard about it, I wished I'd gotten up at the ungodly hour necessary to see a studio showing there" (17 November 1933, PG-SHC).

---

1. For two years Margaret Hewes had held an option on *Potter's Field* and frequently planned to produce it. A few days before the present letter Green received a letter from Clark: "Margaret Hewes has just come to life. She telephoned yesterday saying she planned to open with *Potter's Field* about the middle of January" (16 November 1933, PG-SHC).

2. In December, after returning to Chapel Hill, Green got word from Clark that Hewes could not raise enough money for the planned production and had asked for an extension of her option (21 December 1933, PG-SHC). Green replied that he "had already surmised [the disappointing turn of events]—the usual differences between wish and power to perform. Still maybe she will come through with enough backing. I hope so. The extension of contract with her is all right of course" (28 December 1933).

## 100. To Sarah Gertrude Knott

[Chapel Hill, N.C.]
22 January 1934

Dear Miss Knott:[1]

I am herewith returning your notes on the objectives of the National Folk Festival with a new copy which includes a few minor corrections I have made in the phrasing.

I don't want to make a big matter out of a little matter, and since it is not a little matter I will repeat what I told you here. I think it is a mistake to put the representatives of folk-culture on the back of the stationery and the representatives of finance on the front. Actually it should be the other way around, though I see no reason why the proper balance shouldn't be worked out.[2] I shall write President Roosevelt but should prefer to do it on the new stationery, since my connection with the Festival will be apparent thereon. You know, there is nothing like authority for getting an answer.[3]

Sincerely yours,

1. In late December Knott visited Green in Chapel Hill, and the two went over plans for the National Folk Festival, whose objective, according to Knott, "is to bring together from the many regions of the United States exhibits of the various folk arts which are the richest heritage of our people" ("General Plan," 1934, PG-SHC).

2. The letterhead proposed by Knott displayed down the lefthand margin the names of prominent St. Louis people involved with the festival, such as August A. Busch, Jr., then on the back listed the large national committee of folklorists, such as J. Frank Dobie, G. L. Kittredge, John Lomax, Percy MacKaye, Constance Rourke, and Lamar Stringfield. Knott changed the letterhead so that only her name, as national director, Green's as national chairman, and Maurice Weil's as president appeared on the front. With a show of equality, folklorists and business leaders were listed together on the back.

3. On 7 February 1934 Green wrote to Franklin Roosevelt, inviting him to attend the festival and requesting a brief statement on "the importance of conserving the folk traditions on which a nation's culture ultimately rests" (PG-SHC). Roosevelt replied:

> We in the United States are amazingly rich in the elements from which to weave a culture. We have the best of man's past on which to draw, brought to us by our native folk and folk from all parts of the world.
>
> In binding these elements into a National fabric of beauty and strength, let us keep the original fibres so intact that the fineness of each will show in the completed handiwork. (2 March 1934)

In a letter to Knott, Green suggested that "the first paragraph of President Roosevelt's

## 101. To Charles C. Sikes[1]

[Chapel Hill, N.C.]
22 January 1934

Dear Mr. Sikes:

I don't know when I have ever read a more frankly beautiful letter, and I wish I were able to speak with sudden and Olympian insight with an answer to your problem. The very fact that you are so intricately bothered is proof to me that you are worthy of the deepest thought one is capable of giving. Tentatively I think of three places you might head for in your search—New York, Los Angeles, or Chapel Hill. Before giving any definite advice, I should like very much to talk with you. At this distance though it seems to me that Chapel Hill would be the best bet. Would you be interested in coming up here and taking a course in writing under Phillips Russell[2] or playwriting with Mr. Koch—? Not that either of these men, or anybody for that matter, could provide you with a complete answer. You are wise enough to know that lies within yourself. But they could offer you a means for trying your hand at writing. If that is the career you prefer—it makes no difference if you do feel that what you write now is not so very good—then I would say give yourself a chance. The finest things usually come through long apprenticeship both in technique and in struggle, and Beethoven, Dante and the other great ones of the world stand as witnesses to that truth. We can all learn a lot from trees. The biggest ones, the strongest ones, have a slow and turmoiling growth, and in their youth no doubt feel that they will never arrive to the stature of some of the giants in the forest. But day by day, year by year they keep building

---

letter would make a fine front page statement for your programs" (13 March 1934), and it was so used for the festival, held in St. Louis during the week beginning 6 May 1934.

---

1. Charles C. Sikes received a B.A. from UNC in 1931 and had been a student in one of Green's classes. Now at his family home in Monroe, North Carolina, he wrote to Green about his hopes for his life. For the last several years he had felt something "bubbling and boiling" inside him, always "just on the verge of coming to the surface." Reading brought some contentment but made him "feel like a parasite," and when he tried writing, it seemed bad. He did not "want to go to the dogs" by drinking and knew he "must find some means of self-expression and this must be either through writing, acting, or some of the associated arts." He closed by wondering what Green thought of his idea of "going to the West Coast in the hope of there finding myself" (16 January 1934, PG-SHC).

2. Biographer who taught creative writing in the Department of English at UNC.

towards the light. Yes, trees must be often terror stricken, unhappy and ready to quit, but the life force in them refuses to be whipped. So let it be with you and me. In the recent Mencken and Nathan philosophy Browning stood in bad report.[3] But today he is re-righting himself, and these old crooked lines of his speak the truth—

> Then, welcome each rebuff
> That turns earth's smoothness rough,
> Each sting that bids nor sit nor stand but go!

Wouldn't you like to read this "Rabbi Ben Ezra" poem? Another good book is *The Great Hunger*, by Johan Bojer.[4]

If you are around this way any time call me up. We might have a session about these things. I need it too.[5]

With best regards always,

## 102. To Elizabeth L. Green

[Hotel Somerset], Boston, Mass.
[Monday], 23 April 1934

Dear Honey:[1]

I have treated you like a dog, but I have been too busy to write anybody. We have been working twelve and sixteen hours a day trying to whip this drama

3. In *The Smart Set* and *The American Mercury*, "Victorian," like "Puritan," was a term of reproach.

4. Norwegian novelist whose *The Great Hunger* (trans. 1920) dealt with the struggle for self-fulfillment.

5. A few weeks later Green received word from Sikes that the financial resources of his family had suddenly evaporated and he had taken a job in a department store in Raleigh. Much encouraged by Green's letter, he said he would work on his writing, and he included a sensitive three-page reaction to Bojer's novel (27 February 1934, PG-SHC). Later Sikes moved to Anniston, Alabama, and made his career in the Hudson Department Store chain.

---

1. On Friday morning, 13 April, Green arrived in Boston by train from Chapel Hill to help Margaret Hewes with her tryout production of *Potter's Field*, which would run for eight performances at the Plymouth Theatre, opening on Monday, 16 April, and closing Saturday evening, 21 April. On arrival he found a chaotic situation. With inadequate financial backing, Hewes hardly knew from day to day whether she could

into shape. On Sunday morning,[2] we had to re-do the whole last scene for the opening Monday night. However, publicity was good—newspaper articles—interviews—photographs, etc.

The play was received very well indeed, and now every review may be termed a "rave" with the exception of one.[3] I should have kept some clippings and forwarded them, but actually I have been too rushed to do it.

Tell Paul and Byrd I appreciate their letters and will reply in due season. Kiss the babies for me.

Now as to my plans:—I had bargained with Fox Corporation last week to allow me until April 30 to arrive at their studio in Hollywood, preceding that, Warner Bros. had agreed to let me work for Fox first and then come to them for *Anthony Adverse* afterwards[4]—so I thought everything was set until Mr. Pratt "the Director of the Show" had returned to his school,[5] that left me high and dry with the drove of Negroes on my back and so I have been quote directing ever since he left, and that was three days before we opened.

We plan to move the whole company down to New York on Saturday next,[6] and rehearse in a theatre not yet chosen, for a week, and open on Saturday May 2nd.[7]

Last night, we sent to New York for a new Director to help me out and for Frank Wilson and Rose McClendon to come into the cast.[8]

---

keep the company together. The large, all-black cast consisted of amateurs from schools and theater groups in the Boston area, none with rigorous professional experience. The show lacked a director. And the script, which Green completed several years ago, seemed to him now to need revision.

2. 15 April.

3. The *New York Times* review, which stressed the amateur status of the performers ("Potter's Field," *New York Times*, 22 April 1934, sec. 9, p. 1, col. 1). The rave reviews were in Boston papers (e.g., "Paul Green's Stirring Play of Negro Life," *Boston Evening Transcript*, 17 April 1934, p. 8, cols. 1–2).

4. Popular novel (1933) by Hervey Allen, on which Green planned to base a film script but did not.

5. E. Stanley Pratt directed *Potter's Field* during rehearsals until about the time of Green's arrival, then returned to Choate School in Wallingford, Connecticut, where he taught speech and dramatic arts.

6. 28 April.

7. The Saturday following 28 April was 5 May.

8. For the contemplated New York production. Wilson and McClendon starred in the original production of *In Abraham's Bosom.*

What I would like would be for Fox to give me an extra week so that I could stay right on with the thing until its re-opening in New York, then you could come up to the opening, then we could come home and talk with Weeks about the house plans[9] and I would go on from there to the coast.

I shall wire Julian Johnson[10] to-morrow telling him when I shall start work on his picture, if he will grant me this extra week.

As soon as I know definitely, I will get in touch with you.

Hurriedly and with best love always. Paul

P.S. My address is Hotel Bristol, West 48th St., New York City.[11]

## 103. To A. P. Kephart[1]

[Hollywood, Calif.]
5 May 1934

Dear Mr. Kephart:

I am not entirely against capital punishment as such, for from the true horticulturist point of view there are evil members to be pruned out, but I am

9. H. R. Weeks, of Atwood and Weeks, architectural and engineering firm in Durham, who was drawing plans for the Greens' new home on the 200 acres east of Chapel Hill they bought in 1933.

10. Production head at Fox Film Corporation.

11. Because of inadequate financing, Hewes postponed the New York production of *Potter's Field* until the fall, with Green's concurrence (Paul Green to Margaret Hewes, 7 May 1934, PG-SHC). He returned to Chapel Hill on Saturday, 28 April, then left the next day for Hollywood, arriving on 2 May (Elizabeth Green to Roy W. Cowden, 2 May 1934, PG-SHC). In Hollywood he revised *Potter's Field*, changing the title to *Roll Sweet Chariot*, and for Fox wrote a film script based on Sinclair Lewis's novel, *Work of Art* (1934).

---

1. On the morning of 3 April members of the North Carolina Interracial Commission met with State Commissioner of Parole Edwin Gill in Raleigh in an attempt to have the death sentence of Theodore Cooper, a black man convicted of murder, commuted to life imprisonment. Having gone to Hollywood around 27 March, Green was unable to attend and sent a telegram to a commission member for distribution to the press: "Sorry your invitation came too late for me to attend your meeting this morning. I am absolutely opposed to capital punishment as it is carried out in this State. Any social system which provides such an array of human tragedy as we have on death row today stands condemned with the criminals themselves. . . . The

absolutely opposed to it (as I said in my recent telegram to the press) as it is carried out in North Carolina. I think any steps you can take wiping out the disgrace of death cells overflowing with moaning, ignorant human beings will be an everlasting credit to us all. You can count on my cooperation when I return to North Carolina. I am sorry my absence from the state made it impossible for me to be present at your meeting on April 30 and give voice to my views.

Sincerely yours,

## 104. To J. C. B. Ehringhaus[1]

[Hollywood, Calif.]
20 May 1934

Dear Governor Ehringhaus:

During the winter I was in North Carolina and had occasion to become acquainted with the facts in the case of one Emanuel (Spice) Biddings, or Bittings who is at present under sentence of death for the killing of his landlord, Auffy Clayton, near Roxboro, a year ago.[2]

---

time has come when we should be done with this frightful business of murdering ignorant Negroes. The problem of social betterment is not to be worked out that way" (quoted in "Cooper Given New Lease on Life through Ruling," *NO*, 4 April 1934, p. 3, cols. 1–5). Shortly thereafter A. P. Kephart, on the faculty of the North Carolina College for Women (now the University of North Carolina at Greensboro) and president of the North Carolina Society for the Abolition of the Death Penalty, invited Green to speak at a meeting of the society in Raleigh on 30 April (9 April 1934, PG-SHC).

---

1. J. C. B. Ehringhaus (1882–1949), lawyer from Elizabeth City, was governor of North Carolina, 1933–37.

2. Emanuel Bittings, black tenant farmer and former soldier in World War I, shot T. M. Clayton on the morning of 7 September 1933. According to Bittings, Clayton ordered him to move his share of the tobacco crop into Clayton's packhouse. Bittings started the job, then Clayton told him to stop and Bittings returned home. A little later, "my wife—she had just got up after having a baby—hollered up to me that Mr. Clayton was on the front porch knocking one of our boys up against the house. I came down and told him to leave." Clayton walked into the yard, called his wife, and "told her to listen to the last words he told that God-damned nigger before he shot him." Thinking he saw Clayton reach for a pistol in his pocket, Bittings got his shotgun

A thorough study of the circumstances surrounding the killing and the subsequent trial and sentence convinced me that the defendant, Biddings, received a rather heavy sentence. I won't go into all the details for these have been prepared for submission to the Supreme Court by M. Hugh Thompson, an attorney of Durham.[3]

As a citizen, interested along with you in the welfare of the people of North Carolina, no matter of what race, color or creed, I am making a plea for clemency for the negro in case he is not granted a new trial. Unfortunately, my individual efforts for him have been handicapped by my having to return to California[;] and because I am afraid that in the show-down only public sentiment and your executive power can save Biddings from the electric chair, I am writing you this letter. Of course I realize as well as you and other leading men of the State do, that the majesty and justice of the law must not be handicapped by sentimentality and zeal of a misguided point of view. But when one considers the character and practise of Clayton with his tenants, the oppression and even brutality that Biddings endured, and when one considers the subterfuge methods indulged in by the defendant's counsel, Escoffrey,[4] one can hardly arrive at any conclusion other than that the sentence of death was extreme.

---

from the house and shot Clayton ("Death Row Inmate Tells His Story of Life, Death," *NO*, 5 April 1934, p. 14, cols. 4–7). On 25 January 1934 in Roxboro, North Carolina, Bittings was tried, convicted, and sentenced to death, his electrocution set for late March.

3. Early in March, after spending several days in Roxboro talking with people about the murder, Paul, Elizabeth, Phillips Russell, Louis J. Spaulding (prominent black businessman of Durham), and others formed a Bittings Defense Committee ("See Parallel in Paul Green Play: Playwright's Defense of Spice Bittings Recalls *In Abraham's Bosom*," *NO*, 5 March 1934, p. 5, col. 1). The committee dismissed Bittings's trial lawyer, who refused to appeal the conviction to the North Carolina Supreme Court, and, after unsuccessfully attempting to bring in an International Legal Defense lawyer, replaced him with M. Hugh Thompson, who filed an appeal on 18 April, thus suspending the execution ("Bittings Appeal to High Court Is Filed," *NO*, 20 April 1934, p. 11, cols. 4–5).

4. In addition to refusing to file an appeal, Phillip Escoffrey, a black lawyer in Durham, had failed to bring in witnesses who could corroborate Bittings's testimony, thus creating the impression during "the trial that Bittings killed his landlord without provocation, following a dispute over a division of their crop" ("See Parallel in Paul Green Play," *NO*, *5 March 1934*, p. 5, col. 1).

A few months ago I went over the facts as well as I could—talked with people around Roxboro—had a session with Escoffrey himself—talked to white and black citizens and more than a few of them said, quite openly: "Well, somebody should have killed Auffy Clayton long before Biddings did."

A former attorney of Roxboro told me that if he or any other reliable white lawyer had appeared for Biddings he could have secured a compromise on a second degree verdict. I am sure that Escoffrey was the "nigger in the wood-pile" and I hate for the fairmindedness and prestige of our State, as well as Biddings, to suffer by his connivance.

I sincerely trust that if events should warrant such action that you, by virtue of the power vested in your office, will see that Biddings gets something of a square deal.[5]

Yours very truly,

## 105. To Loretto C. Bailey[1]

[Hollywood, Calif.]
23 June 1934

Dear Loretto—

After such a vivified and earnest letter as your last one, I see nothing but my duty to rally to the cause of Dr. Nelson and his drama.

5. In mid-June the state supreme court denied Bittings's appeal for a new trial (Paul Green to Harriet Herring, 28 June 1934, PG-SHC).

---

1. Loretto C. Bailey (b. 1907), from Winston-Salem, North Carolina, entered UNC in 1927 and quickly involved herself in Playmakers activities as a writer and actress. Several of her plays were produced by the Playmakers and published, beginning with "Job's Kinfolks" in 1928 (Frederick H. Koch, ed., *Carolina Folk-Plays*, 2d ser. [New York: Henry Holt, 1941], pp. 241–64). In the fall of 1933 she began teaching at Shaw University, a Baptist college for blacks in Raleigh, and recently she wrote to Green about a plan by the president of Shaw, William Stuart Nelson, to organize a drama competition for black high schools in the state and hold the finals at Shaw. To the winning school Nelson wished to award a silver cup named the "Paul Green Cup," and Bailey wrote to ask Green's permission (22 May 1934, PG-SHC). In reply Green wondered if they had considered offering a Frederick H. Koch Cup (31 May 1934). Bailey's vigorous response outlined Nelson's position. In addition to a real interest in the drama, he had a desperate need, because of the precarious financial situation of the

Of course I am deeply honored—that's already understood before comment is made—that a "Paul Green Cup" is likely to be of benefit. Therefore I am glad to offer it, and you must know that I am relying on your judgment and kindness in helping it to be a worthwhile thing. But for goodness sakes, how much is it going to cost? It must be a good one, but I have no idea as to the expense. Is it fifty dollars or a hundred? Don't go beyond the latter figure because I have a lot of hungry mouths to feed.[2]

I should like to write the sort of letter you write and tell you all the Hollywood news—such that it is—but I am too tired and too busy.

My best regards to the new doctor in the family.[3]

Ever, etc.

## 106. To Emjo Basshe[1]

[Hollywood, Calif.]
9 July 1934

Dear Emjo—

You perhaps have had copies of *Potter's Field* (the name of which I have changed to *Roll Sweet Chariot*) from Barrett Clark. The new script will answer

---

school, to upgrade Shaw, make it the center of something noteworthy in the state. "Your name stands for something to him," she continued, "and to very many of those students. It would be much more glamorous than offering a prize from Shaw—to offer a Paul Green Award. . . . It's nothing less than your duty. And Prof. [Koch] approves" (9 June 1934).

2. "The cup's not going to be expensive I promise," Bailey answered. "I thought, heaven help me, that cups were five dollars or so, even the football kind" (26 June 1934, PG-SHC).

3. Bailey's husband, J. O. Bailey, a member of the Department of English at UNC, received his Ph.D. in English from UNC at the June commencement.

---

1. Emjo Basshe (1898–1939), actor and director in New York since the early 1920s, had been signed by Margaret Hewes to direct *Potter's Field* in the fall and had written to Green about a technical problem in the staging. The script called for the projection of some speeches as if they were unspoken thoughts, and the microphone and loudspeaker system used in the Boston production caused numerous problems. Basshe had gotten an electrical engineer to develop a new system and now needed to know exactly which speeches were to be projected that way (1 July 1934, PG-SHC).

most of the questions about my intention as to the sound "Voice."[2] I think there will be a little more revision especially in the last part, but generally it seems to me pretty nearly correct.

I appreciate your attitude and understanding of the play and am sure you will give it the best you've got, and I am glad you are determined it shall have adequate rehearsal. Two weeks is certainly not enough.

Some time ago I wrote Barrett quite fully as to my wishes, and one of them is that the play do not depend entirely on the Boston Amateur Organization.[3] The New York papers will call us on it sure as shooting. We should have the cast well sprinkled with the best New York has to offer. As to that best, you and Mrs. Hewes will have to agree.[4]

With best wishes, etc.

## 107. To M. Hugh Thompson[1]

[Hollywood, Calif.]
10 July 1934

Dear Lawyer Thompson:

Your wire yesterday afternoon also gave *me* a ray of hope, and I needed it after the queer news in your letter a few hours before.

2. In the published script no speeches are designated "Voice." Uzzell's lines in the prologue, which are spoken "to himself," or as if "thinking," show the clearest need for some projection system (*Roll Sweet Chariot: A Symphonic Play of the Negro People* [New York: Samuel French, 1935], pp. viii–x).

3. The group (not an organization as such) who did the play in Boston.

4. When *Roll Sweet Chariot* opened at the Cort Theatre in New York City on 2 October 1934, the cast consisted largely of professionals. Frank Wilson and Rose McClendon from *In Abraham's Bosom* had leading parts, and Warren Coleman played John Henry.

---

1. Black lawyer in Durham handling the Bittings case. Following the state supreme court's refusal in June to grant Bittings a new trial, Thompson attempted to win a reprieve for Bittings from State Commissioner of Parole Edwin M. Gill. In a letter Green received on 9 July, Thompson outlined Gill's activity (PG-SHC). Gill interviewed Bittings's two daughters and his wife, all of whom corroborated the testimony at the trial that Bittings shot Clayton in the back following an argument over the disposition of his tobacco crop and that Clayton was unarmed and made no threats

Perhaps there is no need to enlarge upon what I said in my wire, but I will repeat as a matter of emphasis that the staunch loyalty to truth of the Bittings wife and three children at the expense of the condemned man is more than startling—it is downright suspicious. Another thing.—They all seem to agree like Happy Hooligans upon what happened. If you can get from anybody who talked with them something of their first statements, I am sure you will find a great divergence in them. Escoffrey told me that when he talked with the wife (I don't remember as to the children) soon after the murder, she told quite a different story from what she later told him when he was ready to bring her to court as a witness. Have you heard from any source that Mrs. Bittings (who was sick in bed at the time Clayton was killed) said she heard Clayton call out to his wife to "Come here and take a last took at this goddamned nigger before I blow his brains out?" I have. Will you ask Escoffrey if she didn't first tell him that?[2]

---

against Bittings. Gill was surprised by the testimony. He had intended to grant Bittings a reprieve but now could not, and Bittings's execution date remained Friday, 6 July ("Daughters Seal Doom of Father," *Durham Morning Herald*, 4 July 1934, p. 2, col. 2). Receiving this news, Green immediately wired Thompson: "I AM ASTONISHED TO HEAR OF THE TURN OF EVENTS IN THE BITTINGS CASE STOP APPARENTLY COMMISSIONER GILL HAS CO-OPERATED IN EVERY WAY POSSIBLE TO SEE THAT THE CONDEMNED MAN GOT A FAIR CHANCE AT LIFE STOP THE CASE STILL REMAINS VERY MYSTERIOUS TO ME FIRST IN THAT NO REASONABLE PROVOCATION FOR THE MURDER HAS BEEN ESTABLISHED AND SECOND IN THAT THE WIFE AND CHILDREN WHO HAD SUCH AFFECTIONATE FEELINGS FOR THE HUSBAND AND FATHER UNANIMOUSLY SWORE TO EVIDENCE THAT SENDS HIM TO HIS DEATH THIS DEVOTION TO TRUTH AT ALL COSTS IS SO IDEAL THAT MEDALS ARE IN ORDER STOP NO THE ONLY CONCLUSION I CAN COME TO IS THAT EITHER BITTINGS WAS CRAZY OR THAT THE RELATIVES WERE INTIMIDATED STOP I SUPPOSE IT IS TOO LATE FOR ME TO DO MORE AT THIS GREAT DISTANCE AND SO THE SUBJECT IS ENDED BUT WITH THE HOPE THAT THROUGH A BETTER MUTUAL UNDERSTANDING OF US ALL SUCH TRAGEDIES WILL OCCUR LESS AND LESS OFTEN STOP WILL YOU PLEASE WIRE ME COLLECT AT ONCE WHETHER BITTINGS HAS BEEN EXECUTED OR NOT REGARDS PAUL GREEN" ([9 July 1934], PG-SHC). A few hours after sending the wire, Green received a telegram from Thompson saying that Gill had postponed the execution into September to allow more time to investigate circumstances surrounding the murder.

2. At a hearing before Gill on 24 July Thompson presented two men from Roxboro who swore that Mrs. Bittings "told them before her husband was arrested that Clayton had struck her in the face before he was shot by Bittings and that her version of the shooting then was substantially the same as that given by Bittings on the stand"

Another thing.—Is it certain that Clayton was shot in the back? Wasn't he shot in the side? Bittings claims that Clayton was turning toward him with his hand on his hip pocket when he pulled down a shotgun and killed him. From the report of the Coroner you no doubt already know the location of the wounds on Clayton's body, but I was rather reliably informed that he was not shot in the back. If he wasn't, then the wife and childrens' testimony that he was killed while walking away from Bittings, stands partially contradicted.

Can't something be made of the fact that Clayton's reputation as a landlord was bad and that he was a quarrelsome person when drinking?[3]

To repeat once more.—One man doesn't kill another man because he is ordered to move his tobacco. There is more to it than this, and I believe that in view of all these qualifying and uncleared-up matters, Governor Ehringhaus and Commissioner Gill have a clear right and duty to set aside the verdict of the courts and commute Bittings' sentence to life imprisonment.

Will they?—is the question.[4]

Yours very truly,

Copy to: Mr. Daniels.[5]

---

("Bittings' Case Takes New Turn at Clemency Hearing," *Durham Morning Herald*, 25 July 1934, p. 3, cols. 3–4).

3. At the hearing on 24 July Thompson presented a third witness who testified "that Clayton was extremely hot-tempered and frequently had trouble with his tenants . . . [and] that Clayton had ordered him off Clayton's farm at the point of a shotgun only a few weeks before the killing took place" (ibid.).

4. Because Bittings's family adhered to their account of the murder, Commissioner Gill did not set aside the verdict of the court, and Bittings's execution was set for Friday, 28 September. On Wednesday morning, 26 September, Elizabeth Green held a four-hour conference with Governor Ehringhaus, pleading with him to commute Bittings's sentence to life imprisonment. Ehringhaus refused, and the execution took place as scheduled ("Two Victims Face Execution Friday," *NO*, 27 September 1934, p. 1, col. 2; p. 2, col. 2).

5. Jonathan Daniels, editor of the *News and Observer* in Raleigh and supporter of blacks (see Charles W. Eagles, *Jonathan Daniels and Race Relations: The Evolution of a Southern Liberal* [Knoxville: University of Tennessee Press, 1982]), had been alerted to the Bittings case by Green and had asked Green to keep him informed on it (Jonathan Daniels to Paul Green, 21 March 1934, PG-SHC).

## 108. To William Johnson

Fox Film Studio, Hollywood, Calif.
21 July 1934

Dear Billy[1]—

I was surprised to get your letter typewritten. That's a new accomplishment I didn't suspect you of. The news about Uncle Arch was sad,[2] but I still hope for the best. Buie[3] has also written that he is very sick and not expected to live, though nobody is certain as to the immediate outcome. Well, you are young, but you too already understand there is suffering in the world, and fun too. They go together so often and we have to use them both as best we can.

You were very nice to take time to tell me all the news about the crops. It was almost as if I was back there and could see them and everybody around the neighborhood. My ability to return the compliment is handicapped, but I'll do the best I can.

Paul and Byrd[4] are going to school—we had to give them something to do. Byrd goes to a French-American one, and Paul to the Hollywood Military Academy. They seem to like their teachers and are doing fine—so *they* say. Paul's teacher is an army captain and the young man says he walks about with a long stick in his hand ready to whack you if you don't behave. I suppose it's a ruler or blackboard pointer the captain carries. Also Paul is studying clarinet and will be tooting in a band soon.

Janet and Betsy[5] have become water dogs. They love to wade in the ocean's edge and let the waves roll over them. The salt makes their eyes red as a terrapin's but they don't seem to mind it. We have our old cook Grace back, and she does the feeding while Mary handles the children. Aunt Lib[6] and Mrs. Lay[7] do a lot of sewing and knitting and going to flower shows, gardens, etc. As for me I work every day at my office, and the details of that routine—with its conferences, writings, meetings, discussions etc.—would not interest you.

I suppose by this time you are barning tobacco, and I wish I could be helping. Uncle Hugh confirms in his letter the fact you've had a lot of rain. Of course rain here is an unknown quantity.

1. Son of Green's sister Mary, almost fourteen.
2. Archibald Long, husband of Green's half-sister, Alda.
3. Daughter of Archibald and Alda.
4. Ten and eight years old.
5. Nearly three, and four years old.
6. Elizabeth.
7. Dr. Lay had died on 12 August 1932.

Last week-end we took a whole flock to Lake Arrowhead—a place high up in the mountains—Willie, Vernon, and Billy Vaughan Stacy,[8] Mrs. Lay, our crowd and my secretary. We fished and rode horseback and everybody had a good time. Paul and I got a motorboat and fished for hours. He finally caught a little perch as big as a one-cent piece. His chest stuck out and he said "Golly, what a dang good fisherman I am!" We lugged the monster home and cooked it. By that time it was so small you could hardly taste it, bones and all.

We expect to be back sometime in the autumn—maybe the middle of September. We are planning to build our new house when we get back, also the pond. I hope in a year or two you will be able to come up and help me catch fish there. Also I might need a good farmhand now and then. I've bought a twenty-three acre meadow next the farm[9] for a couple of cows, and maybe you could teach me to milk again.

Are you going to the University or to Duke when you finish at Buie's Creek, or have you decided to be a peddler or what—maybe a doctor?[10]

Be a smart boy as I know you always will and give my love to Mother, Daddy and the children.

Uncle Paul

## 109. To Drama Editor, *New York Times*[1]

New York City
3 October 1934

Dear Sir:—

In your issue of Sunday September 30th an article entitled "Conventions in the Theater" appeared under my name. This article was not written by me; I

8. Willie Cutts, Paul's cousin, had married Vernon Stacy, and with their daughter Billie they lived in Los Angeles.

9. An area of Chapel Hill now called Glen Lennox.

10. He attended UNC, receiving a B.A. in 1939 and an L.L.B. in 1941, then established a law practice in Lillington. Later he served as district judge, trustee of UNC, and member of the board of governors of the state university system.

---

1. Green left Los Angeles by plane on Friday, 21 September, the next day met Margaret Hewes and Emjo Basshe in New York for rehearsals of *Roll Sweet Chariot*, and then in the week of 23 September took the play to Milwaukee and back to New York for its opening at the Cort Theatre on Tuesday, 2 October. Arriving back in New

had no knowledge of it, and I do not hold the views which it expressed.[2]

I have since heard from your department that the article was submitted as coming from me and therefore published in good faith. But I am sure you will agree under the circumstances that my disconnection with the matter should be made clear.[3]

Sincerely yours,

## 110. To Elizabeth L. Green

Hotel Bristol, 120–135 West 48th St., New York City
24 January 1935

Dear Old Girl—[1]

I haven't done much toward the play but confer with The Group. We meet again the end of this week or the first of the next. In the meantime I am lying

---

York on the Sunday before the opening, he found in the drama section of the day's *New York Times* an article attributed to himself.

2. The article, clearly a prank, began: "Here it is 1934 in the theatre, and still I am writing plays without conscious regard for their feasibility on the stage." Showing some knowledge of the history and unpublished script of *Roll Sweet Chariot*, the article attempted to ridicule Green for the demands his plays made on the stage, praising the producer of *Roll Sweet Chariot*, for instance, as one "who has found no insuperable obstacle in a stage direction which states: 'A blast is heard near by and the shacks are crumbled' " (see *Roll Sweet Chariot*, p. 79). It ended by declaring that if inventive directors and stage designers ever appear in the United States, "there will be playwrights, now germinating in the fields and cities of this land, ready to spring up, their hands fully armed" ("Convention in the Theatre," *New York Times*, 30 September 1934, sec. 9, p. 1, col. 8; p. 3, cols. 6–7).

3. Slightly revised, the present letter appeared in the letters-to-the-editor column, *New York Times*, 7 October 1934, sec. 9, p. 3, col. 8.

---

1. January was a month of crisis for the Group Theatre. Their season so far a failure and no new play in sight, the three directors (Crawford, Strasberg, and Clurman) were prevented from disbanding the organization only by a protest from the actors, who insisted that they continue the search for a script (Clurman, *The Fervent Years*, pp. 134–35; Cheryl Crawford, *One Naked Individual: My Fifty Years in the Theatre* [Indianapolis: Bobbs-Merrill, 1977], p. 70). Probably Crawford wired Green to come to New York with anything he had. His newest play, *Shroud My Body Down*, produced

back here in a teeny alley room (pretty quiet place) trying to shape the script up. I hope in a day or two to get up nerve to go to see Canfield.[2]

Everything is snowed under—17" of snow and the thermometer around 9. I've cashed one check #234 for $50 and will try to make it last. Be sure to allow for it. If the Group likes my synopsis—or story outline—(that's all I can show them when we meet), then I may stay right on here and work with them until the play is in final rehearsal, or I might return home and do it there,—though the Group wants something to start laboratory working on within the next week or so and it'd be more sensible for me to get a cheap two-room apartment for a month or so and stand by.[3]

Don't put out much money on the house.[4] If the Budd-Piper people[5] send another bill try to pay them a little.

Have seen Erm and Loretto.[6] E. looks a bit tired but seems to be happy. No job yet. Lewis is very kind to her. Maybe he doesn't have these internal storms that lash him about in hope, disappointment, yearnings, stirrings and the

---

in December 1934 by the Carolina Playmakers, was "an experiment in mood and atmosphere" (*Shroud My Body Down* [Iowa City: Clio Press, 1935], p. 3) and hardly the kind of thing to interest the socially conscious Group. His only other possibility was an idea for a play that became *The Enchanted Maze.*

2. About entering his unfinished novel *This Body the Earth* in the 1935 Harper Prize Novel Contest, the award for which was $7,500. Cass Canfield was president of Harper and Brothers, and the deadline for finished manuscripts was 1 February.

3. Around 1 February Green returned to Chapel Hill for concentrated work on *This Body the Earth.* The Group had resolved its crisis by deciding to do a play by one of its members, Clifford Odets's *Awake and Sing!* (Clurman, *The Fervent Years*, p. 136). Canfield extended the deadline of Harper's novel contest until Green finished a draft of *This Body the Earth* in May (Harper and Brothers file, 1935, PG-SHC).

4. In the Glen, which the Greens were planning to sell.

5. Roofing company in Durham.

6. Loretto Carroll Bailey, with a Rockefeller Foundation fellowship in 1934–35 to revise *Strike Song* (written with her husband and produced by the Carolina Playmakers in December 1931), frequently went to New York during the period to work with the Theatre Union, one of the newer social theater groups interested in producing her play about the 1929 strike in the textile mills of Gastonia, North Carolina. In June 1934, Green's sister Erma had married Lewis Leverett, an actor in the Group Theatre.

like—or maybe he does. I guess we all do.[7] The Group play is pretty poor stuff—though well-acted.[8]

Hurriedly
with love Paul

## 111. To Albert Lewin[1]

[The Glen, Chapel Hill, N.C.]
16 February 1935

Dear Mr. Lewin:

I have just returned from New York and found your letter waiting me. This accounts for the delay of answering. What you say about *The Laughing Pioneer* interests me very much, for naturally I want to sell the story to the screen, and in the past two or three years at least two studios have considered it—with strings attached. In the meantime I had decided to use the material as a basis for a play, looking towards a New York production, and have already gone so far as to sketch out a synopsis and confer with possible producers and actors for next year.[2] You can see that if the play is produced—and it looks now as if it certainly will be—it would be unwise at this time for me to tie the story up in such a way as to kill this chance. If Mr. Thalberg[3] and you will except the privilege of dramatization, then I will sell the picture rights. However, I think the option price you suggest is too small in view of the fact that the previous sale of motion picture rights will considerably lessen the enthusiasm of any New York producer. Accordingly, in the light of the above, I will sell the story for your total price of $5,500.00, with $1,000.00 to be paid down as an

7. According to Erma Green Gold, the final guess was true of Leverett, and in the fall of 1935 they were divorced (interview with Erma Green Gold, 14 November 1983).

8. *Gold Eagle Guy*, "the story of a power-hungry robber baron in San Francisco" by Melvin Levy (Crawford, *One Naked Individual*, p. 66), which closed on 26 January 1935.

---

1. Lewin, with Metro-Goldwyn-Mayer, had recently sent Green the studio's offer to buy motion picture rights to *The Laughing Pioneer*.

2. Most recently with Sam Byrd, actor (at the time playing in *Tobacco Road*) who hoped to produce *The Laughing Pioneer* as well as act in it (Paul Green to Sam Byrd, 7 April 1935, PG-SHC).

3. Irving Thalberg, a vice president and the driving force at MGM.

option, and the rest to be paid at the end of four months in case you do the picture.

When I was last in Hollywood I conferred with several people who were interested in *The Pioneer* for either Helen Hayes or Pauline Lord.[4] But I have a better suggestion to make to you. The mysterious romantic woman, living and brooding in a great old Southern mansion—a mansion full of memories and ancient glory[5]—has never had adequate representation on the screen. Therefore—Greta Garbo.[6] Specifically, it would not be stretching matters too far to have Miss Alice speak with a husky touch of accent since her mother could have been a far off foreign kind of woman, and Miss Alice somewhere in the story could answer the boy's inquiry by saying that she speaks much like her mother.[7] If Garbo now has no accent then all the better. Anyway she is the only actress I know of who could give forth the strange fire, the hidden vehemence, the great determination and endurance that characterized the dominant women of the Old South. There has been entirely too much of sweetness and light and the Southern honeysuckle, wisteria vine type of womanhood. Above all she would be worthy of whatever romance came to her and certainly a match for it.

Sincerely yours,

## 112. To Barrett H. Clark

[The Glen, Chapel Hill, N.C.]
8 May 1935

Dear Barrett:

Ever since I saw you in New York a few months ago I have been head over heels in my novel, temporarily entitled *This Body the Earth*. I sent the last chapter off Sunday,[1] and Harper's is now setting it up in galley proofs. It

4. Well-known stage actress who had also done several motion pictures.

5. Description of Miss Alice, major character in the novel.

6. Actress and intriguing personality from Stockholm, now under contract to MGM.

7. The novel develops Miss Alice's relationship with a young vagabond who becomes her lover.

1. 5 May.

proved to be quite a job, some six hundred typewritten pages. I feel pretty good over it, and I am sure by the time I rework it it will be even better.

As to *The Laughing Pioneer*—I've sold it to MGM, but with the reservation of all dramatic rights. The price was rather small so far as movie things go, but at Mr. Sheil's suggestion I closed with them. They have paid $1,000 down and are to pay the remaining $4,500 on or before October 15. My agreement with them is to go out and spend two or three weeks touching up the script, for which duty they will pay me more than the price of the book. Both Mr. Sheil and I thought it unwise to pass up this deal despite Sam Byrd's interest in doing the play on Broadway. And since it seems now that *Tobacco Road* will run forever, I am sure we did the right thing.[2] Still I am working out the stage dramatization—for Sam primarily, and will send it along to you shortly to pass on to him. I have instructed MGM to send the remaining $4,500 to French when due.

Feeling the strain of tearing back and forth to California, I have been trying to wangle a picture job to do here in Chapel Hill. (This is mum except for Mr. Sheil.) Rosalie Stewart[3] has worked out an arrangement with Universal for me to do a picture out of Rachel Field's book, *Time Out of Mind*, for the price of $10,000—$1,500 to be deducted from that if they don't need me for the last week's revision. $3,500 is to be paid on their receipt of the first treatment (no right of refusal), and then $5,000 upon acceptance of the shooting script (right of refusal), and $1,500 for a week's revision.[4] I have instructed Rosalie to send the payments to Mr. Sheil, since I am already down on the books there and need $1,000 more to carry me until the first payment comes due. Will you ask him to accommodate me with this one more amount—sending the check direct to the Bank of Chapel Hill. And many thanks.

Knowing the movies as I do, I am sure they will buy my novel, *This Body the Earth*. And when I have corrected the final galleys, which will be near the

2. *Tobacco Road*, Jack Kirkland's dramatization of Erskine Caldwell's novel (1932), opened on 4 December 1933 and over nine seasons ran for 3,182 performances. Byrd, who wished to act in and produce Green's dramatization of *Laughing Pioneer*, played the part of Dude Lester in *Tobacco Road*.

3. Green's new literary agent in Hollywood replacing Hunter Lovelace, who had gone into other work.

4. Green did a film script (*Time Out of Mind* film script, Paul Green Collection, NCC) of Field's novel (1935), but the picture was not made until 1947 and Green is not listed as its author.

middle of the summer, I will get in touch with you and Mr. Sheil about handling it for the movie sale. In fact I will be in New York again before that time and talk it over with you both and with Harper's.[5]

According to my present plans I will be with the Group Theatre the latter part of the summer, working out my *Enchanted Maze* play. The understanding between the Group and me is for early production—rather I should say between Cheryl and me, as she is right much the Group.

The Theatre Alliance looks like a grand thing and I congratulate you.[6] I don't know whether I ought to seek for a place on the board or not, for I might want to offer a play for production. Suppose I do all I can as a simple member. I am writing Elmer Rice.[7]

The Iowa people write that *Shroud My Body Down* will be out in July. I will see that you get a copy of that poetic heartburn.[8]

By the way, will you send Burns Mantle,[9] personally, a copy of *Roll Sweet Chariot*?

With best regards, as always, to you and Mr. Sheil,

5. No studio bought the novel after its publication in late October by Harper and Brothers, and *Honey in the Horn* by H. L. Davis won the Harper Prize that Green coveted for his novel (Cass Canfield to Paul Green, 20 June 1935, PG-SHC).

6. Clark and a number of others in the New York theater and business community had recently established the Theatre Alliance, a producing organization intended to present plays in repertory and, through its play selection, encourage "development of the native drama" (Barrett Clark, Sam Jaffe, et al., to Paul Green, 4 May 1935, PG-SHC; see also *New York Times*, 22 April 1935, p. 15, col. 1; 6 May 1935, p. 22, col. 2; and 22 June 1935, p. 18, col. 2).

7. Rice, playwright trained in the law and active in the American Civil Liberties Union as well as the Dramatists' Guild, was the main organizer of the Theatre Alliance, which failed to raise sufficient money to produce a season of plays (*New York Times*, 7 October 1935, p. 11, col. 1).

8. *Shroud My Body Down*, verse play produced by the Playmakers in 1934 (opened 7 December), was published in 1935 by the Clio Press, Iowa City, in the Whirling World Series of experimental works.

9. Compiler of the annual theatrical record, *The Best Plays of [Season]*.

## 113. To Herbert Kline[1]

[Chapel Hill, N.C.]
15 September 1935

Dear Mr. Kline—

I appreciate your interest in my work and shall look forward to seeing the article. In accordance with your request I have asked Samuel French to send you copies of all my plays.[2]

It is true that some of my radical friends have at one time or another called me to account for what they describe as a tragic and defeatist attitude towards life. They are entitled to their own opinion of course, but I think their findings are wrong. I hold no such attitude. My concern with tragedy and wasteful suffering as subject matter for drama is and has always been that they are mainly products of man's greed and blindness and are to be eradicated. May my friends of the machine and the loom, my comrades of the plough and the hoe, forget me utterly, as they will, if I ever lose that point of view.[3]

Sincerely yours,

1. Kline, editor of *New Theatre*, magazine of the Theatre Union, a socialist group at the Civic Repertory Theatre in New York City, asked Green for a response to the charge by leftists that his plays showed a defeatist attitude and that "plays like *In Abraham's Bosom* . . . were harmful to the cause of the Negroes." Kline raised the question because he hoped to write an article on Green and the valuable contribution his plays made to "a drama of social protest." For the article he also wanted copies of Green's plays (Herbert Kline to Paul Green, 10 September 1935, PG-SHC).

2. Kline seems not to have published an article on Green.

3. Two days earlier Green wrote out a response to Kline, then marked it "not sent." The initial response is a lengthy defense against the charge of defeatism, the key points being: "My concern with poor-whites, Negroes and other oppressed and poverty-stricken human beings has mainly been, I think, due to the fact that their condition makes me want to tell their story to the world. . . . These ruined, broken, lightless lives move me to say my say as nothing else does. . . . I have long believed, and still do, that the way to a new and better order is to know the failure of the present. And it is in these characters I write about that the failure is most manifest for me. . . . If one doesn't write about what excites his sympathy, stirs him to the heart, challenges him, what's the use of writing at all?" (13 September 1935, PG-SHC).

## 114. To Percival Wilde[1]

[Chapel Hill, N.C.]
[Mid-October 1935]

[Dear Mr. Wilde—]

I agree that the chain-gang is the matter of concern in "Hymn to the Rising Sun," and not any sort of sex vagary. But precisely because that is true, I think it would be a mistake to have Runt's punishment come as a result of some minor infraction of rules. For then the darker, more disastrous nature of convict life would be but once again illustrated by a pathetic and not tragic incident—and tragedy is what I am after in the piece, since the lives I am telling about are tragic. Suppose the Negro were put into the sweatbox because he had been caught smoking in his bunk, or talking back to one of the guards. Then the dramatic result would be to point the finger of accusation at the system the while it put an arm of sympathy around the abused individual. But this would be the old sheep-and-goat method now a little dear to our younger radical writers, and not true to the infinite complexity and shades of difference of human nature. Again, the Runt is what he is because the system is what it is, and the system obtains as it does because of such fellows as Runt. But—and here the higher reality comes in—the observer (you, others, myself)

1. In June 1935 Percival Wilde (1887–1953), writer in Princeton, New Jersey, asked Green to contribute to a projected anthology of one-act plays on social themes (Percival Wilde to Paul Green, 24 June 1935, PG-SHC). The request came as a trial was about to begin in North Carolina of prison officials accused of mistreating convicts in the state chain gangs, especially blacks. The trial was triggered by reports that two black convicts, Shropshire and Barnes, had both legs amputated because their feet froze and gangrene set in after their chain gang boss left them chained in an unheated cell for several frigid days in January. Green hoped the trial would create a climate of opinion in which the chain gang system could be abolished, and in that mood he began a play for Wilde's anthology that became "Hymn to the Rising Sun." Wilde responded enthusiastically when he received the play (Wilde to Green, 25 September 1935) but later objected to the use of masturbation as the reason why Runt, a convict in the play, is locked in the sweatbox, where he dies. Wilde told Green, "Your tremendous play might be even more tremendous if Runt's offense were a triviality which would not be punished anywhere else; . . . [and] its value as propaganda would be definitely increased if the offense were of such a nature that it could be openly discussed in mixed companies. The more people talk about the play, the better you will be pleased; masturbation is not the issue; the chain-gang is" (11 October 1935).

stands outside the vicious circle and sees that we must go back, far, far back, to start growing a different and happier society. And that is true, isn't it? And after all what better criterion than truth?[2]

## 115. To Elizabeth L. Green

[Hotel Roosevelt, Hollywood, Calif.]
Friday [29 November 1935]

Dear Honey—

I got in here yesterday morning (Thanksgiving), as I wrote,[1] and everything at the studios was standing still. This morning Rosalie[2] and I had a short meeting and she is bubbling with enthusiasm as usual—she looked resplendent in nice clothes, new Buick and a chauffeur. Honestly you ought to see this place—wealth, munificence, glitter hanging from the trees. Hotels have been remodeled, including a shiny basalt front for the Montecito,[3] which I passed a few minutes ago on my way down town for my baggage, Highland Avenue has been widened, houses to rent are at a premium (columns in the newspapers for such having shrunk to a couple of inches), Warners and First National all painted over[,] fine curtains, pictures, etc., also ten (10) new stages being built, etc. etc. including Dorothy[4] making $200 a month out on the Zanuck-Fox lot. (But one person seems not to have suffered any benefits from the boom—namely, Vernon.[5] I saw "them" last night and he's still on the status of Uncle Bierny the old car, nor has Willie's salary been raised, she says.) Even the Southern Pacific steward told me they had done a bigger business the

2. Wilde included "Hymn to the Rising Sun" in *Contemporary One-Act Plays from Nine Countries* (Boston: Little, Brown, 1936), pp. 7–37, and introduced it with Green's letter, saying: "The squeamish may object to the reason assigned for 'Runt's' punishment. They should not. It is most logical, and the subject itself is dealt with in the most matter-of-fact way in all modern works on penology. A letter from the author dealing with the point is so interesting that it may be quoted in its entirety" (p. 6).

---

1. In a telegram to Elizabeth on 28 November 1935.
2. Stewart, his Hollywood agent.
3. Where the Greens had an apartment in 1933.
4. McBrayer, Green's secretary at Fox Films when he first went to Hollywood in 1931, who remained a lifelong friend.
5. Stacy, married to Green's cousin Willie Cutts Stacy.

last year than ever before. Rosalie says "things are definitely on the go. Zanuck says he wants you, Paramount wants you,"—everybody wants you, and so on. But in a conference with Warner Bros this morning they wanted me but at the old figure. They say they're entitled to, etc.[6] We finally ended the meeting by their saying that I might do a picture as a job.[7] I told them I had to be home for Christmas, and that I could write a script between now and then. Okay, they said. But the rub was that *Green Light* was the piece—"we've been holding it for you," etc.[8] This afternoon I've been here in my room at Hotel Roosevelt studying the book. Just a moment ago on the phone they said they had got hold of something I might like, *Tales of Hoffmann.*[9] That sounds better. They're sending the book around here to the hotel in a few minutes. Rosalie and I are going over to M. G. M. next week for a meeting with them about the *Laughing Pioneer*, also she says there are three studios interested in *This Body* and will get something put through about that soon. But as always, I only believe when I see these folks writing on the dotted line.

Dorothy's sister is going to type the college play,[10] which I worked on on the way out. I'll send a copy to Cheryl immediately. In reading it I realized more than ever that it's not near right. I need at least two more different scenes. As it stands it's only a one act play. And in my revisions sent on to Sam from Montgomery[11] I divided the play into scenes, not acts, as follows—

Scene 1. Scene 2.

Intermission

Scene 3. Scene 4. Scene 5. Scene 6.

Intermission

6. In 1932, when his salary at Fox was $625 per week, Green had contracted to do a picture for Warner Brothers, a picture continually postponed until now. His most recent Hollywood salary, paid by Darryl Zanuck in 1934–35, was $2,000 per week.

7. That is, at a flat fee for the script rather than on a per week basis.

8. Novel (1935) by Lloyd C. Douglas.

9. Probably not the Offenbach opera of that title but the stories on which it is based—stories of the supernatural by the nineteenth-century German writer Ernst Hoffmann.

10. *The Enchanted Maze.*

11. Samuel Seldon, director with the Playmakers, had *The Enchanted Maze* in rehearsal for an opening in Chapel Hill on 6 December 1935, and Green was still at work on the script when he took the train for Los Angeles on Sunday night, 24 November. He sent the revisions to Seldon from Mobile (Green diary, 25 November 1935, PG-SHC).

Scene 7. Scene 8.
Maybe this and the music will help it to pass, but in cold consideration I was disappointed. A hundred and twenty pages and too little had happened.

Among the changes here, some have been sad—if not all—Berkeley died of an operation—D. says drink, cirrhosis of the liver.[12] He was penniless, friends took up a collection. Don't repeat it. Also Carl Ericson's wife left him and he committed suicide a few weeks ago. A fine fellow, as you know, and he should never have got into the writing game, with no more talent than he had. So—

So as my plans stand now, I will try my best to close a deal on one or two books, finish the Warner job and be home for Christmas for any of the breaks of N.Y. towards a production. I'll let you know everything definitely as soon as I am settled. Address me here at Hotel Roosevelt temporarily. If the Wilde proof of the chaingang play comes send it on immediately.

Love to you all, Paul
A sign of the real good times is that everybody seems to [be] trying to get a divorce—I'm swearing off the newspapers awhile.—Also high-powered armored cars with inside guards have made their appearance on the street—hauling bank money. What a world. I need refuge from my thoughts.

## 116. To Elizabeth L. Green

Hotel Roosevelt, Hollywood, Calif.
8 December 1935

Dear Honey—

It was nice to hear your voice[1] and I wish you all weren't so far away. But—Anyway I'll be back for Christmas and that's better than I expected when I left.

12. Reginald Berkeley, a British screenwriter in Hollywood, was at work on *Carolina* when Green met him in 1933. The Greens remained in touch with Berkeley through his close association with Dorothy McBrayer, who mentioned Berkeley's death, though not the details, in a letter to Green just before he left Chapel Hill: "Mr. Berkeley died ten days after I returned from India. It was very depressing" (8 November 1935, PG-SHC).

1. Following the opening of *The Enchanted Maze* in Chapel Hill on 6 December, Elizabeth called to tell him about the reception of the play.

I am working here in my hotel[2]—a little room, single bed, $3 a day, $18 a week. Have just got (rented) a dictaphone and am going to try to get a rough draft of the picture finished before I leave—bringing the script back and finishing it at home, also I hope [to] do *Tales of Hoffmann* there or a script on Beethoven.[3] No news on *This Body the Earth*. Lovelace thinks there's no picture in it, though Rosalie says "two studios are definitely interested." I can't make heads or tails of Rosalie; she has so many irons in the fire. Hunter L. is talking of going back into the agency business and wants "to handle me." I'd rather have him. He is taking charge of *Laughing Pioneer* and says he'll be able to close a deal on it. I think we have a copy of the book there. As soon as you get this, wrap it up and send it to him—

Hunter Lovelace.
180 South Orange Drive,
Hollywood California

So far I have stuck pretty close here in my room brooding on this *Green Light*. It's a tough assignment, but I'm beginning to see the light—red, I'm afraid.[4]

Dorothy[5] has done a lot of typing for me—"Hymn to Rising Sun," also *The Enchanted Maze*. Last night I read the clean version (The E. M.) over and am sorrier than ever that I didn't let Chapel Hill have my tragic ending—Parker's suicide in lab 8th scene, as well as the wrecking of the bell tower.[6] I am writing

2. On the film script of *Green Light*.

3. Neither of which worked out.

4. Never enthusiastic about the novel, Green finished a film script, but when Warner Brothers released the picture early in 1937 only Milton Krims was credited with the screenplay.

5. McBrayer.

6. *The Enchanted Maze* opened in Chapel Hill on the night of 6 December, and the next day Koch wired Green, in part: "LIB AND ALL YOUR FRIENDS AND CRITICS AGREE ENDING OF PLAY FROM WINFORD'S CONCLUSION OF SEVENTH SCENE THROUGH EIGHTH OBVIOUSLY ANTI-CLIMACTIC STOP UNLESS YOU WIRE US WILL CLOSE PLAY TONIGHT WITH PARKER'S COMMENCEMENT SPEECH AND PRATT'S REACTION IN AUDIENCE" (copy of telegram in Playmakers Scrapbook, 1935–36, NCC). Green acquiesced, and the play as given by the Playmakers on 7 and 9 December ended with a speech by the central character (Parker) denouncing universities for undermining the vision of students and a speech by a disillusioned student (Pratt) declaring he will never set foot on a university campus again (*Carolina Play-Book*, December 1935, pp. 112–17). The

out the ending and sending it all on to Cheryl with the firm statement that this version is only "material." Then when I get to N.Y. after Christmas maybe we can go ahead with it. Honestly I am surprised at the reception (according to yours and Proff's report) the play got in C.H.[7] I was afraid it would be the awfulest wash-out, what with crude actors, etc., etc. Sam is something of a marvel. How he ever got it on at all in such short time is beyond me. Tell him again my hat is off to him.

Today I had lunch over at K. MacGowan's house.[8] His wife looks very old and sad, doesn't like California, evidently broods upon her lost talent as a painter, and so on. K. asked me to try to cheer her up with praise for the climate, your attitude to it all, and so I did. But with no success. "It's all right for you men to like it here" she said with tears welling into her eyes, "but for me—" We had to change the subject. Last night I read again *Madame Bovary* and so at this lunch I felt very superior in my reaffirmed knowledge about women. Their greatest ogre, and enemy, is not their own betraying hearts but the god ambition that steals their men away from them. So they think. But

---

omitted ending had Parker, years later, showing a maze with rats in it to a group of freshmen and assuring them that humans, like the rats, had the power to break out of the maze of custom, and that the purpose of education was to unleash that power (Playmakers Scrapbook, 1935–36, NCC).

7. Koch's telegram opened: "ENCHANTED MAZE GREAT SUCCESS LAST NIGHT STOP REVERBERATIONS OF EXPLOSION STILL ROARING." The play attacks universities for sacrificing their educational mission to the demands of philanthropists willing to give millions to schools that accept the social status quo, and to the emphasis on scientific scholarship, which attaches greater importance to fact than to vision. The play did stir up an "explosion" of controversy on the campuses of UNC and Duke University, both of which had benefited from philanthropists and largely adopted the scientific method in scholarship, and several state and national newspapers joined in. (Newspaper clippings on the controversy fill several pages of the Playmakers Scrapbook, 1935–36, NCC; see, for example, *Daily Tar Heel*, 7 December 1935, p. 1, col. 5; *Greensboro Daily News*, 7 December 1935, p. 9, col. 5; *NO*, 10 December 1935, p. 1, col. 3; 11 December 1935, p. 2, col. 1; *Gastonia Daily Gazette*, 10 December 1935, p. 4; and *New York Herald Tribune*, 15 December 1935, sec. 5, p. 4, col. 6.)

8. Green met Kenneth Macgowan in 1926 when the Experimental Theatre, headed by Macgowan, Eugene O'Neill, and Robert Edmond Jones, produced *In Abraham's Bosom*. The period of *Abraham* was Macgowan's last with the former Provincetown Players group, and by 1932 he was in Hollywood, a film producer with RKO Studios. In August 1935 he joined Twentieth Century–Fox as a producer. He and Edna Behre had married in 1913 in Boston.

they're wrong again, poor things, I thought to myself as I looked at Mrs. M's worry-laden face. Men without ambition wouldn't interest them long, and so the solution ought to be through a unity of ambition. You get me. etc. etc.

Tonight I feel as if I were on the chaingang, quoting to myself Captain Huff's words "This ain't no life for a human being."[9] Sitting cooped up here trying to make enough money to pay this and that. But I keep saying also that it's a very short time and I'll waste as little of it as I can—get it over with—push on—drink the bad dose of medicine and pray it helps, if not one's stomach, his character's fortitude.

Last night I saw Billy Erwin.[10] He looks like a ghost—thin, abstracted, something on his mind—his laugh is a sort of dry stretch of his facial muscles. He ought to leave here. I hope to have a good talk with him soon, try to buck him up. He says he saw Leon[11] Thursday night just as he L. was catching a bus to go to San Francisco to see his girl. Leon has written a book, he says, which he's carrying around trying to get published. All sounds very like Hugo Hoffmansthal's son.[12] He, so Billy says, is not too happy, talks of stowing away on some ship to Japan, China or somewhere.

Dorothy is as pretty as ever and speaks with loathing of India.[13] She asks about the children—especially Byrd. Tell Byrd this, for D. is very fond of her, also Janet comes in for a great deal of praise. Last night Billy and I drove out to Pacific Palisades[14]—the silent dark (two) houses brought a lump into my throat. We stopped and spoke to Mrs. Robinson.[15] She showered me with joy as if I were Jesus come again. She had a thousand questions about you, the

9. Approximates a line near the end of the speech by the chain-gang captain on the meaning of the Fourth of July in "Hymn to the Rising Sun."

10. Young man from Salisbury, North Carolina, who went to Hollywood with the Greens a few years earlier and now worked at Twentieth Century–Fox.

11. Leon Russell, son of Phillips Russell who was now married to Green's sister Caro Mae and taught creative writing at UNC.

12. Hugo Von Hofmannsthal (1874–1929), Viennese poet and playwright, died of a stroke a day after the suicide of his son Franz, a frustrated writer estranged from his father (*New York Times*, 16 July 1929, p. 25, col. 2; 8 September 1929, sec. 4, p. 8, col. 2).

13. McBrayer went to India in September 1934 for work with the Theosophical Society in Madras, then returned to Hollywood in the summer of 1935 (Dorothy McBrayer to Paul Green, 27 August 1934 and 8 November 1935, PG-SHC).

14. Where the Greens rented two houses during the summer of 1934, a small one, as a place for Green to work, across the street from the one they lived in.

15. Friend and former piano teacher of the Green children.

children, and told a flowing story of their visit in England, then switched off to music, sent her regards to Paul and Byrd and also solicitous urges that they keep on with their music at all costs. Then from the back room the captain's bass calls out "Well, I say" and Mrs. R. hurried me in to see him. He was already in bed for the night and looked doubly lean and diabolical stretched out under the sheets. A few words in which I learn that things are just "sliding along" with him and then into another room to see Nancy June, who was sleeping like an angel with a little doll's face close to hers. That Robinson ma'm is certainly a remarkable woman—an overflowing heart and all that goes with it.

I was wrong about Vernon.[16] He does have a job—gets up and goes to work at 5 and stays till seven. He's running a café down town—employs several girls and has already made enough to make it show in his dress and manner. He is talking about a new car and plans for building a little house "some of these days"—etc.

If I don't stop and get to work on G. Light you'll think I'm homesick or something. Really I'm getting along okay, but feel like a race horse temporarily stopped from running. A thousand plays, stories and novels keep bubbling up in me and they seem to bubble the more since I got in the habit of trying to write them during the last year.

My love—Paul

Don't let the potatoes freeze—

The stuff about MacGowan's wife is confidential, of course.

## 117. To Elizabeth L. Green

Warner Bros. Studios, Burbank, Calif.
[11 December 1935]

Dear Honey—

Thanks so much for the letter and clippings about the play.[1] Apparently everything is wrong and most everything is suggestedly right with it. I agree that it's too bad that I couldn't be there during rehearsals, for I could have told whether it was fitting to add the tragic suicide or not. A wire has just come

16. In letter 115.

1. *The Enchanted Maze.*

from Cheryl begging for it—their two plays are reported as flops[2]—and I have sent the script on with a long letter explaining my planned changes. In the next few days I expect to be able to have the whole thing improved, though this picture[3] keeps me pretty busy—day and night.[4]

Please economize until I notify you differently—I mean on Christmas shopping. Money is hard for me to get hold of here—As yet haven't been able to put through a deal with anybody—though plenty of talk. Can get all the jobs I want if I remain here but otherwise it seems slow go. This $625 a week seems so small compared to the former $2,000.

Out of this check pay what bills you have to and do your Christmas shopping. It's about all I'll be able to send until I get home—*Don't think of getting Paul and Byrd new bikes*!

Love, Paul

I wish you would begin preparing a list with addresses of all (1) members of N.C. Legislature and Senate of last year, (2) Superior Court judges in N.C., (3) N.C. newspaper editors and any others you think should receive copies of New Theatre containing play. Am asking Molly Thacher to allow me 200 copies.[5]

2. *Weep for the Virgins* by Nellise Childs, which opened on 11 November 1935 and ran for nine performances, and *Paradise Lost* by Clifford Odets, which the Group opened on 9 December 1935 and, by means of salary cuts and a newspaper campaign, kept going for seventy-two performances (Clurman, *The Fervent Years*, p. 157).

3. *Green Light.*

4. Green left California for Chapel Hill on 20 December (telegram, Paul Green to Elizabeth Green, 13 December 1935, PG-SHC), then on 1 January went to New York City to confer with Crawford and others in the Group about *The Enchanted Maze.* On 4 January 1936 he wrote to Koch from New York saying the Group thought the play not in shape for production and asking Koch not to let out copies of the script since he planned to spend the spring revising the play (letter in Playmakers Scrapbook, 1935–36, NCC). When the play was published in 1939, it was in five scenes, the last scene bringing a version of the tragic ending into the original scene 7.

5. Thacher, drama editor of *New Theatre*, had scheduled "Hymn to the Rising Sun" for the January 1936 issue, which Green would send to numerous state leaders. Percival Wilde objected to having the play appear in the magazine three months before his anthology was to come out, but Green went ahead because of his desire to influence the debate over chain gangs in North Carolina as soon as possible.

## 118. To Elizabeth L. Green

277 Trumbull Avenue, Nichols, Conn.
18 June 1936

Dearest Honey—[1]

Just a note. Your sweet letter came this morning and set me so hungry for you I can hardly stay at my typewriter. Yes, we understand each other now better than ever before, that is, I understand myself better. I do love you so, and realize what a fine golden woman you are—I hope I can always keep that vision in front of me when I get "down." It will give me something to cling to. And when you need me I'll try to be strong enough for your need. But let me tell you this in my arms!—I hope near the end of this ungodly month. No, I don't mean that exactly, for I have begun to enjoy my work a bit. I've moved my typewriter over into an old deserted 200-year-old house near here and work way up stairs by a little window. Looking out I almost expect to see Indians or hear the tramp of the king's men.

That income tax man sounds ominous. I have no doubt they'll figure out something we owe somebody. They always do.[2]

1. In February, during a visit in Chapel Hill by Harold Clurman, Green and the Group decided to drop *The Enchanted Maze* (1936 Green diary, p. 100, PG-SHC; Clurman, *The Fervent Years*, p. 172), and in April Green began to think about "a sort of comic anti-war play" for the Group (1936 Green diary, p. 104, PG-SHC). Kurt Weill, in New York after escaping Nazi Germany, wanted to work with an American playwright; and Cheryl Crawford, finding that "the most American playwright I could think of was Paul Green," in May brought Weill to Chapel Hill, where the three of them planned the "comic anti-war" musical that became *Johnny Johnson*, taking "general inspiration" from Jaroslav Hašek's *The Good Soldier Schweik* (1930), Georg Büchner's *Woyzeck* (1836–37), and Carl Zuckmayer's *The Captain of Köpenick* (1930) (Crawford, *One Naked Individual*, pp. 93–94). Green also "read Woodrow Wilson's war speeches. I still think he was a great man in many ways—his world (religious) view of nations and their mutual and necessary responsibilities" (1936 Green diary, 1–13 May, PG-SHC). He worked on the musical into June and also sold his house in Chapel Hill (in the Glen) and began construction of the new one just out of town (in Greenwood). On 4 June he took a train for New York City, then on 8 June went with the Group to their summer rehearsal headquarters at the Pine Brook Club in Nichols, Connecticut, near Bridgeport. Green, Crawford, Weill, and Lotte Lenya (Weill's wife) stayed about two miles from the club in an old house on Trumbull Avenue. Elizabeth's letter to which this one responds is lost, unfortunately.

2. The Internal Revenue Service claimed that Green still owed $1,758.40 on his 1935 income tax, and Elizabeth $769.25. For tax purposes he had taken California as his

Thanks for the pictures of the house. Save your dollars and let no contracts until I okay them or come home to go over things.

My plans are to come home for about a week—I might have told you—at the end of the month, arrange for a loan with Allen or somebody, let contracts, then come back here and stay until the play is well launched in rehearsals or is dead and discarded.[3]

Hurriedly and with my love and kisses.

Ah, what a mixture of things our days have been. But the peace and stress of creation have stood out foremost. That's good too.

Paul

## 119. To Elizabeth L. Green

Hotel Bristol, 129–135 West 48th Street, New York City
Monday [Late August 1936]

Dearest Honey—[1]

Everybody is tickled with the cowboy ballad. I told Cheryl you wrote it, and Tony sings it beautifully.[2]

---

state of residence, and the IRS based its claim on a denial of that residency status. After correspondence and meetings that ran into January 1937, the IRS reduced the bill to $133.11 for Green and $78.27 for Elizabeth, which Green paid (Treasury Department file, 1936 and 1937, PG-SHC).

3. Green would get home on 18 July (telegram, Paul Green to Elizabeth Green, 16 July 1936, PG-SHC), arrange a construction loan with Charles S. Allen of Durham Bond and Mortgage Company, and spend a few days overseeing work on the new house in Greenwood. At the end of July he returned to Connecticut and wrote to Elizabeth: "I've been thinking about how hard Charlie [Brooks, contractor for the new house] and his men are working—I see their sweat-stained shirts, their arms going up and down sawing, sawing, nailing, nailing. And I think we can afford to increase their wage a bit. (Consider old man Barbour [O. Z. Barbour, doing masonry work on the house] charging 75 cts. an hour.) I've figured that the increase mentioned in the memorandum attached will cost us $120 more and it will mean so much to the men. So if you agree, hand this memo. to Charlie" (30 July 1936, EG-SHC).

---

1. In late August the Group returned to New York City to rehearse *Johnny Johnson* (Harold Clurman directing), and Green took a room in the Hotel Bristol.

2. Elizabeth wrote the lyrics of two songs in *Johnny Johnson*, the cowboy ballad "Oh, the Rio Grande" sung by Tony Kraber in the Group production, and the song of the cannons. Both are in the same scene (act 2, scene 2 in *Johnny Johnson: The*

I'm glad you have "ideas" in your head, and we must both work so that we don't stagnate. In the long run we will be worth more to the children and to the world by keeping on with some sort of career. It's the example—the living image—that affects a child more than the precept and the vague expression of hopes and specific "oughts." Golly, I want you here so bad. Also I need you—four of my one acters are in rehearsal on 63rd St,[3] and I'm so busy with J. J. I can't help out there, you could. Also I've got to do that Stage article—$150—which I'll devote to you for your trip up next week???[4]

Tomorrow I finish the script of J. J. and begin getting it ready for publication. Mr. Sheil is glad, he says, to get out a "different" edition.[5] The Group continues elated, and I try to be, though I'm far from satisfied with the diminutive ending and Johnny's song.[6]

Barrett is thriving. Lamar is here.[7] Erm[8] is living temporarily with a girl friend at 148 E. 27th. She sends her love.

---

*Biography of a Common Man* [New York: Samuel French, 1937] and in John Gassner, ed., *Five Plays of the South* [New York: Hill and Wang, 1963]; act 1, scene 6 in the 1971 edition).

3. Location of the Federal Theatre Project's Experimental Theatre, which had in rehearsal numerous plays, including Green's "In the Valley," "Unto Such Glory," "Fixin's," and "Hymn to the Rising Sun." "Hymn" and "Unto Such Glory" would be produced by the Federal Theatre Project at the Experimental Theatre, opening on 6 May 1937 for a run into July (Hallie Flanagan, *Arena: The History of the Federal Theatre* [1940; reprint, New York: Benjamin Blom, 1965], pp. 393, 428).

4. Emanuel Eisenberg, press representative of the Group, asked Green to do a piece on *Johnny Johnson* for *Stage Magazine* (Emanuel Eisenberg to Paul Green, 11 August 1936, PG-SHC), but Green seems not to have gotten to it, and Elizabeth did not visit him in New York City before the opening of *Johnny Johnson* in November.

5. "Different" perhaps because the play is set mainly outside the South or because it is a musical drama. Samuel French published *Johnny Johnson* in April 1937.

6. The play closes with a quietly ironic scene: as everyone else gives ear to a demagogue in the distance raving about military preparedness and war, Johnny strolls off singing about brotherhood, justice, and peace. Green always wanted something more dynamic for Johnny to do at the end, such as pleading with the crowd himself and thus creating a disturbance, but never thought of anything suitable (Paul Green to Stella Adler, 31 December 1955, PG-SHC).

7. Stringfield, living with his brother, O. L. Stringfield, in Glenbrook, Connecticut, did much conducting in New York with Works Progress Administration (WPA) orchestras and over the radio during the summer and fall of 1936.

8. Who had gotten divorced from Lewis Leverett in the fall of 1935.

I'm saving every cent I can, hoping to get where I can have you up. As for clothes, you could get here and buy a few things after you arrive.

I love you with your ideas and urge to flight from the rut more than ever. I'll try to help. And don't throw off on your abilities as a mother either. They all go together.

Paul

I think "Raleigh Road—8431" is the safest and most honest address, for the time being.[9]

## 120. To Charles de Sheim[1]

[New York City]
13 October [1936]

FOR YOUR SAKE AM TERRIBLY SORRY YOUR PRODUCTION OF PLAY IS BANNED AND AM ANXIOUS TO HELP IN WHATEVER WAY I CAN TO STRAIGHTEN OUT THE TANGLE. WITH KINDEST REGARDS AND APPRECIATION FOR THE WORK YOU ARE DOING[2]

Paul Green

9. Raleigh Road, a little over a mile away, was the closest state or city road to their new house, and 8431 was their telephone number.

---

1. Charles de Sheim (d. 1941), director with the Federal Negro Theatre in Chicago, had in rehearsal "Hymn to the Rising Sun," and the production had just been banned. Richard Wright, press representative of the Federal Negro Theatre, persuaded de Sheim to attempt the play, but on the night of its scheduled opening, 9 October 1936, Robert J. Dunham, Illinois administrator of the WPA, prohibited the production, saying the play was "of such a moral character that I can't even discuss it with a member of the press" (*Chicago Tribune*, 10 October 1936, p. 1, cols. 6–7). Trying to prevent the cancellation, George Kondolf, head of the Federal Theatre in Chicago, appealed to Hallie Flanagan (Flanagan, *Arena*, pp. 136–37) and also wired Green, quoting Dunham as above, giving de Sheim as the person to contact, and asking "WHAT CAN YOU DO" (13 October 1936, PG-SHC).

2. Several attempts failed to lift the prohibition, and de Sheim resigned as director of the Federal Negro Theatre (Flanagan, *Arena*, p. 137). Wright, frustrated first by the lack of enthusiasm for the play on the part of the black cast and now angry about the cancellation, had himself transferred from the Federal Negro Theatre and after a short time went to the WPA Writers Project for work on the guidebook for Illinois (Michael Fabre, *The Unfinished Quest of Richard Wright*, trans. Isabel Barzun [New York: Morrow, 1973], p. 133).

## 121. To Elizabeth L. Green

[New York City]
Saturday night [17 October 1936]

Dearest Honey—

Just a note to let you know I am still here and kicking. The show is going along as well as could be hoped—though now it's announced in the papers to open November 14.[1] I simply can't see how I can stay here that long. No matter if I try to live like a pauper it costs terribly. Monday morning I'm going to send a wire to Rosalie[2] to get busy and find me a picture to do—and quick. In the meantime I'll start combing New York for something. I keep laboring on the script trying to get everything in and yet cut it down into playing time. So far I haven't succeeded. I'm as nervous as a witch with it, but see next Wednesday as a day when almost the last touches will be in. This living without you is a mess for us both,[3] and if we ever get out of these financial doldrums we must arrange things better. Hallie Flanagan up from Wash. to breakfast this morning.[4] She wants—after N.Y. showing—to open Johnny in many W. P. A. theatres throughout the country, using W. P. A. orchestras and actors.[5]

Jim Boyd,[6] Erm and several of us went to Carolina–N. Y. U. ball game today.[7] Jim has just had his eye operated on, "cut open like a watermelon,"

1. *Johnny Johnson* would open on 19 November at the Forty-fourth Street Theatre. Both Clurman and Crawford thought the theater too large, but it was the only one available (Clurman, *The Fervent Years*, pp. 176–77; Crawford, *One Naked Individual*, p. 96).

2. Stewart, Green's agent in Hollywood.

3. Revised from "a mess for me."

4. Green was closely associated with the Federal Theatre Project from its inception. He was on the National Theatre Conference program at the University of Iowa in the summer of 1935 when Harry Hopkins announced the creation of the project and named Hallie Flanagan its director. Flanagan came to the job from Vassar, and *Arena: The History of the Federal Theatre* (1940) is her account of the project and the ideas behind it. She appointed Frederick Koch director of the project's southern region, and when trips from Washington took her to Chapel Hill, she usually visited with the Greens and held meetings at their home.

5. Federal Theatre productions of *Johnny Johnson* were mounted in Boston, New Orleans, and Los Angeles.

6. Novelist and friend of the Greens from Southern Pines, North Carolina.

7. Football game won by UNC, 14–13.

etc.—"didn't hurt a bit." Brave boy. Jim and Kate[8] have had a hard session with Helen and Laurence.[9] Helen left last night for Reno in tears—divorce. Kate says Laurence is off his head, etc., not crazy but wild as a hant. Nobody could do anything about patching their case up, not even the political economist Walter L[10]—I had a strong urge to try to talk to Helen and (also) beg those two not to ruin their lives, but I knew too well that people don't steer with that sort of advice.[11] Well, I'm too tired to describe the pictures that shoot up in my mind, but I feel sad about it, and Jim and Kate are much upset. I'm afraid it's the old story—success came with too much money too soon for them both. Oh hell!—On that basis I ought someday to be a great literary emperor, for I'm getting hammered on the anvil plenty long, and yet I know the hammer's in my own hand. So—

Once again I must tell you how everybody likes your lyrics. Last night Tony (the cowboy part) sang his song for a lot of theatrical people. They were delighted.

If I finish off my part of the play and certain army technique rehearsals which I must do,[12] I'll come home next weekend for a couple of weeks—provided further, I have some money to pay bills with.

Please stop in at Strowd's[13] and tell Bruce I couldn't get by the other day, but I'll send him a check the last of this month.

Don't worry, honey, we'll get our heads above board somehow.

I love you, that's the main thing any way. The only change in me is that I've gradually become aware of the necessity of saying it now and then. And another way in which I've never changed one bit from the first day I met you—that I love you more the nearer the light you are and I am. Of course I may not always judge the right light by what I see shining high ahead, but I must think

8. Boyd's wife, Katharine.

9. Stallings.

10. Lippmann, friend of the Stallings since the early 1920s, when he and Stallings worked for the *New York World.* Lippmann became guardian of their two children following the Stallings' divorce, granted on 1 December 1936 (Joan R. Brittain, *Laurence Stallings* [Boston: Twayne Publishers, 1975], p. 24).

11. Noted in the margin: "For they are the sort whom memory of more beautiful days will harass to death. I don't think they have anything to build on now."

12. Green was the only one associated with the production who had military experience.

13. Chapel Hill's Ford dealership, owned by Bruce Strowd.

I do—nothing can be done about that. And that old practical-ideal dream of our following our talents (be they small or great) the while we paid our "pleasurable and necessary dues to biology" and the old man river of life also remains as constant with me today as it did the day you named the anemones for me there by Horace's hill.[14]

And still another constancy—your letters are as fresh—fresher[15]—today as they were that long ago summer when you wrote "Machiavellian Night"[16] and I was so pleased at your vast learning.

Paul

## 122. To Pierre de Rohan[1]

[Chapel Hill, N.C.]
14 December 1936

Dear Mr. Rohan—

When I consider the gloomy first meeting we all had preparatory to the launching of the Federal Theatre[2] and see today what Hallie Flanagan and you others have done, I take off my hat in astonishment and surprise. The Federal Theatre Project is the biggest thing that's ever happened to the American stage or American drama for that matter. Through it a new and living theatre has been born, and that's enough to justify the project against any and all adverse contentions of whatever voice, sect or creed—as well as against the cash-register which refuses to add up correctly.

As to its potentialities, they are infinite. And here I might get loose for several pages on community play, education, self-expression, and social adjustment, not to mention the vital life-giving art of the theatre itself, if you didn't stop me. However, I will restrain myself in the contemplation of a

14. Hillside near Horace Williams's home, then on the outskirts of Chapel Hill.

15. Noted in the margin: "(inconstancy there—a bit)."

16. Unlocated.

---

1. Rohan, editor of the *Federal Theatre Magazine*, asked Green for a statement about the Federal Theatre Project for his January issue (Pierre de Rohan to Paul Green, 10 December 1936, PG-SHC).

2. Perhaps the first meeting of regional directors, in Washington, 8 and 9 October 1935, which Green attended with Koch, director of the southern region.

brightening dream which I believe will be made possible by this very project—namely, A National Peoples Theatre.[3]

Sincerely yours, Paul Green

3. A "dream" Green outlines in "Nationwide Drama," in Green, *Plough and Furrow*, pp. 1–26.

# IV

## *The Lost Colony* and *Native Son*, 1937–1941

Winter–Spring 1937
In Chapel Hill writes *The Lost Colony.*

June–July 1937
On Roanoke Island for rehearsals and opening of *The Lost Colony* on 4 July.

Fall–Winter 1937
Begins *The Common Glory* for Federal Theatre Project production (project ends before production).

January 1938
Lecture tour to University of Florida and University of Miami.

Summer 1938
Sets aside about 100 acres in Greenwood for residential lots.

June 1938
On Roanoke Island for revision and rehearsal of *The Lost Colony.*

September 1938
Returns to UNC faculty in recently formed Department of Dramatic Art (heretofore drama program was part of Department of English).

18 September 1938
Pallbearer at funeral of Thomas Wolfe in Asheville.

February 1939
Leads unsuccessful campaign to bring Wolfe books and papers to UNC library.

Summer 1939
Writes *The Highland Call.*

23 August 1939
*The Lost Colony* broadcast nationally on CBS radio.

November 1939
*The Highland Call* produced in Fayetteville, North Carolina.

May 1940
Offers to dramatize Richard Wright's *Native Son.* Helps Zora Neale Hurston collect Negro spirituals.

July–August 1940
With Wright in Chapel Hill dramatizes *Native Son.*

Fall–Winter 1940
Revises *Native Son.*

November 1940
Elected to two-year term as first president of National Theatre Conference.

18 January 1941
Inducted into National Institute of Arts and Letters.

February–March 1941
Disagrees with producer John Houseman and director Orson Welles about last scene of *Native Son.*

25 March 1941
*Native Son* opens in New York City with last scene as revised by Welles (published in April with last scene closer to Green's version).

Summer–Fall 1941
Works through National Theatre Conference to establish theaters at Fort Bragg in North Carolina and other military bases.

17 December 1941
Flies to Los Angeles to write film script for *Rumelhearts of Rampler Avenue*, produced by Harold Clurman.

## 123. To D. B. Fearing[1]

Raleigh Road, Chapel Hill, N.C.
18 January 1937

Dear Mr. Fearing—

This is to confirm the agreement made between the Roanoke Colony Memorial Association of Manteo and myself in your office on January 16; namely that—

I am to write and deliver to you for production in July, 1937, a pageant-drama entitled *The Lost Colony*, said pageant to be the sole property of the Roanoke Colony Memorial Association of Manteo, and to be produced and shown only at Manteo;[2] that—

1. D. B. Fearing (1890–1943), state legislator and merchant in Manteo, North Carolina, was chairman of the Roanoke Colony Memorial Association of Manteo, a group planning the celebration in 1937 of the 350th anniversary of the arrival in 1587 of Sir Walter Raleigh's colonists on Roanoke Island. Influenced by the biblical pageant at Oberammergau, Germany, the association wanted to present a historical pageant-drama as the focal point of the celebration, and Green had been interested in writing such a play at least since 1921 (see letter 25). The present letter reflects the first decisive step in the enterprise. On 3 January, according to Green's diary, the "Roanoke Island folks" visited him in Chapel Hill "for conference on the pageant." On 15 January he drove "to Manteo with Proff Koch, Bill Couch [director of the University of North Carolina Press] and Elizabeth. Rain all the way." They got stuck in the mud and did not get to Manteo until 11:30 that night. On the morning of 16 January the group met "with Committee about Raleigh Celebration. Go out to fort, draw new designs for open air theatre. Fear for the looks of the thing, but feel I am in time to keep too much of a monstrosity from being built. Fair and cold. In afternoon a meeting in court-house" (meeting described in "The Beginning of 'The Lost Colony,'" in *The Lost Colony: An Outdoor Play in Two Acts*, rev. ed. [Chapel Hill: University of North Carolina Press, 1954], pp. iv–vi), then in the nearby office of Fearing's wholesale grocery company, where "it is finally decided that I with Elizabeth's help will write the pageant."

2. Green and the others returned to Chapel Hill on Sunday, 17 January, and Monday morning found "E. beginning on research for pageant" (Green diary, PG-SHC). Green began writing the play in early March and by June was able to take a script to Roanoke Island for rehearsals. Meanwhile, on the site of the original colony the Waterside Theatre had been built, a stage at the edge of Croatan Sound, with wooden benches on a hillside sloping down to the stage. "At last," according to the diary, *The Lost Colony*, directed by Samuel Seldon, opened on 4 July, a Sunday evening, 2,500 people in the audience, "agony of rain in first act."

From the sale of the book of the play the author is to receive a royalty of five per-cent, and all other income derived from the production at Manteo or book sale shall belong solely to the above Association;[3] that—

The Roanoke Colony Memorial Association agrees to pay the author the sum of $1,500.00 to write the said pageant-drama—$400.00 on the signing of this agreement ($100.00 already having been paid), $500.00 on March the first, and the balance of $500.00 on the delivery of the script; that—

In the event that at some later date it is mutually agreed between the author and the above association to offer the said pageant-drama for sale to the moving picture, radio, television, magazine or serial publications or to any theatrical enterprise then the proceeds from such sale shall be shared fifty-fifty between the Association and the author; and no contract for so disposing of the pageant-drama can be entered into without the mutual consent of the above two parties; that—

In the event either of the contracting parties fails to keep the terms of this agreement, then all monies and rights shall revert as before.

Signed Paul Green
Signed D. B. Fearing
Melvin R. Daniels, Sect.[4]

3. The first edition of *The Lost Colony*, priced at $2.00, was published by the University of North Carolina Press in August 1937, and for the dates 5–17 July Green's diary notes: "Reviewing proof and last copy of *Lost Colony*. Yield art form to historical fact" (PG-SHC).

4. After opening, *The Lost Colony* played on Friday, Saturday, and Sunday nights through the first weekend of September, then had its final performance on Labor Day (Monday, 6 September 1937). The production attracted national attention from the start. The theater was built with labor from the Civilian Conservation Corps, and its major piece of equipment, an organ, was donated by the Rockefeller Foundation. The Federal Theatre Project supplied actors for the major roles; the U.S. Postal Department issued a commemorative stamp, and the Treasury, a commemorative half-dollar; Brooks Atkinson gave the production a laudatory review in the *New York Times* (15 August 1937, sec. 10, p. 1, cols. 1–2; p. 2, cols. 1–2); and on Virginia Dare's birthday, 18 August, President Roosevelt visited Roanoke Island, gave a speech, and attended a performance sitting in his car. During the summer, over 50,000 people attended performances (William S. Powell, *Paradise Preserved: A History of the Roanoke Island Historical Association and Related Organizations* [Chapel Hill: University of North Carolina Press, 1965], chapter 8).

## 124. To Groff Conklin[1]

[Raleigh Road, Chapel Hill, N.C.]
21 January 1937

Dear Mr. Conklin—

Now that I think back on our meeting the other day I don't feel sure I got your name right—whether you spell it as above or not.[2] But I don't think that matters so much, for right off the bat we seemed to have a great deal in common so far as thinking goes.

A short case of flu has kept me from writing you as I proposed, but I'm back at the typewriter now and I hope to continue so far a good while without interruption.

You remember that I requested an extension of six months on the North Carolina book.[3] Further that I offer McBride my sometime-coming *Little Bethel Caravan* or maybe *Omnibus*,[4] the date of delivery to be one year after the Carolina book, and there to be at the present signing of the contract an advance of $250. This Little Bethel book will run about seven or eight hundred pages and will comprise the life and death of some three or four hundred people from the early settlements in the late 17th century to the present in that particular neighborhood. There will be short stories, short plays, poems, superstitions, folk-lore, character sketches, and so forth and in the back a map and alphabetical list of characters somewhat as in the style of the appendix in *Wide Fields*, a former McBride publication.[5] Please let me know soon what Mr. McBride thinks of the idea.[6]

1. Editor at Robert M. McBride, Incorporated, with whom Green discussed writing projects on a trip to New York on 10–13 January for the closing of *Johnny Johnson.*

2. He did.

3. A book characterizing the state and its people. Green signed a contract with McBride for the book on 6 March 1936, with a completion date of 15 May 1937 (T. R. Smith [McBride editor] to Paul Green, 2 May 1938, PG-SHC).

4. "Little Bethel" was Green's fictional name for the area of the state in which he grew up, the Cape Fear River valley in Harnett and Cumberland counties where most of his work is set. At least since 1935 he had contemplated a new collection of short pieces on the life of the region. A diary entry for 7 May 1935 lists twenty-two subjects for short plays (titles and brief notes) under the heading, "Little Bethel Plays" (PG-SHC).

5. *Wide Fields*, a collection of Green's short stories with an appendix of character sketches entitled "Little Bethel People" published by McBride in 1928.

6. McBride liked it, and Green signed a contract for *Little Bethel Caravan* on 3

Since coming back here I've been doing some work on the Carolina volume, and I've got hung rather strongly in my mind now the picture of doing this book somewhat autobiographically; that is, start from the writer's childhood on the farm and the growing interest that fills him about his native state, how each year he studies and learns more about it, how as he learns more he grows more critical of it, how he finally enters the lists to help correct some of the abuses, etc., etc. This will keep a constant thread of continuity and will still allow, I think, for the depiction of type characters, such as I told you about—the typical poor-white tenant, the Negro laborer, the factory owner, the landlord, the revival preacher, the hound dog,[7] and so on even to include the school teacher and his alma mater, the state university.[8]

I hope you will send me a copy of the New York book.[9]

With best regards,

## 125. To I. Schlanger[1]

Raleigh Road, Chapel Hill, N.C.
12 March 1937

Dear Mr. Schlanger—

I have just returned to Chapel Hill[2] and found your communication of March 4 relative to the tragic death of Ben Leider and the proposed memorial

---

February 1937, with delivery of the typescript set for November 1938. McBride paid an advance on the book of $250 and extended the time on the North Carolina book by six months.

7. Village bum.

8. Green did not write an autobiographical book on North Carolina, nor did he publish *Little Bethel Caravan*, although his later collections of short stories and folklore show the kinds of material he discusses here.

9. Edward Hungerford's *Pathway of Empire: The Story of New York State* (1935), which Conklin sent with Erskine Caldwell's *Some American People* (1935), both published by McBride, hoping they would "be of some assistance to you in planning the state book" (Groff Conklin to Paul Green, 22 January 1937, PG-SHC).

---

1. In mid-February 1937 Ben Leider, a crusading New York City journalist in the mold of John Reed, was killed in the Spanish Civil War (*New York Times*, 1 March 1937, p. 7, col. 2). An amateur pilot, Leider was in the first group of American aviators to volunteer for the Loyalist cause, and when his plane went down near Valencia he became the first American to die in the fighting. Schlanger and other New York City

fund. I say tragic death, because after all these years of doing some fighting myself I have come to the fast and necessary conclusion that to live (for a cause) is better than dying (for it)—that is if the cause is one so commingled in truth and lies as the loyalist ideal in Spain. In other words I think Ben Leider should be alive and at home today. I do not agree entirely with the attitude that must have been his and which seems to be yours—namely, that the war in Spain is between the defenders of right (the loyalists) and the defenders of wrong (the fascists). There are wrong and right on both sides. And the killing follows the old, old pattern of one ideal opposed to another ideal, each being right or each being wrong, depending on which side you are fighting. All around Chapel Hill Tom, Dick and Harry are busy breaking up old wrecked cars, ancient sawmill boilers, busy gathering up all odds and ends of scrap iron and hauling them to the railroad station to be shipped away for making shells and guns for the war in Spain. Even though the countryside gets cleaned up a bit and tidied some, I look at the loaded passing trucks with sorrow. Nor would my sorrow be eased in the least if I were convinced that all this iron were destined for the loyalists' cause, and none of it would ever reach the fascists unless captured. I simply say "too bad, too bad" and go to work the harder to strive to keep the peace. Day in day out I hear of this friend or that friend who has disappeared toward Europe to fight for democracy. I once did the same, but no more now. And I feel it would be a sin against my intelligence to try to memorialize such familiar and shameful examples of youthful violence and wrong. To repeat, let us live for whatever good there is in the loyalist cause—write, explain, the while we make clear the pity and the waste of it all; for the one certain way to ruin whatever good there is there[,] is to sail away, grab a gun and enter into the business of killing men. I'm about to confess to a Christian ideal. Suppose so—No, I don't wish to help raise a memorial to poor Ben Leider and thereby preach by example that he was a

---

friends quickly organized a "Ben Leider Memorial Fund" to buy food and medical supplies for the Loyalist forces, and Schlanger had asked Green for a contribution and permission to list him as a sponsor. Leider went to Spain, "not as a mercenary," Schlanger wrote, "but out of his considered judgment, recognizing the vital relation of the Spanish civil war to the fight against Fascism and for democracy everywhere." To the group initiating the fund he had "already assumed heroic stature" (4 March 1937, PG-SHC).

2. From Roanoke Island for a planning session on *The Lost Colony* (Green diary, 29 March 1937, PG-SHC).

noble hero and it behoves other young men to go and get themselves killed and memorialized likewise. I'm sure you know enough of history to know that men have been killing one another for thousands of years in the name of some ideal or other, and the ideals remain pretty much unaffected one way or the other. Now that I've begun repeating myself, I'd better stop.

Finally, though, rather than hurrah and honor any Ben Leider, I think we all ought to urge everybody to stay out of the Spanish fight. There are too many fighting as it is.

Still with respect for your motives, Paul Green

## 126. To Elia Kazan[1]

[Raleigh Road, Chapel Hill, N.C.]
12 April 1937

Dear Gadg—

Sorry I missed you too. Right at the last moment I was informed that you were spokesman for the Group members in Hollywood and I wanted to ask you whether the Group was to continue and if so whether you felt I was in any way bound to it so far as *The Enchanted Maze* is concerned. No contracts have ever been signed, although they have been ready for signature a long time, and most of my dealings have been with Cheryl and with her as a Group member. Now that she is pulling out and wants *The Maze* for her new organization I thought I ought to make the slate clean before any obscurity of method or motive crept in.[2] Frankly I am as much interested in the future of the Group as

1. The year 1937 was difficult for the Group Theatre. After *Johnny Johnson* closed in January, the company found itself with no scripts to work on and no money. Most of the company went immediately to Hollywood. Elia Kazan (b. 1909), nicknamed "Gadget," who joined the Group from the Yale Drama School in the summer of 1932 and played two roles in *Johnny Johnson*, left Hollywood for New York City in late March to look for work in the theater. Green was in New York 6–10 April to accept the Medal of Honor awarded to *Johnny Johnson* by the New York Drama Study Club at the Waldorf-Astoria on 9 April. While there he conferred with publishers and people in the theater and looked unsuccessfully for Kazan, who later sent a note regretting he missed seeing Green.

2. Unwilling to stay in Hollywood, Crawford returned to New York City and decided to become an independent producer. In a letter of 17 March 1937 (quoted in Cheryl Crawford, *One Naked Individual: My Fifty Years in the Theatre* [Indianapolis: Bobbs-Merrill, 1977], p. 100), she resigned from the Group.

ever and feel that in such organizations the best future of the American drama rests. But just as frankly I think that the kind of organization Cheryl tells me she is starting is better suited to go ahead with preparations for producing the college play than the Group is or may be by the middle of summer. In the first place she is here in the east and we can get together at an early date for work on the script. In the second place I believe the type of Broadway actor she is getting together will give me a production with a professional touch which I need at this stage of my Broadway wars. Accordingly I have promised her the script. Of course the Group might not have wanted the play anyway. For to repeat, all my dealings about it—except one meeting here with Harold[3] more than a year ago—have been with her. She it seemed was the individual most interested and has been all along.[4] However I hope the Group carries on stronger than ever, for it is needed more than ever, and that I shall have the opportunity to write something else for it.[5]

I hope you get a good part in the movies, if you wish it, and I know you'll be a big success on the screen if they give you any kind of a break as to role.[6] Give my love to Molly and to "Hit."[7]

Ever,

Will you pass this word on to Harold and with love to him and Stella.[8]

3. Clurman.

4. But eventually she decided not to produce *The Enchanted Maze.* Published by Samuel French in 1940, it has had no professional production.

5. Although Green did not write another play for the Group, it continued under Clurman's direction until 1941, with Kazan as a prominent member.

6. Kazan would make his name as a director, winning an Academy Award in 1947 for *Gentleman's Agreement* and in 1954 for *On the Waterfront.* In the theater he began by directing Maxwell Anderson's *Truckline Café* in 1946, then Tennessee Williams's *Streetcar Named Desire* the next year.

7. Molly Day Thacher (Kazan's wife) and their son.

8. Stella Adler, member of the Group and Clurman's companion.

## 127. To Robert B. House[1]

Raleigh Road, Chapel Hill, N.C.
13 April 1937

Dear Bob—

The WRITERS' WORKSHOP course which Mr. Stevens and I have discussed, and about which I talked to you yesterday, is pictured in my mind somewhat as follows—[2]

I wish to bring here to the university some eight or ten young creative writers selected from among the best in America and supplemented by any of our own student body who show the requisite talent and set them to work next fall each on his respective project—whether it be a novel, long play, moving picture script, stories or what not,—looking towards what one might call professional disposal of their work when the year is over. I will act as advisor and consultant, but the administrative phase of the course will be handled by Mr. Koch (or anybody you and he designate), with the aid of Mr. William Peery[3] as secretarial assistant. In order to make this course a success, I have already put the following request to Mr. Stevens of the Rockefeller Foundation and he has asked me to have you set it up in the regular form:

1. Robert B. House (1892–1987) was chief administrative officer of UNC at Chapel Hill. After earning a B.A. from UNC in 1916 and an M.A. in English from Harvard in 1917 and service in France during World War I, he returned to North Carolina and in 1926 became executive secretary of UNC. When three state university campuses (in Chapel Hill, Raleigh, and Greensboro) were joined administratively in 1931 to form the Consolidated University, with Frank Porter Graham from the Chapel Hill campus as president, House took charge of administration at Chapel Hill, with the title of dean of administration, an office he held until retirement in 1957. Over the past few years he had arranged Green's leaves of absence from the Department of Philosophy and helped Koch move out of the Department of English to create the Department of Dramatic Art (1936). Now Green was preparing to rejoin the active faculty as a member of Koch's department in the fall of 1937.

2. David Stevens was director of the Humanities Division of the Rockefeller Foundation. On a tour of the South he lunched with Green in Chapel Hill on 25 January 1937, and Green saw him as "a quiet gentle man. The weight of money behind him, and the spectacle of begging professors everywhere" (Green diary, PG-SHC). On 9 April, in New York to accept an award for *Johnny Johnson*, Green talked with Stevens about the course outlined here (Green diary).

3. Graduate student and playwright.

| | |
|---|---|
| Eight creative writing fellowships at $500 | $4,000.00 |
| A fund for ten invited lecturers at $100 | 1,000.00 |
| Books and periodicals for the course | 500.00 |
| Total | $5,500.00 |

As you so well put it in our conversation it is a fine thing to have people around who are doing creative work, for in just such ways as this do universities encourage culture and enlightenment. Or briefly it's fun doing these things. And I will appreciate your getting together with Proff Koch and sending in the requisition—or whatever it's called. I'm attaching a copy of my letter to Mr. Stevens.[4]

Anything you and Proff think should be stated, why put it in.[5]

With best to you as ever,

## 128. To Georgia S. Fink[1]

[Raleigh Road, Chapel Hill, N.C.]
19 May 1937

Dear Miss Fink—

I am in receipt of a letter from you and also one from Miss Farmer[2] relative to the short drill scene which you have found necessary to add between scenes

4. Unlocated.

5. Although the Rockefeller Foundation made grants to UNC during the next several years of over $100,000 (see the foundation's annual reports, 1938 and 1940), it did not fund the course outlined here, the proposal for it coming "too late for consideration" (David Stevens to Frederick Koch, 17 June 1937, PG-SHC). However, Green went ahead with the workshop, beginning winter quarter, 1937, and the class met at his home on Sunday evenings.

---

1. The Federal Theatre Project in Los Angeles, which earlier in the year produced *The House of Connelly*, now had *Johnny Johnson* in rehearsal. On 12 May, Georgis S. Fink, director of the Regional Service Bureau of the project in Los Angeles, requested Green's permission to add a three-page episode to their production script. The episode, designed to provide time for the actor playing Johnny to change from civilian to army costume, showed a sergeant drilling a squad of inept recruits.

2. Virginia Farmer, friend of Green and a supervisor of the Federal Theatre Project in Los Angeles.

3 and 4 of act one—in *Johnny Johnson.*[3] After reading the scene which Miss Farmer so kindly sent me, I do not feel it would be wise to use it. In the first place it is not quite in the style of the rest of the script and in the second it is the old "awkward squad" treatment and serves, I'm afraid, to blur the issue by placing several soldiers in the same light in which we place Johnny. From the story point of view Johnny is the awkward fellow and should stand out thereby the most in contrast to his fellows who are not so green and non-conforming. He is the one whom the sergeant should be inspecting and drilling and not the squad. In the New York production the drill scene opened with Sergeant Jackson alone on the stage shouting orders into the wing—such as were in the old script, and which I presume you are using.[4] These orders were directed to someone out of the scene whom the audience surmises to be Johnny. This heightened Johnny's entrance and also gave him more time to make the changes into his uniform. I hope you can work out your production somewhat in this manner. If not, then I suggest that you let Johnny keep on his civilian trousers and have only the army blouse (coat) and hat on. Such a change could be made in 30 seconds and would be perfectly in line with historical accuracy and would as like as not add to Johnny's comic uniqueness.

Miss Farmer also has written about using the old words of Johnny's song—not the published love version—at the end of the play. This is quite satisfactory.[5]

May I add a note from hard experience: if your actors are not good at singing, please have them do as much of their songs in recitative as possible.[6]

With best regards and hopes for a successful show,

Sincerely yours,

(Copy to Miss Farmer.)

3. Scene 3 ends with Johnny recruited into the army. Scene 4 opens with him on a troop ship for France.

4. In the published texts Green omits the drill scene.

5. Lyrics to the closing song in the Group production have not been published, and the first edition (1937) gives no words for the closing melody. The earliest published text to end with lyrics is the revised edition of 1971.

6. In her letter Farmer mentioned that the woman playing the heroine (Minnie Belle) was a good actress but could not sing (12 May 1937, PG-SHC).

## 129. To Paya Haskall[1]

[Raleigh Road, Chapel Hill, N.C.]
10 September 1937

Dear Miss Paya Haskall—

Thanks for your letter of August 4 which has just reached me. I am sending your request for the music of *Johnny Johnson* on to the composer, Mr. Kurt Weill, and no doubt you will hear from him or his agent in the near future. You mention that a rough translation of the play had been read to a group of theatre workers and that you were about ready with the translation. I presume this is the translation made by Mrs. Norman Hapgood and Leo Bulgakov, which Mrs. Hapgood was to show (and perhaps already has) to Stanislavsky or some of his associates, and that you have taken it over to polish up—or what not.[2] I do not know whether Mrs. Hapgood is in Russia or not. If she is, I wish you would get in touch with her if possible, for she has my authority to handle the play. And of course in the meantime thanks very much for anything you may have done or will do for its production there.[3]

1. Haskall wrote to Green from Moscow about translating *Johnny Johnson* and producing it in Russia (letter unlocated).

2. Elizabeth Hapgood had an extensive background in the theater as well as in Russian studies and in 1936 published the first of several translations of Stanislavsky's work, *An Actor Prepares*. In New York Green had lunch with Hapgood, Barrett Clark, and Leo Bulgakov on 8 April 1937, and his diary describes her as a "highly intelligent woman, clear thinking, honest, dependable. Kindly consented to present 'Johnny J.' to the Moscow Art people. Bulgakov will make a synopsis and translate a few scenes for a sample." On 14 April she wrote to say the play had arrived. "I do not know what I can accomplish in Moscow but I shall certainly do my best for you" (PG-SHC). She would sail on 30 April, she added, and probably return in July.

3. A few years later Hapgood wrote to Green: "I really did deliver your plays (and the synopses in Russian by Leo Bulgakov) [other Green plays not identified] to the hands of Nemerovich Danchenko [associate of Stanislavsky]. But I am afraid that it was at a moment when foreigners and foreign things were rather suspect and I hear you have never heard from them" (22 January 1940, PG-SHC). But a diary entry shortly after the present letter notes receiving a "long letter from translator in Moscow wanting me to revise 'Johnny J.' for production there—giving Johnny a stronger anti-fascist, anti-war scene at the end. Well, I have my own vision about human truth in character and I can't write such an ending. Ergo no production, I suppose" (10–26 November, PG-SHC).

Sincerely yours,
As to the new play I am writing—it is not yet ready but when it is I shall forward you a copy.[4]

## 130. To James Boyd[1]

Raleigh Road, Chapel Hill, N.C.
7 October 1937

Dear Squire—

Elizabeth has just come in with a chuckle in her mouth speaking of a story the while and out of the corner, and I have just read same, called "Civic Crisis." Brother in arms, you have sure gone and done it. It's great. In fact I am ready to say it's one of the subtlest, slickest, comicest pieces of American delineation of these and recent times.[2] We thought of sending you a hail and salute wire and then decided a note would be of better savor and tact seeing as how I am like Ulysses lying under the belly of a ram-Pegasus[3] (and he won't move) and she is playing the Dorcas housewife to my recumbent position.[4] Ergo a slow and dallying letter is our representative. Cum pace laetas.[5]

Wilbur Daniel Steele and Sherwood Anderson and wife are to be with us and the owls next week.[6] Can't you come up for an evening or two of

4. Perhaps *The Enchanted Maze.*

---

1. James Boyd (1888–1944), historical novelist (*Drums* [1925], *Marching On* [1927], *Long Hunt* [1930], *Roll River* [1935]), lived in Southern Pines, North Carolina, and was a close friend of Green, who dedicated *Roll Sweet Chariot* to him. Earlier in the year the two tried to collaborate on a play based on *Laughing Pioneer*, but neither could get to it because of other work (Paul Green to James Boyd, 21 July 1937, Boyd Papers, SHC).

2. "Civic Crisis" (*American Mercury*, August 1937, pp. 468–80) is a humorous but deeply satirical story of a policeman in a southern town who can appreciate a crisis in the life of a dog in the town but not in the life of a black resident.

3. Instead of riding the winged horse of inspiration, Green, like Ulysses escaping the Cyclops, feels like he is clinging to the underside of a ram.

4. Woman from Joppa who "spent all her time doing good and helping the poor" (Acts 9:36).

5. Perhaps *laetare*: Rejoice in peace.

6. Steele, short story writer and novelist, lived in Old Lyme, Connecticut, but was born in Greensboro, North Carolina, and had lived in Chapel Hill during 1927–29. He and the Andersons, from Troutdale, Virginia, visited Green during the week of 11

spreading the bull and the rest of him?[7] A letter from Mrs. Poteat Stallings[8] today says Kate[9] and she are going to Taos, so *and* God knows about you and your whereabouts. We're sending this into the void. I called up your place the other night and a voice said "No, sir, he haven't said when he's coming back."

Respectfully yours,

## 131. To Hector McL. Green[1]

[Raleigh Road, Chapel Hill, N.C.]
6 December 1937

Dear Heck—

Your Cousin Elizabeth tells me I was supposed to have written you long ago about the pony. We have decided to buy him—provided our method of payment is satisfactory and provided, of course, you haven't already sold him or committed him elsewhere. I am herewith enclosing check for fifty dollars as a first payment and would like a couple of months or so in which to pay the balance—for I am going to arrange to have the children work this out by doing odd jobs around the house. They will appreciate the gift more if they contribute something themselves. If the above is satisfactory in every way, then we would like to have the pony delivered some time just before Christmas, so that we can keep him at a neighbor's house and bring him over here as a complete surprise for the children on Christmas morning. If you will let us

---

October for the meeting of the North Carolina Library Association, which focused on southern writers.

7. Anderson met Green and Boyd the previous December. In a letter of 6 December 1936 Anderson tells of visiting Chapel Hill the previous day and meeting "Paul Green, both E. [Anderson's wife Eleanor] and I taking an instant liking to both Green and wife, as evidently, they did to us. . . . I think Green is in a period of disgust with the movies and determined, at least for the time, to try hard to live by the stage. That, of course, putting him up against the New York theatre managers, not so essentially different from the Hollywood gang. We dined [at the Greens' on the night of 5 December], and James Boyd came over from Southern Pines" (Howard Mumford Jones and Walter B. Rideout, eds., *Letters of Sherwood Anderson*, [Boston: Little, Brown, 1953], p. 368).

8. Helen Stallings, whose family name was Poteat.

9. Boyd's wife, Katharine, who needed a dry climate because of asthma.

---

1. A relative who farmed near Lillington, North Carolina.

know the hour and date we'll have somebody down on the highway to meet you and show you where to put him. About eleven o'clock on the morning of Christmas Eve would suit us best, but whatever you decide will be all right.

With love and best wishes to you and all the family.

Paul Green[2]

## 132. To Henry Allen Moe[1]

[Raleigh Road, Chapel Hill, N.C.]
16 December 1937

Dear Mr. Moe:

I am delighted to have your letter of December 14 which mentions a subject I have been thinking a great deal about; namely, the possibility of doing something on a great dramatic scale at the world's fair interpretative of the spirit of this nation—its past, its present, and its future. Last summer I wrote a musical-historical drama based on the accounts of Sir Walter Raleigh's attempts to settle this country, and to my joy, and somewhat surprise considering, it turned out to be a great success. We are repeating it each summer from July 4 to Labor Day at the waterside theatre built for that purpose on Roanoke Island, North Carolina. Right now I am finishing another such drama written around the creation and adoption of the American constitution, for simultaneous production throughout the country by the Federal Theatre.[2] Due to the

2. Hector followed the suggested schedule in delivering the pony. On 24 December "E. got the children off visiting so we could receive the pony," Green noted in his diary, and he hid the pony in a stable in the low land north of their house. "His name is Bill," the diary adds; "It fits him." On Christmas morning: "Children up at four o'clock. Had to go by flash light down to see Bill the horse. Screams, opening of gifts, and running in and out of rooms till breakfast time. Fun all day riding pony, etc. Weather very warm and sultry though fair" (PG-SHC).

---

1. Henry Allen Moe (1894–1975), head of the John Simon Guggenheim Memorial Foundation and acquainted with Green since his fellowship year of 1928–29, approached him on behalf of the committee planning the 1939 World's Fair in New York City about the possibility of writing a play for the fair.

2. On 27 October 1936 the Federal Theatre Project had opened Sinclair Lewis's *It Can't Happen Here* at twenty-one theaters in seventeen states, and the companies would eventually play a total of 260 weeks. Seeing that production as an important step in creating a "People's Theatre" in the United States, Hallie Flanagan and others

many problems involved, its showing may be delayed, but in a few weeks it will be off my hands, and I'd like nothing better than to begin consideration at once of some such plan as that suggested by Dr. Smith's outline.[3] I shall be in New York at Hotel Bristol, West 48th Street, for a few days beginning December 27,[4] and I hope I can get the chance to talk to both you and Dr. Smith.

To give you an idea of at least one approach to our American material I am sending you by separate mail a copy of *The Lost Colony.* Of course the world's fair drama would need to be much vaster and with better choreography in every way.

With best wishes and regards,

## 133. To Elizabeth L. Green

[Hotel Bristol, 129–135 West 48th Street, New York City]
Monday night, 27 December 1937

Dearest Darling—

Proff. has just left the room after seeing *The Star-Wagon* which he reports as very charming, but in his trying to retell the story it sounded very incoherent.[1]

---

in the project wanted another play for simultaneous productions (Flanagan, *Arena: The History of the Federal Theatre* [1940; reprint, New York: Benjamin Blom, 1965], pp. 115–29). After several preliminary discussions with Flanagan, Green, on a trip to New York in September 1937, agreed "to go ahead with Constitution play [*The Common Glory*] for simultaneous openings by Federal Theatre" (Green diary, 9 September–1 October 1937, PG-SHC).

3. With his letter Moe included a three-page outline of a possible pageant by Carleton Sprague Smith, chief of the Music Division of the New York Public Library and member of the Music Committee for the fair. The outline, entitled "America and To-morrow: A Pageant Symbolizing Our Country's Contribution to Civilization," gave a panoramic view of American history from the period before the arrival of Europeans to the present, stressing the superiority of democracy over totalitarian forms of government such as communism and fascism. The pageant was designed for a large theater and called for a ballet, chorus, symphony orchestra, and moving pictures in addition to an acting company (14 December 1937, PG-SHC).

4. For the National Theatre Conference and meetings with Federal Theatre Project officials.

---

1. Koch and Green went to New York City for the annual meeting of the National

Last night on the train coming up he and I spent hours talking about the theatre, and of course he gave me before we were through a complete account of his travels with "The Christmas Carol"—also.[2] This morning we were up early and at it again, then arriving at the hotel we parted. I got some of my rather seedy clothes pressed and then went over to the Century Club for lunch with Dr. Smith and Moe. The latter failed to appear, but a Mr. Olney was there,[3] and we spent an hour or so discussing the possibility of a production in the amphitheatre which is being built. The stage is 200′ long, and Olney says he hopes to have the stage a floating one so that on occasions it can be pushed back and a bit of water can show between the audience and the stage. I am looking forward with a great deal of interest to going out there tomorrow morning to go over the site with him.[4] From what I already see there is a strong mixture of politics, art, and social prestige-or-not in the fair. But all I'm interested in right now is the chance to do something theatrical for it. I have suggested a production committee, the early choice of a director, and the use of contemporary (to the story) American music. I'm sure I was on the right track at Roanoke (for this sort of thing) and on the wrong track with *Common Glory*—unless Kurt in the main adapts Revolutionary Days music.[5]

---

Theatre Conference, 27–30 December. *The Star-Wagon* was Maxwell Anderson's fantasy of time travel that opened on 29 September 1937.

2. Each Christmas Koch gave dramatic readings of Dickens's story in Chapel Hill and other places around the state.

3. Moe, not on the planning committee for the 1939 World's Fair, had contacted Green for Smith and Julian Olney, executive secretary of the Committee on Music for the fair.

4. From here on in the letter, midnight had apparently passed since Green began the letter on Monday night, and now he considered "today" to be Tuesday, 28 December. On Wednesday morning, 29 December, he went with Olney "over to Long Island to look over the site of the amphitheatre. Trucks were hauling and dumping dirt and a great stir and bustle going on. I wanted to get a shovel and fall in with the making. Then I came back to Olney's office in the Empire State Bldg and talked with him about plans" (Paul Green to Elizabeth Green, 29 December 1937, PG-SHC).

5. Most of the music in *The Lost Colony* is traditional English music, for example "Greensleeves" (see *The Lost Colony Song-Book* [New York: Fischer, 1938]). Music is even more fully integrated into *The Common Glory*. Green began by thinking that Weill would compose the music, as he had for *Johnny Johnson*, but at the time of the present letter the script was not finished and Weill had done no work on the music

Saw Hallie Flanagan yesterday and she claims to know nothing as to the future of the Federal Theatre, though if her pleasant babyish face was any index she either did know something good or didn't care. The latter not likely.[6] Also saw Mrs. Isaacs[7] (all at the theatre conference) who is suffering with arthritis and had to shake hands left and upside down. I am meeting with her group tomorrow afternoon at five. Also over to say a few words at Hotel Pennsylvania—at drama group. Haven't seen John McGee[8]—am waiting a call from him now. Today will be our first conference I suppose.[9] What will come of it I don't know. But somehow the thing must be worked out.[10] Then if I do the World's Fair piece the trilogy will finish the story of American Democracy so far as I am concerned.[11]

I love you so and I will pull out of this despond.[12] Hope you will ride "Bill"

---

(Kurt Weill to Paul Green, 14 March 1938, PG-SHC). Historically authentic music was important to Green, however. When *The Common Glory* was eventually done in 1947, its music came by and large from the era of the American Revolution or earlier (see *The Common Glory Song-Book* [New York: Fischer, 1951]).

6. Current difficulties of the Federal Theatre Project are aptly summarized in Jane de Hart Mathews, *The Federal Theatre, 1935–1939* (Princeton, N.J.: Princeton University Press, 1967): "In December 1937, the future of the entire WPA hung in the balance" (p. 159).

7. Editor of *Theatre Arts Monthly.*

8. Longtime director of the southern region of the Federal Theatre Project and now associate national director in charge of selecting plays for project productions.

9. On *The Common Glory.*

10. Originally, Green was to send Flanagan a script of *The Common Glory* by 1 December, when rehearsals would start (Hallie Flanagan to Paul Green, 14 October 1937, PG-SHC). But he did not complete the script by 1 December, and Weill, who was to work on the music during December, instead went to Hollywood for a motion picture job. Green finished some part of the play in time to take it on the present trip—"a poor old piece of script," he called it (Green diary, 28 December 1937, PG-SHC). Then on the way home, on Saturday, 8 January, he stopped in Washington for another conference with Flanagan and McGee, who thought they conveyed their belief that Green was on the right track with the play but actually put him off by what Green took to be a lack of enthusiasm on their part (John McGee to Paul Green, 19 March 1938, PG-SHC).

11. What Green had in mind to write for the World's Fair is not clear. In February 1938, Olney resigned from the Music Committee of the fair. Although his successor, Olin Downes, continued to correspond with Green, nothing came of the discussions.

12. Due at least in part to his inability to complete *The Common Glory* to his

a lot and get a good rest. I may stay right on here until I get these matters settled. See if you can without too much expense figure out some way of planning to go down to Florida with me.[13] Also will you take time to send me those notes about *Common Glory* you were going to make.

Ever my love. Paul

Mr. Stevens wants me to go by Charleston and have a look at the Dock Street Theatre which they have opened[14]—you remember the invitation. I promised to. It seems the theatre has asked the Rock. Found. for money.[15] I would expect to start—if you could go and we drove—about the twelfth of January—spending a bit of time on the way (you know, old houses, etc.) and we could have a good time.[16] I'll get some more money from French somehow.[17] Willis will be glad to come back for that week—or maybe you could get George. It

---

satisfaction. The diary of the period is full of deprecatory notes, for example, "Working on 'Common Glory.' So far plenty of commonness and little glory" (16–20 December 1937, PG-SHC). To some extent this groping resulted from his working arrangement with the Federal Theatre Project, an arrangement in which they and he, as McGee put it, had to *agree* on the script. In the finished play he mirrored some of his own difficulties in the scene where Jefferson drafts the Declaration of Independence. After a visit from a group led by Franklin and the two Adamses, "*Jefferson's spirits*," a stage direction tells us, "*obviously have been cast down, like any sensitive artist, by the visit of the committee of criticism. He rubs his forehead heavily as if to iron away a pain there*" (*The Common Glory: A Symphonic Drama of American History* [Chapel Hill: University of North Carolina Press, 1948], act 1, scene 6, p. 116).

13. For lectures at the University of Miami.

14. Colonial theater in Charleston reopened by Dorothy and Dubose Heyward and others in 1937 with assistance from the WPA.

15. On the afternoon of 30 December Green attended a meeting of the Rockefeller Foundation (Green diary, PG-SHC).

16. When they traveled by automobile, the Greens frequently stopped to look at old houses or unusual trees and flowers and to talk with the people thereabout.

17. To Green's request Sheil replied: "In all sincereness I must tell you that it is not possible at this time to send you all of the $750. advance requested. Our first of the year payments are exceptionally heavy and the very best I can do is to send the enclosed check for $300" (5 January 1938, PG-SHC). The Greens had two loans from the Bank of Chapel Hill, one for $3,000 and another for $2,500. On the second one a payment of $500 was due 13 January 1938. The first one came due in toto on 30 December 1937, but Green had to carry it over for ninety days with an extra interest payment of $45 (W. E. Thompson to Paul Green, 3 January 1938).

might be we could get Mrs. Watson[18] and her husband to come out and stay the time, or somebody. Anyway if you feel you can make it, do plan to go.[19]

## 134. To Elizabeth L. Green

Antilla Hotel, Coral Gables, Fla.
Sunday night, 16 January 1938

Dear Honey—

At last I'm down here and a long way it is.[1] My reading last night[2] seemed to go well in Gainesville. Reception afterward though was pretty heavy for me. Robert Frost was there. What a grand fellow! This morning he drove with me 15 mi[les] across country to catch the train.[3]

It is now 10:30 P.M. I've just been out to Mrs. Orton Lowe's—a white-haired sweet brave woman with a beautiful home which she and Dr. Lowe had just finished. Now she has to sell it, furniture too. She can't keep it.[4] But she smiles and goes right ahead. She told me something of Robert Frost's struggles, and seeing how others live up to their lives I am thus encouraged in my own.[5]

18. Mabel Watson frequently typed and did other secretarial jobs for Green.

19. Elizabeth did not make the trip.

---

1. Green was at the University of Miami as guest lecturer in the Winter Institute of Literature, 17–21 January, where he talked each day on a topic relating to his own or other modern plays (Orton Lowe to Paul Green, 17 August, 4 September, 3 November, and 6 December 1937, PG-SHC). He had taken a train from Durham to Jacksonville, Florida, on 14 January, gone to the University of Florida at Gainesville on 15 January, and thence to Miami on 16 January.

2. From *Johnny Johnson* (H. P. Constans to Paul Green, 23 December 1937, PG-SHC).

3. Frost and his wife spent the winter of 1937–38 in Gainesville. Green and Frost met at the Bread Loaf Writers Conference in Middlebury, Vermont, when both of them lectured there in August 1937.

4. Orton Lowe, organizer of the Winter Institute of Literature who arranged for Green's visit, had died on 6 January 1938 (B. F. Ashe to Paul Green, 10 January 1938, PG-SHC).

5. Frost, guest lecturer at the Winter Institute of Literature in 1936, had a hard personal life in the middle 1930s. His daughter died in 1934; both he and his wife were frequently ill; and his wife was shortly to die—in March 1938 (Lawrance Thompson, *Robert Frost: A Biography* [New York: Holt, Rinehart and Winston, 1982], chapters 30–35).

This poor university here is very shabby and I know it must be a strain to pay me $500. I hear the professors' pay has been about $1,900 a year, the president $3,000, though they're getting a bit more just now.

Deposit this check.

I love you. Paul

I am getting my room as a favor here at $25 a week. Near the university.

## 135. To Frederick H. Koch

Raleigh Road, Chapel Hill, N.C.
1 April 1938

Dear Proff—

Herewith that rough picture for the future of our department:[1]

1. Increased endowment. (As already planned.)[2]

2. The strengthening of the department personnel. At the present the staff is overworked by too many varying and diverging duties.[3]

3. More inclusive courses of instruction, especially in the field of motion picture and dramatic criticism. Nearly every small town paper in the country as well as the large ones has room for this kind of writing. It seems we ought to offer training for such an opportunity. It would help a lot of our young folks get jobs. They all can't be playwrights, actors and directors.[4]

1. Since coming to UNC in 1918, Koch had been a member of the Department of English, but in the spring of 1936 a Department of Dramatic Art was set up, with him as chairman (Dougald MacMillan, *English at Chapel Hill, 1795–1969* [Chapel Hill: Department of English, UNC, [1970]], p. 36). Green had dropped his longstanding affiliation with the Department of Philosophy and joined the new department.

2. Over the next several years much money came to UNC and the Department of Dramatic Art from the Rockefeller Foundation. The foundation's report for 1938, for instance, lists payment of $183,000 to the department: $33,000 for salaries and course development, the remaining $150,000 for a building fund contingent on UNC raising $350,000 (pp. 310–11).

3. When organized, the department consisted of Koch, Green, Samuel Selden, Harry Davis, and John W. Parker. For 1938–39 Koch added to the staff two faculty members and four graduate assistants (UNC Record, 1938–39).

4. Courses introduced in 1938–39 were "The Study of Motion Pictures," "Voice Training for Stage and Radio," and "Teaching Dramatics in High Schools" (UNC Record, 1938–39).

4. Use of motion picture equipment in instruction. (As already planned.)

5. The development of *The Carolina Play-Book* into a regional theatre and drama magazine, with a regional board of editors to aid the editor-in-chief, and the publication of material of higher standards. The Carolina Stage could be developed to take care of the especial needs of the state association and The Playmakers.[5] Or consider the founding of a regional drama magazine with *The Carolina Play-Book* to remain as it is.

6. The establishment of the summer work on Roanoke Island as a going concern. (As already planned.)[6]

7. The development of a dramatic and cultural center at Asheville—the building of an outdoor theatre, the annual production in the summer of a mountain outdoor drama of the festival and folk opera type to be written by myself, the ultimate creation of a summer institute of the theatre and the establishment of a writers' conference there.[7] (The summer repertory company is already being formed under the direction of Danny Reed.)[8]

8. To erect at Chapel Hill with the aid of W. P. A. funds a regional theatre building, primarily for the use of the Carolina Playmakers but secondarily to serve as a home for regional dramatic activities, with an auditorium seating at

5. *The Carolina Play-Book* was published quarterly by the Carolina Playmakers and the Carolina Dramatic Association, a statewide organization headed by Koch. The association was large and needed a vehicle for communication. For example, its Sixteenth Annual Drama Festival in March–April 1939 brought over 3,200 people to Chapel Hill to see 38 plays performed by 406 actors from groups throughout the state (UNC "President's Report," in Playmakers Scrapbook, 1938–39, NCC). *The Carolina Stage* was a newsletter issued as needed to keep up with association business.

6. The department's connection with the *Lost Colony* production was extensive. Koch was advisory director, Samuel Selden the actual director, and several others from the department held production positions. In addition, departmental graduate students regularly acted in the show (*The Lost Colony: 352nd Anniversary Celebration, 1587–1939*, souvenir program, 1939, in NCC).

7. Plans unrealized.

8. Daniel Reed, who would go to New York City as an actor and theater manager at the end of the present summer, came to Asheville from Columbia, South Carolina, where he had founded the Town Theater in 1919. His production for the Asheville Summer Theatre, *The Royal Family* (by George Kaufman and Edna Ferber), ran from 22 June to 31 August 1938 (George Stephens to Paul Green, 5 June and 26 September 1938, PG-SHC).

least 750, with workshops, office space, etc. somewhat as already planned. This is to be worked out in cooperation with the architectural planning board of the Federal Theatre.[9]

9. The appointing of some member of the present dramatic department—despite the reference to duties above—or the securing of a new man to handle the details of cooperation with the Asheville people, Roanoke, Charleston,[10] and perhaps later Williamsburg.[11] I suggest Howard Bailey—with some increase in his salary, of course.[12]

This is hurriedly written down and somewhat lacks that Freshman English principle of parallelism.

More power to you and to us all,

9. The hope, as Green wrote in another letter, was to make "this southeastern region one of the great cultural and dramatic centers of the nation" (Paul Green to George Stephens, 1 April 1938, PG-SHC). A day or two before the present letter Hallie Flanagan had spent "a whole evening at Paul Green's house" conferring with him, Koch, and others about the theater in the Southeast. In North Carolina, she noted in her report to WPA officials, "we have a dramatic pattern very different from any elsewhere in the country." Koch and the Playmakers had built up an "extraordinary statewide interest in drama, . . . [and] both Professor Koch and Paul Green have a definite philosophy of community participation, high standards of theatre production, and great qualities of leadership." She proposed that the WPA "furnish labor and any possible proportion of costs to erect a regional southern theatre in Chapel Hill" (Hallie Flanagan to Ellen Woodward and Lawrence Morris, 7 April 1938, PG-SHC; quoted in Flanagan, *Arena*, p. 112). The plan was for UNC to provide the land and, by 1941, to raise $350,000, the Rockefeller Foundation to provide $150,000, and the WPA to provide the labor. The plan was still being discussed in Washington when the WPA ended in June 1939 (ibid., p. 113).

10. Where the historic Dock Street Theatre had been reopened with support from the Rockefeller Foundation and the WPA.

11. Where Green had begun to negotiate for a production of *The Common Glory*.

12. Howard Bailey was a graduate student and instructor in the department. In the fall of 1938 he became director of dramatics at Rollins College but for several summers returned to Roanoke Island as Selden's associate in directing *The Lost Colony* (*The Lost Colony: 352nd Anniversary Celebration, 1587–1939*, souvenir program, 1939, in NCC).

## 136. To J. B. Johns[1]

[Raleigh Road, Chapel Hill, N.C.]
6 June 1938

Dear Mr. Johns—

This is to confirm the agreement between you and myself to the effect that—

I do hereby appoint the Service Insurance and Realty Company of Chapel Hill, N.C. as exclusive agents for selling and disposing of my real estate consisting of some one hundred acres along the Raleigh Road and adjoining the Gimghoul and Battle Park property,[2] such appointment to run five years from date.

It is understood that for its services the Chapel Hill Insurance and Realty Company shall receive a commission of ten per-cent on its sales.[3]

Sincerely yours,

1. Manager, Service Insurance and Realty Company of Chapel Hill.

2. That is, 100 acres of the 223 acres Green bought in 1933 and 1934.

3. Debts prompted Green to sell this part of his Greenwood property. To buy the property, then to build his home there in 1936, he borrowed from the Bank of Chapel Hill and also took advances on royalties from Samuel French. In early 1938 his notes at the bank totaled $5,500, on which he had trouble making payments (W. E. Thompson to Paul Green, 3 January 1938, PG-SHC; Paul Green to Charles S. Allan, 4 January 1938, EG-SHC). His advances from French, which had rarely exceeded $4,000, now totaled $11,911.79 (financial statement, Samuel French, Incorporated, to Paul Green, 29 March 1938, PG-SHC). Through 1943, when the five years of the present agreement expired, Green sold sixteen lots encompassing almost forty acres for about $20,000—that is, about $500 per acre. (The record of deeds at the Orange County Courthouse gives date and acreage of sales, but not price. But Harry K. Russell, who in 1940 bought the eighth lot sold, consisting of 2.1 acres, paid $1,000 for the lot [Harry Russell to Laurence Avery, 8 August 1984].)

## 137. To Elizabeth L. Green

Hotel Fort Raleigh, Manteo, N.C.
Saturday [11 June 1938]

Dearest Honey—

I haven't had time to write you since I got here.[1] We've had all kinds of meetings and I've had to work on the script and collecting a workable bundle of music in lieu of the song-book material that's in New York.[2] Everything looks fine—the actors are beginning to arrive, Old Tom (new) is here,[3] and the whole caboodle will be in around next Monday. The theatre is much improved—Mr. Gillette did us worlds of good by his short visit.[4] Bell has followed his instructions to the letter—with the exception of the shrubbery, and he hopes to get that in soon. I am writing Mr. G. to come to the opening, also paying my respects to his aid, etc. Lots of people here have asked after you, and it's too bad that you couldn't have come with me and laze around in the water and the sun (not too much of the latter). I miss you too much. I'll try to get back home the latter part of next week, but only if I'm sure everything is going all right.

The islanders are counting a great deal on the show this summer for financial help. Fishing has been bad, potatoes are selling for little or nothing, and a sense of depression has been hanging in the air for weeks. However they're beginning to perk up with hope now.[5] The Negroes here at the hotel

1. Roanoke Island, for rehearsals of *The Lost Colony*, opening on Friday, 1 July, for its second season.

2. With the music publisher Carl Fischer, who would bring out *The Lost Colony Song-Book* in July (Paul Green to Eric Van der Goltz [with Fischer, Incorporated], 27 June 1938, PG-SHC).

3. Donald Somers, who replaced Earl Mayo in the comical role of Old Tom.

4. In February Charles Gillette, friend of the Greens and landscape architect from Richmond, visited Manteo to study the grounds of the Waterside Theatre and to make recommendations to Albert Q. Bell, designer and builder of the theater and grounds (Charles Gillette to Paul Green, 17 February 1938, PG-SHC).

5. D. B. Fearing, business manager of *The Lost Colony*, estimated attendance in 1937 at 60,000 with ticket sales around $50,000, and 1938 would be even better, with attendance around 75,000 and ticket sales of about $65,000 (Paul Green to F. S. Staley, 28 February 1938, PG-SHC). During its first five seasons (1937–41) *The Lost Colony* revived the economy of the island as "some 400,000 people attended [performances], paying approximately $330,000 in admissions, and spending around $3,000,000 in the state" (Powell, *Paradise Preserved*, p. 176).

have come to me wanting us to get Kay Kyser down with his band.[6] "That'll sho' pull the people—people." Paulie would agree.

Take care of your dear self and write me about the chillun and the garden.

I love you, Paul

## 138. To Clyde R. Hoey[1]

[Manteo, N.C.]
21 June 1938

My dear Governor Hoey—

As you know, during the past few years the Honorable Lindsay Warren[2] and many others have labored long and zealously that Fort Raleigh on Roanoke Island might someday be adequately provided for and perpetuated as the site of the first English settlement in the new world. At last it seems that these efforts are meeting with success, for I understand that the National Park Service has at last consented to take over the Fort and is ready to receive a deed to the property from the State of North Carolina.[3]

I am sure we all owe a debt of thanks to Mr. Warren for his splendid work in bringing this about, but it would seem that events have recently come to pass on Roanoke Island which considerably alter the picture and make a new study of the subject necessary.

Three years ago I would have advocated, and did advocate for that matter, that the fort be taken over by the Park Service. And my reasons were the same as those of Mr. Warren and others—namely, the adequate care for and perpetuation of the place as one of historical significance. But since then I

6. Kyser, band leader and radio and motion picture personality, lived in Chapel Hill.

---

1. Clyde R. Hoey (1878–1954), governor of North Carolina, 1937–41.

2. Congressman from the First Congressional District of North Carolina, which includes Roanoke Island.

3. In May 1936, Warren, C. C. Crittenden (secretary of the North Carolina Historical Commission), and others asked the National Park Service to accept ownership of and responsibility for the site. The park service commissioned a study, recently completed, that recommended acceptance (Charles W. Porter III, "Fort Raleigh National Historic Site, North Carolina: Part of the Settlement Sites of Sir Walter Raleigh's Colonies of 1585–1586 and 1587," *North Carolina Historical Review* 20 [January 1943]: 22–42).

have changed my mind. For during these three years and while the Park Service held the matter in abeyance, other things have developed. Through an ever alive community interest and with the help of the Works Progress Administration,[4] the fort has been reconstructed, colony cabins erected, a palisaded enclosure set up, and a theater dug out and fashioned by the Waterside. Today the place is one of great charm and like none other on the American continent. As for the authenticity of the buildings,[5] they are near enough what the colonists might have had to create a fine feeling in the spectator, whether he be schoolboy or art critic, for the life of those far off earlier days. I have done a great deal of reading and studying in the period and I can vouch for their dramatic truthfulness. And after all, that is what is needed most—something that is dramatic and inspiring rather than something that might well prove empty and documentary under another regime.

For instance, I am pretty sure that any scientific agency like the Park Service would in their rearrangement wish to remove the great encircling palisade, for that is not historically necessary. But even to destroy that would ruinously impair the atmosphere of the place and kill the suspense and sense of drama now immediately kindled in any person who approaches the sturdy watchful gates. Again, if the quaint reed-thatched cottages were removed, the same disastrous effect would obtain. And as for the waterside theatre, if that were removed to another site, the spirit would be gone.

I have had some experience in building outdoor theatres and putting on outdoor plays, and I can truthfully say that nowhere do I know of a place so ideally arranged as this for the dramatic representation of the legend and life that once belonged to it. (I can imagine no better set-up possible for a production of *The Lost Colony*.) But worst of all, if the Park Service or any other Federal agency, which must of necessity be rigorous and impersonal in its rules, took the place over, the community participation, the personal feeling of this being ours would depart from the hundreds and thousands who have worked for the creation of what we have. And we all feel that we have only begun this creation. The individual love and responsibility of the people of North Carolina and the nation will increase rather than diminish. That I believe. And I also believe that through this drama and the appeal of the fort

4. Which, beginning in 1934, provided labor through the Civilian Conservation Corps and funds for building material.

5. A sore point. Lack of historical authenticity in its buildings drew the major negative criticism of *The Lost Colony* project at the time (Powell, *Paradise Preserved*, pp. 141–45).

itself we shall be able to provide adequate financial care for this the thing we cherish.

Year by year we wish to make our annual celebration and dramatic production bigger and better until finally it shall become a summer festival second to none in the world. For the material, the ideal, the devotion and the dream are here. And someday *The Lost Colony* and Roanoke Island will, we hope, stand as high in the world of art and music as Oberammergau or the Salzburg Festival.[6] Yes, let us hope even higher.

If I am wrong and the next year or two proves it, then we can take under consideration the advisability of giving the fort and all it contains over to the Park Service. In the meantime I most earnestly request of you that we hold the matter quietly in abeyance until we have had further proof and testing of what we can do. For by no stretch of the imagination can the Park Service give us the freedom and cooperation that we now find among ourselves as The Roanoke Island Historical Association. Furthermore, I see no need for great hurry in the matter, for the historical meaning of the place will remain whether we succeed or whether we fail. That meaning was given to it by the brave colonists of the sixteenth century and not by us.

To repeat in conclusion, your excellency, I feel that the title to the fort should remain either in the keeping of the State of North Carolina or The Roanoke Island Historical Association. What has been done at Mt. Vernon is a case in point.[7]

With cordial regards, Paul Green

P.S. I am sending copies of this letter to Frank P. Graham, Honorary Chairman of The Roanoke Island Historical Association, The Honorable Lindsay Warren, The House of Representatives, Washington, D.C., D. Bradford Fearing, President of The Roanoke Island Historical Association, and Dr. C. C. Crittenden, Secretary of the State Historical Commission.[8]

6. Community performances of medieval plays (*Everyman*, for example) produced each summer by Max Reinhardt from 1920 to 1934.

7. The Mount Vernon Ladies' Association, organized in 1853 by Ann Pamela Cunningham of Laurens County, South Carolina, bought 200 acres of the plantation in 1858 and began to restore the house to its condition during George Washington's last years. The association maintains the house and grounds, including Washington's grave, and makes them accessible to the public.

8. Graham, Warren, and Crittenden responded, none of them agreeing with Green. Crittenden was the most detailed and based his support of the park service on the need to preserve the historicity of the site and keep the grounds undisturbed for the

## 139. To Thomas Wolfe[1]

Chapel Hill, N.C.
15 September 1938

DEAR TOM YOUR OLD FRIENDS DOWN HERE SEND YOU AFFECTIONATE GREETINGS HURRY AND GET FIXED UP AND COME TO SEE US THE TOWN IS YOURS AS ALWAYS

PAUL GREEN[2]

---

sake of archaeological digs. He also assured Green that the park service "has not only shown a willingness to have [*The Lost Colony*] continued but has even based its future program for Fort Raleigh upon such continuance. There seems every reason to believe that you will receive only enthusiastic co-operation" (2 July 1938, PG-SHC). In September 1938 the state and the park service reached an agreement on the transfer of the property in which the park service gained ownership and control of the site, the Roanoke Island Historical Association retained the right to produce *The Lost Colony* at the Waterside Theatre, and the park service agreed to support and publicize the production. The actual transfer of the deed from the state to the federal government occurred on 14 July 1939 (Powell, *Paradise Preserved*, pp. 162–66).

---

1. Wolfe and the Greens had been friends since undergraduate days at UNC, when they all were involved in Playmakers productions. After he graduated in 1920, Wolfe usually visited the Greens when he returned to Chapel Hill from Harvard, New York City, or Europe. After his most recent visit, in 1937, Green noted in his diary: "Tom Wolfe in town. He came out in the evening. We (rather he) talked till 4 A.M. Noticed through all his stories of his travels how factual though rich and intense everything was. He seems to have no feeling for story-telling as an art, that is for plot or construction. A big vital man in all ways" (23 January 1937, PG-SHC). The next day Green mused: "Where is the staying power of our American writers. Tom Wolfe will stay as long as he himself stays for he is his own subject and photographer. But what will happen if his public grows tired of his confessions? Or will it or can it grow tired? I would be surer if he could create and fashion complete and rounded separate works of art to stand alone—cut loose from the matrix of his own emotive-self. But how thankful we should be for what we have" (24 January 1937). The next night he and Wolfe drove in the rain "to Raleigh for dinner at Jonathan Daniels" (25 January 1937). Now Wolfe was in the Johns Hopkins Hospital, and Green sent a telegram—his only surviving communication with Wolfe.

2. The next morning Green received a telegram from Wolfe's brother: "WILL YOU SERVE AS PALL BEARER THOMAS WOLFE FUNERAL SUNDAY AFTERNOON THREE PM WIRE ME ASHEVILLE FORTY EIGHT SPRUCE ST FRED W WOLFE" (TWW-NCC). In July, during a trip to the West Coast and Canada, Wolfe was hospitalized with pneumonia in

## 140. To Frank J. Sheil

[Raleigh Road] Chapel Hill, N.C.
30 September 1938

Dear Mr. Sheil—

I am glad you are back from Europe and I hope you (and I presume Mrs. Sheil) had a good time. Recently I was in New York and called hoping to discuss our present standing and plans for cutting down my account with you[1] but you were away. If it fits in with your wishes at all I'd like to suggest that you take over my one-act plays entirely, crediting my account with the purchase price. This would relieve my sense of obligation to some extent, and I could chip down the rest as fast as possible. The same price you paid for the present-owned fifty per-cent would be satisfactory. This is a suggestion.[2]

Mr. O'Leary writes me that Gollancz wants "The No 'Count Boy" for anthology use and will pay five guineas.[3] Okay with me, and I am sending by separate mail a revised copy of it with easier speech and dialect which will fit the English scene better. Will you please see that the copy reaches Mr. Gollancz. I am anxious that he do not use the old version.[4]

---

Seattle. After an infection in his bloodstream spread to his kidney and heart and finally to his brain, his sister brought him by train across country to Johns Hopkins Hospital, where he was operated on twice, 10 and 12 September, for a cerebral infection. He died on the afternoon of Green's telegram. Wolfe's funeral was held at the First Presbyterian Church in Asheville on Sunday afternoon, 18 September, with Green among the pallbearers (Terry Roberts, "Paul Green Remembers Thomas Wolfe's Funeral," *Thomas Wolfe Review* 12 [Fall 1988]: 4–11).

---

1. Which stood at $11,759.07 (financial statement, August 1938, Samuel French, Incorporated, to Paul Green, PG-SHC).

2. Sheil declined the offer, as he had twice before, saying it would not be in Green's best interest (Frank Sheil to Paul Green, 12 March 1937 and 31 March and 30 October 1938, PG-SHC). In 1937 Green's income from the one-act plays had been $665.05.

3. C. T. O'Leary of Samuel French (to Paul Green, 20 September 1938, PG-SHC) passed along a request to include "The No 'Count Boy" in Constance Martin, ed., *Fifty One-Act Plays*, 2d ser. (London: Victor Gollancz, 1940).

4. The original version of "The No 'Count Boy" is most readily available in *In the Valley and Other Carolina Plays* ([New York: Samuel French, 1928], pp. 175–202), the revised version in *Out of the South: The Life of a People in Dramatic Form* ([New York: Harper and Brothers, 1939], pp. 71–88). The revised version reduces the dialectal spelling of the original; for example, "I des' put on dese heah clothes 'caze it was so hot

The Harper anthology of my plays[5] is now ready except for [a] few revisions. The ms. runs to a thousand pages. I hope to get up soon to arrange with you the matter of credits in the book for French.

I have just finished the new draft of *The Enchanted Maze* and will mail you four copies to reach you either Monday or Tuesday next. The typing is not the best in the world but it's the best I've been able to do.[6] Could you have a copy sent immediately to John Gassner of the Theatre Guild. He is expecting it;[7] also I'd like a copy to reach Jed Harris, maybe Guthrie McClintic,[8] or any other top-notch producer you think of. I am most anxious for an immediate production. (Delos Chappell[9] has money and might be a good bet.) And I don't want to sell the play for a long tie-up. As soon as it gets on in New York I know a lot of colleges and universities will want to do it—at least I think they will. I've had a lot of inquiries from such sources during the past two or three years, and on my desk now is a request from Ohio Wesleyan for permission to produce it as is and at once.[10]

About *Johnny Johnson* and Faustina Orner.[11] Maybe you'd better handle it direct with her, and any price you wish to set and any arrangement you make is okay with me. I am writing her by this mail that you are the person to see.[12]

There are several other business items I'd like to mention concerning my plays and prospects but will wait until I see you.

---

in de house wid my work duds on" becomes "I just put on these here clothes 'cause it was so hot in the house with my work duds on." It also removes explicit statements that the characters are black.

5. *Out of the South: The Life of a People in Dramatic Form*, published by Harper and Brothers in April 1939.

6. French published *The Enchanted Maze: The Story of a Modern Student in Dramatic Form* in November 1939.

7. In his capacity as playreader for the Guild.

8. Broadway producers.

9. Of the New York music publisher Chappell and Company.

10. The play was not produced in New York City.

11. New York literary agent who wanted permission to offer *Johnny Johnson* to motion picture companies.

12. Sheil set the price of film rights to the play at $35,000 and gave Orner the month of October to arrange a sale (Frank Sheil to Paul Green, 3 October 1938, PG-SHC). No motion picture has been made from the play.

On second thought I am enclosing the Gollancz version of "The No 'Count Boy" herewith.

With cordial regards to you and yours as always,

## 141. To James Boyd

Greenwood Road,[1] Chapel Hill, N.C.
8 February 1939

Dear Jim—[2]

Thanks for the letter and reference to general conditions in the shape of a bit of testifying for the Lord. Hallelujah! It always helps me on to hear from you, o struggler *and* reaper in the vineyard fields. I'm sure that in this last testament of beauty you have said sooth and I await the volume with great joy.[3] As for me—as the country correspondent puts it—I'm well as tolerable. The page proofs of my *Out of the South* have gone off and I have begun to sit again by the window watching the snowbirds eat pendulous suet from the plum trees and ponder on a teensy novel all written in the present tense and mostly conversation on spiritual matters for Harper's in the fall.[4] Elizabeth still endures me, the children are growing like bull calves and as clamorously, and day and night I keep dreaming of the right message in Buddhistic terms and hope that each tomorrow will find me not so far from home as I was at sunset just before. Really though don't all of us who practise at the shining

1. Unpaved road from the highway (Raleigh Road, which had been his address) winding northward for about a mile through his property to his home.

2. Boyd, just finishing his novel *Bitter Creek*, had written that "I'm a tired rassler with the Lord and worst of all can't count on having badgered an assurance out of Him. Even when I had Him in a close place once or twice the best I could get was an 'Almost.'. . . When death is on me I'll know it by this sign: I'll see in one belated and apocalyptic vision how to write a book. And yet I would not change my state with kings" (James Boyd to Paul Green, 24 January 1939, PG-SHC). Jacob wrestling with God and winning a blessing is recounted in Genesis 32:24–31.

3. When *Bitter Creek* came out, Maxwell Perkins, Boyd's editor, sent a copy to Green, one of the dedicatees. Green read it on a train to New York City and wrote to Boyd as soon as he got to the Hotel Bristol: "Jim, it's great!—fine and clean and hammered, tempered out into the real steel of living" (20 March 1939, Boyd Papers, SHC).

4. Not done.

word, truth and passion lit, have a hell of an age to stay lit in? Each morning's paper fills me with worse confusion and darkness. I can make no sense of the set up. Here tonight's paper glares at me "England and France will aid Franco"[5] and so it goes with all the premiers and kings and dictators saying to one another "Go f— yourself, for it's me and mine über alles." I love this world, but it means too little unless I can love what men do to it and in it. But on!

I've just read Hemingway's big Fifth Column and Forty Nine book.[6] What a writing man! And yet what a tail-ender in the tradition of Jack London and, strange as it sounds, Sherwood Anderson. He's a bad boy and an evil prophet, or rather no prophet at all. Do you know a story of his—"The Short Happy Life"? It's in this book.[7] Grr-r—That's the lion in it.[8]

Well we miss you all and that's no lie. Let us know when you get back, and let's call a pow-wow. Struthers writes he's coming back to live, and that's fine.[9] Have just seen Helen and David[10] and they're doing good.

Our love to you and yours, Paul

From the press it looks as if old Bill Faulkner has really put on a han't hunt for himself this time.[11] As one fellow put it in Harpers—"I read it in a lather of terror."[12]

5. Leader of the Loyalists in the Spanish Civil War.

6. *The Fifth Column, and the First Forty-Nine Stories* (New York: Scribner, 1938).

7. "The Short Happy Life of Francis Macomber," in ibid., pp. 102–36.

8. On a slip attached to the letter, Boyd noted: "Wonderful criticism of Hemingway."

9. Struthers Burt, novelist and friend of both Green and Boyd, who lived in Southern Pines in the early 1930s, had written to Green from Philadelphia that he planned to return to North Carolina (31 January 1939, PG-SHC). The plan did not work out, however.

10. Helen (formerly Stallings) and her new husband David Cohen.

11. In *The Wild Palms* (1939).

12. In a review of several new books including *The Wild Palms*, John Chamberlain said about one of them that he could "scarcely work himself up into a lather of terror, as he [could] while reading Faulkner" ("The New Books," *Harper's Magazine*, February 1939).

## 142. To Maxwell E. Perkins[1]

[Chapel Hill, N.C.]
[Mid-February 1939]

THE MANY FRIENDS OF THOMAS WOLFE IN NORTH CAROLINA ARE HOPING THAT THE MANUSCRIPT OF LOOK HOMEWARD MIGHT BE SECURED BY THE UNIVERSITY HERE AS A FITTING REMEMBRANCE IS THERE ANY CHANCE OF IT REGARDS PAUL GREEN[2]

## 143. To Frank S. Staley[1]

[Greenwood Road, Chapel Hill, N.C.]
[28 February 1939]

Dear Mr. Staley—

I am very glad that you are getting up information relative to a possible outdoor production at Williamsburg, and I am pleased indeed to send you

1. Maxwell E. Perkins (1884–1947) had been Thomas Wolfe's mentor and first editor at Charles Scribner's Sons and now was executor of Wolfe's estate. On 19 February 1939 several New York City organizations were to hold an auction of books and manuscripts for the benefit of exiled German writers, and one item in the auction was the manuscript of *Look Homeward, Angel* (*New York Times*, 20 February 1939, p. 3, col. 3).

2. Perkins replied that Aline Bernstein, to whom Wolfe gave the manuscript of *Look Homeward, Angel*, donated it for the auction (see Suzanne Stutman, ed., *My Other Loneliness: Letters of Thomas Wolfe and Aline Bernstein* [Chapel Hill: University of North Carolina Press, 1983], pp. 371–76). He added that Gabriel Wells bought the manuscript at the auction (for $1,700) and planned to give it to Harvard University (which he did in March 1939). Perkins closed by telling Green that all the other Wolfe manuscripts were still part of the estate and that "I have always had your university in mind, not only in respect to these manuscripts, but also in respect to several hundred books which Tom owned and which I thought they might want to purchase too" (23 February 1939, PG-SHC).

---

1. Success of *The Lost Colony* stimulated the Rockefeller Foundation to consider an outdoor historical play for Colonial Williamsburg, which the foundation had begun to develop in the 1920s, and in early December 1938 Green met with foundation officials in Williamsburg, where they discussed two subjects for the play: the founding of Jamestown and the founding of the Republic in and around Williamsburg (Paul Green to Kenneth Chorley, 26 December 1938, and Paul Green to Bela Norton, 28 January 1939, PG-SHC). Now Frank S. Staley (1879–1943), in the office of Kenneth

what facts and suggestions I can from my experience with *The Lost Colony* during the last two years. May I take up your questions in order:

1. I hardly know how *The Lost Colony* came to be produced. For many years—in fact since 1921 when I first visited Roanoke Island—I had dreamed of writing something about those tragic first settlers. But time went by and no means of production came to me. However there was some talk round and about on the subject, and some of the Island people themselves became interested. This interest continued in one form or another until I had finished college and gone on to other things. Then one day in 1931 I visited the Island again and talked with Mr. Saunders and Mr. Fearing,[2] two business men of that section, and to my surprise I learned that they had never given up hope of having some sort of celebration to honor the early colonists and had been busy on plans for a long time. Of course there was a lot of commercial instinct behind the plans, and the suggestions that arose out of many committee meetings were rather startling—for instance the idea of having a nation-wide beauty contest to choose the girl who should play Virginia Dare. (They didn't know nor did I at that time that when the play finally came to be written Virginia Dare would be a baby and remain so. There was in all our minds the legend that she grew up to be a beautiful maiden and fell in love with Chief Manteo's son, married him and became the mother of a brave race that somehow evaporated into thin air.)[3] But as we continued to work on the matter, the commercialism fell away, and we all more and more determined to try for the best that was in us and for the best we thought was in the colonists. We went around getting pledges for funds and secured rather a decent amount, but then the depression got worse and these pledges necessarily came to little or nothing. Then the W.P.A. came along and saved us. We got a project approved to build the theatre, and Mr. Warren our congressman[4] with the help of Mr. Fearing and other local business men got the U.S. government to mint 25,000 memorial fifty-cent pieces which were sold (a majority of them) to collectors all over the world for a dollar and a half apiece. Through

---

Chorley, president of Colonial Williamsburg, Incorporated, was studying the feasibility of such a play and had sent Green some questions about *The Lost Colony.*

2. W. O. Saunders and D. B. Fearing.

3. As in Sallie Southall Cotten, *The White Doe: The Fate of Virginia Dare, an Indian Legend* (1901).

4. Lindsay Warren.

this means we were able to pay our proportion in materials for the project. And so we were started at last.

The production was sponsored by The Roanoke Island Historical Association (Mr. Fearing, President), the State Historical Commission, and the Federal Theatre who lent us several key actors to supplement our local talent.

2. One of the main reasons for the success of *The Lost Colony* was that Mr. Fearing, our business manager, was also a confirmed and energetic optimist. No sight of bad luck or fear of failure could stop him. Also another reason was that the local people were interested both as helpers on the side and active participants in the show. And finally the music, color, and movement of the play itself attracted the public, and the public passed that news along by word of mouth.

3. The fact that the local people had pride in their historical background, that they shared in the earnings of the play, and that the tourist trade has completely rejuvenated the island—this has kept their interest alive.

4. According to Mr. Fearing, the attendance for 1937 was around 60,000 and for 1938 around 75,000, a total of 84 performances for the two seasons and some 1,500 average attendance a performance. This seems rather remarkable when one considers that the island is 90 miles from the nearest city—Norfolk, and comparatively isolated.[5] The gross from the play last summer was something over $65,000. I have no figures on the income from the 1937 production, but it was proportionate to the attendance—I should say around $50,000.

5. Our salaries ranged from one dollar per night for children and CC Camp boys[6] to $40 a week for the top actors and technicians. Room and board was had by the visiting actors at about $12 a week.

6. The W.P.A. still pays the salary of a project head[7] who remains on the Island the year round. Only part of his duty is connected with looking after the theatre. There is other local W.P.A. work he has charge of.[8] This is the only additional government help to be added to the statement I sent Mr. Chorley.

5. At the time only a ferry connected Roanoke Island to the mainland, at Manns Harbor.

6. Young men in the Civilian Conservation Corps stationed on the island were used as extras, particularly as Indians.

7. Lee Winslow.

8. A sewing shop in Manteo and other handicraft projects on the island (*The Lost Colony: 352nd Anniversary Celebration, 1587–1939*, souvenir program, 1939, pp. 6, 27, in NCC).

7. I should say that from the sale of programs, books, souvenirs, etc. we received some $5,000 last year. (We had very few souvenirs. Williamsburg could have a wealth of them, as well as books, songs, dances, post-cards, etc.)

8. I estimate the cost of *The Lost Colony* theatre with its palisades, permanent features of huts and dressing rooms to have cost about $15,000 and was financed as stated above in Number 1.

9. The cost of staging *The Lost Colony* for the first time was approximately $17,000—

| | |
|---|---|
| Lighting | $4,000 |
| Costumes | 1,000 |
| Advertising and printing | 5,000 |
| Rehearsal salaries | 2,000 |
| Royalties and music | 3,000 |
| Properties | 1,000 |
| Miscellaneous | 1,000 |
| Total | $17,000. |

10. I feel that there is more dramatic material connected with Williamsburg than Roanoke Island. Whereas the American idea can be said to have had its first faint vision on Roanoke, it came to realization and full statement through Williamsburg and the leaders (Washington, Henry, Randolph, Jefferson, Mason, and others) who made it historically a hallowed place.

11. No doubt the location of *The Lost Colony* theatre on the site once occupied by the colonists had a great deal to do with the success of the play, and the same thing would be true in the Williamsburg production. Except more so, for the whole place and its spirit there are dramatic and imaginative to begin with. The theatre there should be located in some dell or place convenient to the capitol, or on the site of an imagined dwelling where these leaders used to meet and talk over their dreams and plans for the Republic. Then when the play opens and the prologue part is spoken the audience can immediately be conducted into the point of view of witnessing actual events and personages. (I have some definite ideas on this matter which we can take up later.)

12. Yes, I should be able to write such a play and of course am most anxious to do so. The usual royalties per the Dramatists' Guild contract are, 5, 7½, and 10 per cent for the author, depending on the gross. But this is a matter also

we could discuss as we got nearer to setting up the project. In no case would it be more and could be less.

I think it would take me from six to eight months to get the play and music in final shape, and I would hope we could open in the summer of 1940.

13. The music should be an integrated and dramatic part of the play, and I should want the best possible composer for the job. Mr. Stringfield and I have worked together before and are at present doing something for a small production of a play of mine in New York.[9] He is a good man, but for the present I personally should prefer to wait on the matter of composer until the play is pretty clear in my mind and I have the musical feel of the production well established.

14. To build a simple and charming theatre seating from 2,000 to 2,500 people I should consider $10,000 to be adequate. The theatre on Roanoke Island seats nearly 4,000 and is a bit too large. It strains the actor's voice somewhat. This year we are planning to do something to alleviate this trouble. I think the Williamsburg play should open not later than July 4 and should run yearly.

15. As to admission at a Williamsburg performance, I am not qualified to speak. For *The Lost Colony* we charge one dollar for adults and fifty cents for children. Perhaps it should be more at Williamsburg. We'd have to study this matter, I think.

16. Perhaps a joint sponsorship for the play would be best—say, Williamsburg Incorporated and the A.P.V.A.[10] I don't know. However I think we should want to get the people of Virginia as a whole behind us.

17. The College of William and Mary could very well be interested in and benefitted by the play. In fact I have talked with Mr. Cheek, Director of the Little Theatre there, about the idea. The director and the players could be a fine amateur nucleus for the production, just as our Carolina Playmakers here are a nucleus for our *Lost Colony* production. Then the matter of properties, of all sorts of technical and small business details could be taken care of by the organization. (Now on second thought the College itself might well be one of the sponsors.) I think the play would help the dramatic group there to

9. *Shroud My Body Down*, scheduled for production by the Group Theatre. In late March, however, it was dropped, just as Green and Lamar Stringfield finished a musical score for the production (Green diary, 18–26 March 1939, PG-SHC).

10. Association for the Preservation of Virginia Antiquities.

national recognition and give them a boost toward finer productions in the winter months—productions to which the tourist public would like to come. Then too the outdoor theatre might serve as a place for class and other exercises before the historical drama began its regular summer run. There are all sorts of ramifications and possibilities, of course.

I hope this gives you some light both as to problems and as to solutions. Please count on me to cooperate in any way I can. And let me say lastly that if for any unforeseen reason I got stuck in the writing of the play I would call in the best American dramatist or dramatists that I could get and keep on calling until we had a perfect production. But I am sure I can do the play, and I want to very much.

Cordially yours,[11]

## 144. To John Terry[1]

Greenwood Road, Chapel Hill, N.C.
2 May 1939

Dear John—

We have just had a meeting here of several of Tom's old friends and we are preparing to make a drive for funds with which to purchase the manuscripts

11. Later in the year Chorley told Green they could not arrange to open a play in Williamsburg earlier than the summer of 1941 (telegram, 9 June 1939, PG-SHC). Then World War II intervened, and it was late 1945 before discussions resumed, leading to production of *The Common Glory* in 1947.

---

1. John Terry (1894–1953), who received a B.A. from UNC in 1918 and continued as a medical student for two more years, was a school friend of Green and Thomas Wolfe. In 1930 when Wolfe resigned from the Department of English at Washington Square College in Manhattan, Terry took his place there. After Wolfe died, Terry began raising money to buy Wolfe's books and papers and his homeplace with the aim of establishing a memorial to Wolfe in Asheville (Maxwell Perkins to Paul Green, 11 April 1939, PG-SHC). Perkins told Green about Terry's plan because Green, failing to get the manuscript of *Look Homeward, Angel*, had himself asked Perkins how the rest of Wolfe's manuscripts and his books could be obtained for the UNC library (Perkins to Green, 11 March 1939). When Terry wrote to Green outlining his plan for Asheville, Green replied: "Frankly I think the University of North Carolina is the place to have Tom's MSS. and books—anyway his MSS. The old home in Asheville would require a fortune to buy and keep up. . . . Don't you think we'd better go ahead with [the drive

and books which Mr. Perkins has. I've talked to Mrs. Wolfe, Tom's mother, and she is keen for the idea of establishing this memorial to Tom here. The library has promised us space and proper binding, care, and administration of the material for all time to come.[2] Within the next two weeks I shall be in New York to select actors for an outdoor play of mine,[3] and I'd like to talk with you about ways and means. We are not making anything public until we meet at a memorial dinner sometime soon.[4] In the meantime I have asked Mr. Perkins for a five-months option during which time we hope to raise the money needed.

My intent now is to arrive in New York on May 9. Could you give me a ring at Hotel Bristol about ten o'clock A.M. on that day. The number is Bryant 9–8400. Between us we ought to work out a good plan. I'm glad you and I feel—as no doubt thousands of others will—that this is a great privilege we have to honor a *great* artist![5]

Ever, Paul

---

to get the books and manuscripts for the UNC library]?" (Paul Green to John Terry, 23 April 1939, TWT-NCC). Perkins agreed with Green and, after mentioning that at auction the manuscripts should bring between $7,500 and $10,000, asked what offer Green could make (Perkins to Green, 21 April 1939, PG-SHC). Green, Mary Thornton (head of the North Carolina Collection at the UNC library), and a few others decided to offer $5,000 and ask for five months in which to raise it, to which Perkins agreed (Perkins to Green, 4 May 1939).

2. Perkins was offering to UNC "all the manuscripts that Tom ever put into handwriting except *Look Homeward, Angel*," consisting of twenty-nine small notebooks of diary entries, phone numbers, etc.; six large notebooks of miscellaneous writing; complete manuscripts in pencil of *Of Time and the River*, *From Death to Morning*, and *October Fair*; nine large notebooks containing "The City and the Voyage," "Esther's childhood—My Father's Youth," "Cambridge—The City and the Voyage II," "Ship—Catawba—The Father—Mrs. Jacobs," "Hills beyond Pentland," "Esther's life, childhood," "Esther's life—Her father's life," "The barns at sunset—Esther," and "The Western Journey"; typescripts of *The Web and the Rock* and *You Can't Go Home Again*; and "a large collection of letters to relatives and friends" (Maxwell Perkins to Paul Green, 18 May 1939, PG-SHC).

3. *The Lost Colony.*

4. On 13 June 1939 ("Library Seeks Wolfe's Works," *New York Times*, 14 June 1939, p. 27, col. 3).

5. Green publicized the fund-raising drive for Wolfe's papers through the UNC alumni association, newspaper releases, and letters. Even with an extension of his

## 145. To James H. Fassett[1]

[Greenwood Road, Chapel Hill, N.C.]
15 June 1939

Dear Mr. Fassett—

Am glad to know that your plans for broadcasting from *The Lost Colony* are working out, and I hope you will call on me for any help I can give. I notice from your letter of the 13th that you speak of using Stringfield's music for background to the narrative. It seems to me that it would be much better to use some of the madrigal, folk-song, and ballad melodies typical of the Elizabethan spirit—plenty of which can be found in *The Lost Colony Song-Book* put out by Carl Fischer. Stringfield's contribution to the show was three or four ordered or commissioned pieces to fill in a few gaps, and unfortunately it does not fit the play as well as the material mentioned above. So will you please see that music more native to and integrated with the spirit of the piece is used. Among those I especially prefer are—No. 6—English March; No. 7—Old Tom's Lament; No. 8—We Come from Field and Town; No. 9—Milkmaids' Dance; No. 13—O, Farewell England; No. 20—Christening Dance; No. 23—Eleanor Dare Lullaby; No. 24—Christmas 1588; No. 25—O Death Rock Me Asleep; No. 27—Sleep O Pioneers.[2]

---

option into January 1940, however, he raised only $402. Perkins then sold the material to William B. Wisdom of New Orleans, who made it the foundation of the Wolfe collection he gave to Harvard University in February 1947 ("The Thomas Wolfe Collection of William B. Wisdom," *Harvard Library Bulletin* 1, no. 3 [1947]: 280–87). Into the North Carolina Collection of the UNC library, Green put the small black notebook in which he had recorded contributions to the Thomas Wolfe Memorial Fund, and the money he collected was used for a scholarship in creative writing (Mary Thornton to Paul Green, 14 December 1940, PG-SHC). In February 1949, the Thomas Wolfe Memorial Association, with neither Green nor Terry a member, bought Wolfe's former home at 48 Spruce Street in Asheville and later that year opened it to the public.

---

1. CBS radio planned to broadcast a one-hour version of *The Lost Colony* later in the summer, and Fassett, in the music department of CBS and in charge of making the adaptation, had sent Green his ideas, among them the notion that "the routining will be a difficult matter since I plan to have the show completely segue with Stringfield's music as background for narrative" (13 June 1939, PG-SHC).

2. The numbers locate the pieces in *The Lost Colony Song-Book*, and all of the ones

You may wish to have some Indian music, and in that case Stringfield's Indian Corn Harvest Dance could be used.[3] The point is that the public is interested in Elizabethan music, and if composers are mentioned it might be well to class them mainly together—Tallis, Tye, William Byrd, Morley,[4] and add a statement about the modern composer.

Cordially yours,[5]

## 146. To John A. Oates[1]

[Greenwood Road, Chapel Hill, N.C.]
28 August 1939

Dear Mr. Oates—

Once again let me tell you how delighted I am at the prospect of doing a play for you and in that old opera house. That building cries out for new life

---

Green mentions are traditional English airs from the Elizabethan period or earlier. For instance, number 9 is "Greensleeves."

3. Number 5. Lamar Stringfield also wrote another Indian song (number 12), the overture (number 1), a dance (number 19), and the closing march (number 28).

4. Sixteenth- and early seventeenth-century London composers whose songs Green also used in *The Lost Colony.*

5. On Sunday, 20 August, Green drove to Manteo for rehearsals for the coast-to-coast one-hour broadcast on Wednesday, 23 August, at 8:00 P.M.. Wednesday was stormy, and in the afternoon the chief of the CBS crew called New York about contingency plans. "Columbia said put the show on even if lightning struck the stage," Green noted in his diary. "A lot of prayerful looks at the scowling grumbling sky as the day wore on. Rain held up just before broadcast time—8 P.M. Then the wind began to blow. A dog came in and barked at the actors—Got a stick for murder but decided better. Finally got through at 9" (Green diary, 23 August 1939, PG-SHC; see also Paul Green to Douglas Coulter, 11 August 1939, PG-SHC).

---

1. John A. Oates, of Fayetteville, North Carolina, chairman of a committee planning a celebration of the Scottish settlement of the Cape Fear River valley before and during the American Revolution, had contacted Green about writing a play for the occasion. On 26 August Green drove to Fayetteville and met with Oates and his committee to arrange details of the contract for the play that became *The Highland Call.* Green and the committee wanted to do the play in the LaFayette Opera House, an old building in Fayetteville about to be demolished.

to come into it, and I hope we will make a beginning there that will grow into something splendid and lasting. As soon as I got back here from my conference with you and Mr. Rose[2] I got in touch with John Parker[3] and Dean Bradshaw.[4] Other members of the university committee were out of town. Bradshaw agreed that we should go ahead full speed. There are a few details connected with the Playmakers which must await the return of Professor Koch from Canada around the middle of September, but I am assured by both Dean House and President Graham that they will be worked out. In the meantime I have revised the terms of our agreement somewhat and am sending it along for the proper signature and action.[5]

Please let me hear from you now and then if any idea comes into your mind which you think would be of help to me in constructing the play, and also won't you feel free to call upon me at any time for whatever additional service I may give.[6]

Cordially yours,

2. Charles G. Rose, Sr., president of Fayetteville Historical Celebration, Incorporated.

3. Assistant director of the Carolina Playmakers, who would direct *The Highland Call.*

4. Francis Bradshaw, dean of students at UNC.

5. The contract was to have named Parker as director, but that could not be done without Koch's approval (Paul Green to John Parker, 28 August 1939, PG-SHC). As revised the contract bound Green to write a suitable play dealing with the history of the Scottish people along the upper Cape Fear River and bound Fayetteville Historical Celebration, Incorporated, to pay him $1,000 for the job and to provide a suitable place for the production of the play, preferably the old opera house. It stipulated that all income from productions of the play in Fayetteville belonged to the corporation, but otherwise the corporation had no rights in the piece (1 September 1939, PG-SHC).

6. Through September and October Green visited historical sites involved in the play and wrote *The Highland Call* ("Worked all day on . . . play—tied up in knots—few ways or words and even less story came" [Green diary, 30 September 1939, PG-SHC]). In early November the Playmakers put the play into rehearsal in Chapel Hill. On the morning of 16 November Oates called to say that polio had broken out in Fayetteville and the schools were closed. Green and Parker drove to Fayetteville that day and "met with citizens in courthouse—heard scientists, medicos talk of what they didn't know. Decided to go ahead with celebration, keeping children under 15 away" (Green diary). The play ran at the LaFayette Opera House in Fayetteville, 20–24 November, then at Memorial Hall in Chapel Hill, 5–6 December 1939.

## 147. To Cass Canfield[1]

University of North Carolina, Chapel Hill, N.C.
6 May 1940

HAVE JUST READ RICHARD WRIGHT'S TERRIFIC NATIVE SON CONGRATULATIONS TO HIM AS AUTHOR AND YOU AS PUBLISHER I FEEL THE BOOK WOULD MAKE A FINE PLAY AND I SHOULD LIKE TO TRY MY HAND AT DRAMATIZING IT FOR NEXT SEASON PERHAPS PREFERABLY IN COLLABORATION WITH WRIGHT SINCE IN THAT WAY ALL MATTERS COULD BE DISCUSSED AS WE WENT ALONG WOULD YOU LET ME HEAR WHAT HE THINKS OF THE IDEA[2]

REGARDS PAUL GREEN

1. President of Harper and Brothers, which on 1 March 1940 published Richard Wright's *Native Son.* Green's diary for 29 April 1940 says he had just read *Native Son* "at Cheryl Crawford's request. She's interested in getting it dramatized. Found it horrifying, brutal, and extraordinarily vivid. Reminiscent a bit of *Crime and Punishment.* Doubt I could do anything with it. However, I feel it's the most vivid ['mature' revised to 'vivid'] writing I've seen by any Negro author in America" (PG-SHC).

2. Edward C. Aswell, Wright's editor at Harper, replied the same day that he had sent Green's telegram to Wright, who was in Mexico (Edward Aswell to Paul Green, 6 May 1940, PG-SHC). From Cuernavaca Wright wrote to Green on 22 May that his was "the only offer to dramatize the book that has interested me . . . because of the manner in which you handled the Negro character in your play, 'Hymn to the Rising Sun.' It may be surprising to you to know that I had to resign my job as publicity director of the Federal Negro Theatre in Chicago a few years ago because I fought for a production of your 'Hymn to the Rising Sun.' Indeed, I had to fight both Negroes and whites to get them to see that the play was authentic." He added that Bigger Thomas, central character in *Native Son,* "if put on the stage, will be a kind of character that many Negroes *and* whites will not like. But I think that a great deal of the danger can be avoided by making Bigger a character through whom the social forces of Negro and white life flow. Because of the many threads of Negro and white life you caught in your one-act play, and because of the kind of insight you displayed for the Negro character in that play, I think you can handle a boy like Bigger" (Richard Wright to Paul Green, 22 May 1940). From Mexico Wright came to Chapel Hill, arriving around 21 June. John Houseman, who had wanted to dramatize the novel and would produce the play with Orson Welles when it opened in New York City on 25 March 1941, came from New York City. The next day "Wright, Housman and I worked out rough story from the novel for dramatic study. They went on to N.Y. in late afternoon" (Green diary, 22 June 1940, PG-SHC). Then Wright returned about 9 July and "we began work on dramatizing *Native Son.* . . . Finished first draft today, and Wright returned to New York" (Green diary, 12 August 1940).

## 148. To Zora Neale Hurston[1]

[Chapel Hill, N.C.]
[Early May 1940]

HAVE ARRANGED FOR SOUND MACHINE BUT IT WOULD COST RATHER HEAVILY TO SEND A MAN AND CAR DOWN THERE COULD YOU DRIVE UP AND GET THEM SINCE I HAVE TO BE IN NEW YORK THE LAST OF NEXT WEEK[2] GOOD GOING AND SO GLAD TO HEAR FROM YOU

PAUL GREEN[3]

## 149. To Hallie Flanagan[1]

[Greenwood Road, Chapel Hill, N.C.]
23 May 1940

Dear Hallie—

I have just got back to town and received your letter of May 14, also on tonight's mail another note. Thanks for both of them. When I was in New

1. Zora Neale Hurston (1903–1960), folklorist and novelist, taught drama at North Carolina College for Negroes (later, North Carolina Central University) in Durham during 1939–40 and attended Green's writing class at his home on Sunday nights. For several weeks prior to this telegram she had been in the coastal town of Beaufort, South Carolina, with a fellow student of anthropologist Franz Boas at Columbia University, studying black church life. During the work they discovered many fine spirituals, and Hurston wanted to record them for a play she and Green planned to write. But the other student hurried off to New York City for filming equipment and, according to Hurston, would come back to record "the spirituals for *commercial purposes*!" She added: "Now, dont sit there, Paul Green, just thinking. DO SOMETHING! We cant let all that swell music get away from us like that. . . . Cant you get one of the machines from the University and run a man down here for a week?" (Zora Neale Hurston to Paul Green, 3 May 1940, PG-SHC).

2. To cast *The Lost Colony.*

3. No recordings seem to have been made, and *John de Conqueror*, working title of the play they hoped to write together, was not completed. Hurston moved back to New York City later in the summer (Robert E. Hemenway, *Zora Neale Hurston: A Literary Biography* [Urbana: University of Illinois Press, 1977], p. 274).

---

1. The Federal Theatre Project lost its funding and ceased to exist after 30 June 1939. Hallie Flanagan (1890–1969), on leave from Vassar College since 1935 to head the

York I wanted terribly to get up and talk over the Williamsburg plans and see some of the fine things you are doing, but I had to get back here for graduate examinations as soon as we had selected the two or three characters needed for the Lost Colony. And that was a hectic business. Somehow the word had got into The Times about casting going on at Hotel Bristol, and from then on we were in a madhouse. Telephone and letters and calls at the desk! How tragic—all those fine young people, talented, spirited, and nothing to do with themselves. I felt as never before the loss of the Federal Theatre. While in New York I talked with Stevens about the possibility of FT lighting equipment for Williamsburg.[2] He got Porterfield[3] together with me and we put our wits to working. Finally I was on the hunt alone, going from X to Y to Z and hearing again and again—"No, I'm sorry—they've given you the wrong person. I know nothing about it. You should try so and so." At last I found a man by the name of T. J. Young at WPA headquarters on Columbus Avenue who sounded as if he knew something, and I went there to meet him. As I stepped into the elevator a cop came from nowhere and asked where I thought I was going. I told him. He ordered me out of the elevator around to another street to get a pass, and there was another cop. After giving the sad young man at the desk a convincing story, I thought, he gave me a pass to the 7th floor, and after that I suffered scrutiny from another cop and finally arrived at Young's desk. I asked

---

project, spent July 1939 closing down the operation, then, with support from David Stevens of the Rockefeller Foundation, returned to Vassar, where she and a small staff spent a year organizing and cataloging the records and papers of the project. During that time she also substantially completed *Arena: The History of the Federal Theatre* (1940). Green had begun *The Common Glory* for Federal Theatre production, then turned to Colonial Williamsburg with the plan that Flanagan would direct the show at Williamsburg, opening in the summer of 1940. In a recent letter, however, Flanagan explained that she did not have the time. "Paul," she wrote, "you can imagine that at this time I do not give up easily the idea of working with you, or the idea of being at Williamsburg, or the idea of earning money. It is just that my college job and the book have to be done.—If [the production] only were next summer." She urged him nevertheless to come to Poughkeepsie so they could discuss the production (14 May 1940, PG-SHC).

2. In *Arena* Flanagan tells how the lighting, sound, and other equipment accumulated by the Federal Theatre Project, "worth approximately a million dollars, was locked up in government warehouses" (pp. 367–68).

3. Robert Porterfield, director of the Barter Theatre in Abingdon, Virginia.

him what the hell was this—was I in a free or fascist country. With a wan smile he agreed it looked as if we were already at war with somebody and the screws were on. "No, we've had a lot of labor trouble here," he said. "And what are all those people doing sitting in that auditorium down there?" I asked. "Oh, they're waiting on their applications. They sit there for hours." Well, I managed to throw off the despondent environment and get to the matter of the lighting equipment at last. And then mirabile dictu! A long rambling story of this and that and this and that again. I got out a pad and pencil and tried to note down the high-spot individuals as he went along, to tie together as it were a chain of cause and effect. Out of it all I managed to learn that there was some equipment and that it was stored at Pier 4, East River, South and Broad Streets, that I couldn't get admittance there because I was not a government man, that he had no authority to give me entrance, that the matter was out of his hands, that I would have to go to Washington to see Mr. Akridge, etc., etc. I called Mr. Akridge on the phone, but he would not be back till Wednesday, I should see Mr. Aubrey Williams, and no he was not there and wouldn't be till Tuesday, said the sweet young voice. I got all my notes together, staggered out of Young's office and reported to Stevens. He said go to it and he would get in touch with Washington and help prepare for my coming. I finished my other business and drove on down to Washington Monday afternoon. Early Tuesday morning I got busy. I went to the NYA headquarters and found that Mr. Akridge was a myth that had died so to speak. Neither he nor Aubrey Williams was connected with the NYA. Mr. Akridge's place had been taken by Mr. Orville E. Olsen. Was he in? Sorry he was not. Could I see his secretary. I did. She knew nothing. Was there anybody else there who might know anything about FTP surplus properties. Yes, Mr. Cornelius Miller. Could I see him. Sorry, he wouldn't be back till two P.M. At two I was back and did meet Mr. Miller face to face. Yes, he knew about the matter some—I showed him my notes on the letters that had been sent with an inventory of the lighting equipment from Young's office—WPA-SP-1437–29, dated April 4, 1940. He stared at them. "We have no record of any such inventory," he said. He inquired, phoned around, nobody had ever heard of the surplus property stored there on Pier 4. "The letters and inventories must have been lost," he said. "But I saw the letters and the inventory—copies of them—there in New York, and they were signed by one Somerwell—Young had them," I said. "Who is Young?" he inquired. I tried to explain. Maybe I did, for presently he seemed satisfied he knew who Young was, which was more than I did at that time, for my eyes were beginning to set in my brain. I shook my coma off and went heroically and I believe quietly on. "Mr. Cornelius—Mr. Miller, I mean, the picture is clear in my mind. Here on the one hand we have a grand project under way for which we badly need lighting equipment, and there in the warehouse at Pier 4 is a lot of it rotting away. My purpose in coming to you is to see if we can possibly bring the two together." "Are you in any way connected with the government?" he asked. "No, I'm not, I'm sorry, I'm only a poor playwright and college professor who is trying to work in the peoples' theatre by starting several community ventures in the drama. We've already got two underway, though still handicapped for lack of adequate equipment—one down at Manteo, N.C. and the other at Fayetteville, N.C. The first one is a play called The Lost Colony—you might have heard of it, it's been running for three summers." "No, I haven't heard of it," he said. "And we're trying to start another one at Williamsburg." "Yes, I know about Williamsburg," he said, "the town I mean." We talked for an hour or more and at long last he got interested and said he and Mr. Olsen would do all they could to help me get what was needed. "But you'll have to do it through the state NYA administrator for Virginia—a Mr. Walter S. Newman in Richmond. But first we'll have to get busy here and secure new copies of the inventory in New York, then have the equipment stored on Pier 4 transferred to NYA, then your part of it transferred to Virginia and Mr. Newman, to be lent to your project by him. Maybe too we'd better get a project put through to have it reconditioned and re-inventoried there in New York before it is transferred to Virginia." "How long would that take?" I asked. "Quite a time—perhaps months." "And then the transfer?" "Quite a time too." "Please let it come on down as is after you get charge of it, we'll take care of the reconditioning," I begged. He tentatively agreed. And so I came away with instructions to proceed through Mr. Newman with our request. I called Mr. Newman on the long distance and told him that there was plenty of equipment in existence and that I had been the rounds—mentioning names, places, instructions, etc.—and would he cooperate with us in requisitioning it through his office. He replied that he wouldn't like to have all that stuff charged to him, not knowing whether he would be able to use it, he said. I explained that we intended to use it on loan from him. Well, to cut across he kindly relented and said he would cooperate. So, Hallie, I am sending to Mr. Newman on next Monday a request for such and such lighting equipment for the Williamsburg project. I'm sure it will take months to get it, but get it I will if it's to be got under heaven. I have a letter to take to Mrs. Roosevelt as a further resort, also I will enlist Bob Reynolds[4] and plenty of others if it takes that to cut the red tape. Too, tomorrow I am working out another application through the N.C. NYA administrator[5] for lighting equipment for Fayetteville. He is enthusiastic about the prospect and says he will do all he can. Already he has given us NYA help on making the costumes for Manteo this summer.[6] Somehow I believe these things will go through, and with David Stevens interested the way he is, I'm sure that something is going to happen in our favor. I'll let you know the outcome. In the meantime I am working away on the Wmbg play. Last week we had a committee meeting in Newport News, and the consensus of the group was not to open this August or September but continue building our publicity and production plans for opening on June 12, 1941, to commemorate the adoption of the Virginia Bill of Rights. We deferred definite decision, but how does this latter date sound to you? For you know we must have you with us in the creation of this regional theatre somehow. If we opened in June next year we would plan for a full summer run, working out a cooperative scheme of advertising and promotion with The Lost Colony. The Cape Fear Valley Festival play at Fayetteville will not conflict since it is indoors and will be played each autumn. What do you think of the idea of having Wmbg and Roanoke running at the same time? At any time you can I wish you'd send suggestions along about the theatre and this region, and as soon as I can I will get up your way for a round of plans and discussion.

I hope what I said above about the WPA and NYA doesn't sound too bad. You know it all better than I ever can. I wasn't discouraged at all—not about the drama and what we are going to do there. But about democracy and the American dream as I know them I am not so sure. The essence of American democracy as a way of life is the ideal of the individual morally responsible soul, free in terms of that responsibility. It may be we have failed to work out a declaration of independence and a constitution which lays down the philosophy of how that individual soul shall cooperate in a social plan with other souls. Hitler, Mussolini, Stalin, et al [seem to] start[7] from the point of view of

4. U.S. senator from North Carolina and foe of the Federal Theatre Project who nevertheless supported Green's outdoor plays.

5. John A. Lang.

6. Lang did provide lighting equipment for *The Highland Call* (John Lang to Paul Green, 23 October 1940, PG-SHC).

7. Here the original reads: "Stalin, et als to be start. . . ."

cooperation; we with the idea of separateness or aloneness of persons in their basic rights. There is truth in both views, and we must make our individuality find its place in mutuality if we are to survive. Some of this I hope comes out in my play.[8] But I don't have to say much about this, for it looks as if we are in for plenty of naturalistic illustration of this around us in the next few months and years—Be with us God and hold our breaking hearts!

I have been down to see our friends the convicts again. They asked kindly after you.[9]

About the narrator's part in The Lost Colony—we are using the same man of last year.[10] I am making a note of Raymond though and will keep him in mind for another year. Hope you have had a photograph of yourself sent to D. B. Fearing at Manteo for our program.

Best to you ever,

8. *The Common Glory.*

9. In early April Flanagan had been in Chapel Hill for a Playmakers drama festival, and on 14 April she drove with Green to Williamsburg, where the next day they scouted about for a site to build an outdoor theater. On the way, they stopped at North Carolina's "Caledonia prison farm to see Fred Beal—cold sunshiny day. Fred talked of his plan for rehabilitating the prisoners after leaving the gang" (Green diary, 14 April 1940, PG-SHC). During the summer of 1929 Beal had led a strike of textile workers against the Loray Mills in Gastonia, North Carolina, during which he was convicted of murder and sentenced to twenty years in prison. He fled to the Soviet Union, stayed there about nine years, then, disillusioned with communist society, returned to the United States and began serving his sentence in February 1938 (Liston Pope, *Millhands and Preachers: A Study of Gastonia* [New Haven: Yale University Press, 1942]). Green visited Beal, and others in various prisons, frequently and was one of the few who worked for Beal's release until he was pardoned by Governor J. Melville Broughton in 1942 ("Fred Erwin Beal Gains Freedom under Parole," *NO*, 9 January 1942, p. 1, col. 2–3; p. 2, col. 7).

10. Henry Buckler. Flanagan was urging Green to consider another actor for the part, Franklin C. Raymond (Hallie Flanagan to Paul Green, 23 May 1940, PG-SHC).

## 150. To W. A. Stanbury[1]

[Greenwood Road, Chapel Hill, N.C.]
20 August 1940

Dear Dr. Stanbury:

I appreciate your letter with its kindly advice about the dramatization of the Negro novel, *Native Son*, and I am hastening to assure you that I, along with you and many another North Carolinian, am most anxious to foster a growing racial accord among our people.

You are right, I think, in feeling that the novel as it now stands has a great deal of bitterness and racial antagonism in it—qualities which are understandable enough. However, there is a basic human truth in the book, and Mr. Wright and I are doing our best to put that truth into the play—a truth shorn of its surrounding hate and evil. I consider the character of Bigger Thomas as depicted in the novel to be a challenge to all right-thinking people. We cannot ignore him. Rather, we should seek to understand him, and the causes which brought him into being. As authors, we are trying to make the play a sort of biography—a biography of an American youth who through the degradation of our Democratic system is denied the rights, the privileges, the aspirations and the dreams guaranteed to him by the principles of this same government. It is only incidental that he is black. The play will try to speak for the thousands, the hundreds of thousands of frustrated youths in America. And we hope to make it strong with a demand for leadership in building a society where such ruined and degraded souls will occur less and less often.

And of course we have to take account of the individual's moral responsibility.[2]

With cordial regards.

1. Green and Wright finished their dramatization of *Native Son* on 12 August 1940 (Green diary, PG-SHC), and Green revised it through the fall. While the two were still at work, Green received a letter from Stanbury, pastor of Central Methodist Church in Asheville and member of the North Carolina Interracial Commission, expressing his fear that a dramatization of the novel "could tend only to arouse ill feeling between the white and colored races" (1 August 1940, PG-SHC).

2. In a cordial response Stanbury said that "if *Native Son* be dramatized in the manner you indicate, it should do good instead of harm" (3 September 1940, PG-SHC).

## 151. To Betty Smith[1]

Box 107, Chapel Hill, N.C.
1 December 1940

Dear Betty—

While in New York the past few days[2] I spent some time with Louise S.[3] on matters in general, and in particular I mentioned the hope that your (just) dues could be settled and soon. She evidently has some confusion in her mind about it all. Our committee meets the last of this month, and if this is not cleared off by that time, I'll mention it again and something more.[4]

Best to you. Paul

## 152. To Donald Mason[1]

[Chapel Hill, N.C.]
15 January 1941

Dear Don:

Glad to have word of you and your doings. Of course we all would be very sorry to lose you from our summer and fall program, but in the present

1. Betty Smith (1896–1972), playwright and novelist, came to Chapel Hill in 1936, sent by the Federal Theatre Project to work with the Playmakers. After 1939 and the end of the Federal Theatre, she stayed in Chapel Hill on successive fellowships for young playwrights funded by the Rockefeller Foundation and administered by the Dramatists' Guild. Green was on the guild fellowship committee.

2. For a meeting of the National Theatre Conference, 22 and 23 November, at which he was elected to a two-year term as president.

3. Sillcox, executive director of the Dramatists' Guild.

4. Problems with Smith's fellowship ($1,000) were resolved and she received it for 1940–41, then again for 1941–42, during which time she wrote several short plays and her first novel, *A Tree Grows in Brooklyn* (1943).

---

1. From Chicago and an undergraduate at UNC since 1937, Mason had acted in several Green plays, most recently playing Sandy Ochiltree in the December 1940 production of *The Highland Call* in Fayetteville. Ochiltree is a comic role, and Mason had done so well in it that Green said next summer he might try the part of Old Tom, the major comic role in *The Lost Colony.* Earlier in the month, however, he told Green he was "about to be called into the army; of all times too. Ever since leaving Fayetteville I've been thinking about the things you said, and 'Old Tom.'. . . What I'm

emergency it seems to me all of us should do our part in service to the country. I have done a lot of thinking about this matter of personal inclination and public service. Whether we agree wholly with the practice of force or not, still we must rise up and share the burden pressed upon our citizens. You are a citizen, and you owe the country as much as it owes you. Perhaps you can justly say that you could serve better by continuing in the line of your talent. So could most all of us say. But somebody has got to do the job, and taking your talent and mind into consideration I do not see we should be shown any particular preference over others. I hope you will take your years military service and come back to us that much stronger and better man, and therefore the better artist.

Them's my sentiments and I love you still and want you to try the part of Old Tom when you are free to.

With best as always,[2]

---

trying to get at Paul, is that I need a letter; a letter to that doggone draft board. According to the local board, a letter from you would go a long way in getting me deferred till late next fall. And probably by that time, I can look so unhealthy, they'll defer me for life" ([January 1941], PG-SHC).

2. Later in January Mason wrote to thank Green "for a wonderful letter. It really was Paul; and although it didn't aid my own selfish motives, it's a letter I'll always keep and cherish as a most valuable possession" (undated, PG-SHC). Mason was deferred nevertheless and continued as Wanchese in *The Lost Colony* of 1941 (a role he had played since 1938), then was drafted in December 1941 and sent the next year to the South Pacific as part of the buildup of troops under General Douglas MacArthur. "Dear Paul," he wrote on 26 November 1942, "Was thinking back on a certain month almost two years ago when I wrote you a letter asking a note of recommendation for deferment. Lots has happened since then, for here I am in Australia happy to be doing a job that I know is worthwhile" (PG-SHC). Following his discharge in 1945, Mason returned to *The Lost Colony* and played Wanchese for five summers (1946–50).

## 153. To Richard Wright[1]

Chapel Hill, N.C.
30 January 1941

Dear Richard Wright,

A couple of days ago I received a wire from John Housman in which he asked me to hurry up the final script so that he could go ahead. I wired him back immediately that the script we left with him in Philadelphia could be considered the final one except for the editorial changes, cuts, and music to come, and I urged him to go right ahead with the casting and added that I would come up any time to help as needed.[2]

As soon as I arrived home I came down with the flu and have just got on my feet again. I did a little work in bed, and will send off to Housman tomorrow another script cut and refurbished as needs be. I hope you will keep me informed as to how things are developing.[3]

1. After Richard Wright (1908–1960) and John Houseman conferred with Green in Chapel Hill about the dramatization of *Native Son* (see letter 147, n. 2), Green sent them an outline of scenes based on the discussions, to which both responded enthusiastically (Richard Wright to Paul Green, 26 June 1940, and John Houseman to Paul Green, 27 June 1940, PG-SHC). Then Wright returned to Chapel Hill on 8 July, and the two of them drafted the play, finishing all but the last scene by the time Wright returned to New York City on 12 August (Green diary, PG-SHC; see also Ouida Campbell, "Bigger Is Reborn," *Carolina Magazine* 70 (October 1940): 21–23). Through the fall and winter Green revised the play, several times conferring with Wright. In mid-January the two met in Washington to finish a draft, then took it to Houseman in Philadelphia, where he was trying out a production of Philip Barry's *Liberty Jones.* As the script developed, Houseman, having wanted to dramatize the novel himself, objected continually to elements in the play.

2. One thing Houseman objected to was Green's version of the murder of Mary Dalton (John Houseman to Paul Green, 24 December 1940, PG-SHC). Houseman thought the murder should be staged realistically and in the present, as in the novel. Green, on the other hand, wanted to hide the implausible way the killing takes place in the novel and emphasize Bigger's tortured emotions as he is caught in the bedroom of a white woman. In a scene written with Wright in Chapel Hill, he showed the murder after the fact, through Bigger's troubled dream after committing it; and to get a dreamlike effect he called for the scene to be played under colored lights and behind a scrim (*Native Son* typescript, act 1, scene 5, Paul Green Collection, NCC).

3. Green's next letter to Wright (see letter 154) refers to the murder scene "in its present realistic statement." Evidently it was in Chapel Hill following the meeting in

I hear you made a good speech at Columbia.
Good luck. Hope to see you soon.

## 154. To Richard Wright

[Chapel Hill, N.C.]
7 February 1941

Dear Richard Wright:[1]

I am glad to know that you and Houseman are sticking right along with the play. I haven't heard as to how *Liberty Jones* was received,[2] but good or bad, I understand that *Native Son* will be rushed ahead. I will be in New York from time to time, and will cooperate in any way possible in putting across a bang-up show. No doubt as rehearsals proceed there will be certain little editorial touches we can add in line with each actor's capability. Also, don't let's forget that if we need to, the character of Max can be combined with Erlone.[3] Also, if the murder scene comes too much as a shock in its present realistic statement, then it will be easy enough to sickly it o'er with the pale cast of dreaming.[4]

---

Philadelphia that he removed the dream framework from the murder scene and gave it the literal form used in the production and shown in the published text (*Native Son: The Biography of a Young American* [New York: Harper and Brothers, 1941], scene 4). In his autobiography, *Run-Through: A Memoir* (New York: Simon and Schuster, 1972), Houseman gives an unreliable account of this and other aspects of the dramatization of *Native Son* (pp. 461–75).

---

1. Wright responded to letter 153 by saying he and Houseman had started cutting the new script of *Native Son* and that Houseman would begin casting once *Liberty Jones* was out of the way (3 February 1941, PG-SHC).

2. It was a flop. Directed by Houseman, it opened on 5 February, got negative reviews, and closed after twenty-two performances.

3. In early drafts Green and Wright combined two characters from the novel: Boris Max, Bigger's defense attorney, and Jan Erlone, Mary Dalton's Communist boyfriend (*Native Son* typescript, Paul Green Collection, NCC). Houseman objected to the combination, however (John Houseman to Paul Green, 24 December 1940, PG-SHC), and Green wrote Max into the play (first name changed to Edward) as he removed the dream framework of the murder scene.

4. *Hamlet*, act 3, scene 1, line 85.

Congratulations on the Spingarn award. I wish I knew some way of making myself respectable.[5]

Best regards,

## 155. To Orson Welles[1]

Chapel Hill, N.C.
2 March 1941

Dear Orson Welles:

Yesterday morning the final scene of *Native Son* was finished, and Wright agreed that the pistol-renunciation end seemed to him to be in keeping with what might boil up out of Bigger's character. I am sending herewith a copy of this last scene. I left one with Wright to be given to you, and you may need another. You will notice, of course, that some little bit of Max's stuff could be cut out, but the all-important thing, it seems to me, is to keep this play morally responsible to the world and to the individual as well as dramatic. Of course, we all want that.[2]

5. On 31 January Wright received the Joel Spingarn Award from the National Association for the Advancement of Colored People (NAACP), its highest award for achievement in the interest of blacks, and in writing Green about it Wright said the "medal makes me almost respectable!" (3 February 1941, PG-SHC).

---

1. In mid-February Orson Welles (1915–1985) finished shooting his motion picture *Citizen Kane* and returned to New York City to take over the production of *Native Son*. Green had been in New York a few days ending 1 March for work on the script.

2. Before work on the script began, Green reached an agreement with Wright that Wright would collaborate on the dramatization, that communism would be taken less seriously than in the novel, and that Bigger Thomas would develop a sense of personal identity and moral responsibility (Paul Green to Edward Margolis, 15 May 1963, PG-SHC; typescript of Rhoda Wynn interview with Paul Green, 4:10, 13, Paul Green Collection, NCC). During their time together in Chapel Hill (July–August 1940), Green and Wright considered ways to project the development of Bigger's sense of identity and responsibility through the action of the play, especially in the last scene, but found none satisfactory (Campbell, "Bigger Is Reborn," pp. 21–23), and Green continued to try different endings during the fall and winter, usually with Wright's support. Houseman objected to all the ideas, however (John Houseman to Paul Green, 24 December 1940, PG-SHC), and by late February Green, feeling that

I will be back in New York Friday morning of this week and will see you then. Here's to *Citizen Kane* as well as *Native Son.*

Cordially,

## 156. To Paul R. Reynolds, Jr.[1]

[Chapel Hill, N.C.]

Day Letter, 3 March 1941, A.M.

SINCE I AM UNABLE TO BE IN NEW YORK AT THIS TIME, AND IN ORDER TO HELP NATIVE SON TOWARDS AS COMPLETE PRESENTATION AS POSSIBLE, I WISH WRIGHT TO TAKE OVER THE AUTHORITY AS AUTHOR FOR THE PRODUCTION OF THE FINAL SCENE THERE, AND LIKEWISE I WILL TAKE THE AUTHORITY FOR THE PUBLISHED SCRIPT OF THE LAST SCENE, THE REST OF THE PLAY STANDING IN JOINT RESPONSIBILITY AS IS.[2] STOP. IT IS UNDERSTOOD THAT HE AND I WILL CONTINUE OUR MUTUAL AID ON THE SHOW IN ANY AND EVERY WAY POSSIBLE. STOP. PLEASE HAVE ASWELL[3] SEND ME AT HIS EARLIEST CONVENIENCE A COM-

---

Wright now sided with Welles and Houseman, yielded on several points for that reason. "After all," he said, "[it's] his novel, his characters" (Green diary, 1 March 1941, PG-SHC). But Bigger's development was crucial to Green and he agreed only to revise the last scene, evidently with Wright's assistance, into his final version—the "pistol-renunciation end"—in which Bigger snatches a pistol from a guard, then returns it and takes himself into the electrocution chamber, his dialogue making it clear that the action climaxed his personal development (typescript of Rhoda Wynn interview with Paul Green, 4:17–18). As Green later told Welles, "If when the play is over the audience fails to feel a closer kinship between black and white, as well as the sharp antagonism to injustice and discrimination, then we have failed somewhat in our purpose" (Paul Green to Orson Welles, 10 March 1941, PG-SHC).

---

1. Reynolds, Wright's literary agent, had from the first handled much of the contact between Green and Wright, and between them and their publisher, Harper and Brothers.

2. Evidently, between this and the letter of the previous day to Welles (letter 155) Green got word that Wright supported Welles and Houseman in their opposition to Green's final scene. In its place they put a scene showing Bigger in his cell, arms outstretched, a Christ-figure crucified by white society (for the scene as produced, see Burns Mantle, ed., *The Best Plays of 1940–41* [New York: Dodd, Mead, 1949], pp. 61–63).

3. Edward C. Aswell, editor at Harper and Brothers handling publication of the play.

PLETE SET OF GALLEY PROOFS OF ALL SCENES, WITH THE TWO PIECES OF MUSIC ADDED.[4] THIS WILL HELP ME IN GETTING A CLEAR PERSPECTIVE FOR PROOF-READING THE LAST TWO SCENES. SEE YOU SOON.

AFFECTIONATE REGARDS TO ALL, AND HERE'S HOPING FOR A BANG-UP PRODUCTION.

PAUL GREEN

C/C TO WRIGHT

WELLES

HOUSEMAN

## 157. To Hugh F. Hill[1]

Chapel Hill, N.C.
5 March 1941

Dear Mr. Hill:

You are quite right about the similarity between "The Last of the Lowries" and Synge's "Riders to the Sea." My play was written when I was a student at the University of North Carolina and wildly fervent so far as Synge was concerned, so it is natural that some of his emotional impact upon me should have seeped into what I was trying to say. This applies to another play of mine also, "The No 'Count Boy."[2]

I hope this answers your question.

With cordial regards

4. "Hannah's Song," p. 6, and "Death Lament—Bigger," pp. 145–47, in *Native Son* (play).

---

1. A freshman at Roanoke College, Salem, Virginia, doing a research paper on Synge's "Riders to the Sea" and Green's "The Last of the Lowries." He had noticed a "likeness between the structure, characters, and action of the two plays" and wondered whether Green had Synge's play in mind when writing his own (Hugh Hill to Paul Green, undated, PG-SHC).

2. Suggested by Synge's *Playboy of the Western World.*

## 158. To Paul R. Reynolds, Jr.

Chapel Hill, N.C.
[Monday], 10 March 1941

Dear Mr. Reynolds:

It was nice seeing you again, and thanks for the lunch.[1] I turned over to Harpers' early Saturday morning the complete proof for *Native Son.* Wright and I had time to go through the script once more and make little proofreading corrections up to the beginning of the final scene itself. After considering the method—a kind of fierce close-up intensity—which Welles is using in producing the show, I came to the conclusion that the script had best adhere somewhat to that, since the matter of a well-rounded, well-constructed play was already through the window. So I limped the ending across the goal line as best I could.[2] Wright and I agreed that if the critics and the public agreed too strongly that the play let down after the capture of Bigger, we could do something about revision in the acting version, which we hope French will consider issuing later.[3]

I trust you have revised the contracts according to our agreement, and that I will receive a copy for filing soon.[4]

1. Green went to New York City on Thursday night, 6 March, and spent Friday and Saturday there.

2. Green several times mentioned his admiration of the spectacle devised by Welles for the production (e.g., typescript of Rhoda Wynn interview with Paul Green, 4:22–23, Paul Green Collection, NCC). For details of the staging, see Michel Fabre, *The Unfinished Quest of Richard Wright,* trans. Isabel Barzun (New York: William Morrow, 1973), pp. 211–14. Also, Green, Wright, and Edward Aswell of Harper and Brothers were in a rush to have the book ready by opening night (originally set for 17 March, postponed to 25 March; the book came out during the first week of April). A need for haste along with admiration of the staging influenced Green not to go back to his earlier version of any scene for the published text. His main reversion came in the final scene. There he retained a few lines suggesting Bigger's dawning sense of identity and responsibility, then closed the play with Bigger walking independently into the execution chamber (for the staged ending, see letter 155, n. 2). He also changed the name of Bigger's lawyer to Edward Max, rejecting Paul Max, the name used in the production script by Houseman and Welles.

3. No acting edition of the play was published, but French issued a final revised version in 1978.

4. The latest production contract, dated 25 February 1941, defines the authors' royalties as 5 percent of the first $5,000 gross weekly box office receipts, 7.5 percent of

Well, you have done a lot of hard work on this play, and we all appreciate it. May you be well rewarded in a long continuing percentage.[5]

With cordial regards,

## 159. To Paul Rosenfeld[1]

[Chapel Hill, N.C.]
6 May 1941

Dear Mr. Rosenfeld:

I think it is a great thing you are doing in getting up a memorial issue of *Story* to Sherwood Anderson. If I can possibly get the right mood to hit me I will be glad to write a short piece on some phase of Sherwood's splendid genius. The subject you suggest is a good one.[2] Perhaps I could simply restate for you a long monologue which Sherwood gave utterance to late one night standing in front of my house. He was visiting me and we had been down to see Jim Boyd for the evening.[3] We got back late. The night was balmy and full

---

the next $2,000, and 10 percent of weekly gross over $7,000. The original contract between Green and Wright, dated 22 July 1940, calls for them to divide royalties 55 percent to Wright as author of the novel, 45 percent to Green as dramatist (contracts, Paul Green Foundation, Chapel Hill, North Carolina).

5. *Native Son* had a good run. After several previews it opened at the St. James Theatre in New York City on 25 March 1941 and ran into June for 114 performances, then began a tour that included long stays in Boston and Chicago and lasted until January 1942. A few weeks after the opening, Green noted that "*Native Son*, bastard and mutilated as it is, doing well with the public. Can't get much pleasure out of seeing it succeed since one edge of its truth has been chiseled and blunted off" (Green diary, 16 April 1941, PG-SHC).

---

1. On 8 March 1941 Sherwood Anderson died, and Paul Rosenfeld (1890–1946), music critic, magazine editor, and longtime friend of Anderson, was guest editing a special issue of *Story* magazine as a memorial. He had asked Green for an article based on his friendship with Anderson (Paul Rosenfeld to Paul Green, 30 April 1941, PG-SHC).

2. "The Patriot of the Small Towns—would that approach interest you?" Rosenfeld had asked (ibid.).

3. Anderson lived in western Virginia, on a farm near Marion, and since 1936 had visited Green almost yearly, hoping, he indicated in a letter, to generate a sense of community among writers of the region (Jones and Rideout, *Letters of Sherwood*

of fog. Sherwood sniffed the air and said it reminded him of a certain night in a little town in the middle west. And then he started talking about little towns and how he loved them. Maybe I can repeat this for you, but never as well as Sherwood himself stated it.[4]

With cordial regards,

## 160. To David Stevens[1]

Chapel Hill, N.C.
5 September 1941

Dear Dave:

I don't know where you are, and this is just an acknowledgement of your kind letter of some days ago. I was in New York recently and called your office hoping to have a chat with you about the great work ahead of the NTC and other things. But you were reported as being in Wisconsin.[2]

I am getting up some suggestions to send on to Barclay[3] for our fall meeting, and I hope you will give yours plentifully and completely and will likewise be around as a source of information and guidance when the meeting comes off.

This is to report that our season at Roanoke Island has broken all records. On our closing weekend we played to some 8,000 people. One night the

---

*Anderson*, pp. 369–70). Boyd, a frequent party to the visits, lived in Southern Pines, seventy-five miles south of Chapel Hill.

4. Rosenfeld's deadline for submission was early June, and Green did not write a piece for the Anderson issue of *Story* (19 [September–October 1941]).

---

1. David Stevens (b. 1884) directed the Humanities Division of the Rockefeller Foundation (1930–50) and with interest and money supported *The Lost Colony*, the effort to launch *The Common Glory* at Colonial Williamsburg, the National Theatre Conference, and other projects in the "People's Theatre" movement of the day. At the time of the present letter he was especially interested in the National Theatre Conference and had sent Green a brief report on its project to establish theaters at military bases and suggestions for its convention in New York City in November (David Stevens to Paul Green, 9 August 1941, PG-SHC).

2. Where Stevens had a vacation home.

3. Leathem, professor of drama at Western Reserve University and executive secretary of the National Theatre Conference.

overflow was so great that we had to lock the outer gates and give a second show beginning at eleven o'clock and ending somewhat past one. I had done considerable work on the script and production and we had a better production to offer than in preceding years. Each year there are things to be done to the show, and it is never complete and finished. This is only one more proof that the theatre is a vital and organic thing—like a tree or even a burning bush.[4] I always feel lifted up to think that I have the humble privilege of working at such a blood-pulsing art.

Best to you and yours,

## 161. To Emily Wedge[1]

[Chapel Hill, N.C.]
[Mid-December 1941]

Dear Miss Wedge:

Thank you for your letter of December 8. I should think your compilation of quotation titles would make an interesting reference volume.

As to the titles of my two books mentioned, that of the novel *This Body the Earth* is not a direct quotation but one made up of a rephrasing of something biblical—I don't remember just what—about the body of this death.[2] *Tread the Green Grass* is taken from an old folk song whose source I do not remember, but the song goes—

> Tread, tread the green grass, dust, dust, dust,
> Come all ye pretty fair maids
> And trip along with us.[3]

There are two titles of mine which do use direct quotations, one is *Lonesome Road*, a volume of one-act plays, the title taken from the Negro

4. Exodus 3:1–6.

---

1. Wedge, on the staff of the Enoch Pratt Free Library of Baltimore, was compiling a reference book of titles and their literary sources and asked Green the source of two of his titles (Emily Wedge to Paul Green, 8 December 1941, PG-SHC).

2. Romans 7:24: "O wretched man that I am! who shall deliver me from the body of this death?"

3. In Benjamin A. Bodkin, ed., *A Treasury of American Folklore* (New York: American Legacy Press, 1944), pp. 807–9.

song, "Look down, look down that lonesome road,"[4] and the other a collection of long and short plays under the title *Out of the South.* The quotation for the latter comes from Job 37:9—"Out of the south cometh the whirlwind and cold out of the north."

I trust this information can be of use to you.[5]

Cordially yours,

## 162. To Mary G. Johnson

Villa Carlotta, 5959 Franklin Avenue, Hollywood, Calif.
25 December 1941

Dearest Mary—[1]

Today is Christmas day and I know you are happy with the fullness of the earth and hearts and your children around you. I am sitting here in my apartment trying to work out a plot for a story and I've got plenty in me and around me to keep me busy all right—if it all is most unchristmas like. Drop me a note about how things are going—especially as to what Bill[2] has decided to do. I feel for him and all the millions of other young men now tramping uneasily across the earth fighting for some unknown but hoped for tomorrow. Where it's all to end, God knows. Out here the war seems pretty close with the Jap submarines prowling off the coast in sight of land and sinking oil tankers and freighters.[3] Every citizen here has received instructions how to tackle incendiary bombs when they fall. I got mine yesterday. And the traffic lights have been painted black and hooded down to little baleful red crosses of light. Guards are posted at crucial spots (though I must say, not as thick as they were

4. In Carl Sandburg, *American Songbag* (New York: Harcourt, Brace and World, 1927), pp. 322–23.

5. Apparently Wedge did not publish the reference book.

---

1. Green flew to Hollywood from Greensboro over the night of 17–18 December to write a motion picture script from Maude Delavan's novel, *The Rumelhearts of Rampler Avenue* (1937).

2. Her son, a senior majoring in history at UNC.

3. On 20 December Japanese submarines attacked two American tankers within twenty miles of the California coast, disabling one of them, the *Emido* (*New York Times*, 21 December 1941, p. 1, col. 8; p. 22, col. 2).

at the Greensboro airport when I left there the other day),[4] the asiatics wear buttons proclaiming their loyalty to Uncle Sam, and a great many families here in Los Angeles have lost sons and husbands in the Pearl Harbor debacle. Still folks go on their way here as usual and I'm sure that there's such a sense of war universally in the air that even if air raids came and these incendiary bombs fell people would take it all somewhat as a matter of course, grin and bear it—so dumb and patient is the animal man. So brave and wonderful and tragic too.

I've stayed pretty close to my work here in my apartment and haven't seen the friends I knew when I was out here before. Yesterday I spoke to Willie Stacy on the phone and she made me promise to come to Billy Vaughan's[5] wedding which is in the Beverly Hills Presbyterian Church tomorrow (Friday) evening at 6:30. I said I would be there, of course. I've seen Dorothy McBrayer and she sends her love and greetings to "all those pretty girls."[6] She is working herself to death paying for her house and supporting a rather heavy-weighing mother. The movies seem in lower state as to quality than I've ever seen them, and Hollywood Boulevard in the evening—when I go down to eat or get a paper—is filled with the most uncouth and bizarre crowd of movie people, drawn from all refugee corners of the earth, too, I've ever seen. On the corner near here a dashing white-headed mamma's pet boy keeps his old horse and little covered wagon parked day after day. The wagon is all covered with signs which say he the boy and not the horse has all sorts of talent and he will never leave till he gets a chance in the movies. The police will take care of him no doubt. And besides, the long-haired holy men, spiritualists, European impresarios, dancing girls, and mad cow-mothers with their twittering "Shirley Temple" off-spring add to the clutter and confusion. Most of this is surface stuff and plenty of hard work goes on even if the product is poor.

Hurriedly and with love to all, Paul

I guess whatever few words I've said about the defense methods here are supposed to be confidential.

If Bill joins up before I get back or is drafted, let me know his address. Hope

4. In North Carolina police were stationed in airports across the state to monitor arriving and departing planes (*Greensboro Daily News*, 9 December 1941, sec. 1, p. 2, col. 5).

5. Daughter of Green's cousin Willie Cutts Stacy.

6. Mary's three daughters.

some of you can go up to see Elizabeth at least once and help her in her widowhood—so I feel it, though I may be wrong.

## 163. To Elizabeth L. Green

Villa Carlotta, 5959 Franklin Ave., Hollywood, Calif.
[25 December 1941]

Dearest Honey—

This sure has been a dark Christmas day—with no good old brassy California sun at all, nothing but a slow cold drizzle with ice and snow; believe it or not, for I'll be the only one that tells it—yessir, snow and sleet up on the higher passes, though not down below. I've been here in my room all day digging at this, as Jan[1] says, "cuss it" story. I'm making some progress, and as soon as I can break through the underbrush I'll be able to dictate it down somewhat rapidly, I hope. The war weariness hangs in the air here, no doubt about it. As I said in my other letter[2] people go on about their business, but there doesn't seem to be the old feeling among them anymore. There've been several sub attacks near the shore, and so many people have already lost sons or husbands at Pearl Harbor. And to think this is just the beginning of the misery. Every citizen has already had his instructions how to deal with incendiary bombs. I got mine yesterday. Well, as the Pope said in his Christmas message (I hope you read it)[3] it's terrible business and war may not prove anything—won't if character and moral worth don't dictate the peace. He calls for a return to Christ. That's good too, but I noticed he thought that Christ was the source of truth and left out Mohammed, Buddha, Confucius and the other great religious leaders. He too seems to exemplify the same creedal blindness that nationalism does. Of course I think Mohammed could well be left out but hardly the others. The three great phases of human existence—the individual, the institution, and universal humanity—are hard to get lined up the one for the other, in the other, by the other. But that's the challenge and if the Pope can't see it how can a power-hypnotized general? But I'm preaching.

The pictures of the children have just come, but you left out the main person. Where is she? They are grand.

1. Their youngest daughter, who was ten.

2. Of 18 December 1941 (EG-SHC), which also tells of his rough but beautiful trip "on the sky-sleeper from Dallas."

3. Text in *New York Times*, 25 December 1941, p. 20, cols. 3–8.

Tomorrow night Billie Vaughan gets married. I'll try to give her something from you and me.

Haven't been paid yet, but expect to tomorrow or next day. The movies they're making here are certainly sorry—absolutely nothing in this town worth seeing except "Dumbo"[4]—no plays, nothing. The place is full of all sorts of outlandish people, but dead—to me. Got to get back to work.

All my love, Paul

I searched in the big picture envelope but not a word.

4. Animated feature-length picture by Walt Disney about a baby circus elephant, voted one of the ten best films of 1941 by the National Board of Review and in 1947 awarded a Grand Prix at Cannes as Best Animated Film.

Home near Lillington, North Carolina, on State Road 210 just north of U.S. 401, where Paul was born and grew up. (PG-SHC)

Paul's parents, William A. and Bettie Byrd Greene, about 1889. (PG-SHC)

Paul and his sister Mary in 1897, his tie a remnant from her dress, their shoes scuffed (their good shoes were burned in the fireplace, Paul noted on the picture) to the embarrassment of their mother. (PG-SHC)

Paul as a newly commissioned second lieutenant in Paris, 22 June 1919. (Paul Green Foundation, Chapel Hill)

Elizabeth Lay in the arboretum on the Chapel Hill campus, summer 1919. (PG-SHC)

Elizabeth's parents, George W. and Anna Balch Lay, about 1931.

Horace Williams on the front porch of his home overlooking Franklin Street in Chapel Hill about 1920. (PG-SHC)

Abe (Frank Wilson) pledges to lead his people out of the bondage of ignorance as Muh Mack (Mary Carr, holding the baby) and Goldie (Rose McClendon, in bed) listen, thankful for his renewed determination (*In Abraham's Bosom*, scene 2, Provincetown Players production, Provincetown Playhouse, 1926). (Billy Rose Theatre Collection, New York Public Library for the Performing Arts)

Paul and Elizabeth with Paul, Jr., and Byrd behind the house they rented in London, 1929. (PG-SHC)

First and last pages of Paul's letter to Frederick Koch from London about the British theater and his visit with Bernard Shaw, who, he assures Koch, is the "*youngest man in Europe*" (letter 66). (PG-SHC)

Will (Franchot Tone) comes to the realization that he must "let the past die. It's our life now—our house!" Patsy (Margaret Barker) supports him as Big Sue (Rose McClendon) and Big Sis (Fanny de Knight) look on (*The House of Connelly*, act 2, scene 3, Group Theatre production, Martin Beck Theatre, 1931). (Billy Rose Theatre Collection, New York Public Library for the Performing Arts)

Elizabeth with Betsy, Paul, Jr., Janet (*in Elizabeth's lap*), and Byrd (*on floor*) at home in the Glen, 1932. (PG-SHC)

Dust jacket of Green's second novel, 1935. (Laurence Avery)

Johnny (Russell Collins) discovers that the German sniper (Jules Garfield), who had concealed himself in the statue of Christ in a churchyard cemetery, is only a boy and also named John (*Johnny Johnson*, act 2, scene 3, Group Theatre production, Forty-fourth Street Theatre, 1936). (Billy Rose Theatre Collection, New York Public Library for the Performing Arts)

Paul (*left*) studies site of *The Lost Colony* theater on Roanoke Island in 1936 with Melvin Daniels, W. O. Saunders, Frederick Koch, Chauncey Meekins, Martin Kellogg, Jr., D. B. Fearing, and Ike Davis. (PG-SHC)

Paul and Sam Selden (who directed most of Paul's outdoor plays from *The Lost Colony* in 1937 to *The Stephen Foster Story* in 1959) on Roanoke Island at work on *The Lost Colony* script about 1937. (PG-SHC)

Women in hats, men in coats and ties, children dressed as for church watch Reverend Martin (Bedford Thurman) baptize the infant Virginia Dare (Lynn Bailey) at the Waterside Amphitheatre during the first season of *The Lost Colony* in 1937 (act 2, scene 3). (PG-SHC)

Paul (*center*) with DuBose Heyward, Clifford Odets, Frederick Koch, and Barrett Clark on the porch of the Carolina Inn in Chapel Hill in April 1940 during celebration of the twenty-first anniversary of the Carolina Playmakers. (PG-SHC)

Richard Wright with Paul in Bynum Hall on the UNC campus at work on the dramatization of *Native Son*, summer 1940. (Alec Rivera, Durham, N.C.)

The first encounter between Mary Dalton (Anne Burr) and Bigger Thomas (Canada Lee), when she wonders, "How is it that two human beings can stand a foot from each other and not speak the same language?" (*Native Son*, scene 3, Mercury Production, Saint James Theatre, 1941). (Billy Rose Theatre Collection, New York Public Library for the Performing Arts)

Elizabeth and Paul in the library of their home in Greenwood thinking of their trip to Japan and India, 1951. (PG-SHC)

His brother Davie (Wayne Spiggle), a Confederate sympathizer, looks on as John Freeman (Bedford Thurman) is comforted by his sweetheart, Elsie (Gwen Lanier), and one of his students, Neill (Bob Morris), after proslavery nightriders beat him and destroy his school in Berea, Kentucky (*Wilderness Road*, act 1, scene 8, Indian Fort Amphitheatre, Berea College, Kentucky, 1955). (Institute of Outdoor Drama, Chapel Hill)

Paul checks a rehearsal of *Texas* against the script, Pioneer Amphitheater, Palo Duro Canyon, Texas, 1966. (Paul Green Foundation, Chapel Hill)

Overture to *Texas*, showing the spectacular setting of the Pioneer Amphitheater in Palo Duro Canyon. (Institute of Outdoor Drama, Chapel Hill)

Paul with Mary (*to his left*), Elizabeth, and Mary's son William Johnson in 1979 at Pleasant Plains Methodist Church in Harnett County near Lillington, North Carolina, where Paul and Mary's maternal grandparents are buried. (PG-SHC)

Windy Oaks, a few miles southeast of Chapel Hill, where Paul and Elizabeth moved in 1965. (PG-SHC)

Paul in 1979. (PG-SHC)

# V

## Hollywood, Capital Punishment, and War, 1942–1946

January 1942
: Gains gubernatorial pardon for Fred Beal, union organizer imprisoned after 1929 textile strike in Gastonia, North Carolina.

Winter 1942
: Visits Spanish missions in Los Angeles area in search of site and material for outdoor historical play.

Early March 1942
: To Chapel Hill. Revises *Rumelhearts* into June, but film not made.

April 1942
: Lecture tour in New England and Midwest during which he formulates view that victory in World War II is necessary prelude to democratic world federation.

25 May 1942
: In speech at UNC attacks academic profession for devotion to historical research at expense of inspirational teaching.

Fall 1942
: UNC administration publishes speech, "Preface for Professors," and distributes it to the faculty, arousing controversy.

November 1942
: Instrumental in proving innocence and gaining acquittal of death-row inmate William Mason Wellmon.

February–October 1943
: In Los Angeles for work on film script of *Captain Eddie.*

April 1943
: Betty Smith, whose work he has supported for several years, publishes *A Tree Grows in Brooklyn.*

Late 1943

To Chapel Hill, begins novel, *Stormy Banks.*

Early 1944

Meets with state and Roanoke Island leaders about reopening *The Lost Colony* (closed following 1941 season) after the war.

May 1944

To Los Angeles to write film scripts (*The Green Years* and others). Writes foreword to James Boyd's *Eighteen Poems* (1944).

December 1944

To Chapel Hill, resumes work on *Stormy Banks.*

May 1945

Defends UNC colleague against charge of Nazi leanings.

Mid-May 1945

To Los Angeles to write film script for *Red Shoes Run Faster* (not released) and others.

Early 1946

In Los Angeles revises *The Lost Colony.* Encourages novelist Alice Nisbet and secures publication of her *Send Me an Angel* (November).

30 June 1946

*The Lost Colony* reopens on Roanoke Island.

July 1946

For composer Charles Vardell writes text for cantata, *Song in the Wilderness.*

September 1946

To Chapel Hill, then to Williamsburg about production of *The Common Glory.*

## 164. To Elizabeth L. Green

Columbia Pictures Corporation, Hollywood, Calif.
11 February 1942

Dearest Honey—

I haven't any news to write at all but just to send love and—and all that means. The story[1] is my only pain and joy(?) now, and I've written enough pages to make a novel already—Organization! Organization is the bane of my existence. I guess God had just as much trouble making flesh as he did anatomy, but I don't think that is true with the story writer. Anyway not with me. The plot—anatomy (organization) seems just as hard now as it did twenty years ago. The rest easy.

I know you are having a hard time there with all the household matters on you, and I'll be back at the earliest possible moment to help relieve you. Gosh, how long it's been. Night after night in my room, pulling down my bed from the wall and crawling into it—always around 12 or 1—I carry the old story home with me too. I just haven't been anywhere except— those trips to the missions.[2] Haven't seen Dottie[3] since her group carried me down to Ramona[4] some weeks ago, about which I wrote you. She's asked me to dinner but I've had to decline. Also Stella.[5] Sunday Harold[6] asked me to go hear Stravinsky, but I couldn't. My only wish is to get through and get back home. This is not virtue but desire.

I've certainly done a lot of thinking about things along with this story. Solitude breeds it—and usually when I quit work in my room—I read myself into a sleepy mood as well as I can. Two people in the apartment next to mine have got to raising Cain the last week or two during the small hours--don't know who they are—and that has cut into my, er, rest.

1. Movie adaptation of *Rumelhearts of Rampler Avenue.*

2. Several in the Los Angeles area that Green visited hoping to find ideas for an outdoor drama on some aspect of California's Spanish history (Green diary, 24 December 1941–19 March 1942, PG-SHC).

3. McBrayer.

4. Pageant based on Helen Hunt Jackson's novel (1884), presented annually at Hemet, California, which Green found crude but successful (Green diary, 24 December 1941–19 March 1942, PG-SHC).

5. Adler, who with most members of the Group Theatre was in Hollywood.

6. Clurman.

Thanks for the clothes picture for Byrd.[7] As soon as I can get out I will buy them and send on.

Now I want to get you something. What shall it be? Or will you leave it to me? I'd like to get something you'd 'specially like from out here.

I sent $300 two days ago. Will that be enough till I get back?

All my love, Paul

## 165. To Elizabeth L. Green

[Bronsonia Apartments,[1] 1933 Bronson Avenue, Hollywood, Calif.]
Monday night [16 February 1942]

Dearest Honey—

When I got "home" tonight from the office three letters were peeping through the bars. It helped break the gloom of these dreadful times to have the remembrance steady from the real home.—I can't wait to get back—I was sorry those letters were so thin though Bets'[2] valentine was long in being unraveled and that kept me busy for quite a while.

Yesterday the sun shone and I got in an hour's tennis—though the weather was cold and still is. Tonight's paper says this is the coldest weather L.A. has had for seven years.

Well, it's all over at Singapore as I feared and knew it would be.[3] And part of the scrap iron from Harnett County and the old 6th Avenue L in New York helped shoot it from under its defenders' feet.[4] Still in all this grim business the truth remains—that there is a method, a way of right, and departing from it always brings retribution. Maybe men will never be able to live and behave in line with this truth, but still it is there for us to work toward, and the failure is ours.

As you know all right I'm no "expert" on these political matters, but I don't

7. Clipping from the *Hollywood Citizen* (to which Green subscribed for Elizabeth during his stay) showing blouse and skirt she wanted him to get for their daughter Nancy Byrd (Elizabeth Green to Paul Green, 6 January 1942, PG-SHC).

---

1. To which Green moved in early January (telegram, Paul Green to Elizabeth Green, 7 January 1942, PG-SHC).

2. Betsy, their middle daughter, then eleven.

3. The British surrendered Singapore to the Japanese on 15 February 1942 (Sunday).

4. During the late 1930s Japan bought scrap metal collected in the United States for use in its war with China.

see how any of us can expect this war to be over in less than 5 to 10 years. I shudder at it, for you and for me, for us all. Maybe back there on the farm we can walk up and down, plant and harvest and get a little closer to the warm consoling breast that neither guns nor cataclysms can make to shake or tremble in its peace and deep content. (But we've got to try, to dig for it.) Be still, be still my soul.[5]

I'm so busy here I don't hear much talk, but what I do hear is loud in criticism of the way things are handled—Congress, O.C.D.,[6] Churchill, the navy, etc., etc. The Axis powers have some sort of right on their side, don't they? (I mean if you once decide to act toward victory for your point of view), when they shut mouths up by control which otherwise divide and tear up unity. I'm so tired of all the wise-eared columnists and radio spielers who write and write, and talk and talk—and don't know a thing they're saying. They told us this, they told us that—"Japan is so weak"— "so desperate"—"committing suicide," etc., etc. Before that—"the Maginot line is impregnable,"[7] "the Axis is being swept out of Libya in a headlong rush," etc. Out here, and I'm sure it's the same there, nobody knows what to believe—except that we're getting hell beat out of us. Something will have to be done about these amateur field-generals who shoot off nothing but their mouth. They're doing a lot of damage to the morale of the people.

Well, I'm just a-rambling, sitting here at my little table, and I've got to quit and go to work on this story.

Here's a riddle you can try on the kids: Some savages caught a missionary. The chief's custom was to let the condemned one make a statement before dying. If the statement was considered true the prisoner was to die by shooting with a poisoned arrow; if false, he was to die by fire. The missionary, being

5. As a postscript Green wrote out the stanza from the A. E. Housman poem to which he alludes here:

> Be still, my soul, be still; the arms you bear are brittle,
> Earth and high heaven are fixt of old and founded strong.
> Think rather—call to thought, if now you grieve a little,
> The days when we had rest, O soul, for they were long.
> (*The Shropshire Lad*, no. 48, stanza 1)

6. Office of Civilian Defense.

7. Defensive fortifications built in the early 1930s by France on its German border from Luxembourg to Switzerland. Invading France in 1940, the German army simply went around the line through Belgium.

unusual in that he was quick-witted, made a statement so clever that the chief could not put him to death either by the poisoned arrow or fire. So they let him go. What was the statement. (Answer on back of page one).[8] You might have already seen this in the Readers Digest.[9]

Where did you get the idea I liked this solitude!!! I didn't make myself clear.[10]

Please write me what to bring you.

All my love, Paul

## 166. To Elizabeth L. Green

[Bronsonia Apartments, 1933 Bronson Avenue, Hollywood, Calif.]
Sunday night [22 February 1942]

Dearest Honey—

I have just got back from a visit to Olvera Street[1] where I got Willie and Vernon[2] to drive me—Mexican glass the purpose of my visit. I didn't find much—no large glasses and just a handful of pitchers, no bowls at all. I bought a few pieces and the Stacys took them on home and said they'd pack them and mail them to you tomorrow. The Olvera St. people didn't pack or mail anything, they said. Yesterday afternoon I took three hours off and shopped at the Hollywood Blvd. Broadway shop and got a few little gifts for everybody which I'll bring with me. I still plan to leave here Wednesday night, though Harold[3] wants me to stay on a few more days if I can for polishing the script. We will have a conference tomorrow, and since I have worked again today I am hoping he will not want to keep me.[4] I told him I still wanted to do more

8. Note on the back of page 1: "He said, 'I will die by fire.' Now if this was true then they'd have to shoot him, which if they did would make it false. If false, they'd have to burn him which would make it true and not false. So they couldn't do anything with him. I guess he married the chief's daughter after that and converted the old man."

9. February 1942, p. 86.

10. In a letter to him on 11 February 1942 Elizabeth said, "I hate to think of you so solitary even if you like it" (PG-SHC).

---

1. Street of Mexican shops in central Los Angeles.

2. Stacy.

3. Clurman, producer of *Rumelhearts of Rampler Avenue.*

4. Green left Los Angeles by plane on Friday evening, 27 February, then ran into bad weather at Tucson and transferred to a train scheduled to reach Greensboro

work on the story when I got back home—since I can always make things better. He wants me to do that too. I am anxious to get on with my own work, and of course anxious to leave the studio people satisfied, etc., etc.[5]

Willie and Vernon report their young son-in-law (a fine looking fellow if I ever saw one) now on his way overseas. He and Billie Vaughan married just a week when he had to leave to be a soldier. I have been sitting here tonight thinking about the big subject of man and his world, and my new and yet old belief in a union of federated nations heads the list of my wishes ahead. It's got to come, and we've got to unearth statesmen somewhere big enough to see and work for [it].

This is about the last letter I'll write you—if it can be called a letter—from these shores.

All my love, Paul

## 167. To Mary G. Johnson

Chapel Hill, N.C.
19 April 1942

Dearest Mary—

Elizabeth and I have just returned home after a long trip—nearly three thousand miles in fact—up through New England, out beyond the Great Lakes and back through Ohio, West Virginia, and western North Carolina. We went by car, and I'm still feeling the effects of the driving, the speechmaking, the entertainment, and the "scenery." I talked and lectured at several colleges and universities[1] on the cause of art and democracy in general—doing fairly well once or twice, but mostly not so good I'm afraid. We were very sad and yet proud to learn on getting here that Billy had left to serve his country in the hard days ahead. I feel for you and Alton, and I thought I'd just drop you

---

Monday morning, 2 March (telegram, Paul Green to Elizabeth Green, 28 February 1942, PG-SHC).

5. In Chapel Hill Green worked on the script during the early summer of 1942 (Paul Green to Harold Clurman, undated, and Clurman to Green, 24 June 1942, PG-SHC), but *Rumelhearts* seems not to have been filmed. For writing the script Green was paid $7,500, of which he saved about $4,000 after paying his own living expenses and several family bills (Paul Green to Elizabeth Green, undated, EG-SHC).

---

1. Rutgers, Dartmouth, Williams, Western Reserve, and Bowling Green.

this note to say so once more.[2] Proff Koch and his loyal wife have sent their pride and joy and most brilliant son off,[3] and Mrs. Koch is pretty badly hit by it. For years she has been a great reader of Oriental philosophy and has even lived in Japan and China and liked the people and drawn much comfort from their culture and kindliness. Now she sees her world and her beliefs turned upside down, their content spilt and her own flesh and blood arming the point of a bayonet to do further violence to the sanctity of her soul and the earth's soul. She says she has been able to get a mite of refuge by accepting the everlasting fatalism of "what has to be has to be."[4] The university here is doing all it can too to meet the emergency of declining attendance and technological necessity and finding the same difficulties that face each individual in the trying. There are a few people round and about here—no use to mention names—who still deplore war and the foolishness of such waste and grief (of course we all begin with that) but who make no positive suggestion of what to do with the fact of war or with themselves in it. This doesn't seem to me fair either to the personnel or the issues involved. For we are at war. We must fight, are fighting. There is no security in taking one's stance on the side and watching the tragic drama play itself out and then expect to share in the full favor and responsibility that will live and call for our best thinking and doing beyond it when peace comes again. For the chance these non-participants might have had in helping the social re-creation of the new order (or any order) will have been totally destroyed by the fact that they took no share in the prior activity and process leading to it. At least I think so at this present writing.

As for myself—I am in the throes of trying to understand where I belong. For more than a year now I have been doing what I could on the morale side of soldier entertainment, helping organize music, plays, variety shows, etc. in the different camps.[5] Also I've undertaken to write a few radio shows on the ideal and idea of democracy.[6] But it seems so little, and now with the front line

2. Alton and Mary's son had enlisted in the army.

3. Robert Koch (b. 1919), who had enlisted in the army as he completed an M.A. in art at UNC.

4. Robert Koch was discharged as a lieutenant colonel in 1946 and began a long career in art at Princeton University.

5. A major activity of the National Theatre Conference, of which Green was president.

6. See "A Start in Life," in James Boyd, ed., *The Free Company Presents* (New York: Dodd, Mead, 1941), pp. 177–218.

thundering towards us from every horizon less important than before—anyway less immediately needful. Still that may be about the limit of my contribution except to buy a bond now and then and contribute a bit here and there from my slim pocketbook to other causes—and to keep on writing about life, hope and death out of my "innards." Recently I set down a few of my thoughts for Nell Lewis' Sunday column by way of the stage character Johnny Johnson.[7] It was not much of a thirsty fighting statement, but that was the way I saw the matter then and still do, and I simply can't get up any heat of hate against anybody I call my enemy. Yet I may start carrying a gun again before it's all over, for one must act. Inaction is no answer to anything. And of course blind action is just as bad, maybe worse since more of pain and suffering can lie that way. And I do think we have and can have a cause to fight for. And our young men like Bobby Koch and Billy must be helped by all of us to a comprehension of that cause. What is it? Why, none other than the old religious conception of the brotherhood of man. Or more politically—a federated world of human cooperation and benevolence. But how we may be able to help our enemy into a share of this new and good order after we have had to beat the stuffing out of him is one of the mysteries of time itself. But I'm sure this same time will help to solve it into healing if we do our part as men after the guns are silenced. I think I feel as keenly as anyone else that war is today as always the supreme tragedy of man. Intellectually one can make hardboiled and aloof judgments about it, but emotionally he must participate in it if he is a normal man. The nature of this participation is the second great mystery to me—that is, the right sort of participation. Actually, I have no doubt that if some sort of early stalemate were acknowledged and the gentle light of reason could descend upon both camps, then a just peace and sensible reorganization of mankind would be more easily obtained. But—and here again the hard fact—wars don't end that way. They always go on down to the growling horror of dog eat dog and the strongest survives. How we can get up off our all-fours and become men of justice and goodwill after the killing and the bloodiness are finished is going to be the toughest problem of the whole business. But that we must do—or all our sacrifices will be scattered in foolish

7. *NO*, 12 April 1942, sec. M, p. 2, col. 1. Green has Johnny explain that he is fighting in the present war because "if the democracies win this war and win a victory over their selfishness likewise, then the new world of federated states will have a chance to be . . . [but] if the Axis wins it, such a world as he longs for and is willing to die for will be much slower in coming."

vanity, as foolish as the making of them in the first place. And so I am back at the first mystery again. But this I do know—deep down I know it—that all men everywhere, irrespective of race, color, creed or calling want instinctively to draw nearer and live in the god-like, the beautiful and the good and to grow in grace and betterment from the cradle to the grave. So basically we have something to build on, something to found the new order on, and that is the bounden duty of us all to so build, to so found.

(From this whirl-around of words you see that I am in the full thriving of the dilemma. But I don't plan to stay caught in it. And such thinking out loud on the typewriter as this helps me in the thrashing on through.)

The very nature of tragedy—of which this war is again a most awe-filling sample—is to produce a result different from itself. But to repeat, the result here will only be different not better if we fail to win a victory over ourselves as well as over our enemies. And perhaps always the one most powerful enemy is not out there somewhere but here in the very closeness of ourselves. It is this enemy we must coax and grow into brightness and charity—our own individual soul and ego. As a nation I think we have a lot to offer to the world as a daysman[8] guide. We have already set a pattern for the future order of mankind by the creation of our own system of federated states. The machine which brings Tokyo as near to Washington today as Richmond was a hundred years ago makes it possible for this pattern to grow round the world. The machine is actually a functional and factual Sermon on the Mount if we could learn to interpret its true message. Its purpose and logic are cooperation among men, not division. What we need is more preachers and practitioners to make this truth grow into a conviction. Here I can maybe help my bit too.

And so I think myself through to some sort of purpose and peace of mind.

Can't you all come up sometime soon and spend a Sunday? If you can't come we'll try to get down.

Again and always my fondest love, you know. Paul

Paul[9] is taking care of Billy's stuff which he left behind in his room. This our eldest is planning to take up flying this summer. Well, he and Billy and others like them will have much to tell us when the bugle blows to take the colors down.[10]

8. Arbiter.

9. Then eighteen.

10. After a few days at Fort Jackson, South Carolina, William Johnson was discharged from the army because X-rays showed lesions in his chest. He returned to

## 168. To George R. Coffman[1]

[Chapel Hill, N.C.]
8 October 1942

Dear George Coffman—

If I had had the good fortune to take one of your literature courses in the days gone by—even in the early days of those forty years you speak of—I am sure I would still remember the enthusiasm and belief that were yours, whatever of the facts I had forgot. So I appreciate your letter about my little paper more than I would have coming from one who had no such enthusiasm and belief. My words were no doubt too sweeping and exaggerated and perhaps they are therefore unfair. Let them be a query rather than an affirmation. Like everybody else I am seeking to find in what education consists, and I know it ought not to lead to a weakening of zest for life, whatever its nature is. It ought not to purge away, for instance, the vividness of folk speech for precision and abstraction. It ought not to cause a man who possesses it to say simply "He is rather stout" when the unlettered fellow says "He is fat as a mole," or a "thin man" for "thin as a rake," etc., etc. It ought not, I think, to concern itself so much with "causes" behind as with possibilities ahead, nor concentrate upon what others have done as much as upon what we can do. It ought not to posit problems but uncover opportunities, ought not to seek for relations and influences but for emotional and intellectual fire and inspiration, etc. I say this even while querying, and I say it badly.

---

UNC to finish his senior year, then entered the UNC Law School, from which he received an L.L.B. in 1944.

---

1. On 25 May 1942, as a prelude to commencement, Green gave a public lecture in which he attacked the academic profession for its devotion to historical and scientific scholarship at the expense of inspirational teaching (" 'Teachers Kill Students' Enthusiasm,' Says Green," *Daily Tar Heel*, 26 May 1942, p. 1, col. 2; p. 4, col. 1; speech published as "Preface for Professors," in *The Hawthorn Tree: Some Papers and Letters on Life and the Theatre* [Chapel Hill: University of North Carolina Press, 1943], pp. 1–16). In the fall the university printed Green's speech and circulated it to the faculty. George R. Coffman (1880–1958), chairman of the English department, thought the speech a jeremiad and questioned the justice of such a "wholesale indictment of the membership of a profession." In his experience of forty years he had known many professors who excelled as both scholars and teachers and many students who survived a college education without disillusionment (George Coffman to Paul Green, 6 October 1942, PG-SHC).

What I mean is simply that the coming on of years and of learning ought to increase the fruitfulness and significance of being alive and not decrease it. If not, then the primitive has the advantage of us, or there is a maleficent logic in the very heart of the universe. And that I deny—I deny them both—maybe without show of reason but with a call upon the a priori and intuition as a last resort to steady me. The purpose of education is the spiritual enrichment—I almost said enlightenment—of man. For this and this alone a college of liberal arts has reason to exist. The same is true of technical schools too, but with certain varying physical prerequisites as they appertain to the mouth, hands and other bodily members and functions. In other words the nature of education as you and I experience, practice and try to teach it is primarily religious and aesthetic—that is, it seeks to give man an appreciation, an at-homeness, a sense of oneness, a surcharge of glory and wonder, a vision and a dream aspiration of and in and for the world he calls his. And my contention is that too many of us have forgot that, have become conformists to rote and diluted authority, have lazily and frustratedly allowed a substitution of symbol and sign for the rich, naive and passionate reality creatively acting far ahead of those symbols and signs. Can't we catch up, just as children catch up with their play dreams by the process of self-identification in them? I feel that you stay pretty much caught up, but thousands don't.

Well, this is all again too vague, and, yes, querulous. Maybe the war and its chilling shadow of evil have brought out the Jeremiah in me too strong. And there again, God witness it, is proof that a Jeremiad is not entirely out of order. For we have had no little to do with the bringing of this war on the world. At least I think the teachers are that influential. If not then the point is doubly proved in their failure to teach man to love the world above its mutilation—and thereby prevent its mutilation. But I'm saying again what I said in my paper.

To come at it again—our privilege and duty as teachers is to help man to uncover and meet the challenge of creative activity and thus make it impossible and unthinkable for him because of confusion and discouragement to succumb to the challenges and days and drama of destruction. To do that we must first ourselves believe in a reachable Rightness which we used to call God.

Thanks and with cordial best wishes,

## 169. To E. M. Land[1]

Chapel Hill, N.C.
18 November 1942

Dear Mr. Land—

It was kind of you to lend me your transcripts of the William Mason Wellmon case,[2] and I have read them with the closest interest. Apart from your understandable professional attitude as prosecuting attorney in the case, I believe you are as anxious to see justice done to the condemned man as I am. Your record as a citizen and civic leader shows that. So I am sure you won't object to my writing you how the evidence strikes me in these records and won't mind if I call attention to a few points that seem to me to still need clearing up before final judgment is imposed upon Wellmon. For as long as there is the vaguest shadow of doubt that he is the guilty man we ought to do what we reasonably can to get at the truth. Here are some of the questions that have risen in my mind—set down at random:[3]

1. Did anybody check as to whether Wellmon signed for his pay on the pay-day of Feb. 11 (the date of the crime)? Testimony shows that he was supposed to have signed the envelope in which his pay was handed over.[4] What has

1. E. M. Land (d. 1949), UNC graduate (1899) from Statesville, North Carolina, was prosecuting attorney in the trial of William Mason Wellmon, a black man convicted of and sentenced to death for the rape of a sixty-seven-year-old white woman, Cora Sowers, on her farm near Statesville. The rape occurred around 2:00 P.M. on 11 February 1941; Wellmon's trial took place in Statesville on 11 and 12 August 1942; and he was scheduled to die at the state's Central Prison in Raleigh on 2 October 1942. That date was set aside while he appealed his conviction to the state supreme court, but the court denied the appeal and fixed a new execution date of 20 November 1942. On 17 November, the day before the present letter, Green led a group to Raleigh for a clemency hearing for Wellmon before Governor J. Melville Broughton, a hearing at which Land argued against clemency.

2. Throughout, Green spells the name "Wellman."

3. But the text of the letter is marked by Green as "Revised Copy."

4. Raised near Statesville, Wellmon had moved to Washington, D.C., in 1940 and worked on a construction project at nearby Fort Belvoir, Virginia. During his trial he contended that he was at work at Fort Belvoir on the day of the crime, that his presence there was proved by a receipt he signed for his pay, and that therefore he could not have committed the crime that day in North Carolina (trial transcript, Wellmon file, PG-SHC).

happened to the envelope? Was it thrown away? O'Neill[5] says he would have had to sign for his pay. So does Frick.[6] Obviously if he signed for it and it could be proved, his alibi as to his whereabouts would hold—that is, if Feb. 11 was the actual pay-day. And there is no proof to show it wasn't.[7]

2. Gertrude Ingram[8], one of the chief witnesses for the prosecution, says she was sure it was the 11th day of February she saw Mason Wellmon on his way to Mrs. Sowers' place, though she acknowledged on cross examination she couldn't guess "by making three guesses what day of the month today is" even though she had been summoned to court and was a witness at that moment. Like O'Neill she appears to remember what she wants to.

3. Gertrude Ingram also says that on the same day, the 11th, she told someone about seeing the colored man (Mason Wellmon) going towards Mrs. Sowers'. Whom did she tell? And what did she tell? Did she describe the colored man she had seen? She makes a point of being afraid of strange negro men and of observing them carefully. Her talk doesn't suggest that she is afraid of strangers, least of all those of her own race.

4. What has happened to the $1,000 or $1,200 reward offered for the apprehension and so forth of the guilty party? Has it been paid and to whom?

5. Is it possible that the woman Gertrude Ingram could have been motivated by the reward (or have had any other motive) in pressing on towards her identification of the Wellmon clothes (coat and hat), an identification which came nearly three months after the crime, May after February? And why is it that she is more certain as to the matter of clothes than even Mrs. Sowers is?[9]

5. William Robert O'Neill, Wellmon's supervisor at Fort Belvoir (ibid.).

6. Elihu Frick, auditor for Wellmon's employer, the Charles H. Tompkins Construction Company (ibid.).

7. Payday was 11 February, which was also the day of the crime. Although Wellmon and others spoke of the receipt during his extradition hearing in Washington, D.C., and his trial in Statesville, the receipt itself had not been located and Land assumed it was lost (E. M. Land to J. Melville Broughton, 12 December 1942, Wellmon file, PG-SHC).

8. Black woman from Statesville.

9. Following Wellmon's arrest on 27 April 1941, Cora Sowers and Gertrude Ingram, recently employed as a maid in the Sowers household, went to Washington to identify the rapist. At a jail lineup there on 6 May Sowers could identify none of the eight prisoners as her assailant and Ingram thought the man next to Wellmon was the one she had seen. At a lineup on 7 May Sowers still could not identify anyone, but Ingram

6. Is it reasonable to think that Gertrude Ingram could identify these clothes in a "bad light,"[10] having only seen the man once in passing (even though she said he was acting queerly)? You and I couldn't do it. I don't even know what kind of clothes you had on yesterday at the hearing, though I paid a lot of attention to you during your argument. All I remember is that, I think, they were dark. I'm afraid this Gertrude had been inclined towards the identification of a certain kind of hat and coat from former conversation, questions, etc., referring back to maybe Mrs. Sowers' disordered remembrance of the unknown assailant.

7. Is it reasonable to suppose that a man out to commit a crime of vengeance, as the prosecution says Wellmon's crime was,[11] would inquire along the way as to the home of his intended victim? It is claimed that the "strange negro" so did. Is Wellmon feeble-minded? Nobody has said that he is. Rather he was foreman over a group of workmen. He had at least that much sense.[12]

8. The sheriff said yesterday at the hearing that Wellmon offered at the time of his arrest to return to North Carolina to meet whatever the charge might be. Later, of course, seeing how things were setting against him, he naturally fought tooth and claw to keep away. This seems a reasonable reaction on his part.[13]

9. Again, testimony shows that after being arrested Wellmon requested

---

now thought Wellmon's brown coat and dark cap were those worn by the attacker (trial testimony).

10. Reason given by Land at the clemency hearing the previous day for Sowers's inability to identify Wellmon in the lineup.

11. Land argued that the black community of Statesville, backed by the NAACP, planned the rape as revenge against the white community and the court. In January 1941, he said, a white jury had found a black man guilty of simple assault when accused of raping a black woman, and the black community was outraged at the seeming lack of seriousness with which the jury took crimes of blacks against blacks. According to Land, the black woman's lawyer had said in court that the next rape victim would be white (E. M. Land to J. Melville Broughton, 12 December 1942, Wellmon file, PG-SHC).

12. And scored "above the average for members of the colored race" in state prison mental examinations, according to a prison official (J. M. Neese to William Dunn, Commissioner of Paroles, 18 November 1942, PG-SHC).

13. Land had construed Wellmon's fight against extradition as a sign of guilt.

permission to change from his workman's overalls into his street clothes before being taken to police headquarters. Now I ask you is it reasonable that if he had been guilty of the charge—remembering that he had been in the toils of the law before and must have been somewhat "conditioned" to trying to protect himself[14]—is it reasonable that he would go into his boarding house and put on the very clothes which would help identify him as Mrs. Sowers' assailant? To repeat Gertrude Ingram identified him by these clothes as being the man she had seen in the vicinity of the crime the day it was committed.

10. From the record it appears that Wellmon was formerly a good prisoner in the Central Prison at Raleigh, since in his testimony in one place he says he paid the full five years and later says the actual term of service was three years and nine months—this of course was for an old alleged crime some years ago—and I presume that his shortened time was due to good behaviour.[15] Now if he did commit the crime with which he is charged, he is or was either some sort of imbecile or a sadistic pervert. What does his former record show as to his mentality and such possible tendencies? Has anybody investigated?

11. The captain of the (Washington) prison guard testified that neither Gertrude Ingram nor Mrs. Sowers identified Wellmon at the first line-up there. Yesterday you spoke of the light in the prison as being bad. Yet Superintendent Rives of this prison says the light was good—several big windows in that room, etc., and he also says that Wellmon was not identified at this first line-up. Yet apparently Gertrude *could* identify the clothes, light or no light, even if they happened to be worn by another man. Wellmon says she first picked a man next to him, a man by the name of Young. Did she?[16] Also isn't it strange that though Gertrude Ingram had identified the face of Wellmon in the prison photograph shown her by Mr. Scott as resembling the man seen in the vicinity of the crime[17]—that when she came to Washington

14. In December 1934 Wellmon had been convicted of raping a young white woman and sentenced to five years in prison.

15. Green's spelling.

16. Wellmon testified that at the first lineup (on 6 May 1941) Ingram identified Eugene Young, the man next to him, as the one she had seen going to the Sowers house and that at the second lineup (on 7 May 1941) she identified no one. Ingram's testimony is not known on the point, but apparently after the second lineup she identified Wellmon by his clothes and said that Young had worn those clothes in the first lineup. When cross-examined, Wellmon said he had only one set of clothes in jail and wore it at both lineups (trial transcript).

17. Basis of the warrant for Wellmon's arrest.

she first identified clothes and not the face? The more I consider this woman's testimony, Mr. Land, the more I wonder at it.

12. At the second line-up testimony tends to show that none of the men in the former line-up were included except Wellmon. Why not? Was the intent of the "law" already settling against him because it had become generally agreed that he had to be the man? This doesn't sound like scientific and fair criminology methods, does it?[18]

13. Yesterday you introduced copies of two "damaging" letters against the defense. Where are these originals? Why weren't they with the copies? "They have been mislaid somehow" is not sufficient answer.[19]

14. As to Wellmon's having given a false name to the officers in Washington at the time of his arrest, that is perfectly reasonable, for he was trying to save himself from whatever he was wanted for. Again it is reasonable to think that the officers might have misheard him and he gave his right name after all. "William Wellmon" could have been mistaken for "William Williams." You remember that yesterday the sheriff fumbled quite a bit and didn't seem so sure at first that "William Williams" was the name given at the time of the arrest.[20]

15. In his self-description Wellmon says he has a scar under his left eye. Is this scar noticeable? Mrs. Sowers doesn't refer to it in her testimony. Wouldn't she have noticed that scar as much as she would the teeth if it is in any way remarkable?[21] Wellmon also says he is 6 ft. 3 inches high. And Mrs. Sowers

18. Making a suspect the sole common member of different lineups, acceptable practice at the time, has tended since the late 1960s to be judged unnecessarily suggestive and thus a violation of due process (Charles H. Whitebread, *Criminal Procedure: An Analysis of Constitutional Cases and Concepts* [Mineola, N.Y.: Foundation Press, 1980], pp. 356–60).

19. The copies, dated 6 May 1941, were presented as from the wife of Wellmon's brother, who lived in Statesville, and advised members of the family to keep Wellmon away from Statesville because "Sheriff offering reward and good description of him, woman say she'll know him if she see him again and she will and it be to bad for us all" (Wellmon file, PG-SHC).

20. Land had contended that giving a false name was a sign of Wellmon's guilt. Wellmon testified that he always gave his name as William Wellmon and never gave a false name to law officers.

21. In her original description of the assailant (reflected in the reward notice [Wellmon file, PG-SHC]) as well as her testimony during the trial, Sowers stressed that one or two of his upper front teeth were gold. Wellmon had no gold fillings or caps (trial transcript).

when first asked couldn't say that her assailant wasn't about five feet, six inches tall. Have you measured him? Has he grown some since his former prison measurement of years ago[22]—which measurement was introduced yesterday?

16. O'Neill testifies that Wellmon was a foreman of a smaller group of men under him, and he declares that if Wellmon had been away from work on Feb. 11 he O'Neill certainly would have known it. What is the custom with other such foremen? Are any of them white men? What do they say? Has this been checked?

17. Yesterday you called the governor's attention to how cold blooded Wellmon was, illustrating it by referring to Wellmon's words to one of the deputies taking him to death row—"When they say I'm going to die?" (Then the answer.) "Why the hell they wait so long." You remember of course that Wellmon had been through a tough trial, had fought long and hard in the Washington courts, had also lain a year in jail. His words were natural and not cold blooded. I wouldn't mention this trifling point except that you and I know that in a delicate balance sometimes these trifles can take an innocent man's life away. I am sure, however, that this sort of thing won't affect the governor in his judgment, and I am sure you stuck it in "professionally."

18. It seems to me that five days is an all too short time allowed for the defense to prepare a case of this kind. The Supreme Court doesn't say so, still it seems so to me.[23]

I have great sympathy for Mrs. Sowers and her family, and for her son whom I knew as a fine fellow at Carolina.[24] It is a nightmare they have been through. We all share in their suffering and sorrow. But whatever our sympathy is, I still think the case should be further investigated. I believe Wellmon should be reprieved long enough to allow for this investigation. The cause of justice and race relations throughout the South would, I am sure, be bettered by an act of clemency on the part of the governor. As he himself so grandly put it yesterday—"Justice is not a matter of race." Let us all prove it, help to give

22. In 1934 when Wellmon, age twenty-nine, first went to prison, prison records gave his height as five feet, eleven and a half inches (E. M. Land to J. Melville Broughton, 13 November 1942, Wellmon file, PG-SHC). Sowers described her assailant as about five feet, ten inches tall (reward notice). Land had argued that Wellmon, in describing himself as six feet, three inches tall, was trying to deceive the jury.

23. Wellmon's appeal to the state supreme court had been based on the fact that his court-appointed lawyer had only five days to prepare his defense before the trial in August 1942.

24. Neil S. Sowers, UNC class of 1927 and law partner of Land.

the cause for which we are mutually working a little more time to be tested and justified. Sixty days, ninety days soon go by, they don't mean too much to you and me, but now they mean everything to William Mason Wellmon, whether he be guilty or innocent.

With cordial regards, and I hope you'll give me a ring when you're down this way and we can get together for a meal,[25]

## 170. To Betty Smith

Twentieth Century–Fox Studio, Beverly Hills, Calif.
11 June 1943

Dear Betty—[1]

Many thanks, Betty, for your beautiful book which I've just finished. You have written a lovely poem of youth, vitally characterized, human and there-

25. At the hearing on 17 November Green convinced Broughton to investigate Wellmon's claim that he signed a receipt for his pay on the day of the crime (point 1 of the present letter), an investigation neglected during Wellmon's trial. That night Broughton dispatched to Washington two agents of the State Bureau of Investigation, one a handwriting expert, and on 19 November stayed Wellmon's execution until 28 November. By 21 November the agents had located the pay receipt (showing wages of $32.40 for 40.5 hours worked), authenticated Wellmon's signature on it, and developed evidence showing it could have been signed only on 11 February (SBI report, Wellmon file, PG-SHC). Broughton extended the stay of execution to 18 December, then an additional sixty days, saying, "it is quite obvious that the prisoner could not have been working at Fort Belvoir and receiving and receipting for his pay there during the middle of the day on February 11th, 1941, and have committed the act of criminal assault at or about one-thirty in the afternoon of the same day in Iredell County, North Carolina." He added that he would continue the investigation but that "if my present impression of the case should be confirmed during [the period of the reprieve], I should consider it my duty as a matter of justice to release the prisoner" ("Statement of Governor Broughton," Wellmon file, PG-SHC; excerpted in *NO*, 16 December 1942, p. 16, cols. 6–8). On 15 April 1943 Broughton pardoned Wellmon, who thus became the first person in the state acquitted of a crime for which he had been sentenced to death (*NO*, 16 April 1943, p. 1, col. 1; p. 18, cols. 4–5). In 1971, under a law allowing the state "to award damages for pecuniary loss sustained by reason of wrongful imprisonment up to $500 per year," Wellmon, in prison nearly two years, was awarded $986.40 (*NO*, 13 May 1971, sec. 1, p. 3, cols. 1–4).

1. In late March Green went to Hollywood to work on a motion picture script. In

fore deeply touching. Next to what you are *in your book* I cherish the inscription.[2] And as for what you are outside of the book, that too I hold dear. You are brave, gifted, and fine and may you have many other successes like this one. You deserve them long before they come.

My congratulations to Walter.[3] Give my love to the young married ones. I say love and not advice, for the one has meaning in itself and the other none beside the fact, of course.

Paul

## 171. To Norman Förster[1]

[237 Toyopa Drive, Pacific Palisades, Calif.]
27 July 1943

Dear Dr. Förster:

Many thanks for your article reprint from the Journal which reached me a few days ago. I think you get down to fundamentals in it, though I hope you

---

the last week of April Harper and Brothers published Betty Smith's *A Tree Grows in Brooklyn*, a novel she wrote while attending Green's writing seminar and living in Chapel Hill on fellowships he helped her get. Recently she had sent him an inscribed copy.

2. "For Paul Green, whose steady integrity as a man and an artist gave me an awareness of a most valuable thing—that clear honesty in living, thinking and working makes for a sure recognition of the essential loveliness of people and of life. Betty Smith. May, 1943, Chapel Hill, N.C." (Front flyleaf, presentation copy, Paul Green Collection, Rare Books Collection, Wilson Library, University of North Carolina, Chapel Hill).

3. Carroll, Smith's son-in-law and a playwright whose "Comin' For To Carry" recently won the Carolina Playmakers Award for the best play of the year (Betty Smith, compiler, *Twenty Prize-Winning Non-Royalty One-Act Plays* [New York: Greenberg, 1943], pp. 132–43). Carroll had married Smith's younger daughter, Mary, on 27 May 1943.

---

1. Norman Förster (1887–1972), at the time director of the School of Letters at the University of Iowa, was in the Department of English at UNC during Green's student days there. It was Förster who suggested that Green, while a freshman in the spring of 1917, write what came to be his first play, "Surrender to the Enemy," and through the years Green several times identified Förster as his most inspiring teacher. Along with Irving Babbitt and Paul Elmer More, Förster was a leader in the Neohumanist

don't mind my saying that I have to disagree here and there on your interpretation of those fundamentals. A few weeks ago I was pondering on these old matters of man and his relationship to himself, his fellows and his world, and I thought of you and your long service in and search for a proper statement of them and their meaning. So I sat down and wrote you a voluminous letter spieling forth my ideas page after page. Then later I tore it all up. I decided it would be better to find a time to talk with you. And too I have been writing some little pieces which I've sent off to a publisher. When they come out in book form I'll send you a copy.[2]

Cordially, as always,

For instance in your last paragraph "self-respect" seems to be just half of the matter, if I rightly interpret your use of the phrase "the very foundation of a society, as of a person, is self-respect."[3] If by the word "self" you mean something of what the Brahmans meant in their Upanishads[4] then I agree with you. Anyway, it's a dreadful acknowledgment for us to make that the common people are nearer right in their belief in man than the intellectuals.[5]

---

movement of the 1920s and 1930s, one of whose aims was educational reform. They believed, as did Green, that education should focus on the humanities and stress moral and aesthetic values rather than historical facts and influences, the fruits of scientific scholarship. Recently, Förster had sent Green an offprint of his article on the subject, "A University Prepared for Victory," *Journal of Higher Education* 14 (June 1943): 285–89.

2. *The Hawthorn Tree* was published in December 1943. After receiving his copy, Förster wrote Green: "It's a noble book. . . . You are *never* on the low plane of the usual writing of the day—are always digging down into your deepest experience or rising up where you can see things. In a word, the book is you as I have always known you, unspoiled and unafraid" (3 January 1944, PG-SHC).

3. Deprecating the influence of science on the human image, Förster had concluded: "For several centuries now, man has become less and less great, in his interpretation of himself. Should this process of diminution continue, it will be idle to plan for 'the great society,' since the very foundation of a society, as of a person, is self-respect" ("A University Prepared for Victory," p. 289).

4. That the individual self is only an aspect of the universal soul, and the highest knowledge, an understanding of this unity of the many and the one.

5. Following the sentence about self-respect, Förster wrote: "More of this belief in man has been retained by the common people than by our intellectuals. It would seem that higher education, instead of darkening or destroying this belief, should use and enlighten it" ("A University Prepared for Victory," p. 289).

Dreadful in that there has already been such a waste of time and souls, and not so dreadful in that we have an obvious hint there as to what to do about the future intellectuals.

## 172. To James Boyd

[237 Toyopa Drive, Pacific Palisades, Calif.]
16 August 1943

Dear Jim—[1]

Thanks for your letter and we're all glad to get news of the family—at least the male side poetic and martial. Elizabeth and I can't compete in the contribution to the war—you having two sons actually in and we with only one preparing to get in.[2] Still I guess we all feel it pretty much alike and pretty much together. And the way I feel it I've just put down on a few sheets of paper and the individual comes out of my diatribe all right, but I am forced to play some hell about what is happening to that individual in this universal carnage.[3]

No, I won't go mushy with the Hindu brethren,[4] but I am forced to the conclusion that the brown boys have got something too. Have you ever read Lesson 18 in the *Bhagavadgita* for instance?[5] There are a lot of good things—hard-boiled too—in it. E.g. "There is more happiness in doing one's own law without excellence than in doing another's law well. In doing the work assigned by nature one gets no stain."[6] Again, "A mortal wins consummation by worshipping with his proper work him whence comes the energy of born

1. In a recent letter to Green from Southern Pines, Boyd described military-training activities in central North Carolina, noted that his older son was overseas in the U.S. Coast Guard and his younger son had just left Princeton to join the army, and mentioned that he occupied himself by writing poetry (19 July 1943, Boyd Papers, SHC).

2. Paul, Jr., in the naval Reserve Officers' Training Corps (ROTC) at UNC.

3. Perhaps "A Note on Tragedy," in Green, *The Hawthorn Tree*, pp. 130–48.

4. Green's frequent references to Indian literature had prompted Boyd to close his letter: "When you return, over [Rabindranath] Tagore, I will fight you to the death. Meanwhile, I beseech you to turn your steps towards the lucid and sinewy and to avert your eyes from the brown brothers' beguiling masses of opalescent mush" (19 July 1943, Boyd Papers, SHC).

5. Final lesson, or reading.

6. 18:47. Translation unlocated.

beings and by whom this universe is filled."[7] Well, we'll be going home in a few weeks now and maybe E. and I can hitchhike down to see you and Kate and we can talk about the two kinds of imperialism—that of the soul and that of the armed (however tender and stroking) hand. That will seem nearer my proper work. Anyway, Hindus or no Hindus, I am becoming convinced that democracy is an inspiration of the soul and its extension is that of the hand—a blind pragmatic hand at that. Our problem is to learn to move the hand with the true impulse from the soul to which that hand belongs. Even the two sentimental and fumbling Roosevelts—husband and wife—seem to realize that this is a problem ahead. My contention is that the Indian philosophers can give us some help there. I am glad to find out that the erstwhile synthetic T. S. Eliot and his preceding superior F. H. Bradley[8] (Here's a man!) both agree.

As to the doctors with their gouging, I've paid off and fled. I'm all right.[9]

Paul

We're living out here on the ocean shore and quite surrounded by activity of war—machine and anti-aircraft guns practicing day and night and the naval guns in the hills firing over the house to sea—and soldiers on guard everywhere—everything on the qui vive for any invasion that might be in the making at any time. And at night everything blacked out.

I envy you the poetry—I feel as empty of it as a cracked gourd. Go to it![10]

7. 18:46.

8. Oxford idealist philosopher on whom Eliot wrote his doctoral dissertation ("Experience and the Objects of Knowledge in the Philosophy of F. H. Bradley," Harvard University, 1916) and an essay ("Francis Herbert Bradley," in Eliot, *Selected Essays* [New York: Harcourt, Brace, 1950], pp. 394–404), and quoted in a note to line 412 of *The Waste Land.*

9. In an earlier letter Green must have said he was seeing a doctor for sinus headaches, and Boyd replied: "I am disturbed about your conferences with the doctor. If the public is to be admitted to any portion of one's anatomy, it should be to the heart and not the head. From my years of travail I exhort you to select only the most skillful and experienced man in that line of work, and then to avoid him like the plague. But really the sulpha drugs have rendered most tinkering superfluous, and I hope you are cognizant of that fact" (19 July 1943, Boyd Papers, SHC).

10. Boyd had said, "I keep on writing [poems]. . . . It is slow hard work, and of course utterly unprofitable, but I must say uniquely satisfying" (ibid.).

## 173. To Elizabeth L. Green

Twentieth Century–Fox Film Corporation, Beverly Hills, Calif.
Friday, 10 September [1943]

Dearest Honey—[1]

Your penciled letter about your arrival, the house, Caro Mae, gathering, etc.[2] has just come, and I am glad everything is so nice there—and that even the little bugs were present in the old familiar way (maybe).

Yesterday I had lunch with Mr. Sheehan and he was full of the wildest suggestions on the picture.[3] Afterwards Howard and I held a session, and he was mad as hops and full of suspicions about Mr. S's "balance of mind," even threatened to throw the whole thing up.[4] I tried to calm him, and today we're working again harmoniously as best we can.

Sorry to hear about George Denny and Mary.[5]

I worked here at the studio late yesterday, and stopped by the S. M.[6] second hand bookstore and got a Hardy book (50 cents) to read at night. Home, I watered everything before darkness set in—I mean flowers, for Roger had come during the day as agreed on with me and had done a lot—then I went out to pick the vegetables in the gloaming for Willie,[7] Miss S.,[8] and Dotty.[9] Lo

1. Elizabeth and their three daughters, with Green in Hollywood during the summer, left for Chapel Hill about 5 September.

2. Caro Mae Russell, Green's sister, met Elizabeth and the children at the train station in Raleigh and took them to her home, where they were joined by others for a family gathering and supper (Elizabeth Green to Paul Green, undated, PG-SHC).

3. *Captain Eddie*, based on the life of Eddie Rickenbacker, World War I flying ace, owner of Eastern Air Lines, and during World War II a presidential courier. On a mission to General Douglas MacArthur in New Guinea late in 1942, Rickenbacker crashed in the South Pacific and was on the open sea for twenty-four days before a headline-making rescue. Winfield R. Sheehan, who produced *Carolina*, a motion picture based on *The House of Connelly*, also produced *Captain Eddie* and secured Green to write the script with screenwriter Howard Emmett Rogers. The job began in February 1943, and frequently during the year Green's diary notes Sheehan's capricious insistence that some scene be added or deleted.

4. "Again" added later above the line.

5. Who had decided on a divorce. In late July Denny had visited Los Angeles, discussed his marital problems with Green, and received Green's advice not to separate from his wife of twenty years (Paul Green to George Denny, 23 July 1943, PG-SHC).

6. Santa Monica.

and behold everything had been cleaned off. Well, I said, "Louise,"[10] and let it go at that—for I had left her cleaning in the morning when I drove off to work. So back into the living room to read the paper and to hear more of the radiant Italian news over the radio.[11] Along about 9:30 I was ready for my supper and I was all set for some scrambled eggs, corn flakes, and good coffee. So I went into the spotless kitchen (Louise had come twice and had agreed to be there Monday when I moved out and to help Mrs. Theobald)[12] and turned on my gas and pushed up my sleeves in a good culinary manner. I said "spotless kitchen"! It was not only spotless but clean as the palm of a barber's hand—not a scrap, not a crumb—nothing. Search high, search low, nothing. Louise had robbed me—every egg, cornflake, bit of coffee, sugar, eclair, butter, even the salt and pepper emptied out of the containers, everything gone. There I was, too late to go into S. M. or up to the drug store to eat. I was ashamed how mad I got at that huzzy. So I have no idea I'll see her Monday or any other day in my life. She had said I owed her $12.75 which I had paid, and so she had engulfed everything in her arms and kicked up her heels on leaving me. I don't think she stole anything from the house—I have no way of telling. Finally I found a bottle of half-sour milk—how she'd ever overlooked it I don't know—and drank some of it, for I had had no appetite at Mr. Sheehan's lunch and was really empty. And so upstairs to bed. My heart relented when I saw my room all spick and span, my shorts, handkerchiefs and socks laid nicely out, and some of my old Bill Byrd[13] anger dissipated itself. But later in the night I could have kicked her again, for I started going to the bathroom.

7. Stacy.

8. Stewart, his secretary at Twentieth Century–Fox.

9. McBrayer.

10. Their housemaid.

11. Italy's surrender to the Allies had been announced on 8 September as British troops landed in the south around Taranto and British and American forces landed on the west in the area of Salerno. On 9 September German troops moved on Rome (it would fall to them the next day), but the Italian government under Premier Pietro Badoglio and King Victor Emmanuel III escaped to Allied territory. There were also reports that day that segments of the Italian army had joined the fight against the Germans as Allied troops moved up from the south and toward Naples in the west, and the Italian navy surrendered several ships at Gibraltar.

12. Owner of the house the Greens rented, who planned to move back into the house when Green left.

13. Maternal grandfather noted for his temper.

Something was wrong with the milk. Today at the studio where I scribble this I feel a little weak and chastened, but able to say I'm still a friend of the negro race notwithstanding.

About the tax business I'm really disgusted, but there's nothing to that too except to bow down and pay it. Everytime the expert and Miss Stewart figure it it gets bigger.[14] Miss S. says she's going to make me up a sheet (she's now doing so) showing where my money has gone and is going. Well, I hope to be able soon to wire you I'm leaving here for N.Y.[15] and then I'll be down for a week-end anyhow, and then soon thereafter farewell I pray to Hollywood for a while. I love you more than ever, and miss you so! And the children!

Paul

No bobby pins to be found in any drawer. Maybe Louise got them on her first try.

What about Patsy and the pony?[16]

I wrote Paul[17] sometime ago that if he needed any money to get it from you.

Give Erm my love. Last week in a moment of intuition I sent Caro Mae a check for her—not much, $25, but it maybe will help and cheer her (Erm) up.

Don't take my complaints too seriously. You know that these things really don't cut too deep. Only certain other things, and you know what they are, deeply matter!

## 174. To Elizabeth L. Green

[Beverly Wilshire Apartments, Beverly Hills, Calif.]

1 October 1943

Dearest Honey—

Here it is October first and I am still in California and you're there. However, I am now entering my last week, and next Friday I will set forth

14. Green began work on the Rickenbacker picture in the last week of February at $15,000 plus expenses for ten weeks (through April) (Winfield Sheehan to Paul Green, 20 February 1943, PG-SHC). Thereafter his salary increased, and in a recent letter he told Elizabeth that the tax expert at Twentieth Century–Fox said his taxes ran "between 25 and 30 thousand dollars all told. The undeniable facts have just about knocked me out, and I see if I limp home with even enough to pay off our mortgage I'll be lucky" (8 September 1943, EG-SHC).

15. For further work on the picture.

16. The Greens' horses, cared for by a neighbor during the summer.

17. In school at UNC.

either by train or plane. I have reservations on both.[1] Laurence Stallings is here[2]—we've had time together twice, and he has spent several hours in my apartment telling me his experiences over the world—Washington, Canada, Greenland, Iceland, Ireland, England, etc. He now has the itch to go to China and will be setting out, he says, as soon as he can get his back strong enough to stand the trip. He looks much older, grayer, but is the same old charming, clamorous boy, and doesn't seem to be any wiser or any more settled than before. He gave me a long spiel on the pleasures of poverty—"You are now looking at a man who will never chase the dollar again, who will never own any property—not a stick. I'm a changed man. The Laurence Stallings you used to know you will know no more. He is finished, ended, dead. I can sit back now and look at you fellows trying to make money, scrambling and worried, sit back and view it all with a fine indifference. It is meaningless to me," etc. Then the next hour I find out he is here to write a picture for 20th Cent., is getting a big price for it, and has dreams of building himself a house somewhere near Santa Barbara.[3] He is a Georgia Falstaff with a dash of the feminine boy in him. He adds—"A small house, mind you." He takes delight in describing his wife—"She's what I needed," he says. "She's never read a book." And so on.

Hope you've had the lawn grass sown. If not, I shall see to it when I get there. So don't bother.

There's no news, nothing but work. The chances are after I get home, I may have to go up to New York for a few days to work with Rickenbacker on the finishing touches to the script. Don't forget to phone UNC Press that I'll be home shortly—so the proof of my book[4] can wait there.

Love always, Paul

1. Green went by train from Pasadena to New York City, leaving on Tuesday, 5 October, and arriving Friday morning, 8 October (Green diary, PG-SHC), then took another train scheduled to reach Raleigh that night at 9:15 (telegram, Paul Green to Elizabeth Green, 8 October 1943, PG-SHC).

2. In April 1942, Stallings returned to military duty. Stationed at the Pentagon, he traveled extensively (to Africa, Europe, and Great Britain) before retiring in June 1943 and settling in Whittier, California (Joan T. Brittain, *Laurence Stallings* [Boston: Twayne Publishers, 1975], pp. 25–26).

3. Where he had lived following his second marriage, in March 1937, to Louise St. Leger Vance, his secretary at Fox Film Corporation, where he was editor of Fox Movietonews.

4. *The Hawthorn Tree*, which would come out in December.

## 175. To Elizabeth L. Green

Hotel Bristol, 129–135 West 48th Street, New York City
Saturday, 16 October 1943

Dearest Honey—[1]

I sure wish you were here with me tonight. The blues have got me hard and fast—just why I don't know—maybe because of the pleasure of being with you those few days and then having to break everything off and return to this empty foolish job. Do you ever have a dull hungry ache around your heart? Yes. So you know what I mean. I went out to the Drama Bookshop a few minutes ago and found a good book on tragedy.[2] I'll cheer myself up with it tonight as best I can. You would be so much better than a book! My God! I ought to tell you more often—we both ought to talk more together, deeply, intimately—what you mean to me, your loyalty, beauty of spirit—all. Well, in the coming year working together, for each other and our blessed children, maybe we can grow closer together in a common ideal. So many golden months have gone by almost wasted except for more financial security.[3]

I'll go out now and get my cornflakes and stew at the Kellog Cafeteria and come back to my book of tragedy. I love and miss you so!

It would be nice for you to come up next week—arrange with Campbell to go ahead on the house,[4] put the babies with Caro Mae and take the train to do your shopping. I suggest you measure the rooms you want to buy rugs for before you leave. Do what you think is best.[5]

Paul

1. Getting home on the evening of 8 October, Green returned to New York City by train on the night of 14 October for more work on the Rickenbacker script.

2. W. Macneile Dixon, *Tragedy* (1924; 3d ed., 1929). He also bought Demetrius, *On Style*, and Edith Hamilton, *The Great Age of Greek Literature* (Green diary, PG-SHC).

3. Never able to develop the story the way he wished because of Sheehan's interference, Green worked in New York City until 21 November (Green diary, PG-SHC), returned to Chapel Hill for further revisions, then in mid-December turned in what he considered a chaotic script of over 300 pages (twice the desired length) and resigned from the project (telegram, Paul Green to Winfield Sheehan, [13 December 1943], PG-SHC). *Captain Eddie* was released in August 1945, by which time the script had been substantially revised by John Tucker Battle.

4. T. G. Campbell had put in a bid to paint the Greens' house.

5. She decided to go for a few days (unspecified) (Green diary, 31 December 1943, PG-SHC).

At the lunch yesterday with Mrs. Rickenbacker and Mrs. Lou Gehrig[6] the whole talk was about Jews, Negroes, and Communists. "Anti-semitism is growing terribly here in N.Y.C.," they said. I put out a little plea and hope for human-kindness but got no encouragement.

In today's *Times* I read one encouraging piece—an interview with the Italian philosopher Croce. He spoke good words, truth, and it sounded so good after all the nonsense of politics and hate swirling around. E.g. he defined philosophy as "intensified good sense."[7]

## 176. To James Boyd

[Greenwood Road] Chapel Hill, N.C.
29 November 1943

Dear Jim—[1]

Thanks for your note, and I am sad to think that you are having to be away from home on the old occasion and the old need. But immediately to think of your poem which you enclosed helps to dispel that sadness. It is good, Jim—good and healthy and rooted up and out of our tradition like the best verse of Thomas Hardy. It has something of his gnarl and fibre—but a tree in its own right, of course. The title seems to me right.[2] Editorially, I don't like "warm"

6. Widow of the New York Yankee first-baseman, who died in 1941.

7. Benedetto Croce thought it would embarrass Italians if they let American and British soldiers do all the fighting to free Italy from German control, so from his home on Capri he was organizing volunteer units of Italians to join the Allies. " 'In spite of the fact that I am a philosopher,' he [said], laughing, 'I have got some good sense.'. . . [Then] he gave us a striking definition of philosophy which he said had just come to his mind. It is 'intensification of good sense' " (Herbert L. Matthews, "Croce Warns Nazis Await Allied Split," *New York Times*, 16 October 1943, p. 4, cols. 1–2).

---

1. Boyd, a chronic sufferer from sinus problems, sent Green a poem written while he recovered from an operation at Johns Hopkins Hospital (typescript of poem with letter of 23 November 1943, PG-SHC). The poem, in twenty-two lines, cautions "us heavy people [to] hold our noise / Nor cavil at the shining girls and boys / Who, cursed with too much ardor for their weight, / Fly upward to their fate" (lines 1–4).

2. Boyd noted on the typescript of the poem: "As usual, a good title is hard for me to find. Meanwhile I call it 'The Meteorites.' "

(not "eager" enough),[3] nor "smirk"[4] nor "coin" as two syllables.[5] But these are only little thorn-tears on the garment.[6]

I am back home[7] for what I hope is a long stay. My head nods a bit like a loaded nine pin, but I am praying for the steadying vision and the drive to carry on with a couple of things in mind. Recently I've run across a queer glorious fellow—F. H. Bradley the English philosopher. I knew of his work at Cornell some years ago, but mainly as a name. Now in his fifty year old book *Appearance and Reality* he is extraordinary.[8] Just the right amount of salty doubt and pedestrian pessimism, then pushing through it all with a fist of beckoning hope. These Englishmen! When they're good they're very, very good, and when they're bad they're horrid. Then to prove that they win just the same, my reason acknowledges that that's how it should be.

Allen Tate[9] came up to N.Y. to visit Elizabeth and me a couple of weeks ago and reported something of your intent to settle in Princeton for the winter. Well, we hope for the spring and your coming back again here.

I've been thinking a lot lately of Aeschylus and his bones in Gela[10] and the tramp of the unwitting doughboy going by,[11] and of all the bright souls that war has insulted and obliterated—yet, as I was just reading in the Greek

3. Line 5 reads: "Reaching warm hands to catch a beam of light."

4. Line 11 reads: "Incline to smirk because we are, it seems."

5. Line 14 reads: "And those who hoard each coin that they clutch."

6. Boyd revised line 5 to "Reaching quick hands to catch a beam of light," line 11 to "Breathe pious thanks because we are, it seems," and line 14 to "And those who pinch each penny that they clutch." The poem was published otherwise unchanged ("The Meteorites," in Boyd, *Eighteen Poems* [New York: Charles Scribner's Sons, 1944], p. 19).

7. From New York City, where he worked (14 October–21 November 1943 [Green diary, PG-SHC]) on *Captain Eddie.*

8. *Appearance and Reality*, Bradley's "essay in metaphysics," was published in 1893 and was in fact a regular text in the philosophy courses taught by Horace Williams during Green's student days. After assigning texts, however, Williams would "never mention them again" during the term (Albert Coates, *E. K. Graham, H. W. Chase, F. P. Graham: Three Men in the Transition of the University of North Carolina at Chapel Hill* . . . [Chapel Hill: Albert Coates, 1988], p. 94).

9. Then teaching at Princeton.

10. In Sicily, where Aeschylus died and was buried in 456 or 455 B.C.

11. Since 17 August 1943 when the Eighth Army drove the last Germans from Sicily, the Allies had used the island as a troop and supply depot for the invasion of Italy.

anthology[12]—"The earth in her bosom hides here the body of Plato, but his soul has its immortal station among the blest, the soul of Ariston's son, whom every good man . . . honors in that he saw the divine life."[13] And that is what is so hard, so tragic and so hard for me to see along with your young folks

"Who, cursed with too much ardor for their weight,
Fly upward to their fate."[14]

I'm already quoting your lines. That helps.
Love to all—Paul

## 177. To Bela W. Norton[1]

[Chapel Hill, N.C.]
29 December 1943

Dear Bela—

The *future* Williamsburg production is always in my mind, and as time has been passing I have kept conjuring dreams into that future. We must someday do something that will thrill thousands. I brooded on the Roanoke Island venture for years actually, and I'm sure that it is better that the Virginia plans have had to wait—whatever the reasons. Things cannot ripen too quickly. If they do they spoil just as quickly.

You must be a mind reader for I was just about to sit down and write Mr.

12. *The Greek Anthology*, with trans. by W. R. Paton, 5 vols. (London: William Heinemann; New York: G. P. Putnam's Sons, 1917), a collection of short poems, mostly epigrams from the Hellenistic period, in the Loeb Classical Library.

13. Ibid., 2:37–39. Green uses ellipses in the letter (for "even if he dwell in a far land") perhaps because he was near the bottom of his sheet of paper.

14. "The Meteorites," lines 3–4.

---

1. Green had signed a contract in January 1940 with the Virginia Peninsula Historical Association to write and assist in the production of *The Common Glory* at Williamsburg, Virginia, receiving an advance of $1,250, but plans for the production had been suspended since the outbreak of the war. Recently, Bela W. Norton, vice president in charge of public relations for Colonial Williamsburg, wrote to Green that trustees of the association thought the advance, less his expenses, should be returned so the association could reimburse the individuals who originally invested in the project (Bela Norton to Paul Green, 24 December 1943, PG-SHC).

Hall[2] to the effect that maybe we should clean the slate and all of us be thinking of the day when we could resume—*around a more or less finished script.* I spoke to that effect to my wife, even though it might be a little inconvenient on my part to do it. Now I believe and hope that the Williamsburg production will go far beyond *The Lost Colony.* That is a part of the dream. And of course we shall have to have a key man with the driving business flare there to insure our success. And we shall have to have the proper outdoor site. All of these things will come in time. But we should be thinking about them, don't you agree? You people can be making plans on these.

You will notice that the check I am enclosing is for the full amount advanced to me. It doesn't seem fitting that I should use any of it for travel and expenses (your generous suggestion), since the time, thought, etc., I have put into the venture already are far in excess of the whole if charged for in dollars and cents. It seems to me that the important thing here is not in any way to jeopardize our future plans, and so no one should lose a penny. That has been my policy at Roanoke and elsewhere. For if art can't pay out, then there's something wrong. So all I ask is that it be understood that we will resume negotiations after the war and that I will write the script and we will all work together towards pulling the Williamsburg play off. If you'd drop me a note as representative of VPHA somewhat to that general effect, I should be pleased.[3]

I hope you've had a fine Christmas. Give my regards to Vernon[4] and his lady, Mayor Hall and others.

Cordially and with best wishes to you and yours,

I had thought last year that perhaps we ought to clear up the above matter, and then on second thought I feared if we cancelled the monetary phase of the agreement we might find it hard to start up again. Your letter assures me that such will not be the case. Thanks for that assurance.[5]

2. Channing M. Hall, mayor of Williamsburg and member of the association.

3. Norton sent such a letter on 8 February 1944 (PG-SHC).

4. Vernon M. Geddy, assistant to the president of Colonial Williamsburg and interested in *The Common Glory* project.

5. Norton had said: "We have not abandoned the idea of presenting a play such as we discussed with you, but it is, of course, definitely deferred for the duration. Looking to the future, I think it would enhance the prospects of a more successful resumption of your efforts if we could now clear the slate and have an understanding that if and when the association takes up this matter again, we would turn to you for the assistance and collaboration originally intended" (24 December 1943, PG-SHC).

## 178. To Louis Untermeyer[1]

[Chapel Hill, N.C.]
19 January 1944

Dear Louis Untermeyer—

Your "The American Scene: 1890–1940" idea is certainly an intriguing one, and in trying to think of *twelve* books written in that period which would interpret and show influence on that scene in the way you describe I come to the doleful conclusion that we still look mainly towards Europe for our cultural stimulation and guidance. However I have done the best I can and I think the following have had some effect and are still having it—that is, they have made a difference in our writing, thinking, and sometimes even in our behaving. So:

*Winesburg, Ohio*—Sherwood Anderson
*The Rise of American Civilization*—Charles and Mary Beard
*The Red Badge of Courage* and *McTeague* in one volume—Stephen Crane and Frank Norris
Selected Writings[2]—Theodore Dreiser
Selected Writings (including "Pragmatism")[3]—William James
*Babbitt*—Sinclair Lewis
*The Spoon River Anthology* and The Poetry of Robert Frost[4] in one volume—Edgar Lee Masters and Robert Frost

1. Louis Untermeyer (1885–1977), poet and frequent anthologist, wrote to Green about a project (which did not come to fruition) of the Limited Editions Club to publish "a series of twelve books under the general title *The American Scene: 1890–1940.*" As editor, Untermeyer was "asking a committee of one hundred American men of letters to help me select the twelve books which, ranging over fifty years, will focus the present sharply against the immediate past and give readers not only a panorama but an appraisal of These States" (27 December 1943, PG-SHC).

2. As if they were titles, Green underlined this and the other entries beginning with "Selected," "Collected," or "The Poetry of." In his preparatory notes for the letter he specified *Sister Carrie* (printed 1900, released 1912) as the Dreiser work for inclusion (undated, PG-SHC).

3. Probably not the book of lectures of that title (1907), but the second lecture, "What Pragmatism Means," which came to be the representative statement. In his notes for the letter Green listed *The Principles of Psychology* (1890) as the James work for inclusion.

4. Perhaps *Selected Poems* (1938).

*Prejudices*[5] and Selected Papers—H. L. Mencken[6]
Collected Short Stories—O. Henry
Selected Plays[7]—Eugene O'Neill
Selected Writings and Speeches—Franklin Roosevelt
Selected Writings and Speeches[8]—Woodrow Wilson

My two favorites in the whole list are Eugene O'Neill and Woodrow Wilson.

Good luck in the venture.

Sincerely,[9]

## 179. To Robert Lynn Gault[1]

Chapel Hill, N.C.
1 February 1944

Dear Lynn—

Elizabeth and I appreciate your nice and newsy letter last week, and its arrival brought back the days we saw you there in California. Good luck to

5. Perhaps *Selected Prejudices* (1927), which followed the sixth in the series of *Prejudices* begun in 1919.

6. In Green's notes the Mencken entry is *The American Language*, 4th ed. (1936).

7. Perhaps *Nine Plays* (1932).

8. Among those Green admired were *The Triumph of Ideals* (1919) and *The Hope of the World* (1920), Wilson's speeches in support of the Treaty of Versailles and the covenant of the League of Nations.

9. In Green's notes the list includes twenty-seven writers and is less weighted toward literature than is the final list. Paring down the number, he eliminated such titles as Andrew D. White's *A History of the Warfare of Science with Theology in Christendom* (1896) and Sir William Osler's *The Evolution of Modern Medicine* (1921); Booker T. Washington's *Up From Slavery* (1901) and *These Are Our Lives* (1939) from the Federal Writers' Project; and Irving Babbitt's *The New Laokoön* (1910), Frederick Jackson Turner's *The Frontier in American History* (1920), and John Dewey's *Human Nature and Conduct* (1922). The twenty-second item on the original list begins, "Thomas Wolfe, *Look Homeward, Angel*," then ends, "But influence mainly now, after 1940."

---

1. From Brasstown, near Cleveland, Ohio, Robert Lynn Gault came to UNC in 1937 for graduate work with the Playmakers and joined the staff in 1940 as stage designer. Early in 1942 he was drafted, then stationed at Camp Haan near Los Angeles, where he visited the Greens several times. Recently he had written to Green

you in the days ahead and to Lucile, and may you come back to us soon from wherever you go. We see the Princes and Tippetts[2] and other neighbors often, and we think and most times speak of you all—the young men and the girls whose absent forms and voices have hushed our highways, streets, fields and woods hereabouts to a queer and silent peace.

About the piece of land north of the Princes. We are pleased at the prospect of having you two out here in the woods with us. And as I told you in California, I should be glad to hold the lot for you against your return, and then we could attend to the matter of actual purchase. But if you want to own it now, that is okay too. The Chapel Hill Insurance and Realty Company always handles the details of surveying, deeds, payment, etc. for me. And I am sure they will be glad to accommodate you in any way you may require. As you perhaps remember there is a sort of ravine between this lot and the Princes which helps provide a view east for the Tippetts and somewhat for the Schinhans[3] too who have built just north of them. We wouldn't want that obstructed in any way and I'm sure you wouldn't want it. Nor would you want to place your house near the ravine—for aesthetic and convenience reasons. That means the lot will have to be wide enough for you to build, say, some 100 or 125 feet north of the Princes' north line—that is, have that much space between the end of your house and the ravine. So according to Mr. Hornaday of the above company it would be at least 250 feet wide front and back, maybe a little more, and of course it would run the full depth of 600 or 700 feet—I don't remember the exact measurement of this last. And the kind of house to be built I think should generally conform to the surrounding types and be built down the hill from the road far enough for the Schinhans and Tippetts to see over it. From what you have said before I gather that this is what you'd like too, and it should cost around a minimum of $10,000. The electric and telephone connections would have to come off from the Princes' line, and Billy[4] agrees that this matter can be worked out in a way mutually satisfactory

---

about buying a lot in Greenwood, saying he liked the lot north of the one owned by William Meade Prince and asking about its size and "what financial arrangements are necessary to place me in the category of the 'landed gentry' " (19 January [1944], PG-SHC). He added that he was on leave in Brasstown with his wife, Lucile, his "final leave before going somewhere, no one knows where, yet, of course."

2. Mr. and Mrs. James S. Tippett.

3. The Jan Philip Schinhan family.

4. Prince.

when you return, and I agree that I should be responsible for any extra and reasonable expense which might be connected with this item. Mr. Hornaday of the above company will write you, and if the general suggestions I have made are in line with your wishes, then he can get the deed drawn up in accordance therewith, and you and he can settle on the price. The neighboring lots have sold for $1,000 to $1,500, as I remember, depending upon the size and location.

We've just heard from Don Rosenberg (Mason).[5] He has fought through several tough campaigns in New Guinea and is now relieved from line duty and is putting on plays and acting in them in Melbourne, Australia. So he is safe now, if a piece of scenery doesn't fall on him, [and] he will be back with us in *The Lost Colony* again.[6] And about that, we are busy on plans for raising a lot of money, $50,000 actually, and getting everything set for reopening after the war.[7] There'll be a place waiting for you, of course.[8]

With love from us all—

5. Mason, another Playmaker and member of *The Lost Colony* company (see letter 152), had changed his last name from Rosenberg about 1940.

6. After the war Mason resumed his role of Wanchese for five seasons, 1946–50.

7. In January 1944, according to his diary, Green began to meet with people about reopening *The Lost Colony*, and on 6 February, with others, drove to Raleigh for dinner with Governor J. Melville Broughton on the matter. The meeting began a series of events (chronicled in William S. Powell, *Paradise Preserved: A History of the Roanoke Island Historical Association and Related Organizations* [Chapel Hill: University of North Carolina Press, 1965], pp. 170–81) that resulted in financial support from the state government and widespread popular support of *The Lost Colony* when the legislature acted on 20 March 1945 to put it under the patronage of the state. In the meantime Green also began to think about revising the script. On 13 February 1944 his diary lists ten changes he was considering, for instance: "The need to make the love story between Eleanor Dare and John Borden more dramatic, to be touched upon now and then, showing the difficulties between them, the gradual development of self-reliance and strength in John Borden and the change of class consciousness in Eleanor to the pioneer woman spirit, then the coming together of the two after circumstance has molded them to fit each other" (PG-SHC).

8. Discharged in the spring of 1946 (Robert Gault to Paul Green, 6 September 1945, PG-SHC), Gault returned to *The Lost Colony* as assistant choreographer in 1946, then continued as technical director in 1947 and 1948. Green held the lot in Greenwood for him, and Gault bought it in December 1945.

## 180. To Frank J. Sheil

[Chapel Hill, N.C.]
15 February 1944

Dear Mr. Sheil—

Thanks for your letter of some days ago relative to the matter of producing *Native Son* in Argentina. A year or two ago when this matter came up for the first time, as you may remember, I was very much against a production in that country because of the sensitive relationship between America and it.[1] I still wonder if that sensitivity has in any way been resolved.[2] I should hate to have even a small part in helping to create or to continue any misunderstanding which might hurt the world-wide war effort in which we all are now engaged. It might not do the Good Neighbor policy[3] any good for audiences to see how Uncle Sam botches his job of handling the race problem. What do you think? Who are the people in Argentina who want to do the play? What is their politics? Are they Leftists or are they sensible and responsible theatrical [people] who are interested mainly in good plays and not in subversive propaganda? I think we ought to know a little more about them. As you know I am always willing to take your commonsense advice on things and if you still think that it is wise to release the play down there, then I am inclined to agree.[4]

With cordial regards,

1. Officially neutral during World War II, Argentina sympathized strongly with the Axis powers and from early in the war, when it sheltered the crew of the German battleship *Graf Spee*, was a center of German activity in the Western Hemisphere.

2. In January 1944 General Pedro Ramírez, current Argentine dictator, severed diplomatic relations with Germany and Japan and closed a pro-Axis newspaper. However, ten days after the present letter Ramírez was overthrown by a military coup that led to the fascist government of Juan Perón.

3. Name given to U.S. policy toward Latin America during Franklin Roosevelt's administrations.

4. Sheil replied that the writer Francisco Madrid wished to translate and produce the play in Buenos Aires and that his agent was Lawrence Smith, an Englishman who would not "be inclined to further a production of *Native Son* if he felt it were going to be harmful in any way to the United Nations' war effort" (27 April 1944, PG-SHC). Later, Sheil sent Green a letter from Richard Wright's agent expressing Wright's desire "to have the play performed as widely as possible throughout the world" because of his belief "that both for the war effort and for the peace the problems of the Negro and

## 181. To M. M. Marberry[1]

[Chapel Hill, N.C.]
11 March 1944

Dear Mr. Marberry—

The case of Ezra Pound raises again the age-old question of the artist's responsibility as a citizen and a man in the scheme of things apart from his art. I understand that living in Italy as an American citizen and formerly honored by his fellow poets and writers in this country he embraced Fascism some years ago and since that time has been actively working against democracy, and consequently in this time of crisis between the two ideologies of government a great many people feel that he has dishonored them and betrayed his trust, and the National Institute of Arts and Letters, for instance, should expel him from among its loyal American membership. This is, of course the sort of thing that often happens in strife between nations and in fierce group antagonisms. We are familiar with it.

We remember how in 1918 many a college and school throughout the land kicked the German language so beastly vile out of its curriculum and out of doors only later to realize that the kicker was the one who had perhaps not gained anything in the process. No doubt Pound is of much smaller concern than the German language, but I believe he represents the same principle of logic. From your wire I learn that the Institute refuses to expel him at this

---

other depressed races must be brought out in the open and discussed" (Paul R. Reynolds, Jr., to Frank J. Sheil, 16 May 1944). On receipt of the agent's letter Green, who had left Chapel Hill on 1 May, telegraphed Sheil from Los Angeles: "AM IN AGREEMENT WITH TERMS STATED FOR PRODUCTION OF NATIVE SON IN ARGENTINA" (23 May 1944). *Native Son* was a success in Buenos Aires, opening for a long run on 8 March 1945 (royalty statements, Samuel French, Incorporated, to Paul Green, 1 June, 7 August, and 30 November 1945).

---

1. In July 1943 Ezra Pound was indicted for treason for his radio broadcasts from Rome since 1941, but recently, despite the urging of some members, the National Institute of Arts and Letters had refused to drop him from membership, taking the position that as an American citizen he was presumed innocent until proved guilty (*New York Times*, 8 March 1944, p. 21, col. 4). M. M. Marberry, reporter for the Brooklyn newspaper *PM*, wired Green (and probably other members of the institute as well) for his comment on the refusal, adding: "MANY MEMBERS INDIGNANT SAYING FACT THAT POUND BROADCAST UNDER AXIS AUSPICES REASON ENOUGH FOR OUSTING" (8 March 1944, PG-SHC).

time. Well, I for one think it shows good sense and reason in not doing so. For its business is not legal decisions and punishments and penalties—but arts and letters. If he is guilty of civil or military crimes, let the proper authorities haul him into a court of trial and out of the welter of rumors and facts get at the truth, render its verdict and so punish him as he may justly deserve. Then if his evil is proved to be so monstrous that it puts out his light for us as an artist and unduly embarrasses the Institute, he may have to be dropped from the rolls for decency's sake. I don't know. But in the meantime why not defer judgment and give time and the law a chance to handle him. They do such things rather well, I think. Anyway that's what they are for, and the Institute was created for quite another purpose. Or so I believe.[2]

Sincerely yours, Paul Green

## 182. To Katharine Boyd

601 Ocampo Drive, Pacific Palisades, Calif.
27 May 1944

Dear Kate:[1]

I have done some sort of introduction for Jim's poems, but I don't think it is in shape to send along to you. I have arranged to go to the UCLA Library here

2. Pound was taken into custody by the American army near his home at Rapallo, Italy, in May 1945, returned to Washington, D.C., for trial that November, then declared incompetent to stand trial because of insanity and confined to Saint Elizabeths Hospital in the capital until April 1958, when the indictment against him was dismissed due to continued insanity and he returned to Rapallo. Just before leaving the United States, Pound resigned from the National Institute of Arts and Letters, which removed his name from its rolls in 1960 (H. M. Meacham, *The Caged Panther: Ezra Pound at Saint Elizabeths* [New York: Twayne Publishers, 1967], pp. 208–9).

---

1. James Boyd, Katharine's husband, died on 25 February 1944. At Princeton University in a conference on American culture for British officers, he suffered a heart attack on 24 February and never regained consciousness. Struthers Burt, writer and mutual friend in Boyd's hometown of Southern Pines, telephoned Green with the news early on 25 February. "E. and I both were bowled over and stay that way," Green noted that night in his diary. "[Jim's] fine spirit, his grace of living, his character—cut off, gone forever!" (PG-SHC). Best known for historical novels, Boyd had worked at poems since the start of the war, and Katharine asked Green to write a foreword to a projected collection of them.

and read through Jim's writings again, including his short stories. The library seems to have them all. So in the light of that I hope I shall be better able to give my little piece the right kind of authenticity and human appraisal.

It was awful sad leaving you some weeks ago there so lonely looking and yet so brave on our front lawn.[2] And behind you the house into which I had put so many licks of my own looked lonely too. There is a verse of yearning in the Bible which fits it, but I needn't mention it here.[3]

Elizabeth and I are temporarily settled with the children in a house in Pacific Palisades at the above address. It is much too small and we are looking for something larger, but we may be forced to buy a house since there is absolutely nothing to rent. We both hope there is some chance of your coming this way this summer.

Our love to you and to Dan and Jamie and Nancy,[4] and a thousand things which time will never let us say—[5]

## 183. To Robert B. House

[601 Ocampo Drive, Pacific Palisades, Calif.]
24 August 1944

Dear Bob:[1]

The number of Playmakers out here have been terribly shocked by the news of Proff Koch's death. And we have been in a huddle of grief because of it.[2] I

2. On 30 April Katharine drove the seventy-five miles from Southern Pines to Chapel Hill to talk with Green about the foreword. She arrived at noon, then after lunch Paul and Elizabeth with their two youngest children, Betsy and Janet, left to catch a train for Los Angeles, where Green had a contract with Metro-Goldwyn-Mayer to write a motion picture script based on A. J. Cronin's *The Green Years* (1944) (Green diary, PG-SHC).

3. Perhaps Psalms 137, in which the psalmist laments his exile in Babylon and longs to return to Jerusalem.

4. The Boyds' children. Dan was in the army in France, Jamie in the navy, and Nancy at home with her mother (Katharine Boyd to Paul Green, [summer 1944], PG-SHC).

5. In the fall Charles Scribner's Sons published Boyd's *Eighteen Poems* with Green's foreword.

---

1. Dean of administration at UNC at Chapel Hill.

2. Koch died on 16 August 1944. In Miami Beach visiting his son Frederick, he went

know that President Graham,[3] yourself, and Sam Selden too, will have to make plans soon about the Dramatic Arts Department for the coming year. I recently received your fine letter, in which you conveyed to me confirmation for my leave of absence from the university for 1944–45. Naturally I hope this arrangement can continue in force, for I have a book which I am anxious to complete, but if you all find I am needed there to carry on my graduate work in the department, why I will put aside everything and be back in the fall. I leave it up to you folks to say.[4]

I hope everything is going well with you, Bob, and I know you are saddened like the rest of us at the toll time and circumstances are taking among our ranks. But so it is and evermore shall be with man and man's estate, and therefore we have to be more valiant in the lists for what we hold of good.

With best to you and yours as always,

## 184. To Henry Grady Owens[1]

[Greenwood Road, Chapel Hill, N.C.]
1 May 1945

Dear Grady:

Many thanks for your letter of April 25. I am delighted to know that you are finishing up your doctorate job this summer, and of course any sort of cooperation I can give you I am more than glad to. Here are some sort of answers to the questions you ask:

---

to the beach for an afternoon picnic, ventured into the water, then apparently suffered a heart attack (Carolina Playmakers "News-Letter," 27 August 1944, PG-SHC).

3. Frank Porter Graham, who presided over the UNC system, which consisted of three campuses.

4. After typing the letter, Green noted next to the present sentence: "don't use?" Whether he retained the sentence in the mailed letter is not known, but he did retain the sentiment. House replied: "Thank you for your beautiful letter . . . [which conveys] your own characteristic response to the situation, but I would say do not interrupt your plans at present, but carry out what you have in mind there for the time being" (4 September 1944, PG-SHC).

---

1. Henry Grady Owens (b. 1892), on the faculty at Salem College in Winston-Salem, North Carolina, was completing a Ph.D. in English at New York University. For his dissertation, on Green, which he expected to defend during the coming July, Owens had sent Green a list of last-minute questions (25 April 1945, PG-SHC).

1. You ask for a statement about Mr. Mac and the young teacher in "Mr. Mac's History." I am sending a statement about that on a separate page, signed.[2]

2. I shall be glad to sign the copied letter of Oct. 9, 1941, as soon as I receive it from you.[3]

3. Maybe I shouldn't have killed Harvey Eason (or Easom) off in France. No doubt I'd forgot that as per *Wide Fields* he was still supposed to be living in the year 1928 when this last book was issued.[4] I suppose that an esthetic feeling as to a tragic, youthful death for a cause and the resulting affirmation of the idealism which produced the result made me make this mistake in my timing. I don't think my "putting him to death" necessarily meant an increased stature of creativeness on my part.[5]

2. "Mr. Mac, the Folk History of a Neighborhood," a compilation of local history and legend from Little Bethel (fictionalized version of Harnett County) that Green worked on from the early 1930s onward, is organized as a narrative told by the old Scotsman Mr. Mac to a young college professor, who records the stories (typescript, Paul Green Collection, NCC). Owens asked if both characters represented Green, one in the role of historian (Mr. Mac), the other in the role of artist (professor). In a two-page statement accompanying the present letter Green replied that Mr. Mac was based on D. P. MacDonald, auditor of Harnett County for whom Green worked in the summer of 1921 and with whom he often "tramped the Cape Fear Valley . . . looking up old tombstones, sites of long vanished houses, ancient, overgrown and forgotten roads, and other 'tracks' of human hands and feet."

3. When he began work on the dissertation Owens got from Green a lengthy biographical statement dated 9 October 1941. The original (presumably handwritten) has not survived, but in his letter of 25 April 1945 Owens said he had made four typed copies of the statement (seven pages each) and wanted to send them to Green for his signature, three of them then to be returned.

4. Eason, a character Green modeled on himself as a young man and aspiring writer, appears in "The 'Possum Hunt" in *Wide Fields* (New York: McBride, 1928), then in apparent violation of chronology is remembered in "Mr. Mac, the Folk History of a Neighborhood" (where his name is spelled "Easom") as having been "killed in France [in World War I] fighting to save democracy" (p. 138). In his letter of 25 April 1945 Owens asked, "How do you reconcile the two presentations? . . . I suspect you killed him off because you either consciously or unconsciously no longer needed him. You had reached a mature stature of creativeness. How far wrong am I?" (PG-SHC).

5. Green did not remember, nor had Owens noticed, that *Wide Fields*, although published in 1928, is set well before World War I in "the latter part of the nineteenth

4. I made the statement that a man cannot learn to farm by a book.[6] The longer I live and the more I fool with the earth, the more certain I am that that is true. For farming is identical with the processes of nature's creativeness, and those processes are infinitely flexible and variable even as the temperature, the wind, the sun, and the weather are. So a man living in and of the earth consequently must needs develop the sensitiveness of an artist in dealing with these whims and moods and shades and gradations of nature. The "farming sense" comes mainly from the experience of farming. Of course books and theories and teachings help some just as they do in other fields of man's interest and endeavor. After all, can anything really be taught by a book. In the combination of practice and teaching, the true living of a profession is made possible. In my far away tobacco growing experience no doubt I got quite a bit of help from the United States Department of Agriculture bulletins. But where the bulletins' responsibility ended mine as an individual democrat with free will and that will's attendant responsibility began.

5. As I remember, I had to study Virgil in the summer time in order to remove an entrance condition at Chapel Hill.[7] I found the long nights of tobacco curing when I needed to sit up and watch the thermometer's readings ideally suited for this purpose. But in the tug between Virgil's imaginative wanderings, accomplishments and loves with[8] the dull business of watching a furnace in a tobacco flue, imagination and literature won out. I forgot the thermometer again and again, the heat raced up and down according to my remembering to put wood into the furnace and accordingly my tobacco cured out much the color of the proverbial Negro's "old black hat." My total crop, as I might have told you once, brought me nineteen dollars and some cents. It had cost me in hard-borrowed money more than three hundred. I sold the

century and the first decade or so of the twentieth" (p. ix). So in fact there is no violation of fictional chronology.

6. In his recent letter Owens said he remembered hearing Green say "that a man could not learn to farm by a book. Just before making that statement you had told about ordering bulletins on tobacco raising from the United States Department of Agriculture. I inferred from the two statements that your unfortunate experience [as a tobacco farmer] was the basis of the opinion. Did I infer rightfully?" (25 April 1945, PG-SHC).

7. Having read the *Aeneid* in English translation satisfied one of numerous conditions of entrance to UNC in the fall of 1916 (UNC Catalogue, 1915–16). Owens had asked if this reading interfered with Green's farm work (25 April 1945, PG-SHC).

8. As in letter.

crop in Fuquay Springs, paid a man drayage, found Milton's works and Shakespeare's in a little hypothecary[9]-bookstore in the village. And when I returned home that night I had an armful of literature and only fifty cents left in my pocket. And so with Paradise Lost I worked on towards Paradise Regained.

6. I am glad you told me frankly about your wishes for the future.[10] I will do whatever I can and when I can towards helping you get settled. What help I can be to you, I don't know, but count on me for my best efforts. At the present time I don't know what openings are possible in this particular section. I have been out of the state quite a good deal, but I will look into the matter.[11]

I am returning to California on May 10,[12] and shall be associated with MGM studios, Culver City, and you can reach me any time during the summer and fall there.

With cordial regards to you and yours as always,

## 185. To John Harden[1]

[Greenwood Road, Chapel Hill, N.C.]
4 May 1945

Dear John:

Frank Graham has asked me to write you a note to be passed on to the Governor concerning the subject of research—a subject on which there is to

9. As in letter.

10. Owens had said he was leaving Salem College at the end of the present semester and wanted to find a school "where I can think my own thoughts and express them without fear or favor" (25 April 1945, PG-SHC).

11. Owens completed his degree work at New York University in August, including his dissertation, "The Social Thought and Criticism of Paul Green," and joined the faculty of Furman University in the fall of 1945 (Henry Owens to Paul Green, 18 August 1945, PG-SHC).

12. For work on a succession of motion picture scripts, beginning with one based on an unpublished story by Henry Bellaman entitled "Red Shoes Run Faster."

---

1. As part of its sesquicentennial celebration the University of North Carolina held a conference on Research and Regional Welfare in Chapel Hill, 9–11 May 1945. North

be a conference at Chapel Hill opening on May 9 and with the Governor scheduled for the address of welcome. I take it that Frank thinks I might be able to say something herewith which possibly could be of interest to Mr. Cherry in view of the speech he is to make.

This is a kind of command performance you see, but I am nevertheless glad to comply with it, for it gives me a chance once more to say a word or two about the methods and processes of education, and I think those subjects need a lot of talking about.

In my large Webster's dictionary the word "research" is defined as follows—"usually critical and exhaustive investigation or experimentation having for its aim the discovery of new facts and their correct interpretation, the revision of accepted conclusions, theories or laws in the light of newly discovered facts, or the practical application of such new or revised conclusions, etc." Now you will notice that the use and the uses of this research are covered by the words "practical application." Now you and I know, and all other uncontaminated and natural people know, that there is much more to life than practicality alone, and accordingly for us Webster's definition is not sufficient. But it happens that apparently the imagination[s] of our scholars find it sufficient, for their vision and significance of the word are summed up in the results in such well known and necessary findings as dollars and cents, corn and potatoes, balance sheets and cash registers, tax premiums and life insurance policies, and so on and so on. Nobody denies that all of these are important and that man has to have them. Nobody who really thinks and suffers and yearns in his soul likewise denies that the old Bib[l]ical statement that man shall not live by bread alone is representative of a deep and eternal truth.

Now I notice in the program laid out for the "Conference on Research and Regional Welfare" which is to be held here at Chapel Hill next week that the emphasis is on[c]e again on research as a technological or mechanistic process and its mechanical and practical results. We are to be addressed upon such subjects as "Research for Prosperity in the Industrial South," "The Development of Southern Research," "Nutrition and Public Health," "The Place of Literary Research in Modern Life," "History and Social Reconstruction," and so on. True there is an address by Wilson Compton, President of Washington

---

Carolina governor R. Gregg Cherry was to give the opening address, and John Harden (b. 1903), formerly a newspaperman in Greensboro, was Cherry's executive secretary.

State College on "The Power of Ideas."[2] But I am pretty certain beforehand that the whole trend and emphasis of this conference will be on research as a practical ways and means towards an abundant physical life. (In this case I am providing the word "abundant" for I am willing to bet that among the college professors here meeting and here concerning themselves with life and youth and human destiny there will be, as in the San Francisco conference,[3] little abundance other than the abundance of words.[)]

It is this abundant living that I for one would want to hear about. And that abundant living comes of the spirit more than it can possibly come of the body. Naturally the body, that is, the practical, the physical, the everyday world-around-us life must have its proper consideration. But my point is that we continue this nose-grinding concentration of purpose upon it dealing in gadgets and gew-gaws, in stocks and bonds, in measurements and weighings even of human intelligence, and so being eager for the stalk of life we cut it down and the bloom dies unappreciated, and the fruit does not appear because of this "too practical murdering."

Research, like any other of man's real endeavors, is not for the making and handling and trading and bartering in things alone. It is actually and most really meaningful insofar as it has significance to what I don't mind calling the soul of man.

Yes, I am talking about the soul.

And I believe that if we put the soul first, then all these other things will be added. I believe that a righteous, and imaginative, a creative and artistic people, a people who loves beauty, harmony, symmetry of form, a people who is not satisfied until it has decorated its houses, has touched the common ordinary things by which it lives with the caressing hand of endearment—and people who do that sort of living, they seem to me to participate in this, not so-called but real, abundant life.

I am putting this badly, but here is what I mean—(I wrote it down somewhere pretty much as follows.[4])—

Yes, that's what I mean—life as an art;—green winter fields even to the lyric,

2. Published as "The Usefulness of Useful Knowledge" (in Robert E. Coker, ed., *Research and Regional Welfare* [Chapel Hill: University of North Carolina Press, 1946], pp. 16–32), the speech limited itself to the practical and material.

3. Which had opened on 25 April 1945 to inaugurate the United Nations.

4. In *Forever Growing: Some Notes on a Credo for Teachers* (Chapel Hill: University of North Carolina Press, 1945), pp. 27–28.

lazy and indulgent South: paint on the houses, flowers at the door, and care and beauty and love surrounding our bare, pitiful little country schools and churches; lights and water and conveniences for men and their housewives, not that they may snooze the light away and grow fat in greasy ease, but that they may have more time for books and music and drama and singing. And then outdoor plays and festivals and the beauty of maydays and the sweet and tender girl queen with the prideful young king walking by her side; and good health and joy and imagination among our children, and throughout the land a people alive with the sense of celebration—celebration of their past, their present, and their future—with festivals and choruses and orchestras and all the folk arts flourishing for the mutual stimulation and give and take among us everyone! For these are the decorations of life, the inspiration, the fire, and color and drive and depthful meaning of life. And it is now no longer a matter of the pocketbook and gadgets of commerce, if it ever was, but a matter of the soul. It is the soul I'm talking about.

I am talking about the soul.[5]

For instance, last Sunday I was out in the countryside near Chapel Hill. Walking up out of the creek woods I came into a wide field of some forty or fifty acres. This field was dead to God and man—eroded, marked with scraggly impoverished sassafras bushes, with here and there a patch of perishing broomstraw and a spraddled little 'simmon tree showing themselves. In the middle of this field was a falling-down Negro cabin. I went up to this cabin. Three women were sitting in the yard dipping snuff, their old wrappers indelicately unbosomed, their knees wide apart, and their old ragged, misshapen shoes stuck restfully out. Sitting along like a row of little blackbirds on the rotting, sagging porch were eight children. I looked into their bright, peering inquisitive faces. They were intelligent. I looked at their little spindly, knotted legs. They were in need, desperately in need of some of this "research" we talk about. Here on this fly-besieged porch were eleven citizens of our state—three of them citizens of yesterday, eight of them citizens for tomorrow. Within two miles of this group of wasted young people this conference on "Research and Regional Welfare" will be held. Neither the physical findings of this conference nor what little spiritual crumbs fall from the tongues of the talkers will ever likely reach these eleven people. Nor will it likely ever reach those forty acres of eroded land.

You and I have seen the educational institutions in the South flourish for

5. End of passage from *Forever Growing.*

many and many a year, and we have seen them have little or no effect upon the immediate environment surrounding them.

Now of course, they have had some effect. That is, we have made progress slowly, and our teachers and leaders have always cautioned us that "We have to go slow." True, true we go slow all right, but we don't have to go as slow as we do.

One of the main reasons for this slowness, for this failure in lifting up our people, giving them a new light and a new radiance in their faces and in their feet is that our searchings and the results we find are blindered and vizered[6] down to some over-immediate, practical need.

I think I can prove rather easily that if we forgot practicality some and went in for dreams and visions and imaginations which are the poetry, the inspiration and the spirit of man, we would gain fruitfully in dollars and cents and all the practical comforts, and would not only build such citizens as those mentioned above into an abundant life but would save the lives of those citizens both black and white from a too early and a too wasteful death.

I have had some experience doing research to support a dream, and have seen that research provide the dream for a commonsense basis on which to stand, and have seen that dream bring in the wake of its realization many and many an attendant physical benefit.

Twenty-four years ago I went as a student to Roanoke Island to see the sacred bit of sand and woods whereon and wherein Sir Walter Raleigh's lost colony had tramped and where Eleanor Dare had given birth to the first English child. And where many a brave heart and brave hope had perished. I knew very little about the lost colony at that time, other than the fact that men, women and children had set forth to found a permanent settlement in the New World, had lived in their new home for a brief season, and had perished with nothing but three carved letters "C-R-O" on a tree[7] to tell that they had lived and struggled and suffered and died. There came into me a deep urge to somehow memorialize these tragic people. I kept the urge. I wrote a little one-act play on Virginia Dare. I laid it away. The urge still lived. There came a time when it seemed possible to depict these people in some sort of dramatic representation. So I got busy then on the all important matter of *research*. I worked many a day and night and week searching the records, writing to England, to bibliographers, to libraries, getting up every scrap of

6. Green's spellings.

7. Thought to be for Croatoan, a neighboring island.

information available about Sir Walter Raleigh's colonization efforts and this lost colony especially. And the more research I did on the subject the more clearly came to me the shape of the drama to be written. So the drama was written. The proper music was worked up, the theatre was built, the actors were secured, technical equipment was purchased and rented, and so and so on. And finally on the night of the opening Senator D. W.[8] Fearing who had been a benign and patient father to the enterprise told me that he and the local people of Dare County were involved in the venture to the tune of a $75,000 debt.

Well, this dream somehow caught on, people began to come to see this show, and all the practical benefits mentioned above accrued to and around the enterprise as a collateral witness and result.

Before the war came and killed *The Lost Colony* it had been witnessed by up towards half a million people, the town of Manteo had got itself many a new bathtub and new coat of paint, and many a new bank account was opened in the local bank, and all in all the immediate vicinity prospered to the extent of some three or four million dollars.

It was nothing but a dream to start with, nothing but an urge to have itself born. And because it was a non-commercial, non-practical endeavor it paid out in the most practical results possible.

This is only one instance. It could be multiplied by many another as you know.

For example, the rebuilding of Tryon's palace is a dream.[9] It will take a lot of research to make it come to pass. But because primarily the palace is to be rebuilt as a thing of beauty, the richest kind of human profit will result. It will also bring millions of dollars to North Carolina in time.[10]

And if we get our big outdoor theatre going in Williamsburg where the story of the democratic theory of government and its beginning is to be dramatized and acted out, we shall see again the same thing happen.

Well, John, I am writing on quite at length here about this matter, and

8. B.

9. In 1944 Maud Moore Latham began a campaign to purchase and have the state restore Tryon Palace, which had been completed in 1771 in New Bern, North Carolina, as the home of colonial governor William Tryon.

10. In June 1945 the legislature established a Tryon Palace commission, with Latham as chairman, to oversee the restoration, and on 10 April 1959 the commission opened the palace to the public.

maybe I am deluging you with too many words. But I for one—and I am sure there are plenty of others—would like to hear the Governor in his opening address put in a lick and a plea for research as a means towards an imaginative and spiritual way of life as well as for research as a means of practical living.

For there is in mankind a primal impulse and impetus towards the making of a truly beautiful and vital world. Utility and physical benefits do not satisfy the hunger of his soul. And man will eternally struggle and continue to strive towards the making of such a world. However obscured, hindered and detoured by false doctrines and prophets, he will somehow stumble on towards that goal. But he needs help, we all need help, and it is the business of our leaders, our spokesmen, our lecturers from the platform to help us towards this creative living.

Research for the creative life is research for the really abundant life.

I am rushing this off without taking time to correct it.[11]

With cordial regards as always and my best to Governor Cherry,[12]

## 186. To R. Gregg Cherry[1]

[601 Ocampo Drive, Pacific Palisades, Calif.]
17 May 1945

Dear Governor Cherry:

I have just seen in the *News and Observer* which has reached me here in California about your commutation of William Dunheen. I think you did a fine thing in saving this man's life, for there was no doubt in my mind that he

11. So typographical errors have been corrected within brackets.

12. Cherry's speech, "Research for the Commonwealth," using much language from the letter, adopts Green's emphasis on beauty and spiritual fulfillment. The speech ends with the remark that "research for the creative life is research for the really abundant life" (in *Research and Regional Welfare*, p. 11).

---

1. Green, Elizabeth, and his secretary, Gene Steel, arrived in Los Angeles on 14 May 1945, having left Durham by train on 10 May. R. Gregg Cherry (1891–1957), governor of North Carolina (1945–49), had on 9 May commuted the sentence of William Dunheen from death to life in prison. Following a medical discharge from the army in 1944, Dunheen, eighteen, had shot his girlfriend from ambush with a shotgun. In a story carried in the *News and Observer* of 10 May 1945 (p. 5, col. 1), Cherry gave as his reason for the commutation that Dunheen was mentally ill and epileptic, sicknesses that ran in his family.

was and is mentally sick as you say. Accidentally I happened to meet up with him on Death's Row when I was there to interview another man.[2] Immediately it was obvious that Dunheen was not well and, I thought, had a kind of epileptic look about him. I spoke to the Paroles Commissioner[3] and I mentioned epilepsy, and then I learned of the tendency in Dunheen's family towards this disease.

As you perhaps know I am completely opposed to capital punishment as a part of our penal system. I am sure in my heart that it is far beneath the dignity of our commonwealth—not only as we feel her to be but as we hope she will become—to befoul herself with this continual putting to death of our poor, ignorant Negroes and tenant farmers. One only has to imagine himself on Death's Row for one minute to realize how wrong it would be for the state to come and take his life no matter what his own crime preceding that had been. In fact to take a life in payment for a former life only adds a second death to the one that was. To kill a man in judicial cold blood is but to deny any possible development and amelioration in that man's character. This is not only bad science but worse Christianity. For you and I know that as long as there is life, there is hope for improvement. Again, capital punishment as we practice it in North Carolina and most of the states completely fails as a deterrent to crime. A few days ago I was talking to some old colored people who witnessed a triple hanging in Hillsboro, North Carolina, back in the 'seventies. The dreadful "lesson" of that occasion is with them still. But this secret, hugger-mugger method of the gas chamber or electric chair fails to provide even that terror to our populace.

But as I said, I am opposed to capital punishment on any ground, for it is part and parcel of the old Mosaic law and of a perverse and pessimistic philosophy of mankind. I will not live to see it, but perhaps my children will—the relegation of such instruments as the electric chair, the gas chamber (the pellet and the bowl) relegated to the museum as an inspiration to a new age and a warning to our young people as to the blindness in which a former generation walked.

2. Probably Marvin L. Matheson or Ernest Brooks, Jr., both on death row at Central Prison in Raleigh. In April Green had been asked to consider helping Matheson, a sixteen-year-old white boy convicted of murder, and Brooks, a fifteen-year-old black boy convicted of rape and burglary (Joseph T. Spencer to Paul Green, 14 April 1945, PG-SHC).

3. Hathaway Cross.

I for one as a citizen of North Carolina will always commend any action of yours looking towards the alleviation or the ultimate abolishment of this our failure, not only as penologists but as citizens.[4]

Frank Graham had me send you over a long piece the other day.[5] I am sure you understood under what conditions and in what spirit it was sent.

My best to John Harden, and I would like to call in and pay my respects to you on my return to North Carolina.

With cordial greetings and regards,

## 187. To William T. Couch

[601 Ocampo Drive, Pacific Palisades, Calif.]
17 May 1945

Dear Bill:[1]

I was sorry to have to move away and leave you almost single-handedly carrying on the struggle for Friederich. As I told you at the last, I will be glad to help out in anything further you see fit to do—provided of course it fits in with both your and Friederich's wishes. I still am not sure that the "law suit"

4. In December Cherry commuted the sentence of Ernest Brooks (*NO*, 21 December 1945, p. 20, col. 4), and Green wired congratulations (undated, PG-SHC).

5. Letter 185, to John Harden.

1. When Green left for Los Angeles on 10 May, he, Couch (director of the University of North Carolina Press), and Frank Graham were attempting to help a colleague unjustly accused of Nazi sympathies. In March 1945 Werner P. Friederich, associate professor of comparative literature at UNC, was hired by the Office of War Information (OWI) as a translator for the American army in Germany, then fired a month later after several Chapel Hill people protested the appointment. Protesters claimed Friederich had shown Nazi sympathies in a pamphlet he wrote in 1938 ("Political Problems in Present-day Europe," *UNC Library Extension Publication* 5 (October 1938): 1–47). When Green learned about the firing, he telephoned Friederich (who had moved his family to Boston) to offer financial assistance through the summer, an offer Friederich appreciated but declined (interview with Werner Friederich, 23 August 1986). About the protesters Green mused in his diary: "Mussolini dead and mobbed and spat upon, Hitler's hours drawing to a close, and here in Chapel Hill a group of emotional bigots practicing the very thing they claim to hate upon the innocent reputation of a man" ([late April 1945], PG-SHC).

idea is best.[2] But anyway, count me in on whatever expense you may incur in trying to see that Friederich gets a square deal.

I notice in the morning paper the reference to the curtailment of expenses for the OWI, and also I notice that Representative Rankin urges the abolition of the agency.[3] I can say that Rankin at least for once in his life finds my ear sympathetic. My disappointment and disgust at the agency continues unabated—and why not when I read in yesterday's paper that John Houseman has been appointed to a post in Germany by Elmer Davis (Herr Klauber I imagine).[4]

I know you have a lot better ideas for the make-up of my little book *Tree Forever Growing* than I could possibly have. So I leave that to you and will be hoping to receive the proof soon so that we can get the book out, say, in November since I would like to send out some two or three hundred copies for "Christmas cards."[5]

Could you have your secretary forward me any stray copies of *The Tar Heel* of last Saturday, May 12—if it carried any Friederich material.[6]

2. Since the University of North Carolina Press had published Friederich's pamphlet, Couch was especially incensed at the student newspaper, the *Daily Tar Heel*, for calling it "subversive." He urged Friederich to sue the *Daily Tar Heel* for libel (William Couch to Werner Friederich, 14 May 1945, PG-SHC).

3. On 2 May President Harry Truman announced major budget cuts in eight governmental agencies, one of them the OWI (*New York Times*, 3 May 1945, p. 1, col. 1). The OWI was also in the news for the next several days because Truman vetoed an order of its director, Elmer Davis, creating a news blackout in occupied Germany. Truman wanted "a free press in Germany as soon as conditions warranted" ("Truman Lifts News Curb on Reich; Backs Eisenhower against Davis," *New York Times*, 16 May 1945, p. 1, cols. 6–7; p. 5, col. 4). Truman's move was supported by Representative Rankin of Mississippi (a reactionary usually anathema to Green), who urged the president to abolish the OWI (*New York Times*, 17 May 1945, p. 5, col. 5), a step Truman would take on 31 August 1945.

4. Edward Klauber, friend of Houseman and associate director of the OWI. Houseman seems to have been offered a job by the OWI at the time but declined it (Houseman, *Front and Center* [New York: Simon and Schuster, 1979], p. 148).

5. In July Green would change the title to *Forever Growing*, fearing that *Tree Forever Growing* might echo Betty Smith's *A Tree Grows in Brooklyn* (Paul Green to Mrs. Paine, 2 July 1945, PG-SHC).

6. The issue of 12 May carried several pieces (an article, a letter, and an editorial) on

My home address out here is the same as last year—601 Ocampo Drive, Pacific Palisades, California, and my office back at MGM, Culver City, California.

Best to you as always, Paul

## 188. To Katharine Boyd

[601 Ocampo Drive, Pacific Palisades, Calif.]
22 May 1945

Dear Kate:

Your sweet and beautiful letter has reached me out here. To think that during our last few days in Chapel Hill you were there in Southern Pines! All the while I thought you were up in Boston. Yesterday a copy of *The Pilot* arrived and I saw a reference in it to your being at the local town meeting.[1] That made me want to kick myself. And now today your letter adds to that compulsion for self punishment. Well, we'll be back in Chapel Hill within a few months, and maybe by that time this dreadful war will all be over and we can sit down in something of a peaceful world and consider less lamentingly our freshening hopes and our softening griefs.

I returned to Carolina in December for the purpose of getting the plans for rebuilding and reopening *The Lost Colony* settled. And also I did a lot of work

---

the Friederich case, as did later issues throughout the month. Green and Graham did not get Friederich reinstated by the OWI, soon to be abolished by Truman. Nor did Friederich bring suit against the *Daily Tar Heel* but instead allowed Graham to write to the editors urging on them a responsible course (Werner Friederich to Paul Green, 23 May 1945, PG-SHC; "Dr. Frank's Stand," *Daily Tar Heel*, 19 May 1945, p. 2, cols. 3–4; and "To the Student Body from the Editor: Tar Heel's Final Stand Presented in Letter to Dr. Friederich," 29 May 1945, p. 2, cols. 1–4). Graham also decided that Friederich had not resigned from UNC but only taken a leave. In the fall of 1945 Friederich returned to Chapel Hill and continued his distinguished career, being named Kenan Professor in 1957, helping to found both the American and the International Comparative Literature Association, and holding two Fulbright lectureships. He retired from the UNC faculty in 1970.

---

1. The *Southern Pines Pilot*, which Katharine owned and had edited since the death of her husband, James Boyd, in February 1944, in its issue of 11 May 1945 told of her appearance before the local Board of Commissioners to propose a citizens' committee for town improvements (p. 1, col. 1).

on my Negro story which seems to be spreading over innumerable pages towards something of a saga size.[2] My trip home was pretty much in the nature of a leave of absence from the studio here, since I have a contract covering a number of pictures.[3]

We are settled at the same address—601 Ocampo Drive, Pacific Palisades—and are looking for something bigger against the time when the three girls[4] and Mrs. Lay and our colored maid come out.

I have been inquiring for Laurence S.[5] but he has moved from his former address and in answer to my inquiry at the studio today I was told he was not with MGM. He is living somewhere in Brentwood, and I will try to look him up soon.

You are doing a great job with your paper, Kate, and your article in the *Atlantic* was good![6]

I feel the terror and the trembling of the world! And whatever you say about "darkness," there is light in what you write, for there beats through it the feeling and the intent of a loving heart. And that is the only possible cure for this same terror and this trembling. Home and broken from the wars return—that's going to be too familiar a refrain in the days ahead. Oh, but if it were only "too familiar" before the journey outward ever began! And the flag of true internationalism, of brotherhood, of true religion has yet to find the proper hands to raise it high aloft and the proper and willingly humble knees to bend in obedience to it. There are plenty of proper hands—such as yours—and millions of yearning knees, but somehow the leadership keeps out of joint with the time and the needs, and wastage and death keep on mutilating our fields and green human wishes.

Our love to the children, and Elizabeth is writing Paul, Jr. in Boston.[7] It

2. *Stormy Banks*, novel Green began in late 1943 and worked at sporadically for three decades without finishing. The title character is a "poetic and ambitious" black janitor at UNC, an environment that "never feeds Stormy's spiritual needs" ("Note on Stormy Banks," 24 December 1947, PG-SHC).

3. Among them *The Green Years* (based on A. J. Cronin's 1944 novel; released by MGM in 1946) and *Time Out of Mind* (based on Rachel Field's 1935 novel; released by Universal in 1947).

4. Daughters Byrd, Betsy, and Janet.

5. Stallings.

6. "Heard About Jackson Hole?," *Atlantic Monthly*, April 1945, pp. 102–6, which favors governmental purchase of that Wyoming territory for a national park.

7. In a navy training program.

would be wonderful for him if he could meet up with Nancy.[8] He expects to be sent out to the South Pacific in August.

With love from us both,

## 189. To Harry K. Russell[1]

[326 Adelaide Drive, Santa Monica, Calif.]
23 July 1945

Dear Harry:

Many thanks for your letter of some days ago relative to recommendations for a new head of the Department of Dramatic Art there at the university. Naturally I feel honored at being made a member of the committee of selection, and you will hear from me later as to my suggested choice.

I wish, Harry, it were possible for me to consider offering myself for the headship.[2] There is a great opportunity at Chapel Hill for creating a fine dramatic center of the southeast region—with a mother theatre building, a fine staff, a theatre magazine, extension services to dramatic groups, the creating and fostering of outdoor theatres and celebrations, etc., etc. I only have to close my eyes to see in imagination some of the fine and inspiring things that could be done. And if I were free to accept and if the job were offered to me, I would jump to grab it. I can think of no better future for me than such a job—except one, and that is the job of pounding a typewriter. It happens that I am irrevocably bitten by the writing bug, and that stays uppermost in my consciousness and plans whether I wish it or not. Perhaps I should be worth a darn sight more to the world heading a creative dramatic

8. Katharine's daughter, a student at Radcliffe College.

---

1. In early June Dean House appointed a search committee to replace Frederick Koch (who died in August 1944) as head of the Department of Dramatic Art. Green was on the committee, as were Phillips Russell, Robert Sharpe, Archibald Henderson, and Urban Holmes. Harry Russell (b. 1902) of the English department chaired the committee and had written to Green reporting on their first meeting, at which they decided to ask colleagues around the country to suggest people for the job (8 July 1945, PG-SHC).

2. In the same mail Russell sent a second, "unofficial" letter, handwritten, saying he "would like to know personally if there is any chance of your considering the place yourself. . . . There isn't anything that would do the Dramatic Art department more good, and the University and the state" (8 July 1945, PG-SHC).

center there than I ever will as a writer of motion pictures, plays, novels, and stories. But, to repeat, the inclination of my life is towards writing and will have to remain that. "As the twig is bent," you know. It was a fine gesture of friendship on your part to think of me as you did in this matter, and I deeply appreciate it.

Of course, I will hope to continue my interest and participation in the development of drama at Chapel Hill—somewhat as I have in the past—as an advisor and sort of free lance cooperative worker.

I have had to buy a house here in California because that was the only way I could shelter my brood while I did my work here. The buying doesn't mean that we have become Californians, not by a long sight.[3] When the war is over and reasonableness comes back to the world again, I plan to return to North Carolina to help carry on the above suggested dramatic projects as I have done heretofore.

We all send love to you and the family and are glad that the new baby is thriving.[4] I can visualize you folks there, the road, the green trees and the hot quiet summer afternoons with the far off dreamy call of the yellow-billed cuckoo, and the strident cry of the flicker high in some dead pine, and I know homesickness again.

Affectionately,

## 190. To Samuel Cornwell[1]

[326 Adelaide Drive, Santa Monica, Calif.]
30 July 1945

Dear Sam:

This is just a short note to tell you I am delighted at the prospect of having you for a son-in-law. If I have any immediate advice to give you it is this—

3. Russell, an early settler on Greenwood Road (his was the fourth house built, in 1940–41), had written that "we miss you all. Please don't let buying a house in California keep you there any longer than necessary" (ibid.).

4. Jane, born on 12 April 1945.

---

1. Samuel Cornwell (1925–1979), son of Oliver Cornwell, professor of physical education at UNC, earned a B.S. degree at UNC in 1944 while in the naval ROTC, then remained to work toward a medical certificate, which he would receive in the fall of 1945. Recently he became engaged to Green's oldest daughter, Byrd.

prepare yourself for a rather wayward and haphazard father-in-law. About all I can promise you two is that I will let you alone, wish you well, love you, and share anything in the world I have with you. Beyond that I can promise nothing. And it is in that very "beyond" which the Hindus know about that true forbearance and deep affection are born. (I am a great quoter of the Hindus lately.) You see already how haphazard I am—I hardly know just what I mean, but trust to your intuition to receive my intent.

Well, with that out of the way, let me say, Sam, that I for one don't think you and Byrd are too young to get married.[2] In fact I believe that in mentality, emotional stability and logical grasp of things in general, you and she are several years ahead of her parents at their taking off.[3] And as for making a mistake, etc., one never makes mistakes in the future at any present moment. For the future is always what you make of it as you come to it. And your marriage will be a success or failure not because you marry or do not marry young, but because you work or don't work at it as the years go by. Marriage is a romance, but it is also a "job." And it carries with it like a lot of other things that old ethical imperative and apothegm of "Be not weary in well-doing."

I suppose that is enough of heavy artillery for the moment. And we'll have the house all fixed up out here against the big day.[4]

With affectionate regards,

## 191. To William T. Couch

[326 Adelaide Drive, Santa Monica, Calif.]

[23 August 1945]

DEAR BILL,[1] I HAVE JUST SEEN IN A NEWSPAPER HERE THAT YOU ARE MOVING YOUR GREAT TALENTS AND ENERGY TO CHICAGO, AND I AM ANGRILY AND SORROWFULLY REMINDED ONCE MORE OF THE FACT THAT WE NORTH CAR-

2. A concern Sam expressed in a recent letter (unlocated; referred to in Samuel Cornwell to Paul Green, 20 November 1945, PG-SHC). He was twenty at the time, Byrd nineteen.

3. When Paul was twenty-eight, Elizabeth twenty-five.

4. Sam and Byrd would be married on Christmas Day, 1945, at the Greens' home in Santa Monica.

1. Telegram prompted by the news that Couch, director of the University of North Carolina Press since 1932, had accepted a similar position at the University of Chicago.

OLINA SO-CALLED EDUCATORS AND LEGISLATORS STILL DON'T BELIEVE THE CIVIL WAR HAS ENDED AND SO CONTINUE TO VIEW THE WORLD THROUGH THE NARROW SLIT OF PINCH PENNY AND PARCHED PEAS ECONOMY OF OTHER OUTMODED AND LONG AGO DEAD DAYS. AND SO IT IS THAT ONE BY ONE OUR BEST MEN KEEP SLIPPING AWAY FROM US. WE ARE BLIND AND MAD TO LET YOU LEAVE THE UNIVERSITY NO MATTER WHAT THE COST MIGHT BE TO KEEP YOU. AND YET EVEN ON THE DAY YOU RIDE AWAY THE CHANCES ARE THAT SOME ZEALOUS FELLOW WILL BE STANDING UP IN MEMORIAL HALL[2] DECLAIMING ABOUT THE GREAT UNIVERSITY WE HAVE GOT AT CHAPEL HILL. THAT SAME FELLOW OUGHT TO KNOW YOU CAN'T HAVE A GREAT UNIVERSITY WITHOUT GREAT MEN AND THE STATE OF NORTH CAROLINA DOESN'T SEEM TO BELIEVE IN GREAT MEN. FOR AS SOON AS ONE OF ITS SONS GROWS INTO ANY SORT OF GREATNESS IT IMMEDIATELY FINDS IT CONVENIENT TO LET HIM GO ELSEWHERE. YOU HAVE STUCK IT OUT AT CHAPEL HILL AS I WELL KNOW AGAINST INCREDIBLE DIFFICULTIES AND MUCH LONGER AND MORE PATIENTLY THAN MOST.[3] BUT NOW YOU ARE LEAVING. THE UNIVERSITY WILL NEVER BE THE SAME WITHOUT YOU, AND YET I CANNOT BLAME YOU FOR ACCEPTING A WIDER AND MORE FRUITFUL APPOINTMENT FOR CREATIVE WORK AND LIVING ELSEWHERE. WE NORTH CAROLINIANS NOT ONLY BELIEVE IN THE CIVIL WAR AND ITS ECONOMY AND POLITICS BUT WE LIKEWISE AS FIRMLY BELIEVE IN AN EMPTY AND EVANGELICAL NEW JERUSALEM BEYOND THE GRAVE WHERE WITHOUT ANY EFFORT ON OUR PART OUR TROUBLES OF DEATH ROW EXECUTIONS AND MALNUTRITION AND IGNORANCE AND VENEREAL DISEASE AND POVERTY AND RACIAL PREJUDICE WILL BE COMPENSATED FOR IN THE EFFULGENCE OF A DREAMY PARADISE. WELL, I AM NOT INTERESTED IN SUCH A FAR AWAY AND WISHED FOR JERUSALEM MYSELF. WHAT I AM INTERESTED IN IS THE HELPING TO BUILD A PRESENT PARADISE HERE. AND I WISH MY BELOVED NATIVE STATE AND ALMA MATER WERE LIKEWISE SO INTERESTED. IF THEY WERE THEY WOULD NOT TODAY

2. Auditorium on the UNC campus.

3. Couch frequently stirred controversy with his publications. In 1927, while still assistant director of the press and against internal pressure, he engineered publication of E. C. L. Adams's *Congaree Sketches: Scenes from Negro Life in the Swamps of the Congaree*, black dialect stories for which Green wrote an introduction that university officials thought inflammatory. Through the 1930s he published pioneering sociological studies that exposed racism in the South and the plight of tenant farmers and textile mill workers. Although a crusading liberal himself, Couch also published attacks on the modernist movement in the South, most notably Donald Davidson's *The Attack on Leviathan* (1938).

BE LOSING YOU NOR YOU LOSING THEM. YES, I AM MAD AND ALSO SAD TO SEE NORTH CAROLINA CONTINUE TO THROW AWAY HER CHANCES FOR THE FUTURE SO WASTEFULLY, SO CYNICALLY AND SO BLINDLY. GOOD LUCK, BILL.

PAUL

## 192. To Harry S. Truman[1]

[326 Adelaide Drive, Santa Monica, Calif.]

18 October 1945

AS AN AMERICAN CITIZEN I EARNESTLY BEG YOU TO CONTINUE TO DO EVERYTHING IN YOUR POWER AND TO THE UTTERMOST IN THESE DARKENING AND DANGEROUS DAYS THAT THE PRINCIPLE OF INTERNATIONAL COOPERATION MAY PREVAIL BEFORE IT IS TOO LATE AND BEFORE SOME EXPLOSIVE INCIDENT HAS HURLED US INTO A THIRD AND FINAL GLOBAL WAR. THE NEWS FOR INSTANCE THAT THE ADMINISTRATION REFUSED TO SHARE THE ATOMIC BOMB WITH CERTAIN OF OUR WAR-TORN AND WEARY ALLIES SEEMS IF TRUE ONCE MORE AN EXAMPLE OF MISTRUST WORKING TO HARDEN THE HEARTS OF OUR ALLIES AGAINST US AND US AGAINST THEM AND MAKING MORE DIFFICULT THE MUTUAL CONTROL OF THEIR OWN ATOMIC BOMB WHEN THEY TOO HAVE DISCOVERED IT AS THEY CERTAINLY WILL. WE HAVE NO CORNER ON SCIENTIFIC BRAINS HERE IN AMERICA. BUT WE DO HAVE AT THE PRESENT HOUR ONE OF THE PRICELESS CHANCES OF HISTORY. AND WE SHOULD SEIZE THE CHANCE AND ONCE MORE ASSUME THE MORAL LEADERSHIP OF THE WORLD AND HOLD TO IT THIS TIME WITH ALL OUR MIGHT UNTIL PEACE AND TRUST AMONG MEN ARE ACCOMPLISHED OR ACCOMPLISHED AS NEARLY AS POSSIBLE. FOR SOME SINGLE NATION HAS GOT TO BE FIRST IN BREAKING OUT OF AND GOING BEYOND THE OUTMODED CONCEPT OF ABSOLUTE NATIONAL SOVEREIGNTY INTO THE IDEAL OF THE SOVEREIGNTY OF A BODY OF UNITED NATIONS. AND IT SHOULD BE WE, FOR BY POLITICAL PRINCIPLE AND EXPERIENCE WE ARE FITTED FOR IT. AND ALL NATIONAL EFFORTS FOR WORLD PEACE WHATSOEVER APART FROM THIS GREAT

1. For some weeks national attention had focused on the question whether the United States should share scientific knowledge about the atomic bomb with its allies, particularly the Soviet Union. A few days before the present telegram, President Truman announced that he would not authorize sharing the knowledge. He maintained that since only the United States had the resources to build the bomb, the question would not loom large in U.S.-Soviet relations (*New York Times*, 9 October 1945, p. 1, col. 3).

INTENT ARE WORSE THAN FUTILE AND WASTED. THEY ARE CRIMINAL. THIS IS FIRST ON ANY ENLIGHTENED AGENDA OF LAW-MAKING POWERS, AND IT IS FIRST TODAY IN THE DUTIES OF INDIVIDUAL CITIZENSHIP EVERYWHERE. FOR IT IS NOW CLEAR TO ALL THAT A COOPERATIVE WORLD IS THE ONLY ONE THAT CAN HOPE TO SURVIVE IN A SURVIVAL WORTH WHILE. OUR MILITARY PREPAREDNESS HOWEVER LARGE OR SMALL HAS MEANING ONLY INSOFAR AS IT HELPS US TO COOPERATE TOWARDS THIS IDEAL. MANKIND IS NOW AGAIN LOOKING TO AMERICA TO LEAD THE WAY FORWARD. THIS IS ONCE MORE OUR GOLDEN OPPORTUNITY FOR GREATNESS. AND TO HAVE A SECOND CHANCE IN ONE GENERATION IS A MIRACLE INDEED AND WOULD SUGGEST THAT WE ARE FAVORED UNDER HIGH HEAVEN. SUCH A CHANCE WILL DOUBTLESS NEVER COME TO US A THIRD TIME. AND IT IS TERRIFYING AND UNTHINKABLE THAT SO MANY OF OUR POLITICAL REPRESENTATIVES AND LEADERS SHOULD STILL BULLHEADEDLY TRY TO MEET THIS DIVINE OPPORTUNITY IN TERMS OF A MISSOURI MULE TRADE. TO DO SO IS NOT ONLY TO ASSURE THE ULTIMATE DEATH OF THE TRADER BUT THE CERTAIN KILLING OF THE MULE AND ALONG WITH IT THE LIKELY DESTRUCTION OF NEARLY EVERY CUSTOMER IN THE ENVIRONMENT, TO WIT CIVILIZATION ITSELF. THIS IS THE WORLD'S MORAL CRISIS TOWARDS WHICH HISTORY FOR CENTURIES HAS BEEN BUILDING, AND THE CALL RINGS OUT AT THIS HOUR FOR DEDICATED AND UNSELFISH MEN TO MEET IT. AND NO OTHER TYPE OF MEN CAN MEET IT. AS AN AMERICAN CITIZEN OF TODAY AND A WORLD CITIZEN OF TOMORROW OR NONE I BEG YOU TO CONTINUE YOUR EFFORTS UNCEASINGLY.[2] SINCERELY YOURS,

PAUL GREEN

2. Green sent copies of the telegram to several newspapers and government officials, including North Carolina senator Josiah William Bailey, who replied that he saw "no reason why we should give away any of our military secrets" and that he questioned whether the U.S. government could "resolve" the world's moral crisis (24 October 1945, PG-SHC). Green telegraphed back that "WORLD EVENTS ARE MARCHING ON AND UNTIL AMERICA GETS IN THE FOREFRONT OF THEM AND DOES HER ALL OUT BEST TO HELP CONTROL THEM WITH HER MORAL LEADERSHIP I THINK THEY ARE THE MORE CERTAINLY FRAUGHT WITH DESTRUCTIVE POSSIBILITIES NOT ONLY TO YOU AND YOUR LAISSEZ FAIRE PHILOSOPHY BUT TO ME AND MY ACTIVE ONE. NOW YOU MAY BE IN A WAITING STATE OF GRACE, SENATOR, FOR SUCH DESTRUCTION BUT I AM A SINNER AND I WANT TO LIVE" (6 November 1945).

## 193. To Melvin R. Daniels[1]

Metro-Goldwyn-Mayer, Culver City, Calif.
11 November 1945

Dear Melvin:

I have recently received from Brent Drane a copy of the British Museum receipt for *The Lost Colony* material which has been filed there for an eternal memorial to Dr. Drane.[2] I wrote Mr. Drane that I would pass this[3] on to you for permanent keeping in *The Lost Colony* files. I suppose you and Ike[4] will know where to put it.[5] I think of you all often, and even today on this bright Sunday morning I am making plans to be with you all early next summer to work for the reopening of *The Lost Colony.* I am keeping in touch with Sam Selden and Governor Broughton as to the improvements I have made in the script. I am sure we are all going to have a great opening and a great summer season in 1946.

Give my regards to all the folks, and if there is any suggestion you'd like to make as to how I as author could improve the drama I hope you will send it along.[6]

1. Since the 1920s Melvin R. Daniels (1891–1973), of Wanchese, North Carolina (on Roanoke Island), had participated in the effort to launch and produce *The Lost Colony,* and after D. B. Fearing died in 1943 he handled much of the daily business of the Roanoke Island Historical Association, producer of the play.

2. Reverend Robert B. Drane, rector of St. Paul's Episcopal Church in Edenton, North Carolina, from 1889 until his death in 1939, was a charter and always vigorous member of the Roanoke Colony Memorial Association, organized in 1892 "for the benevolent and patriotic purpose of reclaiming, preserving, and adorning Old Fort Raleigh, built in 1585" (charter, quoted in Powell, *Paradise Preserved,* p. 73). To commemorate Drane's work, his son Brent, a civil engineer in Washington, D.C., arranged a memorial collection of *Lost Colony* material at the British Museum. The collection consisted of copies of *The Lost Colony, The Lost Colony Song-Book,* a playbill from 1941, a souvenir program from each season, 1937–41, and issues of several newspapers devoted to *The Lost Colony* (copy of British Museum receipt, 20 September 1945, PG-SHC). Brent Drane established a similar Robert B. Drane Memorial Collection in the Library of Congress (Mortimer Taube to Brent Drane, 12 May 1945, copy in PG-SHC).

3. Formal receipt from the British Museum.

4. I. P. Davis, also of Wanchese and active in *Lost Colony* affairs.

5. They framed and hung it in the museum at Fort Raleigh (Melvin Daniels to Paul Green, 19 November 1945, PG-SHC).

6. Daniels had only one suggestion, that they show the colonists coming ashore

With kindest personal regards,

## 194. To Samuel Selden[1]

[326 Adelaide Drive, Santa Monica, Calif.]
14 November 1945

Dear Sam:

Many thanks for your letter of a few days ago. And first of all, of course, congratulations on becoming head of the Dramatic Art department. I applaud the good sense of the University administration in electing you. You deserve it, you are eminently qualified, and I am sure the future of things dramatic at Carolina will thrive under you. If I can ever be of any help to you as time goes by, you know you can call on me.

About *The Lost Colony*—I am glad to hear that you have got Herbert Andrews interested in working with you on redesigning the stage, for I know you are loaded with more work than you can do.[2] During the past year or so I have indulged myself in some rather fancy images of a more spectacular production than any we have had in the past.[3] However, as time has gone on

---

from boats out in the bay. "Other than this I would not add to or take away one single thing in the play." Remembering the prewar seasons, he added: "Man there was something about this that just held a person spell bound. Why I have actually heard women cry during the performance. It carried one back some 350 years ago and made them live among those early settlers, endure their hardships and trials" (ibid.).

---

1. Samuel Selden (1899–1979), born in China of missionary parents and educated at Yale (B.A., 1922), joined Koch's Playmakers staff in 1927 following five years as actor and technical director with the Provincetown Players (1922–27). He directed all of the prewar productions of *The Lost Colony* and now was making plans to reopen the play in the summer of 1946. On 3 November 1945 he had been named to succeed Koch as head of the Department of Dramatic Art and director of the Carolina Playmakers.

2. Economizing on production costs, Selden did not hire Andrews, probably someone in the theater in New York City (Samuel Selden to Paul Green, 2 February 1946, PG-SHC).

3. For instance, "the matter of backs for the seats in the amphitheatre. I have been to several outdoor theatres here in California and made a careful study of their seating methods. The Hollywood Bowl is a good example. There the banks of seats are bolted into concrete pilings and rise up into a comfortable slatted back—the slats running horizontally. I hope you will get Al Bell interested in thinking about this" (Paul Green to Samuel Selden, 1 September 1945, PG-SHC).

and as the possibilities of reopening the play become nearer an actuality, I have felt more inclined to let well enough alone. This is my attitude at the present moment. I know we are going to have a lot of expense and a lot of construction and production problems. There may be a new mood abroad among the people. It may be that the airport on Roanoke Island will affect us. I don't know. I think then it is wiser for us to try to rebuild the set-up pretty much as it was before. And by that I mean that we should rebuild with wooden materials—plank and logs—waiting the day when we may allow ourselves something more permanent.

Now, when I say "let well enough alone" I don't mean that we shouldn't improve our production over former years. That is my intent so far as the script goes. I have some eight or ten small changes to make in the story, but none of them will necessitate a change in the stage lay-out. Later on I will write you about these more fully. In the meantime I might mention by way of illustration—

1. To strengthen the love story between John Borden and Eleanor Dare.[4]

2. To intensify and keep more alive the threat of the Spanish power to the colonists throughout the play.

3. To better the music in spots.[5]

4. To show some signs of the colonists' actual work and building up the settlement. (Of course it would be fine if in this particular item we could see more obvious evidences of The Lost Colony crowd building up things rather than coming in and inhabiting a milieu already constructed. If in some way when the colonists arrive on the island we could see a pretty dilapidated fort—with the back of the Chapel, say, providing some sense of wrecked palisadoes or gapped vision of the sound waters, and then in the next scene we might see

4. See letter 179, n. 7.

5. During the war Green collected much Tudor music from rare book dealers and the Huntington and Folger libraries. In addition to increasing the amount and historical authenticity of the music in *The Lost Colony*, he hoped to publish a "Roanoke Island Songbook" that would be "a cross-section of Tudor music . . . an imaginative conception of what one might consider to be the musical consciousness of a body of representative Sixteenth (or early Seventeenth) [century] English citizens like those on Roanoke Island" (Paul Green to Adeline McCall, 22 August 1945, PG-SHC). Although the songbook did not work out, Green added three songs to the production of *The Lost Colony* in 1946 and for the first time included the music when he published the second edition of the play (Memorial Edition [Chapel Hill: University of North Carolina Press, 1946], pp. 155–96).

the interior of the Chapel—which so far as the audience would know has been recently constructed by the colonists themselves. This no doubt would mean that the Chapel would have to be worked on a pivot and a track of some sort and swung around. It might be too expensive for us to consider. Anyway, either by word reference or some bits of action we can get in a more actual sense of building-for-permanence—which the colonists no doubt did in the early days of the settlement. For so far as they knew they were beginning a new nation on this land.)

So, to repeat, I suggest that we plan to go ahead with pretty much the same sort of lay-out as before. I am sure you and Herbert will work things out, along with Al Bell,[6] in the most satisfactory manner possible. Money of course will be our big need, and I do hope that the governor and Billy[7] won't be disappointed in the amount of funds that come in.

Good luck to you, Sam, and all our family send affectionate greetings to you and Wautell and the babies.[8]

## 195. To Samuel Selden

[326 Adelaide Drive, Santa Monica, Calif.]
14 January 1946

Dear Sam:

This is just a note to let you know what I am doing about *The Lost Colony* and to make a request of you. I have just finished revising the script of the play for publication and would like to include on a dedication page the names of all our Lost Colony members who have passed away since the project first began. I have written to Melvin Daniels[1] for the Manteo list, and I would deeply appreciate it if someone in your office could supply me (even if it duplicates Melvin's that will be all right) as to names and dates of birth and

6. Designer and builder of the Waterside Theatre, now in charge of rebuilding it for the opening of *The Lost Colony* on 30 June 1946.

7. J. Melville Broughton, former governor and now president of the Roanoke Island Historical Association, headed a campaign to raise $50,000 for the reopening of *The Lost Colony*. William D. Carmichael, Jr., comptroller of UNC, assisted Broughton in the fund-raising drive.

8. Selden's wife; their children were Priscilla (three) and Sam, Jr. (six months).

---

1. In charge of day-to-day operations of the Roanoke Island Historical Association.

death. I hesitate to trouble you, for I know how busy you are, but the truth is I have no one else to turn to.[2]

I would like to call this edition of the play a memorial edition. What do you think?[3] Also I would like to write a poem as best I can commemorating those who have died and have it published in the souvenir program as my contribution thereto—provided there is to be such a program.[4]

I notice in the *News and Observer* some reference to Al Bell's working on the amphitheater and doing something about making it possible for the landing of the colonists to be seen in the production.[5] This may not be an accurate report, and I know you have an eye on everything—good as Al is. I think our imaginative token of the illuminated masts crossing behind the stage in the night was better than any actual landing could be. The imagination of the spectators was able to function, and in addition very little time was consumed in the depiction of this fact.[6] However, as I wrote you quite some while ago, I think if Al can figure out a way to show the fort a little more wrecked than it has been—that will be better, for later when we see the colonists well settled we will see the proof of their industry in the rebuilt chapel, etc.

I have made very few changes in the script—practically all of them editorial and minor.[7] I have here with me the prompt copy which Harry Davis[8] turned

2. The second edition of the play is dedicated to the memory of seventeen members of *The Lost Colony* enterprise who had died since 1941 (p. ix).

3. The second edition, published in June 1946 by the University of North Carolina Press, is designated on the title page as the Memorial Edition.

4. The 1946 souvenir program includes no poem by Green. It does list the names of those memorialized (p. 54, in NCC) and includes on the same page Michael Drayton's celebration of the original colonists, "To the Virginian Voyage" (1606), which Green sent with another letter, thinking it would "add to the historical as well as literary interest of the program" (Paul Green to John A. Walker, 18 April 1946, PG-SHC).

5. Albert Bell, designer of the Waterside Theatre, was presently renovating it and had proposed mounting the back stage wall on a track so its sections could be slid apart, revealing Albemarle Sound and the "colonists" landing each night in small boats (*NO*, 6 January 1945, p. 14, cols. 7–8).

6. The "imaginative token" was retained and, up to the time of the present writing, still signals the arrival of the colonists at Roanoke Island.

7. That is, in comparison with the 1941 production script. In the second edition Green used most of the revisions from the prewar production scripts (1937–41). Thus, the second edition "does not vary too much from the 1941 showing, [but] it does differ

over to me in 1941. It carries pretty complete production changes and notes. If you would like it I will mail it on to you.

I trust the work is going well with you, Sam, and I do hope we can get *The Lost Colony* opened with a flourish this summer.[9] Anytime you can I wish you'd let me know something about how the money campaign is going for the reopening.

With love to you and Wautell and the two babies,

## 196. To Alice W. Nisbet[1]

326 Adelaide Drive, Santa Monica, Calif.
2 February 1946

Dear Miss Nisbet:

No doubt by this time you have received my wire in which I told you I liked your story "Send Me An Angel." It is a very fine piece of work, and I should like to see some first rate American publisher get it out in a book and sell it widely. But first, I think, quite a bit of editorial work will have to be done on

---

quite a bit from the 1937 edition" (Paul Green to Woodrow Price, 16 May 1946, PG-SHC).

8. Associate director of *The Lost Colony* before and after the war and member of the Carolina Playmakers staff.

9. *The Lost Colony* opened on 30 June 1946. When it closed on 2 September, it had drawn a larger audience (52,083) and a larger average nightly attendance (1,132) than any of the prewar seasons (Powell, *Paradise Preserved*, p. 181).

---

1. In December 1945 Alice Nisbet sent Green the typescript of a novel, "Send Me an Angel," addressing it to him in Chapel Hill and asking if he would "read, criticize, and tell me if it is worthy of publication? It is my first finished product and may be very terrible which is what I am trying to find out" (5 December 1945, PG-SHC). When he got the typescript he wired her: "YOUR MANUSCRIPT HAS BEEN FORWARDED TO ME HERE IN CALIFORNIA. I HAVE READ IT AND THINK IT SPLENDID. AM WRITING YOU ABOUT IT. CONGRATULATIONS AND REGARDS" (2 February 1946). The novel focuses on Delilah, a black farm and house worker in South Carolina driven to murder and suicide by the death of her retarded son, Sammy. Its title comes from Stephen Vincent Benét's "John Brown's Body": "I'm feeling mighty poorly / Yes, mighty poorly, / I ain't got no strength, Lord, / I'm all trampled down, / So send me an angel / Just any old angel / To give me a robe, Lord, / And give me a crown."

the manuscript. Don't you think so too? For instance the dialect seems a little overemphasized and difficult. Also the spelling should be corrected. But we can take these matters up in a later letter.[2] In the meantime could you please tell me something about yourself and would you kindly send me anything else you might have written. It is so rare to find a writer of ability, of sensitivity and genuinely expressed emotions that I am keenly interested in you.[3]

Cordially yours,

## 197. To Erma Green[1]

[326 Adelaide Drive, Santa Monica, Calif.]
6 February 1946

Dear Erma:

This is a late day to write you a Christmas thank you letter, but so many things have been happening that I have neglected writing to anybody. By

2. Nisbet replied that spelling "has always been a problem to me. I found the dialect difficult as well. Often the thing that sounded natural would be inconsistent, and I never managed to spell it without a distracting number of apostrophes. As you must know the southern Negro, I am greedy for suggestions. I want the whole thing to be the best it can, and self conscious dialect would be dreadful. How can you make it simple, readable, and right all at the same time?" (13 February 1946, PG-SHC).

3. Alice W. Nisbet (b. 1921) replied that she was raised on a farm near Van Wyck, South Carolina, graduated from Winthrop College in 1940, then taught in South Carolina until the fall of 1945, when she joined the American Red Cross and went first to Finney General Hospital in Thomasville, Georgia, where she sent Green her typescript, then to Welch Convalescent Hospital in Daytona Beach, Florida, where she was at present. She had worked on "Send Me an Angel" for eight years, since she was eighteen, she added, and had only one other piece of fiction, a short story that was not in shape to send out (ibid.). On Green's recommendation Harper and Brothers considered the novel. When they rejected it, Green suggested that Nisbet send it to the University of North Carolina Press, which published the novel in November 1946. When Nisbet sent Green a copy of the book, with warm thanks for his help, she added that she could not write from imagination, only from experience, and that she had taken an overseas Red Cross assignment hoping to make from the experience a "book worthy of your interest and enthusiasm" (27 November 1946). No other publication by her has come to light.

---

1. Green's youngest sister, who lived in New York City.

many things I mean my work at the studio,[2] my work for myself at home,[3] and the preparations and completion of the wedding.[4] Now at least one of the foregoing is finished and I am taking time to dash off a few letters or notes hither and yon.

Elizabeth and I appreciate your taking the time in the past months to write us the good full letters you have. We hope you will continue to do this, for we really enjoy them whether we deserve them or not. I appreciate a lot the book—*The Wisdom of China and India*[5]—which you sent me. It was a thoughtful gift. During the last few years I have been an indefatigable student and searcher among the oriental religions and philosophies. I have got a lot of help from them, although the mass of stuff I have had to work through in order now and then to get a more self-sustaining insight has been pretty terrific. This particular book I had not seen, and I have thoroughly enjoyed its contents and the easy style in which they are presented. I don't suppose I'll live to see such a happening as that of the orient and the occident feeding each other, complementing each other from their mutual wisdoms. There is a little of such inter-feeding going on now, but oh, too little!

Perhaps in the next thousand years the world will witness a strange thing—the orient will discover and adopt and develop even further the thing known as the machine, and the western world will, having tired of it somewhat, adopt the metaphysics of the east. Wouldn't that be something—for them to exchange philosophies rather than interfuse them? So it is rather amusing to consider that some day maybe the descendent of the hardboiled American business man will be a fanatical preacher and practitioner of yogi, and the descendent of the theosophical transcendental Brahmin will be a follower and practitioner of the atomic engine.

Sometimes I am inclined to think that it is the nature of both *things* and

2. In 1945 Green signed "an indefinitely extended contract with MGM . . . to do a number of pictures for them and they are kind enough to give me freedom on and off pretty much as I wish" for his own writing projects (Paul Green to Woodrow Price, 28 June 1946, PG-SHC).

3. In November 1945 Green sent a collection of short stories to Harper and Brothers, which they would publish in September 1946 as *Salvation on a String and Other Tales of the South.* At present he was revising the script of *The Lost Colony.*

4. Of his daughter Byrd and Samuel Cornwell on 25 December 1945.

5. Lin Yutang, ed. (New York: Random House, 1942).

*theories* to complete themselves to exhaustion in a sort of excess which goes with their being what they are.

There are some rather nice poems in the book. These two stanzas I like—

Yellow's the robe for honour,
And green is for disgrace.
I wear the green and not the gold,
And turn away my face.

I wear the green of scorning,
Who wore the gold so long
I think upon the Sages,
Lest I should do them wrong.[6]

We hear from Paul now and then. He is still out around the Philippines and working hard as radar officer on his ship. The last letter from him utters the none too definite hope that he may be a civilian again sometime this summer and with a chance to enter M. I. T. to carry on his electronic research, looking towards a career in that field. Byrd and our new son Sam are of course there in New York and you will have and have had occasion to see them off and on.

We all send love,

## 198. To Thomas J. Wilson[1]

[326 Adelaide Drive, Santa Monica, Calif.]
12 February 1946

Dear Tommy:

First let me tell you that I think the University of North Carolina and the South generally are very lucky in getting you as the new director of the Press. I

6. Ibid., poem 7, "written B. C. 769 by a divorced woman" (p. 874). The third, and final, stanza is:

It is for her he shames me.
I sit and think apart.
I wonder if the Sages knew
A woman's heart.

1. Thomas J. Wilson (1902–1969), professor of French at UNC before the war and recently discharged from the navy, had just succeeded William Couch as director of

wish you all success in the job, and I am sure you will have it. If there is any way I can ever be of assistance to you—and I don't count sending you books to be published as assistance—I hope you will call on me.

Thanks for the wire you sent me about *The Lost Colony* manuscript. I have just mailed it registered mail to you. It will make a larger volume than formerly, and I think a better one. For instance, I am including along in the text the melodies of the lyrics as needed, and I am including in the back of the book the complete musical layout of the play. The last item should help the sale of the book, for I think quite a number of people will want to have the music, especially since it is arranged in a simple piano and singing form.

As to illustrations for the volume—I shall pretty much have to depend on you and your helpers there at the Press. I am sure we should be able to get a better choice than we had before. Literally hundreds of shots have been taken in and around the production and the theatre. No doubt Bill Sharpe,[2] Department of Conservation and Development, Raleigh, North Carolina, has a lot of them on hand. Also at Manteo there should be a perfect storehouse of them. Mr. I. P. Davis there would be able to help you. If the job doesn't turn out to be too expensive—I should like to have twenty or thirty illustrations. What do you think?

Also I should like to have the front cover stamped with the figure of Eleanor Dare holding the baby Virginia in her arms and the back cover stamped with the head of Sir Walter Raleigh. These pictures appeared on the memorial fifty-cent coin which was minted in honor of the 350th anniversary of the "founding" of the Lost Colony.[3] I am sure the dies are available somewhere. Again I think I. P. Davis could be of assistance in locating them. This matter of the stamping is a little extra, and if you think I should, I will be glad to pay for this particular expense.[4]

---

the University of North Carolina Press. In January Green wrote to a staff member at the press saying it had occurred to him that "the Press might not care to take on the expense of a new edition [of *The Lost Colony*] for the reopening of the play this summer" (Paul Green to Porter Cowles, 28 January 1946, PG-SHC), and Wilson wired back that on the contrary the press was most interested (7 February 1946).

2. Who handled the state's publicity of the play.

3. As part of the fund-raising drive to launch *The Lost Colony* in 1937.

4. Wilson replied that the Federal Bureau of Investigation would not allow them to use a facsimile of the coin on the book and proposed that on the front cover they stamp Raleigh's profile from the coin, that they leave the back cover blank, and that on

Again, about the paper for the volume. The original paper was, I felt, too cold. Could you get something a little warmer, say, something of the tintage of that used in a volume of mine—*The Hawthorn Tree*. Maybe you wouldn't have to use as heavy a weight as that, but, as I say, I'd like something warm.[5]

I plan to be back East for the rehearsal and reopening of the play. Since our showings begin on July 1, I think we ought to get the book out, if possible, a few weeks earlier so that we can get some distribution on it ahead of time, as well as have copies available for sale in and around the theatre.[6] As soon as I get the proof I will read it the same day and return it to you. I'd like, too, to have a glance at the pictures chosen and maybe put captions on them.[7]

With cordial best wishes for the coming year, and Elizabeth joins me in love to you and your wife,

## 199. To Percival Wilde

[326 Adelaide Drive, Santa Monica, Calif.]
16 May 1946

Dear Percival Wilde:[1]

What a sorrowful letter you wrote me. Sorrowful, I mean, in what you had to say about your son. I am very sorry that I have not been at Carolina this

---

the title page they use a line drawing of Eleanor Dare holding the baby Virginia (8 April 1946, PG-SHC). The Memorial Edition followed that plan.

5. The paper in the Memorial Edition is creamier in color than that used in the first edition.

6. The book was ready for distribution in early June, a few weeks in advance of the opening on 30 June.

7. Wilson replied that they could not get the book out on schedule if Green did the proofreading because transcontinental mail was too slow. He suggested that Green allow his sister Caro Mae Russell and Alice Paine of the press staff to do the proofreading in Chapel Hill and to select and write captions for the illustrations (21 February 1946, PG-SHC). Green agreed (Paul Green to Alice Paine, 7 March 1946).

---

1. Wilde, friend of Green since publishing "Hymn to the Rising Sun" in 1936, had written to Green about his son's withdrawal from UNC earlier in the year. Roger Wilde enrolled at UNC in November 1945 following discharge from the army, but emotional problems stemming from experiences in the Italian campaign prevented him from continuing in school. "He has nightmares in which he has hand to hand combats with Germans," his father reported. "According to his own estimate, he killed about fifteen of them at close range, and it is not a pleasant thing for a young

year. Maybe I could have met up with him and we could have talked some and out of that talk some mutual understanding might have occurred. An understanding that would have helped both of us, him hurt in physical war and me hurt in the terrors of the imagination. Yes, these last few years have witnessed apocalyptic terrors enough to destroy the confidence of us all in ourselves. But of course where there is a heartbeat there is the dogged persistence of life. And where there is life there is hopefulness as well as the hauntingness of despair. For the first time in my life I find myself ashamed of being an American. I plan a trip around the world and I already imagine myself in India or in Japan and when asked for my nationality for the first time in my life I will hesitate at saying "I am an American." If only there was some way these horrible wars could be fought by the people who generate them, by us oldsters, you and me and the senators and the congressmen and the stuffed abdomens that sit authoritative-wise behind their shining desks issuing orders by which the young and the fine, the straight and the lithesome are sent out to die. The good North Carolina boy who, now with plaudits ringing in his ears, dropped that first bomb on Hiroshima[2] is in for rocky days ahead. There will come a time when people passing along the street will point and say "He lives there." Then later they will say "He lived there" for no doubt the weight of tens of thousands of innocent and helpless ones dead suddenly on that morning of August 6, 1945 will begin to weigh on him like an incubus. And he, poor boy, will come to the realization that perhaps he has the awful precedent honor of being the greatest mass murderer of all time—considering the amount of time it took to do the killing.[3]

---

man to relive such moments." Roger was one of twelve from a company of 180 to survive, and his father summed up his emotional state by reporting "that when his mother asked, 'Roger, did you make any friends in the Army?' he replied, 'Yes, but they're all dead' " (23 March 1946, PG-SHC).

2. Thomas Ferebee of Mocksville, North Carolina, bombardier on the *Enola Gay*, 6 August 1945.

3. The published record shows no compunction on Ferebee's part. Just after the bombing his parents reported that "Tom was not at all reluctant in talking about" it, adding that he said, " 'It was as easy as dusting off a table' " (*Mocksville Enterprise*, 2 November 1945, North Carolina clipping file, NCC). Later he said, " 'Hiroshima was a milk run. All we had to do was drive in and drop—and hope to hell it worked" (*Winston-Salem Journal*, 3 August 1975, p. 1, col. 6). See also Gordon Thomas and Max Morgan Witts, *Enola Gay* (New York: Stein and Day, 1977), where Ferebee is said to look back "on his experience as the world's first A-bombardier without regret, believing it 'was a job that had to be done' " (p. 282).

Well we fellows who try to write words and make books must pray and work for some illumination of the page in order that the darkness of bestiality and hate and ignorance and of barbarism do not extinguish the feeble yet persistent hope of love and brotherhood shining in human hearts.

With affectionate greetings to you and yours,

## 200. To Richard Adler[1]

[326 Adelaide Drive, Santa Monica, Calif.]
17 May 1946

Dear Richard:

I want you to know I deeply appreciate the letters you have sent me recently. It was good to hear from you, for I am always interested in your thoughts, what you are doing and in the news of yourself and your family.

I am glad you got interested in Joe Feldman's play.[2] There is a lot of good stuff in the script and you are right in recognizing it. I also think you're wise in waiting on it for the present. Maybe someday you can get it revised and set on the stage. I say someday.

I had a delightful association here for three or four days with Tyrone Guthrie relative to the *Everyman* project. I am glad you are interested in this too.[3] There is a great challenge, and as great possibilities, in the subject matter.

1. Richard Adler (b. 1921), who later became well known as the composer of such musicals as *Rags to Riches* (1953), *Pajama Game* (1954), and *Damn Yankees* (1955), was a 1943 graduate of UNC, where he worked in Playmakers productions and took Green's writing course. Recently out of the navy (1943–46), he had written several times to Green about two of his enthusiasms: a theater project for Green and a production idea for himself.

2. Feldman, undergraduate with Adler at UNC, had been killed in action in January 1944, but his play *Behold the Brethren* stayed in Adler's mind and from Feldman's father he recently got a script with the hope of having it produced by the Group Theatre, some of whose members he knew. On rereading the play, however, it struck him that four of its six main "characters are unsympathetic Jews. To produce it as such would be a step back for freedom," he felt, "and to eliminate some of these people would be to write another play." Despite the play's potential, therefore, he had decided at least for the present to drop the idea of a production (Richard Adler to Paul Green, undated, PG-SHC).

3. Since the middle 1930s Green had hoped to adapt the medieval morality play *Everyman* for a black cast, making black experience representative of mankind

The visit of Guthrie only confirmed me in this certainty. But I still feel that I have a few other things to do before *Everyman* is right. I am leaving here in a few weeks to go East for final rehearsals and reopening of *The Lost Colony*.[4] At that time I am to have a number of meetings with a group of men in Williamsburg and Jamestown relative to a vast outdoor play in that section dealing with the beginning history and the democratic ideal of this nation and on which I have been working and thinking for some time.[5] The project was originally got underway just before the war. But the outbreak of that madness stopped the ideal, just as war always stops the truly creative and beneficent dreams of men. (That's a devil of a thing to be saying to a man who has just served as much time in the defense of his country as you have. But I am sure you understand my attitude and will forgive my vehemence. But I can never forgive time and circumstance and cruel authority which have robbed us forever of such good boys, such gifted spirits as Joe Feldman, Sanford Stein,[6] and many another.)

I note what you say about Copland and Harris.[7] I am sure the right

---

generally. He discussed such an adaptation first with Max Reinhardt in 1937 (telegram, Max Reinhardt to Paul Green, 18 January 1937, PG-SHC), then with Richard Wright when they collaborated on *Native Son* (*Native Son* drafts and notes, PG-SHC). More recently Stella Adler (no relation to Richard) and Harold Clurman of the Group Theatre urged Green to go ahead with the project (Stella Adler to Paul Green, 12 March 1946, and Harold Clurman to Paul Green, 12 April 1946, PG-SHC). That spring Stella Adler played in Leonid Andreyev's *He Who Gets Slapped*, directed by the Englishman Tyrone Guthrie. She told Guthrie about the *Everyman* idea, discovered he admired Green's work (especially *The Lost Colony*) and would like to direct the production, and arranged for him to fly to Los Angeles to discuss the project with Green for a few days around 25 March (Stella Adler to Paul Green, 12 March 1946; Green diary, 31 March 1946, PG-SHC). Stella Adler had learned of Green's ideas for *Everyman* from Richard Adler, who was enthusiastic about the project and hoped to be associated with the *Everyman* production (Richard Adler to Paul Green, Tuesday Eve, undated, PG-SHC).

4. Green went to Roanoke Island on 20 June, ten days before the opening (Paul Green to Samuel Selden, 24 May 1946, PG-SHC).

5. *The Common Glory*, production of which Green discussed with local leaders in Williamsburg on 24–25 June, then again on 3 July (ibid.).

6. Another UNC contemporary of Adler, killed in September 1944.

7. Adler had heard Green mention Roy Harris as a possible composer in the *Everyman* project but thought Harris could not write theatrically effective music. He

composer will work out right when the time comes for the actual musicalization of the drama.

I know you feel like a bird with new wings, getting out of the service. You have done a grand job in time of war, and now that the days of peace open ahead of you I know you will continue to do even a finer job.

The idea of the job as dramatic director at a boy's camp for the summer sounds exciting.[8]

I could write on and on for pages, but have to stop and get to work. Janet, Betsy and Mrs. Green join me in love to you and yours,

## 201. To Charles G. Vardell[1]

326 Adelaide Drive, Santa Monica, Calif.
23 July 1946

Dear Charlie:

Here's the poem, and I hope it will do. I hope too, you won't have to cut it, for it would show rougher in the gashes, I fear.[2]

If we the world could only follow the Moravian credo—love for one

---

also thought Aaron Copland's music too modernistic for the project (Richard Adler to Paul Green, Tuesday Eve, undated, PG-SHC).

8. Adler had outlined the advantages of his first civilian job: the experience of putting on a show a week, a healthy outdoor environment, and all expenses plus $500 for eight weeks of work (ibid.).

---

1. In 1752 a group of Moravians from Bethlehem, Pennsylvania, moved into the Piedmont of North Carolina at present-day Winston-Salem and by 1772 were settled enough to start a school for girls, Salem Academy and College, which would celebrate its 175th anniversary in 1947. For the occasion the president of the school asked Green and Vardell to provide a cantata, Green to write the text, Vardell the music (David Weinland to Paul Green, 2 April 1946, PG-SHC). Charles G. Vardell (1893–1962), trained in composition at Juilliard and Eastman School of Music (Ph.D., 1938), was dean of the School of Music at Salem College and had collaborated with Green on an earlier cantata, *A Christmas Prayer in Time of War,* sung at the college during the Christmas season of 1944. With the present letter Green sent the text for the anniversary cantata, *Song in the Wilderness.*

2. In several letters over the spring Vardell urged Green to get him the text by 1 June so he would have the summer to do the music, but he did not have to cut the poem to finish his work by December (Salem College folder, 1946, PG-SHC).

another, brotherhood![3] Never was a philosophy, a religion more timely and more needed in the hearts of men than now. I am sure your music with all its power and might will say just that—love one another, that is the way out of our difficulties. It's as simple as that. The Brethren have shown us the path to follow.

I have purposely omitted place names from the poem such as Salem, Wachovia, etc.[4] This seemed better in view of the fact that your composition doubtless will be used in other places and on other occasions in future days.[5]

Affectionate greetings and good luck,

## 202. To Ellis Arnall[1]

[326 Adelaide Drive, Santa Monica, Calif.]
[Late July 1946]

ONCE MORE THE NOBLE COMMONWEALTH OF GEORGIA HAS BROUGHT SHAME UPON HERSELF AND UPON US ALL WITH THIS MOST RECENT LYNCHING OF FOUR NEGRO CITIZENS. YOU HAVE BEEN A LEADER FOR RACIAL JUSTICE IN THE SOUTH, AND AS A CITIZEN AND A SOUTHERNER I BELIEVE THAT YOU WILL

3. Moravians, who call themselves Unitas Fratrum (United Brethren), have as their credo: "In essentials, unity; in non-essentials, liberty; in all things, charity."

4. The settlers named their town Salem and the area, Wachovia, in remembrance of Wachau, estate of the great patron of Moravians, the German count Nicholas von Zinzendorf.

5. *Song in the Wilderness: Cantata for Chorus and Orchestra, with Baritone Solo* (Chapel Hill: University of North Carolina Press, 1947) was presented at Salem College on 31 May 1947, with Paul and Elizabeth in attendance, and broadcast nationally over NBC radio.

---

1. In 1946 Ellis Arnall (b. 1907) was in his last year as governor of Georgia. Racial tensions in the state escalated in June, when the Supreme Court ruled unconstitutional a state law barring blacks from voting in Democratic (the only meaningful) primary elections. One result of heightened racial feeling was the murder of four blacks by a white mob near Monroe, Georgia, on the evening of 26 July. A black farm worker, Roger Malcom, in jail in Monroe for knifing his white employer, had been freed that day into the custody of a friend, Loy Harrison, prosperous white farmer of the area, who posted bond for him. When he came to pick up Malcom, Harrison brought Malcom's wife and two other blacks, George Dorsey, recently discharged from the army, and Dorsey's wife. On the drive back to Harrison's farm, his car was

DO EVERYTHING IN YOUR POWER TO BRING THE GUILTY PARTIES TO TRIAL AND WIPE OUT THIS BLOT BEFORE THE WORLD.[2]

PAUL GREEN

## 203. To Robert E. Sherwood[1]

[Greenwood Road, Chapel Hill, N.C.]

[8 November 1946]

I WISH TO PROTEST AGAINST UNJUST RACIAL DISCRIMINATION WHEREVER IT OCCURS WHETHER IN THE WASHINGTON CITY THEATERS OR ON THE STREETS OF CHAPEL HILL. I APPLAUD YOUR COURAGEOUS STAND ON MANY A PUBLIC

---

stopped by twenty white men, who dragged the four blacks from the car and shot them repeatedly (*New York Times*, 27 July 1946, p. 1, cols. 6–7; p. 32, cols. 1–2).

2. Arnall replied that he was "doing everything humanly possible to ferret out, prosecute and convict the parties guilty of the murder of our Negroes at Monroe, Georgia" (30 July 1946, PG-SHC). Indeed, the day following the lynching he had ordered the Georgia Bureau of Investigation to stay in the county until the crime was solved, offered the maximum reward allowed under state law ($10,000), and requested assistance from U.S. attorney general Tom Clark (*New York Times*, 28 July 1946, p. 1, cols. 2–3). While showing genuine admiration for Arnall's "sense . . . of justice and your energetic leadership," Green unobtrusively criticized the residual racism implicit in Arnall's reference to "our Negroes" by using Arnall's phrase without the possessive pronoun when he praised Arnall's determination to bring to justice "the parties guilty of the murder of the four Negroes at Monroe, Georgia" (Paul Green to Ellis Arnall, 21 August 1946, PG-SHC). Despite Arnall's efforts, no one was tried for the crime. The Justice Department investigation led to an inquiry by a federal grand jury, but the inquiry identified none of the lynch mob (*New York Times*, 20 December 1946, p. 3, col. 7; 5 January 1947, p. 54, col. 2).

---

1. Robert E. Sherwood (1896–1955), who spent the war years in Washington, D.C., as speech writer and emissary for President Roosevelt, returned earlier in the year to New York City, his playwrighting career, and participation in the Playwrights' Company. At the time of the present telegram, the Playwrights' Company, a producing organization directed by several playwrights, had in production in Washington a play by another member, Maxwell Anderson's *Joan of Lorraine*, and the star of *Joan*, Ingrid Bergman, had stirred a controversy by criticizing Washington theater managers for operating racially segregated theaters. Immediately Sherwood telegraphed Green inviting him to add his name to those of Sherwood and eight other playwrights who wished to "protest against the practice of racial discrimination in legitimate theatres and auditoriums in Washington, D. C." (8 November 1946, PG-SHC).

QUESTION AND AM GLAD TO ADD MY VOICE TO YOURS WHENEVER I CAN. CORDIAL REGARDS.

PAUL GREEN[2]

## 204. To Channing Hall[1]

[Greenwood Road, Chapel Hill, N.C.]
19 November 1946

Dear Mr. Hall:

Pursuant to our conversation in Williamsburg the other day, I am sending you this letter which may serve as a statement of facts on which a letter-contract can be drawn between me and the organization which is to produce the play I am to write for the theatre there in the William and Mary woods.[2] (You notice that I do not give the name of the producing organization—which at the present time is, I understand, The Jamestown Corporation, Inc. I feel

2. Thirty-three playwrights signed the statement by the time Sherwood released it to the press on 13 November. The next day he thanked Green for his response ("It was particularly valuable to have the name of such a distinguished Southerner as yourself on this list" [PG-SHC]) and sent an article on the protest from the *Washington Evening Star* ("Race Issue Threatens to Close National Theater Before Jan. 1," 13 November 1946, p. 1, col. 4).

---

1. Channing Hall (1890–1953), longtime mayor of Williamsburg, Virginia (1934–47), was vice president of the Jamestown Corporation, which earlier in the year helped revive the prewar interest in producing an outdoor historical play in the Jamestown area. Throughout the spring and summer Green corresponded with members of the group ("No one could have a keener interest or higher hopes for this play and its success than I," Green told G. P. Arnold, who initiated the correspondence [4 April 1946, PG-SHC]), and in June when he came east for work on *The Lost Colony* he met with them twice. On 16 October Green left Santa Monica with his family by car for the move back to Chapel Hill. They took a northern route to visit one of Elizabeth's sisters, Ellen Hodgkinson, in Minneapolis and another, Virginia Hawkins, in Racine, Wisconsin, and got home in the evening of 22 October (Green diary, PG-SHC). After two days of rest Green was in Williamsburg on 25 October for a meeting about the play and thereafter, into February 1947, returned to the area almost every week for planning sessions, research, and oversight of construction of the theater (ibid.).

2. In late October the group switched from Jamestown as the site of their theater to a wooded area belonging to the College of William and Mary near Williamsburg (Green diary, PG-SHC).

that in view of our possible need for future funds and sustaining memberships that this name may be changed to something more educational and smacking more of the public weal—such as, for instance, The Jamestown-Williamsburg Historical Association. I mention this only in passing.)[3] I suggest the following set-up:

1. I hereby agree to write the historical drama and provide the musical score for the first production in the Jamestown-Williamsburg outdoor theatre sometime in the late summer of 1947.[4] Also I will keep artistic oversight over the project.

2. For these services I am to receive a total royalty commission from the gross box office proceeds of ten (10) per cent.

3. The ownership of the drama and its collateral theatrical, radio, television, motion picture and mechanical rights whatsoever shall be the property of the producing organization and myself as author in the proportion of Sixty (60) percent and Forty (40) percent—Sixty percent belonging to the producing organization and Forty percent to me as author. (This in terms of the usual Dramatists' Guild contract, copy of which is herewith attached.)[5]

4. Accounts and payment of commission or royalty due the author from production in the Jamestown-Williamsburg theatre shall be made weekly to the author's agent, Samuel French, Inc., 25 West 45th Street, New York City. (The usual procedure under the Dramatists' Guild contract.)

5. I, as author, agree to pay all of my personal, secretarial, travel and communication expenses as they arise, with the understanding that the producing organization will advance me, if I so desire, against my future royalties from the play, a sum not to exceed $2,500.00.[6]

6. It is agreed that the author shall retain all literary rights to the play and the music, such as the right to publish and republish.

3. The producing organization retained its original name, the Jamestown Corporation.

4. *The Common Glory* opened on 17 July 1947.

5. Exploring contract terms with the president of the corporation prior to this letter, Green outlined two ownership clauses for consideration: the 60-40 split included here and sole ownership by the corporation for payment to Green of $25,000 (Paul Green to Colgate Darden, 23 September 1946, PG-SHC).

6. Sentence deleted here: "In the event that through some responsibility of my own, the production should fail to materialize, I hereby agree to return the said $2,500.00, or any part thereof which has been used, to the producing organization" (for background, see letter 177).

I hope the above information will be sufficient for you and your committee to write me a letter which will embody these points and therefore can serve as a contract between us. I suggest it be made in quadruplicate so that Governor Darden may have a copy,[7] you may have a copy, I can have one and I can send the fourth to my agent, Samuel French.[8]

With sincere regards, and I'll be seeing you soon,

## 205. To David H. Stevens

[Greenwood Road, Chapel Hill, N.C.]
19 November 1946

Dear Dave:

I have just got back from a visit up to Jamestown and Williamsburg and found your nice letter of the 14th waiting for me. I was delighted to get news of your doings and especially pleased to hear that your "carrying the torch" not only reaches towards the rising sun of Japan but towards the now twilight of Europe.[1] It must give you great satisfaction to be one of the elements constantly energized against the ever surrounding and threatening darkness of barbarity. Such it is, apart from the singing and the gold, to be a stalwart worker for enlightenment.

7. Colgate W. Darden, Jr., president of the Jamestown Corporation and soon-to-be-named president of the University of Virginia, had been governor of Virginia, 1940–44.

8. The final contract, with the terms outlined here (except the fifth—the Rockefeller Foundation covered Green's travel expenses), was signed in June 1947 (Paul Green to William A. Wright, 3 June 1947, PG-SHC).

---

1. Stevens's letter of 14 November has not been located, but perhaps it referred to several Rockefeller Foundation programs announced the previous August to revive libraries and schools in Europe and help European scientists reestablish contact with scientists in other parts of the world (*New York Times*, 3 August 1946, p. 7, col. 1; 24 August 1946, p. 13, col. 7). Stevens had spent the month of March in Japan as part of an American Education Mission appointed by President Truman to revamp the Japanese educational system. Stevens said their purpose was to eliminate "militaristic indoctrination" and make the educational system "a democratic medium for individual growth," an aim that included everything from language reform to the admission of women into the schools on an equal footing with men (Stevens, "Office talk on Japan," typescript of speech given at Rockefeller Foundation, 16 April 1946, PG-SHC).

The Jamestown-Williamsburg dramatic project is prospering apace. We have run into one or two snags during the last few months, but though we tripped, we haven't fallen—yet. After I had worked out a good dramatic story line for the play to be done in the theatre we were to build on Jamestown Island, we ran into difficulties both with our relationship with the park service and with the matter of building a sewage disposal plant—the last lowly item necessary as a sort of basic wherewithal for our more aery dream.[2] At last, after plenty of deliberation and after we had already begun the clearing of the site on Jamestown, we decided to put the whole thing over on the mainland. William and Mary College has been so kind as to give us the use of some twelve to twenty acres of wonderful woodland adjoining the campus itself.[3] Here on Lake Matoaka (Lake Pocahontas fittingly!),[4] we have begun the construction of our theatre. The difficulty I spoke of just above lies in the fact that I have had to recast my drama.[5] This, along with the oversight of the construction and constant watchfulness against some certain architects and

2. The National Park Service was reluctant to permit the rearrangement of roads and wooded areas necessary for building an outdoor theater on the island (Paul Green to Charles B. Borland, 16 September 1946, PG-SHC), but the last straw was the discovery that Jamestown Island was too low for proper drainage of a sewage system (Green diary, 25 October 1946, PG-SHC).

3. John E. Pomfret, president of the college, offered the land when the sewage problem made Jamestown Island impossible, and the offer was formally accepted at a meeting of the directors of the Jamestown Corporation in Richmond on 1 November 1946 (Green diary, PG-SHC).

4. Although better known, "Pocahontas" was only the title (equivalent to "princess") of the several daughters of Powhatan, Algonquian chief in the area of Jamestown during its settlement. "Matoaka" was the personal name of the young woman, daughter of Powhatan, who may have saved John Smith's life and certainly married John Rolfe in Jamestown in 1614.

5. The site of a historical play was crucial to Green because he could not count on "an adequate substitute elsewhere for the emotion our audiences will feel when they witness the drama on the very spot where our forefathers dreamed and struggled and endured and died" (telegram, Paul Green to Colgate W. Darden, Jr., [mid-August 1946], PG-SHC). For the Jamestown site, Green had developed a plot focusing on John Rolfe (Green diary, 1 November 1946, PG-SHC). The change of site to Williamsburg meant a change of dramatic focus to Jefferson and the framing of the Declaration of Independence. "What the *Lost Colony* shows as trying to get started—namely, a settlement and a creed of government taking root in the new world—[*The Common Glory*] will show as not only getting started but actually coming to fulfillment in Democracy" (Paul Green to George Prince Arnold, 4 April 1946, PG-SHC).

builders who seem to hate trees and want to cut down every one in sight—all of this has kept me on the hump.[6] (Of course, we are all working together in a great good gaiety and fellowship, but still I have to watch these formalists.)

I have asked Robert Edmond Jones to come down and be with us a few days to help us get through the initial stages of our building. I am going up to Richmond tonight to meet him, taking him over to Williamsburg, and we will be there the rest of this week working in the woods.[7] The Governor[8] has generously assigned to us a number of his young American honor convicts. And already we have struck up good camaraderie with them—so much so that recently, one of the convict bosses gave me a little nice but firm lecture on how "it don't do to be too goddamed familiar with the convicts!"—etc.

Financially—we are working on a wing and a prayer. And that is a good way to work too, until all muscle has been strengthened and all excess fat of loose thinking and loose endeavor has been sweated away. I do hope I will be working around Williamsburg when you are there for the meeting.[9] I'd like to take you out and show you the disgorged entrails of the fair body of our theatre which is to be. For by that time, I hope we will have steam shovels going good.[10]

6. In Green's estimation the architect in charge of preparing the Lake Matoaka site was an unimaginative and insensitive fellow, and they had a running (albeit half-humorous) battle about preserving trees. Green would be in Williamsburg a few days each week into spring 1947 and frequently on arrival would find that "several lovely trees which I had made the architect swear to heaven he would save for me had been dug up." On such occasions Green "blasphemed a bit under the moon and excoriated the empty night"—and continued to exact the promises (Green diary, 8 December 1946, PG-SHC).

7. According to his diary, Green telephoned Jones on 19 November (Tuesday), met him at the train station in Richmond the next evening, and the two spent Thursday and Friday going over the theater site at Lake Matoaka and discussing design possibilities (PG-SHC). Jones and Green had known one another since the Macgowan-O'Neill-Jones Experimental Theatre produced *In Abraham's Bosom* in 1926–27. After Jones returned to New York City Green thanked him for "giving me the benefit of your vast and subtle and sensitive experience in making houses and the integuments [for] dreams" and hoped Jones could work with him on another of these "lyrical peoples' theatre projects" (24 November 1946, PG-SHC).

8. William M. Tuck.

9. Of the board of directors of Colonial Williamsburg, of which Stevens, as director of the Humanities Division of the Rockefeller Foundation, was a member.

10. *The Common Glory: A Symphonic Drama of American History* (Chapel Hill:

You and the Foundation have been wonderful about the theatre fund here.[11] To have kept it intact for us for these eight years was a fine gesture of trust and belief in us. It is all too bad that we haven't been able to measure up to this trust and belief.[12] But we are a public institution and we are running as a trinity now—State College at Raleigh and the Women's College at Greensboro being attached. So our progress in securing state funds is slowed down in proportion to our increased mass.[13] Still, I am hoping for a miracle. And of course miracles always come. The trouble about them is that they so often come so late that the dead heart that has died praying for them to happen is beyond the power of either appreciation or resuscitation.[14]

Our love to you and Ruth and the children and grandchildren and we must get together soon and—talk! We are looking forward to having you both here with us sometime during the coming winter.

---

University of North Carolina Press, 1948) contains a photographic essay (captions by Green) on the building of the theater (eight leaves following p. 260), including those scenes Green wished to show Stevens.

11. At Chapel Hill.

12. In 1938 Green and Koch had received a grant of $150,000 from the Rockefeller Foundation to furnish a dramatic arts building to be built by the state on the Chapel Hill campus. The building still had not been built, however, and recently the foundation had canceled the grant (Paul Green to I. P. Davis, 19 December 1947, PG-SHC).

13. Consolidation of the three campuses into one administrative unit took place in 1932. During the Depression, however, university building funds came primarily from foundations and such governmental agencies as the WPA. During World War II the state reinstituted a campus building program, but it involved mainly war-related buildings—a naval ROTC building, dormitories for cadets, and the like (Louis Round Wilson, *The University of North Carolina under Consolidation, 1931–1963: History and Appraisal* [Chapel Hill: University of North Carolina, Consolidated Office, 1964], pp. 93–94).

14. In 1978, three years before Green died, the state built a theater on the UNC campus and named it for him.

# VI

## Symphonic Drama, UNESCO, and the East, 1947–1951

Early 1947
Oversees construction of theater in Williamsburg and revises *The Common Glory.*

31 May 1947
*Song in the Wilderness* performed at Salem College, with Greens in attendance, and broadcast nationally over NBC radio.

17 July 1947
*The Common Glory* opens at Williamsburg.

Fall 1947
Resumes weekly meeting of writing group at his home. Begins negotiations with National Capital Sesquicentennial Commission for *Faith of Our Fathers* in Washington, D.C., in 1950.

November 1947
Renews attack on the death penalty.

9 February 1948
Speaks at William and Mary College (Charter Day) on importance of dramatizing democratic ideals in American heritage.

Spring 1948
At Manteo and Williamsburg working on scripts and productions of *The Lost Colony* and *The Common Glory.*

5 June 1948
Speaks to UNC alumni on importance of extending equal rights to blacks, attacks UNC trustees for refusing to admit black applicants to law and medical schools.

July 1948
To Los Angeles to write film script for *Roseanna McCoy* and explore possibilities for outdoor historical play.

Early October 1948

To Chapel Hill.

18–19 November 1948

In Washington for meeting of Fellows in American Letters of the Library of Congress. Votes with minority against giving Bollingen Award to Ezra Pound for *The Pisan Cantos.*

December 1948

Rescues Lander statue of Virginia Dare (in 1953 places it in Elizabethan Garden on Roanoke Island).

Summer 1949

In Williamsburg revises and rehearses *The Common Glory.*

30 August 1949

In Chapel Hill attacks anti-Communist loyalty oath newly required for employment at UNC.

Fall 1949

Begins drafting *Faith of Our Fathers.*

Winter–Spring 1950

Finishes *Faith of Our Fathers* and arranges production.

Summer 1950

Often in Washington overseeing rehearsals of *Faith of Our Fathers,* which opens on 5 August in Rock Creek Park.

Fall–Winter 1950

Adapts Henrik Ibsen's *Peer Gynt* for producer Cheryl Crawford.

January 1951

In New York City for rehearsals of *Peer Gynt,* which opens on 28 January.

May 1951

Appointed by President Truman to U.S. National Commission for UNESCO.

June–July 1951

With daughter Betsy in Paris for Sixth General Conference of UNESCO. Attracted to Indian and Far Eastern delegations. Sees musical spectacle in Roman amphitheater in Lyons and visits Paul Claudel (10–11 July).

October–December 1951

With Elizabeth on lecture tour in Japan and India sponsored by Rockefeller Foundation. In Japan enthralled by Kabuki. In India attends Conference on Western and Eastern Philosophy at Delhi University (11–14 December).

## 206. To Paul Green, Jr.[1]

[Greenwood Road, Chapel Hill, N.C.]
7 January 1947

Dear Son—

You and your friends have given me quite a job—in asking me for an appraisal of *This Is My Beloved* by Walter Benton.[2] I say "quite a job" because this long poem seems to be written somewhat along the flowery and be-meaded furrow dividing sensuality from true love, though clearly enough the plough wing is turned toward the physically erotic, that is, not so much away from sensuality after all. Of course when I use this figure of speech I am telling you what I think—right off.

It is hard to define good poetry. No less a writer than A. E. Housman ("The Shropshire Lad," etc.) shrank away from definitely defining the nature of it. He said the problem was like that posed by a rat for a terrier: the terrier might not know the nature of a rat, but when one appeared he knew it was a rat by the effect the creature had upon him. Just so he H. knew good poetry from the effect upon him.[3]

Now from the effect of Mr. Benton's poem on me, I feel, yes, I think I know, he is much more interested in celebrating sex as such than he is of[4] a higher, more lasting love.

He may be honest in his intent and in what he writes. But many an honest man is a misguided man, and Mr. Benton seems to be limited to a one-sided view not only of love but of life likewise. He is too much concerned with stimulating the physical emoluments of manhood (and womanhood) by a vivid yet repeated-until-his-poverty-of-imagination-is-revealed roll call of dandlings and dawdlings, kissings and wallowings in the bed, on the bed—or any place level enough for lying down.

Well, this is not enough for you and me and the future of our race to live by! Not hardly.

1. At the time a graduate student in electrical engineering at North Carolina State University in Raleigh.

2. Published in 1943 by Alfred A. Knopf.

3. Such as his hair standing on end, his skin bristling, a shiver running down his spine, his throat constricting, and water welling up in his eyes (A. E. Housman, *The Name and Nature of Poetry* [Cambridge: Cambridge University Press, 1933], pp. 46–47).

4. As in letter.

x . . . . . . . . .[5]

I'm afraid this is not much help. I suggest again you read Shakespeare's "Venus and Adonis," "Solomon's Song," some of Walt Whitman's poems in praise of the body, and I think you will agree that Mr. Benton is far behind them, not only far behind but on the wrong track.[6]

Also there are other fine poets—Shelley, Keats, Tennyson, Wordsworth, Coleridge—who have written about love and done it beautifully.

Ever, Doog[7]

## 207. To James Holly Hanford[1]

[Greenwood Road, Chapel Hill, N.C.]
10 January 1947

Dear Dr. Hanford:

I am delighted that you are putting down some of the happenings of your own life, and I know others will be. You have had a rich experience, and your sharing it in published form will enrich many additional lives—thus your teaching goes on and on.

You have asked me some questions I am afraid I can't answer—Why did the

5. As in letter.

6. Green first made this suggestion on the night of 15–16 December 1946. Returning on 15 December from Williamsburg and Manteo, he found that Paul, Jr., had arrived for the Christmas holidays, and that evening they "had a session in his room on the nature of pagan love." Paul, Jr., showed him Benton's poem and said some school friends, unable to decide if it was good poetry, had appointed him "a delegate to lay the matter before me." Green judged it a poem "in praise of the body delicious," prescribed the reading suggested here, and concluded his diary account with the fear that "this is the last time they will ask me for a verdict" (PG-SHC).

7. His nickname within the family.

1. James Holly Hanford (1882–1969), in the English department at Western Reserve University, taught at UNC 1914–21, during which time Green attended his course on Romantic poetry. Recently he told Green that he was "writing an autobiographical chapter on my experience at Chapel Hill" and instead of reminiscing wanted "to try to say what in essence was happening culturally there and why." He asked Green's help with a series of questions, beginning with: "Why did the University and the State take a sudden leap forward in about 1912–18 or did [they]?" (8 December 1946, PG-SHC).

University and the state here take a sudden leap forward about 1912–18, by what reason and what agency were certain men such as Dr. Greenlaw, Dr. Branson (and yourself certainly) brought to Chapel Hill, etc., etc.?[2]

Accounting for any phenomenon of culture or of sterility among a people or any section is almost a matter of metaphysics or perhaps meteorology—I don't know. What I am going to say below may not make much sense, but if you don't mind I'll ramble on a bit in my inclination and urge to make some reply to the challenging queries you have sent.

Some two or three weeks ago I was talking to the Governor of Virginia.[3] He happens to be interested in a dramatic project which I now have in the making at Williamsburg. During the course of our talk he spoke out with quite some vehemence. "North Carolina is a great state," he said. "If I could only help to wake Virginia up, get her stirring, moving forward the way your state is moving, I would feel I'd done a job of absolute value to my fellow citizens."

"But if North Carolina is on the move now," I replied, "she was long fast asleep while Virginia and South Carolina on either side of her carried the strong bit of leadership far and wide. I need only to start calling the roll—way back—Washington, Jefferson, the Randolphs, the Lees, Richard Bland,[4] the Blairs,[5] the Nelsons,[6] the Pages,[7] the Tylers,[8] the Harrisons[9] and"—

2. Edwin Greenlaw came to UNC as chairman of the English department in 1914. Greenlaw, who hired Hanford, rebuilt the departmental faculty, helped found the University of North Carolina Press, and played a large role in numerous other university developments. Sociologist Eugene C. Branson also came to UNC in 1914 and pioneered the study of rural economic and social problems.

3. Colgate W. Darden, Jr., at a meeting about *The Common Glory* (Green diary, 14 December 1946, PG-SHC).

4. Colonial leader and author of the earliest statement against British taxation (*Inquiry into the Rights of the British Colonies* [1766]).

5. James Blair founded William and Mary College in 1693 and served as its president until he died in 1743. Francis Preston Blair, journalist in Richmond, was prominent in national politics from the Jacksonian era until his death in 1876.

6. Influential family during the revolutionary era. Thomas Nelson, member of the Virginia House of Burgesses and the Continental Congress and signer of the Declaration of Independence, commanded the Virginia militia during the American Revolution and became governor in 1781.

7. John Page succeeded Thomas Nelson as governor. Thomas Jefferson Page, naval explorer in Paraguay prior to the Civil War, served in the Confederate navy.

"I know, I know," he said, "but they're all dead. What I'm talking about is the present and especially the future. Look at your University down there—your sociological work under Odum.[10] Your fine University Press. Your dramatic work. Your extension projects. Your great manufacturers—the Haines,[11] Grays,[12] Reynolds, Duke University, your recent movement in good health, your schools, your hospitals, your fine race relationship, and the flood of creative writing that is being done at Chapel Hill for instance—think of that. Dozens and dozens of books are coming out of that little village. Almost yearly. Charlottesville where our University is situated is many times as large as Chapel Hill, and yet a book rarely comes from there and when it does it is likely not to have the bite of life's teeth in it"—I'm giving him the figure of speech here. And so on, so on he went. "I could keep calling the roll. You see, I'm talking in the present and looking to the future in reference to your state's accomplishments, and you and I in speaking of Virginia have to do it in the past tense."

Well, anyway, as I told the governor, I can see that Virginia is now beginning to stir, and I prophecy great things for her people.

I believe that about the time you refer to there began to be a gathering of enthusiasm, inspiration, creative scholarship and creative living together in Chapel Hill. To be able to say why is, to repeat, a different matter. It is the custom these days to derive matters by way of historical description—a custom which of course is old and hallowed enough to be just that. Deep down I believe in constant and ever appearing newness, and in any description of causality as well as in the causal process itself, there is always an X either of form or substance which appears fresh[,] new[,] and cannot be accounted for. This X perhaps is essential to and one with the nature of the mind's awareness. Whatever it is, I believe it is, has been and will continue to be. So with this reservation I will continue.

8. Family of the tenth president.

9. Family of a signer of the Declaration of Independence (Benjamin Harrison), the ninth president (William Henry Harrison), and the twenty-third president (Benjamin Harrison, grandson of William Henry although born in Ohio).

10. Howard Odum, influential scholar who came to UNC in 1920 and as an outgrowth of his study of rural sociology founded the Institute for Research in the Social Sciences.

11. That is, Hanes, textile manufactures in Charlotte.

12. Prominent in the R. J. Reynolds Tobacco Company in Winston-Salem.

The restless bodies and spirits of the various people who settled this country of ours moved mainly through the medium of ships on water to get here. It happened that Virginia on the north of this Tar Heel commonwealth had deep and easily traveled rivers penetrating up into the heart of the seaboard to the very edge of the Blue Ridge Mountains—such as the Potomac, the York, the James. South Carolina, below us, likewise had the same sort of advantage in the Ashley and the Cooper. So accordingly the tide of moving men and trade entered at two deep seaport places. Norfolk was built and even in the time of the Revolution was a flourishing town of five or six thousand people. Charleston grew up to be a leading metropolis in the colonies. Up the James at the falls, Richmond was built. Halfway between Norfolk and Richmond the cultured little center of Williamsburg grew—here where the early bill of rights and many a document and deed for freedom was made manifest.

Now drawn like a barrier—and it was that—across the eastern seaboard of North Carolina was a stretch of treacherous sandbars and shallow inlets, complicated with the raging and diabolical weather of Cape Hatteras. So a tradition of talent and leadership grew up on either side of us. Virginia and South Carolina furnished ten important men to the early history of our country to every one North Carolina furnished. And even as late as the Civil War most of our Confederate generals came out of those two states and North Carolina furnished more private soldiers than any other southern state. In fact for generations North Carolina was a sort of hewer of wood and drawer of water commonwealth compared to her swiftly risen aristocratic neighbors north and south. When I was a little boy I heard the old description of Tar Heelia—"A valley of humiliation between two mountains of conceit." I remember with what admiration, awe and twinges of envy I would hear stories of the great plantation houses along the James and Potomac and along the Ashley and Cooper rivers. There were few if any of this sort in North Carolina. My grandfather, John Green, was pretty typical of the yeoman North Carolinian—his grandfather came down out of Virginia in the early 18th century as thousands of others did. In fact North Carolina, I would guess, was settled in great part by indentured servants who had run away, by restless almost criminal young sons, by proguing hunters and now and then a wagon train of religious emigrants—infiltrating, wandering and pouring in overland from either side—and not from the ocean, since the sandbars mentioned shut the door in the face of ships of any size. (I recall now that the failure of the Lost Colony was attributable mainly to the fact that the treachery of the Carolina seacoast made it almost impossible to supply the settlers from ships.

And Sir Walter Raleigh himself gave John White and Ananias Dare instructions that they should only come by Roanoke Island, pick up some men who had been left there by Sir Richard Grenville and go up further north and make their settlement on the deep waters of the Chesapeake. They ignored Sir Walter's orders, and so we know that group as the Lost Colony.)

I am being a little emphatic when I say that North Carolina was, up until nearly the end of the 19th century, rather much of a lost colony herself. But things get grown, institutions demand their submissives, and the eager forward spirit gets slowed down by the objects of its own creativity, and finally there comes a day when even the look of Robin Hood himself "turns again homeward."[13]

So did it happen with Virginia and South Carolina. In time a second-hand quality began to pervade their constituency. The fathers were greater than the sons and the grandfathers greater still and so over the meridian mark the process went and life began to get into reverse. (As I say, I am emphasizing a little heavily to brad the point.)

As you see, North Carolina has no such history of pride and attainment to look back to. She was a poor white state so long that all of her yearning, her urges, such as they were, were towards the future. So you might expect that if she ever did get started, she would be like a self-made man on the make—she would really go to town with a vengeance. And every inch of accomplishment was a hundred per cent on the plus side and was that much, generally speaking, an advance over his immediately preceding progenitor.

You know something of the story of the Dukes[14]—how old Wash Duke as a bare-footed married man twisted up his home-made tobacco and sold it to the occupying Federal troops around Durham.[15] I don't say that this was the

13. Echo of Alfred Tennyson, "Crossing the Bar," line 8.

14. Tobacco family headed by Washington Duke (1820–1905), then by his youngest son James Buchanan Duke (1856–1925).

15. When Lee surrendered to Grant at Appomattox, Virginia, on 9 April 1865, large Confederate and Federal armies were still in the field. General William T. Sherman with 50,000 troops in Raleigh was opposed by a Confederate army of 30,000 under General Joseph E. Johnston forty miles west in Hillsborough, and it was not until 26 April that they arrived at terms of surrender. Their conferences were held midway between Raleigh and Hillsborough, at the Bennett farmhouse near Durham. Following Lee's surrender, Washington Duke, Confederate artilleryman, walked home from New Bern, North Carolina, where he was released, and on his farm north of Durham

beginning of North Carolina's development, for the seeds of progress, the thistledown from the wings of high-flying ideals were in the air, but I think it illustrates my point. Here was old Wash Duke face to face with the miracle that the superior Yankees wanted something he had. The miracle that his handiwork was good enough for them to pay good money for. So he got busy with that bit of esthetic and economical stimulation. He did some mail order business with these Yankees after they had returned to Ohio, Indiana, Illinois or wherever they went. He got his son Buck working with him at the grinder, chopping up the leaves of tobacco into Duke's Mixture.[16] And so he got started. It wasn't long until he got stallion-proud in his mind and one of his co-workers developed the trademark of Bull Durham, the he creature, the mighty symbol of virility and invigoration.[17] (Of course the phrase "the worm will turn" is a good way to account for the phenomenon of this state's waking up. But that takes care of itself.)

Washington Duke, his son Buck, began to make good, and the American Tobacco Company came a-borning.[18] Where two men come to accomplishment, you will likely find a third or a fourth or a fifth attracted in that direction even if they have stopped in the bushes to reconnoiter. So we had other men who began to dream the economic dream in textiles, lumber, mines.

Pushing back the enemy on one front emboldens others to attack him in still other places. The stimulation appeared in the field of public education and in politics. The liberation of knowledge was heard of as a fact—but mainly in terms of economic liberation. The more education you have, said

---

found nothing to support his family (his wife was dead) but a barn full of tobacco. With the help of his sons he shredded and sacked the tobacco, labeled the sacks "Pro Bono Publico," loaded them in a wagon drawn by two blind mules, and began peddling his ware among the Federal troops and others in the area (William K. Boyd, *The Story of Durham* [Durham: Duke University Press, 1925], chapters 3 and 5).

16. Later name for Pro Bono Publico.

17. John R. Green (not a close relative of Paul) owned Bull Durham, the most famous and best-selling tobacco in the post–Civil War decades, with its trademark, the picture of a bull. He was a coworker with Duke only in the sense that they were both in the tobacco business. In fact they were bitter rivals (Boyd, *Story of Durham*, chapters 4 and 5).

18. In 1890, when Duke and Sons absorbed four of its rivals in Durham and reorganized under James B. Duke's leadership. In 1898 the American Tobacco Company also acquired Bull Durham from Green's successors (ibid., chapter 5).

the speakers, the more earning power in dollars and cents will be yours. Once started, acceleration was sure. Charles Brantley Aycock stumped the state speaking about the power of books—reading, writing, arithmetic, the Bible, Geography—and down with illiteracy. In the early years of the present century he was our governor[19] and one of our best. He was the "education governor"—perhaps our first, if we exclude Governor Jarvis[20] who was somewhat imbued with the philosophy of learning but lacked the dynamism and selling power of Aycock. There were other men who talked the same language. Walter Hines Page,[21] later ambassador to the Court of St. James, Professor McKiver, at Greensboro,[22] and numerous county superintendents of public instruction took up the chorus of their leaders. We had a movement known as moonlight schools in which the hard effort was made to wipe out illiteracy among the whites, young and old, in North Carolina. (Again a phrase like "the time was ripe" could be invoked to explain a lot of things. But that will take care of itself too.)

The carpetbaggers, poor forlorn and misguided zealots, had been rebuffed finally before the terrible undertaking they found here in the south, and the last of them had long ago gone home.[23] But some of the echoes of their teachings, some of the books they had left behind had done a little bit of leavening work among the people. Anyway there was the sense of their impress upon us—even as most of us deplored and hated them and their memory. Also the presence of Yankee soldiers up and down the length of the state, drawn from all strata and places of the Union—they too had made some mark upon us. Also, for some reason or another, a few "foreign" teachers from the north, a graduate here and there from Harvard or Yale or Princeton, had happened into the faculties of our state university and colleges. Also I think the rise of Woodrow Wilson, a North Carolinian by residence and friendship, even though Virginia-born, helped the state towards a feeling of pride in his

19. 1901–5.

20. Thomas J. Jarvis, governor, 1879–85.

21. Journalist in Raleigh in the 1870s, then in New York and Boston (*Atlantic Monthly*, 1895–98), partner in Doubleday, Page publishing company from 1899, and Wilson's ambassador to Great Britain, 1913–18.

22. Charles Duncan McIver, who persuaded the legislature to establish the first state college for women in 1891 in Greensboro, over which he presided, 1891–1906.

23. Albion Tourgée, best known and most influential of the carpetbaggers, left North Carolina for New York in 1878, after thirteen years in the state.

scholarship and the place of education in public life.[24] It may be worth noting that the University of North Carolina was the proud host to him as commencement speaker in 1912.[25]

Whatever currents, connotations, facts, tendencies, were in the air, there were enough for a sensitive man to get their impact. Such a man was Edward Kidder Graham. As president of the University of North Carolina[26] he became a man afire with a zeal for service, for true progress, for scholarship, for enlightenment, in short for true civilization. He, I think, represented the sensitive and feeling fingertips of the state. And not only was he all fingertips, he was also the strong, reaching, grasping, friendly and encouraging hand.

And he was not alone, of course. There were other sensitive young men who could hear the song on the wind with ever so slight a cocking of the ear—men like L. R. Wilson—he especially,[27] Roulhac Hamilton,[28] E. C. Branson (who was sent, called for, and got by these eager men),[29] Edwin Greenlaw, yourself, Dr. Hanford—one of the best of them all—(I make my bow with thankfulness!), Norman Förster,[30] Marvin Stacy,[31] Addison Hibbard[32] and so

24. Born in Staunton, Virginia, Wilson attended Davidson College in North Carolina (1873–74), and his family then resided a year in Wilmington (1874–75).

25. 1911.

26. From 1913 until his death in 1918.

27. While heading the UNC library (1902–32), Louis Round Wilson with Edwin Greenlaw established the University of North Carolina Press, becoming its first director (1922–32), then spearheaded creation of the School of Library Science and was its first dean (1931–32). In 1932 Wilson went to the University of Chicago to develop a School of Library Science, then returned to UNC in 1941.

28. UNC historian (1906–45) and indefatigable collector of unpublished papers and records throughout the Southeast, founded and directed the Southern Historical Collection (manuscript department of the UNC library), 1930–45.

29. In 1913 Branson, from the Georgia State Teachers College in Athens, spoke to a conference in Chapel Hill on the problems of rural life and his efforts to study and improve rural economic and social conditions. The speech so impressed leaders at Chapel Hill that President Graham, in his zeal to "carry the University to the State," brought Branson to UNC as head of a new Department of Rural Social Economics (Louis Round Wilson, *The University of North Carolina, 1900–1930: The Making of a Modern University* [Chapel Hill: University of North Carolina Press, 1957], pp. 207, 219).

30. Member of the English department (1914–30), stimulating teacher, and leading Neohumanist, helped establish the study of American literature with a series of books beginning with *Nature in American Literature* (1923).

on and so on—and not forgetting Frederick H. Koch, one of the most message-carrying of stimulators.

And so as in the active yearning sky, when after a long drought a feel of rain comes in the air, a yeastiness, a gathering of intensity, of mood and sultriness, until finally there is a whiff of a cloudlet and then others and then a combining of these cloudlets into one bigger, blacker, and procreant one, then a flash of lightning, then finally the coming of the enriching, pouring rain—somewhat like this was the gathering of the creative actuality here at Chapel Hill. In terms of weather, the rain is continuing, and the thirsty crops are not satisfied. Even now as I write these words there are some hundred books underway here in Chapel Hill—ranging from volumes of stories through plays, novels to huge humanitarian and sociological tomes. And on other fronts the endeavor is mightily continuing—in dramatic productions, in the University Press, in the extension work, library science, business foundation, medicine, etc., etc.

But alas, I am afraid I glimpse yonder in the distance the breaking of the cloud and a sign of dry weather to return. I hope to God I am mistaken. But our educational leadership seems to me to be weakening here. To change the figure—Watch a flock of birds flying across the land, say they are blackbirds, bluebirds, or robins—whatever they are, they follow and swerve and tend rhythmically after their leader. I have seen flocks of birds mill around in the sky—just milling, energized but in frantic indecision. I hope our faculty flock resembles the first figure and not the last. But as I say, I am apprehensive.

To repeat, you have done your part in helping this "cultural" phenomenon to be actualized here, and I always look back to the days you used to read Bobby Burns and Wordsworth to us. And I look back with the same sort of thankfulness too to that day when you took me aside on your front porch down on Cobb Terrace and gave me a bawling out for triflingness.

With affectionate greetings,[33]

Among the clippings Harpers sent me about my recent little volume of stories,

31. From the mathematics and engineering department, was chairman of the faculty (1910–19) and acting president (1918–19) following Graham's death.

32. Member of the English department (1919–30), pioneered the study of southern literature and coauthored the influential *Handbook to Literature* (1936) with W. F. Thrall.

33. Hanford thanked Green "for the interpretation of the flowering period of Chapel Hill which you so generously wrote out for me" ([1947], PG-SHC) but did not publish an autobiography.

*Salvation on a String*, was yours. It was very fine and flattering and I thank you.[34]

## 208. To Norman Förster

[Greenwood Road, Chapel Hill, N.C.]
23 March 1947

Dear Norman Förster:[1]

I had a big time at your house last night, and I hope the bigness of my pleasure didn't squeeze down that of someone else. But when such tremendous and mighty subjects as that under discussion last night rise to the fore I always want to fling myself headlong into the turmoil of their fermentation. Maybe I am over-hasty in my grabbing at certain conclusions, but I must repeat—it seems incredible to me that any absolute should be charged with having precedence over another in any hierarchical arrangement which would appear appreciably true to human requirements. When Walter Pater says that poetry in its higher reaches aspires to music, I think he can only mean, if he has real meaning in his statement, that all arts in their essentialness share a quality of identity.[2] Of course I know he has reference to "sound" in poetry, but this use of the word is arbitrary. Could a wonderful Chippendale chair aspire to be a Fifth Century figurine, or vice versa. Not at all except in "aspiring" to be in and of the nature of beauty itself. (And I am using the word beauty here in the Platonic sense.)

Moreover, it seems so obvious to me that the high priests of literature and the arts can "sell" their commodity to the world in terms of utility that the

34. "A Master Spins Yarns from Folklore," *Cleveland News*, 5 October 1946.

---

1. Förster had retired to Chapel Hill from the University of Iowa in the spring of 1946. The evening before the present letter Green sat up "most of the night over at Norman Förster's with a group of English teachers and estheticians . . . talking about the place of literature and the liberal arts curriculum" and had "found out . . . from the professorial ranks that literature and the arts specifically and generally are being put to it to defend themselves from the on-rush of pragmatic group activities" (Paul Green to Howard Mumford Jones, 23 March 1947, PG-SHC).

2. In "The School of Giorgione," in *The Renaissance* (New York: Macmillan, 1905), Pater, arguing that form and material are indistinguishable only in music, said, "All art constantly aspires towards the condition of music" (p. 140).

wonder to me is how they can all prevent themselves from immediately taking to the highway and roads as Jeremiahs of burning eloquence.

Long ago I fastened upon one of many truths—namely, that the beautiful is not only the true and the good but it is also the truth truly and righteously useful. An extreme illustration—an Indian's tomahawk—is most a tomahawk when he has cherished it unto himself sufficiently to have decorated its handle and even its blade with cosmic interpretations and appreciations of his own.

The humanists can stand up on any day, on any box or in any pulpit or pour forth their statements in any pages of books and magazines whatsoever to the affect that the way of life by bread alone leads but to destruction. The true humanists of the world never concert their acts to the destruction of the Cassino Abbey[3] or Bach's ancient organ squatted awesomely in its own churchly home.[4] They never by putting their heads together lead a nation into three hundred billion dollars bankruptcy indebtedness for shells and guns and poison gases and pensions and atomic bombs and psychiatric wards for the maimed and undone on the fields of battle. The battle fields of the humanists are the places where joy and song and good health and abounding vitality live—not die. It is only the fellows who in their own narrow scientific and technological fields are forgetful of the deeper and more cultural loyalties and principles of existence who lead us into such disastrous temptations and degrading results. What more spontaneous doctrine could be yours and your confreres'! To allow pedestrian and plodding blinded men to push the humanities into a defensive position is a great and unutterable sin on the part of the defenders of thc faith. Now, not tomorrow, today, all of us should leap to action and carry our banner—and I say our banner even if I believe in certain excesses beyond the envisaging of the golden-meaned liberalists—proudly and dramatically high. And it is easy to dramatize our doctrine, for, to repeat, it can be shown that not only does our religion fee the spirit but it helps keep the

3. The Abbey of St. Benedict at Monte Cassino, reduced to rubble by Allied bombers on 15 February 1944 during the invasion of Italy because it was erroneously believed that German troops were using the abbey as an observation post.

4. Perhaps the organ in the Marienkirche at Lübeck, destroyed by the British fire bombing of Lübeck, a U-boat port, on the night of 28–29 March 1942. Bach spent nearly three months in Lübeck at the end of 1705 under the inspiration and tutelage of Buxtehude, organist of the Marienkirche (Charles Sanford Terry, *Bach: A Biography* [London: Oxford University Press, 1933], pp. 68–69).

body healthy, well-housed, and well-clothed. In other words ours is a religion and should be so carried abroad.

Rather than finding discouragement in the present setup, I find encouragement. I am glad for example to find that the world itself, humanity at large, is faced with the same sort of problem of catastrophe or salvation which today and tonight faces the individual man. It is good for the world to be brought sharp up against the question of whether it shall restrain its appetites and cruel selfishnesses and follow a deeper ethic of brotherhood which leads to survival and practical and worthwhile accomplishment or whether it shall under whatever guise of narrow nationalism or shibboleths of honor and greed cast itself headlong over the precipice and perish into everlasting nothingness. It is good that we have reached this pass. We have a moral decision to make.

So I count it just as good in their way that the liberal arts must come forth out of their schematism and cloistered bindings and fall afoul of the enemy in the broad open daylight upon the dusty highway of traffic. And I believe they will so come forth and in louder voices—even such voices as H. L. Mencken and Miguel de Unamuno[5]—cry out its virtues and its wears[6] even as it lays on in the battle.

So welcome each rebuff that turns life's smoothness rough![7]—lines I learned under you long ago, though perhaps you don't remember that they meant much to anybody at that time, since in those days Browning and certain of the Victorians were being poisonously and scathingly attacked from certain high windy places.

As everybody knows, you have been doing your part in the establishment of civilization on this globe for many a year. Right now all the wisdom you have accumulated during these years needs to be somehow packed up and discharged against these erring traitors who have risen up in the true State. This is a bad figure. Maybe I should say they need to be bathed, baptized and blessed with the wisdom of your spirit. How can that happen. The new intuition!—and with the proper loudness!

I am sending you by separate mail a copy of my latest findings—a book of intensely local stories titled *Salvation On A String*. I don't mean the title to be funny. I simply wanted to call a bit of attention once more in an impractical

5. Spanish existentialist, whose *Del Sentimiento Trágico de la Vida* (1913) shows the primacy he attached to individual experience.

6. That is, wares.

7. Robert Browning, "Rabbi Ben Ezra," stanza 6.

practical surrounding to the instability of matters including the salvation of souls.

Ever affectionately,

I hope we can get some walks in now and then. It is not far from your house to mine and from mine to yours, and most of it is woods, which is not a bad item.[8]

## 209. To William Sharpe[1]

[Williamsburg, Va.]
8 July 1947

Dear Bill—

I am glad we had a chance to talk some matters over there in Manteo even if briefly. And I am in your debt too for a good supper.

I have been thinking further as always about *The Lost Colony* and ways and means to improve its quality and reach as time goes on. And I want to repeat that I shall never let up one lick in my efforts for its welfare either from the point of view of hard and unremitting toil or from the point of view of author with artistic oversight over it. Also I shall work likewise and in the same spirit of dedication to see that *The Common Glory* with its ideal of democracy cooperates to the fullest to increase the crowds coming to Roanoke Island where the spiritual birth of our nation took place. I'm sure we both agree that the key word, Democracy, is what we're all striving for in these later days. The voice of John Borden in *The Lost Colony* and the voice of Thomas Jefferson in

8. Förster lived on Gimghoul Road, a short street running east from the UNC campus toward Green's home about a mile away across a wooded valley.

1. As chief of the News Bureau in the North Carolina Department of Conservation and Development, William Sharpe (1903–1970) headed the publicity committee for *The Lost Colony.* Green went to Roanoke Island for the opening of *The Lost Colony* on 1 July and in a conversation there with Sharpe on 4 July suggested a cooperative advertising campaign with *The Common Glory* in which the ads for each play would include information about the other. The suggestion triggered the disturbing revelation that Sharpe and other supporters of *The Lost Colony* resented *The Common Glory.* With Rockefeller Foundation money behind it, its promotion could dwarf *The Lost Colony* and threaten attendance on Roanoke Island. After returning to Williamsburg, where *The Common Glory* was being readied for its opening on 17 July, Green wrote to Sharpe, using stationery of the Jamestown Corporation.

*The Common Glory* speak out, each in his different and dramatic way, this our American theme. And each voice is the stronger because they speak together. (Who in this world would want to weaken one child because another had been born?)[2]

This is to me a thrilling fact, Bill. And there can be only real and vital cooperation in this fact—only increased strength—and never knifing competition. And I shall strive with all my might to see that this is so.

I'd like to come over soon and sit down for a long talk with you. Also I hope to get together with Governor Broughton[3] and Bruce Etheridge[4] and Billy Carmichael[5] and others before our board meeting in August.[6] There are many things the production staff and myself need help and advice on[7]—looking to the continued development of the play there on Roanoke Island—a play you have done so much to help and strengthen.[8]

Affectionately,

2. Parenthetical sentence added in revision.

3. Chairman of the Roanoke Island Historical Association, producer of *The Lost Colony.*

4. Director of the Department of Conservation and Development and member of the board of directors of the Roanoke Island Historical Association.

5. Comptroller of UNC and chief fund-raiser for *The Lost Colony.*

6. Originally this and the previous sentence read: "I'd like to come over soon and sit down for a long talk with you, and talk also with Billy Carmichael and Governor Broughton and Bruce Etheridge and others, before our board meeting in August." The revision arranges the names in order of political prominence.

7. Originally the clause read: "There are many things Sam Selden as director and the production staff and myself as author need help and advice on."

8. Green sent a copy of this letter to Broughton, Etheridge, Carmichael, Selden, and others. Although brochures on each play were made available at the site of the other, no joint advertising campaign developed. "It is very difficult to do these things satisfactorily," Sharpe explained in a letter to Green, "and unless and until *Lost Colony* is a bigger financial success than it is at the moment, we do not feel that we should spare any efforts in another direction. This is not, I hope, selfishness on our part, but there is no point in our trying to be all things to all peoples at this stage in an enterprise which is, frankly, in much need of such feeble help as we can give it" (11 July 1947, PG-SHC).

## 210. To William A. Wright[1]

[Greenwood Road, Chapel Hill, N.C.]
3 August 1947

Dear Billy Wright—

I felt like apologizing for my declamation concerning the tickets the other day, but I didn't find it opportune to do so. I later had a serious talk with the responsible parties, and I hope matters will be mended by the time I meet with Mr. Darden tomorrow or next day.

This note is neither an apology nor a bellyache, just a statement of fact for your further information solely. We have had our play open now more than two weeks and yet day after day from 5:00 to 6:30 P.M. the public is still unable to buy a ticket in Williamsburg to it. Day after day complaints arise from people who wander around wanting to know where and how one can buy a ticket—(There is still no adequate sign announcing our headquarters. Yesterday I learned the sign had been made more than a month ago and was still lying in behind Phi Beta Hall. I authorized its being put to use at once. I mention this only as one of many illustrations of how triune and multiple-headed authority works to frustration.)

At the same time I hasten to say I am humbly and devoutly thankful that we—all working in harmony and good fellowship—have been able to accomplish so much. And I look forward next year to a great and triumphant undertaking. But to go back to the tickets—there simply is no sense in all our complaints being met with the gentlemanly explanation that "we're counting up"—"please come back later" or "go to the theatre box-office after 6:30" or "it takes time for us to get organized," etc. My answer to this last is that it doesn't take time, it takes intelligence. And intelligence has not yet been applied in selling tickets in Williamsburg to *The Common Glory*.

Well, I'm counting on all these matters being straightened out this week. And in the meantime of course my business is to keep making the play better and better.

Cordially,

1. *The Common Glory* opened on 17 July. Wright was secretary of the Jamestown Corporation, producer of the play, and responsible for daily operations.

## 211. To Julian Johnson

[Greenwood Road, Chapel Hill, N.C.]
2 September 1947

Dear Julian:[1]

This is just to let you know I deeply appreciated the nice letter you sent me about *The Common Glory.* The play will finish its summer run at Williamsburg on September 14. We have had a rather spectacular success with it so far as crowds go.[2] Next year I hope to have both it and *The Lost Colony* down at Manteo (just ending its tenth year) flourishing out in the kind of productions I have dreamed of for them both for quite awhile. It looks as if we will have enough money to do the job up right for both the plays.

I hope everything is going well with you and that you and Darryl Zanuck[3] and the other brains in the organization there are planning some real dynamic, hard-hitting pictures about American democracy and he-men in America and American ideals—and things of this sort. Hollywood has for so long fed and fattened the youth of this land on easy success, passionate and senseless love, bedroom and sly appraisal of women's bodies, etc., etc. that the time has come for the great interpretative mediums of American genius to show forth something for people to live by. In other words—what is the meaning of America? If there ever was a time when this meaning ought to be spoken forth in ringing terms that time is now.

In a few weeks I am going up to Washington to meet with some of the Congressmen and Senators about doing a big show right there in the middle of the country's capital in which I try to set forth some of the ideals that have made us great as a people and without which ideals we are certain to grow

1. Brooks Atkinson reviewed the opening night performance of *The Common Glory* (*New York Times,* 19 July 1947, p. 11, cols. 2–4), then devoted his Sunday column to the play as well, saying it "creates a mood of reverence and wonder" and "is a religious rite. Without being pompous or sanctimonious, it serves the American tradition" (*New York Times,* 20 July 1947, sec. 2, p. 1, cols. 1–2). Julian Johnson, story editor at Twentieth Century-Fox and friend since Green's earliest Hollywood days, was "thrilled" by the Sunday article and wrote that "the scope and vision of your dramatic imaginings continue on a high plane. And, an original one. No man in America can write the things you are writing, nor do them half as well" (4 August 1947, PG-SHC).

2. Attendance during the eight and a half–week run of *The Common Glory* was about 90,000 (Paul Green to H. P. Caemmerer, 18 September 1947, PG-SHC).

3. Head of Twentieth Century–Fox.

more and more weak and ultimately fall into second-ratedness without ever having reached the true greatness for which our forefathers died.[4]

I remember not so many years ago urging Darryl Zanuck to make a picture about Boulder Dam—the dam was then a-building.[5] He laughed quite easily and said nobody would be interested. What a drama that was—the harnessing of a great river, the splurge and outpouring of muscle power and brains and energy, the triumph of men's will over indomitable masses of stone and water and earth! If it had been made right, everybody would have liked it.

Of course as we all know, one of the great weaknesses of our Democracy is the constant urge of our leaders to give over the hard grind of leadership and claim to find leadership among the people. The people don't give leadership, they require it. So Mr. Zanuck says—"The people wouldn't like such a picture."

Hollywood still has great leadership to give. The time gets shorter.[6]

Ever affectionately,

## 212. To Bette Odets[1]

[Greenwood Road, Chapel Hill, N.C.]
8 November 1947

Dear Bette:

Many thanks for your special delivery which has just come relative to Hanns Eisler and his wife. I can think of nothing more dismal and discourag-

4. The sesquicentennial of Washington, D.C., as the national capital would be in 1950, and during the summer of 1947 President Truman appointed a committee to plan the occasion. In early August 1947 Green met with the committee and began looking for a site for an outdoor historical play, and he would return to Washington for a meeting on 7 October.

5. Constructed between 1933 and 1937, Boulder Dam (now Hoover Dam) was the highest dam in the world at the time (over 700 feet).

6. Johnson replied that "you are the only playwright I know who puts patriotism above personal ambition. The sincerity and honesty of your productions has spoken so loudly of this that I am sure this is the reason for the great contemporary success of your pieces" (5 September 1947, PG-SHC).

---

1. On 26 September 1947 the House Un-American Activities Committee (HUAC) recommended deportation of Hollywood composer Johannes (Hanns) Eisler, who

ing to them both than the prospect of deportation. Of course as you know I am by profession and effort a thorough-going American democrat. I happen to believe that the Declaration of Independence, the Bill of Rights and the Constitution of the United States are documents generous and wide-reaching and inspiring enough to absorb the best activities of all of us. If Hanns Eisler and his wife happen to believe differently or—happen to believe that the truth resides in Moscow and not this side of the Atlantic—even so my sympathy goes out to them. If the world were normal now and there were havens and refuges of average comfort I would not be so moved to work in their cause. But these are abnormal times. A home is hard to find—a good home—even in these United States. And I wish all people on this earth good homes. So I will do what I can to help. If Eisler lied about his passport, if he got into the United States by false pretences, if he fails to appreciate the past characters of Thomas Jefferson, Washington, Lincoln, and my friend the unknown folklore philosopher who lives in almost every and any American hamlet—even so, to repeat, I will reach out my hand to help however weak it be. This is no time for grudges or for tit-for-tat remembrances. These are the days of the open friendly hand and not the clenched fist in order that you and I may live, our children may live and flourish, and Cliff[2] may continue to write good plays.

And of course my best love to him.

As you know I have no use at all for the kind of politics, un-American politics, being practiced by Messrs. Rankin and Thomas.[3] The recent farce in Washington[4] was just that, and the above two gentlemen came off much worse in the show than they expected. But I will add too that the politics of

---

had been convicted of passport fraud in August 1946. Eisler and his wife, Louise, fled Germany in 1933 and in 1940 entered the United States from Mexico on a nonquota visa granted on his claim to be a professor, a claim disputed in the 1946 passport trial. Bette Odets (ca. 1921–1954), feeling that Eisler was being harassed by the HUAC because he was a member of the Communist party, sent Green a petition, directed to U.S. attorney general Tom Clark, which protested Eisler's deportation on the grounds that he was a respected and productive composer and had been politically inactive during his years in the United States. She urged Green to sign it (4 November 1947, PG-SHC).

2. Odets's husband, whom Green knew from the Group Theatre.

3. John E. Rankin, representative from Mississippi, vocal member of the HUAC, and J. Parnell Thomas, representative from New Jersey, chairman of the committee.

4. The HUAC opened its hearings on communism in the motion picture industry on 20 October 1947.

Sam Ornitz, Charlie Chaplin, John Howard Lawson, Dalton Trumbo,[5] and others seem to me to be just as un-American at the other extreme. Now whether a man's political beliefs and thinkings are his own personal and sacred property is a deep question. I am inclined to think they are. But to use freedom of speech and assembly to foster movements which would destroy those very freedoms and rights makes a fellow put on his thinking cap—and so on and so on.

Again by the way, the letter[6] which the Composers' Guild of Great Britain sent to the Ambassador of the United States strikes me as being rather sassy[7] and would I should think tend to prejudice the ambassador against Mr. Eisler and his wife rather than softening him towards their cause.[8]

Ever,

## 213. To Mrs. Clyde M. Kelly[1]

[Greenwood Road, Chapel Hill, N.C.]
10 November 1947

Dear Mrs. Kelly:

I appreciate your kind words about my little whirling dervish talk the other afternoon at the Bull's Head Book Shop. Yes, I did say, as one of the elements

5. Hollywood figures charged with Communist affiliation during the hearing.

6. Included with Odets's petition.

7. In tone the letter is shrill (denying Eisler an exit permit for work on a film in France "amounts to a sentence of death, a non-judicial sentence of death, upon this outstanding musical artist") and condescending ("Your Government's action in refusing an exit permit on the mere instigation of a press campaign suggests that it may be compliant to the demands of the House Committee for Un-American Activities") (PG-SHC).

8. Green did not sign the petition even though Odets asked him a second time to do so. "It was my impression from your letter [the present one] that despite your reservations you would sign the petition," she wrote. "Since it was not inclosed, I am wondering whether its omission was an oversight . . . or was my impression incorrect?" (18 November 1947, PG-SHC). In March 1948, Eisler and his wife were deported to Austria, later becoming citizens of Czechoslovakia.

1. On Wednesday afternoon, 5 November 1947, Green gave a talk on *The Common Glory* at the Bull's Head Bookshop on the UNC campus (*Daily Tar Heel*, 4 November 1947, p. 1, cols. 7–8). The talk, attended by Mrs. Kelly from Durham, was wide-

of my moving belief, that I prefer to think of man as having created God rather than God man. By that I simply meant to put the hard fact into the face of my listeners that each individual in this world bears on himself ultimate responsibility not only for his behavior but for the ideals that energize such behavior—at least I think so. Of course I am talking about a grown-up normal people and not about mishap personalities and little children who have not got dry behind the ears.

I believe with the Gospel of St. John that there was a Light that came into this world, the word made manifest, a logos, a Tao (to change the terminology), a Way, a principle of righteousness which permeates the awareness, the intellectual activity, the being of man. Now I don't think animals and plants and vegetables have this awareness, have this sense of a principle of guidance and behavior. The essence principle—and here I would spell it with a capital P—I call God. Now if all human beings were obliterated and there was no human awareness in the great eternal stretches of time and space, then for me there would be no God nor godliness. God is a concept, a methodology, a logos (to repeat) of rich and optimistic creativeness. The word rich is obvious in its meanings, and by "optimistic" I mean the upward lift in man's aspirations and thinking and efforts. For instance, there have been deposited along the reaches of past time numberless golden truths—truths wrapped up in words, made manifest in statements—such as, "A soft answer turneth away wrath," "Overcome evil with good," "The law came and I died," "Only the slayer is really the slain," "This is the accepted hour," "Only in death does life have its source," "In the gateway of death man has set up his shining dream of immortality," "The basis of civilization is ethical," "Except ye believe ye shall likewise perish," etc., etc.

Man gives birth to these principles and these words and only man. Man grows in grace insofar as he identifies his person with such principles, and it is in that process of identification that the creative power of man is expressed in its most intense and free expression. Now good to me being such a principle as I described above, then only in men's souls, hearts, persons—whatever you call it or them—can God live. A corollary fact to this statement can be put forth as

---

ranging, and she described it as "the most enlightening and inspiring talk I've ever heard, even from a pulpit." But she "understood [Green] to say that: Man created God, not God who created man! That, to me was astounding and confusing. I believe you didn't say that there is no God. What I should like to know is your conception of God. And His relation to man" (7 November 1947, PG-SHC).

follows: Just suppose that every human being forgot Jesus Christ entirely, his name meant nothing, his history meant nothing, he had no significance to humanity at all. Then he would be truly dead. So it is in our remembrance and our efforts to make him a living force that he may be said to survive. Thus it is that we create him daily—or not. Thus was he created as a spiritual leader from the very beginning—that is, through his effect upon his hearers. Thus you might say without the ear to hear there is no sound. And so the ear creates sound. If there were a God preceding man's awareness of him then I would call him a chaos waiting for the formative power of the human design.

In commentation let me repeat what I said in my talk that each thing makes itself, each thing is itself, the heavy sleet is its own self, my elm trees are their own selves, the two meet, the weaker suffer disorder and breakage. Now obviously though the baby grows itself in the sheltering umbrage of its mother and later expands into further growth with its food and drink and play, still it is always first its own master. It is the source of its own process of growth and the process of growth is its true self as child. I believe that this fact of self-growth applies likewise to spiritual matters—to use a term that makes the physiological psychiatrists shudder in their unstable neural systems.

I didn't mean to add confusion to confusion and pile up so many words. I hope you can make sense out of part of the above.

And so I end by repeating that for me man created and will continue to create God rather than God being the creator. I'm sure all this sounds know-it-all.

With cordial greetings and regards,

## 214. To M. B. Andrews[1]

[Greenwood Road, Chapel Hill, N.C.]
29 November 1947

Dear Mr. Andrews:

I am glad to have your letter of a few days ago relative to the two matters of capital punishment and an epilogue for *The Common Glory* play. I respect

1. On Friday morning, 14 November 1947, three men convicted of rape were put to death in the gas chamber at Central Prison in Raleigh. The state had already executed twenty-three men that year, and ten remained on death row. On 14 November Green drafted a protest against capital punishment and sent it as an open letter to the *News and Observer*. Paying for one crime by committing another "seems senseless," he said,

your feeling in the first item, and I presume that by your statement, "I think capital punishment is wise at the present time" you mean that if the death penalty were abolished now and some horrible crime, for instance, were committed in North Carolina then the outraged feelings of the people (realizing that the guilty criminal would not be put to death) would pour themselves out and cause a lynching. This is to say from your point of view that capital punishment may destroy a guilty one and by so doing prevents the people generally from misbehaving. As I say, I respect your point of view as to this but I cannot agree that your reasoning is sound. By any test of civilization, punishment should be of a conditional sort—that is, if we ever hope or expect to climb in the scale of quality of living. I sometimes bet for fun with my friends on football games and I wouldn't mind betting with you on this matter—that you cannot possibly by any degree of logic prove that the gas chamber and the electric chair do not belong in the same category of cruelty and blindness as the medieval instruments of torture and punishment such as the rack, the screw, the wheel, the iron tongs, the stake, and the iron virgin. We look with amazement, disgust and scorn at those ancient means of human "betterment." If the chamber and the chair are not identical with them, what are they? In fact, I could come nearer proving by logic that they are even more horrible than the long ago methods and means.

I love North Carolina. I believe in the scriptures that men should put down their buckets where they are, fish in their own home waters. I would like to see a program of betterment for this state—something definite laid out in items, 1, 2, 3 to work at. Certainly one of the items would be a thorough and scientific

---

"and is only a continuance of the old Mosaic law of an eye for an eye and a tooth for a tooth outmoded by Jesus of Nazareth two thousand years ago." He denied that the threat of execution is a deterrent to crime and maintained that the way "to build the lives of our illiterate and misguided citizens into a better future is to start at the bottom with education and encouragement and understanding one with another. The use of the grotesque and horrible gas chamber in our penal system is only a further proof of our failure to measure up to the problem" (*NO*, 18 November 1947, p. 4, cols. 4–5). M. B. Andrews, owner of an insurance agency in Goldsboro, North Carolina, wrote to Green about the piece and also about *The Common Glory*, which he saw during the summer. "Capital punishment is wise at the present time," Andrews thought, "especially in certain rare cases. However, I appreciate your feeling, and I think you made a strong case against this type of punishment. Though I have never met you personally, I have long known something of your deep feeling for the fundamental things in life" (26 November 1947, PG-SHC).

study made of our penology. I am so sure that our scientific findings would be identical with those instincts of humaneness in all of us that amelioration and positive action as to this question would result.

I like your imaginative depiction of a possible epilogue interpretation for *The Common Glory* and I will think about it.[2] However, I have so much of democratic drama to cram into two hours that I am pushed for time and I don't see just how I could work out such an epilogue. But as I say I will think about it and I most cordially thank you for your interest in writing me.

Sincerely yours,

## 215. To Jonathan Daniels[1]

[Greenwood Road, Chapel Hill, N.C.]
23 December 1947

Dear Jonathan:

Just a note to welcome you back to North Carolina and to wish you and Lucy[2] and the family a happy Christmas. We have started up our regular Chapel Hill writing group here, meeting each Sunday evening at 8:00 o'clock at the home of one of the members. We would all love to have you come over

2. Andrews suggested an epilogue "pointing toward world peace, based upon world understanding under law, and under world government." On the night he attended *The Common Glory* the audience was deeply moved, and he visualized just such an epilogue: "A young girl, age 10, dressed in shining white silk, crowned with diadem trimmed with gleaming silver stars, reminiscent of the Star of Bethlehem. I saw her standing in an attitude of prayer, with eyes and hands lifted to high Heaven. Behind her in the shadows, I visualized a trumpeter who, after sounding his horn, spoke a few brief words to the end that world government might be established to promote and guarantee world peace."

1. Jonathan Daniels (1902–1981) was a friend since college days at UNC (B.A., 1921). During the 1930s as owner and editor of the *News and Observer* in Raleigh he advocated New Deal programs, then held several high positions in President Roosevelt's wartime administration, and in 1946 went back to his family newspaper. At the time of the present letter he had recently returned to Raleigh from Geneva, Switzerland, where he went in November as the U.S. delegate to the United Nations Subcommission for the Prevention of Discrimination and the Protection of Minorities.

2. Daniels's wife.

some time and read from or talk about that novel of yours.[3] The group consists of Daphne Athas,[4] Noel Houston,[5] James Street,[6] James Childers,[7] Betty Smith, Clare Leighton,[8] Frances Patton,[9] Joe Jones,[10] Walter Carroll,[11] Jessie Rehder,[12] Josephina Niggli,[13] Phillips Russell (when he will come), Foster Fitz-Simons,[14] and two or three others who are coming in after Christmas. A Chapel Hill group has been meeting off and on since 1932 or -3. Of course Hollywood and other excursions have interrupted things. I hope now for some months we will be able to stick together pretty well. Our next

3. Daniels's most recent book was *Frontiers on the Potomac* (1946), based on his experience in Roosevelt's administration (he was press secretary when Roosevelt died in 1945), and his next would be on Truman, *The Man of Independence* (1949). His only novel, *Clash of Angels*, was published in 1930. In an interview he said: "I'm always writing a novel. I'm afraid I'm a frustrated novelist." He also feared, however, that "I operate best when I have to meet a deadline; with a novel you don't" (*New York Times*, 15 October 1950, sec. 7, p. 41, col. 2).

4. A 1943 graduate of UNC whose first novel, *The Weather of the Heart*, was published in 1947.

5. From Oklahoma, a novelist (*The Great Promise* [1946]) and short story writer, and neighbor in Greenwood.

6. Journalist and novelist from Mississippi, whose *The Biscuit Eater* was published in 1941.

7. Novelist from Alabama (*Mumbojumbo* [1941]) and colonel in army intelligence during the war (*War Eagles: The Story of the Eagle Squadron* [1943]).

8. From England, an artist (*Sometimes—Never*, drawings [1939]), writer, and engraver (*Four Hedges: A Gardener's Chronicle*, text and engravings [1935]; *Southern Harvest*, text and engravings [1943]), then completing a biography of her mother, *Tempestuous Petticoat: The Story of an Invincible Edwardian* (1947).

9. A 1926 UNC graduate and Playmaker, then at work on the Miss Dove stories that would be published in 1954 as *Good Morning, Miss Dove.*

10. Newspaperman and 1931 graduate of UNC whose *1-B Soldier* (1944) was a humorous account of the foot soldier in World War II.

11. Newspaperman and playwright, whose *Tin Top Valley* was produced in New York City by the American Negro Theater in February 1947.

12. Friend of writers and teacher of creative writing at UNC from 1947 until her death in 1967 (*The Nature of Fiction* [1948]; ed., *Chapel Hill Carousel* [1967]).

13. From Mexico, joined the Carolina Playmakers in 1935, wrote numerous Mexican folk plays and stories.

14. Formerly a dancer with Ted Shawn, on the Playmakers staff and at work on a novel, *Bright Leaf* (1948).

meeting is on Sunday night January 4 at my house. Maybe you and Lucy could plan to come over and have dinner with us before-hand.

Elizabeth and I are taking the children up to New York the day after Christmas for a week's seeing of shows[15] and we will be back on January 3. We will give you a ring about the dinner and the meeting.

Hope you spoke some light and had some fun there in Switzerland!

Ever,

## 216. To Gerald W. Johnson[1]

[Greenwood Road, Chapel Hill, N.C.]
4 January 1948

Dear Gerald:

I certainly appreciated that nice letter you sent me sometime ago. Since then I have had further dealings with the Washington group relative to the sesquicentennial celebration and the George Washington drama which I had

15. *Brigadoon* (Lerner and Loewe), *Allegro* (Hammerstein and Rodgers), *Finian's Rainbow* (Harburg, Saidy, and Lane), *Antony and Cleopatra* (with Katharine Cornell), *Medea* (Jeffers's adaptation, with Judith Anderson, directed by John Gielgud), *Oklahoma!* (Hammerstein and Rodgers), *The Mikado* (D'Oyly Carte production), *Crime and Punishment* (adapted by Rodney Ackland, with John Gielgud and Lillian Gish), and *Ice Time* (ice show featuring Sonja Henie) (Paul Green to Erma Green, 27 November 1947, and Erma Green to Paul Green, 17 December 1947, PG-SHC).

---

1. Gerald W. Johnson (1890–1980), historical writer, commentator on the South in the tradition of H. L. Mencken, and longtime friend of Green, had been an editorial writer on the *Greensboro Daily News* (1913–24), professor of journalism at UNC (1924–26), then colleague of Mencken on the *Baltimore Sun* until 1943, when he turned to free-lance writing. Recently he wrote to encourage Green on the George Washington play Green was contemplating for the sesquicentennial celebration in Washington, D.C. In dealing with our great historical figures, Johnson mused, "we have gone through the hero-worshipping phase, and the debunking phase and, to a large extent, through the fact-finding phase. . . . But only in rare instances have we as yet attempted the esthetic approach. Sandburg's *Lincoln* is an instance, . . . and so [is] your Roanoke Island thing. Yet what is scholarship for, if not to supply art with reliable material? It is the artistic treatment that assimilates a hero into the very tissues of the nation. I hope you will have the opportunity to make Royal George a genuine emotional experience" (31 October 1947, PG-SHC).

in mind. Some difficulties seem to be developing there, and I am not too certain that the whole project will not fail so far as I am concerned. I found a spot in Rock Creek Park,[2] sequestered, aloof, beautiful and unique for building the outdoor theatre. General Grant[3] and others okayed my wishes with thorough good will, but of late the political boys have expressed a contrary wish about the play. They desire to build a temporary set-up down near the Washington monument and there put on the "pageant" where everybody will find it of easy access. Of course all along I have pointed out the two great enemies of these symphonic drama activities—city turmoil and airplane noises. But the boys don't seem to be too much disturbed by those disturbances. They consider the matter from the point of view of the eye and not from the ear. In a conversation yesterday with Representative Sol Bloom[4] I made it quite clear that I could not be interested in doing the drama in such a place as has lately been talked of. This sort of project takes a great deal out of a man, and under the best circumstances the results hardly are surcease enough for falling hair, puffy eyes, stomach ulcers, and physical dyspepsia.

Our Williamsburg venture last summer flourished amazingly.[5] I have revised the drama and been over plans for the re-opening of it on July 2 next. I would certainly be glad to have you down to see the thing and enjoy what Colgate Darden calls "the damn snobbery of the 18th century" here in Williamsburg. As for me I love it, being fed on corn, peas and after-the-Civil-War thinned soup.

Congratulations on the Paul Jones book.[6] You keep putting in the licks for light, uplift, entertainment and the promised land. I salute you and shake your hand.

As for the recent Washington show[7]—Parnell Thomas, Sam Ornitz, John

2. In the northwest section of Washington, D.C.

3. Major General Ulysses S. Grant III, chairman of the Park and Planning Commission for the district.

4. Of New York, member of the Sesquicentennial Commission.

5. In its first season *The Common Glory* attracted national attention (Brooks Atkinson, "Virginia's Glory," *New York Times*, 27 July 1947, sec. 2, p. 1, cols. 1–2) and large audiences ("According to the figures I have just received, 81,877 people attended the show during its 8 week run" [Green diary, 3 October 1947, PG-SHC]).

6. *The First Captain: The Story of John Paul Jones* (1947).

7. Hearings of the Hollywood Ten before the House Un-American Activities Committee, chaired by J. Parnell Thomas of New Jersey, opened in October 1947. Johnson's letter to Green began with the teasing lines: "Are you really any good? The

Howard Lawson, Alvah Bessie, Albert Maltz, and other good friends of mine—they are being taken care of as many an absurd anomaly is—by the passage of a few weeks of all-powerful corrosive and easing time. I know the Hollywood boys well, have been in their homes, heard them talk about giving a thousand dollars a week per to the Communist party, have warned them against continuing in ignorance of the Jeffersonian tradition and their keen affirmation of Lenin and Stalin by contrary, etc., etc. The last time I saw John Howard Lawson he was sitting on the steps of the administration building at UCLA. He and I had an argument. Quoth John—"Heads are going to roll."—"Yes," I replied with some heat, "and Goddammit, you mean my head, and I don't like it!"

Well, it all was rather dumb. It had better be forgotten, hadn't it? The truth is I don't like the politics of Charlie Chaplin, Albert Maltz and their buddies any better than I do the politics and methods of Parnell Thomas, Monsieur Rankin[8] and their friends. I do happen to like Thomas Jefferson. So I keep telling the fellows when we meet—"Go read Thomas Jefferson." Is that right?

More power to you, and best wishes and affectionate greetings for the new year to you and yours. Elizabeth joins me therein.

Ever,

## 217. To John E. Pomfret[1]

[Greenwood Road, Chapel Hill, N.C.]
31 January 1948

Dear Jack:

I have just mailed you at Miss Hunt's request a statement concerning the proposed theatre institute for the summer.[2]

---

question has been raised in my mind by the fact that I have seen no notice of your arrest, and I submit that a Hollywood writer who hasn't yet been arrested for contempt of Congress has much to explain" (31 October 1947, PG-SHC)

8. John E. Rankin of Mississippi, influential member of the HUAC, called throughout 1947 for the deportation of Charlie Chaplin, whose latest motion picture was *Monsieur Verdoux.*

---

1. John E. Pomfret (1898–1981) was president of William and Mary College and had cooperated extensively in the production of *The Common Glory.*

2. In 1948 William and Mary inaugurated an Institute of the Theatre to run each summer in conjunction with *The Common Glory* and consist of classes and workshops

Now about my talk for 11:00 A.M., February 9.[3] I thought maybe you would give me a little guidance thereon, but your letter magnanimously seems to leave the field to my own skirmishing.

I have a sort of address worked out and written and with a rough poem spiced in.[4] But I think it is a little over-philosophical for reading, and I should like with your indulgence to use the Charter Day motif for a short talk, well, on DRAMATIZING OUR HERITAGE. The essence of my paper already written deals with what I as a writer think we as citizens should be doing today in our arts, letters, music, theatre, movies, about our heritage. I could speak from this, I believe, with some pleasure and I hope not too much boredom to the audience. May I go on for a few more paragraphs.

You as head of a college are sitting in a place of great fun and opportunity. You might holler to throw out the fun as a misnomer, but still I'd want to stick to the word. Every day you are up against matters of idealism, personal faith, duty, destiny, life's work, etc. among your nearly two thousand young people. In my way too I am constantly dealing with young American boys and girls, though not to the extent you are, and I am bothered not a little by their lack of understanding of the principles on which this country was founded.

Last night I was reading that great trilogy of Aeschylus—*Agamemnon*, the *Choephori* and the *Eumenides*. Also I read again the comment of the great German scholar, Dindorf[5] I think it was,—to the effect that this work of art

---

in various aspects of the drama. Althea Hunt of the Department of Fine Arts at William and Mary (and codirector of *The Common Glory*) organized the institute and asked Green to send Pomfret a statement supporting the institute that he could use in applying to the Rockefeller Foundation for funds (Althea Hunt to Paul Green, 27 January 1948, PG-SHC). Green did so, praising such institutes as "beachheads for the culture and artistic development of our people" (Paul Green to John E. Pomfret, 30 January 1948).

3. February 9 is Charter Day at William and Mary, and 1948 was the 255th anniversary of the royal charter establishing the school in 1693. Pomfret asked Green to speak on the occasion. The present letter was not mailed (noted in Green's hand atop the first page: "Not sent") because it turned into material for the speech.

4. Notes on the theme of the present letter, with some of the same language, appear in Green's diary for early October 1947 (PG-SHC). They are notes for a talk he gave in Chapel Hill at the Carolina Dramatic Association on 18 October and at a Faculty Club luncheon on 21 October (*Daily Tar Heel*, 17 October 1947, p. 1, cols. 4–5; 19 October 1947, p. 4, col. 4).

5. Wilhelm Dindorf, nineteenth-century editor of Aeschylus.

was perhaps the greatest product put forth so far in the history of man's spirit. Maybe the statement is an exaggeration. I don't know. But I do know that one of the reasons for its greatness was that the author loved his subject, found it important. Aeschylus loved Greece and the heroes of his country's past. And in writing about his native land and these heroes, he the more made manifest the greatness and importance of both.

Now I along with many another—and I am sure this applies to a vast number of our people—have sometimes found it hard to keep faith in my country.—(And too often I have not admired our leaders. Today, at this hour, where is admirable leadership? Also I have found it a saddening fact that most of the writing in America which has had vitality and importance in this twentieth century has mainly been energized out of hate, anger, evangelical fervor against some inimical cause, or has been fired into passion by a one-sided mission of quick and arbitrary social improvement.)—Still, from my earliest boyhood I have felt that the principles of democracy which underlie our form of government are identical with principles of truth. And as time has passed, I have come to believe that they possess the righteous reality of a true religion likewise.

I could make a roll-call of these principles here, but they are old familiar friends to you—such as the rule of the majority, trial by jury, freedom of the press and speech and assembly, protection of the minority, the solution of problems by thought rather than by force—(There are no concentration camps in a democracy. The liquidation of the opposition would mean the liquidation of democracy itself.)—inviolability of the person, of conscience and rightful possessions, the acceptance of public responsibility as a measure of one's liberties and guarantees, the state to be a product of the citizenry and not the citizen a chattel of the state, etc., etc.

Well, these may sound a little dull in the roll-call. The problem is not to let them be dull in their activated use. In fact the problem now is how to get them widely working among our people so that we can cohere into a unity of vision, of determination, fit to meet the times.

In these days of crisis—and I am sure I don't know when there were not times of crisis—I find myself turning more and more to these elements and constituencies of our democratic philosophy. I am going back to the characters in our nation's past history and trying to put my ear in tune to their speaking. And just as in Greece her literary workers reinterpreted their heroes—their Ulysseses, Menelauses, their Agamemnons and gods and goddesses and with each interpretation raising them into more vivid reality—just so should we in this nation seek to interpret and re-interpret, dramatize and re-dramatize the pioneer figures of Franklin, Washington, Jefferson, Adams, Lincoln and others. And as we work to make them live again, so much more will they live in the lives of our children and the generations of the future—generations who in turn can reinterpret and redramatize them for their children.

I don't mean that this is ancestor worship. I simply mean that if we can make real and manifest and dramatic in our thinking, feeling and doing the lessons and meanings of our forefathers, just so much stronger and more stimulated can we be for the future. And in moments of weakness as now, times of uncertainty and wandering as now, we can look back for a moment to their figures standing there in a close-up actuality, can cup our hand to our ear and listen to the words of Jefferson riding on the wind—"We have declared for the equality of men, for the freedom of men, the responsibility of men."—"The purpose of the state is to see that the talents of its citizens reach their fullest expression."—"A nation can only be as strong and healthy as its citizens are strong and healthy."[6] Etc., etc.

And thus it will be that from a backward look and a backward listening we can turn squarely to the future and face that future more reassured, more certain of the way we should and must go, of the things we should and must do, of the leadership we need to take and must take.

When we consider, for instance, the mediums of entertainment and instruction now active in the American scene, I think we must acknowledge that they are failing to do a good job in interpreting ourselves to ourselves, our past to the present, and our present to the future.

Here I could talk quite a lot about the failure of the motion picture, of the radio, of the tabloid newspapers, of the slick magazines, and how the pap indulgences, the ever-repeated and sly credos that physical comforts somehow produce spiritual strength (Be sure to smoke Camels for your windpipe's sake!) are misleading and disorganizing to our young folks.

It seems to me that the outdoor theatre production of historical plays offers a good chance for the reinterpreting of America to herself. (The dedicated spot, the inherited event.)

6. Paraphrase of lines spoken by Jefferson in *The Common Glory: A Symphonic Drama of American History* (Chapel Hill: University of North Carolina Press, 1948), particularly his closing speeches (pp. 252–53).

And here of course I could talk a lot about the possibilities in such a form of drama, with special emphasis upon the meaning of festivals and celebrations—a people joyous and happy, celebrating their past, their great men, the ideals that made them great. Etc., etc.

So you see I could get wound up on this subject, concluding with some poetic synopsis such as the following, recently written out.

1

Man is the eternal worker and creator,
Like God himself.
Upbuilding enterprise is his
Or else he dies.
To work, to make, to shape, to form
In thought and deed and fact
With the feel of the hand,
His hope and plans; to conjure up
And set them forth for serving and beholding
Are his delight, his solace and his dream.
And in that dream a richer fact,
A prior and primordial motive—
The need to know, to know the truth
That makes him free.

2

In mire and murk of seas and rain
And sightless slime a million timeless years
He crawled his lightless way
Till in a darkened hour his miracle was born—
The first himself—
A starbeam out of heaven fell
And flickered on his brow
To wake him where he slept.
And slothful eyes were raised to see
The tiny bright intruder from on high.
And in the seeing, wonder grew,
And wild amazement, worship, awe.
And prayer was born—
Stiff awkward prayer that breaks from those dumb lips

And spills the vocables outflying
Through the enclosing soundless universe.
And liberation comes.

3

He moves to reach and reaching moves,
And thus begins his fate, his destiny and dare—
The upward climb, the outward grasp
And following feet to where the vision leads.
And now the calling summons in the sky,
The truth writ clear which he must know—
In starry globules, whirling orbs of light,
And myriad frozen stars and floods of cosmic fire,
Vast worlds that flame and flare and burst and die
In glory effulgent and splendor illimited.
And faith is born.
A living faith forevermore
In that eternal Being in whose mind all beings are,
And all things alike whose essence is.—
—The dreamer dreamless while he slept
Awoke in dreaming to his dream.

With cordial greetings and regards to you and Mrs. Pomfret, and we will be seeing you soon,

Elizabeth and I appreciate the invitation to spend Sunday night[7] at your house. We shall be delighted. We will be arriving sometime in the afternoon and will be busy with meetings[8] until late evening. So you mustn't have us on your mind at all.[9]

7. 8 February.

8. About the coming production of *The Common Glory.*

9. Later Green revised paragraphs five ("Last night I was reading that great trilogy . . . ") through eleven ("And thus it will be . . . ") as "Dramatizing Our Heritage," in Paul Green, *Dramatic Heritage* (New York: Samuel French, 1953), pp. 49–51.

## 218. To Owen Dodson[1]

[Greenwood Road, Chapel Hill, N.C.]
14 May 1948

Dear Mr. Dodson:

I had to leave the other night without seeing you. But I wish to thank you for your kindness in providing me with three tickets to your *Bayou Legend* show. I found the whole production very interesting, especially the script. I think you improved dramatically in many ways on Ibsen. Your poetry was good too, and your folk images I found delightful.[2] For several months some New York actors and theatre people have been thinking about doing *Peer Gynt* on Broadway. I was especially interested in seeing your show from the point of view of such an eventuality. Of course the New York production would be Ibsen's play and not an American version of it, but I am sure that I as adapter of the Ibsen drama will have to work mighty hard to equal what you did in your interpretation. More power to you.[3]

I tried to pay the young man at the desk for my tickets, but he wouldn't allow it. Again my cordial thanks.

Sincerely yours,

1. Owen Dodson (1914–1983), professor of drama at Howard University, was directing his play *Bayou Legend* in a production by the Howard Players. Green saw a performance on 4 May, having gone to Washington that day from Williamsburg, where he was casting *The Common Glory*. *Bayou Legend*, an adaptation of *Peer Gynt*, focuses on a black voluptuary from the Louisiana swamps (in Darwin Turner, ed., *Black Drama in America: An Anthology* [Greenwich, Conn.: Fawcett Publications, 1971], pp. 206–95).

2. Green, one of a handful of whites in the audience, especially enjoyed a scene (act 2; ibid., pp. 278–82) featuring ape characters "dressed in white suits—'white apes.' The symbolism was obvious. . . . Well turn about [is] fair play" (Green diary, 4 May 1948, PG-SHC).

3. In January 1948 Cheryl Crawford began discussions with Green about adapting *Peer Gynt*. She wanted to produce the play with Lee Strasberg directing and John Garfield in the title role. Such a production became part of the American National Theatre and Academy season for 1950–51, when the play opened on 28 January 1951 (*Peer Gynt* folders, 1948–51, PG-SHC).

## 219. To Roy Ald[1]

[Greenwood Road, Chapel Hill, N.C.]
26 May 1948

Dear Mr. Ald:

Yassuh, in my ignorance it looks like I will be left out of your book. Then maybe I deserve to be, for I am totally ignorant of the wherefores, the whethers and the whys of cocktails. I say this truthfully even though I was born and have been raised in the land of the mint juleps. The greatest drink innovation I can think of—and it's not really an innovation but my favorite—is a jug of cold water out of the spring below my house. Here the Indians drank and the deer and the furtive night possum long, long ago. I get a good animal kinship from drinking there likewise. And I reach a hand to civilization by using a jug.[2]

Cordially yours,

## 220. To Ward Morehouse[1]

[Greenwood Road, Chapel Hill, N.C.]
4 June 1948

Dear Ward Morehouse:

I am very glad to hear that you are writing a book on the American drama. It is bound to be good, and I am looking forward to seeing it.

You ask about an anecdote connected with my play *In Abraham's Bosom.* I remember something connected with the genesis of the play, but perhaps you wouldn't call it an anecdote. Rather it might partake of the nature of what the late philosopher Alfred Whitehead called an event. Anyway there were several

1. Roy Ald, editor at Fawcett Publications and later author of such works as *Sex Off Campus* (1969) and *Jump for Joy!* (1971), had just completed his first book, *Favorite Recipes of Famous Men* (1949) and was at work on a companion volume, "Favorite Cocktails of Famous Men," "a collection of the drink preferences of distinguished men in Art, Music, Science, the Theatre and other prominent areas of endeavor." He wondered if Green would "be kind enough to contribute a recipe for a cocktail or other drink innovation which you favor" (Roy Ald to Paul Green, undated, PG-SHC).

2. "Favorite Cocktails of Famous Men" seems not to have been published.

---

1. Ward Morehouse (1898–1966) was drama critic for the *New York Sun.*

people involved in the happening—and I am sure that ever since then it was remembered as an event.[2]

It was many, many years ago. I was a little boy come to the neighboring town of Angier[3] on a bright spring day to get a load of fertilizer for our farm. I wanted to see the train come in. I stood by the little shack of a station waiting along with several others, among them an old Confederate soldier leaning on his walking stick, for the train to put in its appearance. Soon it showed its round black moon of a locomotive end around the bend. It puffed and wheezed along toward us and finally drew in with a rusty squealing of its brakes. It was an old wood-burner, and the climb into town had been tough. The engineer piled out of the cab, grease-marked outside and full of spleen and frustration inside. He began to work on the old locomotive and squirting grease here and there into its aged joints. I looked down the track and spilling out of the Jim Crow car—there were only four in all, a white car, a Negro car, a freight car and a caboose—spilling out was a swarm of little Negro school children all dressed in their pink and white and blue picnic garments and with ribbons in their hair. Also there was a sprinkling of young Negro boys all ironed and pressed and scrubbed clean by their mamas for this great day. At the head of them was a tall yellow Negro man wearing gold-rimmed glasses and with a white expanse of white slick-ironed shirt front and wing collar and big black bolster tie. The little Negro children twittered and chirped in the sunny air, looking about them, happy as only children can be happy. They were on their way to Durham, North Carolina, on what was called in springy parlance of those days "a 'skursion." The big yellow man was the teacher and he was taking the children on this jaunt as a wind up for his year's school teaching. He came strolling forward toward us and toward the irate and working engineer. He felt good. He was expansive. The world was sitting to his hand.

"Good mawning, gentlemen," he said graciously to us. The old Confederate soldier blinked up at him, continued leaning on his stick, said nothing. I a little boy naturally said nothing. But I was already in my heart admiring this gracious, this genial, this successful and respectable representative of the

2. Whitehead stressed that an event consists of a unified group of elements calling to mind past events that follow the same pattern and presaging future instances of the pattern (see Alfred North Whitehead, *Science and the Modern World* [New York: Macmillan, 1925], pp. 106–7).

3. About six miles north of his father's farm.

Negro race. (Even as I looked at him there echoed in my mind one of the Southern commandments on which I was raised, oft repeated by my father even—"A Negro is like a mule. Treat him fair, work him hard, feed him good and you get the right results." Even then that morning—as much as I loved my father—I knew he was wrong. Here was a fine Negro man that showed he was wrong. No, Negroes were not mules, nor were they animals as our old local preacher was wont to say, generating them in his mind out of the loins of Cain and the woman he married in the land of Nod—even as the Scriptures themselves do tell.)[4]

"What time do the train get to Durhams, suh?" the Negro teacher asked of the engineer.

"None of your damned business," called the engineer behind him, still bent over one of the drivers with his oil can. Then he looked around. He straightened spasmodically up and glared at the colored man.

The Negro already had taken a shocked and rebuffed step backward.

"Sorry, suh, sorry," he said, and he was beginning to bob his head up and down a bit, bending his body at the waist.

"Take off your hat," the engineer suddenly squealed. Off it came in the culprit's hand. The little children down at the other end of the train began to see something was wrong, and in the blink of my eye I saw them begin to huddle together a little closer as if some fearful threat were beginning to be felt in the air.

"Take off your specs," the engineer snapped.

"But I ain't done nothing, white folks, ain't done nothing," said the colored man, and he backed away a couple of more steps.

"Don't white folks me," the engineer shouted. He flung the oil can behind him, snatched the walking stick from under the old Confederate soldier's resting hand and quick as lightning struck the Negro teacher a terrific wham across the face. Before the engineer pulled the stick away the blood had already rushed out and stained its splintered wood.

A little babble of shrieks and moanings rose from the school children, and like a gang of pursued goats they bounded up the steps of the Jim Crow car and inside to safety. The old Confederate soldier had almost fallen on his face when his support was jerked away. He righted himself with spread-out legs, the engineer handed his walking stick back to him. The old soldier took it and resumed his resting without a word. I couldn't look at the dreadful stick. I

4. Genesis 4:16–17.

couldn't look at the colored man. I shivered as if some bitter freezing chill had overspread the world. It seemed—as I remember it now—that a darkness overspread the sky—just as I'd seen it one morning when the sun was eclipsed and the chickens began to cluck uncertainly and start strolling toward their roost down by the garden.

A low whimpering moaning sound came from the Negro school teacher. And what did he say? What was his accusation there for a moment in time and space? He simply said—

"Lawd, white folks, you done ruined my shirt."

"All aboard," yelled the engineer. He climbed hastily into his cab, pulled the whistle cord a couple of times. The Negro school teacher turned, still holding his big white handkerchief, now dyeing itself all over crimson, against his face. . . .

Yes, that was a sort of anecdote. Years later when trying to speak a word for the Negro people, the scene haunted me and I sat down and wrote the story of a school teacher who tried desperately to help his people and failed.[5] It wasn't a Confederate veteran's walking stick that laid my hero low. It was something more up-to-date and final—a shotgun.

The school teacher of that spring morning long ago still lives—now a very old man. A bad scar still shows on his face, running from his forehead down across his chin. And there must be a scar in his heart too. There is in mine, and always will be.

Good luck to you in your venture.[6]

Cordially and sincerely yours,

## 221. To Jonathan Daniels

[Greenwood Road, Chapel Hill, N.C.]
21 June 1948

Dear Jonathan:

I've just got back from Williamsburg and Manteo and to my neglected correspondence. I'm darn sorry for the delay in answering your note of some days ago. And I regret not being able to get in my two-cents worth on the

5. *In Abraham's Bosom.*

6. The letter narrates its event "with such poignance" that Morehouse reproduced it nearly verbatim in *Matinee Tomorrow: Fifty Years of Our Theater* (New York: Whittlesey House, 1949), pp. 211–14.

South as Economic Problem Number One.[1] About my speech the other day to the reunion groups here[2]—I stood up on my hind legs and talked about a fact as obvious as a preacher's shirt front, to the effect that all this emphasis upon man as a scientific unit in a universe of things and thing-processes is a piecemeal interpretation of the truth. Civilization is ethical first of all and scientific somewhere later down the line. But when it happens that ethics and science come to an identity of contention about the way forward—then I for one feel that this truth is pretty well demonstrated and science has received its real justification. Theory without practice is empty, and practice without a controlling idealism is blind. It is so obvious that equality of humanity for the Negro, for instance, is both an ethical must as well as a scientific must that I am constantly astonished at the remissness of our leaders in failing to push forward toward its realization. A state which has a third of its citizens in a weakened condition is certainly that much the weaker state. Here science and religion agree. A fine and self-reliant Negro citizenry is a first on the agenda of North Carolina progress. Behavior of the trustees of the University recently in refusing even to consider the ideal of justice and fair play to be worked for is another one of those blind myopisms so cynically and blithely indulged in in the south. The invoking of points of order, this and that and the other to elide the responsibility is still the old hypocritical Sunday long face of the Monday trader.[3]

1. In June 1938 President Roosevelt issued a report and made a speech on "The South as Economic Problem Number One," and now Daniels, editor of the *News and Observer* in Raleigh, planned "to devote considerable space to a ten-years-after reconsideration and re-evaluation showing progress made and such lags as remain." For the issue he wanted a statement from Green (Jonathan Daniels to Paul Green, 1 June 1948, PG-SHC), but the issue appeared the day before the present letter (*NO*, 20 June 1948, sec. 4, pp. 1–3).

2. On 5 June Green spoke at a reunion supper for the UNC classes of 1937, 1938, 1939, and 1940. His task was to help these newly emerging participants "in the conduct of the University and public life" to "see the University in relation [to] our lives and our time" (Fred H. Weaver to Paul Green, 24 May 1948, PG-SHC). Daniels asked for a copy of the speech, saying he was "very much interested in seeing what you had to say" (Jonathan Daniels to Paul Green, 9 June 1948).

3. During the spring two black students applied to the UNC School of Law on the ground that their law school, North Carolina College in Durham, was not recognized by the American Bar Association, and a third black student applied to the UNC School of Medicine. The response of the UNC Board of Trustees was to announce,

Well, I could go on raring around on the lack of leadership in our beloved state—but yesterday riding along and noticing new paint on so many farmhouses, flowers in the yard, electric lights, and the glimpsed refrigerator now and then in a tenant farmer's kitchen gave me an elation and lift and a belief that the better life, both material and ideal, is possibly under way in our borders.

I go back to Williamsburg and Manteo tomorrow. Can't we get together some evening and sit around and talk some of these things out? What about a program of progress for North Carolina—a few first things to be done first. It ought to be easier to get such a thing started now that the Republicans are going to give us back our states' rights.[4]

My love to Lucy and the girls,[5]

## 222. To Elizabeth L. Green

Chateau Elysée, Hollywood, Calif.
30 August 1948

Honey—[1]

The meeting in Santa Barbara Saturday night was most enthusiastic. I talked—addressed the crowd—for more than an hour, open forum, etc., and I left the group of key people to see what they can do. I said ½ million dollars

---

through its executive committee, that "the matter of admission of Negro students to professional schools of the University of North Carolina was not considered by the executive committee on a point of order that the matter is beyond the authority of the executive committee and/or the Board of Trustees, under the law" ("Negro Applications Get No Action from Trustees," *Daily Tar Heel*, 18 May 1948, p. 1, cols. 7–8).

4. States' rights, championed by the Republican party, was a major issue in the 1948 presidential campaign, and because of a split in the Democratic party (the Dixiecrats, who called themselves the States' Rights party, withdrew and ran their own candidate), it was widely believed that the Republican Thomas Dewey would defeat the incumbent Harry Truman in the November election.

5. Jonathan and Lucy C. Daniels had two daughters, Lucy and Adelaide.

---

1. In late July Green flew to Hollywood to write a film script for Metro-Goldwyn-Mayer and to explore possibilities for an outdoor historical play in southern California. Santa Barbara was one area where he found considerable interest, and Hendley Klyne, president of the Santa Barbara Arts Council, had arranged for Green to meet with community leaders on Saturday, 28 August.

would be needed. They are going to have other meetings—a sort of town one, all kinds of clubs, etc. represented on Sept. 20. I have promised to fly back out here in the fall if things come to a head. A committee is to wait on Gov. Warren[2] soon and see if the state will furnish any funds.[3] So I've done about all I can do at S. B. I'm going to have a talk with Gilmor Brown of the Pasadena Playhouse and Kenneth Macgowan[4] before I come back.

Tomorrow I finish my script[5] and hand it in to Goldwyn the next day. It is due the day following that. I'll be 24 hours ahead of schedule. I think it's good so far. Of course Goldwyn may want to throw it out the window, squealing about what's happened to the sex in it.[6]

Please get all available and necessary forms and data relative to the Obenaus matter.[7] I'll sign up everything as soon as I get back. I've just got a statement from the C. G.[8] Last week with one night rained entirely out the royalty was $1,587.00 (mum!). This all helps. I do wish I had some sort of setup with the L. C. likewise.[9]

2. Earl Warren.

3. The centennial of the admission of California to the union would be 1950. Already a Centennial Committee was planning a state celebration. Klyne and others in Santa Barbara hoped a play in their area could be inaugurated as part of the celebration.

4. In the Department of Theater Arts at the University of California at Los Angeles, who, along with Gilmor Brown, was interested in the outdoor drama project.

5. *Roseanna McCoy*, based on a novel of the same title by Alberta Hannum.

6. *Roseanna McCoy* is a Romeo and Juliet story in the context of the Hatfield-McCoy feud. When Green began work on the script, Goldwyn wanted Roseanne and her boyfriend "to love each other physically before the question of marriage comes up. 'To cement things,' says Goldwyn in his quaint way. I refused to do it that way. Why not try some self-control on the part of screen lovers for a change? I asked" (Paul Green to Elizabeth Green, 4 August 1948, EG-SHC). Green worked on the script until he returned to Chapel Hill around 5 October. When the picture was released in August 1949, John Collier was credited with writing the screenplay.

7. Erna Lamprecht was nanny to the Green children during the family's stay in Berlin and London in 1928–29. Now married to Willy Obenaus, she and her family wanted to immigrate to the United States from Germany, and the Greens had been trying to arrange it through the U.S. State Department for several months.

8. *The Common Glory*.

9. For *The Lost Colony* Green never received royalty payments.

I'll put John Bauer out of misery soon. I may go once more in farewell to Ojai—if I can find time.[10]

The papers here today made quite a spread of Henry Wallace's misadventures in Carolina. Think of Mary Price for governor—and you get egg yolk on Wallace's hair! 2=2 right on![11]

Always, Paul

## 223. To Christopher Crittenden[1]

[Greenwood Road, Chapel Hill, N.C.]
24 December 1948

Dear Chris:

This is to acknowledge receipt of your letter of December 14 in which via

10. Bauer was director of Ojai Festivals, Ltd., an organization created to promote concerts, exhibitions, performances, and other artlike activities in the Ojai Valley of Ventura County, California. Throughout the year Green corresponded with Bauer and went to California thinking Ojai Festivals was a solid prospect to sponsor the outdoor historical play he hoped to write for southern California. After meeting Bauer (on several treks into the valley hunting a theater site), however, Green decided that Bauer was unreliable and that he would have to look elsewhere for a sponsor (Paul Green to Elizabeth Green, Friday Night and Monday Night, undated, EG-SHC). Green had written a letter informing Bauer "that we'd better drop any plans for an Ojai Symphonic Drama—so far as I am concerned" (Paul Green to John Bauer, 6 August 1948, PG-SHC), but he did not mail it. Although Green would do a play in Santa Barbara in 1953, for the present he shifted his attention to the sesquicentennial project in Washington, D.C., and the production there of *Faith of Our Fathers* in 1950 (Paul Green to Hendley Klyne, 15 October 1948).

11. Wallace, presidential candidate of the Progressive party, attended the state convention of the party in Durham on 29 August, the day the convention selected state chairman Mary Price as its gubernatorial candidate. The convention nearly turned into a riot as anti-Wallace demonstrators marched with signs, exploded firecrackers, and pelted Wallace with eggs ("Near-Riot Results as Anti-Wallace Crowd Demonstrates at Party Rally" and "Mary Price Is Nominee for Governor," *Durham Morning Herald*, 30 August 1948, p. 1).

1. Christopher Crittenden (1902–1969), of the North Carolina Department of

the Attorney General's ruling you transfer to me the statue of Virginia Dare.[2] I accept it with many thanks and trepidations.

A couple of years ago down in Manteo I stumbled on the white-souled creature[3] back in a storage room.[4] The talk was that she was to be broken up by hammers and so on because she was unsuitable to the world for which her sincere creator had designed her. "Good gracious alive," I said, "that would be a sin." I still think it would have been. So it was I said before any harm should come to her, give her to me—somebody. I'll shelter her against breakage as best I can, though I can't say the same as to the weather. The landscape man who has been working on my place considered that she might be suitable for a garden niche, planted deeply in and behind and snuggily some thick box-[wood]—where she can be visited with the right approach. I'll see.[5]

Again thanks, and best wishes to you and yours for a happy Christmas,

---

Archives and History, was secretary of the Literary and Historical Association of North Carolina.

2. Carved by Louise Lander in Rome in 1859 and, because of her friendship with Sallie Southall Cotten, memorializer of Virginia Dare and prominent in North Carolina literary and historical circles, willed by Lander to the Literary and Historical Association in 1926. The attorney general ruled that the association had the right under the will to make a gift of the statue.

3. The statue is carved in lovely white Carrara marble.

4. After coming to Raleigh in 1926, the Dare statue stood in the state historical museum until the late 1930s, when its space was taken for offices. It was moved to the office of a supreme court justice, but after a few weeks, because it embarrassed his secretary (Lander depicted Virginia Dare as a lithesome young woman wearing only a fishnet), the justice sent the statue to Roanoke Island for storage. In the winter of 1946 the shed where it stood was blown into Roanoke Sound by a storm, and the statue had been rescued from the water only recently when Green spotted it during a visit to Manteo for work on *The Lost Colony* (William S. Powell, *Paradise Preserved* [Chapel Hill: University of North Carolina Press, 1965], pp. 59–61).

5. Green kept the statue by a reflecting pool in his yard until 1953, when he gave it to the Garden Club of North Carolina for permanent display in the formal Elizabethan Garden adjacent to the Waterside Theatre on Roanoke Island.

## 224. To Byron Bray[1]

[Greenwood Road, Chapel Hill, N.C.]
25 January 1949

Dear Mr. Bray:

Thanks for your most interesting letter. The questions you raise are indeed important ones and require patience and growth to cope with them. I am sure that a young tree growing often feels completely discouraged at the difficulty of pushing its roots through hard soil and shale and gravel to reach the sustenance needed for itself. Well, with luck, which is generally cooperative, you see the results of not losing faith—here and there great big fine trees that have reached maturity and abounding fruitage.[2] I feel that the first step in dissolving away apparently adamant frustration is to recognize that time and growth are a process at work. And what seems so blue and doleful today, tomorrow with good effort will not so seem.

I am here most of the time—though I see by my calendar I will be away on the weekend of February 4, 5 and 6.[3] I will be glad to see you most any time. I do hope though you will drop me a line or telephone me a day or so ahead.[4]

With cordial greetings and regards.

1. Byron Bray, a student at Campbell College, near Green's childhood home, asked if he might come to Chapel Hill for a talk. His recent reading of *In Abraham's Bosom* deepened his sense of the menacing threats of society, threats that "not infrequently . . . make me wish that I had whatever it takes, or doesn't take to do away with myself. But that may not be the solution. Surely we all have an idea (Christian [at the start of his journey in *Pilgrim's Progress*] could not see Wicket Gate, but he said he thought he could see the light shining about it) that there is hope. But is there, Mr. Green? Is there any real hope for a world so full of frustrated individuals?" (23 January 1949, PG-SHC).

2. When Christian finally reaches Heaven's Gate, he sees written over it in letters of gold: "Blessed are they that do his Commandments, that they may have right to the Tree of Life, and may enter in through the Gates into the City."

3. For a planning session on *The Common Glory* in Williamsburg (Paul Green to Roger Boyle, 31 January 1949, PG-SHC).

4. In mid-February Bray visited Green, then wrote him about it. Green replied: "I am delighted to have your note of some days ago and to hear that you are doing so well" (8 March 1949, PG-SHC).

## 225. To Harrison Smith[1]

[Greenwood Road, Chapel Hill, N.C.]
12 May 1949

Dear Mr. Smith:

I am not surprised that you have been receiving letters and essays from your readers on the subject of the Bollingen Award to Ezra Pound. I have been getting some communications myself, since I am supposed to have been a guilty participant in the making of the award. In fact some of my communications have been rather terrifying. My nearby neighbor who is the local editor and a friend of some twenty-five years standing[2] came forward recently with the resolution that I along with the other Library Fellows in American Literature be shut up in the mental sanitarium where Ezra Pound now resides. And there we could continue writing drivel and fanning the air with mutual salutations and huzzahs, he said.[3]

I was opposed to giving the award to Pound. And so were some two or three others of the group.[4] But in the news release sent out from the Library we were all lumped together in a ridiculous unanimity.

1. On 19 February 1949 the Library of Congress gave the first Bollingen Award (for the best book of poetry by an American in the previous year) to *The Pisan Cantos* by Ezra Pound. The award angered a wide spectrum of people, from patriots who took it as a national affront, to literary traditionalists who saw it as partisan support for modernist poetry. Since December 1945, Pound had been in Saint Elizabeths Hospital, confined as mentally incompetent to stand trial for treason for his support of Italy and Germany during World War II. The cryptic and allusive cantos themselves had been written during the final months of the war while Pound was held in an American army prison near Pisa, Italy, awaiting transportation to the United States for trial. Judges for the Bollingen Award had been the Fellows in American Letters of the Library of Congress, of which Green was a member since its creation in 1944 by then librarian Archibald MacLeish. *The Saturday Review of Literature* led the charge against the award, and Harrison Smith (1888–1971), president and associate editor of the weekly, wrote to Green (probably to each of the fellows) that many readers were bewildered by the cantos. "Since you were one of the judges who in secret ballot voted for the Award," Smith continued, "it has occurred to us that you might be kind enough to interpret Mr. Pound's poetry, since the value of it, as poetry, is often in question" (6 May 1949, PG-SHC).

2. Louis Graves, editor of the *Chapel Hill Weekly*.

3. See "Suitable Place for Jurors," *Chapel Hill Weekly*, 25 February 1949, p. 2, col. 1.

4. Which in addition to Green included Leonie Adams, Conrad Aiken, W. H. Auden, Louise Bogan, Katherine Garrison Chapin, T. S. Eliot, Robert Lowell,

The Pisan Cantos which won the prize strike me as being a volatile fever-fret of wordage. And I am bull-headed enough to believe that most any loquacious and smattering-languaged literary practitioner hereabouts could fire off a volume of equal worth within a few weeks.

This is not to deny the beauty and poetic quality in some of Pound's other and earlier works.

When asked at our last meeting just what was the reason for the existence of the Library Fellows, one of the number in authority made answer as follows—"The best proof that the Fellows have a reason for being," he said, "is that they exist at all." This no doubt was profound as well as quaint.

Well, since I can't make heads or tails of the Pisan Cantos—suspecting they are all tail and no head—I am unable to interpret them for the reading public. The ravings in Pound's volume are as unintelligible to me as was the voting of the some eight gifted men who declared they were good.[5]

Sincerely yours,

## 226. To Gerald W. Johnson

[Theta Delta Chi Lodge, William and Mary College, Williamsburg, Va.][1]

25 August 1949

Dear Gerald:

I see you have pulled off another good book[2] and I am looking forward to reading it within the next week or so.

Thanks for your words about the Bollingen Award.[3] I think you are darn

---

Katherine Anne Porter, Karl Shapiro, Theodore Spencer, Allen Tate, Willard Thorp, and Robert Penn Warren. Of these fourteen, twelve attended the meeting of the fellows at the Library of Congress on 18 and 19 November 1948, when the vote on the award was taken. Eight of the twelve voted for *The Pisan Cantos.* Green and Shapiro voted against it, and two abstained (Statement of Procedure of the Jury for the Bollingen Award, July 1949, PG-SHC; see also Karl Shapiro, letter to the editor, *Baltimore Sun*, 25 February 1949, p. 16, col. 4).

5. In an editorial attacking the award, Smith and Norman Cousins, editor of the *Saturday Review*, quoted extensively from the present letter ("Ezra Pound and the Bollingen Award," *Saturday Review of Literature*, 11 June 1949, pp. 20–21).

---

1. Green rented the lodge for the summer for his frequent visits to *The Common Glory* (Paul Green to George P. Lyon, 20 August 1949, PG-SHC).

2. *Our English Heritage* (1949).

3. During the summer of 1949 the *Saturday Review of Literature* continuously

right—the artist as prophet is sure playing heck with his followers when he sets up whimsy and insanity for deriving his standards of beauty and creativeness.

The whole thing has puzzled me a great deal. In the meeting where votes were taken and inclinations expressed, I found myself ill at ease and homeless. "Allen," I said—to Tate—"I can't get on to what is happening." I looked across at Eliot and he was suave and apparently profound. Ted Spencer, poor fellow,[4] was sleek and well-groomed and the best of Harvard. Conrad Aiken was silent and contemplative and seemingly solid of weight and thoughtfulness—all true men and good. And yet I kept hearing the refrain—"A crazy man is their prophet and they have come to crown him seer."

Well, I am glad that the *Saturday Review* came stepping in. Maybe this fulmination of mouths will serve strangely to clear the air somewhat.[5] Anyway I appreciate the confirmation your letter gives me that I was not thrown out trying to steal second.

Ever to you,

---

attacked the Library of Congress for giving the Bollingen Award to Ezra Pound for *The Pisan Cantos.* Citing letter 225, the *Saturday Review* revealed that voting on the award by the Fellows in American Letters had not been unanimous ("Ezra Pound and the Bollingen Award," *Saturday Review of Literature,* 11 June 1949, pp. 20–21), then ran, along with other pieces, two diatribes by Robert Hillyer ("Treason's Strange Fruit," 11 June 1949, pp. 9–11, 28, and "Poetry's New Priesthood," 18 June 1949, pp. 7–9, 38). In a recent letter Johnson told Green that "ever since Hillyer exploded his stink-bomb I have been meaning to write to congratulate you on being clear of the Ezra Pound mess." He added that he was "much less disturbed by the idea of giving a prize to a traitor than by the idea of giving one to a nut. Some good poets have gone insane, to be sure, but by the time they went insane they were no longer good poets. Art is, or ought to be, the highest form of sanity; to admit that insane stuff can be art is to surrender the citadel. That strikes me as worse than any possible political implications of the award" (20 August 1949, PG-SHC).

4. Spencer died on 18 January 1949.

5. Following the *Saturday Review* pieces, a group headed by Representative Jacob Javits of New York called for a congressional investigation of the award to Pound. On 19 August 1949, however, Senator Theodore Green, chairman of the Senate-House Library Committee, while declining such an investigation, forbade the Library of Congress to award any more literary prizes. On the same day Librarian of Congress Luther H. Evans canceled all library awards in the arts (in addition to the just-inaugurated Bollingen Award, the library had for several years given awards in music and painting) (*New York Times,* 20 August 1949, p. 13, col. 7).

## 227. To Erma Green

[Greenwood Road, Chapel Hill, N.C.]
8 September 1949

Dear Erma:

Both *The Common Glory* and *The Lost Colony* closed on September 4. I am sorry you weren't able to get down,[1] but we all understand how busy you are. The plays had a good season, being some 15% ahead of last year both as to attendance and income. Kay Kyser[2] came down to Roanoke and helped us out a lot with his publicity and with acting in the show. He played the master of ceremonies a number of times and the public responded to his talent and his generosity.[3]

There is no news here much. Our house is gradually quieting down. Anne[4] and her two daughters have gone off to Racine to live with Virginia.[5] This morning I took Betsy[6] and her Oberlin friend, Lydia Johnson, over to the airport. Betsy is going home with Lydia to visit her a few days in New Hampshire, thence out to Detroit to see Dorothy (McBrayer) Stahl,[7] thence back to Oberlin to settle down for the long year of work.

Janet[8] as you know is back home from her dancing season in Connecticut and is head over heels in preparations for going out to the University of Wisconsin. Sam[9] has arrived and is enjoying his wife and two daughters.[10] Mrs. Lay is with us and will be until Miss Stevens[11] returns on October 24.

1. From Manhattan, where she worked in the Publications Department of Bethlehem Steel.

2. Band leader and radio star who lived in Chapel Hill.

3. Kyser acted the part of the queen's master of ceremonies for several performances beginning on 9 August, and his wife, Georgia Carroll, played one of the colonists.

4. Elizabeth's sister-in-law, whose husband Henry Lay died in 1948.

5. Virginia Hawkins, Elizabeth's youngest sister.

6. One of Green's daughters.

7. Friend of the family who had been Green's secretary during his early years in Hollywood.

8. Youngest of the Green children, who spent the summer at the School of Modern Dance at Connecticut College in New London.

9. Cornwell, husband of Green's oldest daughter, Byrd, at Creighton University during the summer in a medical training program.

10. Elizabeth, born on 6 February 1947, and Janet, born on 6 August 1949.

11. Alice A. Stevens, retired schoolteacher, Mrs. Lay's boarder and companion for many years.

All in all we have had quite an active summer. Elizabeth and I had a house in Williamsburg which we have just released.[12]

I needn't talk about the expense!

I hope everything is going well with you and you are enjoying your work. I plan to be up to New York sometime this fall and hope we can see some shows and an opera or two together.

Herbert Graf (and I hope his wife), Stage Director at the Metropolitan, is coming down to visit us about a week around October 1.[13] We will put them up here somewhere in our domicile and get in a lot of good talking about the future of opera and musical drama in America. He is a good man and has already written a good book entitled as I remember, *The Future of Opera in America.*[14] I met him out in Hollywood some years ago when he had Lauritz Melchior out there doing a picture for MGM.[15]

Everybody says Byrd's new baby is pretty.

Hugh's two little boys[16] have been up here visiting us and we [had] quite a time. They did a lot of work for me on the yard with the tractor. We all ate in relays. It really was fun.

12. Rented until Labor Day from the Theta Delta Chi fraternity at William and Mary College for his frequent visits to work on *The Common Glory.*

13. Graf saw *The Common Glory* on 25 August and discussed it with Green, then wrote that he would like to talk further about the staging of "musical festive plays" because they represented "a good deal of my hopes for the 'Opera for the People' " (2 September 1949, PG-SHC).

14. Graf came from his native Vienna in 1934 to stage a season of opera in Philadelphia, then went to the Metropolitan Opera in New York City. His outlook on the theater had much in common with Green's. Graf's *The Opera and Its Future in America* (New York: W. W. Norton, 1941) treats opera as one phase in the history of musical drama, which he traced back to the Greeks, and develops the point that "opera [of the future] must be folk theater—expressing the emotions of the people in musical drama" (p. 272). At *The Lost Colony* he had experienced "one of the most moving performances of the musical theater it has ever been my privilege to know" (p. 255).

15. Melchior, Danish tenor who debuted with the Metropolitan Opera in 1927, made three motion pictures for MGM: *Thrill of a Romance* (1945), *Two Sisters from Boston* (1946), and *This Time for Keeps* (1947). The Grafs came to Chapel Hill on 5 October for a visit of a few days (telegram, Herbert Graf to Paul Green, 2 October 1949, PG-SHC).

16. William, sixteen, and John, fourteen.

We've had a little stir-up around here about freedom of speech in the University. As usual I fired off my mouth and have received quite a bit of congratulations and abuse mixed.[17] Why do college professors let the pragmatic voice run over them the way they do. A long time ago I wrote a line in a play somewhat as follows—"There is something in this academic life that works on a man's manhood."[18] It might even be true.

I miss my old fellow fighter, Bill Couch,[19] though Phillips is stepping in pretty well.[20]

Love,

17. In May 1949 it came to light that Hans Freistadt, from Austria and a graduate student and teaching assistant in physics at UNC, was a member of the Communist party. Immediately the board of trustees began considering whether to require job applicants to pledge that they had never been Communists but voted unanimously against the requirement ("Trustees Vote Unanimously Not to Start 'Witch-Hunt,'" *Daily Tar Heel*, 25 May 1949, p. 1, cols. 6–8). Then over the summer Robert B. House, chancellor at Chapel Hill, in a step not taken by chancellors of the other campuses of the university at Raleigh and Greensboro, added such a pledge to applications for employment at Chapel Hill. Green heard about House's action in late August and criticized it sharply in a speech in his hometown, Lillington, on 30 August ("Green Scores Loyalty Paper Required of Faculty at UNC," *NO*, 31 August 1949, p. 9, cols. 1–2). In several state newspapers Green soon published a lengthy defense of academic freedom (e.g., "Professor Hits UNC Order Requiring 'Loyalty Oaths,'" *Greensboro Daily News*, 26 September 1949, sec. 2, p. 1, cols. 1–3).

18. In *The Enchanted Maze: The Story of a Modern Student in Dramatic Form* (New York: Samuel French, 1939) the local madam, when asked if any professors from the nearby college frequent her house, says no, "the married ones don't need it and the single ones ain't able to stand it. . . . You know, academic life seems to do something to men—seems to work on their—(*Laughing.*)—hardihood" (p. 92).

19. Formerly head of the University of North Carolina Press, at present in a similar position at the University of Chicago.

20. Phillips Russell, in the journalism department at UNC and married to Green's sister Caro Mae, was helping to organize a Chapel Hill Committee on Freedom of Thought and Speech, consisting of faculty members from UNC, Duke University, and Wake Forest College ("Move Is Launched to Cease Anti-Red Pledges at U.N.C.," *Durham Morning Herald*, 3 November 1949, final edition, p. 1, cols. 1–2; p. 5, col. 5). Despite continuous protest, however, the question about Communist affiliation remained on job applications until 1959, when William C. Friday, president of the university system, and William B. Aycock, chancellor of the Chapel Hill campus, removed it ("UNC Officials Rap Loyalty Pledge on Applications," *NO*, 6 January

## 228. To Paul Green, Jr.

[Greenwood Road, Chapel Hill, N.C.]
11 October 1949

Dear Son—[1]

We've all been hoping to hear from you from day to day, but so far we haven't been lucky.

How are you, and how is the work going? You know I'm as interested as I can be in how the year is working out for you and Skip.[2] Write us how Jenny[3] is.

Your car[4] is here, sitting idle, its front and nose all shiny and new. The brake has given us no end of trouble, so we just don't drive it at all now. Poe-Mangum[5] fixed it several times, and Sam[6] drove it some when here. The last time he did, the brake gave out suddenly (though fixed the day before by P-M.) and he crashed into the back of a car and tore both up pretty bad. The insurance company paid for the other car—$112.00 (a hundred and twelve),[7] but I have a bill and will pay for the damage done to yours—I don't see how Sam can—which amounts in all to some $120.00. It has already been repaired—new bumper, new front fenders, headlight repaired, radiator, etc. I haven't let Sam know about the damage, since he went away with the impression that insurance would take care of it. But the Service Insurance & Realty Co. says your policy carried no self-protection. There's no hurry about disposing of your car. It can just wait here until you send orders what to do with it.[8]

---

1959, p. 9, cols. 3–7; "UNC Trustees Board Adopts Bill of Rights for Faculty," *Durham Morning Herald*, 26 May 1959, sec. B, p. 4, cols. 4–6).

---

1. Paul, Jr., entered the doctoral program in electrical engineering at Massachusetts Institute of Technology earlier in the fall.

2. Dorrit Gegan Green, known as Skip, who married Paul, Jr., on 20 October 1948.

3. Skip's mother, who lived in Boston.

4. The old Plymouth Paul, Jr., drove while in graduate school at North Carolina State University in Raleigh.

5. DeSoto-Plymouth dealer in Chapel Hill.

6. Cornwell.

7. A leaky pen made the figure look like $412.00.

8. Later in the month Green bought Paul, Jr., and Skip a new Ford as a "long-delayed wedding present," getting a credit of $400 for the Plymouth against the cost of the new car, $1,923.50 (Paul Green to Paul, Jr., and Skip Green, 4 November 1949, PGJr).

I'm very busy with all sorts of work, including a fierce effort to keep the State of N.C. from putting a four-lane by-pass truck highway right through Greenwood. The present surveyed right of way goes right over the lot you and Skip picked out and on right along behind the Prince's. All the Greenwooders are upset and are looking to me for protection. I'll do all I can, but the matter looks dark. It will damage me thousands of dollars. Whatever is right, of course—I'm using a lot of "rights"—must be done.[9]

For the last few weeks we've been trying to push the Obenaus project ahead, after hearing from a German doctor friend that that family were in desperate circumstances.[10] To-day an ecstatic note from Erna announces success at last. The Counsel at Hamburg has finally informed them that they are to come. So I've got little lumps in my stomach about the expense and responsibility. But here again it must be done.[11]

9. Earlier in October Greenwood residents were shocked when, without notification, state highway engineers began surveying a 200-foot right-of-way through Greenwood. Since August state and town officials had discussed the need for a by-pass east (where Greenwood lay) and south of Chapel Hill in order to carry through-traffic away from congested city streets, but the route had been talked about only in general terms. After several conferences with Green, highway officials moved the route eastward to the line between Greenwood and the adjoining property owned by William Muirhead, who shared the right-of-way contribution with Green (*Chapel Hill Weekly*, 26 August 1949, p. 1, cols. 7–8; 14 October 1949, p. 1, col. 8). Green then joined others planning to landscape the highway coming into Chapel Hill from Raleigh and the bridge over it required by the by-pass in order to "make a beautiful approach from the political capital to the intellectual capital of North Carolina" (*Chapel Hill Weekly*, 21 October 1949, p. 1, col. 8).

10. For over a year Paul and Elizabeth had been trying to gain government permission for Erna Obenaus and her family (husband and three children) to immigrate to the United States. The frustrations of the effort are clear in Green's remark to a friend that "there is no fixed procedure" for arranging immigration. "Each case seems to be unsettled and continuously deferred on its own demerits. . . . In a nutshell, I advise you to write to your Congressman and get him to put you on to the proper person (and of course he will prove to be the wrong one), in the State Department at Washington, D.C. From then on you will need no prompting from any of your friends. Your own irritation and frustration will be sufficient to keep you going" (Paul Green to Evan P. Ford, 29 December 1949, PG-SHC).

11. Sponsored by the Greens (who paid travel expenses and guaranteed support), the Obenauses sailed from Cherbourg on the *Queen Mary* on 8 February 1950 and on 14 February docked at New York City, where the Greens met them. In Chapel Hill the Greens installed the Obenaus family on a chicken farm northwest of Greenwood and

I hope Janet[12] and Bets[13] are writing to you. They seem to be happy and flourishing—as we hear from them.

My love to Skip and Jenny too.

I'm enjoying music at night no end. I still bless you for giving me the phonograph.[14]

Get Skip to write to Grandmother.[15] She's pretty blue most of the time—now that her twilight is falling fast, as it will fall for all of us including you. You write her too.

Love, Doog

## 229. To Hilda Lee Walker[1]

[Greenwood Road, Chapel Hill, N.C.]
25 February 1950

Dear Miss Walker:

I am grateful to you for your letter of February 17 explaining the attitude of the District of Columbia Daughters of the American Revolution relative to

---

provided them a monthly stipend of $200 (Erna Obenaus to Elizabeth and Paul Green, 12 January 1950, PG-SHC; Paul Green to Janet Green, [11 February 1950], JG).

12. Freshman at the University of Wisconsin.

13. Junior at Oberlin College.

14. Just before leaving Raleigh for Boston.

15. Mrs. Lay, seventy-nine and an invalid in Chapel Hill.

---

1. Green asked Jan Sibelius to compose an overture for *Faith of Our Fathers*, the play he was writing for the sesquicentennial celebration of Washington, D.C., as the capital of the nation, and Hilda Lee Walker, corresponding secretary for the District of Columbia chapter of the Daughters of the American Revolution, sent him a resolution adopted unanimously by the chapter's executive committee. The resolution called on Congress to withhold all money from the celebration if it was not "kept All-American through the employment of all program participants." "Only a native born or long-time resident could feel and understand sufficiently the spirit of the homeland" to write the overture, the resolution maintained, and Sibelius, an "octogenarian Finnish Composer," had "paid this Country but one short visit back in 1914." To choose him, or any other foreigner, for the commission would be "disparaging not only to our American composers . . . but also . . . to our American culture as a whole" (Hilda Lee Walker to Paul Green, 17 February 1950, PG-SHC). In addition to Green, she sent copies of the resolution to President Truman, the National Capital Sesqui-

Jan Sibelius' being invited to write an overture for the proposed Washington Sesquicentennial drama.

I had hoped to have for our dramatic occasion in the nation's capital a salute to America for her greatness and justice as a democratic nation—a sort of Europe to America greeting which would say, "Good luck to you, our hopes are in you and the hopes of the world. Do not fail us." Yes, I had in mind a sort of hymn to democracy, a paean of musical praise to the abiding character of George Washington and the principles of self-government which lived in him and in our forefathers and which must be kept alive and strengthened if we are to fulfill our destiny.

I believe that nothing is ever lost by a statement of honest opinion, whether in agreement or in difference. So I have thought that in all fairness to you personally and to the D.A.R.—which has evinced so vital an interest in this project—I ought to thus explain my point of view.

I know we all are working for a common cause and that cause is the nobility and the strength of the American dream. And as long as we all keep that determination and vision before us and work hard for it, we will not go far amiss.

Naturally I do not mean that the American dream should ever be a hidebound and nationalistic concept. Rather I believe with Jefferson, Washington, Adams, Madison and others that the principles of our democracy are universal and have in them the potentiality for increased universal human happiness.

And though it may be true that specific and idiomatic inspiration of peoples are closely connected with nationalistic and ethnographical boundaries—still goodness, truth and beauty as such spill beyond these boundaries and are universal in their meaning and in their application.

So in thinking of a musical salute from Europe to America I naturally thought in terms of true beauty, not a limited beauty. And therefore it was natural that my mind traveled toward the greatest living European composer as worthy of giving that salute in an overture—Jan Sibelius.

Unfortunately I must report that Mr. Sibelius is ill at the present time. The chances are he will be unable to say to us on the occasion of the opening of our drama in Rock Creek Park—"Hail America, Mother of Democracy! Hail George Washington, mighty man—a man for the ages! Hail to you, Ameri-

---

centennial Commission, the National Society of the Daughters of the American Revolution, and editors of local newspapers.

cans all—keep fighting ahead—that your nation may live, that your dream may not die!"[2]

With cordial greetings,

## 230. To Igor Stravinsky[1]

[Greenwood Road, Chapel Hill, N.C.]
8 April 1950

Dear Mr. Stravinsky:

I am enclosing herewith some words for your use. Yesterday I talked with Mr. Watson[2] and told him about my efforts to work out the extra item of expense which would be incurred by the use of additional musicians beyond the organist. I am in high hopes that I can settle everything early in the week. I will send you a wire the minute I get the matter cleared. In the meanwhile you perhaps can make use of the words I am enclosing. If there are too many for your purpose, then use those that suit you best.

With cordial greetings and regards,[3]

2. Sibelius, who was not sick, said he was "greatly honoured by your invitation to compose an overture for the play regarding George Washington. . . . I very much regret, however, to inform you that I am not able to consent to your request as I do not any more write music needed for some special occasion" (telegram, Jan Sibelius to American National Theatre and Academy, 30 January 1950, PG-SHC).

---

1. Failing to get Sibelius, Green turned to Igor Stravinsky (1882–1971) for an overture for *Faith of Our Fathers*. The Russian-born composer had lived in the United States since the late 1930s and became a citizen in 1945 but still seemed appropriate for the European salute to American democracy that Green wanted for the play (see letter 229). Stark Young, who lived near Stravinsky in Manhattan, visited him for Green and found him interested in the project (Stark Young to Paul Green, 15 March 1950, PG-SHC). Green talked with Stravinsky by telephone on 6 April, liked his idea of adding a choral group and some brasses (trombones and trumpets) for the overture (Paul Green to Robert Breen, 7 April 1950), and promised to send him a text (unlocated) for the music.

2. Warner Watson of the American National Theatre and Academy, Green's point of contact in discussions with composers.

3. In addition to the financial problem caused by additional musicians beyond an organist (a problem Green did not resolve), he also ran into the nationalistic bias he had encountered in connection with Sibelius. Edward Boykin, director of the Sesqui-

## 231. To Gerald W. Johnson

[Greenwood Road, Chapel Hill, N.C.]
15 January 1951

Dear Gerald—[1]

I am glad you have found equanimity. Buddha and Schopenhauer found it too. I am still hopeful—and lost.

Right now I am busy rehearsing a fable which I have concocted in an adaptation of Ibsen's *Peer Gynt.*[2] John Garfield is playing the lead and we have a fine cast.[3] Valerie Bettis is doing the choreography. I am trying to say something relative to the huge swollen tragedy of the world—say a tiny vocable of reason. My faith is like that of the old woman's. You remember when she wee-weed in the sea, she said, "Every little bit helps." We open in New York on January 28. And I already see the critics with their shillelaghs

centennial Commission, on learning about the talks with Stravinsky, wrote Green that "this Igor Stravinsky idea is loaded with dynamite." Boykin and Congress were being flooded with resolutions that any composer engaged for the production be of American birth. "The Sibelius incident produced much publicity. It was adverse . . . [but it showed] that there is a deep interest in this task in which we are engaged. Should we now come forward with the idea of using a composer who is only recently naturalized, I believe it would produce another deluge of publicity that could well be fatal to our plans. So, I urge you, insofar as this project is concerned, to drop the idea of using Stravinsky" (Edward Boykin to Paul Green, 17 April 1950, PG-SHC). When *Faith of Our Fathers* opened for its first season (5 August to 30 September 1950), its overture was by Richard W. Dirksen from Freeport, Illinois, assistant choirmaster and organist at Washington Cathedral and musical director of the play.

1. Johnson closed a recent letter to Green by saying he was "facing the New Year with great equanimity. I figure that all is lost, including sanity, so nothing that happens from now on can matter much" (6 January 1951, PG-SHC).

2. Green cut Ibsen's long and varied play, dispensed with Edvard Grieg's music, and brought the script into focus as a satire on Western materialism, presenting Peer as "the wastrel, the selfish ego-centric seeking to find his life in outside things" (Paul Green, "Modernization of *Peer Gynt,*" *New York Times*, 21 January 1951, sec. 2, p. 3, cols. 1–3). Cheryl Crawford was producing and Lee Strasberg directing the adaptation for the American National Theatre and Academy at the ANTA Playhouse in Manhattan. Green got home on 13 January from a week of rehearsals, and on 18 January returned for rehearsals until the opening on 28 January.

3. Which also featured Mildred Dunnock, Pearl Lang, and Karl Malden.

raised, each sitting by his respective rat-hole, ready to kill any touch of experiment and imagination which emerges.[4]

About the poem[5]—I disclaim any connection with it. My wife wrote it for a play on which we were collaborating—"Blackbeard." She is a much better poet than I am and I hope you will talk about her. I will ask her to get a copy of it—and I will enclose it here-with.[6]

Greetings, sir,

4. Green really feared critics would attack the production for lacking pace and intensity. Under Strasberg's direction, *Peer* "moves like a slow-motion film," he noted in his diary, and to no avail he urged Crawford "to get after Strasberg to get some pep and zip into *Peer.* The critics will kill us as we huddle and mumble Stanislavski." With Elizabeth and their daughter Janet he attended a cast buffet before the opening performance, then while they went to the theater he returned to his hotel "and read proof on the play for the publisher. I couldn't face the opening" (Green diary, 12, 15, and 28 January 1951, PG-SHC). While none of the reviewers was harsh, most agreed with Brooks Atkinson that the production was "nebulous [and] desultory" (*New York Times*, 4 February 1951, sec. 2, p. 1, cols. 1–2). Arriving home, Green noted in his diary, "A tough trip! The end of a dream. Tomorrow to begin dreaming another" (30 January 1951, PG-SHC). *Peer* closed on 24 February after thirty-two performances and was published in May by Samuel French.

5. Johnson wrote to say he was preparing a talk and wanted to discuss Green's poetry but could not locate one poem he needed, "a bit from long ago called 'Black Bill's Song,' or something like that, and dealing with the drowned men off the coast. Besides being sparkling verse it has the flavor of North Carolina ghost stories, and the flavor is what I am trying to isolate and identify. I have seen it in print, but in what volume?" (6 January 1951, PG-SHC).

6. "Blackbeard," Elizabeth's conception with revisions by Paul, was produced by the Carolina Playmakers in March 1922, then published in Green's *The Lord's Will and Other Carolina Plays* (New York: Holt, 1925), pp. 47–96. With the present letter Green sent Johnson a copy of the poem he wanted, Bloody Ed's song from the opening of "Blackbeard" (ibid., pp. 53–55).

## 232. To Doris Falk[1]

[Greenwood Road, Chapel Hill, N.C.]
17 February 1951

Dear Miss Falk:

I like your letter very much. You come straight to the tragic point and seem to keep your humor.

I have a very capable secretary,[2] and I am lying propped up on the sofa, my feet against a hot pad—all very comfortable—and so maybe you won't mind if I comment a bit at length on this question you are dealing with—tragedy.

You speak of "the Aristotelian glass darkly."[3] Thank you for being frank about it. This ipse dixit authority[4] continues still to hold people's minds in thrall. It would seem to me that with the new Einsteinian concept of the moving continuum, since the development of biochemistry and the commonplaces of "growth" and "process" and the Bergsonian elan vital—in short

1. Doris Falk (b. 1919), later a teacher and scholar of modern drama at Rutgers University, was at the time of the present letter a graduate student at Cornell University completing her Ph.D. in English. Her dissertation focused on "some religious themes in American drama," and Green's plays were "therefore . . . tremendously important" (Doris Falk to Paul Green, 21 January 1951, PG-SHC). She initiated the correspondence by asking about the different versions of *The Field God*: the produced and first published version (in *The Field God and In Abraham's Bosom* [1927]), in which the central character resolves to live at the end, and the version in *Out of the South* (1939), in which he ends the play by committing suicide. Green answered that he preferred the second, tragic, version. "The suicide of [the central character] Gilchrist seems to me right. This ending seems to give better dramatic effectiveness both as to story and human meaning." After mentioning that another of his plays, *The House of Connelly*, also had different endings, he concluded by saying, "You can see I still don't know what tragic drama really is. More than that, it seems I don't know just what to believe about this life we live. Generally I do though" (Paul Green to Doris Falk, 1 February 1951). Falk "was delighted to receive your letter answering my questions so directly and honestly. Your acknowledgement of doubt as to the real nature of tragic drama has encouraged me to talk over with you some of my own confusions on the subject"—which she did in two packed and sparkling pages (14 February 1951), to which Green here replies.

2. Sara Gene Steel.

3. Falk began by saying, "Maybe I am still seeing through an Aristotelian glass darkly, but I can't help looking for indications of justice—moral order—and inevitability in tragedy."

4. Authority based merely on assertion.

process, motion, organic change—it would seem that the formalism of the great Stagirite[5] would have less hold on us all than it does.

About the protagonist Gilchrist in *The Field God*—you are right.[6] It could be said that the traditional God did have the last word. If so, why not? Why should we keep "looking for indications of justice—moral order— and inevitability in tragedy"? Certain kinds of tragedy—yes. But other kinds, maybe not. Do a man's death and failure always have to seem just? It may be their very injustice that wrings our hearts.

I guess Gilchrist's struggle is simply to save his values—those he counts realest to himself. When he fails there is nothing much worth living for. So it seems to him. That is one way of putting it.

Your suggested ending for the play sounds good too—the dogged continuation of existence, tending the sick hog and in loneliness.[7]

The tragic ending I once planned for *The House of Connelly* was cued out of life. Patsy Tate representing creative life and optimism for a new day was set upon at the procreative moment of her existence (her wedding night) and murdered by the household ignorant and jealous spirits (the two old Negro women) as protectors of the old way of life and enemies to the new. God knows this sort of killing off of good and new movements below the Mason and Dixon line has occurred often enough. The ending I used was also cued out of life.[8] Often in the south new ways have taken hold and produced new and better conditions. Consider the present dairy movement. May I suggest that a great deal of our perplexity over such matters as these comes from applying the logic of the content to that of the form, or vice versa. You mentioned the word "pessimistic." That is a sample of what I dare to mean.[9]

As I remember, somewhere Hegel says that a character which is dramatic

5. Aristotle, who was born in Stagira.

6. Falk had argued against the tragic ending preferred by Green, saying Gilchrist's suicide implied no moral order and only affirmed the puritanical god against which he struggled.

7. Falk had said she "expected Gilchrist neither to affirm his [humanistic] faith exultantly at the end nor to commit suicide, but to pay the price of his convictions—spiritual and social isolation—and go out to tend that sick hog, alone." (For a reversal of Green's view that such an ending is appropriate, see Paul Green, *Dramatic Heritage* [New York: Samuel French, 1953], p. 82.)

8. The optimistic version in *The House of Connelly and Other Plays* (1931).

9. Amplified in Green, *Dramatic Heritage*, p. 83.

plucks for himself the fruit of his own deeds.[10] Again, yes and no. For often a dramatic character has to eat the bitter fruit which someone else has plucked for him.

And then there is always Jesus Christ and the sufferings of Buddha— and of any and all the martyred saints. And to completely lariat-tie myself, let me add that the tragic flaw which you mentioned[11] may often turn out to be the lack of any tragic flaw—thus putting the character out of joint with the times which have their flaw. The jut of his more perfect personality, say, failing to fit into the warp and curve of error waiting for him. And so against the power of this surd, this wrinkle of fault in an overpowering and marred environment, our blessed protagonist wrecks himself.

A character who is awry with any or all of his three worlds—himself, his neighbor, the outside universe—is the subject matter for drama if he struggles to dissipate this awryness. If he fails or pays too big a price, we have a tragedy. If he wins without too great a struggle, we have less tragedy, and so on.

And of course here we are talking always about tragedy as an art.

In all tragedy, whether classical, romantic, naturalistic, realistic, expressionistic—to use the scholar's hated labels[12]—the problem of evil raises its head. And that means good raises its head also.

Some say that dramatic tragedy is essentially a depiction of the struggle between a right and a wrong, between truth and untruth, between good and evil.

Hegel's theory as everybody knows differs from this. The highest type of tragedy is never an exhibition of the struggle between good and evil, right and wrong, but between two goods, two rights. His illustration is as you will remember, *Antigone*.[13]

Maybe there should first be a definition of drama. How do you define it? I will hazard a definition—"Drama is a story acted."

To paraphrase Hegel again, he speaks somewhat as follows—Drama in its

10. *The Philosophy of Fine Art*, trans. and with notes by F. P. B. Osmaston (London: George Bell and Sons, 1920), 1:252–53.

11. Falk had said that with tragedy "the audience feels a sense of justice in the downfall" of the central character "probably because of the 'tragic flaw.' "

12. Modified to "the scholar's empty terms" in Green, *Dramatic Heritage*, p. 84.

13. *Lectures on the Philosophy of Religion*, trans. E. B. Speirs and J. B. Sanderson (London: Paul, Trench, Trubner, 1895), 2:264–65.

best sense is the presentation of human actions, relations and aspirations in their actually visible form to the sensuous and imaginative consciousness, exhibited in the spoken speech, behavior, pantomime and habiliments of living persons who in this way give expression to their intents, hopes and dynamic will—the plunging forward, the moving on, the realization of the self concerned. The dramatic action then depends on conditions of collision, human passion and character, leading to actions and reactions which in their turn call for further resolutions of conflicts and disruptions.[14]

Let me make another definition—Drama then is the representation of will working toward its fulfillment.

Must tragedy as such have an unhappy ending? What is meant by an unhappy ending? Why do people in a theatre take pleasure in the spectacle of unhappiness. Why?

We all know Aristotle's answer,[15] which seems to me only half right.[16]

What do you think the Christian answer is? Wherein does the Christian esthetic differ from the classic or pagan Aristotle? Which do you think is nearer the truth? (Now I find myself asking you this rainfall of questions.)

I hope in your thesis you will give a lot of good discussion to the matter of "pleasure in the spectacle of suffering" and the unhappy ending.

What do you yourself consider to be the highest type of dramatic tragedy? (Please give an example.) (And what a crazy word "type" is!) Would you place *Macbeth* at the top or *Agamemnon*? Or the Book of Job? Or *Hamlet*? Or parts of Dante and Milton.

What about the protagonist himself. Can we have pity and fear and einfuhlen[17] for the essentially evil? Can we? What about Milton's Satan?

Perhaps you will say at once that the true protagonist must be truly human—human enough, like us other mortals enough, to excite in us a fellow feeling.

Can innocence be truly tragic? Perhaps you will say no. Then can ignorance be tragic? What about knowledgeful guiltlessness.

I keep wondering—Must there always be a certain justness, a matter of receiving one's deserts in a true tragedy—at least from some sound point of view or another? Did Macbeth deserve the fate that fell upon him? Suppose he

14. *Philosophy of Fine Art*, 4:248–50.
15. Catharsis, mentioned in *Poetics*, chapter 6.
16. Amplified in Green, *Dramatic Heritage*, pp. 85–86.
17. Empathy, sympathetic understanding.

had won his wild intent, made his purpose prevail. How would we, the spectator, the reader, feel about him?

No doubt you will say that only in the fact that Macbeth received the death he deserved because of the crimes he had committed in his fell and fearfully purposed ambition—only because he received his death could we accept him as a tragic human being.

All right then, if a totally evil man is not properly tragic, then, to repeat, what about the totally innocent one? Does he stir in us tragic emotions if some undeserved fate falls upon him? Perhaps you will say that his case is pathetic, piteous, like a child being accidentally killed by an automobile, but not truly tragic.

All right then, what about Jesus Christ. (I keep going back to this.) Does his story excite in you this feeling of pity and fear, this sympathy, this yearning, this desire to help? And so on.

It is obvious that there are many kinds of dramatic tragedy—perhaps as many kinds as there are specimens of it—*Macbeth* is a kind, *Hamlet* is a kind, *Oedipus* is a kind, *Antigone* is a kind—and all kinds are specific individuals and there is no group or type among them except insofar as we arbitrarily and uncritically say so. (Maybe there are as many kinds as there are separate instances—as in the case of human individuals.)

Perhaps we might quote from an ancient Oriental who said there is only one way into the world, but an infinite number of ways out of it—birth is one, but death is infinitely varied.[18]

I believe there can be a tragedy written about a totally evil man, either beginning as such, or ending as such. Here I would define evil as the self-ruined individual. There can be tragedy of the evil-good man, the weak and volatile. There can be tragedy of the perfect man. There can be tragedy written about the struggle of evil against evil and tragedy written about the struggle of good against good. And so on through all the wordage combinations.

The skill of the artist, plus his ethical intuition, his poetic fervor—all would help determine the greatness of the art product.

For me, Shakespeare has always lacked the ultimate kind of greatness—that is, a religious intuition of existence. Where Aeschylus lacks some of the human warmth, the tender particularity, the rich foliage of life—there is in him a sense, an awareness of man as an ethical creature which satisfies me

18. Probably from the South China oral tradition.

better than Shakespeare's miraculous power as a sensory and romantic writer. For me the highest subject matter of tragic drama is the struggle of man to reach, to discover the self within him (and therefore outside of him likewise) as an abiding reality. And that reality of itself is identical with the good.

I feel, I think, that this reality is the true fountain of youth, the secret of life—propelling itself ever outward in waves of life, mystic, germinal of creative being.

When the effort toward self-realization is so fierce and strenuous as to destroy the self—in the very terms of goodness, the very principle of righteousness which the protagonist labors to reach—then there is basically and as subject matter the richest and realest drama possible.

I am not a pragmatist in the William James sense. (I knock on wood.)[19] But I am a pragmatist in the Alfred Whitehead sense, or even in terms of Plotinus. (I knock on flesh.)[20] And of St. Thomas Aquinas and Aristotle insofar as he, the latter, accepts his forms and types as coming created out of, say, a platonic ideal of reality.

I do not believe in the academic image known as "a body of truth." But I do believe in truth as a creative process which real men, which important protagonists of our potential dramas can create and sustain, and whose importance and reality lie only in such creativity and such sustaining.

Tragedy deals with free men, or men seeking to be free or with slaves struggling to break their bonds or free men passing in spite of all activity into slavery—their greatness depending upon the struggle they wage against their enslaving fate or destiny or chance—call it what you will.

Another question—Is the universe maleficent or beneficent? Or is it neither—simply neutral?

Finally, would this sort of thing stand up:—Tragedy is a sad story acted out—Comedy is a funny story acted out—Farce is a ridiculous story acted out.

And each kind or type or example—can it not—can incorporate some of the nature of the others in it—though each must be in a completed work of art essentially in and of itself.

19. James said the truth of an idea was determined by its usefulness in practice, but Green believed that "each and everything is more than what it is used for" (Green, *Dramatic Heritage*, p. 90).

20. Both Whitehead and Plotinus, an early Neoplatonist, thought that intuition was the source of knowledge about ultimate reality and that the imagination determined the form of human experience.

I guess I'd better stop or I'll get more mixed up than ever. But with your critical and creative acumen, I hope you can see a thread of continuity, of process-logic, running through it all.

By separate mail I am sending a copy of the little essay *Forever Growing.* On page 33 I speak some more about this subject.[21] I know it will all sound a little jumbled to you—but I am still doing the best I can.

I am sure your thesis will make a fine book. If after reading it, I feel inspired to write more and better plays, then it will be a success for me. If it discourages me—not. I am hard to discourage.

If you would be interested, perhaps the University of North Carolina Press here might like to publish the work. Or is it bespoke elsewhere?[22]

With cordial greetings and regards,

## 233. To Elizabeth L. Green

Hotel La Pérouse 40, Rue La Pérouse, Paris, France

21 June 1951

Dearest Honey:[1]

I am up here at Hotel La Pérouse where Betsy is living—Hotel La Pérouse—Room 60—waiting for her to get up and come down stairs. I got up and dressed and rushed up here and found with my poor eyes I read 7:30 for 6:30,

21. The pleasurable response to suffering depicted in tragedy.

22. After receiving this letter Falk stayed up until "four o'clock in the morning" working on her reply, then at the end of its five pages apologized for the length. "My only excuse for such verbosity is that as Whitman said to Emerson: I was simmering, simmering, simmering, and you brought me to a boil" (Doris Falk to Paul Green, 21 February 1951, PG-SHC). Later, she narrowed the focus of her dissertation to the plays of Eugene O'Neill and published it as *Eugene O'Neill and the Tragic Tension* (1958). Green used the present letter as the basis of "Tragedy—Playwright to Professor," in Green, *Dramatic Heritage*, pp. 81–91.

---

1. In May President Truman appointed Green to the U.S. National Commission for UNESCO, and on 17 June Green and his daughter Betsy, a rising senior at Oberlin College, flew to Paris for the Sixth General Conference of UNESCO. They arrived about 7:00 P.M. and stayed that night at the Hotel Raphael, headquarters of the U.S. delegation. That elegant hotel seemed ostentatious to Green, however, and the next day he moved Betsy to the Hotel La Pérouse, himself to another hotel and later to the Hotel D'Iena at 28, avenue D'Iena.

so I'm an hour early—and glad of it, since I get time to scribble you at least a note before we get breakfast(?) and start the grind. I am working night and day trying to keep my head above the flood of directives that pour in on me by the hour and understand what all this gathering is about. Alas, already I'm beginning to see why Archie MacLeish feels the way he does about the organization at present.[2] To put it boldly I find that the two strongest powers physically and financially—G.B. and the U.S.—are obviously the weakest, most cautious and uncertain spiritually, to use this term again. The entire delegation with the exception of Mr. Stakman of Minn.[3] seems to be completely overridden by paper work and technical wordage. Luther Evans[4] might be a first-rate man if he'd forget his statistical and bibliographical conditioning for awhile. By far the richest in wisdom are the oriental delegates—of whom I'm getting to know a few and I hope to know them all before I leave here, or most of them. They are troubled by the U.S. ways, manners and means, seeming to wish to reconcile our material power with some undiscovered *rightness* which they hope, nay even suspect, lies within us. For after all they that love the Lord shall prosper and they that don't won't—has for a long time been good oriental doctrine.[5] I'm afraid they're going to *continue* to be troubled at these Unesco[6] meetings as long as the U.S. sends the type of delegation she does. And of course she will send no other.[7] So: I fear for the

2. In remarks to the U.S. National Commission on 10 May Archibald MacLeish, a founder of UNESCO in 1946, said the organization was falling away from its purpose. UNESCO's responsibility was to uphold the ideals of civilization and represent the cultures of the world. Instead, the organization was giving in to pressure to propagandize for the West in the current East-West conflict, particularly to support United Nations military action in Korea. The cause of civilization would not be helped, he feared, by this emphasis on political differences and divisions around the world (*New York Times*, 11 May 1951, p. 19, col. 1). Green had responded to the speech with a note: "More power to you in your thundering idealism. Down the stretch of history the witnesses for the Lord have always been right!" (Paul Green to Archibald MacLeish, 18 May 1951, PG-SHC).

3. Elvin Charles Stakman, professor of plant pathology at the University of Minnesota and president (1949–51) of the American Association for the Advancement of Science.

4. Librarian of Congress.

5. See Psalms 122:6.

6. At the time Green consistently wrote the acronym UNESCO as "Unesco."

7. Because, Green thought, the National Commission was a branch of the Department of State.

future of Unesco. Unless some new intuition and power hit it its days are numbered. Maybe it will last 2 years, 5 years, 10 years—but ever with increasing weakness until its funds are withdrawn. I am searching in myself for some idea of what the way forward is. And so are many of the delegates further to the east. But no one yet has seen the begriff,[8] anyway not given utterance to it. Maybe I won't be so pessimistic when I have worked here more and seen more of the people—other than my U.S. politically instructed and civil-serviced-to-death confreres. (This attitude is not to be repeated to anyone of course.) I yet may be able to send you a te deum letter.[9] And after all it's a great privilege for me to meet these people here and get a close hot sense of the world's turmoiling[10] and aspirations embodied in living actuality around me.

Betsy is thriving and working her little efficient self very hard. She's an assistant to Howard Vickery[11] and is doing a lot of liaison work among the delegates, setting up dates for photographic appointments, taking notes on a lot of the speeches from the conference floor—she looks real cute sitting up with Mrs. Paul Douglass[12]—wearing her translating ear phones and writing away. Her French is improving fast. Tomorrow she is taking time off to go with some of the delegation girl friends to Versailles.

Paris is very, very beautiful though sobered by her late experiences[13] and present world conditions. Tell Jan[14] Bets is already looking to the day when

8. Idea, concept.

9. Green was never able to write in praise of the conference or the U.S. delegation. His report at the end of the session complained of "too many programs, papers, and directives for what is being done [and] too much time taken in full Conference discussion of meticulous budget matters." It stressed the "danger of too much political control and civil service efficiency in which the inspiration and freshness of the Unesco dream may be blighted to death" ("Report to Howard Vickery: Sixth General Conference," [9 July 1951], PG-SHC).

10. Originally "a close hot sense—even scent—of the world's turmoiling," then "even scent" was marked through.

11. Assistant director, UNESCO Relations Staff.

12. Emily Taft Douglass, wife of Senator Paul Douglass of Illinois and a member of Vickery's staff.

13. Several times in his diary Green noted "obvious marks of the fighting in 1944—the liberation," such as "roofs off of houses, a church damaged, and walls blown in" (10 July 1951, PG-SHC).

14. The Greens' youngest child, who was spending the summer at home following her first year at the University of Wisconsin.

the two of them can come back here for a visit. Also tell Gene[15] I'll write her some news and instructions when I can—and for her *not* to work too hard. Also tell her to write me about what she is doing—all the news from her secretarial end of the line. Much love and pantomime of delivery to go with it. P.

Dear Jan: Thanks, honey, for your sweet Father's day note. Bets delivered it punctually on the 17th. I'm already missing you very much, and right now I can see you humming and doing about the house. I hope the summer will be great fun for you, and remember I'm depending on you greatly to sort of keep your protective arms around the lady of the house. Write me when you can. You would love some of the figures of speech let loose here by the oriental delegates in their "speeches"—beautiful. A heartful of love to you! Doog.

Give Grandmother and Miss Stevens[16] my love. Will write them something, a card or two at least.

## 234. To Elizabeth L. Green

[Hotel D'Iena] 28, avenue D'Iena, Paris, France]
[6 July 1951]

Dear Honey:

Note the above address.[1] Bets and I will be at that Hotel next Wednesday and remain there a day or two or more. Then we shall be going about England and Scotland with Paul and Skip and Jenny.[2] So I guess I'm going to have the mournful fact of no letters from you. But if you could still write, send your missives on to the Hotel above. I'll ask them to hold any mail—after I leave—and I'll pick it up on my return.[3] I got a sweet note from you this morning

15. Sara Gene Steel.

16. Alice A. Stevens, Mrs. Lay's boarder and companion for many years.

---

1. Across the top of the page Green had written "Hotel Mount Royal, London, England."

2. Jenny Gegan, mother of Skip.

3. On 12 July (Thursday) Green and Betsy flew to London, where for a week he worked in the British Museum on Walter Raleigh, Elizabethan garden designs (for the projected Elizabethan Garden on Roanoke Island), and Pocahontas; watched Queen Elizabeth II lay the cornerstone for the National Theatre (13 July); and went to Gravesend to visit the grave of Pocahantas and the church dedicated to her there (15

telling about the hog-wire for the pool, etc.[4] I know you're going to love little Dorrit and won't Skip miss her!

Bets and I are still plugging on here. She's having a wonderful time going to concerts, shows, etc. I'm doing all I can for Unesco, which is not too much. I've tried to get the delegates interested in introducing a consideration of comparative religions and the great ethical systems of the world as part of Unesco's program for world understanding. I've just this morning met with the Pakistan delegates and sounded them out. They were 50-50. They're afraid of the explosive nature of religion as a subject of "inquiry." Also I've found the Roman Catholic point of view against it. My plan would be for a humanistic[5] consideration, a philosophical dealing with the matter. It seems to me so obvious that the religious/humane and ethical principles[6] of the great religions could be studied to much profit, and that this would lead to better understanding among us all. Well, the philosophical congress in New Delhi in December ought to be a great treat for us.[7] I've already made a few suggestions to the program committee here which is planning it. I've been over their prospectus and found that they too were crowding in a multiplicity of subjects, tending to divide *man* up rather than not. I'm having a lot of fun meeting and talking with Radhakrishnan[8] and other members of the Indian

---

July). On 20 July he and Betsy went by train to Southampton to meet Paul, Jr., and his wife and mother-in-law, with whom they toured until 23 July, when Green left Betsy with the family party and flew home, arriving in Chapel Hill the next day (Green diary, PG-SHC).

4. While Skip and Paul, Jr., were in England, Elizabeth and Janet kept their daughter Dorrit (born 20 May 1950) and put up a strong fence (hog-wire is a welded wire fence with 2″ × 4″ meshes) around the reflecting pool in the yard to keep the baby from crawling into it.

5. In the midst of this cursive letter, Green printed "humanistic," separating the letters to emphasize the word.

6. Green first wrote "religious and ethical principles," then without crossing out "religious" added "humane" directly above it and inclosed the double-decker result in parentheses, pairing "religious" and "humane."

7. Conference on Western and Eastern Philosophy at Delhi University, 11–14 December 1951, which Green (accompanied by Elizabeth) would attend during a lecture tour of the Orient sponsored by the Rockefeller Foundation (1 October 1951–1 January 1952).

8. Sarvepalli Radhakrishnan, leader of the Indian delegation to UNESCO (1946–52), was an organizer of the Conference on Western and Eastern Philosophy. Before

delegation. They say R. loves nothing better than to get seated in his bed at La Pérouse hotel each night and then have four or five maidens sit around on the bed and talk to him and he discourse to them. More power to him, forgiving this dolce-far-niente weakness,[9] if it is that. Yesterday we had a good talk about the Soviet system versus ours—you may know he is the Indian ambassador to Moscow—and though Marc Connelly[10] who had called by was quite talkative, I enjoyed my bit of sitting at the feet of Hindu wisdom.

I am sitting here in the lobby of Hotel D'Iena waiting while the desk clerk tries to reach Paul Claudel in the South of France. He is living in his Chateau there—a very old man now,[11] and I do so want to see him. It will be the only chance I'll ever have. His son is here in Paris and says he's sure his father will see me. He is a great spirit and I want to shake his hand and hear him talk some—even for a few minutes—about the world and man's place in it as he conceives it. Of course I've read his thoughts in many of his books.[12] But I want to meet him face to face. It will mean a train trip of nearly 800 miles—uhm.

Bets has lost her camera, so we'll be back without any picture record of our sojourn. She left it in the Opera Comique[13] and when we went back no trace could be found of it. Poor child, she's been really hurt by the loss.

Give my love to Ginger.[14] I've never been much of a brother-in-law to any

---

his diplomatic career Radhakrishnan taught at several Indian universities and at Oxford and published extensively on the topic of the conference, particularly *East and West in Religion* (1932) and *Eastern Religions and Western Thought* (1939). In 1952 Radhakrishnan became vice president of India, then president (1962–67).

9. Weakness for pleasant inactivity.

10. Fellow playwright and member of the U.S. delegation.

11. Eighty-three.

12. On the flight to Paris Green "spent most of the time reading *Pages de Prose* of Paul Claudel [André Blanchet, ed., (1944)]. I always enjoy him, feel lifted up, even when his religious mysticism offends my common-sense" (Green diary, 17 June 1951, PG-SHC). On 23 and 24 June (Saturday and Sunday), having caught a cold, Green "crawled into bed for my cold's sake and read a lot of the correspondence between Claudel and Gide [*Correspondence, 1899–1926 de Paul Claudel et André Gide* (1949)]. I found myself all the time interested in Claudel's letters to Gide and not Gide's to him" (Green diary, 24 June 1951).

13. Where they saw Rossini's *The Barber of Seville* on 30 June (Paul Green to Elizabeth Green, 1 July 1951, EG-SHC).

14. Elizabeth's sister Virginia Hawkins, visiting in Chapel Hill.

of my folks, but my heart has been good. My love too to your mother and tell her Bets and I are thinking of her. My love to Jan, bless her, I know she's busy, and to Gene, who I'm sure is working too hard, but then women are like that. Bets is just walking in the door, gay and chic. She's taking a friend out to dinner and I'm tagging along as soon as my call comes through—if it ever does.[15] On en retard![16]

Love, P. G.

## 235. To Paul, Jr., and Dorrit Green

Grand Hotel, Calcutta, India
5 December 1951

Dear Paul and Skip:[1]

Herewith are some snaps we took here in the orient. Please send them on with our love to Miss Stevens and Grandmother. They can keep them. We are

15. It did, and Claudel invited Green to visit. On 10 July at 12:55 P.M. he and Betsy took a train (the "Rapide," and "rapid it was. It really flew") for Lyon and arrived about 6:00 P.M. (Green diary, PG-SHC). Green went straightway to "see the old Roman amphitheatre and take some measurements. But it was closed" (Paul Green to Elizabeth Green, 12 July 1951, EG-SHC). At supper, however, he saw a notice that two cantatas, Arthur Honegger's *King David* and Igor Stravinsky's *Les Noces*, would be performed with dancers that night at the amphitheater, so he and Betsy "got a taxi and went back to a wonderful evening of music, oratorio-effect, chorus, orchestra—and the ghosts of 1,800 years ago walking in the ruins. That one evening was worth all the sweat—and it was hot in Lyon—of getting there" (ibid.). The next morning he hired a taxi to take them to Claudel's Château de Brangues at Morestel, sixty-five kilometers east of Lyon. "I had a lot of good talk with him and came away feeling fine. I liked his Thomistic dogmatism and optimism about the world" (ibid.). That afternoon he and Betsy returned by train to Paris. Later, Green wrote an account of his visit: "Paul Claudel," in Green, *Dramatic Heritage*, pp. 132–46.

16. Until later!

1. Of his present trip Green said, "The Rockefeller Foundation asked me to go into Asia on a lecture tour dealing with the arts in the United States. I was to be an ambassador of culture as it were—a voice however one and single in support of a sort of Yankee creativity different from the old commerce and trade and the usual dollars and cents diplomacy" (Preface, "Diary Notes of a Round-the-World Lecture Tour," PG-SHC). Elizabeth went with him, and their trip lasted three months (1 October

working hard and know you are too. And how's the family growing?[2] Our experiences are quite weird, and our hearts are always aching at the poverty and suffering we see. But we are learning a lot and I am doing quite a bit of lecturing and writing articles for the papers out this way as I go. What good it all does, I don't know.[3] Tomorrow night a dinner is being given for us—these social functions are always painful.[4] On Friday I lecture at Calcutta University.[5] And on Saturday we fly to Delhi.[6] We will be there until Dec. 14 and then fly to Istanbul, Turkey. The security situation is causing us to revise our itinerary somewhat. Down in Malaya, Thailand and Burma we weren't always too certain of our safety. Guerrillas and bandits are making life miserable for a

---

1951–1 January 1952). Before going to India, they were in Japan (9–29 October) as guests of Waseda University in Tokyo and visited numerous other places for four or five days (Okinawa, Jakarta, Denpasar, Singapore, Bangkok, and Rangoon). They arrived in Calcutta on 30 November and remained until 10 December ("Diary Notes" and Itinerary, Asian Tour, PG-SHC).

2. Skip was four months pregnant with their second daughter, Nancy, born on 25 May 1952.

3. Among his lecture titles were "Broadway," "The Educational Theater in America," "Symphonic Festival Drama," "Movies in America," "The Carolina Playmakers," and "Folk Drama in the United States" ("Paul Green Describes Trip," *NO*, 10 December 1951, sec. 1, p. 5, cols. 1–4). Green interpreted in the other direction too, sending back accounts of the oriental theater and his trip (ibid., and "Tribute to the Kabuki Theater of Japan," *New York Times*, 27 January 1952, sec. 2, p. 1, cols. 4–7; p. 2, cols. 5–6). Green recounts the trip and his impressions in three essays in Green, *Dramatic Heritage*: "Asia and the American Dream," pp. 155–63; "The Japanese Theatre," pp. 164–69; and "The Indian Theatre," pp. 170–77.

4. At this buffet supper, however, given in Green's honor by George Mann, public affairs officer for the U.S. Information Service, "we had a very wonderful evening. . . . A number of interesting people came to the dinner," among them Saumyendra Nath Tagore, head of the Communist party in Calcutta, and Mrs. Kiddo Mukherjee, head of the Theatre Guild of Calcutta ("Diary Notes," 6 December 1951, PG-SHC).

5. On "The American Drama." But the lecture was canceled because of the death on 5 December of Abanindra Nath Tagore, painter and professor of fine arts at Calcutta University ("Diary Notes," 4 and 7 December 1951, PG-SHC).

6. Uncertainty about their reservation at the Hotel Imperial in Delhi prevented the Greens from flying there until Monday, 10 December, for the Conference on Western and Eastern Philosophy at Delhi University. During the conference Green renewed his acquaintance with Sarvepalli Radhakrishnan, conducting an interview with him that served as the basis for "A Sound Heart," in Green, *Dramatic Heritage*, pp. 147–54.

lot of people out this way. We'll be a bit relieved when we get to Athens—past Cairo and the smoulderings in the near east.[7] Calcutta is something to see with babes and little folks lying out at night—chilly nights—on the sidewalks, up against walls, everywhere—mute, helpless, and hungry, no home, no care, no protection. And goats and sacred cows and calves wandering about by the thousands not fit for anything but used as pets and the patty-cake dried dung used for fuel. Every afternoon late the city is a stench of nose-burning smoke from the people cooking their supper.[8] Your mother is standing up fine as you can see, and I am doing my best. All our love to all of you, and Paul, I hope you're past the hardest of your research.[9]

Doog

7. Later the Greens decided against visiting Cairo, where since 27 October an unofficial state of war had existed between Egypt and Great Britain over control of the Suez Canal. Leaving New Delhi on 14 December, they flew to Istanbul, then to Athens on 17 December, to Rome on 23 December, and to Madrid on 29 December. On 31 December they left Madrid for Boston, where they were met by Paul, Jr., and Skip on the morning of 1 January (Paul Green to Paul Green, Jr., 24 December 1951, PGJr).

8. Green's diary includes several accounts of the pathetic sights on the streets of Calcutta (30 November, 1 and 5 December, PG-SHC). One morning he even "got up early to take a walk in the town to see if the poor people were still lying on the sidewalks. A weeping heart" ("Diary Notes," 2 December 1951).

9. Paul, Jr., in his second year of doctoral work in electrical engineering at Massachusetts Institute of Technology, was beginning research for his thesis on "spread spectrum communication" (Paul Green, Jr., to Laurence Avery, 10 November 1987).

# VII

## Symphonic Drama and Integration, 1952–1955

February 1952
: Urges UNESCO to take stands on behalf of morality in world affairs.

Spring 1952
: Often in Washington, D.C., trying to arrange summer production of *Faith of Our Fathers.* Despite attendance of over 100,000 in 1951, which made the play self-supporting, National Capital Sesquicentennial Commission votes in May to discontinue it.

Summer 1952
: Writes *Hoedown*, a folk musical.

Fall–Winter 1952
: Begins *The Seventeenth Star.* Translates and adapts Henri Meilhac and Ludovic Halévy's libretto for Georges Bizet's *Carmen.* Collaborates with Josephina Niggli on *Serenata.*

April 1953
: In New York City with director Herbert Graf and conductor Kurt Adler accommodates colloquial libretto to rhythms of Bizet's music.

27 June 1953
: *Carmen* opens at Central City Opera Festival in Colorado.

Summer 1953
: In Santa Barbara, California, for rehearsals of *Serenata*, which opens on 8 August. In Columbus, Ohio, for rehearsals of *The Seventeenth Star*, which opens on 27 August in celebration of the sesquicentennial of Ohio statehood.

Fall 1953
: Begins *Wilderness Road.*

Early April 1954
: Visits Berea College in Kentucky, sponsor of *Wilderness Road.*

Summer–Fall 1954

Because of intense but diverse feelings about the play at Berea, outlines two versions of *Wilderness Road.*

December 1954

Visits Berea to oversee construction of theater and win acceptance of version of play he prefers.

Winter–Spring 1955

Writes *Wilderness Road.*

5–6 June 1955

Carl Sandburg visits.

29 June 1955

*Wilderness Road* opens first season at Berea College.

8 August 1955

Attacks North Carolina governor for attempting to prevent integration of schools in the state.

Winter 1955

Plans *The Founders.* Makes several trips to Jamestown and Williamsburg for construction of theater and research.

## 236. To Luther Evans[1]

[Greenwood Road, Chapel Hill, N.C.]
2 February 1952

Dear Luther:

This is to tell you I think we are to be congratulated on having you head our UNESCO National Commission. George Stoddard did a great job, and I am sure that you will create and carry on your fine leadership in your individual and stimulating way.

It seems more important than ever that UNESCO take more dynamic leadership in not only national but in world affairs than it has heretofore. I know there are plenty of answers and reasons why the organization should work smoothly and quietly and persuasively behind the scenes more or less. I think the world situation is too serious for that. The American democracy has got into the fiery and suffocating grip of militarism. Our State Department has no realistic or imaginative foreign policy. If I am not a blind man hobbled and can't run, its policy is played by ear and from day to day and flung into being by the "stop Russia" game.

UNESCO is of course a child of our State Department. But must a child be conditioned by its parent that it must continue to ape its ineffectual behavior. I hope under your leadership that UNESCO will come out more boldly for the needed virtues among men and against the evils that are now obvious everywhere.

I have just completed a trip around the world—visiting Hawaii, Japan, the Philippines, Southeast Asia and up through Thailand, Burma, India, Iran, Lebanon, Turkey, and on through Europe home. My business was the theatre and the collateral arts of music and dance. But it was clear to me that we are not winning the millions of people in Asia to our cause—the cause of a free and self-reliant democracy. In fact we are losing friends every day, and Russia is gaining them. I saw it true in Malaya, in Thailand, Burma and especially in India. And if we lose India, then we in truth have lost Asia.

UNESCO's work in fundamental education and technical assistance is

1. Luther Evans (1902–1982), Librarian of Congress (1945–53) and member with Green of the U.S. National Commission for UNESCO, succeeded George Stoddard, president of the University of Illinois, as chairman of the commission on 1 February 1952. Green did not mail the present letter (atop the first page he wrote, "Not sent") but sent a shorter one instead, which consisted of the first two paragraphs of this draft and a brief closing paragraph: "UNESCO has much to do, and if there are any errands you trust me to run, I'll try to do them" (20 February 1952, PG-SHC).

good. But it is not good enough, for there is no authoritative moral voice speaking a great vision and enough unselfish dream with it.

I think Archibald MacLeish was more right than wrong![2]

I wish UNESCO would get so fired up with its responsibility and privilege that its uncouth and physiological pedagogy of terminology would be fused and burned away into living language and fervor of spirit. I have been struck again and again in listening to the talks and in the meetings [by] the confusion of tongues—quantitative and spatial terms being used when qualitative and psychological (or spiritual) meanings were intended.

The other afternoon we gave a television show there in Hunter College[3] and afterwards we held an open forum. I got hit between the eyes when one of the lady delegates from the middlewest stood up and wanted to know from us fellows sitting on the platform how we could make UNESCO better known. "Out in the Mississippi Valley where I come from," she said, "when the people do hear of it, they think it's some kind of cereal."

I needn't take up your time. You need it for something better. But let me repeat—can't UNESCO stand for things in the public press—openly condemn abuses which are ruining us in Asia, the flood of bad gangster, crime, violence and cheap sex pictures that are being poured into the Oriental world from Hollywood,[4] the dynamiting of innocent Negro citizens in Florida,[5] the cynical military support being given to effete colonialisms and certain heavy-handed dictatorships, etc., etc.

2. When he said UNESCO was failing its purpose by becoming partisan and should focus on concerns that unify mankind (see letter 233, n. 3).

3. A discussion with illustrations of ways to visualize the objectives of the United Nations (a scene from *The Common Glory* was one of the illustrations), featuring Green, Malcomb S. Adisesiah, head of UNESCO Technical Assistance, and Mab Ingalls, head of the World Health Organization, was broadcast live from Hunter College in New York City on Sunday, 27 January (Rehearsal notes, 26 January 1952, PG-SHC).

4. At a dinner party in Calcutta Saumyendra Nath Tagore told Green that "the leaders in your country make the dreadful mistake . . . of failing to reach the heart of humanity. All we hear from America is power, power, machinery, machinery, armaments, war, atom bombs—and then there are your movies which contaminate the people" ("Diary Notes of a Round-the-World Lecture Tour," 6 December 1951, PG-SHC).

5. Since 23 September 1951 several dynamite blasts had occurred in Carver Village, a black apartment complex near a white residential area in Miami.

Maybe I am off-base. Maybe UNESCO is not supposed to take such stands. But if the organization continues as is with its civil service and protocolic mindedness, it will not too long from now cease to be of any effect at all in the world scene. And the worst accusation of all will be leveled against it in Congress—"it does nothing"—and its funds will be withdrawn. It will close up shop.

Maybe what I advocate would bring it to a closed door sooner. But even so it would have perished with some glory and its empty filing cases and meeting halls thereafter would still be haunted by voices at least that would keep repeating something worth saying.

How can we folks down here in North Carolina organize a branch of UNESCO and help along more swiftly the abolition of race discrimination, segregation, and general ignorance. For instance, down here at my university we ought to be setting up a great plan for the humanities—by which our young college students here could be trained for world citizenship. We ought to have Buddhistic and Hindu psychology brought into our curriculum, the Oriental religious epics, the ethical systems and philosophies made available for study. We ought to bring scholars out of Asia to hold seminars down here in our benighted south. There is much, much work to do. You can give us some good advice.

Don't take time to answer all this. We can talk about it all over a luncheon when I am up your way some day.

Much power to you.

Ever,

## 237. To Dorothy E. Shue[1]

[Greenwood Road, Chapel Hill, N.C.]
19 February 1952

Dear Mrs. Shue:

I congratulate the people of Cumberland County and all such civic-minded leaders as yourself on the opening of your library. From long experi-

1. Shue, librarian of the Cumberland County, North Carolina, Public Library, asked Green for "a few words of greeting—or anything you would like to write" for display in the new county library building scheduled to open on 22 March 1952 (11 February 1952, PG-SHC).

ence in trying to create books and loving and associating with the books of others, I know something of what it means to have this dream of yours come to realization.

I never get tired of saying—and please forgive me for saying it again here—that the greatness of a people lies in its devotion to the arts of beauty, of truth and, yes, of goodness. These arts and these principles are the fire and fervor of a nation's soul, and however mighty the arm of strength and physical power may be, it ultimately will avail little unless this strength is equaled by these creative productions of the soul!

And whatever and whenever a new symphony orchestra is brought into being, a fine new play is produced, or a good book written, or a library such as yours built and furnished forth for feeding the spiritual hunger of man—then just so much more surely does the nation in which these great things occur move closer to the fulfillment of the rich destiny meant for it.

More power to you and your associates. And I hope someday to come and sit down at a table in your new library building and read for awhile and meditate on the fine thing you have done. Yes, a library too, like a church or cathedral, is for meditation—as well as study and learning.

Sincerely yours,

## 238. To Dorothy McBrayer Stahl

[Greenwood Road, Chapel Hill, N.C.]
29 April 1952

Dear Dottie:[1]

I got back from Washington, D.C. this morning—where I had been haranguing with politicians and shysters for two or three days trying to get my outdoor play *Faith of Our Fathers* out of the grip of their strangling fingers[2]—

1. McBrayer, Green's secretary at Fox Film Corporation in 1932 and since then a friend of the family, married Marvin Stahl in 1945 and moved with him to Grosse Pointe Park, Michigan. Recently she sent Green John Tettemer's autobiography, *I Was a Monk* (1951).

2. The play had become entangled in presidential election-year politics. Democrats on the National Capital Sesquicentennial Commission wanted to continue *Faith of Our Fathers* for a third summer, believing its popularity would help their party in the November elections. For the same reason Republicans on the commission wished to kill it. Green's only hope, his friend Jonathan Daniels advised him playfully, was to put a song in the play called "I Like Ike" (campaign jingle for Dwight Eisenhower, Republican candidate for president) (Green notes on telephone conversation with

and found your copy of John Tettemer's book waiting for me. Tonight after supper I lay down on the sofa and now have just finished it. Thank you for sending it, and I'll return it right away and have the bookstore here order me a copy. I want to have it around, and I'm sure Janet and Elizabeth will want to read it. It is a good thing! I know because it made me feel good, better, lifted up. I can't write you fully about it now—but can I later?—but I especially like the latter part, from Chapter XV on. I was glad to see you had marked the best part.[3] He's right—so right. And when I can I'll dictate a splurging epistle, if I'm not intruding on your time, and try to say why. What he said in the late chapters is so identical with that profundity of the orient, the part of it I love, which evokes reality, experiences reality, oneness, monism, God—any name you wish—and doesn't try to define, syllogize it, or crust it over with judgments and logic.[4]

Please write me all about his life—both its practical everyday part and his religious and human attitude. You know, tell me about the man after he left the monastery or ceased being a monk rather. I know about his marriage, children, etc. from the prefaces and from California.[5] My love to Marvin and the children too.

---

Jonathan Daniels, 24 April 1952, PG-SHC). In June the commission voted to discontinue the play despite the fact that attendance of over 100,000 in 1951 made it self-supporting (press release, undated, PG-SHC; *Washington Post*, 11 June 1952, sec. I, p. 19, cols. 1–2).

3. Chapter 15 (the final chapter) is a moving account of Tettemer's development as a mystic and consequent resignation from the Society of Jesus.

4. Later Green said he agreed with Tettemer "that all the manifold explanations of reality made by the scholars somehow never explain reality—at least to me, in such a way that I can experience it—the way I do with, say, the Second movement of Brahms's Number Four, or in some wonderful poetry like Wordsworth's 'Ode on Intimations of Immortality.' Reality must be experienced, and I agree too that all of man's training and working will, if they are right and fruitful lead to that experiencing—more and more" (Paul Green to Dorothy McBrayer Stahl, 17 May 1952, JG).

5. In Hollywood in the early 1930s Green met Tettemer, who supported himself with small roles in motion pictures (*Lost Horizon* and *Meet John Doe* among them). Tettemer, born in St. Louis, resigned from the Society of Jesus, in which he held high office, in the mid-1920s, married a British woman and moved to Los Angeles in 1928, there wrote *I Was a Monk*, and died in 1949 (Dorothy McBrayer Stahl to Paul Green, 19 August 1951, PG-SHC; Jean Burden, "Foreword," *I Was a Monk* [New York: Knopf, 1951], pp. 9–12).

Paul

Janet seems happy and has a good analyst here to whom she goes regularly. She has a job, also is keeping our now extensive lawn mowed.[6]

## 239. To William and Betsy G. Moyer

[Greenwood Road, Chapel Hill, N.C.]
2 May 1952

Dear Bill and Bets:[1]

I have just come from the concert of the N.C. Symphony,[2] and I couldn't go to sleep without writing you. You would have loved it all—wonderful for a people's orchestra[3] like this! (the concert was). And Bill, I thought of you especially during the second movement of the Brahms IV. I guess I agree with you about the greatness of this melody.[4] It made me know—well, in the words of Hegel—reality, know it in the sense of experiencing it. Beauty! Yes, in listening to it, "filling" it and being filled by it I knew that *Something* also knew and I felt drawn to It as It was drawn to me. Isn't that the finest thing can happen in an art experience?[5] Write us. Jan is OK, has a job. She'll write you fully, or mom will. Love. Doog. (ouch)[6]

6. Following a period of depression at the University of Wisconsin earlier in the spring, Janet now lived at home and had weekly sessions with Dr. George C. Ham, head of the Department of Psychiatry in the UNC School of Medicine. She enrolled at UNC in the fall, taught modern dance through the UNC Extension Division, and in 1954 graduated Phi Beta Kappa with honors in English.

---

1. Betsy and William Moyer married on 4 April 1952 at Oberlin College where both were students. After graduation they moved to Boston, where Moyer took a position as trombonist with the Boston Symphony Orchestra.

2. At Aycock Auditorium in Greensboro, North Carolina.

3. An orchestra that travels around the state playing in towns small and large.

4. In an early letter to Green, Moyer gave as the reason for his shaky handwriting that he had just performed Brahms's fourth symphony with the Tanglewood student orchestra and was too excited to write legibly (6 July 1950, PG-SHC).

5. In the margin to the left of the passage beginning "It made me know" and ending here, Green wrote: "On reading this over I find it sounds sentimental, but you understand."

6. In Green's handwritten letters, both margins tend to shift to the right as he

## 240. To W. D. Weatherford[1]

[Greenwood Road] Chapel Hill, N.C.
23 June 1952

Dear Dr. Weatherford:

I have received your fine letter of June 18 with its proposal relative to the drama of the Scotch-Irish people of the Southern Appalachian Mountains. I have read and studied them both very carefully, and first let me congratulate you on your vision and your hopes. You have a great dream, and I am glad to see that you realize the importance of the practical phase of it and have thoroughly visualized ways, means, and methods of procedure.

I have been associated with a number of outdoor festival dramas—dramas celebrating our heritage—and I am now working at still another which will tell the story of the Pilgrims and their piety and unyielding self-reliance.[2] But I have not yet met with any of the founders of these dramas who has had, it seems to me, quite your thoroughness of foresight and preparation. Because of this, if for no other reason, I would guess that this Berea dream of yours will be a first rate success. The affirmation and even glorification of the theme of education appeals to me very much as a teacher, for I have taught school myself off and on since I was about seventeen years old. In fact I did my first

---

moves down the page. "Ouch" is crowded into the bottom right corner and may be his reaction to the tight spot he was in, with no more room to write.

---

1. W. D. Weatherford (1875–1970) had a phenomenal career promoting education and better race relations and studying life in the southern Appalachian region. Long a trustee of Berea College (1915–64), he chaired the committee charged with planning a celebration of the school's centennial in 1955, and as the main event of the celebration he envisioned a play focused on the people of the region and their thirst for education (Weatherford, "A Drama of Mountain Life," typescript, PG-SHC). In a letter of 18 June 1952 Weatherford invited Green to write the play for the 1955 celebration, and the letter with its accompanying typescript, "A Drama of Mountain Life," provided Green a unique experience. For the only time in his career, he was approached to write a play by somebody who had already imagined every phase of the project, from general purpose to practical details. In the letter of 18 June Weatherford presented himself as a dreamer like the leading characters in *The Lost Colony* but added that he wanted "to be a dreamer whose dreams come true" (PG-SHC).

2. Projected for Plymouth, Massachusetts, but never produced or completely written.

teaching in an old log schoolhouse in Harnett County when I was sixteen years old. I filled in for a teacher who as I remember had gone off and got drunk and was unable to function for awhile.

I shall be glad to write the drama for you[3] and to participate in bringing this dream to completion in any way I may be needed. The terms you offer me are quite satisfactory.[4] They are pretty much the same as obtain in my other plays. I am receiving this year the same amount per performance—$25.00—for *The Lost Colony*,[5] and for *The Common Glory* I get a straight royalty figure.[6]

I am pleased to note that you will be coming to Manteo and Williamsburg around July 1. Would it be possible for you to attend the opening of *The Common Glory* the night of July 1? I shall be there and would like very much to see you. If you could be my guest that night for dinner and the opening I would appreciate it.[7]

*The Lost Colony* opens on the night of the 28th.[8] You could go on down to Manteo from Williamsburg and see that drama on the 2nd—or at your pleasure.[9]

I find your typescript statement—"A Drama of Mountain Life"—full of good stuff for pondering. So I am keeping it—unless you want it returned. If

3. It became *Wilderness Road.*

4. $1,000 on delivery of a full play outline, due no later than the third week of April 1954 (time of the spring meeting of Berea's trustees); $1,000 on delivery of the completed script, due no later than November 1954 (time of the fall trustees meeting); $25 for each performance, with 75 anticipated during the summer of 1955; and a royalty of 15 percent on the sale of published copies of the play (18 June 1952, PG-SHC). In the margin of Weatherford's letter Green added the payments mentioned here and noted: "Totals up to $5,875 . . . only $4,000 guaranteed."

5. The only year the Roanoke Island Historical Association paid Green anything approaching a royalty for performances of *The Lost Colony* was 1952. The association reduced the fee to $20 a performance, then stopped paying that during the last weeks of the season (Paul Green to William Hardy, 26 April 1952; Hardy to Green, 2 May 1952; and Green to Martin Kellogg, 2 October 1952, PG-SHC).

6. Ten percent of gross proceeds.

7. Weatherford accepted (Paul Green to W. D. Weatherford, 24 June 1952, PG-SHC).

8. Of June.

9. Weatherford did, and wrote that "I am back from Manteo where I saw your *Lost Colony*. It is the best of all the outdoor dramas I have seen. You did a magnificent job on that" (W. D. Weatherford to Paul Green, 5 July 1952, PG-SHC).

so, I will have copies made of it. It will prove of great importance to me in my research, which research will be most admirably facilitated by the plans in your letter as stated in paragraphs 5, 6, and 7.[10] But we can talk further on these matters if you can come over to Williamsburg for the opening.[11]

With sincere greetings and regards, Paul Green

## 241. To Charlotte Palmer Timm[1]

[Greenwood Road, Chapel Hill, N.C.]
9 August 1952

Dear Mrs. Timm:

I am very glad to have you include any statement you wish to make about my play *The Lost Colony*. I would like to suggest, however, that it be designated as a bit more than a pageant. Actually I consider it a drama—in my terminology a "symphonic drama." And may I presume upon you by enclosing a copy of a little article I wrote on the subject.[2] The other outdoor plays I write are likewise not pageants only. In each of them I try to tell a straight and connected story, interweave characters, and build toward a psychological

10. Which asked Green to spend "a week [accompanied by Weatherford or a member of Berea's faculty] in each of four deep mountain states [West Virginia, Kentucky, Tennessee, and North Carolina], studying the native life of Berea's constituency," for which Berea would pay Green $1,000 and expenses, and to spend a month at Berea "studying our method of education through a work study program," for which Berea would pay Green $1,000 and expenses. Weatherford also offered Green the use of his own extensive collection of historical material on the region.

11. The major change in the terms outlined by Weatherford was that the text of *Wilderness Road* did not become the property of Berea College. Green retained the copyright himself, as his experience in dealing with the Roanoke Island Historical Association caused him to do with every play after *The Lost Colony*. He published *Wilderness Road* through Samuel French in 1956, dedicating it to Weatherford.

---

1. Timm, of Ann Arbor, Michigan, was at work on a book, *Let's Do a Pageant*, and wished permission from Green to devote a section to *The Lost Colony*, which she considered "the apex of American pageantry" (Charlotte Palmer Timm to Paul Green, 22 July 1952, PG-SHC).

2. Probably "*The Lost Colony*: A Dialogue at Evening," later published in Paul Green, *Dramatic Heritage* (New York: Samuel French, 1953), pp. 42–48, which recently appeared in *Theatre Arts* 36 (July 1952): 72–73.

climax. This is not usually the case in pageantry. It seems that other writers who are now producing outdoor plays strive to make them more dramatic than pageantal.

And many thanks for the mimeographed material.[3] I have read it with a lot of interest.

And congratulations too on your doing such a book. It is very badly needed.[4]

Sincerely yours,

## 242. To Herbert Graf

[Greenwood Road, Chapel Hill, N.C.]
17 September 1952

Dear Herbert:[1]

I have just returned to town from a meeting out in Ohio where the people are interested in doing some sort of an outdoor drama[2] and have therefore been delayed in getting your letter of September 14. I am delighted that you are still interested in going ahead with the *Carmen.* For I am. So you can count me in—understanding of course that you and Don[3] and I ought to get together soon for some discussion of ways and means and the over-all picture.

3. A summary of her teaching and writing (among which were three pageants for the Ann Arbor Board of Education and Parks Department).

4. *Let's Do a Pageant* seems not to have been published.

---

1. Stage director of the Metropolitan Opera in New York City but at the time working with the San Francisco Opera, Graf had been invited to stage Georges Bizet's *Carmen* in Central City, Colorado, during the annual summer opera festival there in 1953. For the production he wanted a new translation of the text that, "without being *Carmen Jones,*" was "an interesting *Carmen* for American ears" (Herbert Graf to Paul Green, 16 March 1952, PG-SHC), and he wanted Green to make the translation. He asked Green to let him know quickly whether he could do the job because the deadline for accepting the Central City offer was 1 October (14 September 1952).

2. On 11 September Green met in Columbus with a committee planning the celebration of Ohio's 150th anniversary as a state in 1953, for which he would write *The Seventeenth Star,* produced at the state fair in Columbus, 27 August–7 September 1953.

3. Oenslager, stage designer for the project, who had worked with Green on *Peer Gynt* and *Johnny Johnson.*

I have just finished an American folk opera which I entitled *Hoedown.*[4] I used native music and native lyrics wherever possible—my main purpose being to sell great music among the people. It has been bought by a young New York producer,[5] and I hope him success with it.[6]

So I will be coming up to New York off and on during the fall and winter. You and Don set the date for our discussion and I will be there.[7]

Elizabeth joins me in sympathy to you and your wife over her illness. I am glad to know that she is recovered now, and please give her our best greetings and love.

Ever,

## 243. To David Andrews[1]

[Greenwood Road, Chapel Hill, N.C.]
4 June 1953

Dear David Andrews:

My sincere admiration to you for your efforts at Raleigh the other day. You did a noble thing, and I only wish I had been over there sitting down by you,

4. Set in Green's fictional Little Bethel, featuring a county singing competition, with folk music and lyrics from the collection of Winnifred Minter Moon (*Hoedown*, Paul Green Foundation, Chapel Hill).

5. Charles Christenberry, Jr.

6. Because of its music, *Hoedown* was expensive to produce, and Christenberry could not raise sufficient money. By early 1954 Green thought of the play as "indefinitely postponed" (Paul Green to Samuel French, 21 September 1954, PG-SHC). It has not been published or produced.

7. Graf staged *Carmen*, in Green's translation and adaptation of Henri Meilhac and Ludovic Halévy's libretto, at the Opera House in the old gold-mining town of Central City, Colorado, opening it on 27 June 1953.

---

1. On 29 May 1953 two black men, Raleigh Speller and Clyde Brown, sentenced to death for rape, were executed at Central Prison in Raleigh, and David Andrews, on the American Friends Service Committee in Greensboro, North Carolina, protested the executions (David Andrews, letter to the editor, *Greensboro Daily News*, 31 May 1953, Feature sec., p. 5, cols. 5–6). After futile pleas to Governor William B. Umstead for intervention, he had fasted on the steps of the capitol in Raleigh during 28 May, the day before the executions (David Andrews to Paul Green, 15 July 1953 and attachment, PG-SHC).

protesting with you this inhumanity to man which our state continues to practice over there under the garb of a generous and even-handed justice. We are a brutal people still, and our climb out of barbarity must continue even as it is difficult to be continued. I cannot for the life of me understand this cynical and careless and even intended killing which goes on and on and on. The only answer is animal barbarism. And the sooner we realize the condition of our souls and our senses—if such a realization is possible—then the more quickly we can begin to understand and indulge in acts of human kindness. I hate the Death House. I hate all of the paraphernalia attached to it, and I especially hate its anesthetic sanitary quality.[2] To think that a second killing makes the first killing right is the thought of an insane man. But then too this barbarity I speak of is a kind of madness.

I hope you will keep in touch with me as time goes on, and I know that your persistence in the way of right will carry you forward in this world—carry you far in spite of man's too easy sensual cruelty. For my philosophy is that mixed in with and sometimes underneath these barbarities there is a streak of rational logic which is the essence of man's true being—a logic which he cannot deny and which in his thoughtful moments he must always believe, namely that his challenge is to creative beneficence and not to malign and destructive malignance.

My best greetings,

2. Following two more executions later in the year, Green sent a letter to leading state papers in an effort to disabuse people of the notion that modern methods of execution had an "anesthetic" quality. He pointed out that "we shudder at the sight and even the thought of the ancient barbaric instruments of torture and justice—the rack, the wheel, the garrote, the screw, the iron spike, the heated tongs, melted lead or the headsman's bloody axe. But cruel as these were five hundred years ago, their pain was hardly equal to that of death by gas today. In North Carolina's house of horrors the condemned culprits are slowly strangled—yes, by degrees are smothered to death. The writhings and convulsions of the dying criminal often last as long as eight minutes, or ten, or twelve and even fifteen minutes before finally the strangling lungs burst with blood and the stopped heart brings relief in extinction. We call it asphyxiation, but it is a fiendish suffocation just the same" (8 November 1953, PG-SHC; see *NO*, 10 November 1953, sec. 1, p. 4, col. 6).

## 244. To Stark Young[1]

[Greenwood Road, Chapel Hill, N.C.]
3 September 1953

Dear Stark Young:

I got back from Columbus last night[2] and on my arrival here received your wonderful token of thoughtfulness—the new edition of *So Red the Rose.* I will read your fluent words and experience your colorful images again on this a second reading of the story. And this is to thank you too for your nice letter of some weeks ago.[3] I have been out on the west coast and in the middlewest putting on a couple of symphonic dramas[4]—as I lovingly and bullheadedly call them—and that accounts for my delay in responding to your message of friendship. I am having a lot of fun going up and down the world writing and putting on these plays of the people's heritage and hope. But truly I am anxious to get back with one or two things I have in mind for Broadway.

I continue to hope for you the best of everything and I trust that I shall some time soon have the privilege of coming by and shaking your hand.

Ever more joy and therefore strength to you—

1. In a review of Eric Bentley's *In Search of Theater* Green praised Bentley for, among other things, his appreciation of theater critic Stark Young (1881–1963), whose long career as reviewer for *The New Republic* is represented by *Immortal Shadows* (1948) ("A Quest for Honesty and Integrity," *New York Times*, 15 March 1953, Book Review sec., p. 6). After returning from Europe, Young thanked Green, saying, "The first thing that delighted me when I got home on March 16th from Rome was the Sunday *Times* with your article on Eric Bentley's book. I was very appreciative indeed of your comment on me and my writing. A good opinion from you—especially one so happily put—has an extra value for me, since I have long held you in high esteem, your work and what I have learned of you personally" (27 May 1953, PG-SHC). A little later he sent Green a copy of *So Red the Rose*, best known of his novels and newly reprinted from its original publication in 1934.

2. Where *The Seventeenth Star* was in production.

3. 27 May 1953 (see n. 1).

4. *Serenata* and *The Seventeenth Star.*

## 245. To John Gassner[1]

[Greenwood Road, Chapel Hill, N.C.]
9 September 1953

Dear John:

I have just got back from some playmaking out in California and Columbus[2] and am settling down for the fall and winter's work here in Chapel Hill. Too bad I missed you on your trip. Someday we must get together for a lot of good talk about the theater. Many thanks for the kind words you say[3] and I am delighted that you are writing some pieces on the symphonic drama work here on the eastern seaboard.[4] (The term "symphonic" is about the best I can get for this sort of theater in which all theater arts can be and are used to "sound together"—music, dance, poetry, mental speech, masks even, dynamic and vital lighting, color, pantomime, etc.)

I don't know where the original ending of *The House of Connelly* is, but I will try to find it and send it to you.[5] It was a tragic conclusion and cued out of—well, an art intuition rather than a life recollection.[6]

1. John Gassner (1902–1967), longtime play reader for the Theatre Guild, anthologist, and teacher of drama, spoke to the Southeastern Theatre Conference in Chapel Hill on 8 March 1953 (published as "An American National Theatre," in *The Theatre in Our Times* [1954], pp. 549–57), then returned to the area in July to see *The Lost Colony* and *The Common Glory.* In a recent letter he expressed regret at not seeing Green during the trip (27 August 1953, PG-SHC).

2. For *Serenata* and *The Seventeenth Star.*

3. *The Lost Colony* "stirred my wife and me greatly," Gassner wrote. He added, "The other week I reread, actually studied, *The House of Connelly* and *Potter's Field.* What a fine poet wrote those plays" (27 August 1953, PG-SHC).

4. In *The Educational Theatre Journal* Gassner devoted part of his regular "Broadway in Review" to *The Lost Colony* and *The Common Glory* (5 [October 1953]: 235–39) and in a later number planned to write about *Unto These Hills* (by Kermit Hunter in Cherokee, North Carolina) and *Horn in the West* (by Hunter in Boone, North Carolina) (5 [December 1953]: 349–50).

5. Gassner read the play in *The House of Connelly and Other Plays,* which has the comic conclusion used in the Group Theatre production, but on Gassner's visit to *The Lost Colony* Sam Selden told him there was another ending that Green preferred, and Gassner asked to see it (27 August 1953, PG-SHC).

6. Later Green found the script used at the University of Iowa in July 1939 (the first production of the play with the original tragic ending) and sent it to Gassner, who found it "tremendously effective. I have given *Connelly* a lot of thought from time to

I guess one reason I changed *Potter's Field* to the *Roll Sweet Chariot* version was in order to get it produced.[7] It had been bought and re-bought by various managers and never came to the stage.[8] Finally it was bought by a person who said she would produce it if I could make certain changes.[9] Anyway that is how I remember it.

With sincere greetings and regards,

## 246. To Eugene Richard[1]

[Greenwood Road, Chapel Hill, N.C.]
16 September 1953

Dear Father Richard:

You will not remember me perhaps, but one night up at a little movie theatre in New York I got you to help me on an item in a proposed production of *Carmen*—a prayer for a priest in that play.[2] The production opened in

---

time, as I believe this play has stature; with the original ending . . . the play has grown for me a good deal. In a sound professional theatre, *Connelly* (with the *original* ending) and *Desire Under the Elms* would be in repertory year in and year out" (8 July 1954, PG-SHC). When he edited Green's *Five Plays of the South* in 1963, Gassner included *Connelly* with the tragic ending.

7. Gassner wondered why *Potter's Field* had not been produced. "It's a superb work; stirred me deeply. Why the *Roll Sweet Chariot* version?" (27 August 1953, PG-SHC).

8. In the early 1930s several people attempted a production of *Potter's Field*: Sidney Ross, Jasper Deeter, Harry Moses, and Walter Hart.

9. Margaret Hewes, who produced *Roll Sweet Chariot* in 1934.

---

1. Eugene Richard was priest of the Holy Name Catholic Church on West 96th Street in Manhattan.

2. During the first few days of April Green was in New York City with Herbert Graf, who staged *Carmen*, and conductor Kurt Adler working to accommodate the language of his text to the rhythms of Bizet's music. The three of them wanted a moving production for American audiences, so Green made a colloquial version of the Meilhac/Halévy libretto, expanded the dialogue to clarify the story, and added a scene. In Prosper Mérimée's "Carmen," the source of the libretto, religion was important to Don José, and Green's new scene at the beginning of act 4 showed Don José visiting a church at night and meeting a priest, who prays for him—a scene intended to raise suspense for the final encounter with Carmen (Paul Green to Franco Colombo, 19 May 1953, PG-SHC).

Central City, Colorado, and was a fair success, I understand.[3] This is just to thank you for your kindness on that night.

Sincerely yours,

## 247. To Mary (Mrs. Roark) Bradford[1]

[Greenwood Road, Chapel Hill, N.C.]
25 September 1953

Dear Mrs. Bradford:

I am glad you are loyal to the memory of your husband for he was most worthy of it. I loved his work too and continue to love it. About the John Henry matter: You should not be alarmed over any possible infringement.

Some thirty years ago when I was a student at the University of North

3. Donald Oenslager, designer for the production, wrote Green that "you would have been very pleased with how well your libretto came off, only favorable comments on all sides. I think the Church scene is definitely an addition to the libretto and score" (9 July 1953, PG-SHC).

1. In 1952 Everyman Opera Company produced a highly successful revival of George Gershwin and DuBose Heyward's *Porgy and Bess* (for the Russian leg of its world tour in 1955–56, see Truman Capote, *The Muses Are Heard* [1956]), and the company's organizers, Blevins Davis and Robert Breen, hoped to continue as a black repertory company for musical plays on black subjects. As their next production they had arranged for Green to write a folk musical with composer Harold Arlen ("Stormy Weather," "That Old Black Magic," "Blues in the Night," score for *The Wizard of Oz*) based on the John Henry legend (Paul Green to Robert Breen, 12 June 1953, PG-SHC), and on 6 September 1953 the *New York Times* ran an article about their plans (sec. 2, p. 1, cols. 6–7; p. 3, cols. 4–6). Mary Bradford, who moved to Santa Fe following the death of her husband, Roark Bradford, on 13 November 1948, read the article with "surprise and alarm" and wrote to Green forthwith, reminding him of her husband's novel, *John Henry* (1931), and the folk opera he based on it (1940). The world at large, thinking he had merely written down a preexisting legend, did not appreciate her husband's achievement, Bradford thought. In fact, "his research turned up almost nothing" about John Henry, so the popular image of Henry along with the events associated with his life were, she was sure, "largely the product of [Roark Bradford's] own fertile brain." She concluded: "It's going to be interesting to watch how . . . another folk opera about John Henry comes out. It'll be another 33 years before Roark Bradford's copyright will be in the public domain" (9 September 1953, PG-SHC).

Carolina I was very much interested in the legend of John Henry. I got all the phonograph records I could of the folk ballad which told of that muscle man's exploits. Howard Odum and Guy Johnson of North Carolina also were interested. And Johnson himself wrote a book about this folk hero—gathering together all the versions he could find of the ballad.[2]

It was about this time that I tried my hand at writing a Negro play.[3] I brought a character into that drama who called himself John Henry. It was an alias, but the play made a point of the Henry story.

And when I come to write a John Henry play, it will be a piece celebrating the place of the Negro in the building of America. And I find the legendary John Henry—apart from the work your husband did—to be a good representation of that building.[4] As I conceive the drama now, the action will be laid in a railroad labor camp. John Henry comes into the scene looking for a job, he gets a job, falls in love, marries, fights, struts his stuff, and dies in a contest with the steam drill.

Actually the reports about my drama are a little ahead of the game. For right now I am working on another project,[5] and it will be quite awhile before I sit down to the Henry writing.

I appreciate your writing to me. Stick to your guns. Like you, I want dear Roark to get the acclaim he deserves![6] And I remember when I heard the sad news of his death. Our family all gathered in the library and we read aloud a number of his wonderful dialect pieces. And my wife said, "Children, a wonderful man is gone."[7]

Sincerely yours,

2. *John Henry: Tracking Down a Negro Legend* (1928), which grew out of two books Johnson coauthored with Odum: *The Negro and His Songs* (1925) and *Negro Workaday Songs* (1926).

3. *Potter's Field.*

4. Bradford's story is a tall tale (at birth John Henry weighs forty-four pounds) about a roustabout on the Mississippi River who dies loading bales of cotton onto a riverboat in competition with a steam winch. The theme of the story is Henry's love life.

5. *Wilderness Road.*

6. In addition to *John Henry*, Roark Bradford wrote numerous dialect stories based on black folk material, such as *This Side of Jordan* (1929) and *Ol' King David an' the Philistine Boys* (1930). Perhaps he is best known through Marc Connelly's *The Green Pastures* (1930), which was based on Bradford's *Ol' Man Adam an' His Chillun* (1928).

7. Probably because of a threatening letter from Mary Bradford similar to the one

## 248. To Francis S. Hutchins[1]

[Greenwood Road, Chapel Hill, N.C.]
16 April 1954

Dear Dr. Hutchins:

I had to go directly from Berea to Williamsburg, Virginia, for tryouts of *The Common Glory* outdoor play there. And this is the first chance to thank you and your wife for your kindness and hospitality to Mrs. Green and myself during our recent visit to Berea. Our whole trip there remains sweetly in our memory, and my admiration for the work you and your associates are doing continues to deepen. If the Berea concept of education is not the right one, then I never expect to find it on this earth.[2] Just how much this concept can come into the Berea outdoor drama, I don't yet know. Maybe it will have to be dealt with indirectly. Naturally I will always welcome any suggestions from you and your staff on this subject.

The Friday night meeting in the Anna Smith dormitory to which Mr.

---

Green received, Davis and Breen had already thrown in the towel on the project and so informed Green (Robert Breen to Paul Green, 11 September 1953, PG-SHC), and Everyman Opera Company had no production beyond *Porgy and Bess.* Green, however, wanted to disarm Bradford and keep his options open. He continued to think about a musical drama focused on John Henry (Paul Green to Robert Breen, 16 September 1953), or at least on the role of blacks in the development of American society (Paul Green to Charles S. Johnson, President of Fisk University, 21 October 1955).

---

1. In preparation for writing *Wilderness Road,* Green spent 30 March–3 April 1954 at Berea College talking with faculty and students about education there, the centennial of the school, and the play that was to celebrate the school's heritage. Francis S. Hutchins (b. 1902), president of Berea College (1939–67), strongly supported the centennial drama. W. D. Weatherford, responsible for organizing the production, operated out of Hutchins's office, and on Green's visit Hutchins arranged for him to speak to the student body at chapel and meet with the faculty on several occasions.

2. Berea charged no tuition and offered a variable work/study plan by which students must work at least ten hours per week in the school-owned farm, dairy, bakery, or craft shops and could increase their hours of work and earn up to all college expenses. Hutchins, Weatherford, and others emphasized that Berea was not therefore a vocational school but rather a liberal arts college attempting to "prepare a student for life" (W. D. Weatherford to Paul Green, 14 May and 21 March 1953, PG-SHC).

Cronk[3] took me seemed to me quite in order.[4] I taught philosophy and comparative religion here at the University of North Carolina for many years, and during that time I spent many an hour in session with young people who were working out problems or trying to. One of your student leaders wrote me some days ago apologizing for her group's lack of hospitality, etc. She said she was sorry to learn that I had become discouraged over the project because of this meeting. But as I have hastened to assure her, I have not in the least. In fact I was stimulated by the discussion. I wrote Mr. Cronk as follows—"I wish you would most optimistically when occasion arises assure any and all students that I thought the Anna Smith Friday night meeting was okay. I did not object then and I never remember objecting in the past to an honest airing of opinions among people. These young students wanted to put questions and get answers about a project that vitally concerned them. I was glad to cooperate."[5]

With sincere personal greetings to you and yours,

3. Ted Cronk, business manager of the Berea drama.

4. Scheduled as an informal discussion between Green and students, the meeting became quite emotional. Green talked about his admiration for John Fee, leader of the small group of abolitionists who founded Berea in 1855 out of a conviction that education was essential to freedom and political democracy. The students who spoke up, however, were opposed to the planned centennial celebration. Some feared that any depiction of Berea people, most of whom came from comparative isolation in the Appalachian Mountains, would expose them to ridicule by outsiders. Others resented spending $200,000 on a play when there was a crying need for a hospital and radio station in the area. Still others thought, if there must be a play, it should not be historical but should focus on the present struggle for civil rights for blacks. The meeting became tumultuous and ended with no apparent agreement about the celebration (Tinsley Crowder to Paul Green, 3 April; W. D. Weatherford to Green, [4 April]; Peter and Martha White to Green, 9 April; Beth Meyer to Green, 9 April; and Betty Ruth English to Green, 14 April 1954, PG-SHC).

5. 13 April 1954, PG-SHC. Cronk replied with assurances that "the Berea family in general is not represented by the small minority you heard. Practically speaking, we could not have staged an event which would unify the campus behind our project in a more substantial way than this has done" (16 April 1954). From the student council Green had already received a resolution of support: "BE IT HEREBY RESOLVED that the Student Council, representing the student body of Berea College, expresses its full faith and confidence in Mr. Paul Green and the work he is producing for the recognition of Berea's century of achievement" (7 April 1954, with Simon Perry to Paul Green, 8 April 1954).

## 249. To W. D. Weatherford

[Greenwood Road, Chapel Hill, N.C.]
3 July 1954

Dear W. D.:

I hope you don't think I have fallen into a river or something worse and got drownded.[1] But Elizabeth and I have been up north in New England,[2] to New York and to Williamsburg, and I have necessarily neglected my correspondence. But that doesn't mean I have been neglecting the Berea drama. It has been in my mind all the time.

I have looked over the contract, and of course generally it is okay. I have some suggestions to make about specific matters here and there, but they can wait until I have given them a little more thought and until I am more certain of the final shape of the play. We both already agree on the amount to be paid and the method of payment and the requirements that I will have to fill as to manuscript delivery.[3] I think the September date for a finished script will have to be revised. But I will telephone you or write you a little later.[4] The music and dance people will be able at that time to start ahead with some of their endeavors,[5] though I am sure that it will be the spring of 1955 before we can all

1. Green's spelling.

2. Where they attended graduation ceremonies at Massachusetts Institute of Technology on 11 June, when Paul, Jr., received a Ph.D. in electrical engineering, and remained to visit with Betsy and Bill Moyer, whose first child, Ellen Elizabeth, born on 29 April 1954, they had not seen.

3. Green and Weatherford worked out the terms in early May, when Weatherford visited Chapel Hill. Berea College would have production rights to *Wilderness Road*, while Green retained literary rights. Beginning with the second summer, 1956, Green would get a royalty of 5 percent of gross box-office receipts from the college's production of the play. For writing *Wilderness Road* Berea would pay Green $7,500: $3,000 when he finished a preliminary draft, due on 15 September 1954; $3,000 when he completed the script, due on 1 April 1955; and $1,500 from box-office receipts during the run of the play in the summer of 1955 (29 June–5 September) (Paul Green to W. D. Weatherford, 28 May 1954, PG-SHC).

4. Weatherford replied that Green misread that part of the contract. "My rough notes for the lawyer said a 'rough draft with music'—Sept. 15. See if your contract does not say that—and Apr. 1, 1955 for final script" (W. D. Weatherford to Paul Green, 12 July 1954, PG-SHC).

5. Rolf Hovey, choral director on the Berea music faculty, wished to begin rehearsing the songs in the play with the aim of recording them (W. D. Weatherford to Paul

get seriously down to the matters of production. Of course we want to have everything ready well ahead.

I am sending you enclosed herewith an article which has just come out in *Theatre Arts.*[6] It seems to me to be a thoughtful piece and is in line with my own long-ago conclusions about the esthetics and philosophy of these outdoor dramas.[7] It has all the time been my hope that because we are suiting ourselves at Berea with a somewhat small and intimate theater that I could in this drama pay due respect to requirements of characterization, dialogue, and plot movement for the story. I want this Berea play to be good literature, good drama, good theater art. And I am sure you agree. John Freeman, the protagonist of the play as I now see it, is a young man on fire with the vision of service to his people. He believes in the power of education, the right sort of education. So like another John the Baptist, a Savonarola,[8] like John G. Fee himself,[9] this young man dedicates his life to make this vision prevail. He believes that his Scotch-Irish ancestors came into the Appalachian country to find a better and more ideal life for themselves and their children and their descendants. He believes that this heritage is a sacred one and that he and his people must give of the best of themselves to measure up to it. And heritage apart, he has his own ideals. Peace, brotherhood, true knowledge, hard work, courage and determination—all of these he believes in. In the midst of his endeavors the nation starts breaking apart, proving his point for the need of

---

Green, 5 January 1955, PG-SHC), and Frank Smith, also of the music faculty, wanted to begin work on the dances.

6. John Gassner, "(The South Shows the Way) Outdoor Pageant-Drama: Symphony of Sight and Sound," *Theatre Arts* 38 (July 1954): 80–83, 89.

7. One of Gassner's points was that open-air staging encouraged episodic structure, and in episodic structure character development was a problem (ibid., pp. 81–83). Green wrote Gassner that "you put the case [for symphonic drama] admirably—both as to its possibilities and the difficulties. All along we have been wrestling with the proper dividing line—if that is the right phrase—between spectacle demands and characterization—these two mainly." He added that at Berea "we are trying an experiment. . . . We have decided to keep the amphitheater small, to seat 1,500, and see what we can do with the more intimate type of play for the outdoors. I am working on the play now and I hope to get in some good dramatic writing" (Paul Green to John Gassner, 5 July 1954, PG-SHC).

8. Fifteenth-century Dominican reformer noted for democratic sympathies and moral fervor.

9. Founder of Berea College.

right education, of right understanding. His people are divided among themselves, the horror of the Civil War is sweeping over the land. There is no escape from the challenge and from the evil itself. John Freeman must go forth to fight with physical force for the peaceful dream in which he believes. Every blow he strikes whether of inspiring word or fearful thrust of the sword is for the true cause. "In the beginning was the word—and the word was with God and the word was God."[10] That's it. The right word, the right thought, the right idea—true education—the Berea type of education.

I continue to feel that the play should open just before the outbreak of the Civil War and continue through to the peace that follows and the beginning of a school which exemplifies John Freeman's ideals—the same as John G. Fee's ideals. In fact in the final scene I put John G. Fee as a sort of memorial spokesman over the dead body of John Freeman.

Therefore the problem of going back chronically and showing the coming of the Scotch-Irish people into the mountains as an actual physical fact on the stage, their struggles and wars and killings that followed proves very difficult for me. This pageant type of prologue would, I fear, land us in the very dilemma of oratory and skimpy characterization which we all need to shun. I suggest that the prologue matter remain in abeyance. If we find we have to later, we can put it in.[11]

I will get a full continuity off to you before too long.

Thanks for your nice address at the Eagan Day services,[12] also for your

10. John 1:1.

11. Weatherford always favored such a prologue. He was "absolutely sure . . . that people will never see the real struggle of the present mountain people, nor will they be able to appreciate their heroic qualities, unless we do give them, through a prologue or in some other way, a glimpse at the long slow trek into the mountains with their isolation and eternal silence which has made these mountain folk into a silent, but heroic group" (W. D. Weatherford to Paul Green, 14 May 1953, PG-SHC). In a cordial reply to the present letter, he "confess[ed] just a little fear of running too much into the Civil War struggle" (12 July 1954, PG-SHC).

12. Each year the American Cast Iron Pipe Company in Birmingham, Alabama, held a memorial service for its founder, John J. Eagan, who put all of his company stock in a trust to be administered for the benefit of the workers. Weatherford said the address "embodies my philosophy of labor" (W. D. Weatherford to Paul Green, 13 June 1954, PG-SHC).

suggestions for the opening of our play. You are always on the side of the most high Lord.[13]

Ever,

## 250. To Edward Herbert[1]

[Greenwood Road, Chapel Hill, N.C.]
5 August 1954

Dear Mr. Herbert:

I have been out of the state for awhile and that accounts for my delay in answering your letter of July 14. I don't know what influence O'Neill has had on my work. Certainly he has stimulated me a lot, as any worker in a medium is inspired by a fine worker in that medium. I remember when the *Emperor Jones* first appeared in *Theatre Arts* magazine.[2] I picked it up at the university library here, read it through, walked around the building all excited, returned to the reading room and went through it again. Later when I was working on a Negro play of my own entitled *In Abraham's Bosom*, I no doubt still kept some of the feeling I had first felt for O'Neill's piece. As I remember it, I wanted to reach some high point of frustration, shame and despair in Abraham's life, and in a sort of delirium brought on by excessive passion of hate and murder, there appeared before his eyes a vision out of the past—a vision where he saw the white man and his mother creep into the bushes and do the business of his, Abraham's own procreation—and Abraham rushing forward and yelling for

13. The particular suggestions are lost but most certainly involved Weatherford's constant theme—"the heroism of my mountain people" and their thirst for education (W. D. Weatherford to Paul Green, 13 April 1954, PG-SHC). The cover letter he sent with the suggestions reveals Weatherford's preoccupation with the play: "Now I have been thinking so constantly of that prologue that it has written itself out in my mind. Don't laugh at its crudeness but I am sending it inclosed" ([June 1954], PG-SHC).

---

1. Edward Herbert (b. 1919), later professor of English at Northern Illinois University, was at the time a doctoral student at the University of Wisconsin and planned to write a dissertation on Eugene O'Neill, whose influence on American drama he wished to consider. "I have read your plays with much pleasure," he wrote to Green, "and with no discredit to your originality or independence of thought, I wondered whether you were at all influenced by the work of O'Neill" (14 July 1954, PG-SHC).

2. *Theatre Arts* 5 (January 1921): 29–59.

them to stop that, stop that—it's me![3] This is of course only a rephrasing out of Job which says "Let the day perish wherein I was born, and the night in which it was said There is a manchild conceived."[4] No doubt there are influences of J. Millington Synge in my work—in the one act plays "The Last of the Lowries" and "The No 'Count Boy."[5] I am sure too I felt the shocks of Gerhart Hauptmann in his so-called naturalistic period of *Drayman Henschel*[6] and *Rose Bernd*.[7]

And think what Strindberg and Wedekind meant to O'Neill—a good thing. Life after all is a sort of rope, isn't it, splicing itself on through time and space and into eternity; or a never ending symphonic movement, constantly replenished out of old motifs and themes into new ones—"I in thee and thee in me."[8]

With best regards for your project,[9]

## 251. To Samuel Selden

[Greenwood Road, Chapel Hill, N.C.]
23 December 1954

Dear Sam—[1]

I have just got back from Berea. We had a good meeting there. The theatre[2] is coming right along and everybody seems proud of it. President Hutchins

3. Scene 6.
4. Job 3:3.
5. See letter 157.
6. Produced in 1898; published in 1899.
7. Produced and published in 1903.
8. John 17:23.
9. Herbert switched from O'Neill and wrote his dissertation on "William Gilmore Simms as Editor and Critic" (1958). Later he published excerpts from this and other letters as "Eugene O'Neill: An Evaluation by Fellow Playwrights," *Modern Drama* 6 (December 1963): 239–40.

---

1. Since Selden was to direct *Wilderness Road*, Green kept him posted about the composition of the play—which was complicated. W. D. Weatherford, tireless in his efforts on behalf of Berea's centennial celebration, wanted the play to focus on the pioneer era in Kentucky leading up to statehood in 1792 (e.g., W. D. Weatherford to Paul Green, 21 March, 14 May, 6 November, and 4 December 1953, and 13 April, 17 May, and 12 July 1954, PG-SHC). But Green leaned toward the Civil War era and a

and his group put down as much as an ultimatum—no pioneer play. One of the board was quite vehement, the others agreeing.[3] W. D. was there, and he and I accepted cheerfully the issued instructions. So now I continue with the civil war drama, trying to forget the other one which I had brought so far along. I'll do my best of course to have some sort of script for you to work with by Feb. 20.[4] Hutchins is quite willing to stand by truth, peace and brotherhood as our subject, even if we should lack the popular success of a colorful pioneer. So I say bless him.[5]

Hurriedly and with good Christmas greetings to you and yours,

---

plot focused on education, integration, and pacifism. Over the summer of 1954 he outlined both plays (Paul Green to W. D. Weatherford, 5 August 1954), and during a visit from Weatherford in the fall he agreed to go ahead with the pioneer play (Paul Green to Francis S. Hutchins, 6 October 1954). He went to Berea for a meeting about the play on 19 December with Weatherford, Hutchins, and Berea's trustees.

2. Being built on Indian Fort Mountain about three miles from the Berea campus.

3. Hutchins wanted the play "to deal with ideals and principles for I believe that it is ideals and principles plus practice which have enabled Berea to grow and have strength and be of significance" (Francis Hutchins to Paul Green, 27 September 1954, PG-SHC).

4. When Selden was to begin casting the play.

5. Probably Green had promoted Hutchins's "ultimatum" against a pioneer play. The Civil War story gave him a chance to write not only a dramatic rather than pageantal play but also "a parable for modern times," as he subtitled *Wilderness Road.* By late 1953 he had anticipated the Supreme Court decision of 17 May 1954 in *Brown v. Board of Education of Topeka, Kansas,* that separate school systems for blacks and whites were unconstitutional (Ted Cronk to Paul Green, 18 December 1953, PG-SHC), and he knew the turmoil the decision would generate in the South. During May he took time off from *Wilderness Road* to write an open commencement address for southern schools, not for delivery at any particular graduation ceremony but for publication in leading state papers (see "The Goodliest Land Under the Cope of Heaven," *NO,* 30 May 1954, sec. 4, p. 1; p. 2, cols. 3–6). In the address he tried to provide a calming perspective by placing equal opportunities for blacks in the context of the overall development of the state. He wanted *Wilderness Road* to help in the same direction, to be an "instrument for helping Americans renew the ideals and purposes that had guided the destinies of their forefathers," particularly the ideals of brotherhood and free inquiry ("Play Dares South to Face Problems," *New York Times,* 30 June 1955, p. 20, cols. 8–12).

## 252. To William A. McGirt, Jr.[1]

[Greenwood Road, Chapel Hill, N.C.]
12 January 1955

Dear Bill McGirt:

Thanks for the wonderful letter and for the two poems.[2] They are good. I'm interested in your talent and I wish I could see you more often. You've got a lot to say, and I believe you will say it. I can't fully answer and talk over the typewriter as I would want to. Let's leave most of it for easier mouth words someday.

I delight in your statement that you regard the USSR as a challenge not an obstacle.[3]

What is the creative power of fear? Where does hate come in? And where—what—is the creative power that lies beyond—behind—fear and hate? Let us search our hearts and be sure that our fear, our hate of sin, of evil, is not directed more to the sinner and evil-doer than to the vices themselves.

I do not know what energizes and inspires Junius Scales. I wish I did.

1. On 18 November 1954 Junius Scales, head of the Communist party in North and South Carolina, was arrested by the FBI and charged under the 1940 Smith Act with membership in an organization advocating overthrow of the U.S. government by force and violence, a felony carrying a sentence of up to ten years in prison. Arrested in Memphis, Scales, a longtime resident of Chapel Hill, was extradited to North Carolina on 24 November and jailed in Winston-Salem. William A. McGirt (b. 1923), a poet working at a fish market in Winston-Salem, visited Green on Scales's behalf on 6 January (William A. McGirt to Paul Green, 3 January 1955, PG-SHC), then wrote a lengthy letter urging Green to "do something" to help Scales: "The case of Junius Scales is the ultimate test for us in this State. . . . His conviction and jailing without a struggle of the broadest sort—would be a grievous setback. You can do something about it because you are immaculate" (11 January 1955).

2. "Asheville, October 3" (in *NO*, 3 October 1954, sec. 4, p. 4, col. 3) and "Star in the Millions' Eyes" (in *NO*, 25 December 1954, sec. 1, p. 4, col. 6). In the tradition of William Wordsworth's "London, 1802," "Asheville, October 3" (birthday of Thomas Wolfe) calls on the spirit of a great writer from the past to cleanse the present of a great evil, in this case McCarthyism. "Star in the Millions' Eyes" is a Christmas poem with a similar theme.

3. McGirt said that "to find the creative necessities of the American destiny and to push them, to exercise our spirits and hands toward liberation of soul and society, THIS IS OUR TASK regardless of the existence of the USSR or any other nation. Indeed, I see the USSR as a challenge, not as an obstacle" (11 January 1955, PG-SHC).

Maybe I can hear some of the trial and find out. Do you suppose he could be persuaded to put some of his vision down on paper?[4] I'd like to see it. And how I wish I were out of this present hard and firm commitment in writing an anti-war play,[5] so that I could hear all the trial, keep a diary perhaps, and publish a long statement. But I shan't be done this job in time. Even so, I wish his dilemma had been brought about by other causes than those that seem so tangled and obscure and ex-parte—if dilemma like this it had to be. Every rebel against an order he disapproves of may consider himself not only a rebel but a prophet or even a martyr. This is understandable. I have known only a few Communists in my time, and without exception they have all seemed to me more taken with psychic difficulties than actually with the challenge of emendation necessary to get a proper social job done. Self-indulgence, bad thinking, fascination with cruelty, frustration—all kinds of things come in too often. And after all so much of this business is pure childishness—nothing adult and responsible about it. Fellows like McCarthy,[6] like the millionaire house-builder I told you of, are just as silly as most of the Communist devotees. There is silliness on both sides. And there is plenty of work to be done by all of us in the full sunlight of the hot ploughfield, and these shrieks and jumpings up and down and loyalty oaths and protestations and hearings and trials and suspicions and fear—all are scum and wash and upheavings of half-sick neurotic people—sick mainly, I believe, because they don't honestly seek for the truth and try to rest in it—or rather work hard in it when they find it.

I don't look back to the founding fathers as saviours and sacrosanct philosophers—as maybe you think I do. I consider them as part of the tradition—most of them are—which I find refreshing.

The tree of civilization, Bill, has roots that go back on down, much deeper than any of these. They are branches of that tree, fruit sometimes of it. Behind them are the New Testament, the Greek civilization, the Hebraic, and now the Orient. See, Bill, we have a tree of life. And most of these misguided young people don't do much except maim it, spray it—or try to in their too-often

4. Much later he did, in Junius Scales and Richard Nickson, *Cause at Heart: A Former Communist Remembers* (Athens: University of Georgia Press, 1987).

5. *Wilderness Road.*

6. Joseph McCarthy, chairman of the Senate Internal Security Subcommittee, most sensational of the witch-hunters then trying to expose Communists in society and government.

boy-impishness—with weed killer. Question: why are young people like Scales the way they are? Does he have his own answer? If not, the first duty to himself and the present hysterical and confused authorities who waste their time and the public's money on this matter is to find it. I warn you, Bill, I advise you rather, try soon to find out in such matters as these what is part and what is whole, what is particular and what is universal, what is real and what unreal, what is passing and what remains, what is true and what is false? Maybe there is no clean-cut dividing line between the two so that you can say to yourself, right here wrong begins and right here right begins. But on the left hand and on the right hand you can feel the direction, the emphasis as it were.

I know the flux of human action and the wheeling of the world makes us all too often feel that nothing is constant, nothing is to be sighted by the soul and measured as being there—there to stay, there to be believed in today, tomorrow and always. So where all is change, all relativity, the fanaticism of the church, of the state, of a party or ism will often stand out as the fixed and reliable, the truth, often be seized on as offering some immediate stability, and so we join these fanatics for the very same reason that made them come together in the first place—self-incompleteness. And so to complete ourselves, to prove our manhood the easy way, we join in the parade of the idols, the common consent programs, and we march to the house of the hated one—and always somebody is hated in this business in order to drum up the proper emotions—and try to overthrow his dwelling, or his temple, or seize him and put him in jail with an impossible $500,000 bail set for him.[7]

If Scales actually worked for the overthrow of this government by violence and hoped to see the Russian system substituted for it then he is too big a fool to bother with—just as big a fool as Joe McCarthy, who worked against him, worked to overthrow him and his kind by violence and punish them therefore.

Aren't the methods of Scales and of McCarthy the same—if you can call what Scales has undertaken as a method? Totalitarianism is bad, whether German, Italian, Russian, American or any kind.

If Scales actually wanted to help the lot of the poor Negro, the poor worker—wanted to help wipe out injustice, and who doesn't, even if for no other reason than that he himself may be safe!—wanted to bring brotherhood

7. A false start, probably deleted before the letter was mailed, occurs here: "If Scales—and he seems to have been McCarthy in another camp—a."

and world unity and abandonment of war to pass as he claims, he took a mighty poor way to do it when he turned Communist.

Maybe the truth is he too is just a spoiled non-conformist and gets satisfaction and mental stimulation by opposing the established order of authority. If he had been a Russian citizen these years and kept the same temperament,—and I don't see why he wouldn't—wouldn't he if he could, have been against that government? He could have found plenty of reasons to wish it bettered. And again, shouldn't a revolutionary if he is honest think the thing on out, ask himself how the revolution can complete itself into a growing social system?

How would Junius Scales run this country? I'll tell you how. Crazy, that's how. The evils we now have are small indeed to the evils such fellows as Scales would bring upon a nation—if they had the power to do it.

But of course, Bill, that doesn't mean that by realizing the half-baked schemes of such fellows as these, that we should become fanatics of hate for them and go to witch and youth baiting and thus find a good excuse for ignoring our own shortcomings by persecuting others who differ from us.

No. Let us work harder than ever to make our people—help make them—into the nation they should be as part of a cooperative and inspired world. The true enemies of us all are neither Communist nor Capitalist, neither politicians nor priests, but ignorance, prejudice, hate, fear and personal childish selfishness. Yes, poverty too and one-sided nationalism.

Fear and hate may give a man a lot of words, stir up his emotions and make him speak easy, help him to improve his style. Richard Wright, of *Native Son*, and I used to talk a lot about that.[8] But at the same time these evils fill him with the pus of corruption, they help degrade his soul and blind his senses.

Come out from behind that rock, Bill. I'm not afraid of you, and you have nothing to fear from me. Nor have you anything to fear from any man unless you fear first.

I do hope this too-brief, honest statement of the matter as I believe it to be will not discourage you or confuse you. Even if for the moment you are bothered, remember your talent and that will clear you up.

Come to see me.

Sincerely,[9]

8. In 1940–41 when they collaborated on the dramatization of *Native Son*.

9. McGirt continued to send Green poems. In 1956 he was subpoenaed by the

## 253. To Carl Sandburg[1]

[Greenwood Road, Chapel Hill, N.C.]
24 January 1955

Dear Carl:

I have read your jostling, active life-filled words to the opening section of the coming "The Making of America" with a lot of pleasure. How much you are our voice—America's voice, now, yesterday, and on. Keep doing it, good man, keep right on—strong, tough, enduring—

And it's wheel her, wheel her, wheel
  And it's roll her, roll her, roll,
God's mercy on the steel
  No mercy on my soul.[2]

---

House Un-American Activities Committee, convened in Charlotte, North Carolina, where he was accused of succeeding Junius Scales as head of the Communist party in North and South Carolina (*Charlotte Observer*, 14 March 1956, sec. A, p. 1, col. 5; p. 2, cols. 5–7). Later McGirt changed his name to Will Inman and with *I Am the Snakehandler* (1960) published the first of numerous books of poetry. Moving around a great deal, he continued as a poet, teacher, and editor, then settled in Tucson, Arizona. Scales was convicted at his trial during April 1955 in Greensboro and sentenced to six years in prison—the heaviest sentence ever given for a Smith Act violation. After an unsuccessful appeal to the Supreme Court in July 1961, Scales (who became disillusioned with the Communist party and resigned from it in 1957) began serving his sentence on 2 October 1961 at the federal penitentiary in Lewisburg, Pennsylvania. Green, declaring he had "known Junius since he was a little boy and he's not going to harm anybody" (noted on Norman Thomas to Paul Green, 30 June 1961, PG-SHC), signed a petition to the Supreme Court in July 1961, then was among those who worked for a presidential pardon. On 24 December 1962 President John Kennedy freed Scales by commuting his sentence to parole on his own recognizance (Scales and Nickson, *Cause at Heart*, p. 368 and chapters 16–25).

---

1. In 1955 Harcourt, Brace published the third edition of a textbook, *The Story of American Democracy* by Mabel Casner and Ralph Gabriel, for which Carl Sandburg (1878–1967) provided an introduction, "This America," that linked passages from several of his books of poetry to celebrate the role of the common man in the development of the United States. Calling the textbook *The Making of America*, Sandburg, who had lived in North Carolina since moving to Connemara Farm south of Asheville in 1945, sent Green a copy of the introduction.

2. Green's extemporization suggested by Sandburg's introduction.

But doesn't mercy fill the soul as we roll, doesn't it?

Come to see us, Carl, and bring your guitar. We want you to come down and tell us about these days and the country, anything that might be on your mind and sing some to us. We would like to work up a little recorded program of some 25 minutes of you. The university here tells me as a token of gratitude it will pay you an honorarium of $400. Please say you'll do it, and come when you can.[3]

Thanks for your kind words about my visit to GBS.[4]

Ever,

## 254. To Luther H. Hodges[1]

[Greenwood Road, Chapel Hill, N.C.]
[8 August 1955]

AS AN OLD FRIEND I WANT YOU TO KNOW THAT I WAS ONE OF THE MOST DELIGHTED PEOPLE IN NORTH CAROLINA WHEN YOU BECAME OUR GOVERNOR. I

3. Sandburg came on 5 June and that night made his recording for the UNC Educational Radio and Television Center, which was developing a series of recordings by well-known writers (among them Arthur Miller, Robert Frost, Allen Tate, Randall Jarrell, Archibald MacLeish, Sandburg, and Green) for broadcast over the National Educational Radio network. The next night Sandburg gave the commencement address as UNC awarded him an honorary degree. Staying with the Greens, "he had rehearsed his talk to us and made it a kind of ironic attack on America's craze for 'More, more, more.' But up before the audience, he settled for a short fifteen minute, almost polite little word of greeting and admonishment to youth. . . . [Afterwards] we had a banjo player and ballad singer and guests who stayed till midnight, after which he talked on till 2:30 A.M. again with drinks. . . . Next day he slept late and we saw him off at the air port" (Elizabeth Green, "Description of Carl Sandburg's Visit, June 1955," PG-SHC).

4. Sandburg had written: "Today gave a slow reading to your 'G. B. S. The Mystic' in *Tomorrow* [8 (August 1949): 29–35]. A great keen piece of writing and portraiture. I say this as an Old Reporter who knows craftsmanship" (23 November 1954, PG-SHC).

---

1. Luther Hodges (1898–1974), graduate of UNC in 1919 and textile executive until retirement in 1950, was elected lieutenant governor of North Carolina in 1952, then succeeded to the governor's office on the death of William B. Umstead in November 1954. In May 1955 the Supreme Court reaffirmed the illegality of separate school

FELT THAT ONCE MORE WE WOULD HAVE A LIBERAL FORWARD-LOOKING CHIEF EXECUTIVE WHO WOULD LEAD THE STATE IN THE WAY OF PROGRESS SO ABLY BEGUN BY CHARLES B. AYCOCK TWO GENERATIONS AGO.[2] IN A TIME OF CRISIS HE TOOK A BRAVE STEP FORWARD AND THE PEOPLE FOLLOWED HIM.[3] I BELIEVED THAT IN THIS TIME OF PRESENT CRISIS YOU ALSO WOULD TAKE A SECOND STEP, CARRYING ON WHERE AYCOCK LEFT OFF AND FACING WITH COURAGE, PATIENCE, TACT AND GOOD FAITH THE DIFFICULT EDUCATIONAL TASK SET BEFORE YOU.

FROM WHAT I KNEW OF YOU IN COLLEGE AND OVER THE YEARS I EXPECTED THAT. THEREFORE, I WAS VERY MUCH SADDENED AND SURPRISED TONIGHT IN YOUR RADIO AND TELEVISION ADDRESS TO HEAR NOT THE VOICE OF LEADERSHIP AND BRAVE IDEALISM BUT RATHER THE OLD FAMILIAR MESSAGE OF AN ANCIENT AND REACTIONARY SOUTH. FORGIVE ME BUT THAT IS WHAT I HEARD THOUGH I LEANED OUT HARD TO LISTEN FOR SOMETHING ELSE.

TRUE, THE JOB OF CARRYING FORWARD HOWEVER SLOWLY BUT STILL CARRYING FORWARD THE CHALLENGING DIRECTIVE OF THE UNITED STATES SUPREME COURT IS A TOUGH ONE. WE ALL KNOW THAT. BUT MEN GROW GREAT ON

---

systems for blacks and whites and urged the seventeen states with dual systems to comply with haste. Over statewide radio and television on 8 August, Hodges gave North Carolina's response, which was to note that the Supreme Court outlawed only forced segregation of the schools and to ask that black citizens now send their children to black schools voluntarily. He had hard words for the NAACP, which he feared would stir up blacks to integrate the schools, and warned that the state might abandon public education altogether if his request for voluntary segregation went unheeded ("Address on State-Wide Radio-Television Network," in *Addresses and Papers of Governor Luther Hartwell Hodges* [Raleigh: Council of State, State of North Carolina, 1960], 1:199–214). The next day the governor's office reported that he received hundreds of wires and letters about the speech, all of them warmly supportive except two, one of which came from a prominent person whose name the office withheld ("Hodges Hears from Speech—Most Favored Plan," *NO*, 10 August 1955, sec. 1, p. 1, cols. 2–3). The following day the state's major newspapers printed the present wire (e.g., *NO*, 11 August 1955, sec. 1, p. 4, col. 4, and *Charlotte Observer*, 11 August 1955, sec. B, p. 1, col. 4).

2. Aycock became known as the "education governor" when he made universal public education the major theme of his administration (1900–1904).

3. In 1903 he successfully opposed a bill in the General Assembly that called for division of school taxes by race, a move that would have severely damaged black schools because of the impoverished condition of blacks.

TOUGH JOBS AND SO DO STATES AND NATIONS. THE NAMES AND DEEDS REMEMBERED IN HISTORY PROVE THAT.

NO DOUBT FOR THE TIME BEING YOU WILL RECEIVE MANY LETTERS AND TELEGRAMS AND HANDCLASPS OF PRAISE FOR WHAT YOU SAID AND THE PROGRAM YOU LAID OUT. BUT TRUTH STILL REMAINS THE TRUTH, RIGHT STILL THE RIGHT, JUSTICE STILL REMAINS JUSTICE, AND HUMAN HEARTS STILL ASPIRE UPWARD.

I AM SAYING THIS PUBLICLY FOR CONSCIENCE SAKE.

REGRETFULLY, PAUL GREEN[4]

## 255. To Francis S. Hutchins

[Greenwood Road, Chapel Hill, N.C.]
21 September 1955

Dear Dr. Hutchins:[1]

Thanks for the letter from Mr. John Freeman. I have read it carefully and as

4. A few days later Green noted in his diary: "What a tragedy Luther Hodges has involved himself in and all North Carolina with him. No leadership, none. . . . Of all the naive propositions—his plea for voluntary segregation. He asks the Negroes suddenly to give over their long fight for freedom and complete self-expression as becomes and belongs to all citizens of this country—a fight they have been waging these many decades. . . . I have had a number of letters about my wire to Hodges after his 'Voluntary Segregation' speech. [One from Hodges, who said: "We are not facing at this time in North Carolina a theory or an ideal, but a realistic problem" (16 August 1955, PG-SHC).] Some very scurrilous, threatening me with mulatto grandchildren, a boycott on *The Lost Colony*, etc. The usual understandable but unforgivable prejudices. Reading Einstein lately for comfort" (25 August 1955).

---

1. *Wilderness Road*'s first summer (29 June–5 September 1955) was a success. The *New York Times* reviewed it enthusiastically on opening night ("Play Dares South to Face Problems," 30 June 1955, p. 20, cols. 8–12). W. D. Weatherford, always partial to a pioneer version, graciously acknowledged that "I think you have a great play—not my play—but a great play" and reported enthusiastic reviews in Kentucky newspapers (W. D. Weatherford to Paul Green, 6 July 1955, PG-SHC). And attendance was strong. Several people did question the climax of the play, however, where the central character, John Freeman, seeing Confederate forces destroy his school, joins the Union army. They thought the play would be more effective if Freeman remained faithful to his pacifist principles, and Hutchins passed along a letter from one of them

soon as I can find time will write him fully on the dramatic problem he raises in the continuity of *Wilderness Road*.[2]

I agree with him that there is some work to be done on the play still. My problem, as I have known it from before we opened, is to find some way in a page or two of additional dialogue to make dramatic and obviously understandable the "metaphysics" of sacrifice. John Freeman in the play is called upon—from without and from within—to prove the integrity of his beliefs. To adduce such proof, he must make a sacrifice. Obviously it is not enough for the voice of his father to speak from the void, saying, "except a grain of wheat go into the earth and die, it shall not produce" etc., or words to that effect.[3]

I am looking forward to a much better production and a greater success of *Wilderness Road* next year. I always appreciate any suggestions you have to make or send along looking towards this eventuality.[4]

I trust you have had a big opening for your college year.

Sincerely yours,

---

(also named John Freeman)—a six-page defense of his belief that "the place for a Christian in time of war is in the ranks of the unarmed combat medics" (John Freeman to Francis Hutchins, 3 September 1955).

2. Letter unlocated.

3. Act 2, scene 5, where Freeman's father echoes John 12:24. To another correspondent Green explained that "by sacrifice I don't mean negation in a bad sense. Rather perhaps I mean devotion to an ideal, a purpose, a thoroughly self-felt need and prerogative. Yes, sacrifice which means the chance to fulfill the personality. I certainly have no interest in burnt offerings and puritanical ascetic deeds. And maybe law comes in here, something of the kind of law Saint Paul talked about along in Romans, the 7th chapter" (Paul Green to Florence Cairns, 28 September 1955, PG-SHC).

4. Before the second season, Green expanded act 2, scene 5 so that it develops more fully the idea of sacrifice implicit in John 12:24–26. The published text (1956) is the revised version.

## 256. To Elisabeth S. Peck[1]

[Greenwood Road, Chapel Hill, N.C.]
28 October 1955

Dear Dr. Peck—

Many thanks for sending me the copy of John G. Hanson's letter. How the man must have suffered, and really how needlessly! I count it one of the mistakes of mankind that we fail to realize the finality of our acts. Most of us live in a queer sentimentality of second and third chance possibilities. There are no such possibilities. Cruelty is finally and irrevocably cruel when it occurs. Oppression the same, blindness the same, ignorance likewise. The new deed and the new trial are just that—new. The past error and the past sin are forever that—old and done. St. Paul with all his good works could never bring back to life one of the martyrs he had cheated of life.[2] But then good deeds in turn also are eternal in their reality. We the living can gain strength and confidence in this latter truth too. Right now we in North Carolina and most of the South are turmoiling over an evil fiction, namely, that deeply sunburnt men (Negroes) are not of the same soul's worth as bleached-out men (Whites) and do not deserve the same rights of opportunity and personal

1. Elisabeth S. Peck (b. 1883), retired chair of the history department at Berea College and author of *Berea's First Century, 1855–1955* (Lexington: University of Kentucky Press, 1955), sent Green a copy of a nineteenth-century document recently sent to her. In December 1859 a large group of armed proslavery men drove out leaders of the abolitionist Berea community to Cincinnati. In March 1860 one of the abolitionists, John G. Hanson, returned to Berea to work his sawmill but was met by a drunken mob bent on hanging him. They wrecked his mill, and he hid in the mountains for several weeks before escaping again to Cincinnati (*Berea's First Century*, pp. 15–20). While in the mountains Hanson wrote an eloquent "Appeal to the Citizens of Madison County & to the State of Kentucky." Making clear that he had violated no law or moral principle, Hanson (echoing Jacob in Genesis 31:36) asked, "What's my crime? What have I done that I should flee out to these mountains as a beast, to be hunted as a partridge of the mountains, and again I cry, what have I done and against whom?" Peck said the appeal "was sent to me by a great granddaughter of John Hanson. When she saw *Wilderness Road* this summer, she was greatly moved by it. As a result, I received this morning by mail—not a copy, but the original letter for Berea's files. As soon as I had deciphered it, I realized how close your John Freeman [in *Wilderness Road*] was to John Hanson. John Freeman might have written just such a letter as this" (25 October 1955, PG-SHC).

2. Acts 7–8.

dignity. The governor of my state and I have had some public argument. It will continue. I will never yield to his prejudice. Do we count in the scheme of things? I maintain we all do, whatever color, calling or kind we may be. Question—do we count for good? We should, we must[.][3] Thus the program of work and striving is obvious and imperative. It is always good to hear from you.

Elizabeth and I send our love, Paul

Forgive my preaching. I've got into the lamentable habit lately, maybe because time seems to be running out.[4]

3. A question mark, evidently a typographical error, appears here in the original.

4. Handwritten postscript to this typed letter.

# VIII

## Symphonic Drama and the Civil War, 1956–1961

April 1956
With Charles S. Johnson and Arna Bontemps at Fisk University in Nashville, plans symphonic drama on blacks in the United States (project halted by Johnson's death in October).

Fall–Winter 1956
Often in Jamestown and Williamsburg for work on *The Founders* and *The Common Glory.*

13 May 1957
*The Founders* opens at Jamestown, plays in the afternoon while *The Common Glory* plays in Williamsburg at night.

Fall–Winter 1957
On state and national committees to plan centennial celebrations of Civil War. Stirs controversy with stand that Civil War was a tragedy and should be celebrated only as a step toward national unity. Drafts *The Confederacy.*

February 1958
Urges state to celebrate Civil War by publishing letters of Zebulon Vance, North Carolina leader during the war.

1 July 1958
*The Confederacy* opens at Virginia Beach, Virginia.

Fall–Winter 1958
Drafts *The Stephen Foster Story.*

June 1959
In Bardstown, Kentucky, rehearsing *The Stephen Foster Story* for its opening on 26 June.

Summer 1959

*Wings for to Fly* (one-act plays on wastefulness of segregation) published, copies sent to state legislators, judges, and newspaper editors.

July 1960

Visits St. Augustine, Florida, and neighboring Anastasia Island in preparation for *Cross and Sword.* Margaret Harper begins correspondence with Green that leads to production of *Texas* (in 1966).

Fall 1960

Raises money for Lumbee Indian children denied access to high school in Harnett County.

Fall–Winter 1960

Works at novel, *Stormy Banks.*

April 1961

Corresponds with Carl Sandburg about Abraham Lincoln and Civil War.

September–October 1961

In Spain for background work on *Cross and Sword.*

Fall 1961

Works at redesigning the Waterside Theatre (home of *The Lost Colony*), destroyed the previous year by a hurricane.

## 257. To Paul, Jr., and Dorrit Green

[Greenwood Road] Chapel Hill, N.C.
10 January 1956

Dear Paul and Skip:[1]

We had such a good time Christmas as no doubt Mimi[2] wrote you. We are back here settled down to work while Polly the dog[3] lies out on the front lawn with her head and ears up guarding us from sparrows, tom tits and a single mocking bird that might threaten us. The "King of Instruments" has arrived[4] and I have enjoyed it greatly with now and then some goose-pimples along my *hips* at the mighty blowing of the great pipes. Someday we must go to St. John's the Divine and hear that organ.[5] I'm glad you liked the van der Post book on Africa,[6] even keeping some healthy criticism of it the while. He is a mystic of course,[7] and maybe that's all right, for who knows but that all factuality and pragmatic actuality have a glow and glory at their beginning

1. Following a planning session on *The Founders* in Williamsburg, Paul and Elizabeth drove to Manhattan on 21 December 1955 for a visit with Janet and her husband, Herbert Lauritzen (married 6 November 1955), then to Boston, where their other three children lived, on 24 December. That night all four families gathered at the home of Bill and Betsy Moyer. On Christmas day they convened at the home of Paul, Jr., where he played the organ and they all sang carols. On 26 December Paul spent the afternoon playing pool with Paul, Jr., Sam Cornwell, and Bill Moyer. Then on 27 December Paul and Elizabeth left for Chapel Hill and drove straight through (Green diary, PG-SHC).

2. Elizabeth's nickname in the family.

3. The family collie.

4. Record sent by Paul, Jr. (amateur organ builder), volume 8 in a series published by the Boston organ company Aeolian-Skinner to demonstrate the range of tone qualities available on organs (interview with Paul Green, Jr., 3 May 1988).

5. To demonstrate the trumpet stop, the record included Henry Purcell's "Trumpet Voluntary" (actually by Jeremiah Clarke) and Purcell's "Trumpet Tune and Air" played on the Aeolian-Skinner organ at the Episcopal cathedral in Manhattan.

6. Laurens van der Post, *The Dark Eye in Africa* (London: Hogarth Press, 1955), which Green gave them for Christmas.

7. A white South African, van der Post wrote about the problems in his country "from what I regard as the centre of myself, from a point in total awareness where my experience of the past and my intuition of the future, where my conscious knowledge of life, Africa, the world and my own urgent feeling about them, meet" (ibid., p. 27). In a recent letter to Green, Paul, Jr., confessed that he found some of van der Post's "theories . . . nothing short of supernatural" (6 January 1956, PG-SHC).

and their ending? What can be more mystical, say, than a scientific physics which defines matter as fields of force? Or such a term as a finitely-infinite universe? What I mean is that statistics, readings, controls of physical power, interpretations thereof too, bring us up again and again short and breathless with wonder. And the very nature of that wonder is religious, poetic, and laden with a pervasive sense of goodness and love for all mankind. It *is* hard for us—a nation of builders and engineers—to consider that in the naive folk life of masses of people like the dark folks of Africa or of India there may reside a sense of world-reality which is to be thoroughly respected. The Greeks for instance long ago found it hard to think that an ugly man (i.e. Socrates) might also be a good man—since they identified truth, goodness and beauty pretty much as one. Mimi has just come in and we are hurrying off to Durham to see *Red Shoes* again.[8] Kiss the three angels[9]—four with Skip—for us.

Love, Doog

We sure hope, Paul, you can get down to see us on your next Washington trip.[10]

## 258. To Abbott Van Nostrand[1]

[Greenwood Road, Chapel Hill, N.C.]
3 March 1956

Dear Abbott:

Thanks for your letter about *Wilderness Road*, and I'm glad to note that I will be receiving proof soon and the book will be out in time for our

8. A British film (1948) playing at Duke University and featuring music and a ballet based on the Hans Christian Andersen story of the title.

9. Daughters of Paul, Jr., and Skip: Dorrit Carolyn (five), Nancy Elizabeth (three), and Judith Joanna (one).

10. In connection with his research for the armed services at Massachusetts Institute of Technology's Lincoln Laboratory, Paul, Jr., visited Washington, D.C., frequently and had mentioned that on one of the trips he might "swing down to N.C." (Paul Green, Jr., to Paul Green, 6 January 1956, PG-SHC).

1. Abbott Van Nostrand (b. 1911), with Samuel French, Incorporated, since 1934 and president since the retirement of Frank J. Sheil in 1952, recently wrote Green about two matters: an upcoming production of *Johnny Johnson* and publication of *Wilderness Road* (29 February 1956, PG-SHC).

immediate use by the first week in June.[2] Thanks also for information about Stella Adler and the planned *Johnny Johnson* revival. A special delivery has just come in from her telling that she is working full steam ahead on it.[3]

Mr. Davis—Lotte Lenya's husband (Lotte was Kurt Weill's wife as you no doubt know)[4]—telephoned me last week saying MGM Recordings want to put out an album of the songs from *Johnny* within the next few weeks. He said they would be in touch with you about it. He said also he was getting off a letter to me right away about some small revisions here and there in the lyrics. Haven't heard from him yet. This is just to keep you informed—no action needed yet, I presume.[5]

Also I'm enclosing a letter from Dr. Klein of Westminster Recordings with my reply for your information.[6] I took it for granted that you would agree to the royalty terms he offers,[7] and at the proper time we can take up the matter of a contract. If you have any difference of opinion on this please let me know. It seems okay to me.

The latter part of this month I meet with the Jamestown Corporation on

2. When the play began its summer run at Berea College, which placed an initial order for 400 copies (Abbott Van Nostrand to Paul Green, 11 April 1956, PG-SHC).

3. Adler, member of the Group Theatre when it produced *Johnny Johnson* originally in 1936–37, eventually could not get permission from the Kurt Weill estate for a Broadway revival (ibid.). She produced the play for two weeks at the off-Broadway Carnegie Playhouse in Manhattan, opening on 21 October 1956.

4. Lenya married George Davis shortly after Weill's death in 1950.

5. MGM Records released the recording in 1957 with Burgess Meredith singing the title role (also featuring Lotte Lenya). The lyrics are closer to the revised text published by Samuel French in 1971 than to the original 1937 version, especially at the end, where words are added to Johnny's musical theme.

6. Arthur Luce Klein's letter (27 February 1956, PG-SHC) outlined his plan for a series of records of American playwrights reading from their plays and discussing their ideas of the drama, and Green's reply (3 March 1956) accepted Klein's invitation to join the series. Arthur Miller had just made the first record, Klein said, and Green would go to Manhattan for his recording session on 10 May (Arthur Klein to Paul Green, 11 May 1956).

7. "Five hundred dollars advance on a royalty that is predicated at 8% of the net price, which is the wholesale price, and comes to approximately twenty cents per record. A sale of twenty thousand, a not unlikely figure, would yield a royalty of four thousand dollars" (Arthur Klein to Paul Green, 27 February 1956, PG-SHC).

plans for the production of the Jamestown play I am writing and at that time we will bring the contract into final form and I will return it to you for your approval.[8]

I am in correspondence with Associated Music Publishers about bringing out a *Wilderness Road Song-Book*—comparable to *The Lost Colony Song-Book* and *The Common Glory Song-Book* which Carl Fischer published some years back. I don't think I need trouble your office about a contract for this until negotiations are further along, but I'd like your opinion on this firm. I presume they are first-rate.[9]

A southern university[10] is in touch with me about a big Negro Symphonic Drama to be built around the Fisk Jubilee Singers and the old Negro spirituals and to be produced within the next year or two. It sounds like a wonderful thing, and I am meeting with a group of educators and promoters on April 27 in Nashville, Tennessee to consider ways and means. If we get as far as talking contract I'll send the rough terms on to you for your suggestions.[11]

Best regards as ever,

8. To celebrate the 350th anniversary of Jamestown in 1957, the Jamestown Corporation, producer of *The Common Glory*, planned to add a play to its schedule, and on 30 March Green went to Williamsburg to discuss the play he was writing for the occasion, *The Founders*. Green's original interest, before problems about the location of the theater forced him to shift to the revolutionary subject of *The Common Glory*, had centered on Jamestown and John Rolfe. *The Founders* opened on 13 May 1957 at the Cove Amphitheatre outside Williamsburg toward Jamestown and played its first summer in the afternoon while *The Common Glory* ran at night at nearby Lake Matoaka Amphitheatre.

9. No *Wilderness Road Song-Book* was published.

10. Fisk University.

11. Charles S. Johnson, president of Fisk University, and Arna Bontemps, writer and librarian there, invited Green to Fisk, and following his visit on 26–28 April Green wrote to Johnson: "Bontemps and I had some extended talk about the possibilities for an outdoor symphonic drama dealing with Fisk history and the contributions of the Negro people to the life and culture of America—in the direction of your correspondence with me earlier" (30 April 1956, PG-SHC). He added that "the prospects look good," but Johnson's death on 27 October 1956 brought an end to the project.

## 259. To Leroy Collins[1]

[Greenwood Road, Chapel Hill, N.C.]
14 January 1957

Dear Governor Collins—

Your state, the nation and all the yearning world are indebted to you for your fine inaugural address. I have just read a shortened version of it in *The Christian Science Monitor,*[2] and I wish it were possible for you to have your secretary send me a complete version. Better still I hope you will publish it in some national magazine, say, *The Atlantic* or *Harpers.*[3] It is good to have wisdom like this sounded out of our present-day South.

Sincerely yours,

## 260. To Francis S. Hutchins

[Greenwood Road, Chapel Hill, N.C.]
7 May 1957

Dear Dr. Hutchins:[1]

I am highly honored and deeply touched by the news in your letter. It has been my good luck to receive a few honorary degrees here and there from

1. Leroy Collins (1909–1991), who became governor of Florida on the death of Dan McCarty in 1954, then was elected to a term of his own in 1956, devoted his inaugural address (8 January 1957) to the matter of racial integration. He urged all citizens to admit the rule of law, all whites to recognize that blacks had been denied equal opportunities, all blacks to realize that they must earn advancement, and both races to work together in practical and constructive ways. He remarked that James Russell Lowell's "Once to Every Man and Nation" had always inspired and challenged him and concluded by quoting the third verse:

> New occasions teach new duties,
> Time makes ancient good uncouth:
> They must upward still and onward
> Who would keep abreast of truth.

2. " 'New Occasions Teach New Duties,' " *Christian Science Monitor,* 12 January 1957, p. 18, cols. 5–6.

3. Collins did not publish the speech but sent Green a copy (23 January 1957, PG-SHC).

---

1. Hutchins notified Green that the faculty and trustees of Berea College had voted

other colleges and universities,[2] but I get a special thrill from your announcement. I believe so heartily in the Berea philosophy of life and education that to have her president and faculty recognize in me something kindred to them makes me feel, well, reaffirmed.

If you could please have me supplied with a cap and gown, I'd be thankful.[3] My height is 5 feet, 10½, weight 180, and hat size 7½.

Mrs. Green and I will arrive on the morning of June 2 and return the next day. I am pretty strenuously tied up these days with our Williamsburg doings,[4] but I'll want to confer at length of course with Ted Cronk on our drama.[5] I am writing him about reservations.

With all good wishes to you, Mrs. Hutchins and the children.[6]

Sincerely yours,

## 261. To Arthur Gelb[1]

[Greenwood Road, Chapel Hill, N.C.]
26 June 1957

Dear Mr. Gelb—

I have been away from home for several weeks working at a number of outdoor summer productions, and that accounts for my delay in getting to

---

to confer on him a doctor of letters degree at commencement on 2 June, an action that gave Hutchins "the utmost personal gratification" (1 May 1957, PG-SHC).

2. Western Reserve University, 1941; Davidson College, 1948; University of North Carolina, 1956; and University of Louisville, 1957.

3. Hutchins had offered to do so if Green sent his measurements.

4. Opening a new play, *The Founders*, on 13 May as well as *The Common Glory*.

5. *Wilderness Road.*

6. The citation accompanying the award at the six o'clock ceremony read in part: "By word and by deed Paul Green has always been a vigorous enemy of such darknesses as injustice, inequality, intolerance, war, and despotism. He has dipped his pen deeply into the heart of America's past to remind us that men today and tomorrow may be, and should be, guided by the spirited pioneers in the American dream of liberty and justice and brotherhood. His dramatic spectacles have brought to the people and to our country a national theatre and a historical consciousness" (PG-SHC).

---

1. Arthur Gelb (b. 1924) and his wife Barbara, both on the staff of the *New York Times*, were at work on a biography of Eugene O'Neill (*O'Neill* [New York: Harper,

your letter of May 11. It is good news that you are going to do a thorough study of Eugene O'Neill. As you say, such a book is long overdue, and I wish you all success with it.

As to my impressions of O'Neill, I would need space for a long essay, of course, to put them down. To begin with let me say that I felt the strength of his personality and talent from the very first day I began writing plays. A traveling company came to the University of North Carolina when I was a student there back, I think, about 1921 with a production of *Beyond the Horizon.* I was gripped and inspired by the powerful and sombre truth of this play, and so I the more strongly resolved to write plays too with something of the same honesty and sincerity as his. (Ridgely Torrence with his three short Negro plays[2] had already been an encouragement to me.)

Later while I was writing a play about a Southern Negro school teacher,[3] a copy of the old *Theatre Arts Magazine* arrived with its version of *The Emperor Jones.*[4] I read the drama through and without getting up from my seat in the library read it through again. The reach of its imagination sent me tingling and whooping along to increased effort on my plays. "What a thing! What a thing!" I kept saying to myself.

This was back in 1924, I think.

Later—around 1927, 8 and 9—I was in New York working on the production of some of my dramas,[5] and I used to run into O'Neill around the Theatre Guild. He was always interested in what I was doing and would ask how things were getting along with me. He seemed to be like this with everybody—kind-hearted, encouraging, sympathetic, ever modest and with no frills.

Then one night James Light—the director and long-time associate of O'Neill along with Kenneth Macgowan and Robert Edmond Jones—took me

---

1962]), and Gelb asked Green for his "impressions of the dramatist . . . the time you first met O'Neill, how long you knew him, whether you corresponded with him" (11 May 1957, PG-SHC).

2. "Granny Maumee," "The Rider of Dreams," and "Simon the Cyrenian" (1917).

3. *In Abraham's Bosom.*

4. *Theatre Arts* 5 (January 1921): 29–59.

5. *In Abraham's Bosom,* produced by the Provincetown Players in the 1926–27 season; *The Field God,* produced by the Experimental Theatre (successor of the Provincetown Players and directed by O'Neill, Kenneth Macgowan, and Robert Edmond Jones) in the spring of 1927; and *The House of Connelly,* accepted by the Theatre Guild in 1929 (see letter 63).

up to O'Neill's apartment and we talked theatre. And such talk! The only occasion I can think of equal to it was the time I spent with Bernard Shaw in London when that soaring, playful and gibing spirit carried on a flood of theatre talk for three or four hours.[6] O'Neill, unlike Shaw, was a quiet-spoken, reticent man. But on this particular night he talked freely of his hopes and dreams for a new kind of American theatre—a theatre of the imagination unbounded and one in which the audience especially might participate more vitally and fully. He hoped, he said, someday to write plays in which the audience could share as a congregation shares in the music and ritual of a church service. "There must be some way that this can be brought about," he said. "As it is now there is a too cold and cut division between the stage and the auditorium. The whole environment of the piece—stage and auditorium, actors and spectators—should be emotionally charged. This can only happen," he went on, "when the audience actively participates in what is being said, seen and done. But how, that is the problem. Still there must be a way."

Then he told about his recent efforts somewhat in that direction, the play *Lazarus Laughed.*[7] He seemed to set a lot of store by that play—more I think than it deserved—but it was wonderful to see his enthusiasm for it and to catch something of his visioning of a new kind of theatre he felt it portended. "What I would like to see in the production of *Lazarus,*" he said, "is for the audience to be caught up enough to join in the responses—the laughter and chorus statements even, much as Negroes do in one of their revival meetings."

I only met O'Neill once more in passing, after this. But I went to see every one of his plays as they were put on and I read them all, not once but several times. And I continue to read them. I remember that I was disappointed on the opening of *Mourning Becomes Electra.*[8] The play seemed pompous and its grand manner a bit phoney at that time. But as the years have passed by and I read it over and give it my own mental production I like it better and better. Perhaps it is his greatest accomplishment. I don't know. He has done so many fine things it is hard to choose. And then after all—why choose. O'Neill remains our greatest pioneer in the American Drama. He has opened the barred door on a boundless future for it. His inspiration will continue.

I remember having only one letter from him and that I passed on years ago

6. See letter 66.

7. Written in 1926–27, produced in Pasadena, California, in April 1928 (never produced in New York City).

8. In 1931.

to Barrett Clark for his drama collection. Clark and I were planning a volume of *One-Act Plays for the American Imaginative Theatre*,[9] and I asked O'Neill to contribute. He replied, as I remember, that he would be unable to, for he had lost his touch for one-acters and doubted he would ever write any more of them. I suppose he didn't.

With best regards,[10]

## 262. To Herman Alexander Sieber[1]

[Greenwood Road, Chapel Hill, N.C.]
[Late August 1957]

I DO NOT KNOW ALL THE FACTORS INVOLVED IN THE EZRA POUND CASE BUT SO FAR AS I CAN SEE THERE IS NO GOOD REASON TO KEEP HIM LONGER AT ST. ELIZABETHS. I HAVE NEVER HAD ANY SYMPATHY WITH HIS ATTITUDE TOWARD THIS COUNTRY. HE HAS ALWAYS BEEN ABUSIVE OF IT AND NEVER REALLY TRIED TO HELP IT LIKE OTHER HONEST AND HARDWORKING AMERICANS. FOR THAT I CONDEMN HIM AND TELL HIM TO STAY OUT OF MY HAIR. STILL I DON'T HAVE ANY INTEREST IN SEEING HIM PUNISHED FURTHER IF PUNISHMENT IT IS. HE IS SICK AND SORRY NO MATTER HOW GOOD A POET SO KICK HIM OUT, GET HIM OUT, I SAY, AND LET HIM ROOT HOG OR DIE. BUT THEN WOULD THE MOVIES OR TELEVISION SNAP HIM UP AND EXPLOIT HIM AND MORE MESS RESULT! THERE

9. Perhaps *One-Act Plays for Stage and Study*, 4th ser. (1928).

10. In *O'Neill* the Gelbs quote extensively from the present letter (pp. 602–3).

---

1. On 21 August 1957 Congressman Usher L. Burdick of North Dakota introduced a resolution calling on the House Judiciary Committee to investigate "the sanity of Ezra Pound, in order to determine whether there is justification for his continued incarceration in Saint Elizabeths Hospital" (House Resolution No. 403). Herman Alexander Sieber, graduate of UNC (B.A., 1949), poet, and senior specialist in the Legislative Reference Service of the Library of Congress, was asked to prepare a report on Pound's case, and on 28 August he called Green to talk over the matter. The next day he wrote to Green: "We've got to make the report an objective one, that is, one which quotes facts, figures and comments without weighing the validity of the arguments, one way or the other. The comments we are quoting, of course, reflect differing views, although—frankly—they mostly indicate that we ought to take a good look at Pound's predicament to see whether we are doing the right thing. The question is: Should Ezra Pound be released from St. Elizabeths? I'd appreciate a short (2, 3 paragraphs) statement of what you think" (29 August 1957, PG-SHC).

ARE WORSE TRAITORS IN THE AMERICAN SCENE THAN POUND AND THEY'RE NEITHER SHUT UP NOR PUNISHED.[2]

PAUL GREEN

## 263. To Kermit Hunter[1]

[Greenwood Road, Chapel Hill, N.C.]
13 November 1957

Dear Kermit—

I have hesitated to write you in a follow-up of our telephone conversation some weeks ago until I was absolutely sure of our Norfolk project.[2] Now at last today everything is settled and we are going forward with it as fast as we can. Sam[3] has finally received a contract, and he told me this afternoon he is accepting my invitation and is signing to direct the show. I have signed a

2. Following maneuvers among politicians, lawyers, and writers (traced in Harry M. Meacham, *The Caged Panther: Ezra Pound at Saint Elizabeths* [1967]), Pound's case was brought before the U.S. District Court in Washington on 18 April 1958 and his indictment for treason dismissed. Sieber's report was read into the *Congressional Record* by Congressman Burdick on 29 April 1958 ("The Medical, Legal, Literary, and Political Status of Ezra Weston (Loomis) Pound," *Congressional Record* [1958], appendix, A3894–A3901). Pound left Saint Elizabeths on 30 April 1958 following twelve years of confinement and in July returned to Rapallo, Italy. Sieber's first book of poems (*In This the Marian Year* [Chapel Hill: Old Well Publishers, 1955]) included "In Defense of the Poet Laureate of St. Elizabeths" (p. 16).

---

1. Kermit Hunter (b. 1910), who completed his doctorate in dramatic arts at UNC in 1955, was the second most prolific author of outdoor historical plays, his longest-running works being *Unto These Hills*, which had its forty-third season in Cherokee, North Carolina, in 1992, and *Horn in the West*, which had its forty-first season in 1992 in Boone, North Carolina. At the time of the present letter he taught at Hollins College near Roanoke, Virginia, and had been asked to write a Civil War play for Appomattox. Knowing that Green had been approached by a group from Norfolk also to write a Civil War play, he called Green to talk over the situation (Kermit Hunter to Paul Green, 17 November 1957, PG-SHC).

2. For over a year Henry Clay Hofheimer II and Sidney S. Kellam of Norfolk corresponded with Green about the project that became *The Confederacy*.

3. Selden.

contract too, and between us we will work to turn out something worth while. But of course as you and I know from hard experience sometimes the best of intents don't result in the successful thing—yes, and the important thing—that we yearned and hoped for.

As is always the case with me I am writing a lot of pages and having to throw most of them away in favor of a new idea or scene that flares in from the outer shadows, that in turn so often to give way to still another relentless successor. I have never yet learned the art or skill of playwriting and I doubt I ever shall. Sometimes I think Dunsany's method was as good as any.[4] He got a whiff of a beginning, he used to say, and then simply began. He pushed the story along. I have always wanted to have my drama story pulled along, that is, have some goal out there ahead of me acting somewhat suction-like. Anyway I have at least always needed to know what my big (or showdown) scene was to be. Right now I haven't yet got that big scene for General Lee and the Civil War tragedy and am accordingly moving very slowly with the job.[5]

We all missed you here at our get-together of the outdoor theatre people.[6] We needed your inspiration, yet I thought all in all the meeting was very much worth while—if for no other reason than to tell one another our troubles and difficulties.

It looks as if Berea College is going to drop *Wilderness Road* even though through Ted Cronk's hard promotion work we had a successful season last year—more successful than that of *The Lost Colony*, and we have no intention at all of giving up that play. President Hutchins told me recently over the phone that the board of trustees meeting on November 22 will decide about *W.R.* He didn't sound hopeful. I am keeping my fingers crossed.[7] And I want you to know that we all appreciate the boosts you have given that play. You helped us immensely.

4. Lord Dunsany, Irish writer best known for the one-act fantasies he wrote for the Abbey Theatre.

5. *The Confederacy*, which opened for its first season in Virginia Beach, Virginia, on 1 July 1958, focuses on Robert E. Lee, and its big scene came to be the final one (act 2, scene 7), where Lee, as president of Washington College (now Washington and Lee University), represents national unity and courageous idealism.

6. Conference sponsored by the Carolina Playmakers, 26–27 October 1957.

7. Hutchins called after the meeting on 22 November to say the trustees decided to continue *Wilderness Road* in 1958 (Paul Green to Abbott Van Nostrand, 26 November 1957, PG-SHC).

I am sure your head is teeming with new ideas and I send you my best wishes for their good bringing-off—and my sympathy too.[8]

Much love to you both,

## 264. To Richard Walser[1]

[Greenwood Road, Chapel Hill, N.C.]
27 February 1958

Dear Dick:

I am glad you have in mind the possible publication of Sam Morphis' story, and I do hope you'll do it—along with a good biographical account of Sam. It is a pathetic piece and would be good for people to read in these times. At least I think so—in so far as anything does people good.[2] Why don't you sound the

8. Hunter did not do a Civil War play at Appomattox. At the time he had two new plays running—*Chucky Jack* (1956–59) at Gatlinburg, Tennessee, and *Thy Kingdom Come* (1957–60) at Salem, Virginia—and was at work on *Heart of a City* (1958) for Roanoke, Virginia.

---

1. Richard Walser (1908–1988), in the English department at North Carolina State University in Raleigh, was at work on the book that became *The Black Poet; Being the Remarkable Story (Partly Told by Himself) of George Moses Horton, a North Carolina Slave* (1966), and Green sent him the autobiography of another impressive Chapel Hill black, Sam Morphis. Walser found the thirty-page manuscript (dictated by Morphis to Horace Williams about 1900, when Morphis was seventy) "too valuable to let lie" and asked Green's permission to publish it (Richard Walser to Paul Green, 24 February 1958, PG-SHC).

2. Born into slavery on a plantation outside of Chapel Hill, Morphis grew up playing with his master's sons but in his early teens realized they had a future while he did not. Fearing he would be sold, he ran away to Chapel Hill, where college students gave him enough money to buy his "time," and in 1858 he petitioned the state legislature for freedom. Failure of the petition made him feel "less of a man" ever afterward. During the twenty years following the war, with the backing of a white friend, Morphis developed a hackney business in Chapel Hill and built a two-story home for his family. His holdings were all in his white friend's name, however, and on the death of the friend his heirs began demanding money from Morphis, who was soon ruined. During his last bitter years, he took some comfort from the observation that younger blacks were developing a "clear race-consciousness" and making themselves independent of whites. He concluded: "There is some gladness that comes to

editor out about using it in the *Historical Review*?[3] It has enough carapace of documents-and-history about it to take away some of the social finger-pointing—a thing that usually frightens institutional souls fluttering into the bushes.

I remember when I first read the MS. some thirty-odd years ago I was so touched by it that I dreamed up a play about it and made the note you mention to that effect then.[4] (I once saw a Negro man, a school teacher, beaten by some white toughs down in Harnett County. I was a little boy at the time.[5] That teacher and Sam Morphis coalesced into one character for me, I guess, in the *Abraham's Bosom* play.)

As I recall it, Horace Williams a long time ago handed Sam's account on to Louis Graves for his use in a New York paper or magazine. (Louis was on *The Times* then, I think.)[6] He couldn't use it. Later Louis came to UNC as the journalism professor.[7] One day we were talking about the Negro and the South and he passed it on to me. I talked with Horace about it, and he said for me to keep it and do what I could with it. Now after these years maybe you'll bring it out. I hope so.[8]

Ever,

---

me when I see that my type of Negro will be soon gone from the face of the earth" ("Autobiography of a Negro," PG-SHC).

3. *North Carolina Historical Review*, edited by Christopher Crittenden, who, Walser feared, might find "the talk about race . . . too strong" (24 February 1958, PG-SHC).

4. Attached to the manuscript is Green's note that Morphis's story was a source of *In Abraham's Bosom.*

5. Recounted in letter 220.

6. 1902–6.

7. In 1921, following military service in France.

8. The Morphis piece remains unpublished.

## 265. To Marie F. Rodell[1]

[Greenwood Road, Chapel Hill, N.C.]
9 October 1958

Dear Miss Rodell:

We are delighted down here in Chapel Hill that Dr. King is on the road to health again. What a terrible thing it was that happened to him! He has suffered, he has endured, and how wonderful it is that he is still spared to carry on his good work of brotherhood and understanding among men.

When I read *Stride Toward Freedom* I was so moved by the heroic story that I had the urge to try some sort of dramatization based on it—though I wasn't sure what form such dramatization would take nor just when I could get to it. I know though that when Dr. King is available I'd like to discuss the matter with him and consider ways and means. Will he be coming back South in this direction any time within the next few weeks or months?[2]

Sincerely yours,

1. Harper and Row notified Green of its intention to publish *Stride Toward Freedom*, Martin Luther King's account of the Montgomery bus boycott in 1956–57, and on the day of publication (8 September 1958) Green wrote the publisher that he wanted to dramatize the book. The publisher was excited, believing "there is material here as vital as that contained in Richard Wright's *Native Son*," and turned over Green's letter to King's literary agent, Marie Rodell of the Rodell and Daves Agency in Manhattan (James S. Best to Paul Green, 16 September 1958, PG-SHC). Rodell, herself "awfully pleased with the idea," reported that King "very much likes the idea of your dramatizing *Stride Toward Freedom*" and asked Green to "let me know what sort of arrangement you have in mind." She added that it would be some weeks before King could discuss the project. He was in Harlem Hospital recovering from stab wounds inflicted by a crazed black woman while he autographed copies of the book at Blumstein Department Store in Harlem on 20 September (22 September 1958).

2. On his return to Montgomery, King replied that "Marie Rodell informed me of your interest in placing my book, *Stride Toward Freedom*, in play form. I was certainly happy to hear this and knowing your great reputation in this field my delight was increased even more." Saying his health still forbade much travel, King invited Green to Montgomery to discuss the project (19 November 1958, PG-SHC). For unrecovered reasons, Green declined: "My admiration for your fine book is as strong as ever," he replied, "but events have moved in such a way and nature since my first letter to you that I believe a dramatization of it would better wait" (26 November 1958).

## 266. To Edwin S. Lanier[1]

[Greenwood Road, Chapel Hill, N.C.]
6 February 1959

Dear Ed:

I think your questionnaire is a fine thing to do, and I wish I knew more to say in reply. About item 3: I don't think any money should be appropriated to "celebrate" the centennial of the Civil War if the sense of states' right, cleavages, etc. in our national fabric is to be heightened thereby. I am a member of the national and state Centennial Commission groups and have attended a number of meetings, and I have been saddened by the fact that half-sleeping antagonisms reared right up in some of these meetings on the smallest of provocations.[2] Of course I think it would be fine for the legislature to appropriate money for documentation work, say, the accumulating of records, publication of sound historical volumes, etc., etc. which would have as their aim the telling of the real story of North Carolina's contribution to the great heroic struggle—"First at Manassas, last at Appomattox", etc.[3]—a story

1. Edwin S. Lanier (1901–1989), state senator from Chapel Hill, sent Green a questionnaire (unlocated) on how the state should celebrate the centennial of the Civil War. Item 3 on the questionnaire had to do with the appropriation of state money for the celebration.

2. For instance, at a meeting of the North Carolina Confederate Centennial Commission in Raleigh on 10 October 1958, Green wanted it resolved that the purpose of their effort was to celebrate the Civil War as "a great national tragedy" out of which "the union was forged," not as a glorification of slavery or states' rights. But several at the meeting, led by Mrs. R. O. Everett, lawyer and former president of the North Carolina United Daughters of the Confederacy, did not believe the issue of states' rights had been settled ("States' Rights Battle Breaks Out As Civil War Centennial Planned," *NO*, 11 October 1958, p. 1, cols. 6–8). A few days later one man told the commission chairman "that he would take four months off from his work if necessary and do all he could to see that the legislature didn't appropriate one cent for the celebration if it was to be put on the way Paul Green wanted it," and another said, "Paul Green had made him so mad that he was ready to fight." "Good gracious," Green continued in his diary, "I thought my little talk had been harmless enough. It is all very melancholy, very saddening. See how we are drifting into evil in the South for lack of leadership" (Green diary, 13 October 1958, PG-SHC).

3. While First Manassas, 17–21 July 1861, was the earliest major battle of the war, a skirmish occurred at Big Bethel, northwest of Newport News, Virginia, on 10 June

which has never been told. U.N.C. and its press, the State Archives people, newspapers and others could get behind this. As the subject was studied, other ideas of memorializing would come forth. The North Carolina people could be stirred to help—old attics and trunks searched for letters and documents which could be offered to add to the stock of our heritage, to be preserved actually or in micro-film (which would take some money). Also perhaps a field consultant via the Carolina Playmakers could be arranged for to give advice and help on local pageants and memorial occasions,[4] but I don't think a dime should be appropriated for such pageants and occasions themselves. Let the local people in each case do it. For instance—to go back to my first items—Virginia has appropriated, I understand, $25,000 for the publication of the Robert E. Lee papers.[5] We have in North Carolina a number of good Civil War names—Zebulon Vance,[6] Pettigrew,[7] Ransom[8] and others—which have never been properly dealt with. Suppose money were appropriated to back a number of good volumes and monographs, an editorial board set up, and a few chosen scholars and historians put to work to really tell our Civil War story—then we'd have something worthwhile to result, I think. And always the point of view of the Centennial is important. The national office in Washington has well given that in advance—pointing out the tragedy as a

---

1861, where Henry Wyatt of North Carolina was one of eight Confederate casualties. Thus the full form of the phrase is: first at Bethel, farthest at Gettysburg (where two North Carolina regiments headed General George Pickett's charge up Cemetery Ridge), last at Appomattox (where North Carolina troops under Captain David Allen were among the last to surrender) (Glenn Tucker, *Front Rank* [Raleigh: North Carolina Confederate Centennial Commission, 1962]).

4. In 1961 the commission sponsored the writing of three plays with Civil War settings for community production: "Durham Station" by Betty Smith, "Many Are the Hearts" by Manly Wade Wellman, and "No Bugles, No Drums" by George Bernholtz.

5. The Virginia legislature appropriated $25,000 that year for its Civil War centennial commission, without specifying its purpose, and no Lee papers seem to have been published by the Virginia commission.

6. Hero of the Seven Days Battle in June 1862; later governor of the state and U.S. senator.

7. James J. Pettigrew, a field officer mortally wounded leading Pickett's charge up Cemetery Ridge on the third day of the battle of Gettysburg, 3 July 1863.

8. Robert Ransom, Jr., who distinguished himself at the Seven Days Battle and Harpers Ferry.

testing time of our democracy, a testing out of which the unified nation was born and not born until then, and in which brave and heroic men on both sides gave their lives for the right as they saw the right to be.

If the "celebration" should serve, as I say, to arouse antagonisms and emotions better left quiet, then we ought to forget the whole thing. And I think there is a danger of this if we are not careful, especially in view of the school and race situation in the country.[9]

Regards,

## 267. To Evelyn Foster Morneweck[1]

[Greenwood Road, Chapel Hill, N.C.]
27 April 1959

Dear Mrs. Morneweck:

Dr. Van Grove has kindly forwarded your letter of April 10 on to me here, since so many of the matters you mention have to do with the actual writing of the play.

Let me say right off that your thoroughgoing two-volume *Chronicles of Stephen Foster's Family* is being of great help to me in composing—I guess that is a good word to use—the script.

I am afraid though you are going to be very much surprised, and maybe even disappointed, when you see what I have done to Foster's biography. But in order to get a dramatic shape instead of a loose chronicle to Foster's life, I am having to interpret the facts rather freely, preferring the "spirit" of Foster to the actual space and time events. But in the main the piece will be historically authentic.

Since so much uncertainty surrounded this venture for so long a time, I

9. National Guard troops still patrolled Little Rock, Arkansas, sent by President Eisenhower in September 1957 to maintain order as blacks entered the city's white high school. As yet no southern state had integrated its school system.

---

1. With his musical collaborator Isaac Van Grove, Green was at work on *The Stephen Foster Story*, which would open in My Old Kentucky Home State Park at Bardstown, Kentucky, on 26 June 1959, and Evelyn Foster Morneweck (1887–?), niece of Foster and family historian (*The Birthplace of Stephen C. Foster* [1936] and *Chronicles of Stephen Foster's Family*, 2 vols. [1944]), wrote to Van Grove about the rendition of several Foster songs.

have been delayed in getting the play script finished.[2] Right now I am about two-thirds through. I hope within the next week or so to come to the last page. Then the matter of quick revisions and mimeographing. As soon as the play is ready I will ask Mr. Cronk[3] to send you a copy.

And all of us deeply appreciate your kind and considerate suggestions and helpfulness.[4]

I have especially made a note of the pronunciations and interpretations of the six songs you mention on page two of your letter.[5]

I am very glad to have your suggestion of substituting "darky" for "nigger."[6] I had already come to the same conclusion and am affirmed by your corroboration.

And another thing you will have to prepare to forgive me for is the lack of proper emphasis upon the different members of the Foster family in my story. But when one has only two hours for his play, then things have to move in a

2. Laban Jackson of the Kentucky Department of Conservation first contacted Green concerning a play in 1957, and along the way the project experienced delays due to fluctuating state and local interest and a threatened lawsuit by a jealous Kentucky author (correspondence files with Laban Jackson, Ted Cronk, and Earl Hobson Smith, 1957–58, PG-SHC).

3. Prime mover and general manager of the Foster project.

4. Morneweck thought her suggestions would help with "the authentic singing of the songs. Not because I know anything about music but because I am the last of the Foster family . . . who learned Foster melodies from one who sang them with Stephen Foster himself" (Evelyn Morneweck to Isaac Van Grove, 10 April 1959, PG-SHC).

5. Saying her points reflected Foster's intentions, Morneweck wrote that "Oh! Susanna" is a comical "nonsense song" with playful pronunciations as in the line, "And when I'm dead and buried," where the final word "should be pronounced in *three* syllables 'bear-eye-ed' to rhyme with 'dead,' " that a similar thing occurs in "Way Down in Cairo" where the name of the town should be pronounced "kay-eye-row," that "The Glendy Burk" and "Nelly Was a Lady" should not be sung in a choppy staccato, that "doo-dah" in "De Camptown Races" should not be pronounced "doo-daw (as in jackdaw) but doo-dah with a short 'a' as in 'daddy,' " and that "Old Black Joe" is not a bass solo but was "written in two sharps for baritone or tenor" (ibid.).

6. Morneweck was "with the State of Kentucky in objecting to the changing of Stephen Foster's words with one exception, 'nigger.' I thoroughly believe this should always be changed, because Stephen changed it himself in 'Old Uncle Ned.' 'Darky' is a term of affection, but 'nigger' is cruel, offensive and insulting" (ibid.).

hurry and often he can only give a character who deserves a great deal more just a line or two here and there.[7]

I remember with good feeling still the meeting with you and your husband in Bardstown last year.[8]

With best greetings and regards to you and yours,

## 268. To Elizabeth L. Green

[Bardstown, Ky.]
9 June 1959

Dear Honey—[1]

I am here at rehearsal at the school house—we've been all mired up at the theatre with rain, and as usual everything is far behind there[2]—and while the folks are resting a few minutes I'll scribble you a note. I've been a poor correspondent, but gosh I've been busy as can be. The play is still formless. (Sam is so slow and indefinite with his workers as he smiles and is gracious.) As soon as we have got the script fitted to the actors and correctly timed I will get out of everybody's hair, and I know there'll be great relief wider than the

7. In the play Stephen's older brother Morrison Foster, Morneweck's father, appears only in a crowd scene and has no lines.

8. Evelyn and Alfred Morneweck, from Detroit but recently retired in Stuart, Florida, visited Bardstown frequently because of their involvement with My Old Kentucky Home State Park, and they may have met Green in early July 1958 when he was there for an organizational meeting of the drama project (Paul Green to Ted Cronk, 15 July 1958, PG-SHC).

---

1. Since the first day or two of June, Green had been in Bardstown for rehearsals of *The Stephen Foster Story.* On 22 May he had sent the script to Ted Cronk for duplication, with a copy to Samuel Selden, who had become head of the drama department at the University of California at Los Angeles in the fall of 1958 but was returning east for the summer to direct *Stephen Foster.* The play was to open on 26 June, and Selden planned to arrive in Bardstown on 5 June, but Green wrote to him that "for the life of me I don't see how we can get this play on in twenty days. The music, the music, and the singing, the singing! So is there any way we can get something at work by June 1?" (5 May 1959, PG-SHC).

2. Work on the theater, near the Federal Hill mansion in My Old Kentucky Home State Park, was not finished until the afternoon of the opening.

woods and higher than the trees. But really these are a fine group of young people, talented and anxious to work.[3] And you and Janet[4] will love the music.[5] Faxie[6] has surprised me with lovely costumes.[7] Van[8] is here working hard, and everybody loves him too. My hope is to get away home this weekend, arriving Sunday sometime. I'll let you know.[9] My present purposed duty (for financial future hopes etc.) is to start on the round—Manteo, Va. Beach, Wmsbg—for one night rehearsal oversight and attention at each play,[10] and then from Wmsbg straight back here in time to be of use in a final shaping of *Stephen Foster* for opening night. I ought to be here not later than the evening of June 21 for that rehearsal.[11] Then perhaps I could start back the afternoon of June 22, the next day. I hope both you and Jan can go on the whole tour. If necessary maybe Jan could fly to N.Y. from here if she had to get back in a hurry. So you better work hard getting vegetables into the freezer. Even better work out the itinerary as to days also—when we should leave C.H. etc. It will take one day and part of the next to drive from Wmsbg here. They're starting again.

Love, love, Paul

3. Stephen was played by James Morris, Jane (Jeanie with the lovely brown hair) by Barbara Lockard, and E. P. Christy by Martin Ambrose.

4. Their daughter, visiting from Manhattan.

5. About forty Foster songs woven into the play. "As we all know," Green told Cronk, "the success of our project depends first of all on the beautiful way we sing and give forth Foster's music" (22 May 1959, PG-SHC).

6. Fairfax Proudfit Walkup.

7. As she began work on costume designs, Green told Walkup "costumes for this play must be 'out of this world.' Let us theatricalize to the point of exaggeration in colors, contrasts, etc. . . . You can hardly overdo the minstrel costumes. . . . And the costume of E. P. Christy should be a dream" (27 March 1959, PG-SHC). He mentioned two books with helpful pictures and notes.

8. Isaac Van Grove, arranger of the music.

9. Green did get home on Sunday, 14 June.

10. *The Lost Colony*, *The Confederacy*, and *The Common Glory*.

11. The Sunday before the opening on Friday, 26 June.

## 269. To Samuel Selden and Ted Cronk

[Greenwood Road, Chapel Hill, N.C.]
14 June 1959

Dear Sam and Ted:[1]

I think you have got our play and theatre project off to a promising start. The ripples of differing opinions were to be expected under the circumstances, I guess, and perhaps we'll all know better next time. They resulted no doubt from the author's care for his play and from the fact that the staff had not had time to acquaint themselves with the needs and possibilities of the script before plunging into their varying rehearsals. But I believe that our planning conferences (which I had felt were of prime importance [from] the very start along with a get-together reading of the play) finally helped us to unify our intent into a common vision and purpose, and from now on all should go well.

There still remains the finalizing of the job which I hope we can do when I come back.[2] (Of course it would be wonderful if when I came back everything was so beautifully accomplished that nothing remained but to give loud applause and thankful embraces.)

One thing we did not get worked out before I left—the time length of the overtures. This should be done at once to save further wastage. There is no use in Ralph[3] and the chorus working hard to learn stuff we don't have time for. The full length of the first act overture should be no more than three and one-half minutes. That of the second act should be two and one-half minutes. The length of the first overture now is well over four minutes. It should be cut at once, and such cutting will have the further advantage of keeping back some of the song material later used in the play. At present too much of one or two songs is given in this overture. Ralph will know where to cut it. I spoke to both him and Van about it before I left—and of course I have mentioned it to you, Sam, also. Maybe by this time this has been taken care of.

As to the overture for the second act—I didn't have a chance to check it before I left. But here, too, the time length controls.

1. On reaching home Green immediately sent director Sam Selden and producer Ted Cronk the ideas about *Stephen Foster* that ran through his mind during the drive from Bardstown.

2. About 21 June.

3. Musical director Ralph Burrier.

I hope Harry[4] has been able to build the minstrel scene to its dramatic point[5] and likewise the nightmare scene.[6] I think he agreed on the story needs of those two scenes at the last conference.

And for your information also, Ted, I would like to say that there doesn't seem to be any need to go to further expense to construct the Old Kentucky Home vision paraphernalia up on the hillside at the rear.

The height of the "crosswalk" under which the speakers are to be housed would require a structure so far up in the air that I am afraid the appearance of our amphitheatre from the front of the house for visitors during the daytime would be badly marred. Tommy[7] seems to have done very well indeed, with his problems.

And, Ted, you have worked miracles. At that meeting of the businessmen with yourself and Jackson[8] the other evening I was impressed with the interest and determination the local people have in the project.

I think you have there at Bardstown one of the greatest art and community news stories this country has ever afforded. I can see *Time*, *Life*, the *Reader's Digest*, and other magazines and newspapers featuring this town and its play during the coming years. For one thing, the name Bardstown is a stroke of genii luck in itself. I think you also are lucky in having the project finally become a purely local one.[9] Now American critics and writers can tell, as the play continues year after year, about a little American town which turned its mind and soul to memorializing a musician, a sweet singer, a folk minstrel, etc., etc. Music![10]

I think also Faxie has done a stupendous job on the costumes. All praise to her. And I hope I have made my enthusiasm apparent to her. Just before I left,

4. Choreographer Harry Coble.

5. Act 2, scene 2, where Christy is forced to acknowledge Foster's authorship of the popular "Old Folks at Home" and hold out the promise of payment for Foster songs—thus the possibility that artists can support themselves with their art.

6. Act 2, scene 3, section C, in which Foster, crushed and unable to compose because Jeanie has denounced him, is tormented by grotesque fantasy figures singing snatches from his songs but in distorted harmonies and rhythms.

7. Stage designer Tommy Rezzuto.

8. Laban Jackson from the Kentucky Department of Conservation.

9. After building the J. Dan Talbott Amphitheatre in My Old Kentucky Home State Park, the state left the project in the hands of a local group, the Stephen Foster Drama Association.

10. In 1992 *The Stephen Foster Story* played its thirty-fourth consecutive summer.

on the way out of town, I went by the costume shop to be available for any last-minute queryings she might have. We discussed the matter of Jeanie's dress for the groundbreaking ceremony.[11] She was in complete agreement that this first appearance of Jeanie should be cute, adorable—enchanting! So she plans to give her a dress suitable in every way to the occasion.

She has some fine ideas, Sam, as to quick costume change for the last scene;[12] let Dr. McDowell, when he comes out with Mrs. McDowell and surprises the two lovers, wear his rather capacious nightshirt over his suit, and Jeanie in her upstairs room likewise can have her negligee over her wedding dress, and so on.

Also, Ted, I forgot to check to see whether the devil in the show[13] is billed on the program as His Satanic Majesty. He should be.[14]

Affectionately, as always,

cc: Ralph Burrier, Thomas Rezzuto

## 270. To Harold C. Fleming[1]

[Greenwood Road, Chapel Hill, N.C.]
19 June 1959

Dear Mr. Fleming:

Thanks for your letter of June 8 and for the motion picture script, "Wealth of Violence," which were waiting for me here on my return home. I have just finished reading the script and am hurrying along my impressions of it.

11. Act 1, scene 2.

12. Changes between act 2, scene 3, section D, where her parents surprise Jeanie (who has come down from her bedroom) and Foster on the front steps at midnight, and act 2, scene 4 (the next and final scene), where the two young people are cheered following their wedding.

13. The Christy minstrel show.

14. And is.

---

1. Harold C. Fleming (b. 1922) was executive director of the Southern Regional Council, formed in 1944 to bring to bear on public issues such as race relations the views of leaders in business and the professions. Green was a member of the council, and Fleming asked him to evaluate a motion picture script for possible funding by the council. The script, "Wealth of Violence" by Jim Larkin, was a fictionalized account of the strife in Clinton, Tennessee, over integration of the local high school. In the fall of 1956 Clinton, eighteen miles north of Knoxville, became the first town in the Deep

The author has done a good solid *reporter's* job, it seems to me, even if the story is supposed to be fictionized.[2] He takes us right into the midst of things and lets us see prejudice and misunderstanding fully stewing and turmoiling. But, to come quickly to the point, I think the country has, alas, already seen so much of this sort of thing that a reporting of it again, even in a film, will simply be doing once more what the newspapers, television, radio and word of mouth have already done to repletion. (And at the end of the script things are as bad as they were to start with.) Further, I doubt that the public would care enough about seeing such a picture to make it financially profitable to anyone. Of course, I may be wrong here.

But I don't think I am wrong when I say that if the Council embarks on the sponsorship and support of a full-length film on this sensitive and "loaded" subject, it should be a film which leads somewhere, which has more of the spirit of reaching hands across the divisioning, of illumination, of the final and basic solving of something, or at least the suggestion of solving, so that we can feel at the end that a bit of the plus side of living has been added to—that the job has been worth doing.

Integration in the schools is not only a Southern but is something of a national dilemma, as everybody knows. Race relations are our American tragedy right now, and any film dealing with them should, I think, give us some of the heartache and heart-hunger of that tragedy. I find these lacking in the script. I find too much peckerwood violence and rush and wash and go of mobbery throughout. And to use that old abused Aristotelian word—there is no purgation out of this bleeding and sound and fury. As I say, we already know all we need to know of this kind of behavior. I, along with most everybody else, am tired of hearing about it.

---

South to undergo court-ordered integration when twelve black students were admitted to the previously white school. Unlike the situation at Little Rock, Arkansas, however, state and local officials in Clinton, supported by a large majority of the population, worked to implement the court order, and it was only with the arrival of John Kasper, a white racist from Camden, New Jersey, that trouble began: marches, riots, beatings, and finally the demolition of the school by three dynamite blasts in the early morning of 5 October 1958 (*Christian Science Monitor*, 1 September 1956, p. 8, cols. 1–2; 7 September 1956, p. 14, cols. 1–4; 4 December 1956, p. 5, cols. 2–3; 5 December 1956, p. 1, cols. 4–5; p. 4, cols. 7–8; 6 October 1958, p. 3, col. 1).

2. Larkin spent about a month in Clinton in 1957 doing research for the picture (Borden Mace to Harold Fleming, 27 May 1959, PG-SHC).

But I am *not* tired of hearing about those who are earnestly trying to accomplish something.[3] If the author had written about such people and had thrown out most of the scenes dealing with Bud Saunders, Kyle Foreman[4] and their mob followers (a reference to them now and then would almost be enough), I believe his script would be more worthwhile and would have a better chance at financial success. But from Hollywood and TV experience I too know how much more easy it is to get an effect by violence than by rational behavior and thinking. But that is exactly the challenge here. And it should be met. The matter is too important for the usual documentary or Hollywood treatment. It requires vision, objective and even benign understanding and a sense of moral value. (Racial violence is a far different thing from the *violence* in our popular westerns.)

The present script seems to me a good first draft but with the main thing left out—a warm, human story. In revision, the author might well consider, I think, the possibility of concentrating more on two families—one Negro and one white. We could get to know the members of the two as we go along—especially the young folks. As it is now, the action dances on so fast with so many characters, and most of them worthless, that we are never allowed to stay with anyone long enough to get down into their hearts and minds. So suspense is lacking—except for the suspense about possible violence and physical hurt to someone. And for the Council's purpose this is the most unimportant suspense of all. Also I think the author could do more with the churches.[5]

The kind of picture I am suggesting is, I know, harder to do than the one the present script calls for. But it should be harder. It should require not only

3. D. J. Brittain, Jr., principal of the high school, supported by the school board and the teachers, began planning for integration in January 1955, as soon as the court order came down. Mayor W. E. Lewallen tried to reason with Kasper and his followers, saying the question of integration had been settled in the courts and the town intended to obey the law (*Christian Science Monitor*, 1 and 7 September 1956).

4. Fictional characters.

5. The school was closed on 4 December 1956 because sixteen whites, two of them women, beat a white minister, Reverend Paul Turner, pastor of the First Baptist Church in Clinton, for escorting six of the black students to school. And following the dynamiting of the school on 5 October 1958, the churches of Clinton offered their buildings as emergency classrooms (*Christian Science Monitor*, 4 and 5 December 1956 and 6 October 1958).

the best creative power of the author but of both the Council and Louis de Rochemont,[6] as well. "Wealth of Violence" does not quite do that.

And to start with, the title is wrong. Wealth of violence is not what we want, but rather a wealth of the creative spirit. To keep on repeating—a film mostly devoted to violence is the easiest and least worthwhile thing in the world to do in the present situation. But the right film should be done, I think, and the Council could find no better producer for it than the Louis de Rochemont organization.[7]

With best greetings and regards, Paul Green

## 271. To Gerald W. Johnson

[Greenwood Road, Chapel Hill, N.C.]
11 August 1959

Dear Gerald:[1]

Thanks for your good letter of a few days ago. I read it with the usual fun when I got back from my outdoor drama doings in Kentucky. (With the help of one Happy Chandler[2] and the Kentucky state legislature we have built a

6. New York City firm producing the picture.

7. The council turned down the script for Green's reasons: too much violence, unworthy characters (Harold Fleming to Paul Green, 3 August 1959, PG-SHC).

---

1. In 1959 Green published a book consisting of three one-act plays: "The Thirsting Heart" (from the story "Education South," in *Dog on the Sun* [1949]), "Lay This Body Down" (from the play "The Hot Iron," in *Lonesome Road* [1926]), and "Fine Wagon" (from the story of the same title in *Salvation on a String* [1946]). His purpose in the book was to show the misery and wastefulness of human potential inherent in current race relations, and, as he told his publisher, he wanted to send out "two or three hundred copies of the book in the Southern political and social scene as early as possible" (Paul Green to Abbott Van Nostrand, 6 January 1959, PG-SHC). He entitled the book *Wings for to Fly* (from Chaucer's "The Squire's Tale," in which people wonder if the magical brass horse of the story "was lyk the Pegasee, / The hors that hadde wynges for to flee" [lines 207–8]), and with this title suggesting human aspiration he coupled the sobering epigraph: "For what sin can be greater than to cause a man to miss his own life." Johnson was one of those to whom Green sent *Wings for to Fly* in the summer of 1959, and Johnson responded that in general he was delighted with the book (24 July 1959, PG-SHC).

2. A. B. Chandler, governor of Kentucky, who had declared 1957 to be Paul Green

gem of an outdoor theatre in the edge of Bardstown near the old Southern mansion of "My Old Kentucky Home," and there with a lot of fighter Churchill's sweat and tears we have got another show going.[3] This time I tried something different—no wars, no stump speeches, no "American dream" philosophy, just a play, and of all things about a young fellow who wanted to have a normal life, win his girl, pay taxes and write music and songs—one Stephen Foster. Dramatic question in the play—can he do it? The audiences seem to like to see him try. We have been selling out nearly every night and the crowds come from everywhere. The little village is jubilant with the cash registers jingling in all the stores. Ah, Caesar!)

About the race problem and the futile white man[4]—many years ago[5] I was so sore at the ignorance and brutality in a certain North Carolina chain gang that I wrote a play against the system, "Hymn to the Rising Sun" and sent published copies to every legislator, political leader, newspaper editor, and prominent educator in the state, hoping to do some good at my own expense.[6] To this day I have not had a word or line in response from any recipient. Talk about futility! (The occasion of the play was the loss of four feet frozen from exposure belonging to two chain gang members named Shropshire and Barnes. You may remember those gentlemen. I tried by tongue-pleading to get our commonwealth to do something for them in reimbursement. "What," said Capus Waynick,[7] "that would mean the state acknowledged responsibility—er—a kind of guilt. No sir." Etc.)

---

Year in the state because of *Wilderness Road* (Paul Green to A. B. Chandler, 28 February 1957, PG-SHC).

3. When Winston Churchill presented his war cabinet to the House of Commons on 13 May 1940, he had nothing to offer the British people, he said, "but blood, toil, tears and sweat."

4. Johnson had said, "The impotence of the civilized minority of the white South is not wholly due to inertia. In part it is attributable to the high tragedy of man's isolation from his fellows. You can't do much for people. You can't do much for your own children, let alone children of a different race. . . . The civilized white man . . . can't give to either [the racists or the blacks] any of his valuable possessions, to wit, discretion, foresight, historical perspective, poise. He would, gladly; but he cannot. And he, too, is pathetic" (24 July 1959, PG-SHC).

5. In 1935.

6. See letters 114 and 117.

7. Chairman of the State Highway and Public Works Commission (1934–37).

You are right—the giving of the humiliated Negro one dollar by the white professor (which in this case was me) meant nothing.[8] But the showing in the little drama that it meant nothing was part of the point of the piece. Which reminds me of the same Russian point of view as yours here when some years back too the Moscow Art Theatre wrote me asking for permission (why I don't know, since they took what they wanted in those days) to do an anti-war play of mine, *Johnny Johnson*, saying that they hoped I'd rewrite the ending and have Johnny take some positive action, lead a movement in protest or fight or something rather than stand pitifully on the street selling toys and dolorously singing his credo of pacifism. I couldn't comply, for then—even as now it seems—I was rapt in a sense of pathos and felt it sufficient to show man in a posture of futility due to his sins, feeling that this showing ought to suggest and urge the reality of what should be different. (I hope to grow beyond this.)[9]

So with the three little plays in *Wings for to Fly*. And I had them cheaply printed for wide distribution in the south. This time a bit of progress—for I've had a few words of acknowledgement from friends like you but none from the White Patriots, the hardened sinners.

Yes, down here we too are full of Nixon's doings.[10] Even tonight he's on television again.[11] I'm out in my office and Elizabeth is in the house listening

8. In "Fine Wagon" a black man and his son set out with high hopes and a team and wagon to haul wood for a white professor, but under the load a wagon wheel breaks. The professor, frustrated at what he takes to be their incompetence, dismisses the black man but gives him a dollar, then returns to the house fuming about the "helpless—hopeless" black man (*Wings for to Fly* [New York: Samuel French, 1959], p. 31). At home the black man, unable to contain his humiliation and anger, beats his mules and threatens his wife and son.

9. Johnson had not urged Green to give "Fine Wagon" a positive ending and in fact had "long maintained that you got more of the American Dilemma in that yarn than [Gunnar] Myrdal did in two volumes" (24 July 1959, PG-SHC).

10. On the day of Johnson's letter, Vice President Richard Nixon, in Moscow for the opening of an exhibition of U.S. consumer products, got into a public shouting match with Nikita Khrushchev, head of the Soviet government, over the merits of capitalism and communism. Johnson said, "My head is full of Nixon in Moscow. The evening papers carried the account of his collision with Khrushchev . . . and I verily believe that right then and there the sonofabitch made himself President of the United States!" (ibid.).

11. Reporting on his trip to Moscow and urging that the United States needs "a policy of 'stand your ground, talk tough and don't retreat' in dealing with the Russians" (*New York Times*, 12 August 1959, p. 3, col. 2).

and seeing. Today I heard one of his former enemies, a democrat, say—"If that fellow was running for president right now I'd vote for him." You may be right—that he has by his Russian trip made himself our next president. But I couldn't call him a sonofabitch, for I admire a pretty woman too much, and he's married to one.

Eheu, this American scene! I have been reading a lot of you, Commager, Nevins, Schlesinger[12] et al. for a piece I've got to write this week, and I shake my head.

But not as much as I did—and this is the real purpose of this note—for I've just read your recent book, *America Is Born* which Morrow sent me.[13] Man, it's good. It clears up a lot of things for me as it will for thousands of other children, and all of us wait happily for the volumes to follow.[14] I'm saying this and more to Morrow.[15]

Bless you evermore,

## 272. To Barbara Davidson[1]

[Greenwood Road, Chapel Hill, N.C.]
30 August 1960

Dear Miss Davidson,

Thanks for sending me Guy Owen's *Season of Fear*. I have read it word for word and find it good sensitive writing. The book is full of sweat, the smell of

12. Social historians Henry Steele Commager, Alan Nevins, and Arthur Schlesinger.

13. In September 1959 in its Junior Books series William Morrow would publish Johnson's account of early American history and had sent Green a copy for comments.

14. *America Grows Up* and *America Moves Forward* (both 1960).

15. Frances Phillips, friend and editor at Morrow, sent Green the book, describing it as a "history for young'uns" (9 July 1959, PG-SHC), and Green replied that he "loved Gerald Johnson's first volume. . . . I read most of it twice right off and found it fine not only for young younguns but for this old youngun too. His free chatty style is just right. And how clear and interesting and well-reasoned as to causes is his account of this country's early history" (13 September 1959).

---

1. Davidson, in the publicity department of Random House, sent Green an advance copy of *Season of Fear*, the first novel by North Carolina writer Guy Owen. Set in a farming community along the Cape Fear River, *Season of Fear* focuses on Clay Hampton (Hamp), whose repressed sexuality leads him to dynamite the husband of

sour clothes, the pain of thorned bare feet, and southern poor white rotgut shiftlessness—as well as spurts and gleams of beauty here and there.

The characterization of Hamp is wonderfully realised.

Maybe this is enough! Maybe this is enough!

But like heroic and confuted Robert E. Lee I ask myself, "What's it all worth?"

And in this querying I am repeating what a Hollywood producer's wife once said to me after she had read a collection of my southern poor white and Negro plays—"What's it all add up to?"

Isn't it too bad after all that so many fine and lyric talents in the South have to do their do with characters and events not worth the doing?

Or are they?

With best greetings and regards,

## 273. To Marshall L. Locklear[1]

[Greenwood Road, Chapel Hill, N.C.]
10 September 1960

Dear Professor Locklear:

I appreciate very much your letter of September 9 which I received yesterday. From personal experience I know that people often have an impulse to

---

the girl of his fantasies. As lawmen close in, Hamp is shot by a friend bent on protecting him.

---

1. In North Carolina the Lumbee Indian population is concentrated in the southeastern part of the state, where several counties operated three school systems: one for whites, one for blacks, and one for Indians. But Harnett County, where Green grew up, had no high school for Indians and bused Lumbee students to East Carolina Indian Institute in nearby Sampson County, a daily round-trip of about seventy miles. In the fall of 1959 several Harnett County Lumbee children applied for admission to the high school nearest their homes, the white school in Dunn, but were turned down. Denied again in the fall of 1960, seven students and the parents of two staged a sit-in at Dunn High School on 31 August and 1 September and were arrested for trespassing (*New York Times*, 1 September 1960, p. 18, col. 1; 2 September 1960, p. 19, col. 1). Marshall W. Locklear, a Lumbee with a master's degree in education from UNC (1956), was director of guidance and counseling at Pembroke High School in Robeson County, center of the Lumbee population, and he wrote to Green for help. He knew Green felt that "without regard to race . . . our American youth is entitled to

write about something which happens to be touching them at the moment and then after that moment is past the impulse to action fades away. I am glad you didn't wait but sent me a note out of your real and immediate feelings.

Thus encouragement is made mutual.

The failure of our democracy to find its working in the hearts of all our people is a constant source of sadness to millions of our citizens. But of course democracy like any credo, principle, or religion does not live and work by itself. Human hearts and minds and souls must make it work, or it is empty, dead and nothing. We must all, wherever and whenever we can, keep up our determination to speak and carry on that the truth, that justice, that the right may prevail. And let us do so without ill-feeling, without animosity, without the poison of bitterness, which is perhaps the hardest part of the job.

So we must not weaken, we must not yield, whatever kindness may be needed, whatever gentleness is required.

The educational authorities in Harnett County are so completely off the beam, so far wide of the mark of both Christianity and sound sociology, so contrary to the bent and drive of the modern world that it is piteous. I hope you and those close to you will go on with your efforts for a democratic and equal-opportunity education for your children. To fail to do so would not only be to fail yourselves and our nation, but the cause of humanity in the world itself. And in fact it would be failing the final best interests of the very people who in their ignorance and misguided sincerity are opposing you.[2]

Sincerely yours,

---

and should be provided with an education," and he knew as well that Green's "comments and views will have much weight not only in Harnett County, but here in Robeson County also, and even the United States" (9 September 1960, PG-SHC).

2. When it became clear that the Lumbees would not be allowed to attend Dunn High School in 1960–61, the American Friends Service Committee placed eleven of them in private homes in Raleigh, Greensboro, and High Point, and Green undertook to raise money for their expenses as they attended high schools in those cities (William Bagwell to Paul Green, 13 June 1961, PG-SHC). Contributions arrived from Dunn, from throughout the state, and from such notables as Eleanor Roosevelt and the American Baptist Convention. In the fall of 1961 the Harnett County school board admitted the Lumbees to Dunn High School (*New York Times*, 1 September 1961, p. 18, col. 7).

## 274. To Margaret Freeman Cabell[1]

[Greenwood Road, Chapel Hill, N.C.]
17 September 1960

Dear Mrs. Cabell:

The other day in St. Augustine, Florida, a lady brought me a copy of your husband's *The First Gentleman of America.*[2] I read it that night and was completely taken by it. When I had finished I struck the side of the bed in frustration, thinking to myself—"if the author were only alive so that I could write him and tell him how much I enjoyed this book!"

It is grand!

From what I gather from the smart boys, your husband's name at present doesn't shine as brightly as some of the muck, the malformed and the wastrel crew. But you watch. There is going to be a great rebirth into public awareness and appreciation of James Branch Cabell's writings.

With affectionate greetings and regards,

1. In November 1959 Green began to correspond with W. I. Drysdale about the play that became *Cross and Sword,* first produced in 1965 to celebrate the 400th anniversary of St. Augustine, Florida. In July 1960 he signed a contract to do the play (Paul Green to W. I. Drysdale, 21 July 1960, PG-SHC) and for a few days at the end of the month visited St. Augustine and Anastasia Island (where the amphitheater was eventually built) to discuss plans and consider theater sites. Although at the time of the present letter Green had not settled on a plot or central character for *Cross and Sword,* he eventually focused the play on Pedro Menéndez and his struggles to establish St. Augustine. Margaret Freeman Cabell, from Richmond, Virginia, was the widow of James Branch Cabell, who died in 1958. The Cabells spent many winters in St. Augustine.

2. Novel (1942) in which Menéndez and the founding of St. Augustine are major concerns.

## 275. To Burnet M. Hobgood[1]

[Greenwood Road, Chapel Hill, N.C.]
10 October 1960

Dear Hob,

Thanks for your note of September 30. I am glad to have news of your doings, and I congratulate you on the good job out in Decatur.[2] Elizabeth joins me in love to you all.

Right now I am doing research for a symphonic drama down at St. Augustine, Florida. No opening date is set yet, but I am trying to get a good start ahead of the deadline. I want to make use of the Catholic church, the friars, the wonderful religious music, and the relationships of the church to the Indians in the new world. The Franciscans had a philosophy of love and brotherhood, the church itself a philosophy of institutionalism, and the Spanish nation in the sixteenth century had a philosophy of aggrandizement. All of these points of view were at work there in the early history of Florida. Right now I am considering a drama which embroils them all one with the other. Of course you might know where my heart would be—with the peace-loving friars who got conked in the head by the very children of nature they hoped to save, aided on the side quite cold-bloodedly by the Englishmen from the Carolinas and Georgia.

Ever since I was a young Sunday school teacher in my teens I have been fascinated by the philosophy of non-violence. Maybe this time I will be able to get out a dramatic piece which will say my say on this subject. Whether this would be a lucky thing to do at this time of burning and poisonous nationalism I can't say. But wouldn't it be a wonderful thing if one of these outdoor dramas could reach the people through a character who made the vision of brotherly love stick under the eyelids of the prejudiced and blind and thus give them sight?

1. Burnet M. Hobgood (b. 1922), who acted in *Wilderness Road* and *The Confederacy*, was chairman of the drama and speech department at Catawba College and editor of *Southern Theatre News*, journal of the Southeastern Theatre Conference. For the journal he was collecting information on the 1960 season from those involved with outdoor plays and asked Green for a report on his "new shows for future years" (30 September 1960, PG-SHC).

2. During the summer of 1960 Hobgood played in Kermit Hunter's *The Golden Prairie* in Decatur, Illinois.

Then I am pecking out a novel on the side.[3]

I know you both are busy as always.

Affectionately,

## 276. To Grace Smith Surles[1]

[Greenwood Road, Chapel Hill, N.C.]
11 November 1960

Dear Mrs. Surles,

To think of you remembering and writing me about that long-ago acquaintance in Lillington, North Carolina. Your words brought the image of you a little girl with your arm full of "Grit" newspapers standing there on the street in that town.

I am glad to know that life has been good to you, and I have no doubt that you have deserved its goodness.

My best greetings to you and your husband,

3. *Stormy Banks.*

1. Grace Smith Surles (b. ca. 1909) wrote Green that each time she saw his name in newspapers over the years, she had wanted to write and ask if he were the person of that name she had known when she was a child. She lived now in Birmingham, Alabama, but had grown up in Lillington, North Carolina, where for a few years around 1920 she sold a newspaper, the *Dunn Grit*, on the street in front of the courthouse. At the time a young man named Paul Green, who played baseball and (in the summers of 1921 and 1922) was in and out of the courthouse often, called her " 'The Little Paper Girl.' " Her father "only had one leg and was not a rich man, and lots of times you helped to buy my school books. You were always nice to all the children, especially to me, and a child never forgets anyone who has been nice to them." Finally the suspense became "too much for me. I had to find out [whether Green was that person]. So won't you please let me know if I am right or wrong. Either way I wish for you much happiness and success" (Grace Smith Surles to Paul Green, 6 November 1960, PG-SHC).

## 277. To John Ehle[1]

[Greenwood Road, Chapel Hill, N.C.]
17 March 1961

Dear John:

This is a hurried note.

I am glad to have a copy of your letter to Dean Carlyle Sitterson about the state of creative writing—of course all writing is creative more or less, but I know what you mean—here on the campus of the University of North Carolina, and I would apply your remarks equally to the more inclusive subject of arts totally. From what I know of Carlyle Sitterson's thinking and intentions I am sure he too is anxious as you and I to see our university hitting on all cylinders. And as long as the arts are neglected some of the cylinders are dead. He knows that.

To change the figure of speech—it is most a matter of climate, isn't it? And though we have had some climate here for the arts and continue to have some on this campus, we need more and better. Or still another image—create a pulpit and some morning you are likely to wake up and find a preacher in it talking away, or build a bird-house and a bird is likely to come and live in it and lay its eggs, if there are any birds around, and there are always birds about. And when we build neither of these, then both the preacher and the bird are apt to be more scarce and take up residence elsewhere. And as everybody knows preachers are a necessity and birds are beautiful.

Yes, let us create a better climate for writing here—and again I say the same goes for thc other arts.

And how can we do this simple but mysterious thing? Well, I know of no better way than for the University to evince a keener and more solid interest in creative writing, to show that it believes creative writing is important in the life of the students, important here in their life and important in their life out yonder. And how in the world can it do it better than by having good courses offered and college credit given for them?

1. John Ehle (b. 1925), novelist from Asheville on the UNC faculty at the time, did his B.A. (1949) and M.A. (1952) work at UNC, then stayed in Chapel Hill to write his first novel, *Move Over, Mountain* (1957), under Green's guidance. Recently he wrote an eight-page letter to Carlyle Sitterson, dean of the College of Arts and Sciences, deploring the decline of the creative arts on campus and urging a reinvigorated program (with additional courses, scholarships and prizes, and faculty with national reputations), and sent a copy to Green (John Ehle to Carlyle Sitterson, 24 February 1961, PG-SHC).

Some of this is being done—some.

A few writers have come out of this university in the past—and every one of them got their first start and inspiration from writing courses given here, and given by vital and encouraging teachers—Tom Wolfe, Betty Smith, Josephina Niggli,[2] Frances Patton,[3] Jonathan Daniels, John Ehle, William Hardy,[4] Richard Adler, Daphne Athas,[5] Legette Blythe,[6] Robert Finch,[7] Jessie Rehder,[8] Bernice Kelly Harris,[9] Kermit Hunter, Paul Green, Kate Porter Lewis,[10] Gwen Pharis Ringwood,[11] Arnold Schulman,[12] Max Steele,[13] and many others. All of these came mainly from the playwriting course and then from

2. Novelist and playwright from Monterrey, Mexico, who began her long career as student and teacher in the Playmakers organization in 1935.

3. An early Playmaker (1923–25) from Durham best known for her novel *Good Morning, Miss Dove* (1954).

4. Novelist (*Lady Killer* [1957], *The Year of the Rose* [1960], *The Jub Jub Bird* [1966]) and playwright (*Sword of Peace* [1974]) from Norfolk, Virginia, who entered the Playmakers program in 1953.

5. Novelist (*Entering Ephesus* [1971], *Cora* [1978]) from Carrboro, North Carolina, who entered UNC in 1939 and began a long career as teacher of creative writing there in 1967.

6. Early Playmaker (B.A., 1921), author of several symphonic dramas, among them *Shout Freedom* (1948), *Voice in the Wilderness* (1955), and *The Hornet's Nest* (1968).

7. Playwright from Montana (with Betty Smith, *The Professor Roars* [1938], *Gentle Youth* [1941], "Miracle at Dublin Gulch" [1942]), who came into the Playmakers program in 1937.

8. Who began a long career as teacher of creative writing at UNC in 1947.

9. Novelist (*Purslane* [1939], *Hearthstones* [1948], *Wild Cherry Tree Road* [1951]) from Seaboard, North Carolina, who wrote several plays produced by the Playmakers in the 1930s.

10. Playwright from Greenville, Alabama, who entered the Playmakers program in 1938 and edited *Alabama Folk Plays* (1943).

11. Novelist and playwright from British Columbia, Canada, who entered the Playmakers program in 1939.

12. Playwright (*A Hole in the Head* [1957]) and screen writer (*Love with the Proper Stranger* [1963], *Goodbye, Columbus* [1969]) from Philadelphia, who came to UNC in 1942.

13. Novelist (*Debby* [1960]) and short story writer (*Where She Brushed Her Hair* [1968], *The Hat of My Mother* [1988]) from Greenville, South Carolina, who graduated from UNC in 1946 and began a long career as teacher of creative writing there in 1966.

the journalism courses[14] came Robert Ruark,[15] Hoke Norris,[16] and others and from Jessie Rehder's class Doris Betts[17] and others.

Why is it that no composers, for instance, have come out of the music department here over all these years? And think of the tremendous folklore storehouse full of raw music material waiting to be used here in North Carolina—the mountain ballads, Negro work songs, folk hymns, etc., etc. Sibelius, Moussorgsky, Dvorák and their brethren would have had fits of creativity if they had had such a heritage. And from us what? And from Chapel Hill what? Nothing—nothing except the loud blowing of the athlete's tuba in the daytime and the rat-tat-tapping of the musicologist's typewriter going at night as he searched and gimletted out his notes—which as regards the body of living art could have been set down as "obits" and left at that, yes, pretty much at that, though of course I exaggerate here some—exaggerate for truth's sake. What a shame, what a tragedy—when we might by this time have had some dozen or more young composers loose in the world and spreading plenty of joy and inspiration abroad and helping to build a solid and rich American civilization out of their fertile souls—composers who had got their start here at the University.

(I like the head of the music department as a man,[18] but I still say it is a great tragedy that during his tenure nothing really creative has come out of it—the best being his own fine musicology studies perhaps[19]—a tragedy that during this time his own specialty has specialized others around him to pretty

14. Taught by Phillips Russell.

15. Journalist and novelist (*Horn of the Hunter* [1953], *Something of Value* [1955], *Uhuru* [1962]) from Wilmington, North Carolina, who graduated from UNC in 1935.

16. Journalist and novelist (*All the Kingdoms of Earth* [1956], *It's Not Far but I Don't Know the Way* [1969]) from Holly Springs, North Carolina, who entered the UNC graduate program in 1946.

17. Short story writer (*The Gentle Insurrection* [1954], *Beasts of the Southern Wild* [1973]) and novelist (*The River to Pickle Beach* [1972], *Heading West* [1981]) from Statesville, North Carolina, who entered UNC in 1954, then began a long and varied career on the faculty there in 1966.

18. Glen Haydon (Ph.D., University of Vienna, 1932), was head of the music department from 1934 to 1966.

19. *The Evolution of the Six-Four Chord: A Chapter in the History of Dissonance Treatment* (1933), *Introduction to Musicology: A Survey of the Fields, Systematic and Historical, of Musical Knowledge and Research* (1941), and numerous articles.

much the same like interest and the fine creative talents that came his way—and many of them came, just as many I would say as ever came by Professor Koch's door—had the singing in their hearts and brains gradually discouraged away for lack of guidance and help, and more and more—in the vivid language of our late Billy Carmichael[20]—became academaniacs.)

I keep hearing a Negro refrain beating in my head—"They ain't nothing wuss than to cause a man to miss his own life."

And alas the University has, at the same time it has been helping young people to find their true lives, also been helping a lot of others to miss their best lives. It is these latter, I take it, we all are especially concerned about at this time.

I have happened over the years to meet many American writers, and from talking with them and hearing them talk I know that most of them got great inspiration in their writing from the courses they had in college. Actually it was impossible for these courses not to help them for it gave these aspiring young writers a better chance to work at what they wanted to do—that is, write.[21] Think of the numerous playwrights Professor George Pierce Baker from Harvard and Yale helped on toward a career—Eugene O'Neill, Sidney Howard, Philip Barry, and many others. Some of these I have heard declare most emphatically that Professor Baker's courses were a godsend to them.

There have been some funny notions about writers loose in the world, funny notions loose on this campus—such as that they are a special breed of humanity and being so the usual stimuli of living don't apply to them—such as to say for instance that a fellowship in creative writing has nothing to do with producing a writer. This is nonsense.

Writers, painters, composers are human beings and as such they must react like human beings—be discouraged by the usual things that discourage human beings, be inspired by the usual things that inspire human beings.

Again to say that a good engineering teacher can help produce a good engineer but that a good creative writing teacher can't help produce a good writer—well, again that's nonsense.

It is a matter of appreciation of values, isn't it? Right now, as you say, the University of North Carolina doesn't seem to have as much appreciation of

20. Who died on 27 January 1961.

21. In his letter to Sitterson, Ehle noted that "there are often arguments, as you well know, about whether the arts can be taught" (John Ehle to Carlyle Sitterson, 24 February 1961, PG-SHC).

creative writing, or the arts, as it should have. Let us all get together then, work together to help remedy this situation.

As for me, I believe that the arts are the soul and fervor of a nation, are in the main the fire and glory of a people and a nation may produce all kinds of bankers, dizzying engineers and inventors and builders and yet miss the full greatness that might have belonged to it if it had properly encouraged its poets, its composers, its novelists, its essayists—in order to bring forward the full frontage of its significance.

Can't a group of us some night get together with Sitterson and others and talk about this most important subject?[22]

I refer you to a significant for our purpose text in an old book which we aspiring writers neglect to our loss, a text which says "where two or three are gathered together in my name."[23] Selah.

As I say, hurriedly,

## 278. To Carl Sandburg

[Greenwood Road, Chapel Hill, N.C.]
3 April 1961

Dear Carl:[1]

That was a fine piece you said at the one-hundredth Anniversary of Lincoln's inaugural in Washington, and many thanks for remembering me with a copy of it.

22. Sitterson, who shared Green's and Ehle's concern, remembers "a number of multiple-hour wide ranging conversations" with Ehle about the creative arts on campus. He supported the efforts of Ehle in the radio, television, and motion picture department, Jessie Rehder in English, and Wilton Mason in music to do such things as expand appropriate course offerings, increase the number of artistic awards, and enlarge artist-in-residence programs (Carlyle Sitterson to Laurence Avery, 21 June 1988).

23. Matthew 18:20.

1. On 4 March 1961 the 100th anniversary of Lincoln's first inauguration was celebrated with a reenactment in Washington, D.C. In the morning, when no public event occurred historically, Carl Sandburg, introduced by Speaker of the House Sam Rayburn (himself the son of a Confederate soldier), spoke from the east steps of the Capitol on the significance of Lincoln's inauguration. Then Sandburg, the actors

I like not only your words but Lincoln's too—those you quoted[2]—though I wouldn't quite subscribe to the statement you made on page 8 that the eyes of youth are "strange and baffling," except poetry-wise.[3]

Yay, go to it, dreamer, and that is what counts—your dreaming helping us to dream better and more golden dreams and thus to build ye republic the better and more shining. How wonderful to have had the experience of having lived! You prove it.

And so as we consider this Civil War centennial let us lament and never celebrate, let us lament the blindness of our leaders that keeps tumbling our young folks into the spasm of death on the battlefields and causing them to miss that lengthened wonder.

Yesterday I passed through Salisbury, North Carolina and stopped off and went out to the site of the old Federal prison.[4] A marker there spoke above a little plot of ground not even an acre big saying, "Here 11,700 Federal soldiers lie buried." And they lie there "unknown" buried. Let the imagination x-ray

---

playing Lincoln and Chief Justice Roger Taney, and the rest of the official party retraced Lincoln's steps on that day, first with a similar lunch at the Willard Hotel, then to the Capitol steps for the swearing-in ceremony and a reading of Lincoln's address, and finally with an inaugural ball that night. In his morning speech Sandburg characterized Lincoln's inauguration as "a great day in American history of which we might say it was sunset and dawn, moonrise and noon sun, dry leaves in an Autumn wind and Springtime blossoms, dying time and birthing hour—and birthing hour" (p. 8, PG-SHC). Recently he sent Green a copy.

2. Mainly from the inaugural address, in which Lincoln gave theoretical and practical support for his intention to preserve the union, and from the 1858 senatorial campaign, where he developed his opposition to slavery.

3. Sandburg said, "Youth when lighted and alive and given a sporting chance is strong for struggle and not afraid of any toils, punishments, dangers, or deaths. What shall be the course of society and civilization across the next hundred years? For the answers read if you can the strange and baffling eyes of youth."

4. Former cotton warehouse used by the Confederacy throughout the war as a prison for captured Federal troops. It served as a holding ground for Federal troops awaiting exchange until August 1864, when the Federal government stopped exchanging prisoners. At Salisbury over the winter of 1864–65 the prison population skyrocketed. Many died from hunger, cold, and disease and were buried in trench graves (Louis Brown, *The Salisbury Prison: A Case Study of Confederate Military Prisons, 1861–1865* [Wendell, N.C.: Avera Press, 1980]).

on down a few feet through the ground. What a horror of bones piled yards deep!

And now while I am weeping and talking, thinking of the rot and the gangrene and the sobs and mother-calls through the long night there in that prison a hundred-years-near ago, I say loud that I hold your idol Abraham Lincoln too one of the tragic participators in and creators of this maelstrom of pain and shame. It was he—sucked along by the party pull and bestrid by the radicals that, like Ikie and the pregnant gentile girl "couldn't vait"[—who] pushed on toward Sumter and the call for volunteers and the blockade and thus drove the border states in cement together with the hard-core cotton group and so on into the blazing holocaust.

But then when I read again his words you use on pages 4 and 5, beginning at the bottom of page 4 thus—"These representatives in old Independence Hall" and ending on page 5 with "take courage to renew the battle which their fathers began"—a battle not of bayonets and fists now but of ideals and open reaching hands—then I almost love him entirely once more.[5]

There is great danger of apotheosizing Lincoln so much that his life-giving inspiration as a noble, yearning struggling man may be lost to us in a sort of stony deity. We have seen this happen to Jesus Christ, poor like Abe and a carpenter's son—and happened to such an extent that the more the American people, for instance, join the church and go Sundays to chant his praise and bow down to him the more aloof he becomes and we a lost and wandering people religiously.[6]

Think of the twisted bloody crucifix that hangs in front of millions of children's eyes every day of the year. What for? Well, no wonder it becomes an

5. Sandburg quoted one of Lincoln's 1858 campaign speeches in which he extolled the framers of the Declaration of Independence as farsighted statesmen who, knowing the tendency toward tyrants, " 'established these great self-evident truths, that when in the distant future some man, some faction, some interest should set up the doctrine that none but rich men or none but white men, were entitled to life, liberty and the pursuit of happiness, their posterity might look up again to the Declaration of Independence and take courage to renew the battle which their fathers began' " (pp. 4–5, PG-SHC).

6. Sandburg was presently in Los Angeles serving for a few weeks as consultant on *The Greatest Story Ever Told*, a motion picture based on Jesus' life. (Later postponed by Twentieth Century–Fox, the film was released in 1965 by United Artists.)

empty symbol and good that it does, otherwise we would have a whole race of little hallucinated sadists and masochists—and maybe we do have too many of them at that because of this. Whadda you know?

Elizabeth and Janet send love, and when are you going to pay us that owed visit? If you see Julian Johnson around the lot, give him my regards—Henry King[7] and Clifford Odets too.

## 279. To Emma Neal Morrison[1]

[Greenwood Road, Chapel Hill, N.C.]
24 October 1961

Dear Emma Neal:

I think we had a good meeting about the theatre remodeling plans, and I look forward to our getting together the Thanksgiving week-end when we can finalize matters.

I understand things better now. Evidently Mr. Bell[2] and Mr. Gibbs[3] worked on the assumption that what they agreed on would be satisfactory to all. And

7. Who directed *Carolina*, motion picture adapted from *The House of Connelly* and released in 1934.

---

1. On 11 September 1960, a few days after the final *Lost Colony* performance of the season, Hurricane Donna struck Roanoke Island and obliterated the Waterside Theatre. Over the winter the Roanoke Island Historical Association sought funds to rebuild the theater, and in the summer of 1961, as the show played in a makeshift setting, reached an agreement with the National Park Service to finance the reconstruction. Emma Neal Morrison, a member of the association board of directors since 1956 and its chairman beginning in 1962, headed the Theatre Reconstruction Committee. During late September and early October 1961, Green was in Spain doing research for *Cross and Sword* (Paul Green to W. I. Drysdale, 20 January 1962, PG-SHC). On the day he got back to Chapel Hill he saw a photograph in the newspaper of construction work at the Waterside Theatre and immediately wired Morrison: "OF UTMOST IMPORTANCE THAT THE THEATRE RECONSTRUCTION COMMITTEE . . . CONFER WITH THE ARCHITECT AND BUILDER BEFORE ALL PLANS ARE FINALIZED AND ADVANCED TOO FAR FOR POSSIBLE CHANGE IN IMPORTANT FEATURES" (17 October 1961). Morrison called a meeting of the Theatre Reconstruction Committee for 23 October in Manteo.

2. Albert Bell, original builder of the Waterside Theatre, now in charge of the reconstruction.

3. Robert Gibbs, National Park Service superintendent on Roanoke Island.

apparently the Park Service authorities in Washington who approved their plans thought they were approving what all of us had agreed on previously. (But there had been no chance for such an agreement, since the theatre committee of which you are chairman had had no chance to see the plans.) Too bad that this mixup occurred, but I'm sure that with your definite leadership in the matter we can straighten things out.

Al Bell is a good builder—none better. But he is not a theatre architect in the real sense, and his present plans—to speak discreetly—are inadequate in many important particulars.[4]

Way back in 1937 Sam Selden and Al and I worked up ways and means for building the amphitheatre, and Al put down on paper and in scale for us what we were able to afford to build at that time—having one mule and a scoop and only wheelbarrows and shovels for moving earth. We ran out of money, time and patience and, among other things, left the slope of the auditorium flatter than we wished, flatter than good acoustics and good sight lines required. We all knew that, but we said we were building for the one season. If we should by chance be successful and run more than one season we would later amend such matters as these. Yes, later if we continued our play we would build the theatre right, we said.

Now after all these years we have a chance to do things right. So let's do it—at least do right what we do do.

As we mentioned—I am getting up some outdoor theatre engineering information which I will get to you for the committee's consideration at the meeting.

In the meantime, you remember, Al said he had plenty to do on basic center stage construction, and the problems of light towers, side stages, wiring, seating, auditorium sloping and control booth could wait till our meeting in November.

4. Whereas Bell planned to rebuild the theater pretty much as it had been, Green saw an opportunity to improve it. To bring the audience closer to the action and enhance acoustics and sight lines, he wanted to decrease seating capacity from 2,500 to 1,750, move center and side stages closer to the audience, and increase the degree of incline so the last row of seats would be not eighteen but twenty-five feet above stage-level. For the comfort of spectators he wanted to substitute armchairs on a paved floor for the former wooden benches over sand. Also, to strengthen technical support of performances he wanted to move light towers closer to the stage and relocate the control booth so its operators had a better view of the stage (Paul Green to Albert Bell, 3 July 1961, and Paul Green to John Cauble, 24 October 1961, PG-SHC).

Of course I'm all for Al Bell and count ourselves lucky to have him. And I'm sure that with your and the committee's help he will cooperate in every way in getting the best possible theatre plant in which to produce our play.

Again Elizabeth and I thank you and Fred[5] for your sweet hospitality.[6] And all of us owe Fred (and always you) a special debt for the trouble he is taking for our project.[7]

Affectionately,

## 280. To Paul R. Reynolds, Jr.

[Greenwood Road, Chapel Hill, N.C.]
25 November 1961

Dear Paul Reynolds:[1]

Alas, I have long been saddened over the death of Dick Wright as I know you have. I always admired him and counted him a friend, though to my sorrow and regret he often seemed not to understand my intent nor me his need—and vice versa. Both of us failing—in an environment which then as now murks up the truth by which men try to live. God rest him—no, I won't say that, for that's part of the trouble with that environment, us calling on God to do this or that and thus obviating responsibility when we ought to be kicking our own behinds (it can be done) to spur us into humane and intelligent action—So I say may he rest well from his labors, for they were strong and fine, and he will. And I say too that as for me the light of his talent and his soul was so bright that it blinded away entirely the crazy question of color. I'm sure it did that for many thousands of others.

5. Morrison's husband, a lawyer in Washington, D.C.

6. The Morrisons had a vacation home at Kill Devil Hills, near Manteo, and the Greens were their guests for the meeting of the Theatre Reconstruction Committee.

7. The new theater, ready for the summer of 1962, was dedicated by Governor Terry Sanford on 14 July. It incorporated most of Green's ideas, but capacity was reduced only to 2,000 and wooden benches were retained, but with a back rail added and the floor paved.

---

1. Paul R. Reynolds, Jr., Richard Wright's agent, passed along to Green a request to use a scene from the dramatization of *Native Son* on a television program. He added, "There's no money in it. I don't really care, and Dick's no longer alive," and suggested that Green just write yes or no at the bottom of his letter and return it (20 November 1961, PG-SHC). Wright had died in Paris on 28 November 1960.

About Konigsberg and the TV quote for an educational program:[2] Like you I don't much care, since Dick is dead, but I do care a bit. For I think the integration question is dead, and only the funeral is waiting. The body already stinks, and so shoveling is soon in order. That is, if the program in any way treats of old hat and dead cat, I think *Native Son* better be left out. Could Konigsberg drop me a line as to the nature of his show?[3]

Many thanks,

2. Franklin Konigsberg, a New York City attorney, was trying to secure permission to use a scene from *Native Son* in a program being developed by Hazel Barnes for an educational television station (KRMA) in Denver, Colorado (Franklin Konigsberg to Paul Green, 5 December 1961, PG-SHC).

3. The show dealt with existentialism rather than integration, and Barnes wanted to use scene 3 of the play, Bigger's introduction to the Dalton household (ibid.). Green replied, "Go ahead, it's okay with me—though I don't give a whoop in this world about existentialism. It is just another one of these fads, like the spike heels women wear these days—and I wish to goodness it couldn't do any more harm" (28 December 1961).

# IX

# Symphonic Drama, the Soviet Union, and Integration, 1962–1967

Late May–June 1962
: Visits Leningrad and Moscow to acquaint himself with the Soviet people, then in Athens for UNESCO conference on Drama for Mass Audiences.

July 1962
: Begins collecting James Boyd's books and papers for UNC library.

August 1962
: Begins successful campaign to have death sentence for Robert Lee Case changed to life in prison.

Summer–Fall 1962
: Works at dramatizing *Stormy Banks.* Begins putting into book form the folklore he has collected since 1920s.

December 1962
: In newspapers, attacks capital punishment.

Winter–Spring 1963
: In Chapel Hill writes film script based on John Howard Griffin's *Black Like Me* (released in 1964).

Summer–Winter 1963
: Disputes claim of Roanoke Island Historical Association that it controls text of *The Lost Colony.*

12 October 1963
: In University Day speech at UNC attacks state law prohibiting Communists from speaking on campus.

Winter–Spring 1964
: Revising *The Founders,* explains nature of historical drama to producers of the play (Jamestown Corporation), some of whom prefer historical pageant.

Summer 1964

Begins *Cross and Sword.*

Spring 1965

Visits St. Augustine for theater construction and rehearsals of *Cross and Sword.*

May 1965

Moves to Windy Oaks, farm a few miles southeast of Chapel Hill.

27 June 1965

*Cross and Sword* opens on Anastasia Island near St. Augustine.

Fall–Winter 1965

Visits Canyon, Texas, and begins *Texas.* Revises *Native Son* for production in New York City (canceled after producer dies).

Summer 1966

In Canyon, Texas, for rehearsals of *Texas,* a sound and light spectacle that opens on 1 July 1966 in Palo Duro Canyon.

Fall–Winter 1966

Works on *Stormy Banks* and folklore collection.

Winter–Spring 1967

Begins work on *Trumpet in the Land.*

October 1967

Protests American military action in South Vietnam.

## 281. To Irving E. Carlyle[1]

[Greenwood Road, Chapel Hill, N.C.]
10 March 1962

Dear Irving:

Thanks for your letter of about a month ago concerning the letter of W. C. George published in the local state papers. Absence from home has delayed my answer. I am sure that the professors in our Southern universities would be encouraged to stand a little more to the front in liberal matters if they could feel in a public way the backing of such people as yourself—I mean the sort of backing which you give the cause of free speech in your note to me. Of course I believe they do feel your unafraid strength, but they need a whole army of you. And maybe even that would not be enough for these timid and institutionalized souls. And I hurry on to say that if we professors showed as much zeal for what we believe as George does for what he believes, we'd all be a darn sight more civilized.[2]

1. Irving E. Carlyle (1896–1971), lawyer in Winston-Salem, trustee of Wake Forest University, prominent in the liberal wing of the Democratic party, and at the time chairman of the Governor's Commission on Education beyond High School, sent Green a clipping from the *Winston-Salem Journal*. The clipping was a letter to the editor by W. C. George, head of the Department of Anatomy in the UNC School of Medicine until retirement in 1960 and a leading opponent of integration. His status as a scientist lent authority to his white supremacist views, and in 1961 Governor John Patterson of Alabama commissioned him to write his major statement on the subject, *Biology of the Race Problem* (1962). In the clipping sent to Green by Carlyle, George took up an assertion by a UNC administrator that the school's scholarly stature had declined over the past thirty years and argued that "the 30 year period of our decline coincides with the period during which we have shifted from an emphasis on scholarship and search for truth to a policy of promoting social and political ideologies—especially to working up a lather over integration" (*Winston-Salem Journal*, 3 February 1962, p. 4, col. 5). George ended with the complaint that freedom of speech, once the norm in Chapel Hill, was no longer practiced there, since campus classrooms and auditoriums were frequently closed to him. In his letter to Green, Carlyle noted that "if there ever was academic freedom on the grand scale it occurred when the University allowed Dr. George, while a member of the faculty of the University, to promulgate his decadent ideas." Carlyle himself was worried by the reluctance of enlightened scholars to speak out on social issues (Irving Carlyle to Paul Green, 5 February 1962, PG-SHC).

2. When *Biology of the Race Problem* appeared, George and his supporters showed their zeal by placing a large advertisement in the *New York Times* in the form of an

Over the years I again and again as a professor here at the University of North Carolina have for one reason or another fired off my mouth considerably, and you'd be surprised and pleased if I could tell you the strong support I have received from a huge number of the faculty members for many of my contentions against race prejudice, discrimination, McCarthyism, political witch-hunting, anti-communist job oaths, etc. But—and here's the point—you'd be unhappy to know how that support came to me. I'll tell you—it came secretly. Only in one exception has any faculty member ever stood out in public print and spoken on my side.[3] But, Lord, again and again I've been stopped on the street, or been told over the telephone, as follows—"Paul, that was a good statement I read of yours. Go to it. I'm for you in this matter—yes, sir, a hundred percent." Etc. And then I've usually answered back as follows—"But, John, if you'd only say that in public. Rise up in faculty meeting even and say what you stand for, that would be worth much more than anything I can say." Etc. He—"Oh, I can't do that. After all I'm a scientist—and a scientist just can't get into controversial matters." I—"But you're already in controversial matters. You've just said so, and after all the place of the university in humanistic free thinking—" etc. He again—"Oh, I mean publicly, I can't get involved publicly." Etc. again and again.

Institutionalism is a necessity for ideas to live and have shelter and housing, no doubt, but how often it smothers by too close hen-setting the very idea it should tend and develop. Let me mention in this connection the murals in the Institute of Government here—paid for by the Knapp Foundation (and legislative appropriation in the whole).[4] Maybe you've seen them. I saw quite a lot of Kughler the artist who painted them when he was down at Manteo doing the early sequences.[5] Later in Chapel Hill I saw him.[6] One day he

open letter to President Kennedy urging him to read the book and delay implementation of recent Supreme Court school decisions until new cases could be tried with *Biology of the Race Problem* as evidence (3 October 1962, p. 33, cols. 3–8).

3. Probably William Couch (see letter 187).

4. A series of fourteen large murals depicting key points in the development of North Carolina, painted by Francis Vandeveer Kughler on commission from the Joseph Palmer Knapp Foundation, which gave $500,000 (a sum matched by the state) for construction of the Knapp Building to house the Institute of Government at UNC. The building was dedicated on 28 November 1960, when the murals were unveiled in its auditorium.

5. The second mural depicts Ralph Lane's expedition on Roanoke Island in 1585.

showed me his educational panel he was working on—Aycock and the others standing in the light and welcoming the coming children[7]—all white children and all white teachers. I mentioned to Kughler some of the leading state Negro educators and further suggested that in this picture of public education in North Carolina some item or items should be given to what we'd done in that direction. I suggested a Negro student or two somewhere, even in the background, also maybe the figure of Dr. Shepard of N.C. College with a book in his hand as showing among the teachers.[8] He thanked me for the suggestions. "For after all," I urged, "I know you as an artist want to represent the facts, and Negro public schooling has been a big fact in the life of the State," etc. Later on he called me and suggested I have another look. I did, and sure enough he had the figure of Dr. Shepard in the background, but no Negro children. "I'm not just sure of Dr. Shepard even," he said. He said he'd talked the matter over with the committee,[9] and he had decided that he as artist had to stay out of controversial matters. When later the murals were hung, even Dr. Shepard had disappeared.[10] So that panel is untrue to Aycock

---

Kughler began work on the murals in 1956 and did sketches for the second mural on location in the summer and fall of that year.

6. The twelfth mural, "Pageant of Dreamers," shows Frederick Koch directing an ensemble of Albert and Gladys Coates (founders of the Institute of Government), Benjamin Swalin (first director of the North Carolina Symphony), the Wright brothers, the actor Andy Griffith, and a host of others including a group of writers: O. Henry, Thomas Wolfe, and Green. Green and several others posed for Kughler.

7. The tenth mural shows Charles B. Aycock, "education governor" at the turn of the century, standing in the glare of a photographer's light in the state legislative chamber surrounded by children and several dozen of the state's educational leaders through the decades.

8. James Edward Shepard, educated at Shaw and Selma universities, from 1910 until his death in 1947 presided over the school that in 1925 became North Carolina College for Negroes in Durham and now is North Carolina Central University.

9. In identifying important points in the history of the state and people associated with them, Kughler consulted a Committee of Thirty drawn from state historical societies (such as Christopher Crittenden, Edwin Gill, Robert Lee Humber, Dudley Bagley, and A. T. Dill), the UNC faculty (such as Hugh T. Lefler and William Powell), and the Knapp Foundation (Margaret Rutledge Knapp and others).

10. Actually, Shepard is clearly visible in the upper right section of the mural, and there is no record of the mural having been revised after it was hung.

himself[11] and untrue to the people of North Carolina who have over the years, Negro and white, taxed themselves for public education for all. How Goya would have spat and fumed and been "controversial" and painted a great picture! Kughler did none of these. I have not been interested to know who in the University made Kughler's "Education" all white and the artist thus to mock himself in the next generation. Just an example of what I mean.

Hurriedly and with best greetings as ever,

P.S. So you see I am more concerned with what the University does to itself than what weak fellows like George can do to it.

## 282. To Gerald W. Johnson

[Greenwood Road, Chapel Hill, N.C.]
23 July 1962

Dear Gerald:[1]

I finally got so tired out trying to get the truth—at least some believable truth—about Russia from the U.S. press that I recently decided to go over to that country and see a few things for myself at first hand. I went alone—got a driver, a car, interpreters, special lecturers there when I wanted them and really bore down on the subject. In a little over two weeks I learned a lot—not all I wished to but a lot. I studied day and night, went to the big cities, out among the peasants, into libraries, schools, shops, theatres, bookstores, etc.—talked freely, was talked to freely, had every help I asked for, had complete

11. Who insisted on full state support of education for blacks.

1. Under the auspices of UNESCO, several cultural organizations and the Greek government sponsored an international conference in Athens, 13–27 June 1962, on Drama for Mass Audiences. Green was among several from the American theater invited to attend (Harold Clurman, Tyrone Guthrie, Elia Kazan, and Allardyce Nicoll were others). During the conference he talked about special problems faced by the writer of plays for large audiences, saw a moving performance of Euripides's *The Bacchae* at the ancient amphitheater near Epidaurus with an audience of 10,000, and "got some ideas of how to mix recorded and actual song and speech" in his own outdoor plays (Paul Green to Samuel Selden, 2 August 1962, PG-SHC). Before going to Athens, he visited the Soviet Union for two weeks, arriving in Leningrad from Helsinki on 28 May, flying to Moscow on 1 June, and leaving on 9 June for three days of rest in Vienna (Paul Green to Paul Green, Jr., 12 May 1962).

freedom of movement, picture-taking, what-not. So as I say I know more now than I did. And God help us—(just a figure of speech, of course, for he's in no position to help)—the future looks bleaker than ever to me!

The psychotics and paranoiacs in both countries are hurrying and harrying us helpless "freemen" on to destruction. Neither country will tell the human and humane truth about the other. Lies, lies, lies! I bought some five newspapers in Leningrad and Moscow every morning—*Pravda*, *Izvestia*, the *Moscow News*, *L'Humanité*, *The Berliner* (east) *Zeitung*—and never once did I read anything complimentary to the U.S. And Lord knows it's almost as impossible to read anything in our newspapers really favorable to the U.S.S.R.[2]

Have you any glimpse of an idea in your wisdom as to how the stampeding of us Gadarene swine (quite a name for Jeffersonian Democrats) can be stopped before we plunge over the cliff of total folly?[3] I am back in my garage study now working at my Negro plays[4] and stories and folklore,[5] and it's a queer gray cold going, with this black political incubus and delirium tremens nightmare of nationalism whickering in the air behind and above my head.

Another query—by what process, metamorphosis or osmosis, has it happened that the Bible has become the most popular escape literature for us in the west and the church nothing more than a mouthy pious social club?

2. Johnson's playful response: "Back up, man, back up! Wothell, have you, a playwright, forgotten Falstaff's observation of 300 years ago: 'Lord, Lord, how this world is given to lying'?" (*Henry IV*, pt. 1, act 5, scene 4, line 146) (26 July 1962, PG-SHC).

3. After expelling evil spirits from two Gadarenes, Jesus sent the demons into a nearby herd of swine, who promptly rushed over a cliff and drowned in the Sea of Galilee (Matthew 8:28–34).

4. Primarily a dramatized version of *Stormy Banks* (unfinished).

5. A lifelong collection of "the folklore of my people [primarily inhabitants of the lower Cape Fear River valley]—noting down their speech, beliefs, customs, anecdotes, ballads, epitaphs, legends, proverbs, stories, superstitions, herb cures, games and the like" (*North Carolina Folklore* 16 [December 1968]: iii). Green used the material in many stories and plays, and a small portion of it was published by the North Carolina Folklore Society in 1968 as a special issue of *North Carolina Folklore* (ibid.) entitled *Words and Ways*. The entire collection is available as *Paul Green's Wordbook: An Alphabet of Reminiscence* (1990).

Neither has the slightest influence now on the onward hurling world. A fact, by soul!

You might be interested in the enclosed editorial by Kate Boyd[6] and the passing appraisals I made on the Russian scene which she got from my notebooks when she visited us recently.[7] You remember her husband James Boyd—one of the gallant best.

We once thought, didn't we, that Nixon by his argument in the kitchen with Khrushchev had made himself president?[8] But no, we have the Kennedys. I worked hard for JFK.[9] I'm glad we don't have Richard, but I get no gladness from having John. Something stinks in Denmark, and each day the smell is worse. Wouldn't it be something if before long our two-party system turns out to be a misfit in the modern world?

Best greetings as always,

6. "The Press and the People," *Southern Pines Pilot*, 5 July 1962, p. 2, cols. 1–2, which attacks one-sided reporting with examples drawn from the coverage in state newspapers of Green's European trip, in which his favorable impressions of the Soviet Union are slighted.

7. Green's notes on the trip to the Soviet Union and Greece fill two large notebooks ("Diary Notes of a European Journey," PG-SHC), which Boyd, editor of the *Pilot* since the death of her husband in 1944, used as the basis for a balanced article, "Much to Admire, Much to Reject Found by Green in Soviet Union," *Southern Pines Pilot*, 5 July 1962, p. 16, cols. 1–2. In *Plough and Furrow: Some Essays and Papers on Life and the Theatre* (New York: Samuel French, 1963) Green himself published an essay on the Soviet Union developed out of his notebooks, " 'We Have Suffered' " (pp. 115–32), in which he allows a lively and articulate young woman (based on one of his guides) to explain her view that the Soviet Union's goals are peace and happiness in the world and that progress toward these goals is continually hampered by the United States.

8. See letter 271.

9. In the 1960 presidential election.

## 283. To Katharine Boyd

[Greenwood Road, Chapel Hill, N.C.]
26 July 1962

Dearest Kate:[1]

We had a good evening at your house, and as always the restfulness of those trees and your gracious home were amplifications and extensions of your own personality.

Elizabeth said you called up here to say there was some more material of Jim's to come. It hasn't arrived yet, but I am hoping it will be here when we get back from Kentucky next week. She and I set off tomorrow.[2] Each year I have to appear for a while at these different outdoor plays and mingle with the young folks—they expect it and it is good for me and the spread of the people's theatre idea which I have of recent years given my devotion to. August 4 I have to be in Williamsburg.[3]

I have been through the material you let me have, and I have some very strong ideas about it.[4] I want the University here to make a big thing of it, and I see a good book coming from it under the title of, say *James Boyd and His Friends*, or *A Novelist at Work*, or whatever. This is real laboratory and creative source doings, and young writers and students can draw inspiration from it

1. Probably on 21 or 22 July (Saturday or Sunday), Paul and Elizabeth drove to Southern Pines to visit Katharine Boyd and during the evening talked with her about the possibility of establishing a collection of her husband's manuscripts and papers in the UNC library. When they left, she gave them a bundle of the papers to take back to Chapel Hill.

2. On a trip to Bardstown for *The Stephen Foster Story.*

3. For *The Common Glory.*

4. Library records describe this batch of James Boyd's papers as "a suitcase full." Probably it consisted of about 400 letters to his parents from Princeton and Cambridge (1906–12), about 100 to his wife from Italy and France where he commanded an ambulance unit during World War I (1918–19), a sizable file of correspondence with writers (Maxwell Anderson, Archibald MacLeish, William Saroyan, Robert Sherwood, and others) and theater people (Burgess Meredith, Orson Welles, and others) in connection with the Free Company of Players (which Boyd organized to present a series of radio plays nationwide during 1940–41), and letters to Boyd from about a dozen friends and fellow writers (Sherwood Anderson, Robert Bridges, Van Wyck Brooks, Bernard De Voto, Scott Fitzgerald, John Galsworthy, Green, Maxwell Perkins, Laurence Stallings, Thomas Wolfe, and others).

for decades to come. We have here a small Thomas Wolfe collection,[5] and I want to see Jim's larger. Tom was an alumnus and Jim was too by adoption and interest.[6] Numerous graduate students in English can find material for their theses in this[7]—I'm just talking at random but factually just the same. We must put our heads together when you get back.[8] In the meantime I have talked confidentially to the head librarian here, Jerrold Orne, and he is keenly interested. Naturally I have made no commitment other than to take the material—all of it—up to the library and have it put into the vault, waiting for the other to arrive. Now it is safe from fire or any disaster until we call for it and make a decision. I hope you will like my hope to make this *big*. There must be a multitude of Jim's letters resting with divers people and firms. Could we get these back? Eleanor Anderson, Sherwood's wife as you know, years ago called on us all for Sherwood's letters. I sent her quite a lot which I think she returned. (I will look and see later.)[9] I would be glad, if you all wanted me to, to help get all of Jim's together we could. Those he wrote to Max Perkins,[10] for instance, ought to be available. And think of those he wrote to Laurence[11] and John Thomason.[12] Of course you are the perfect one to call for them. But I really am fired up on the idea of creating here a storehouse of James Boyd letters, publications, books, etc., for the future. It would help too I think in getting more intense reading and study and enjoyment of Jim's novels—and above all the young people would have a better chance to walk here under these old trees with a rare and gallant spirit if we do this. Of course too when and if it happens, we must get a real play in the press about it.

5. See letter 144.

6. Reared in Harrisburg, Pennsylvania, Boyd for reasons of health spent the better part of four years (1913–16) on a family farm at Southern Pines, then in 1920, on deciding to write, made the farm his permanent residence. In 1938 UNC awarded Boyd an honorary doctorate.

7. First to do so was David E. Whisnant, "James Boyd, 1888–1944: A Literary Biography" (Ph.D. dissertation, Duke University, 1965).

8. From Sorrento, Maine, where she regularly spent the summer.

9. Green sent Eleanor Anderson sixteen letters written to him from Sherwood Anderson, which she returned after making photocopies for the Anderson Collection at the Newberry Library in Chicago.

10. His editor at Charles Scribner's Sons.

11. Stallings.

12. Career U.S. Marine Corps officer and friend since he and Boyd served together in World War I.

Have a good summer, and all is safe and in the vault until you give the word to bring it out.

Love,

I would love to have a note from you with your reaction and suggestions on this widened scope plan.[13]

## 284. To L. Lyndon Hobbs[1]

[Greenwood Road, Chapel Hill, N.C.]
30 November 1962

Dear Lyndon—

I have been beating the bushes trying to get up money in connection with your work for Robert Case. And I have had help from others. For instance,

13. Katharine Boyd thought Green's ideas were "wonderful" and promised to "do all I can to help" (Katharine Boyd to Paul Green, 30 July 1962, PG-SHC). In January 1963 she gave her husband's papers to UNC, which prompted a lengthy press release noting the scope of the Boyd Collection and outlining its values for research (e.g., "Library Receives James Boyd Letters," *Chapel Hill Weekly*, 10 March 1963, sec. B, p. 3, cols. 1–2). Over the years, through her efforts, Green's, and others', the Boyd Collection grew considerably. Now it includes (in the manuscript department) most of his correspondence and drafts of his short stories, poems, and essays, along with (in the North Carolina Collection) the various editions of his published novels and other books, his published short stories and essays, and the typescript (with revisions) of his second novel, *Marching On*.

---

1. In April 1960 Robert Lee Case, a white mill worker from Gastonia, North Carolina, and a companion were convicted of robbing and raping Janette Black the previous January near Lincolnton, North Carolina. On 3 January the two entered Black's home, tied up her husband and two sons, took forty dollars and forced her to leave with them, raped her six times in the car, and then left her on a country road (*NO*, 4 January 1960, p. 1, cols. 1–3; p. 2, col. 4). At the trial, 4–9 April 1960, Case's companion, William Shedd, twenty-five and illiterate, was sentenced to life in prison. Case, twenty-eight, was sentenced to death. When Green heard about the situation in July 1962, perhaps from a prison chaplain, Case's execution date following three postponements was only a month away, on 24 August. After visiting Case at Central Prison in Raleigh and studying his trial record and biography, Green on 14 August called L. Lyndon Hobbs, an attorney in Shelby, North Carolina, who agreed to ask the governor to commute the sentence to life in prison (Paul Green to L. Lyndon

Rev. W. W. Finlator, pastor of the Pullen Memorial Church in Raleigh,[2] some weeks ago got out a mimeographed sheet appealing for funds. I have written a number of letters here and yon too and am continuing to write. The response has been terrifying in its absence. To date I have been able to collect only $70.[3] I had already sent you my personal check for $100 as a token payment on the wearying work you did sometime ago to get a stay of execution for Robert. Now in order to get another like amount off to you I am adding my check for $50 more to the present $70. I wish I could treble it. I have asked my secretary, Mrs. Mary Kiser, to act as treasurer for any monies we take in. She is sending herewith this check for $100, which leaves us with a balance of $20 in the bank as seed money. I will keep begging.

I hope you will continue to do all you can for Robert. However guilty and ruined and undone he has proved himself to be, he deserves a better showing before the bar of justice than he had.[4] And of course to begin with, the sentence of death he received is too severe. The plaintiff is still alive and well for all her mistreatment, etc. And besides, he has been rotting on Death's Row for some two years already. And again besides everything else—capital punishment is a brutality this beloved North Carolina of ours should abolish forevermore and soon.[5]

---

Hobbs, 14 August 1962, and Hobbs to Green, 16 August 1962, PG-SHC). With an analysis of the trial by Green ("Robert Case," 22 August 1962, PG-SHC), Hobbs met with Governor Sanford on 22 August but gained only another postponement to allow time for an appeal through the federal courts. Green himself paid Hobbs ($100) to approach the governor, and since then had asked widely for funds to cover the cost of the appeal.

2. And a leader in the movement to abolish capital punishment.

3. Ten of which came from Finlator, and ten from Robert Seymour, pastor of the Binkley Memorial Baptist Church in Chapel Hill (Paul Green to William Finlator, 31 October 1962, PG-SHC).

4. Green thought the court-appointed lawyer concentrated on the other defendant in the trial, William Shedd, whose mental incapacities made emotional appeals effective, and neglected Case's defense. Through his own correspondence with Case's brother and sisters, Green had established that on the day of the crime Case was under the influence of drugs ("goof balls") (Wilma Case Dupree to Paul Green, 30 August 1962, PG-SHC), yet during the trial the lawyer did not bring out that circumstance, nor did he call witnesses favorable to Case or allow Case to testify in his own defense ("Robert Case," 22 August 1962, PG-SHC).

5. With Hobbs in charge, the appeal wound its way to the Fourth Circuit Court of

Best greetings and regards,
Copy to Governor Terry Sanford

## 285. To John Howard Griffin[1]

[Greenwood Road, Chapel Hill, N.C.]
3 December 1962

Dear John Griffin—

Many thanks for your note. Again I say I like *Black Like Me*, and I hope I'll write a script out of it you will like. For the present I don't see any real need for us to get together on it, especially since you are so heavily worked otherwise. I've just finished some writing on another project and am writing Carl Lerner and the fellows.[2] I'll start pondering your book tomorrow. If I get hung on anything I'll telephone you somehow. Right now all seems clear as to point of view if you agree that I may have some leeway in creating a few more experiences and jobs of work for the hero. Years ago I dramatized Richard Wright's novel *Native Son*, and at that time I asked to be allowed to keep the violence down as much as possible. It was okay, and I did as best I could. I am

---

Appeals, which on 25 March 1963 granted Case a new trial on the grounds that in the original trial his court-appointed lawyer had a conflict of interest (*Durham Morning Herald*, 19 July 1963, sec. B, p. 7, col. 1).

---

1. Motion picture rights to *Black Like Me*, John Howard Griffin's 1961 diary of his travels from New Orleans to Atlanta in 1959 disguised as a black man, had been bought by independent producer Julius Tannenbaum, who asked Green to write the screenplay. Tannenbaum wanted to make the film because it would "touch upon areas [of experience] that concern [Americans] deeply" (Julius Tannenbaum to Paul Green, 24 October 1962, PG-SHC), and Green accepted because he liked the material and thought the job "a good way for me to put in another lick down here in a cause I believe in" (Paul Green to Harold Franklin, 12 November 1962). When Griffin (1920–1980) learned that Green would do the script, he wrote to say how pleased he was and promised full cooperation. He also sent along his lecture schedule, heavy through March 1963, "in the hope that our paths will cross somewhere along the way" (8 November 1962).

2. Carl Lerner and Norman Kantor, associates of Tannenbaum in the producing organization. Early in November the three visited Green for several days as they planned the film. Lerner, himself a writer, was Griffin's friend and chief contact among the producers (Carl Lerner to Paul Green, 27 November 1962, PG-SHC).

glad there is little or no violence in your book. What I want and what you work for—is more and more understanding. Yes, that's the word—understanding. Given that, we all are going somewhere.[3]

Best greetings and regards,

## 286. To Ruby E. McArthur[1]

[Greenwood Road, Chapel Hill, N.C.]
25 January 1963

Dear Mrs. McArthur:

What a wonderful and touching long letter you wrote me! You had my deepest sympathy and I hope something of understanding in every word of it.

3. Green finished the script and sent it to Tannenbaum on 4 March 1963, then revised it following suggestions from Lerner and returned it in mid-April (film script, *Black Like Me*, 10 April 1963, and Paul Green to Julius Tannenbaum and Carl Lerner, 7 May 1963, PG-SHC). Revised and directed by Lerner, the film was released in 1964 with actor James Whitmore in the central role.

---

1. In a recent Sunday issue of the *News and Observer* Green attacked capital punishment ("Let Us Outlaw the Gas Chamber," 2 December 1962, sec. 3, p. 2, cols. 1–8), claiming that it did not deter crime (when people murder, they are in the grip of unreasoning passion), that lawmakers did not really believe it deterred crime (if they did, they would televise executions with fanfare and close-up shots), and that it was inflicted only on the poor and ignorant, some of whom were innocent. Capital punishment was only an emotional response to the problem of crime, not the response of an enlightened Christian society. After reading the article, Ruby E. McArthur, of Grifton, North Carolina, wrote Green an eleven-page letter narrating the day on which her husband was murdered. On Sunday, 10 September 1961, after they attended church in the morning and visited children and grandchildren in the afternoon, her husband, a retired farmer, went at dusk to check on the roadside store he operated next to their house. There he was beaten and shot repeatedly by two twenty-year-olds from the neighborhood, who then ran off with the cash register containing three dollars. At the trial it came out that the two were drunk and decided to kill McArthur because he kept a large dog in his store at night to prevent them from stealing cigarettes and candy. Sentenced to death, they were presently awaiting a decision on their appeal to the U.S. Supreme Court. "Now, Mr. Green," Ruby McArthur concluded, "what do you think should be done with those two?" She felt his answer might contradict his newspaper article if he "had been beside me thru every step of that horrible night [when she found her husband's body in a pool of

You have suffered so much, your family has suffered so much, that any argument on my part against capital punishment seems not only useless but cruel. I guess we both view this matter from our own experience and long-developed religious attitude and so have to go along as best we can friend to friend. I would dearly love to drive down some Sunday afternoon and get acquainted with you. Would this be possible? If you have a phone number I could call. I would check with you ahead of time.[2]

With affectionate and heartfelt greetings,

Sincerely,

## 287. To Robert Lee Case[1]

[Greenwood Road, Chapel Hill, N.C.]
13 May 1963

Dear Robert—

I have heard by way of your former appeal counsel[2] that you are going to ask for a new trial—maybe you already have—there in Gaston County. I have pondered this matter quite a lot, weighing possibilities pro and con as well as I could. So with the best judgment that I am capable of, I have come to the conclusion that you would do far better to plead guilty, accept the consequent sentence, begin serving your time and move on toward the day of parole. Of course I don't know whether the solicitor now would accept such a plea, though I have understood that he was willing to some time ago. You see, Robert, by dragging the case through the court again you will start with three strikes against you. So I believe. I have read the record carefully, and I see no

---

blood]; and seen the anguished faces of my children when they got home to me; and watched my poor old father as he broke apart and finally passed away from the sheer shock of that awful hour . . . and the confusing and heart-breaking days and weeks up to now as I have tried to hold my sanity and my home together and carry on the business of living, alone" (2 January 1963, PG-SHC).

2. McArthur seems not to have replied.

---

1. Robert Lee Case (1930–1976), in prison for rape in Gaston County, North Carolina, was awaiting a new trial granted by the Fourth Circuit Court of Appeals on 25 March 1963 (see letter 284). His options were to plead guilty in exchange for a life sentence or go to trial again, with possible outcomes ranging from acquittal to a repetition of his earlier death sentence.

2. L. Lyndon Hobbs.

chance of an acquittal. I understand your former counsel feels the same way. I am your friend in this matter—as I have been since I first met you. I am in general opposed to capital punishment, and I am specifically committed to wishing the best for your welfare.[3]

Sincerely yours,

## 288. To Clifford Odets[1]

[Greenwood Road, Chapel Hill, N.C.]
27 May 1963

Dear Cliff—

It is warming and good to hear from you again. Yes, I got that nice book from you last Christmas, and I will have to back up to the kicking machine if I didn't write to thank you for it.[2] Any word or token from you is always appreciated and in the special sense that it brings back the warmth of our old and long-continued friendship and association.

3. Case replied that he agreed with Green's advice but could not comply with it (Robert Case to Paul Green, 24 May 1963, PG-SHC) because, as his court-appointed lawyer explained, the victim would not accept the guilty plea (Bob W. Lawing to Paul Green, 24 May 1963). She "wants Case to die in the gas chamber," Green noted on the lawyer's letter. Case was retried in Gaston County on 22–23 July 1963 and given a life sentence. He became an honor grade prisoner (trustee) in August 1968 but escaped and remained at large a few months in 1969 and in 1974–75, then died in prison on 30 June 1976 (Paul Green to Blanch McDonald, 13 February 1969; North Carolina State Parole Commission to Laurence Avery, 25 August 1988).

---

1. Clifford Odets (1906–1963), who came into prominence as a playwright with *Waiting for Lefty* (1935), was a member of the Group Theatre and began his friendship with Green when the Group produced *The House of Connelly* in 1931. At present he was at MGM Studios in Los Angeles (with an acting company of twelve headed by Richard Boone) developing a series of one-hour plays for the 1963–64 season on NBC Television and asked Green if he had an idea for one of the plays, "something contemporary and meaty." He closed by asking if Green got the book (unidentified) he sent last Christmas (Clifford Odets to Paul Green, 22 May 1963, PG-SHC).

2. In 1937 Thomas W. Haywood of Croatan, in eastern North Carolina, attracted attention by setting up on main street (U.S. highway 70) a coin-operated self-kicking machine, which applied a kick "to any part of the body placed in front of it" (*State Magazine*, 16 October 1937, p. 3).

I am glad too that you would like me to do one of your TV plays. I had read about the project, of course, and was hoping for you and it the best of success. Naturally I have a number of "meaty" ideas beating in me, and in these upboiling and fermenting times how could one not have? For instance the struggle of our Negro minority groups for fair and right freedoms at this time is a dramatic and challenging subject.[3] (I have just done a full-length film script on one phase of this.)[4] Again the tragedy of the Civil War in these centennial years is quick and jabbing in our national consciousness. It might be that neither of these subjects would suit the program. I know how difficult it is really to put forth on the American TV the blood-heart drumbeat of muscled and breathing human drive.

Then too, I have some other subjects in mind, especially folkish ones and tinged with some comedy.

I would love to hear more about your series. I had planned to be out your way sometime this summer, and maybe I could have a good chat about it with you then. Or better still, maybe you will be in New York before too long and we can get together there. In the meantime could your office send me some press releases or brochure material about your planning which would help me to focus and orientate my thinking? Or could you write me more about it?

The pay you mention is generous and sufficient.[5]

And the best thing of all—Baird Shuman came over the other night and

3. The spring of 1963 was the time of mass demonstrations by blacks in Birmingham, Alabama, with the bombing of black churches and the jailing of Martin Luther King, Jr. Sit-ins as a method of protest had begun in Greensboro, North Carolina, in February 1960, when black students from North Carolina Agricultural and Technical State College occupied the lunch counter at a local dime store. In Chapel Hill demonstrations against segregation began in early April 1963, when a few white students at UNC picketed a segregated café on Franklin Street, the main street of town. Then on 25 May 1963, two days before the present letter, Chapel Hill saw its first large demonstration, as about 350 people, half of them black, marched from Saint Joseph's Church, up Franklin Street, over to Rosemary Street, and back to the town hall protesting segregated businesses (John Ehle, *The Free Men* [New York: Harper and Row, 1965], pp. 38–50). A few months after the present letter, on 28 August 1963, King addressed the throng gathered on the Capitol Mall during the People's March on Washington, D.C.

4. *Black Like Me.*

5. "The fee would run in the $5,000 to $6,000 range," Odets had written (22 May 1963, PG-SHC).

spent the evening with us and brought his new book on you.[6] I am pleased that a biography has come out. You may not like it.[7] But whatever differences of opinion I have with the author don't seem too important in light of the importance of this sort of accumulating recognition.[8]

Elizabeth joins me in much love,

6. Baird Shuman, in the School of Education at Duke University, had dinner with Paul and Elizabeth at the Carolina Inn on 24 May and brought them a copy of his *Clifford Odets* (1962) (Green diary, 25 May 1963, PG-SHC).

7. Green was not impressed by the book. At dinner Shuman talked incessantly about his travels and his three cats, and Green found him and his work boring and confused (ibid.).

8. Odets replied that "Shuman's book on 'Odets' rather puzzles me, but, as you say, it was written and published." Concerning Green's ideas for a play, he said, "Negro subjects I am afraid of for TV today—wouldn't know how to handle." He wanted Green to outline "an idea or two in the area of what you called, 'folkish ones and tinged with comedy' " (Clifford Odets to Paul Green, 11 June 1963, PG-SHC). In reply Green outlined several ideas, one a nonfolk play on the post–Civil War years of Robert E. Lee, when he rejected numerous attractive business offers and accepted the presidency of Washington College (now Washington and Lee University), hoping "to do a little good for his fellowman before he died." The idea that caught Odets's eye was the folk comedy "Bernie and the Britches," in which a wife's infidelity stimulates her husband's economic and psychological development. Green outlined the story and sent Odets a copy of the book in which it appears (*Dog on the Sun* [Chapel Hill: University of North Carolina Press, 1949], pp. 71–94) (Paul Green to Clifford Odets, 20 June 1963). That book sent Odets to the UCLA library for Green's other collections of stories, *Wide Fields* (1928) and *Salvation on a String* (1946). The earlier one he particularly liked, thinking the stories "not only beautiful, but as fresh and touching and authentic as they were when written." He liked "Bernie and the Britches" but wanted to think about all of the stories before deciding which one to develop into a play for the television series (Clifford Odets to Paul Green, 10 July 1963). Then on 23 July, shortly after writing to Green, Odets underwent an operation for an ulcerated stomach, cancer was discovered, and on 15 August he died. The television project collapsed.

## 289. To William C. Friday[1]

[Greenwood Road, Chapel Hill, N.C.]
2 November 1963

Dear Bill:

Thanks for sending me Deputy Attorney General Moody's brief on the Speaker Bill. I have read it with interest, irritation and finally a mixture of sorrow and dismay.[2] He misses the entire matter of our concern, I think. No one doubts that the Legislature had the authority to pass such a bill. The matter of pain is the nature of the bill—along with the kind of parochial thinking that produced it.

There is an old Hindu saying that whatever can be thought, man will think

1. On 26 June 1963, the day before adjournment and with its rules suspended, the state legislature passed "An Act to Regulate Visiting Speakers at State Supported Colleges and Universities" (House Bill 1395) prohibiting speeches at such schools by Communists or anyone who advocated overthrow of the United States or the state constitution or who had taken the fifth amendment in refusing to answer questions about Communist involvement. On 12 October, at the annual University Day celebration commemorating the founding of UNC in 1789, Green was the speaker. In "The University in a Nuclear Age" he dealt mainly with the need for a value-laden education but closed by chiding the faculty for failing to protest "House Bill Number 1395, which we now call the Speaker Ban Law or in more homely and accurate parlance the Gag Law." Declaring that "it's not going to gag me," he criticized the law on the basis of Jefferson's notion of the power of truth in a free environment (p. 24, PG-SHC). Newspapers the next day focused on the closing attack (e.g., "Green Raps Reaction to Speaker Ban Law," *NO*, 13 October 1963, sec. 1, p. 22, cols. 1–2), and William C. Friday (b. 1920), who became president of the University of North Carolina in 1956 and proved himself a skillful opponent of the act, wrote Green that "your address on Saturday was splendid." Friday also included a brief on the act by Ralph Moody, deputy state attorney general, saying "I know [it] will be of interest to you" (William Friday to Paul Green, 14 October 1963, PG-SHC).

2. Moody stated at the outset his conviction that the act was constitutional. Then he emphasized the "basic right of the General Assembly to reasonably control its creatures, that is, the various institutions of higher learning of the State . . . [because] there has been developed by certain administrators in these institutions concepts that these institutions are autonomous, can make their own rules of conduct and can in fact do anything they wish" (p. 1, PG-SHC). He concluded with the claim that opponents of the act, who said it infringed academic freedom, were "doctrinaire liberals [who] are very skilful in capturing words without thoughts and turning them to their own purposes" (p. 28).

it. And another one which declares that all that can happen will happen. So we have to ride along with time, don't we?

But time also is energy at work. And the best working is toward a good end. The program ahead then is clear in its provocation and challenge. This I believe.[3]

Always best greetings and regards.

Sincerely,

## 290. To Jonathan Daniels

[Greenwood Road, Chapel Hill, N.C.]
4 November 1963

Dear Jonathan:[1]

I am sending herewith a copy of a recent contract I drew up and submitted to Emma Neal Morrison and Martin Kellogg relative to the settlement of our

3. In 1965, saying the act constituted political interference with the educational process, the Southern Association of Colleges and Schools threatened to revoke accreditation of the state's universities. The legislature, in a special November session, responded by transferring responsibility for enforcing the law from the state to the chancellor on each campus. In January 1966, when a student group at Chapel Hill invited two Communist speakers, the new chancellor, Carlyle Sitterson, denied permission for them to appear on campus. The two came anyway and, standing on the town side of a low stone wall, spoke to several thousand students on the campus side of the wall. In March 1966 the speakers and several students challenged the speaker ban by filing suit against Sitterson and the UNC trustees, and on 19 February 1968 a panel of federal judges declared the law unconstitutional ("Speaker Ban Still around for Fourth Birthday," *NO*, 25 June 1967, p. 7, cols. 2–8, and "Federal Court Rule Puts End to Speaker Ban," *NO*, 20 February 1968, p. 1, cols. 6–8; p. 2, cols. 3–4). Sitterson (who in the meantime regularly permitted invited speakers, Communist or otherwise, to appear on campus) and the trustees quickly announced that they would not appeal the court's ruling ("State Won't Appeal Speaker Ban Ruling," *NO*, 23 February 1968, p. 1, cols. 2–8; p. 2, col. 1).

---

1. Early in the year William Free of the University of Georgia and Charles Lower of the University of North Carolina completed *History into Drama: A Source Book on Symphonic Drama*, and it was scheduled for publication by Odyssey Press. The book included *The Lost Colony* along with historical documents and other material relating to it, and the editors got permission to include the play from Green, copyright holder,

*Lost Colony* matters.[2] This contract seems to me eminently fair, and I do hope the Board at their next meeting in early December will approve it and those of us who have been concerned with this "thing" can forget it and go on with our otherwise knitting.[3]

The Viet Nam imbroglio bothers me a lot.[4] There's something rotten in the

---

and the University of North Carolina Press, publisher of the play since 1937. Just as Odyssey was going into production, however, the company received a letter from Martin Kellogg, Jr., general counsel of the Roanoke Island Historical Association, advising that "the text of *The Lost Colony* is the sole property of the Roanoke Island Historical Association" and that any publication of it "must be with the permission of and under contract with" the association (Martin Kellogg, Jr., to Odyssey Press, 17 April 1963, PG-SHC). Much of Green's time for the rest of the year was spent negotiating, sometimes heatedly, with Kellogg and Emma Neal Morrison, chairman of the association. Over the years he had prodded the association to enter into a new contract with him that included payment of a royalty, and he thought Morrison and Kellogg were using *History into Drama* as a hostage to force him to relinquish his rights in the play. For their part, Morrison and Kellogg thought the original contract (see letter 123) gave ownership of the play to the association, saw no reason for a new contract, and would not agree to publication of *History into Drama* unless Green assigned the copyright on the play to the association. With Green on the point of suing to force the association to agree to publication of *History into Drama*, Jonathan Daniels began mediating the dispute. By September he had persuaded the association to allow publication of *History into Drama* with the copyright notice, "Copyright 1937, 1946, 1954, 1963 by Paul Green. Reproduced with permission of the copyright proprietor," a notice he then had to persuade Green to accept because of its slight indefiniteness about the "proprietor" (Paul Green to Jonathan Daniels, 5 September 1963, PG-SHC). This freed the book for publication but left up in the air the matter of a contract between Green and the association.

2. Green discussed this contract (unlocated) with Morrison and Kellogg in Chapel Hill on 2 November and in sending a draft to Morrison said it "spelled out the Association's full ownership of the drama and my future connection with it" (3 November 1963, PG-SHC). Probably the contract stipulated the payment of some royalty.

3. The directors of the association met in Raleigh on 3 December 1963 but did not approve a new contract.

4. The United States supported democratic South Vietnam in its struggle against Communist North Vietnam, and on 2 November news came of a coup d'état in the south in which General Duong Van Minh, promising stronger action against the north, overthrew President Ngo Dinh Diem. U.S. officials "insisted with some heat

CIA. Power, power, must be the philosophy and the result, bless the Lord, to these weary and blinking watchful eyes ends ultimately in national weakness.

You see that, pagan soul whatsoever, I have some belief in what might be called the righteous bent of the universe. And I believe these power boys go contrary to it and thereby hold back joy and hosanna doings the more. Yea, there are such!

Always love to you and Lucy,

## 291. To Dolphe Martin[1]

[Greenwood Road, Chapel Hill, N.C.]
6 February 1964

Dear Dolphe:

Many thanks for your letter of some days ago with the copy of yours to Margaret Hewes. Your suggestions and advice seem to me eminently right, and I shall await with interest her reaction.[2] Of course I am still in the dark as to just exactly what she intends. Certainly the expense of carrying over a lot of actors from here to London or to anywhere in Europe would be a whopping

---

that they neither organized nor signaled the coup. The Central Intelligence Agency, whose covert operations were widely blamed—or credited—by the diplomatic corps for the plot, maintained its customary silence" (*New York Times*, 2 November 1963, p. 1, col. 5; p. 3, col. 3).

---

1. Dolphe Martin, teaching and working in television in Boston, composed the music for the unsuccessful production of *Roll Sweet Chariot* in 1934, and he and producer Margaret Hewes never gave up the idea of staging the play again. Hewes, now living in London, felt "*Roll Sweet Chariot* is a great piece of work and MUST be done as soon as possible. Somehow I feel it is my Destiny to make this a success" (Margaret Hewes to Paul Green, 18 February 1964, PG-SHC). Accordingly, she had arranged a production in Paris in the spring of 1964 and another in London in the fall and asked Green and Martin to revise the script and score and to recruit the all-black cast in Boston and New York City.

2. Martin advised Hewes there was not enough time to prepare a production for the spring, so the Paris production should be canceled, and that it was economically unfeasible to transport a large cast from the United States to England, so he and Green should try to fill only the leading parts in this country while she found the bulk of the cast and chorus in London (Dolphe Martin to Margaret Hewes, 24 January 1964, PG-SHC).

thing. What sort of backing she has is a question, etc., etc. I am busy as I can be overseeing a number of outdoor dramas[3] and working on three more with octopus fingers,[4] but I am planning a break in the spell for some fair weather doings with you on *Roll Sweet Chariot* when and if the plans come through. Like you, I am leaving everything in the hands of Samuel French. They told me Margaret had sent along an advance[5] in line with my starting to work, but naturally I asked French to hold it up until we knew more about contracts and the kind of production we might expect. Certainly I will never go through another experience if I can help it like the one we all endured there in New York in that long ago time.[6] That nightmare was one of the main things that drove me to working among the people and writing plays for them far from Broadway. I wish it were so you could come here to work. I have plenty of space, a piano waiting, and rooms for sleeping or pacing about. If you could get off I'd take a piece out of the advance and send it up to you for round-trip plane fare. But of course if interviewing actors is in order so far ahead, then I'll have to come up that way. I'll keep my fingers crossed and spit in four directions of the wind for good luck in the total venture.

Hurriedly,

I'm returning herewith the copy of your letter to Margaret.[7]

3. *The Lost Colony, The Common Glory*, and *The Stephen Foster Story.*

4. *The Founders* for Williamsburg in 1964, *Cross and Sword* for St. Augustine in 1965, and *Texas* for Palo Duro Canyon in 1966.

5. Of $1,000 (Abbott Van Nostrand to Paul Green, 11 March 1964, PG-SHC).

6. For that production, see letters 102, 106, 109, and "Symphonic Drama," in Paul Green, *Dramatic Heritage* (New York: Samuel French, 1953), pp. 14–26.

7. Hewes accepted Martin's argument about insufficient time to prepare a spring production and canceled the Paris commitment. During the first days of March, Green visited Martin in Boston for work on the music and story line of the play (Paul Green to Margaret Hewes, 7 March 1964, PG-SHC), then on his way home, to scout black performers for leading parts, he stopped in New York City to see Martin Duberman's *In White America* and James Weldon Johnson's *Trumpets of the Lord.* Eventually Hewes was unable to raise backing for a London production of *Roll Sweet Chariot*, and all plans were off (Harold Dyer to Abbott Van Nostrand, 3 April 1964, and Van Nostrand to Dyer, 21 August 1964, PG-SHC).

## 292. To Lewis McMurran, Jr.[1]

[Greenwood Road, Chapel Hill, N.C.]
12 February 1964

Dear Lewis:

That was a good letter you wrote me sometime ago relative to certain historical items in the Jamestown drama source material, and I appreciate—we all do—your always helpful point of view. Roger and Sue Sherman,[2] Howard Scammon[3] and Russ Hastings[4] were here for a week-end a short time ago, and we put in quite a lot of hours going over *The Founders* script in order first of all to see to it that the conjoining of history into drama was done without violating or invading the citadel of either too much. We sweated over the matter and I think our work would please you and the Board.

Now it is a fact, I believe, that there is nothing more interesting to human beings than others of the same species, and the highest interest is always directed toward individuals first and groups second. So when bodies or groups of human beings are in action or conflict there is always the urge and compulsion on the part of the spectator or auditor to fasten on a single person for hero or one on whom he "puts his money." This is a "law" of human nature and the reason it is a law is that the auditor or the spectator is himself

1. The Jamestown Corporation, producer of *The Common Glory* at Williamsburg each summer since 1947, decided to substitute *The Founders* for the summer of 1964. *The Founders* depicts the settlement of Jamestown (1607–22), and Green wrote it for the 350th anniversary of the settlement in 1957, when it played in the afternoons and *The Common Glory* at night. For the last several weeks Green had worked at revising *The Founders* for the 1964 production. Lewis McMurran, Jr. (b. 1914), from Newport News and prominent in state and national Democratic party politics, was president of the Jamestown Corporation and among those on the board who always seemed to Green to make a fetish of historical accuracy. McMurran was sure, for instance, that departing governor Thomas Gates in 1610 would not include the name of a traitor as he called the roll of colonists who had died and that during the attack on Jamestown of 22 March 1622 Indians did not make their way into the fort—both of which occurred in *The Founders* (Paul Green to Lewis McMurran, 11 June 1964, PG-SHC). The present letter responds to an unlocated list of such presumed inaccuracies and McMurran's call for a pageantlike chronicle of all the chief events in Jamestown's early history.

2. General manager of *The Founders* and his wife, its costume designer.

3. Director of the play.

4. Technical director.

an individual and thinks and wills and imagines as an individual and cannot do otherwise. The things we remember most vividly about the Philistines are Goliath, Delilah, and so on.[5]

So in writing the drama of the Jamestown colony I am faced with this human requirement. I simply cannot and must not divide the audience's attention too much between too many leading characters. My playwriting aesthetics agrees with Dr. Samuel Johnson who said in one of his essays that a play "must always have a hero, a personage apparently and incontestably superior to the rest, upon whom the attention may be fixed, and the anxiety suspended. For though of two persons opposing each other with equal abilities and equal virtue, the auditor will inevitably in time choose his favorite, yet as that choice must be without any cogency of conviction, the hopes and fears[6] which it raises will be faint and languid. Of two heroes acting in confederacy against a common enemy, the virtues or dangers will give little emotion, because each claims our concern with the same right, and the heart lies at rest between equal motives."[7]

And I'm sure that in the Jamestown struggle there factually were many heroes. It may be that John Smith was most heroic of all, or George Percy,[8] or John Martin,[9] or Thomas Dale[10]—during those harsh and bitter days and years of *founding*. But choice had to be made for dramatic purposes. And the facts of history so far as I can read them have pointed to John Rolfe as the main man in the final success of the venture. He actually hit upon the economic salvation of the colony in his tobacco, and without economic stability the enterprise would have perished like the one at Roanoke. And then lucky for our dramatic needs he married Pocahontas and so gave us a main love interest for our play.[11]

5. 1 Samuel 17 and Judges 16.

6. Johnson has "hopes or fears."

7. "Rambler 156," in *The Works of Samuel Johnson*, ed. W. J. Bate and Albrecht B. Strauss (New Haven: Yale University Press, 1969), 5:70.

8. Military leader.

9. Leader in establishing the House of Burgesses in 1619.

10. Autocratic governor who got the colony on its feet, 1611–16.

11. The Jamestown story with John Rolfe as central character was Green's first choice when he began postwar discussions with Colgate Darden and others about doing a play in the area of Colonial Williamsburg. Unable to build a theater at Jamestown, however, the group moved to the William and Mary campus at Williams-

Then too, we have only about two hours total in which we can hold our audience. If I had plenty of time—hours and hours—like Schiller with his *Robbers* I could pay my respects more thoroughly to a lot of historical Jamestown names.[12] But I haven't. So we must go to business as soon as possible—and that means we must get our theme and our leading character moving at once. In working as best we could here, we all felt we should try to approximate our 1957 opening and have the fort pretty much completed when the action gets under way, and so charge right in. I think you will like the way we start things as well as the way we carry them on.

In order to cooperate with history and not violate it, as mentioned above and yet hold to our stage dynamics, we fit the scene where Smith is saved by Pocahontas, for instance, into a re-call on the part of the narrator.[13] And then as for the Indian massacre, we have it occurring in the woods on either side of the fort, and not in the fort, since the Indians actually did not attack Jamestown.[14] (Thanks to Riley[15] and all for setting me straight on this bit of history.) But we do have the people who remain in the fort energized and psychologically as well as physically involved in barricading, strengthening their positions, etc. during the attack, so that the effect is that they are "participating." And since the fort suffered much from fire at different times, it might not be too a-historical to have a fire break out during the outside battle. And again so on and so on. We have, as I say, sweated hard to make

---

burg, and in Green's theory the new location required a new story, one involving events at that place. *The Common Glory* resulted, but the change of direction was not easy for Green. On the day in 1946 when it was decided to build the theater at William and Mary, he complained in his diary: "There is something so artificial about the 18th century! . . . When I found that in the heart of John Rolfe was the vision of righteous labor, the philosophy of earning one's world by 'these two hands' I felt I had something right and solid to build a play on. But here in the 18th century squirearchy, I search for something more meaningful than the rimed couplet, the silver buckle, the sniff of snuff" (1 November 1946, PG-SHC). In *The Founders* he took the opportunity to focus on Rolfe.

12. Although of conventional length, *The Robbers* is episodic and changes focal characters frequently.

13. *The Founders: A Symphonic Outdoor Drama* (New York: Samuel French, 1957), act 1, scene 3.

14. The concluding scene, in which Rolfe is killed.

15. Unidentified.

things jibe, and I believe we have a good historical document and a very fine chance for a dramatic success this summer.[16]

With best greetings and regards,

cc. to Samuel Bemiss[17]
Russell Hastings
Howard Scammon
Roger Sherman

## 293. To Frances Phillips[1]

[Greenwood Road, Chapel Hill, N.C.]
18 March 1964

Dear Frances:

Last night I got in late and found the Woodrow Wilson book waiting. There was no sender's name available, but I guess I can thank you for the thoughtfulness of providing it, for it came from Morrow. I hurried to my room and to read it in bed. It was past midnight when I finished. Smith has done a fine, fine job. He makes you *feel.* The part dealing with Wilson's trials and sorrows in France was especially vivid to me. For I was in Paris during the President's stay there, a young eager soldier. In fact I was standing near the Madeleine Church that day of his riding by like the Savior of the world.[2] And was I proud of him! And so proud to be an American! I still am. I was at Suresnes cemetery when he made the speech which Smith quotes so much from.[3] And in the photograph in the book of that scene I can see myself there,

16. *The Founders* opened on 22 June 1964 and barely made expenses. Reviewers found it diffuse because of its numerous characters and events (e.g., "'Founders' Effect Lost in Crowd," *Norfolk Pilot*, 24 June 1964). For the 1965 season, the Jamestown Corporation returned to *The Common Glory.*

17. Chairman of the Jamestown Corporation, also much concerned with historical accuracy.

---

1. Frances Phillips, longtime friend and editor at William Morrow, sent Green a recent publication, Gene Smith's *When the Cheering Stopped: The Last Years of Woodrow Wilson* (New York: Morrow, 1964).

2. On 14 December 1918, Wilson's tumultuous welcome to Paris following the armistice.

3. Wilson spoke at Suresnes, at the American military cemetery on the outskirts of

for I was standing as close to the speaker's stand as I could get.[4] Yes, I admired and loved Wilson long ago, and still venerate and love his memory. Just a few years ago I drove up to Washington to a peace memorial in the Washington Cathedral.[5] Mrs. Wilson came—very weak and feeble,[6] still heart-hurting in the touches of girlish finery about her which only served to heighten the ruins of her large and broken beauty the way, say, springing flowers do around a desolated and roof-fallen mansion—where once the fires of life burned warm and bright. I had the privilege of helping her back into her car—she wordless, I too—aching and wordless.[7] I am writing Allan Nevins a word too for his fine though short introduction to the book. I loved such as his final words about Wilson—"an understanding of his powers and objects will yet fill the earth."[8] Morrow is to be congratulated on this volume. It is one more step—and a big one—in the rehabilitation and reaffirmation of a great man and his rightful vision in a tangled world—but a world which the more certainly can grow into rightfulness because of that man and his vision. Thus the witnesses of history are the guideposts too as we make our painful wondrous way along.

With love,

---

Paris, on Memorial Day, 30 May 1919. Compared by some to the Gettysburg Address, his speech urged the living to be inspired by the dead to finally secure world peace and justice through the creation of a League of Nations (Smith, *When the Cheering Stopped*, pp. 51–53).

4. The book includes a photograph of the throng before the Madeleine church (plate vii), the picture Green must have in mind. There is no photograph of the scene at Suresnes.

5. On 6 February 1924 Wilson was buried in the Bethlehem Chapel, completed portion of Washington Cathedral. In 1956, the cathedral finished, his sarcophagus was moved to the main level of the sanctuary in a ceremony commemorating the 100th anniversary of his birth. The service, planned by his grandson, the Reverend Francis B. Sayer, dean of the cathedral, occurred on 12 November, with an address by Bernard Baruch and a reading from *Pilgrim's Progress* by Eleanor Roosevelt (*New York Times*, 11 November 1956, sec. 1, p. 125, cols. 4–8).

6. She was then eighty-four.

7. Mrs. Wilson would be buried next to her husband on 30 December 1961.

8. Smith, *When the Cheering Stopped*, p. xi.

## 294. To Joe Layton[1]

[Greenwood Road, Chapel Hill, N.C.]
27 June 1964

Dear Joe Layton:

I looked for you the other night after the opening of *The Lost Colony*, but you were already gone. Well, these few words at a distance must repeat in shortened form what I wished to say in longer in praise of the staging you have given the play for this season. It is grand! So many, many things I have long hoped would be done you have done. The play has been freed from its narrow confines and sent on its flowing, yes, soaring way. So my thanks devoutly and deeply! This seems to me to be the people's theatre, the mass-theatre approaching top form. I have one or two suggestions—more editorial than esthetically functional or anatomical maybe. The transition to the queen's chamber scene seems a little abrupt.[2] It comes flying into the audience's mental lap when it, the audience, I feel, should have a bit of prelude preparation for it in order to share it most fully. The splicing of it fast on the Indian action on the center stage without interpretative statement would appear to cause some self-robbery on the part of the play. I believe we should say farewell to the one through the Historian and so move into the other.[3] Another thing I have pleaded for for twenty years is the passing of the play's ending on earth into a sort of heavenly echo on high. I've talked to sound

1. During the winter Joe Layton (b. 1931), director and choreographer in the professional theater, was engaged by Emma Neal Morrison to direct *The Lost Colony*. He thought it " 'an excellent play,' " and in a letter mailed with contracts told the 1964 cast they " 'should be the first to know that there will be major changes in the physical production. . . . *The Lost Colony* has continually been made better by the Author. So, the written word is ready! . . . I know how high the standards of Broadway are, generally, but the outdoor theatre can measure up to them with your help and mine' " (quoted in John Fox to Paul Green, 13 June 1964, PG-SHC). Paul and Elizabeth went to Williamsburg for the opening of *The Founders* on 22 June, then to Manteo for the opening of *The Lost Colony* on 25 June, where Green made a brief talk at intermission (Paul Green to Emma Neal Morrison, 27 May 1964).

2. At the end of act 2, scene 3, Layton inserted an Indian attack on the colonists on Roanoke Island, played on center stage, then cut the Historian's transitional remarks and went directly to a scene in Elizabeth's throne room set on a side stage (1965 production script, mimeographed, 1966, Laurence Avery).

3. Layton reinstated a portion of the Historian's speech at the beginning of act 2, scene 4 (ibid.).

engineers both in Hollywood and New York and they have assured me it could be done and done cheaply—most simply, say, by shooting a column of sound upward toward the sky from behind the chapel and letting it spill down over the audience from the stars as it were. I refer to the going-away song with its "We walk this way of death alone." If after the colonists pass into the dark on their way into "the vast unknown" and as the spot light comes on the flag (and would to Jesus we had a spot that could really iris in on the flag!) the heavenly voices could repeat out of the sky—or re-echo from the sky—the last few bars of the song, it would give us a goose-pimples-talking effect. I'm sure of that. The logic here for this, it seems to me, is the same that motivated the artistic soul of Augustus Saint-Gaudens in his Shaw Memorial bas-relief where unknown to the marching Negro soldiers but known to us he placed over them the huge and hovering angel of death.[4] There are many examples of this of course in literature and art—among the most beautiful being from the *Greek Anthology*[5] or even the *Spoon River Anthology*.[6] And how I liked the way you've woven some of the songs into the production, how you showed a care for the music! I loved the way you used the little thing—"O once I was courted!"[7] And then the fine doings with "Sir Walter Raleigh's ship went a-sailing on the sea."[8] And so on. Many, many more examples.

Bless you,

I'm sending a copy of this note to Mrs. Morrison as producer. Maybe there will yet be some way to get the recorded heavenly angel voices sprinkling through the night as a benediction over the doomed ones—being like the

4. Saint-Gaudens's memorial to the Civil War colonel Robert Gould Shaw, who led the black Fifty-fourth Massachusetts Regiment in the bloody assault on Fort Wagner, South Carolina, with the figure of death and fame floating protectively above him and his regiment, stands on Boston Common.

5. Collection of tombstone epitaphs and other epigrams for the dead from ancient Greece.

6. Collection of poems (1915) by Edgar Lee Masters (in form similar to the *Greek Anthology*) in which the dead in the cemetery of a small Illinois town confess the hidden details of their lives, thus providing their own epitaphs.

7. Old Tom's love song to his Indian wife, based on a British folk tune with words by Green. The song was placed variously in different editions, and Layton used it as Tom stands guard at the fort midway into the closing scene (1965 acting script, mimeographed, 1966, Laurence Avery).

8. Sixteenth-century ballad used at the end of act 2, scene 1, as the colonists repair and settle into the fort on Roanoke Island.

voices that clustered exquisitely around the mast of the Ancient Mariner's ship:[9]

> And now 'twas like all instruments,
> Now like a lonely flute,
> And now it is an angel's song,
> That makes the heavens be mute.[10]

## 295. To A. Lincoln Faulk[1]

[Greenwood Road, Chapel Hill, N.C.]
28 September 1964

Dear Mr. Faulk:

I have been running around the country this summer attending to a number of outdoor drama projects and have neglected my mail. Many thanks

9. In Coleridge's poem, after the Mariner blessed the living things of the sea, the albatross fell from him, he was able to pray, and—his crew all dead—angelic spirits sailed his ship along. Their sweet sounds "darted to the Sun" (line 355), then came "a-dropping from the sky" (line 358).

10. Lines 363–66. Layton directed *The Lost Colony* until 1984 but never managed a heavenly echo of the concluding song.

---

1. Shortly after attacking the speaker ban in his University Day speech of 12 October 1963 (see letter 289), Green came under attack by Jesse Helms. Later elected to the U.S. Senate from North Carolina in 1972, Helms was at the time a vice president of Capitol Broadcasting Company in Raleigh and political commentator on its television station, WRAL. The attacks began on 15 October, when Helms told viewers that in the University Day speech Green "merely pulled the trigger on an overworked pop-gun." Green "has turned out some very fine plays in his day," Helms continued, "and has been duly rewarded for them. But he has never been impressive in any practical sense when it comes to government and politics." Helms spent the body of his commentary linking Green to Communists and liberals, then concluded: "Mr. Green made some headlines on Saturday when he attacked the Communist-ban law. If he should wonder why North Carolina is inclined to turn a deaf ear to his voice, he might find it helpful to take a look at his own record. Sadly enough, it speaks for itself" (WRAL "Viewpoint no. 710," 15 October 1963, PG-SHC). Such attacks continued, and A. Lincoln Faulk, manager of radio station WCKB in Harnett County, wrote to assure Green that "there is some recourse for you" against "the

for your kind note of July 1 last with its generous suggestion re the local backwoods apostle Jesse Helms, etc. I did take time from my running to go over and sit down for a long chat with Brother A. J. Fletcher[2] whose great knowledge of and interest in music always provides us a common field for take-off and to voice my displeasure at Jesse's continued distortion of the truth not only as it affected me but the cause of democracy too. Fletcher was most affable and spoke as follows. "Why, Paul, I'm sure sorry you feel that way about Jesse. We think he is doing a good job for the state and for us all. Yessir, and it hurts me to think that my good friend Paul Green who I'm always glad to see does not agree that this is so." And so on. "Now I tell you what," he went on, "you come over some evening and appear on my station—you're welcome to, just name it." "Why, A. J.," I responded, "that's real nice of you, but I can't do it. I'd have my little bit of time, and the next evening and all the evenings thereafter good old Jesse would be in there whaling the lard out of me and whooping it up for his cause. I tell you what—give me and Jesse about an hour to debate face to face on your TV. I'd love that. We'd have fun and I believe the viewers would have fun." Etc. "I can't do that, Paul, I just can't. That wouldn't be in line with our policy," he said. So I said I guess I'd still have to go to Washington with my unfair practices complaint. (Later I did.)[3] "Good Lord," he said, "good Lord!" We talked on quite a bit—all in good friendship, though I was careful not to turn my back. A. J. took me out and showed me his azaleas, landscaping, and fountain.[4] He is something of a real artist, that fellow. I always enjoy talking to him. And sing! He's got a good voice and can haul off and please you with "La ci darem"[5] or Faust's "Rien—rien."[6] But he and the hedge-priest Jesse make an unholy couple in our

rantings of one Jesse Helms." Faulk had heard from Green's relatives that Green was "unable to get any kind of response from Mr. Helms in the interests of fair play," and he advised Green to petition the Federal Communications Commission against renewal of WRAL's license to broadcast. "The FCC does not look with any favor on the use of a public facility for biased and prejudiced views," Faulk said, and "where demand for equal time is made it has to be granted" (1 July 1964, PG-SHC).

2. Founder and president of Capitol Broadcasting Company.

3. Documentation unlocated.

4. The grounds at WRAL are famous for their beauty.

5. Duet in Mozart's *Don Giovanni*, act 1, scene 9.

6. Aria in Gounod's *Faust*, act 1. In 1948 Fletcher founded the Grass Roots Opera Company (now the National Opera Company), a training company for young singers that performs operas in English at schools throughout the country.

government. And too I have hated to see my good friend Sam Beard[7] suffering a gradual hardening of the spiritual arteries under their influence.[8] Another good friend Jonathan Daniels always breezily tells me that somehow democracy will survive—he believes it will—that fellows like Jesse, Lake[9] et al. can't kill it. I believe it will not only survive if we work in charity and dedication to make it survive. Golly, we need a lot of hard work! I've just driven two thousand miles through the South and the multitude of Goldwater car stickers I saw was frightening.[10]

Best wishes and regards,

## 296. To Loucille Plummer[1]

[Greenwood Road, Chapel Hill, N.C.]
15 March 1965

Dear Mrs. Plummer:

I have delayed in answering your very sincere and clearly stated letter of some weeks ago concerning the participation of the Negro citizens of St.

7. Director of public affairs at WRAL.

8. A few years earlier Beard arranged an hour program for Green to express his opposition to capital punishment (Sam Beard to Paul Green, 23 March 1963, and Green to Beard, 13 April 1963, PG-SHC).

9. I. Beverly Lake, conservative Democratic politician and state judge.

10. Barry Goldwater, conservative Republican nominee for president, was defeated in the fall election by Lyndon Johnson.

---

1. In 1965 St. Augustine, Florida, the oldest city in the United States, celebrated its 400th anniversary, and the centerpiece of the celebration was Green's *Cross and Sword*. For two years, however, St. Augustine had witnessed some of the bloodiest racial turmoil in the country: blacks marching to the old slave market for rallies, Klanlike whites beating, shooting, and bombing to intimidate blacks and any whites who called for obedience to the law. By June 1964 the governor had to send in state troopers to keep order. Then in July President Johnson signed the 1964 Civil Rights Act, and through the fall an uneasy peace settled on St. Augustine as NAACP lawyers began taking Klan leaders and city officials into federal court and gaining injunctions and restraining orders (Larry Goodwyn, "Anarchy in St. Augustine," *Harper's Magazine* 230 [January 1965]: 74–81). On 8 and 9 January 1965 Green was in St. Augustine for tryouts of *Cross and Sword* and gave a radio interview there in which he "was careful and deliberate in saying that the anniversary celebration was a people's celebration

Augustine in the 400th Anniversary celebration because I have been away from Chapel Hill quite a lot lately and because I wanted to be sure that what I would have to say would help matters rather than hurt. We all have our problems, don't we? Mr. Tommy Rahner, the manager of the St. Augustine drama *Cross and Sword*, was here over the week-end,[2] and he read your letter with I think the same understanding and response with which I had read it. I'm sure that the people connected with the production of our play are wholeheartedly hoping to make the anniversary one for not only all the citizens of St. Augustine but for the citizens of America. For truly this our oldest city is an American heritage and therefore as such is the common possession of the American people. Surely there will be ways in which we can fruitfully share one with another the responsibilities and challenges and opportunities for fine civic service which the anniversary occasion offers. No doubt Mr. Rahner and other of the committees will welcome any further suggestions from you as to how this can be helped along. Maybe since you wrote me, much progress has been made in this. I hope so.[3] I expect to be in St. Augustine on April 23.[4]

Sincerely yours,

---

and that meant all the people and I hoped that all the people would share in it" (Paul Green to Isaac Van Grove, 30 January 1965, PG-SHC). Later in the month Loucille Plummer, a black resident of St. Augustine and field secretary for the Southern Christian Leadership Conference, wrote that she was "very happy to hear your appeal on the radio for the participation of all of the citizens in St. Augustine in the celebration." She wanted to know how she could "help in making the participation of the Negro people a reality." She also asked Green to "kindly use your influence in bringing about some kind of interracial communication in the city." Without improved communication, the city, she feared, "is going to suffer greater losses," and she said she "would not like to see the many years of preparation that you put into the celebration smothered by renewed demonstrations" ([before 30 January 1965]).

2. For a planning session along with director L. L. Zimmerman, musical director Elwood Keister, and choreographer Frank Rey (Paul Green to W. I. Drysdale, 15 March 1965, PG-SHC).

3. *Cross and Sword* includes no black characters because no blacks were involved in the founding of St. Augustine during 1565–67, the period covered by the play. Green insisted, however, that black singers be hired for the chorus. "The artist is also a citizen," he told the music director, "and has full responsibilities as a citizen to do his part in practical relationships like anyone else. We have a chance here, I think, to repair a tiny bit of the race damage done in and around our dramatic project by

## 297. To Philip Lee Devin, Jr.[1]

[Windy Oaks, Old Lystra Road,[2], Chapel Hill, N.C.]
6 September 1966

Dear Lee—

I am back again from the drama wars in Texas. We've had a big success there as to crowds, and in one or two places in the drama I was able to say my

---

getting a few good Negro voices in our recorded group. Get six or seven or eight. They are there somewhere. Also let's have a picture of this chorus to put into our souvenir program" (Paul Green to Elwood Keister, 11 January 1965, PG-SHC). *Cross and Sword* does include Indian characters, and Green urged the general manager to find Indians for the parts. From the U.S. Interior Department he got the address and telephone number of the Everglades National Park, which includes a Seminole reservation, and sent the manager there for tryouts (Paul Green to Tommy Rahner, 16 January 1965). The souvenir program for 1965 does not include production photographs. Production photographs from 1968 are the earliest to show a black in the cast, as one of the Indians, and Indians cannot be identified in the pictures. (*Cross and Sword* photograph file, Institute of Outdoor Drama, University of North Carolina, Chapel Hill).

4. For a meeting of the Florida Historical Society at the Ponce de Leon Hotel, where Green spoke on "the trials and tribulations encountered in researching and writing" *Cross and Sword* (Albert Manucy to Paul Green, 20 January 1965, and Green diary, 4 May 1965, PG-SHC). Rahner had already written to assure Loucille Plummer that the nonprofit organization producing *Cross and Sword*, which included two blacks, "has *not* had the perpetuation of segregation as one of its aims. Indeed, the amphitheatre . . . will be fully integrated. Only one set of facilities has been constructed for the use of all, and every performance will be open to anyone who cares to attend. There will be no de facto segregation in the sale of tickets, for everyone will be able to choose the seat he wishes and all seats will be reserved." Rahner was now filling staff positions and invited Plummer to encourage blacks to apply (copy of Tom Rahner to Loucille Plummer, 24 March 1965, PG-SHC). *Cross and Sword* played its first season, 27 June–5 September 1965, without racial incident but to small audiences. In 1992 it completed its twenty-eighth season.

---

1. Philip Lee Devin, Jr. (b. 1938), later in the Department of English at Swarthmore College but at the time technical director in the theater at the University of Virginia, was writing his dissertation on Green ("Form and Structure in Paul Green's Tragedies," Indiana University, 1967). During his research he visited Green several times, most recently in August, when he left a draft of the dissertation with the Greens. Later in the month Elizabeth returned the draft to him, with her notes on it.

2. In 1963 the Greens bought a farm, Windy Oaks, fronting Old Lystra Road, about

say about man and his habitancy in this universe. At least my characters were able to and in the wings and shadows I applauded.[3] As to the long-ago play "The Lord's Will," my remembering goes thus in answer to your query:[4] One day I got a note from the U.N.C. president, Harry W. Chase, asking me to drop into his office to see him. I went in student fear and trembling wondering what was wrong. He showed me a letter. It was from a big N.C. mill owner[5] who said he'd heard that the Carolina Playmakers were maligning his mill by touring the state with a play known as "The Lord's Will" and which claimed through one of its pallored, emaciated, and coughing characters that his consumption was due to the lint he breathed into his lungs from working in the mill. "This is false," said the letter, "and I wish you as president of our institution to have this play stopped, withdrawn"—or words to that effect. Dr. Chase looked at me, and I looked at him. (He had great doe eyes, eyes that smiled too at times.) "What do you want me to do?" I stammered. "Nothing," he said. "I thought you might be interested in hearing something of the effect your play is causing." "And you, sir?" I queried. He laughed, took the letter and laid it aside. "Keep on writing," he said. And so Hubert Heffner kept on night after night during the run coughing and maligning the mill owner,[6] who by the way was a trustee of the university, and into whose lower berth once in a little train wreck near Hillsborough, N.C., Elizabeth, pregnant, fell from her upper one.

"Good morning, Mr. Erwin."

---

five miles southeast of Chapel Hill. In December 1964 Watts Hill, Jr., bought their home on Greenwood Road (for $75,000). During the winter and spring of 1964–65 they fixed up the house at Windy Oaks and moved there in May 1965.

3. Green's new play, *Texas*, had completed its first season in Palo Duro Canyon, Texas, on 5 September.

4. "The Lord's Will" was one of the plays taken on statewide tour by the Carolina Playmakers in May 1922. In his dissertation Devin said the play aroused so much opposition that the Playmakers had to drop it from the tour, and Elizabeth, in her notes on the draft, said he was mistaken, that the Playmakers did not drop it. Devin wrote to her, asking for "the facts of the matter" so he could make the point that Green "broke away at the very beginning from convention and conventional practice" (Philip Devin to Elizabeth Green, 22 August 1966, PG-SHC).

5. An earlier draft of the present letter identifies him as William Allen Erwin of Durham, owner of Erwin Mills in Durham and elsewhere in the state.

6. Hubert Heffner played the lead in "The Lord's Will," but the character is a fanatical preacher (and healthy), not a consumptive mill worker.

"Good morning—well, bless my life, Elizabeth Green!"

Mr. Erwin and we became friends. He sent us $25 to buy a baby carriage.[7] Selah. He is long dead now, a grand millionaire church-goer and -maker gone to flourish by the River of Life.[8] Requiescat in pace!

Ever, Paul

By the way Chase was a strong defender of freedom. If he had been here I doubt the Speaker Ban law would ever have been passed.

## 298. To Margaret Harper[1]

[Windy Oaks, Old Lystra Road, Chapel Hill, N.C.]
9 September 1966

Dear Margaret—

Thank you for your kind letter and for the good news about the generous-minded sound consultant. Now I'm sure that with your concern and determi-

7. For Paul, Jr. (in earlier draft of letter), born on 14 January 1924.

8. William Erwin (1856–1932), prominent Episcopalian, had known Elizabeth's father when Dr. Lay presided over St. Mary's Episcopal School in Raleigh. Erwin opposed child labor and supported shorter working hours for mill hands. He built St. Joseph's Episcopal Church in Durham and a new sanctuary for Chapel of the Cross Episcopal Church in Chapel Hill.

---

1. Margaret Harper (1904 1991), of Canyon, Texas, read an article on Green, "His Theatre Is As Big As All Outdoors," *Reader's Digest* 77 (July 1960): 229–32, and immediately wrote to him: "The attitudes, the geography and the history of this part of the Panhandle of Texas would make a stunning symphonic drama, and the article about you in the *Reader's Digest* gives me courage to ask how such community creations are produced" (3 July 1960, PG-SHC). Thus Harper began a lengthy correspondence with Green along with arduous organizational work in Canyon, Amarillo, and other West Texas communities that led to the production of *Texas* in 1966. Over the years Green came to focus on the opportunity offered by the site of the theater for the use of sound and light effects. He helped locate the theater in Palo Duro Canyon, the stage backed by a curving canyon wall 600 feet high, and for the spectacular setting wrote a play incorporating the son et lumière techniques he first experienced in the old Roman amphitheater at Lyons in 1951 (see letter 234, n. 15) then studied more closely at a UNESCO conference on drama for large audiences in Athens in 1962 (see 282, n. 1). *Texas* opened its first season on 1 July 1966 and closed on 5 September. Green was present for a few days of work at the opening, then went back

nation some way will be found to bring the lighting effects too to a superb functioning. We really do want to leave our audiences gasping next year at the two finales.[2] We foremost and first put the amphitheatre at its present site with the express purpose of making this wonder background of nature participate theatrically and organically in our dramatic offering. Let's not stop until we do that. I guess I'll hear from Ray[3] soon as to final figures etc. for August and the few days in September.[4]

Love to all Paul

---

on 20 August to check the production. Other elements were in good shape, he reported to Harper on his return to Chapel Hill, but the sound and light effects disappointed him (25 August 1966). She replied that the sound was already better. Before the show closed she had flown out a sound expert from Arlington, Texas, who located the source of the problem. The man was so impressed by the show that he waived his $100 fee and brought his wife back for the closing performance. Harper felt "much relieved to have him interested and working" and only wished she could find a comparable expert with lights (Margaret Harper to Paul Green, 5 September 1966).

2. Act 1 closes with a thunderstorm in the canyon. A character has described such storms as "com[ing] up all of a sudden and break[ing] like a great—well, exploding battlefield of firearms." He remembers "hearing a piece of music back east that had a big symphony in it and a great chorus singing about the world and joy and about God." A friend tells him it was Beethoven's Ninth Symphony, and he continues: "That's the way I hear these storms out here . . . voices singing, a great orchestra going" (*Texas: A Symphonic Outdoor Drama of American Life* [New York: Samuel French, 1967], p. 60). Then the storm arrives, and Green's intention is suggested by the stage direction: "*The chorus and music serve as a background . . . for the light and sound display of the summer storm. The storm is filled with a lot of heat lightning as well as some long vertical zig-zag spearings of bolt lightning, intermittent bawlings of terrorized cattle, the surflike pounding of their hooves against the ground, the sporadic bursts of six-shooters as unseen cowboys strive to turn the flying herd. . . . The whole canyon at the rear . . . lights up in one great final burst and flare of flame and thunder. The chorus and orchestra conclude*" (ibid., pp. 68–69). The second finale is at the end of the play when all of the characters, their difficulties overcome, face "the great canyon background and out of their full hearts sing with the chorus and orchestra the praises of nature and God, as a light and sound display builds up. The display grows into a great deluge of flame and thunder. And then the spectacle fades out on the final word, 'Amen' " (ibid., p. 104).

3. Raymond Raillard, executive vice president in charge of business for the play.

4. Total attendance in 1966 was 61,100 (Institute of Outdoor Drama, University of

## 299. To Janet G. and John S. Catlin

[Windy Oaks, Old Lystra Road, Chapel Hill, N.C.]
17 October 1966

Dear Jan and Jack—[1]

We think of you a lot and look forward to the time you'll be coming for a visit and can tell us in more detail about the many things you are doing.[2] Mimi[3] and I have been very busy, she typing and seeing after her family correspondence. (Is this the way to divide this word?)[4] I've mailed off the revised script of *Texas* finally to the publisher—French.[5] Also I've sent about ¼ of a negro novel to Harpers.[6] If "they" like it, I'll go on with it, I suppose. If not, then I'll consider.[7] Already three symphonic drama projects are holler-

---

North Carolina, Chapel Hill). *Texas*, one of Green's most popular plays, completed its twenty-seventh season in 1992.

---

1. Janet, the Greens' youngest daughter, and John Catlin married at the Greens' home on 15 August 1964, while both were graduate students at the University of North Carolina, she in English, he in classics. They now lived in Norman, where Jack was a member of the classics department at the University of Oklahoma.

2. Janet came for a week in late November to take the comprehensive examination for her Ph.D. in English.

3. Elizabeth's nickname within the family.

4. Lacking space on a single line for "correspondence," Green divided the word after the first "e."

5. In the spring of 1967 Samuel French would publish *Texas*, as well as the songs from the play in *Texas Song-Book*.

6. "Tomorrow Will Be My Dancing Day," a portion of *Stormy Banks*.

7. "Tomorrow Will Be My Dancing Day" (title from the traditional carol "My Dancing Day") deals with the boyhood of Stormy Banks (for an episode, see "Fine Wagon," in Paul Green, *Salvation on a String and Other Tales of the South* [New York: Harper and Brothers, 1946], pp. 264–78), a black man hungry for education in a town like Chapel Hill during the early decades of the century. Never able to attend the university (for an episode, see "Education South," in Green, *Dog on the Sun*, pp. 155–69), he is eventually executed for murder and is discovered to have willed his body to the university medical school (Paul Green to Cass Canfield, 13 October 1966, PG-SHC). After reading "Tomorrow Will Be My Dancing Day," Canfield, president of Harper and Row, replied that he liked the material but preferred to wait for the whole novel (Cass Canfield to Paul Green, 22 November 1966). Green did not complete *Stormy Banks*. His next project was *Trumpet in the Land*, a symphonic drama about

ing.[8] You help create a movement and the movement recreates you—in its own image if you don't watch out. I'm trying to watch.[9]

We both send heartfuls of love! Doog

All goes well in Byrd and Sam's lovely beehive.[10] The bees are busy making honey—for what guests and at what feasts time the stage manager will say in his season, or maybe it is for their own repast. And this is good too.

## 300. To Constance Webb[1]

[Windy Oaks, Old Lystra Road, Chapel Hill, N.C.]

9 May 1967

Dear Miss Webb:

By separate mail I am sending you a copy of a local publication, *The North Carolina Anvil*, in which the original ending I wrote for the play *Native Son* is published.[2] You may be interested in having it.[3]

---

Moravian missionaries among Indians in Ohio around the time of the American Revolution, which he began to consider in the spring of 1967 (Paul Green to Rachel Redinger, 24 April 1967).

8. From the mid-1950s onward Green was swamped with invitations from throughout the country to write historically commemorative plays. At the time of the present letter the most active correspondence concerned a play about Billy Mitchell for the Milwaukee World Festival, a play about Andrew Jackson to commemorate his 200th birthday in 1967, and a play for Fort Macon on an island near Morehead City, North Carolina.

9. Despite his commitment to outdoor historical drama, Green retained an interest in the commercial theater. During the previous winter he revised *Native Son* for a Broadway production in the fall of 1966, but the producer, Sidney Bernstein, who staged Jean Genet's *The Blacks* in 1961 and Athol Fugard's *The Blood Knot* in 1964, died on 22 July 1966, and the production did not take place.

10. The Greens gave each of their children a lot in Greenwood, and their oldest daughter, Byrd, and her husband, Sam Cornwell, recently built a home there.

---

1. In preparation for her *Richard Wright: A Biography* (New York: Putnam, 1968), Constance Webb asked Green about his association with Wright during the dramatization of *Native Son* (2 March 1967, PG-SHC), and in a brief reply Green said he was too busy at present but would send her a full account "within the next few weeks. I'd

I have had to delay writing somewhat fully to you concerning my association with Richard Wright here at Chapel Hill because of the pressing of outside matters.[4] And even now I have to restrain my wordage for lack of time.

And I am sure that I don't remember too accurately many details of this association. I guess, however, that in the main things were as I report them here.[5]

Sometime after Wright's novel came out and was making a success, one of the producers of the Group Theatre[6] approached me about dramatizing it. I glanced rather hurriedly through the book and reported that at that time I wasn't in position to undertake it. Later Paul Reynolds, Wright's agent, got in touch with me about it and said that he had talked to Wright and he, Wright, would like for me to do it. Then I read the book pretty closely and was somewhat horrified at the brutal part in it dealing with the burning of Mary

---

like to go back and remember it and also have a copy for my files of that remembering" (14 March 1967).

2. *North Carolina Anvil* 1, no. 3 (2 May 1967): 4–5.

3. In its various versions the last scene of the play brings into focus the difference between Wright and Green on the central character, Bigger Thomas. The novel presents Bigger as a victim of racial oppression while in the play Green makes him aware of his partial responsibility for his fate. The *Anvil* text, a fourth or fifth version of the scene written over the winter of 1940–41 in consultation with Wright, exemplifies Green's interpretation. The first published text of the play (New York: Harper and Brothers, 1941) suggests the conclusion used in Orson Welles's production, a conclusion exaggerating Wright's view (for the produced ending, see Burns Mantle, ed., *Best Plays of 1940–41* [New York: Dodd, Mead, 1941], pp. 61–63). In 1966 Green revised the play for an aborted production (letter 299, n. 9) and in the final scene presented a striking example of his view, then published that version in William Brasmer and Dominick Console, eds., *Black Drama, An Anthology* (Columbus, Ohio: C. E. Merrill, 1970), pp. 69–177. The final version of the scene, the *Anvil* text with cuts, is in the script used for the inaugural production of *Native Son* in the Paul Green Theatre on the UNC campus on 29 September 1978 (New York: Samuel French, 1980).

4. During the past month and a half Green spent much time trying to win support for a bill in the state legislature to abolish capital punishment, a measure defeated on 27 April 1967.

5. For details of the collaboration, see letters 147, 150, 153, 154, 155, 156, and 158.

6. Cheryl Crawford.

Dalton's body.[7] But I was deeply interested in Wright's Dostoevskian character-digging (the dialogue between him and the lawyer Max)[8] especially in the last pages.[9]

I finally told Reynolds I would undertake the job but I had some requests of my own to make, namely, that I be allowed freedom in making the Communist matter in the book more comic than Wright had it, and further that I have freedom to introduce some new characters if needed, and still further that before Bigger Thomas died he should come to some sort of recognition that he too as a human being had participated in his own fate.

The requirements were agreed to, and I asked Wright to come to Chapel Hill, if he would, and be available for discussion as I proceeded with the dramatization.

He came up from Mexico, as I remember, and arrived pretty much upset due to his rough inspection handling at the border.[10]

Meanwhile I had arranged with the University of North Carolina to have good working quarters on the campus[11] where, with my secretary,[12] Wright and I could get down to concentrated work. The Chancellor[13] readily agreed and said he was glad to have Mr. Wright visit the University and he knew that the color question in my handling would not arise.

My house was somewhat crowded with my wife and four children, and so I got Dick a place to stay in a good boarding house where a lot of the Negro teachers stayed.[14] He seemed satisfied. And so we went to work.

He was most cooperative, and we got along very well together. My secretary was much taken with his talent. She aspired to some sort of literary career for

7. To dispose of it after Bigger kills the drunken girl in a moment of panic.

8. Who takes on Bigger's defense and sees him as a product of class and racial discrimination.

9. Where Max visits Bigger on death row, the setting of the play's final scene.

10. Using Wright's notes, Webb gives a vivid account of his humiliating train trip through the South in the summer of 1940 (*Richard Wright*, pp. 199–205).

11. In 201 Bynum Hall (Ouida Campbell, "Bigger Is Reborn," *Carolina Magazine* 70 [October 1940]: 22).

12. Ouida Campbell.

13. Robert House.

14. In Sunset, on the western edge of town near the intersection of West Rosemary Street and Sunset Drive (Daphne Athas, "The Wrong Side of the Tracks," *Spectator*, 30 April 1987, p. 5).

herself and was watchful and greedy for every creative discussion he and I had about writing in general and the book in particular.

An amusing item came in. One day I happened to realize that the names of too many of the characters in the book began with the letter B—Bigger, Bertha,[15] Boris,[16] etc.

"Now I wonder why I did that?" Dick laughed.

Yes, we had a good time together.

Now and then we would get in touch with John Houseman in New York. He and Orson Welles were to produce the play—if they liked the script—as one of their Mercury Theatre productions. Welles was in Hollywood or Europe or somewhere.[17]

Once or twice I asked Dick to try his hand at writing a scene. He wrote two, I remember. They were beautiful but lacking in any dramatic climb so I couldn't use them.

We got the first draft finished in about four weeks.

During the last week trouble arose—not between Dick and myself—but about him. (It may not be wise to report this in your book, but I put it down for my record.)

My secretary who was literarily inclined, as I say, and also had a strong social consciousness decided to give a party for Wright in her home. She lived in a mill town suburb of Chapel Hill,[18] and the attitude of her neighbors was not quite so liberal as that of some of the faculty closer to the university campus. She didn't let me know she was giving this party and I only learned of it a day later because of the reaction that followed the gathering at her house, attended by some of her "literary" white friends—"a mixed party." Whether the party was a loud one or not I don't know, but the next day some of her neighbors complained to the University about her action and the complaint came on to me by way of the Chancellor. Wright and I were working on the last scene of the play that day. Late in the afternoon the phone rang. It was the Chancellor.

"Paul, you've just played thunder," his voice said.

"What is it now, Mr. Chancellor, what have I done?"

15. Bigger's girlfriend.

16. Max.

17. In Hollywood finishing *Citizen Kane*.

18. Carrboro.

"Well, your white secretary entertained this colored writer in her house last night, and a lot of people are up in arms about it."

"Good gracious!"

"Yes, it's so, and Paul, you've got to do something about it."

It so happened that we were right on the last part of the play and Wright had a reservation on the train to go to New York the next afternoon. I told the Chancellor this.

"But tomorrow afternoon is a long ways off," he said.

"What do you want me to do?" I queried.

"I want you to get him out of town. When you asked me for office space for you and him to work here, I knew that students and faculty would see him going and coming out of Bynum Hall and might wonder what was going on, but I trusted you to handle everything and not let anything like this happen."

Fortunately the phone was in the room adjoining the one we were working in. I closed the door and the Chancellor and I continued our talk, Wright not hearing any of it or suspecting anything. (I never did let Dick know of this disturbance and how his visit might have had unhappy circumstances.) The Chancellor then told me over the phone that several fellows—not students—were at that moment gathering in the local drugstore down the street[19] and were conferring as to what to do about and with Wright.

"They are talking about running him out of town and doing it tonight," he said. "The drugstore owner, a good alumnus,[20] has just phoned in here and told me what is happening. Paul, you have got to go down there and meet with those fellows and do something, do something, I tell you! This thing could get out of hand and give the University a black eye."

"I'm not thinking so much about the University," I replied hotly. "I'm thinking about Richard Wright. I don't want anything bad to happen to him. We have been getting along well together and for this to come up right at the last is rough, mighty rough. I will do everything I can. I will go down there right now."

I went back into the room where Dick and my secretary were chatting and told them that since it was five o'clock, quitting time for the day, we might as well knock off.

I took him to his boarding house in my car and then hurried down to the

19. Eubanks' Drugstore on Franklin Street, a block from Bynum Hall (typescript of Jennie T. Hall interview with Paul Green, 28 February 1970, p. 63, NCC).

20. Robert A. Eubanks, Jr.

drugstore. Four or five men were still there. One of them, a 6-foot 6-inch former University boxer, was in charge.[21] He had a pistol in his pocket. I could see the handle of it. When I walked in, he met me with blazing eyes. I got him by the arm and finally persuaded him to come outside where he and I could talk alone.

I pleaded with him to let everything remain quiet and let Richard Wright go back to New York free and unharmed and with no knowledge of this intended plan to get rid of him. The sullen giant refused to promise anything but said he would think about it, and he did agree to send the other fellows in the drugstore on about their business.

I went with him back into the store and he kept his word, saying, "You fellows go on. Paul and I have got some more talking to do. I'm not promising him a thing, you understand, but we've got some more talking."

They left and the giant later left also.

As soon as it became dark, I drove across town to a side street near where Wright was boarding. I spent most of the night concealed in a hedge near the house ready to do what I could in opposing any possible nightrider action. No action came.

You may ask why I didn't go to the local police and ask for protection for Wright. The answer is simple. I wasn't sure of their "protection."

The next day he and I finished our job and I took him to the train. He had been so helpful that I asked him to share the credit with me for the dramatization. Paul Reynolds suggested that my name appear first and that Wright receive 55 percent of the royalties since it was his original story and that I receive 45 percent. So it was.

Later in New York we had to do some revising of the script here and there and I invited Dick to work in the hotel on 48th Street[22] with me. I spoke to the manager and he said it was all right. About the third or fourth day the phone rang and this irate manager called up from below wanting to see me. I went down and he bawled me out.

"Mr. Green," he said, "this has got to stop. This Negro man comes here every day and rides up in the elevator with our guests and all kinds of complaints are being voiced. I don't want the gentleman to come here anymore—please."

21. Hugh Wilson, a relative of Green (Jennie T. Hall interview with Paul Green, 28 February 1970, p. 64, NCC).

22. Hotel Bristol, at 129 West 48th Street.

"But we are working on a script and we need a few more days."

"Not another day," he said. "When you first asked me, I thought it was just for one meeting, but this constant thing won't do, won't do."

Evidently Dick had suspected something, for at this moment he appeared and the manager took him aside and put the matter squarely up to him. Dick came over to me and laughed—a deep down bitter laugh no doubt.

"Let's go back to Chapel Hill," he said, "where a man is free."

We went over to Harper Brothers who were publishing the play and finished our work in one of their offices.[23]

Rehearsals began, and then I ran smack into Orson Welles' theory of tragedy—pathos rather than *true* tragedy.

"I want this play to end," he said, "with Bigger Thomas behind the bars standing there with his arms reached out and up, his hands clinging to the bars—yes, yes, the crucified one, crucified by the Jim Crow world in which he lived." And so on.

Wright then agreed with Welles. I argued but finally yielded to Dick since it was his book and so took the train back home alone.

As my cab took me to Pennsylvania Station, I noticed a sign painter working up on the outer wall—as I remember—of the St. James Theatre.[24] He had already painted *Native Son* in big letters and under that the splashing names of Green and Wright as authors of the drama. I learned that a day or so later Orson saw this and let out a scream. He had our names erased and in still bigger splashing letters "Orson Welles' NATIVE SON" was put up.

Now that I look back on my short association with Dick Wright I groan inside that I didn't have more understanding of what he was suffering in the white man's world. Maybe we could have got closer together, maybe not.

We used to talk a lot, even so, about America and the people in it and the future. One day he told me he was planning to leave this country and move to Russia. Then for the first time I learned of his membership in the Communist Party. It happened that on that same day, or about that time, he got a notice concerning his income tax. He opened his purse to show me the notice and I saw he had it stuffed with fifty and one hundred dollar bills. As I remember he said he owed $8,000 more in income tax.

And then I sort of blew my top at him. I called attention to the fact that the American people appreciated his literary ability, they bought his book by the

23. At 49 East 33d Street.

24. Where the play opened on 24 March 1941.

thousands of copies, he was honored, and so on and so on. And that already he was a leader of his race and if he fled the scene, he would let so many of them down and he would let people like me down too—and so on.

I don't think my argument made any impression on him. He didn't go to Russia but later he did move to Paris[25] and issued a statement that there was more freedom in one block of that city than in all of the United States—or words to that effect.[26]

Yes, as I say, I wish I had understood our mutual world involvement a little better than I did.

How shocked I was to have the phone ring one night prior to the opening of the play in New York and have Brooks Atkinson[27] tell me that he had a piece from Wright which they had hoped to publish in the *Times* the Sunday before the opening and a lot of it was an attack on me.

"What!"

"Yes," he said, "it's a long piece, several thousand words long."

I gulped once or twice and then went on hotly—"Well I know it's beautifully written—and what the hell! If Wright attacks me in it, okay! I guess I failed him somehow—"

"We're not certain about publishing it," said Atkinson.

"Go ahead and publish it!" I almost shouted.

"We may," said Atkinson, "we may not."

The following Sunday I eagerly and yet forebodingly looked through the theatre section of the New York *Times*, but couldn't find it. The next Sunday the same.

If it was ever published I didn't see it.[28]

I have chatted too long. But once more I say I loved Richard Wright as a man and an artist, and I continue to grieve that it takes so long for us as a

25. In early August 1947.

26. Probably the 1950 essay "I Choose Exile," unpublished but circulated (Michel Fabre, *The World of Richard Wright* [Jackson: University Press of Mississippi, 1985], p. 149).

27. Drama critic for the *New York Times.*

28. Apparently it was not. Wright's only newspaper article relating to the production is "Theatrical Folk Seem Odd to the Author of *Native Son,*" *New York World-Telegram,* 22 March 1941, p. 6, cols. 1–3, in which he playfully ridicules theater people in general and Welles in particular, then ends by dissociating himself from the theater, a medium he as a novelist finds uncongenial.

people to get over our prejudices and reach out a helping hand and receive the same sort of hand in return.

I'm sure your book will do a lot to make Wright live even though he is dead. But like the fallen and too early dead young men in any brutal war, he will know nothing of it! Alas, alas![29]

Sincerely,

## 301. To Donald Gallup[1]

[Windy Oaks, Old Lystra Road, Chapel Hill, N.C.]

19 June 1967

Dear Mr. Gallup:

I am delighted that Mrs. Barrett H. Clark has sent the papers of her husband to your university. As to my letters in the collection, I think Mrs. Clark in her kindness, and maybe it is just that, is in error. I have no objection whatever to anyone's consulting them. No doubt there are personal matters in them, but what the heck!—all of us make our records on earth such as they are and they are irrevocable anyway and why try to control them after the fact. So, so far as I am concerned they are wide open.[2]

With best greetings and regards,

29. In her biography Webb only mentions the dramatization of *Native Son* (*Richard Wright*, p. 189) and makes no reference to the present letter.

---

1. Green's longtime friend Barrett Clark died in 1953, and recently his wife had turned over his books and papers to the Beinecke Rare Book and Manuscript Library at Yale University. The largest author file in the Clark collection was Green's, with forty-one published works, several typescripts, and 293 letters (1925–52). Donald Gallup (b. 1913), distinguished editor and bibliographer and curator of American literature at the Beinecke Library, wrote to Green: "Mrs. Clark tells me that you are concerned about the possible future use of your letters to Mr. Clark at Yale. I have assured Mrs. Clark . . . that the Yale Library will consider your letters . . . as restricted and not available for use without specific written permission from you in each instance. If there are any additional safeguards you wish us to impose to insure the continued privacy of this correspondence, please do not hesitate to let me know" (12 June 1967, PG-SHC).

2. Gallup replied: "Thank you very much for your letter about the Barrett H. Clark papers. Would that all authors were as sensibly philosophical about their letters! The lives of librarians would be enormously simplified and our dispositions would certainly improve" (20 June 1967, PG-SHC).

## 302. To Dean Rusk[1]

[Windy Oaks, Old Lystra Road, Chapel Hill, N.C.]
13 October 1967

Dear Mr. Rusk:

Last night a group of us heard your strong and determined defense of America's Vietnam policy with your proportionate attack on the critics of the present administration. After we had cut off the TV, we all rather woefully considered your call for honoring our compact with Vietnam, the while we remembered a more solemn and prior compact made by our country with the United Nations which renounced war as a method of settling quarrels between countries.[2]

Alas, alas for America—when day after day and night after night our people are subjected to a rain of violence and shoddy Madison Avenue declarations of values along with half truths and the full duplicity of complete untruths memorandaed forth from the desks and the mouths of our leaders there in Washington!

I have just been looking at a picture of President Johnson holding up his little grandson,[3] his face alight with love and pride. But this love and pride become a mockery to me as I recollect that at the same moment he holds his little grandson aloft he is through our obedient young war pilots blowing other little sons to quivering morsel bits there in Vietnam. Of course the little Asiatic babies are of a different color, and according to you, their fathers and brothers are a threat to the security of this mighty nation. No sir!

This country was meant for better things than this!

I know the sharp reply could be a pleading of the cause, the cause, the

1. The previous evening Green and a group of friends had watched a televised speech and press conference in which Dean Rusk (b. 1909), U.S. secretary of state, vigorously defended U.S. military action in Vietnam. Rusk said treaty obligations under the Southeast Asia Treaty Organization (established February 1955) and U.S. national security (threatened by Communist China) forced the United States to support South Vietnam. He added that critics of U.S. policy were ignorant and naive (like "a baby in politics"), were prolonging the war by giving North Vietnam hope of American withdrawal, and were increasing the danger of nuclear catastrophe by misleading China and the Soviet Union about American resolve (text of speech and press conference, *New York Times*, 13 October 1967, pp. 14–15).

2. U.N. Charter (1945), chapter 1, article 2:3.

3. Patrick Lyndon Nugent, two months old, son of Luci Baines and Patrick Nugent (*New York Times*, 12 August 1967, p. 11, cols. 2–3).

cause! Namely, the threat to our security. This is the way it always goes, always a cause for killing people whether armed or helpless. But the true cause is the cause of man himself. Is it not that? Take any young man we are helping to murder in Vietnam. Is there any cause greater than the sanctity of his own life?

I have traveled and lectured all around in Southeast Asia, I have visited in Russia and studied and roamed through much of Europe on Guggenheim Fellowships, and I have seen the fermenting and mixing of man manifold on this earth, and I know now if I know anything that the time is long past for the settling of arguments by wars and mutilations.

If this nation of ours would tend to its business at home—build up a just and vibrant society of its own—we could become the moral admiration of the world. And the urge to friendship and imitation would be completely compelling. But we are now the fear of the world.

As Paul Claudel, the French Ambassador, agreed when I visited him in the Alps—America is by far the most physically powerful nation on earth. "But my fear and the fear of much of the world is," he said, "that your great nation will not have wisdom enough to go guidingly along with its power."[4]

As I say, alas, alas for our poor country![5]

Sincerely yours,

## 303. To V. R. Osha[1]

[Windy Oaks, Old Lystra Road, Chapel Hill, N.C.]
20 October 1967

Dear Mr. Osha:

You wrote me quite a hot letter about my communication to Dean Rusk, and though I can't agree with what you say, I do appreciate the fact that you

4. For the visit, see "Paul Claudel," in Green, *Dramatic Heritage*, pp. 132–46.

5. Green sent this letter to leading newspapers throughout the state (see letter 303).

---

1. Green's letter to Dean Rusk (letter 302), published in state newspapers, drew numerous responses, most of them sympathetic. But the *Greensboro Daily News* ran a biting parody of him as Saul Serene of Chapel Hill by letterwriter Thomas A. Schmidt (21 October 1967, sec. A, p. 8, cols. 4–5). V. R. Osha also disagreed with Green. He saw the letter to Rusk in his hometown paper, the *Asheville Citizen*, on 18 October 1967 (p. 4, cols. 6–7) and sent Green a hot response. "Alas! What stupidity can come from so much 'education,' " he began. "Alas! That some rich Americans left money to the Guggenheim Foundation to be wasted on such as you. You have been a freeloader,

took time enough to speak up for your belief. I guess the basic difference between us is that I don't believe in killing people to establish a power base in Asia, and you do. I read over and over words that fell from the lips of a young man named Jesus of Nazareth, and they continue to make sense as to the brotherhood of man and the squalling infantilism that sees a communist threat everywhere one turns. I guess I needn't go on, for I have no intention of spanking back at you for the spanking you sent to me.

If you are down this way sometime, give me a ring and let's have a good friendly talk on these matters that mean so much to us the living who before too many years will be the dead.[2]

Sincerely yours,

---

now you come back from your pointless peregrinations to bite the hand that has been feeding you." After that the letter got nasty (in the Vietnam conflict Osha wanted "to negotiate after we have whipped the sonsofbitches") and continued for a page and a half before ending (with perhaps unintended ambiguity): "You say, alas for our poor country. I say, alas poor Paul Green, with so much education he cannot see the trees from the forest" (18 October 1967, PG-SHC).

2. No record suggests that Osha came for a visit.

# Symphonic Drama, Vietnam, and Folklore, 1968–1981

Winter–Spring 1968

Supports Eugene McCarthy, antiwar candidate for Democratic presidential nomination. Also revises *Tread the Green Grass* as *Sing All a Green Willow* and *Shroud My Body Down* as *The Honeycomb.*

Summer 1968

Revises *Johnny Johnson*, antiwar play to which producers are turning with renewed interest.

28 March 1969

*Sing All a Green Willow* opens in Chapel Hill to commemorate fiftieth anniversary of Carolina Playmakers.

29 March 1969

Holds forum in Playmakers' Theater (built in 1850, used as a theater since 1924) to launch drive for new theater on Chapel Hill campus.

Summer–Fall 1969

Works on *Trumpet in the Land.*

3 July 1970

*Trumpet in the Land* opens in New Philadelphia, Ohio.

September 1970

Visits Scotland and France.

Winter–Summer 1971

Works on revisions and production matters for the seven plays running during the summer: *The Lost Colony, The Common Glory, Wilderness Road, The Stephen Foster Story, Cross and Sword, Texas,* and *Trumpet in the Land.*

Fall–Winter 1971

Works on folklore collection. Begins *Drumbeats in Georgia.*

30 June 1973
Drumbeats in Georgia opens on Jekyll Island, Georgia.

October 1973
In Mexico for research leading to *Louisiana Cavalier.*

1974–75
Works on folklore collection. Writes *Louisiana Cavalier* and *We the People.*

26 February 1976
*The Highland Call* revived in Fayetteville, North Carolina, to celebrate the national bicentennial.

7 April 1976
North Carolina School of the Arts holds a convocation in Green's honor, and Governor James Holshouser proclaims the day Paul Green Day in North Carolina.

19 June 1976
*Louisiana Cavalier* opens at Natchitoches, Louisiana.

6 August 1976
*We the People* opens at Columbia, Maryland.

Fall–Winter 1976
Writes *The Lone Star.*

29 June 1977
*The Lone Star* opens at Galveston, Texas.

October 1977
Visits Moscow, Leningrad, and Helsinki (where *Johnny Johnson* has played in repertory of Finnish National Theatre since 1974).

29 September 1978
The Paul Green Theatre at UNC dedicated with production of revised *Native Son.*

June 1979
Begins correspondence with U.S. Senator Jesse Helms on disarmament and relations between the United States and the Soviet Union.

10 May 1980
Senator Helms visits Green at Windy Oaks, and they spend the

afternoon talking about their common background and differing views on world affairs.

April 1981

At Memorial Hospital in Chapel Hill for ten days because of heart irregularities.

4 May 1981

Dies of heart failure during afternoon nap at home.

## 304. To Lois Ann Hobbs[1]

[Windy Oaks, Old Lystra Road, Chapel Hill, N.C.]
22 March 1968

I AM VERY SORRY PRIOR COMMITMENTS KEEP ME FROM BEING WITH YOU. ALL OF US WHO HAVE WITNESSED OF RECENT YEARS AND DAYS THE GREED OF AMBITIOUS AND SELFISH MEN BUYING AND SEIZING POSITIONS OF LEADERSHIP FOR THE SAKE OF POWER AND NOT FOR THE SAKE OF SERVICE TO MANKIND AND WITH WOEFUL WASTE AND SUFFERING TO THE WHOLE WORLD[2] NOW WELCOME THE APPEARANCE OF SENATOR EUGENE MCCARTHY ON THE AMERICAN POLITICAL SCENE. HE IS AN HONEST AND COURAGEOUS MAN, A TRUE IDEALIST IN THE BEST AND MOST PRACTICAL SENSE OF THE WORD. HE IS A STATESMAN, AND THIS COUNTRY WILL BE LUCKY TO HAVE HIM ITS PRESIDENT. SO WILL THE WORLD FOR THAT MATTER. AND THAT HE CAN BE IF THE PEOPLE WHO BELIEVE IN HIM WORK HARD ENOUGH. I BELIEVE IN HIM AND WHAT HE STANDS FOR, AND I AM WORKING AS HARD AS I CAN.[3]

PAUL GREEN

1. On 30 November 1967 Senator Eugene McCarthy of Minnesota, an opponent of American involvement in Vietnam, announced that he would challenge President Johnson for the Democratic presidential nomination in the 1968 election. The first test of McCarthy's strength was the New Hampshire primary on 12 March 1968, and Green and others considered it an exciting moral victory when McCarthy lost to the president by only 300 votes (28,721 for McCarthy; 29,021 for Johnson). Lois Ann Hobbs of Greensboro, a Quaker whose husband was president of Guilford College, also supported McCarthy and invited Green to a private meeting designed to secure endorsements and money for the campaign (Lois Hobbs to Laurence Avery, [19 December 1988]).

2. Green was thinking of Robert Kennedy of Massachusetts, who in 1965 took up residence in New York to run for the Senate from that state, then jumped into the Democratic presidential race on 16 March following McCarthy's strong showing in the New Hampshire primary. In a press release sent to McCarthy headquarters Green called Kennedy "a political opportunist of the most cynical sort" (11 April 1968, PG-SHC).

3. Green sent money with this statement (Lois Hobbs to Laurence Avery, [19 December 1988]) and continued to speak out for McCarthy through the turbulent Democratic National Convention in Chicago, 26–29 August 1968, from which Vice President Hubert Humphrey emerged as the presidential nominee to face Richard Nixon in November.

## 305. To Abbott Van Nostrand

[Windy Oaks, Old Lystra Road, Chapel Hill, N.C.]
31 May 1968

Dear Abbott:

It was good seeing you even for a short time the other day,[1] and I was pleased to see you looking so well. Now and then I get rumors of *Johnny Johnson* productions here and there about the country. They are rare.[2] In this time of anti-war feeling maybe we could arrange it so that the play could have more productions. I didn't think of it while I was with you, but what do you think of my going through the play and taking out the musical difficulties and leaving a script that could be produced as a straight play. I see in different catalogues that the musical version is advertised as "Kurt Weill's *Johnny Johnson.*" This is okay from the point of view of the music, just as the ads covering DuBose Heyward's *Porgy* speak of it as "George Gershwin's *Porgy.*" *Johnny Johnson* as a musical drama is very difficult to produce, requiring an orchestra, etc. As a straight play, I don't think it would be too difficult. I could prepare the straight version in a short time. What do you think?[3]

I will within the next few months be able to get to you the two somewhat avant garde plays I mentioned to you. They are both completions of half-finished jobs of long ago. The title of one of them, the 50th Anniversary play for the Carolina Playmakers, is *Sing All a Green Willow.*[4] I haven't yet got a title for the second one.[5]

There is plenty to do. I have staked out my future quite a bit as to outdoor dramas to come—Sam Houston in LaGrange, Texas, (collaborating with Kermit Hunter),[6] a Jekyll Island musical on the "robber barons" for which I

1. In New York City.

2. Green was aware of two in California during the year, in Los Angeles and in Sacramento (folder 2028, PG-SHC).

3. Van Nostrand liked the idea (Abbott Van Nostrand to Paul Green, 20 June 1968, PG-SHC), and later in the summer Green sent him "the new and revised non-musical version of *Johnny Johnson*" (Paul Green to Abbott Van Nostrand, 3 August 1968). This version has not been published.

4. A revision of *Tread the Green Grass*, produced for the anniversary celebration on 28, 29, and 30 March 1969, but not published.

5. Later entitled *The Honeycomb*, a revision of *Shroud My Body Down.*

6. Became *The Lone Star*, which Green wrote alone. It played each summer at Galveston Island State Park, Texas, from 1977 until 1989.

am thinking of getting Richard Adler to collaborate,[7] and the Ohio religious drama on which I am now working.[8] As I said, I hope within two or three years to have a sort of steady royalty income into your office of $25,000 annually.[9]

I am sorry you are losing some of your old reliable standbys[10] but there are always good men coming on, the training of them being the problem of course.

Best greetings as always,

P.S. Could someone in your office tell me who Douglas Turner Ward is and how I can get in touch with him. I have just read two of his little plays put out by the Dramatists Play Service, "Happy Ending" and "Day of Absence." They are terrific. Is he a Negro?[11]

7. Became *Drumbeats in Georgia* (unpublished), which focused on James Oglethorpe and the founding of the colony. Green wrote it alone, and it played at the Jekyll Island Amphitheatre during the summers of 1973 and 1974.

8. *Trumpet in the Land*, which focuses on David Zeisberger, eighteenth-century Moravian missionary to the Delaware tribe in Ohio. The play has been produced at the Tuscarawas Valley Amphitheatre in New Philadelphia, Ohio, since the summer of 1970.

9. Green's royalty income for the previous year was $19,368.16 ($960.86 from amateur productions, $18,407.30 from *The Common Glory, The Stephen Foster Story, Cross and Sword*, and *Texas* (Samuel French financial statement for 1967, PG-SHC).

10. In the Samuel French office staff.

11. Douglas Turner Ward, black playwright from New Orleans, with two associates produced his companion one-act satires "Happy Ending" and "Day of Absence" for a long off-Broadway run in 1966. Out of the experience Ward wrote "American Theater: For Whites Only?," *New York Times*, 14 August 1966, sec. 2, p. 1, cols. 1–5; p. 3, cols. 6–8, which prompted a grant from the Ford Foundation that allowed Ward and others to organize the Negro Ensemble Company on Manhattan's East Side as a training school and producing organization for blacks in the theater. When Green read Ward's description of the company ("Being Criticized Was to Be Expected," *New York Times*, 1 September 1968, sec. 2, p. 1, cols. 4–6; p. 3, cols. 6–8), he was eager for French to offer them the revised *Native Son* for production. "They call mainly for Negro authors," he recognized, but "if any question should arise . . . you could tell them that I am almost as dark as Richard Wright himself and for all I know may have the common blood of humanity in my veins along with all races whatsoever" (Paul Green to Abbott Van Nostrand, 9 September 1968, PG-SHC). The Negro Ensemble Company did not do *Native Son*.

## 306. To Romulus Linney[1]

[Windy Oaks, Old Lystra Road, Chapel Hill, N.C.]
20 July 1968

Dear Rom—

I have been traveling up and down the country these past weeks[2] and have been away from my mail. Now I am back again. Among the books and letters is your *The Sorrows of Frederick* with its beautiful and much appreciated inscription.[3] I've just finished reading the play and sit astonished at the reach and vividness of your imagination. What a thing you've pulled off! And then there are mergins[4] of punch thoughts like sparklers caught in the fabric of the whole piece. Its New York production ought to help stretch the boundaries of the modern theatre a whale of a lot. I'll see it wherever it comes on.[5]

Affectionately,

1. Romulus Linney (b. 1930), playwright and novelist and long a friend of Green, sent him an inscribed copy of *The Sorrows of Frederick* (1966), a play he began in 1961 at Manteo where he spent the summer following a year of teaching at UNC.

2. To the various outdoor plays.

3. "Dear Paul, I don't know whether or not you will approve this play of mine, but I do know that there is a great deal of you and *The Lost Colony* in its bones, for it was conceived one summer in Manteo. For your kindness to me, and for your work, which is a part of me, many many thanks. Rom" (flyleaf, *The Sorrows of Frederick*, Paul Green Collection, Rare Books Collection, Wilson Library, University of North Carolina, Chapel Hill).

4. Dialect term pronounced (with accent on the first syllable) *mer-* (as in *mur*der) *-gins* (*g* as in *g*et) and meaning many, or millions. Also spelled "murgins" (*Paul Green's Wordbook: An Alphabet of Reminiscence* [Chapel Hill: Paul Green Foundation with Appalachian Consortium Press, 1990]).

5. *The Sorrows of Frederick*, first performed at the Mark Taper Forum in Los Angeles in July 1967, was not done in New York or London, but would have a run in October 1969 in Düsseldorf, West Germany. Its second production was at the East Carolina University Theater in Greenville, North Carolina, in February 1969, where Green saw a performance on Saturday night, 15 February (note on Edgar Loessin to Paul Green, 31 January 1969, PG-SHC).

## 307. To Gerald W. Johnson

[Windy Oaks, Old Lystra Road, Chapel Hill, N.C.]
22 January 1969

Dear Gerald:

I am back to my mail again and find your most dynamic and ever-youthful words put on a letter page to me coming all with the same fervor and drive with which you put them down on pages in a book.

You are more than kind to take time to write me about the issue of the little *North Carolina Journal of Folklore*[1] which printed quite a wad of my huge folklore collection entitled *Words and Ways*.[2]

I have had a lot of fun in times past writing down the customs, superstitions and so on of the Cape Fear Basin people—the Basin containing some 8,000 square miles and reaching up toward Greensboro, Hillsboro and Chapel Hill and on around to the edge of the Neuse River crest close by Raleigh and with enclosing arms on out to sea.[3]

The above journal, so Dick Walser[4] tells me, has some 250 subscribers. The reaction to what was published—not only from you but from other people,

1. *North Carolina Folklore* 16 (December 1968).

2. Johnson said he picked up *Words and Ways* the night after Christmas and "read a few pages with, I must admit, only a mild interest, but then the damned thing grabbed me by the scruff of the neck and took off down the road, and I wound up breathless at 3 o'clock in the morning! Lord, how it cavorts and prances! It knocks the dust out of the floor-boards and rattles the window-sashes. . . . Such a burst of exuberant vitality I have not encountered in many a day. I realize, of course, that the effect is heightened by a literary craftsmanship so smooth that it vanishes quite, but the best artificer can't do much unless he applies his tools to good material, and you certainly had it. You have embedded in amber a gaudy winged creature that will be a sight for sore eyes long after you—

with the angels stand,
A crown upon your forehead, a harp within your hand."
(Gerald Johnson to Paul Green, 27 December 1968, PG-SHC)

3. Since the 1920s Green had jotted down unusual words and phrases, folk cures, customs, beliefs, and stories he remembered or encountered from the Cape Fear River valley. Most of his own plays and stories grew out of that material, and in the early 1960s he began concentrated work on it, adding and fleshing out entries and giving them a loose alphabetical organization.

4. Who selected the items for *Words and Ways*.

though yours was much the best for me—has been such as to indicate that I might well go ahead and publish a volume of this anecdotal and customs material without waiting to have Duke University Press (which has expressed interest in the whole) or The University of North Carolina Press take a stab or not at it. What do you think? Who might be a likely publisher?[5]

Long may you continue in your light-giving and life-giving work!

Elizabeth joins me in best love to you and Kathryn,[6]

## 308. To Frank Durham[1]

[Windy Oaks, Old Lystra Road, Chapel Hill, N.C.]
13 March 1969

Dear Frank:

I am delighted that you are doing something about Julia Peterkin. She was a good writer and a good friend to me, and I rejoice in any life-giving happening for her memory. If you could persuade her son down there at Fort Motte Plantation[2] to let loose of her letters and manuscripts, including the manuscript of an unfinished novel, for placing in our archives here or the archives at the University of South Carolina or somewhere, we all would be even more in your debt. I have urged on him the need for some sort of preserving action, but he smiles and says that if his mother had wanted such a

5. Both university presses wanted to reduce the size of the collection, which had grown to over 2,000 typed pages, but Green wanted it published complete and at his death had not found a publisher. In 1990 the Appalachian Consortium Press in cooperation with the Paul Green Foundation published the complete text as *Paul Green's Wordbook: An Alphabet of Reminiscence.*

6. Johnson's wife.

---

1. Frank Durham (b. 1913), on the Carolina Playmakers' staff (1935–37) after graduating from UNC, then in the English department at the University of South Carolina, edited the *South Carolina Review* and asked Green for a play or article for the journal. He suggested a piece on Green's association with *The Reviewer* and to jog Green's memory mentioned his own forthcoming book, *Collected Short Stories of Julia Peterkin* (1970), which included two stories ("Maum Lou" and "Manners") first published in *The Reviewer* during Green's editorship in 1925 (Frank Durham to Paul Green, 4 March 1969, PG-SHC).

2. Lang Syne, the Peterkin plantation, lay along the Congaree River near Fort Motte, South Carolina.

thing done, she would have said so before she died.[3] Pfui! His wife is on our side. She used to be on the library faculty here at UNC.[4]

Congratulations too on *The South Carolina Review.* You are very kind to ask me to contribute to it. I simply do not have time now to sit down to write anything new or recall my association with *The Reviewer.* When I get back from a trip I have to make now,[5] I will look in my files and maybe I will find something already written and unpublished which I could touch up and you would find palatable.[6]

Hope to see you more and more.[7]

Affectionately,

## 309. To Howard Richardson[1]

[Windy Oaks, Old Lystra Road, Chapel Hill, N.C.]
3 April 1969

Dear Howard:

It sure was good to see you again. Your face still so young and fresh brought back memories of our happy association long ago—and not too long, of course—here at Chapel Hill. Congratulations on all the fine work you have been doing and continue to do.[2] If the madmen in the Pentagon and Kremlin

3. In 1961.

4. Genevieve Chandler, wife of Peterkin's son, William, earned an M.A. in library science from UNC in 1951. Peterkin's papers are now housed in several libraries, the largest group in the Lilly Library at the University of Indiana.

5. To New York City for a few days around 20 March.

6. Green published nothing in the *South Carolina Review.*

7. On leave from the University of South Carolina, Durham was in Chapel Hill during 1968–69.

---

1. Howard Richardson (b. 1917), playwright with B.A. (1938) and M.A. (1940) in dramatic arts from UNC, returned to Chapel Hill from New York City during the last week of March as the Carolina Playmakers celebrated the fiftieth anniversary of their organization with a production of Green's *Sing All a Green Willow,* various talks, and a banquet.

2. Most of Richardson's writing during the 1960s, done while he taught at various places, was for television.

don't murder us all, we will yet see the main images of our dreams come to actuality in a beautiful and cooperative world.

I was much amused by the "dialogue" between Wilbur Dorsett and Howard Bailey at the Playmaker banquet last Saturday evening, and I'm sure you were.[3] Their humorous reference to your and my mutual plagiarism was funny a sight.[4] I'm sure too that in our dramatic pieces we both go back to life and not to the work of each other. Some 35 or 40 years ago I wrote about a wild boy and a disturbed poetic girl named Tina, a Church of God preacher and a congregation after them to purge away their sins, especially the girl's, and I slovenly let it be published unfinished.[5] The recent *Willow* piece is its fuller form, and the girl is here Christina. How many times in my childhood have I witnessed the weird doings as Sam Selden[6] well-staged them in the revival scene. And so have you. I had two uncles and two aunts who were Holy Rollers at times, and so I actually was writing about my own relatives in this play. I'm pleased in turning to your fine drama to see that your interpretation of this sort of religion is right and solid—poetically solid, and that's the main thing—and that you, like me, went back to life itself as certain people live it for your story material.[7] Good news about your movie, which Dick Adler mentioned![8]

The main point of this letter, Howard, is to ask whether you'd ever be

3. At a banquet at the American Legion Hall in Chapel Hill former Playmakers Dorsett and Bailey, on the faculty of Rollins College, followed Playmakers tradition by staging a "Caper"—a burlesque of the group's serious work. They focused on *Sing All a Green Willow*, the title of which Green took from Desdemona's plaintive song about a girl whose lover went crazy and killed her (*Othello*, act 4, scene 3), and Richardson's *Dark of the Moon* (1945), a dramatization of the "Barbara Allan" ballad set in the southern Appalachians. In each play the catastrophe is brought on by tyrannical religious fanatics.

4. As in letter.

5. As *Tread the Green Grass*, published in 1931.

6. Director of *Sing All a Green Willow*.

7. Richardson "wasn't a bit upset by the jokes they pulled about our stealing ideas from each other. If anything I felt honored to be in the same bag as my betters!" (Howard Richardson to Paul Green, 4 April 1969, PG-SHC).

8. At a forum on Saturday afternoon (see n. 12 below) Adler introduced Richardson as the "author of *Dark of the Moon*, now being made into a fabulous motion picture" (transcription of forum, p. 11, folder 2040, PG-SHC). The film was not completed.

interested in joining in on writing an outdoor drama. Amphitheatres are popping up all over the land, and Mark Sumner, Director of the Institute of Outdoor Drama here,[9] is busy as a one-armed paper hanger with the itch trying to keep up with their demandings. Our biggest demand though is for playwrights, and for *good* playwrights who can write good plays to go into these amphitheatres. Some of these plays already written have proved and continue to prove very successful and worthwhile—*The Lost Colony, Unto These Hills*[10] (tremendous), *The Common Glory, Texas, Stephen Foster*, etc. I hope you'll consider joining in in this now a great movement, Howard.[11]

A stenographer took down the proceedings of our Saturday afternoon symposium, and I am sending you a copy by separate mail.[12]

9. Institute organized at UNC in 1963 to provide support and guidance for the outdoor drama movement. Sumner had been its director since 1964.

10. By Kermit Hunter.

11. Richardson wrote Green that in 1937 he "thought life was not worth living" when he "wasn't chosen to be in that first production [of *The Lost Colony*] in Manteo," and since then he had dreamed of writing an outdoor play (4 April 1969, PG-SHC). He has not written one, however.

12. For Saturday afternoon, 29 March, Green organized a forum in the old Playmakers' Theater (where Federal troops stabled horses during the Civil War) to stimulate the drive for a new theater on the Chapel Hill campus. On the panel were Richard Adler (who presided), Sidney Blackmer, Hubert Heffner, Robert Dale Martin, Richardson, and other prominent alumni of the theater program along with William Friday, president of the state university system, and Carlyle Sitterson, chancellor at Chapel Hill. Green began the meeting: "Forty-four years ago we got this building and since then we've gotten nothing." He called the present assembly a group of dreamers who will make their dream come true (transcription of forum, p. 5, folder 2040, PG-SHC). At the end he pointed to the audience: "Right over here on the fourth row sits my . . . wife, [who] wrote the very first play ever produced by the Playmakers." Elizabeth then reminded everyone that the first Playmakers plays were done in the old town high school and closed the meeting with a hope that "we'll get a wonderful building soon" (ibid., p. 52). Afterward Green sent copies of the transcript to all participants. Over the next two years he led delegations to see the governor and legislators with influence on appropriations and encouraged the writing of articles sympathetic to the cause in state newspapers. In 1971 the General Assembly appropriated $2.25 million for the theater, and after several delays it was completed in 1978 (at a cost of $1.8 million). The theater was named for Green and dedicated on 29 September 1978 with a production of *Native Son.*

All affectionate greetings to you and yours and good luck on your next play,[13]

## 310. To Betsy G. and William Moyer

[Windy Oaks] Old Lystra Road, Chapel Hill, N.C.
31 October 1969

Dear Bets and Bill,[1]

Just a note to remind you that we are still alive and kicking and being in that condition are able as always to speak our love again across whatever distance lies between us and however briefly. Mimi, I know, keeps the details of our existence here and news about other members of the "clan" pretty well covered from time to time in her family letters. She's an indefatigable public relations woman so far as her brood or clan is concerned—and I'm counted in as a member and accordingly suffer a bit of ego embarrassment from her news items. But when I demur, she blithely says, "Behave yourself, you and your son Paul," and so I try to behave. I don't know what he does.

I am working away on different projects and ideas, mainly the Ohio missionary drama,[2] and am making a bit of progress here and there. I should be making more considering what fine secretarial help and over-all assistance I have.[3]

Anyway, I continue to be bemused though not amused by our human race performances and doings on this globe.

And now to add to the bemusement and confusement comes the news of the Nobel literary award to Sam Beckett,[4] a fellow whose nihilism and personally stupid, do-nothing characters—and that means both stylistically and philosophically—are a continuing diarrhetic pain in a certain tubular lower part of my distressed anatomy. You may have seen or read one of his plays, *Waiting for Godot.* Last night I picked it up again and had another go at

13. *Ark of Safety,* first produced in July 1975 by the Southern Appalachian Repertory Theater in Mars Hill, North Carolina.

1. Green also sent a copy to Paul, Jr.
2. *Trumpet in the Land,* which opened on 3 July 1970 in New Philadelphia, Ohio.
3. From Rhoda Wynn, Green's secretary since 1967.
4. Announced on 23 October 1969.

reading it. Then I tried several others, including "Endgame," and finally gave up on the belly-wash muck. For a while I amused myself in chattering forth the same sort of nonsensical and pseudo-profound dialogue that he Beckett and the Nobel Prize Committee found so important—(Pardon the vulgarity of this sample—say Sam is to blame—his characters speak all alike whether named Vladimir,[5] Nagg, Nell, Hamm[6] or what-not. So for me, A and B.)—

A: (As B's stomach growls.) What was that?
B: A voice from the beyond.
A: Beyond?
B: Yes, de profundis. I don't know Latin.
A: The primeval slime?
B: Exactly.
A: There is nothing we can do. Let the subject rest.
B: If it only could rest.
A: Could, would, should, can't—I grow tired.
B: Then let us rest.
A: True, true—pax vobiscum.
B: Mea culpa—Here we go again. I wish we knew Latin.
A: Yes, yes, why not?
B: (Sucking his forefinger and shouting.) Why!
A: Because we don't know any Latin, I tell you.
B: We speak it, don't we?
A: But what does that signify—specie aeternatatis.
B: All—all.
(Whining now and sucking his thumb and forefinger.)
You, you pubis pubescum—ayeh.
A: True, true again in your perverse lying of the truth.
B: (Scratching his crotch.) Latin is a dead language, say you?
A: Except when we revive it. Aye.
B: Revive it, wherefore?
A: Because we two only can revive it.
(A pause.)
B: Uhm—uhm—the graveyard cough in place of the fuehrer's voice.
(Another pause.)

5. In *Waiting for Godot.*
6. Three of the four characters in "Endgame."

A: Excellent! Oh my soul, most excellent.
B: (Suddenly sobbing.) Nay, nay! (Shudder) I mean no, no.
A: Since we are already both dead.
(A long pause, B's sobbing gradually dies away.)
B: (Finally, and clapping his hands together.) Oui, oui.
A: (Pointing.) Your fly is undone, wee-wee.
B: (Buttoning his fly.) I opened the door that old Adam could escape.
(Fondling old Adam dressed.)
He prefers it so.
A: (Fondling his old Adam dressed.) Yes, so he does—so they do.
BOTH: (Chanting as they fondle.)
Erectum, erecti, sic semper tyrannis! Down, Fido, down.
(Another pause.)
A: Well, shall we stay?
B: Yes, let's stay.

(They move off toward the rear where a thicket of shrubbery awaits them. Suddenly the great eye of the world lifts its lid and glares down on them in a blinding light, but they are so concerned with each other's spiritual-Adam that they do not notice it. Nor do they bother to ask why they should care to go secretly into the thicket, and no wonder, for to have this latter bother they would have to find a new and humanistic Freud born into their universe and become disciples of him, both impossibilities. And so we leave them, "leaving them to stay," saved to damnation and damned to salvation as their daddy Beckett conceived and birthed them to be. O mirabile dictu!—the silly and wasteful mystery to be born from such awkward use of homosexually used semen of life. O, like the rose that grows a-rot in June, let them be.)

And so I call out my Sam Beckett twang-doodle refrain, taking some gleeful and malicious joy that from now and on through eternity he will have to wait for Godot, a Godot that never comes. And now I hear borne in on the sombre drifting wind the little refrain, the little squeaky, squishy homunculus refrain—"Nothing to be done."

Thank you, Bill, for your sweet letter and thank you, Bets, for yours and Paul for his—and as Tiny but healthy Tim, even when he was sick, used to say,[7] And God bless *you* every one.

7. In Dickens's *A Christmas Carol.*

Mimi and I are enjoying the autumn. We have dug our potatoes, got in the last of the tomatoes and peppers and are preparing for our snug winter. Now and then we get pleasure too from our stretch of woodland some miles away.[8] Recently I have opened up an old, old road out there—cutting out the sprouts and stubs that had grown up and trimming off the ends of limbs protruding in. Yesterday we were able to drive this old road from boundary to boundary of the some 350 acres of woods—deep, delightful woods, warm and glowing in their autumn colors—maples, oaks, hickories, sourwood, black gum and the ever, ever present dogwoods. And then dark and enfolding over it all the great tall pines. To go there for us is like going to church. When you come this way again we must go out and walk among these trees. Bill, I have been reading some more of Zen, and it is a great relief from such ex nihilo nihil non fit.[9]

When the forts of folly fall
Find my body by the wall.[10]

As always, love,

## 311. To Jonathan Daniels

[Windy Oaks, Old Lystra Road, Chapel Hill, N.C.]
2 February 1970

Dear Brother in the Cause—[1]

The cause I mention here is not the one the foolish, boy-minded, run-crazy Othello spoke of when he was getting ready to kill sweet willow-song Desde-

8. About ten, south of Chapel Hill off of Mt. Gilead Road, which Green called Pipsissewa Hills for the tiny flowering herb that flourished there.

9. Perhaps *ex nihilo nihil fit*, meaning nothing is made from nothing.

10. Concluding lines of Matthew Arnold's "The Last Word," "my" substituted for "thy" in the last line.

---

1. On the Christmas card the Greens sent the Danielses in 1969 Paul added a somber note: "All under and under the leaves of life we keep grabbing for sustaining goodness, but the hogs of greed-for-power keep rooting the ground ahead of us. (Amen!) I wonder how long the American hog raisers are going to let them keep getting fat and over-fat in the Pentagon pen." Daniels replied, "Pack up your pessimism! Of course the world is in a hell of a fix, but there is nothing unusual about that. Your trouble is that you carry a noble vision into history. . . . You're still looking with the Presbyterian eyes of Woodrow Wilson at a vision last glimpsed in Paris in

mona.[2] Nor is it the cause of Oral Roberts, nor his Honor Billy Graham,[3] nor George Wallace,[4] nor Ted Kennedy of the bridge-crossing,[5] et al. No.

It is the cause, say, for which old Zeus fastened Prometheus to a rock and set a vulture to eat on his ever-renewing liver there in the wild Caucasus back in the dank sweatings of hoary-locked time.[6] It is the cause which the rubber-lipped trumpet-mouthed politicians of today betray when above the cross-studded graves of the rotting young men they howl forth the old cliché-refrain that they did not die in vain for they died to keep America free.

Nuts to the nutty! And oh the dark blood on the ground!

It is the cause, the same, which old pagan Benjamin Franklin inadvertently defended when he said to the martyr-minded revolutionary Sam Adams who was ready to die for liberty too—"And what liberty is there in six-foot of earth, Sam Adams?—Go ahead and die, but I want to live. I'm seventy years old but I still want to live."[7]

Yes, it is the Cause of Life, of Life creative, more abundant, the Good Life—and the good life means the true, the beautiful and the useful life—the heart-beating life. And I'm all for that in my small way, and seeking that I shall not falter, not weaken, never give over.

Thus I declare against pessimism.

In your lovely recent N. & O. published letter, with my "complaint," you spank my rear part somewhat and do it with the rhythm and skill of an inherited paternalism and because of the art shown I don't mind. I deny the

---

1918. The pigs surprised you then but by now you ought to be accustomed to if not immune to their smell" (29 December 1969, PG-SHC). Daniels published the exchange in his Raleigh newspaper, the *News and Observer* (31 December 1969, p. 4, cols. 5–6).

2. Desdemona's supposed unfaithfulness "is the cause, it is the cause, my soul— / Let me not name it to you, you chaste stars!— / It is the cause" (*Othello*, act 5, scene 2, lines 1–3).

3. Popular revivalist preachers.

4. Segregationist former governor of Alabama and third-party presidential candidate in 1968.

5. U.S. senator from Massachusetts who, on 18 July 1969, swam to safety after driving his car off of a bridge on Chappaquiddick Island near Martha's Vineyard. A young woman companion in the car drowned.

6. When Zeus thought of destroying the human race, Prometheus stole fire from heaven and gave it to humans for their salvation.

7. *The Common Glory*, act 1, scene 7.

charge though. And I keep singing my little up-beat song about man's job—yours and mine. And if I moan out against our leaders and say they are bent on ruining us—that is, their bent is such as to ruin us—I don't think that is pessimistic. And if I sing on about the darkness ahead—that doesn't mean I've given over to it.

Will Rogers and I were once standing on the Twentieth Century lot watching a scene being shot,[8] and something of the same sort of accusation against our leaders was in our conversation. "Good old hypocrites," he said. "Like Oklahoma, they'll vote dry as long as they can stagger to the polls," or "shout optimism with the tears running down their cheeks." Etc.

My main quarrel is and ever will be with such men as those now occupying the Pentagon and the Kremlin—bad men, evil men, blind men—along with their tribal head-hunters in the CIA. They spell damnation to you and me and our children's children, and Dick Nixon with his increased push with his enlarged ABM[9] system spells the same—spells it unless reason from somewhere intervenes. That's what I'm calling for—that reason. And thus my little song—as per some Harnett County doggerel which becomes the matter—[10]

When man was first created
  I'm sure his Maker[11] meant
  Him for some good intent,
Kind heart and love, forgiving wrong,
And though through ages fated
  To climb a wandering way,
  At last he'd find the day
When joy should be his song.

But now they say that's all baloney,
The world's a might cruel place,
With tooth and claw and promise phony,
And old Hard Guy, he wins the race.

8. In the mid-1930s Green wrote three film scripts for Rogers: *State Fair*, *Dr. Bull*, and *David Harum*.

9. Antiballistic missile.

10. Concluding song from *Johnny Johnson*, linked with Harnett County because Johnny grew up in a similar rural environment.

11. Noted on right margin: "I use the capital M figuratively, suh."

But you and I don't think so,
   We know there's something still
   Of good beyond this ill
Within our heart and mind.
   And we'll ever strive
   While we're alive
That better way to find.

As up and down I wander
My weary way and long
I meet all kinds of folks
Who listen to my song.

Yes suh, my bosom friend of these many years and many more I trust, I keep singing my song of hope and dedicated effort—singing even louder when the head conductor exchanges his baton for a rifle and calls the death march toward oblivion—my loudness being then no longer singing but a cry and an about face in the march and hollering for others to turn likewise.

And now from under the big wash pot which I see shaking out in my front yard I hear a smothering voice muttering to itself, and going out there and leaning down I recognize old Jeremiah and his monologue.[12] And do I dig down in the soft dirt and under to join my friend the prophet in the pot? No, I do not. I overturn the pot to let him out, and side by side and marching up the hill, not down, we raise a louder song in a louder unison now, hailing the cruel but fated coming of the bears on the mocking children[13] and the rising of the smiling sun thereafter. Yes suh, even so.

Elizabeth and I love you and Lucy,

12. A lamentation over the sins of his people and a prophecy of their destruction. (But Diogenes the Cynic, who went around with a lantern in broad daylight looking for an honest person, is the scold of mankind who lived under a tub.)

13. Children who mocked the prophet Elisha were torn to pieces by bears (2 Kings 2:23–24).

## 312. To John Houseman[1]

[Windy Oaks, Old Lystra Road, Chapel Hill, N.C.]
30 June 1973

Dear John:

In passing through Atlanta the other day I picked up a copy of your *Run-Through*, and read it on my long drama-working trips to Kentucky, Georgia, Texas and elsewhere. It is in the main for me a good book and will be a source of information and encouragement to drama people for a long time to come. I so prophesy.

I regret though the marring of the book by the one-sided account you give of the *Native Son* collaborating and producing and my part in the venture. Your statement is full of inaccuracies and gapped with omissions. I understand your subjective seeing and telling, for you put your whole soul into the project and emotionally so, as is the way of good creative artists of course. But this does not excuse the errors in your story.[2]

I shan't go into the matter of your claimed authorship in the drama for

1. John Houseman (1902–1988), active in the theater, motion pictures, and television from the 1920s until his death, produced *Native Son* when Green's dramatization of Richard Wright's novel was staged in 1941 under the direction of Orson Welles. In 1972 Houseman published *Run-Through* (New York: Simon and Schuster), first volume of his autobiography, and Green bought a copy in mid-June on a trip to five of his plays: *The Wilderness Road* in Berea, Kentucky, *The Stephen Foster Story* in nearby Bardstown, *Texas* in Canyon, *Drumbeats in Georgia* on Jekyll Island, and *Cross and Sword* in St. Augustine.

2. Green does not exaggerate the inaccuracy of *Run-Through*. For instance, on a single page (p. 466) Houseman twice misrepresents Green's script of *Native Son*. First, he quotes three lines from a thirty-one-line monologue in scene 8 of Green's script as if they are an entire speech in scene 10 (for the whole speech, see Paul Green to Abbott Van Nostrand, 20 August 1971, PG-SHC). Second, he suggests that Green changed the name of an important character to Paul, when in fact Houseman and Welles changed the name—perhaps as a joke, since the character, the lawyer Max, is the one who articulates the theme of environmental determinism in the play. The various published texts show that Green called the lawyer Edward Max; only the acting script, controlled by Houseman and Welles, names him Paul Max (see Burns Mantle, ed., *Best Plays of 1940–41* [New York: Dodd, Mead, 1941], pp. 29–63). The whole *Native Son* story in *Run-Through* is similarly unreliable, but because it seems authoritative and is entertaining, *Run-Through* is the basis of most later discussions of the play, which is unfortunate.

instance,[3] but I might repeat here for at least one illustration what I told you in one of our early meetings about the dramatization of the book—that one part of my agreement to do it was that in the play Bigger Thomas should come to the realization that he was at least partly responsible for the character he was and therefore had some responsibility for the fate that fell upon him.

You and I know that something of such realization is true of all human beings. Otherwise there is a self-consciousness of non-entity and lack of sense of choice or being chosen, and self-consciousness doesn't work that way. For me it doesn't. And so I felt that in the original book-ending (And what wonderful almost Dostoevskian writing is there!) Wright's material was failing this truth and if I was to dramatize the book I would require that Bigger Thomas grow through his stretch of endurance and not just suffer. You left out any mention of this agreement in your account. Perhaps you forgot it.[4]

As you know, I finally gave in to you, Welles and Wright—though you and Welles were more demanding than he—and let you end the play in a piece of pathos rather than in tragedy.[5]

I wish you long life and happiness, John.[6]

Paul

3. Houseman says Green's script "exasperated" him (*Run-Through*, p. 465) and that with Wright in New York City he rewrote it, then for the production "used the text Wright and I had worked on" (ibid., pp. 469, 471). But only in the last scene does the produced script differ substantially from Green's text.

4. Houseman mentioned other elements of the agreement but said he heard about this condition only in 1970 (ibid., p. 462n).

5. For the concluding scene as staged, where Bigger is depicted as being crucified by society, see Mantle, *Best Plays of 1940–41*, pp. 61–63.

6. In 1974 the Institute of Outdoor Drama held its tenth annual conference in Chapel Hill, and Houseman gave the main address at a banquet at the Carolina Inn on 22 March. Green introduced him, outlining Houseman's career and saying he had "the wide reach, the far view." Then Houseman spoke, praising the outdoor drama movement as one of the few dynamic areas of the American theater at present (notes, program, and newspaper clippings of conference, folder 2321, PG-SHC).

## 313. To Janet G. Catlin

[Windy Oaks, Old Lystra Road, Chapel Hill, N.C.]
19 March 1974

Dearest Jan—[1]

Many, many thanks for that beautiful poem on my birthday. I was sorry not to receive it from Mimi's hands while the "crowd" was here.[2] It would have been my prideful pleasure to read it for all to hear. Anyway Aunt Ellen[3] and others close in have had a chance at it and have enjoyed its imagery and its "reach." (Once more the quote marks for emphasis.) The thanatopsis touch in the poem pleases me in its beauty, and where beauty is rich solace is. All is still go, go with me, but I can tell you that if fanged pain should seize upon me you would hear this eldish cow-lot urchin call for the calf rope and yell "somebody

1. Green was eighty on 17 March 1974, and for the occasion his daughter Janet sent him an allusive poem, "For My Father on His 80th Birthday":

> What kind of song do poets sing this day?
> No rondel, pretty ditty, nor a dirge,
> For you are there—not I—on that "sad height,"
> Though I would say with my last breath, stay, father yet a while,
> Yet it must come: "the readiness is all."
> "Rage, rage, against the dying—of the light."
> Do you feel old-man-Yeats' "astringent joy"?
> Pose Browning's glorious question: What, "Fear Death?"
> What dead-of-night thoughts now you have who knows?
> Truth in a diary? Who will turn that page?
> Old Oedipus at Colonnus spoke not what he saw
> As he prepared for his last hour in all its shining.
> "No casement slowly grown a glimmering square, to dying eyes
> While unto dying ears, the earliest pipe of half-awakened birds"
> For Oedipus. But the "living light that leapt"
> And grandeur, terror, battle for the strong,
> Wrought out by his soul's light. He had no eyes,
> But "true experience from this great event."
> Thus he "in calm of mind, all passion spent,"
> Went forth at last to be one with his gods.

2. Thinking the poem "might be a bit too serious for a celebration," Janet sent it to her mother "for her discretionary timing" (Janet Catlin to Paul Green, 27 March 1974, Green Family Papers, SHC).

3. Ellen Hodgkinson, Elizabeth's sister, visiting from Minneapolis.

get this monkey off and out of me!" I yet hope to go over and off without such a noise. And, dear Jan, I am very thankful to have had as much time as I have. I have tried to cooperate with the process of the universe by caring for my body and honoring it as a trust allowed me—and so all the rest makes me an object of substantive forces—and so on. . . . Anyway it seems to me obvious and to be early accepted that life-in-death is the sum-up of the above-mentioned process. The instant the first pulse-beat of life occurs in the mother sac the twin brother of death pulseless beats too. And from then on the front-footed march of life reality carries on to the accompaniment of the "muffled drumbeat" to the grave. Plato, as Jack well knows,[4] deals with this as emphatically as any petrographic or petroglyphic statement might try to.[5] To have life requires death-to-be. So rather than saying from the point of view of sensation[6] that life is an interruption of death, can't we say and accept the fact that one is in and of the other. Thus the beneficence or even the solace mentioned above.

Thanks for the fine letter telling of your and the family's doings. It all sounds good, very good. When you folks arrive here in May for a long stay we can do a lot of talking on a mess of subjects. Amen!

I look forward keenly to Jack's treatment of that most difficult term ἁμαρτία—error, tragic flaw, sin, failure or what not.[7] I don't remember what assignment Aristotle made as to the cause of it in human character, how much inner cause, how much outer. It would be interesting to contrast his interpretation with that of Freud, the—ahem—pseudo-scientist. Kiss sweet Virginia[8] for us and much, much love to you both and the "apple of your"—our—eye.

Doog

4. Jack Catlin, Janet's husband and professor of Greek at the University of Oklahoma.

5. As in the *Phaedo.*

6. Green noted in the margin here: "Sensation is the rub, isn't it?"

7. Catlin published nothing on *hamartia*, which Aristotle in the *Poetics* treated not as sin or tragic flaw but as miscalculation or mistaken judgment on the part of a good person (chapter 13).

8. Five-year-old daughter of Janet and Jack.

## 314. To Cheryl Crawford

[Windy Oaks, Old Lystra Road, Chapel Hill, N.C.]
22 April 1975

Dear Cheryl:[1]

It's good to have a word from you, and I am pleased that you are planning to bring out your autobiography.

During these last years I have been so much taken up with building amphitheatres and writing and helping produce plays in them in different parts of the country—the theatre of the people as Romain Rolland used to vision it with many bright words[2]—I have been so busy that remembrances of the past New York theatre are accordingly somewhat obscured. I fear I can't be too much help to you in my items of recall, but I'll do the best I can.

First let me say there is no dimming in my remembrance as to the help you gave me in both *The House of Connelly* and *Johnny Johnson*—especially in the latter—and in other plays.[3]

As you know, *Connelly* was first written with a tragic ending and was sold to the Theatre Guild thus. Then the Guild turned the play over to the Group Theatre for production. At the time—as I found out later—the young Group members were taken with the communist ideology and knew more about and felt closer to Joseph Stalin than, say, they did to our own Thomas Jefferson. This riled the heck out of me. I had a number of arguments. I remember a beautiful-eyed choreography member looked at me blazingly one day and said that in the revolution of the proletariat that was coming in America before long she would take great delight in cutting my throat. And another member shivering with delight of dedication one day said that heads were going to roll in America and Paul Green's would be one of the first to be bounced along the rocky earth by avenging hands. So it was out of this fervor of conviction, I guess, that a decision was made to change the ending of the *Connelly* play to—in Harold Clurman's words—to a yea-saying statement instead of a nay-saying one. I accepted the decision and rewrote the tragic ending, for actually in life

1. Crawford, a founding director of the Group Theatre, was at work on her autobiography and asked Green to reminisce about *The House of Connelly* (first Group production in 1931) and *Johnny Johnson* (collaboration between Green and Kurt Weill, produced by the Group in 1936) (Cheryl Crawford to Paul Green, 5 April 1975, PG-SHC).

2. In *The People's Theatre* (trans. 1918).

3. In 1951 Crawford produced Green's adaptation of *Peer Gynt.*

the new South (Patsy Tate[4] represented this) rose dynamically out of and above the ruined old South (Will Connelly and the Connelly family stood for this). So let life take over, I agreed.

—(I might mention in this connection that following the New York production of *Johnny Johnson* there was some interest expressed from Moscow in doing that play in that city. It was suggested from there that I rewrite the ending into a yea-saying statement, a push-ahead, up-to-the-barricade doing. End with a scene, say, where Johnny grabs a red flag and charges the battlement of the capitalist-military enemy. Sure, let him get shot down if need be. The thing that mattered was that he acted, he did something in leadership toward the new day to come. The original tragic scene as I wrote it for the Group production seemed right, and I am glad it was kept. So far as I know, the play has never been done in Russia. It was done last year in Germany and is now running successfully in a National Theatre production in Helsinki.[5] By the time of your opening of *Johnny* in New York the young members of the Group had begun to see Stalinism for what it was. So no particular argument for an ending different from the one I wrote came up. I remember, though, that I struggled hard—you too—to find a bigger and better statement of man's dilemma of war and peace to conclude with. But I failed. Since then I have written several plays on the subject of peace—*Wilderness Road, Trumpet in the Land, Cross and Sword*—and I have yet to dispense with force, armed might, when ideals are threatened to death. I have heard that the dedicated pacifist Martin Luther King himself said he would pick up a gun against a Hitler threat. In the recent rewrite of *Johnny* for French's paperback edition I improved Johnny's final peace song a bit—in that I have him sing it dynamically and in opposition to the distant harangue of the military demagogue inclining the people to war, the harangue gradually weakening as Johnny sings out his message of good will.[6] The words of this

4. Character in the play.

5. The Finnish National Theatre performed *Johnny* in repertory 1974–78, and in October 1977 Green with his wife and Rhoda Wynn would visit Moscow and Leningrad, then go to Helsinki for a performance and some talks at the National Theatre (Paul Green to Charles Vann, 24 June 1974, and Paul Green to Hubert Heffner, 23 February 1978, PG-SHC).

6. In the original version Johnny exits whistling the theme tune as a military demagogue harangues a crowd ([New York: Samuel French, 1937], p. 175). In the revised version (1971) the harangue weakens as Johnny sings: "When man was first

song are not too good, and Weill's fine melody is too difficult for easy singing. Kurt used to say he wanted the audience to go out of the theatre humming or singing the melody. Good as it is, its reach from low to high is much demanding, and the second-part development complex. But it is a fine thing. The fact that the melody was written long before we started on the play and I had to fit my words to its uniqueness maybe helped account for my trouble with getting the right ending.)

To go back to *The House of Connelly*. From my experience with its production, I became convinced more than ever that life should not control art but that art in its interpretation of life will the more work its control over life. The original tragic ending of the play was the right one. It came out of the nature of the material, out of the author's seeing and feeling, and it should have been kept. In a recent anthology it has been put back.[7] But I am thankful to you and the Group for all things even so.[8]

I gave this play the wrong name, I think. Connelly doesn't in the least suggest the old aristocratic South, but Heyward, Hampton, Rutledge, Pinckney, Ravenel, etc. do. *The House of Hampton* would have been okay. The original title was *The Lady with the Flower in Her Mouth*—or some such phrasing. I paid a visit one day many years ago to a ruined old Southern place in eastern North Carolina—a rambling two-story house with a driveway lined by storm- and sleet-broken cedars leading up to it. I was always out collecting old books, manuscripts, folksongs, folklore, diaries, letters, photographs, etc. for our university library in those days. A wrinkled, blear-eyed woman was sitting in a rockingchair in the desolate, shadowed wide hall of the old house, her palm-leaf fan leisurely moving back and forth sweeping away the flies. Her mouth was raw with a big sore to one side that looked like some sort of mushy bloom, and now and then as we talked she wiped its oozings away with a dirty rag. No, she didn't have any letters, no books, no diaries, all had been sold to Duke Library long ago by her daughter. They had needed money so. We had

---

created / I'm sure his life was meant / To be of good intent— / To seek the right, oppose the wrong, / And though through ages fated / To climb a wandering way / At last he'd find the day / When joy would be his song. / . . . We'll work and strive / While we're alive / That better way to find" (p. 121).

7. *Five Plays of the South*, ed. John Gassner (1963).

8. In her autobiography Crawford explains how she helped convince Green to change his original ending (*One Naked Individual: My Fifty Years in the Theatre* [Indianapolis: Bobbs-Merrill, 1977], p. 55).

some talk about the past days, the proud days, the good days. There she sat waiting for final death.

I went away, and as I rode through the land in my old Ford runabout I said to myself, "I'm going to write something about this old house, this old South. The woman there is the South that's dying, that is dead, the woman with the sore, the flower, in her mouth." Later I learned that Pirandello had a story or play with much the same title.[9] So I changed it. While I was working on research for the play my cousin married a man named Connelly.[10] I thought it a fine name, it sounded good, and so I used it.

You ask about versions of the drama. There were several, more or less, anyway all sorts of rewrite patches and cuttings. And I think I definitely had two full versions, the difference being mainly in the endings. From one of the cuttings—a whole scene where Uncle Bob goes over to the Tate tenant house to have a look at Patsy—I later with changed names and nature made a sort of little folk dance drama called "Saturday Night."[11]

I remember that at a lunch or dinner once—you might have been with us—Theresa Helburn[12] mentioned that she thought the *Connelly* script could be improved in spots and she'd like me to study it and see what I could come up with. Maybe I could cut it some also. About this time I went to Europe on a Guggenheim Fellowship to study the drama there. Theresa wrote that she was waiting for the revised version. I got busy. The more I rewrote and cut the more the words poured out—finally to well over two hundred pages. (You mention 250. Okay.) I sent the version in, and word came back, "For goodness sake stop writing. We'll do with what we have." I stopped. But I worried—saying to myself, maybe I'm like my classmate Tom Wolfe at Carolina—both of us cursed with too much old Southern oratory of flooding words and fervid exhortation for the lean and compressive demands of dramatic form.

To go back to *Johnny Johnson*—I don't know who got the idea for the play first. But to repeat, I know you were the sparkplug that kept firing off the

9. Luigi Pirandello wrote a story about a man with a cancerous growth on his mouth, then made a play of it (1923), both entitled "The Man with the Flower in His Mouth."

10. In 1916, well before Green began to write the play, his cousin Martha Green, whose father was the brother of Paul's father, married Willard Moss Connelly (interview with Erma Green Gold, 14 May 1989).

11. In Paul Green, *In the Valley and Other Carolina Plays* (New York: Samuel French, 1928), pp. 103–21.

12. A director of the Theatre Guild, which first optioned the play.

whole thing.[13] And I know too that I have been an anti-war and pro-peace man for most of my life. Long, long ago I believed in Woodrow Wilson's idealism and I still do. Like Johnny, I listened to his speeches, and in the "disordered time," as Anguish Howington described them in the play,[14] I finally agreed with Wilson as to the war. It was a war to end war, to make the world safe for democracy. So I would step out and do my part. I enlisted and took up the gun to "fight fire with fire."

The use of force to bring non-force didn't work, and I doubt it ever will.

As to influences—when I was studying the European theatre in 1928–30, I saw a movie of Carl Zuckmayer's play *Der Hauptmann von Koepenick*, in which the power of the military uniform is shown and at the same time mocked. Then there was *The Good Soldier Schweik*[15] and also Carl Buchner's[16] *Woyzeck* which I read and enjoyed. Maybe whiffs of these show in *Johnny.* I don't know. My association with Will Rogers in Hollywood though strengthened me in my dislike of stuffed shirts and military uniforms, especially those of high officers with the brutal bragging shows of medals spread across their breasts. Not that Rogers was a pacifist, no, but that he especially deplored the mess our leaders make of handling the affairs and lives of John Q. Citizen, of the Jeffersonian common man, of Johnny Johnson, and of me, and spoke out about it. I wrote several pictures for Rogers, and now and then we did a lot of talking. In some ways the character of Johnny is like Rogers—with a good sense of humor, clear thinking, and despising sham and hypocrisy always.

*Johnny Johnson* then is a sort of morality play, an *Everyman* if you will. At least I intended it so.

Well, I see my remembrances are not over-much obscured after all, and I have run on quite at length in answering your brief questions.

Ever,

13. Crawford brought Weill to Chapel Hill and worked with the two of them until the play was finished (Crawford, *One Naked Individual*, pp. 93–97).

14. *Johnny Johnson* (1937), p. 167.

15. Bertolt Brecht's dramatization of Jaroslav Hašek's novel played in Berlin in 1928.

16. Georg Büchner.

## 315. To W. Charles Park[1]

[Windy Oaks] Old Lystra Road, Chapel Hill, N.C.
17 February 1976

Dear Charlie:

Your brochures have just arrived and all of us have had an eager look at them. All in all the wording and color seem to be effective. But being a man of peace and the play itself emphasizing the need for trading goods, one people with another, instead of exchanging bullets, blades and resultant killings, I am saddened by the frontispiece—a rather awkward rendering at that—of a lifted tomahawk and the threatening sharp sword, one man against another. I suggest if you have a re-run of these that you substitute something more peaceful and poetic for that cruel cover.

And I hope you won't repeat it on posters or *anywhere* else. Couldn't you have a lovely illustration of St. Denis, the Cavalier, bowing over the hand of the beautiful Manuela,[2] or at least some lace and velvet and charm in evidence—or St. Denis swinging Manuela in a dance—or a Spanish couple doing the flamenco—a senorita with a tambourine—a Carmen touch. You know what I mean, Charlie.

As you damn well know, the soul and character of this country are terribly threatened by up-spilling and out-spilling violence and human ruin. Your first illustration adds to it. We don't want to do that.

If we in the arts can't give illumination and inspiration to the strugglers and

1. W. Charles Park was managing director of *Louisiana Cavalier*, the latest of Green's outdoor plays, which would open on 19 June 1976 in the Grand Ecore Amphitheatre at Natchitoches, Louisiana. The oldest European settlement in the Louisiana Territory, Natchitoches was established in 1715 when Frenchman Louis de Saint-Denis built a fort and trading post there. The play focuses on Saint-Denis's efforts to develop the town and maintain peaceful relations with neighboring Creek and Shawnee tribes and Spanish outposts in Texas. In a recent letter Park told Green that theater construction, auditions, and other production matters were coming along nicely, and he included a few copies of the new advertising brochure. The brochure featured a Frenchman and an Indian in hand-to-hand combat, the Indian with raised tomahawk, the Frenchman with a rapier at the Indian's chest, the whole bordered by a large broadsword. Park said he had ordered 200,000 copies of the brochure and was busy distributing them throughout the state (W. Charles Park to Paul Green, 12 February 1976, PG-SHC). Across the top of the letter Green wrote "not sent." For the mailed letter, see letter 316.

2. His Spanish wife from Mexico.

the pilgrims in this world, who can! I count the theatre an art—a great art. (Now don't quote *Titus Andronicus* or *Hamlet* back at me.) And my original hope for these historical productions was that they were pioneer efforts preparing the way for greater people and things to come—an Aeschylus, a Sophocles, an Epidaurus creation,[3] etc. Alas, it seems that the whole "movement" tends to weaken down rather than to develop in quality and inspiration of man. As you know, all sorts of pitiful scripts are popping into existence, and nearly all of them reach out to attract the childish part of the common mind with Indian battles and murder.

Rhoda[4] wrote you about Van Grove's sad loss.[5] I had just sent him a sizeable check. I hope it helps and I hope the mailman will deliver me one from you this week—as promised.[6]

With best greetings,

## 316. To W. Charles Park

[Windy Oaks, Old Lystra Road, Chapel Hill, N.C.]
20 February 1976

Dear Charlie:[1]

Thanks for your full letter of February 12 and the new brochures. In the main they seem to say that everything is moving right ahead for an historic and successful opening for the *Louisiana Cavalier.*

I was especially taken with the colored picture of a cavalier (for transfer) in

3. In classical Greece the worship of Asklepios, son of Apollo and widely venerated god of healing, centered at Epidaurus, and each spring people from throughout the Mediterranean world went there for a great festival that included performances in a large and beautiful amphitheater dedicated to Asklepios.

4. Wynn, Green's secretary since 1967.

5. Isaac Van Grove, friend and composer living in Hollywood, had arranged the music for all of Green's outdoor plays since *The Seventeenth Star* in 1953. When Green phoned him on 12 February to check on the music for *Louisiana Cavalier,* Van Grove told Green that his wife, Joan, had died two days before (note on Isaac Van Grove to Paul Green, 8 February 1976, PG-SHC).

6. Green sent Van Grove $1,000 on 15 February, and Park was to reimburse him out of production funds budgeted for music (ibid.).

---

1. Green sent this letter instead of letter 315, in which he shows his unhappiness over the brochures for *Louisiana Cavalier.*

the Sunday, February 8, issue of *The Natchitoches Times.*[2] This is a striking figure, and I do hope you will be able to feature it more and more in your advertising matter, especially on your posters, magazines, news articles and any and all sorts of advertising. After all, the word "cavalier" is half of our title and perhaps more than half of the subject matter. Then too the ingredients of the play have to do with peace and good will—the trading of goods among peoples instead of the exchange of bullets and blows.

I hope you all are pleased with the music Van Grove has been sending in from his most creative work.

My sympathy and admiration march strongly in the direction of all you good people there, and my hat is off to Arthur Watson[3] for his financial accomplishments in our behalf.

Best as always,[4]

## 317. To Dorothy and Marvin Stahl

[Windy Oaks, Old Lystra Road, Chapel Hill, N.C.]
16 March 1976

Dear Dottie and Marvin—

The days go by, the years slip over the hill of time and fall soundlessly into the "abyss" of history, and yet friendship and lovely memories in that friendship persist. We all send love once more—and some natural regretting goes with it, in that we can't see you more often and talk our challenges ("mistakes") and failing leaders over face to face.[1] I always loved our religious and philosophical talks too, Dottie.

2. A large, dashing figure in plumed hat, cape, wide belt, and soft boots standing beneath the title of the play, the entire picture given in mirror-image for ironing on a sweater (sec. A, p. 9).

3. Lawyer in Natchitoches in charge of fund-raising for *Louisiana Cavalier.*

4. *Louisiana Cavalier* ran through 1979, and its stationery, souvenir programs, and advertisements continued to feature the hand-to-hand combat drawing. No further use seems to have been made of the cavalier in the plumed hat.

---

1. The Stahls lived in Belmont, Michigan, and in a recent letter Dorothy said her husband had a long acquaintance with Gerald Ford, also from Michigan and president since Richard Nixon resigned in August 1974, and would support him in the fall presidential election. Her favorite, she added, was Jimmy Carter (28 January 1976, PG-SHC).

The nature descriptions in your letters are vivid enough, and I could feel the snow and ice of your habitat.[2] Spring has long been here in Chapel Hill—flowers everywhere, Elizabeth keeps the house stocked—and we are caught with the old disease of planting-itis—onions, cabbage, peas, lettuce, etc., etc. I have a tractor I play tunes and hallelujahs on now and then, much to the horror of underground mice and moles. Our recent drama raid in Fayetteville brought me some prizes and honoring,[3] and on April 7 in Winston-Salem is to be a statewide saluting.[4] I count all these as generous and kind-hearted, well, yes, loving obituary outreachings. If I walked with a cane or stick like the man in Chaucer, my exit-tappings might say "Dearest mother, let me in."[5] But nay!

Love, Paul

## 318. To Maxim Tabory[1]

[Windy Oaks, Old Lystra Road, Chapel Hill, N.C.]
12 April 1976

Dear Maxim—

Thanks for your good letter. You are so right to raise a question about a man of peace depicting killings in his plays. I'm sure you must know I struggle for

2. In another recent letter Dorothy said, "We have had a severe winter here. Icicles hang from the roof to the ground all around the house. Our shrubbery is wrapped in ice. And the snow on the golf course is so deep, our dogs have to leap out of one spot to another to keep from being buried in it" (2 February 1976, PG-SHC).

3. To celebrate the national bicentennial, the city of Fayetteville staged a three-week run of *The Highland Call*, and on opening night, 26 February 1976, Congressman Charlie Rose eulogized Green for generating an inspiring sense of American history through his plays (*Congressional Record*, 1 March 1976, p. E 935). Green had included the Stahls on his invitation list, but Dorothy's letter of 2 February conveyed her regret that they could not come and her fond memories of the original production in 1939.

4. On 7 April 1976 the North Carolina School of the Arts in Winston-Salem held a convocation in Green's honor, and Governor James Holshouser declared 7 April Paul Green Day in North Carolina.

5. As the old man says in Chaucer's "The Pardoner's Tale," speaking to the earth (lines 727–31).

---

1. Maxim Tabory, who fled Hungary after the Soviet Union imposed a Communist government in 1956, was medical librarian at Cherry Hospital in Goldsboro, North

an answer to the dilemma. Two thoughts—actuality of historical fact and the nature of the ideals to be defended. As per Hegel's theory of tragedy when two rights—and that's the only kind I am interested in as to forces in opposition—face each other in unyielding contrariety, then the human *all* must, if the drama is to be complete, fight it out to victory or defeat. And the *all* is the all—the living breathing organism, man. And yet, as I say this, I feel that something *main* has been left out. In *Wilderness Road*—if you wish I'll send you a copy and ask for your comment[2]—my man of peace "picks up a gun" (metaphorically) at the last and dies carrying the U.S. flag he believes in as a symbol for human equality up a hill. In *Trumpet in the Land* my Moravian hero refuses the gun, but many of his innocent followers die because he does.

Dr. Kirkconnell is wrong about Johnny J's saying "Sir" to a non-commissioned officer.[3] That's exactly what he would do. Charlie Chaplin when bumping into a table is likely to say as he tips his hat, "Excuse me, sir." Johnny had a double significance in his words when he said "sir" to a corporal. He snickered inside himself too. No doubt Johnny owes a lot to Chaplin.[4]

Good greetings, Paul G—

---

Carolina, and a poet and translator (*Frost and Fire: Collected Poems and Translations* [1986]). After seeing a recent performance of *The Highland Call* in Fayetteville, he wrote to Green that "the battle scene appeared frighteningly real. The public applauded the victory of the Whigs, *one* of whose achievements was that they killed *more* Loyalist[s] than their own losses. . . . It depressed me. I sometimes wonder if it is the irony of fate that *you* write these Dramas, or the hand of Providence, which lets a man of Peace write about some major bloody conflicts in American History" (9 April 1976, PG-SHC).

2. Tabory was eager for a copy (Maxim Tabory to Paul Green, 23 April 1976, PG-SHC).

3. Tabory had given a copy of *Johnny Johnson* to Watson Kirkconnell, staff physician at Cherry Hospital. Kirkconnell liked the play but still "would protest (after three years in the armed forces in World War I) that a private would never address a Corporal or a Sergeant as 'Sir' " (Maxim Tabory to Paul Green, 9 April 1976, PG-SHC).

4. Johnny frequently says "sir" to his corporal, as in, "All right, sir, you're the boss, as the ox said to the yoke" (1971, p. 52).

## 319. To William W. Finlator[1]

[Windy Oaks, Old Lystra Road, Chapel Hill, N.C.]
5 December 1976

Dear Bill—

Elizabeth and I were sorry we missed your "party," but there was no help for it. Now I have your good sermon, and it *is* good. I note your fondness for St. Paul, that fervid and eloquent neo-platonist—your quotations show it.[2] My mother adored the "postle" and named me for him. What a contradiction! He, the author, I suppose, of Romans 7, 8 and 9 would be amused, and patiently so.[3]

In reading your pro-life and forward-shoveling eloquent words,[4] I kept thinking of Reinhold Niebuhr and his doctrine of man the ambivalent one, man the eternal ironist so far as his situation in time and space went. I worked with him a bit in UNESCO, both being delegates to an international conference in Paris several years ago.[5] He had had a heart attack and yet continued

1. William W. Finlator (b. 1913) was pastor of Pullen Memorial Baptist Church in Raleigh and became acquainted with Green through their joint efforts to abolish capital punishment. On 14 November 1976, Finlator's twentieth anniversary at Pullen Memorial, the church held an afternoon reception in his honor and invited the Greens.

2. Finlator had sent Green a copy of his three-page anniversary sermon, in which he quoted St. Paul three times.

3. In those chapters St. Paul depicts human beings as ambivalent creatures, their physical nature inclined to evil, their spiritual nature inclined to good (the dualism that links him with Neoplatonism). And in St. Paul's pessimistic view, which Green "can't buy" (see n. 6 below), unless a person is made new by Christ, he or she is doomed to pursue the physical: "I don't do the good I want to do; instead, I do the evil that I do not want to do" (Romans 7:19).

4. The sermon rehearsed Finlator's activities during the previous twenty years in support of school desegregation, migrant farm workers, civil rights for blacks, and the American Civil Liberties Union and in opposition to capital punishment and the Vietnam War. Such social activism led his "not too respectful son-in-law" to suggest a tombstone epitaph:

> In this grave lies W. W.
> He is no longer here to trouble you, trouble you.
> (Copy of sermon, 14 November 1976, PG-SHC)

5. In 1951, when Niebuhr was about to publish *The Irony of American History* (1952) and *Christian Realism and Political Problems* (1953).

to be a heavy cigarette smoker. We talked some about "purpose" and about the U.S. and its future. "The country is in an ironical situation," he said. "Please tell me Dr. Niebuhr just what you mean by that word—you use it a great deal?" "I mean," he answered, "that whatever the U.S. tries to do to solve its dilemma will only make it worse." And so on. "There is no solution to man's tragic position on earth. So let him make music, attend conferences, etc. if he is happy doing it," etc. Old Schopenhauer back again.

The people love you! Paul

I hold that if man can get himself in a bind, he can get out of it. I know you agree. Selah.

I attended Dr. Niebuhr's funeral in NYC and the oration stressed his philosophy.[6]

## 320. To Raymond Lowery[1]

[Windy Oaks, Old Lystra Road, Chapel Hill, N.C.]
6 September 1977

Dear Raymond Lowery—

I had a good time at our meeting the other day, and I am glad to have another note from you. I haven't seen many movies recently that I liked. *The*

6. Niebuhr died on 1 June 1971 in Stockbridge, Massachusetts, where his funeral was held. But on 10 December 1971 the American Academy of Arts and Letters held a memorial service in New York City for members who had died during the year (Igor Stravinsky, Allan Nevins, and Niebuhr), and Green attended. "George Kennan spoke well of Niebuhr's tragic irony," he noted in his diary. "I remembered N's talk when he and I were working in UNESCO somewhat together. He had had one heart attack but continued his cigarette chain smoking. Maybe this to him was an illustration of 'man's ambivalence.' Old fanatical St. Paul in his lyric diatribes spoke the same sort of stuff—'When I would do good evil is present with me.' St. Paul had a way out, Niebuhr none. St. Paul's I can't buy, and I would respond to Niebuhr again as I did one day at a meeting back in 1951 that the very dilemma he sees man caught in is the source, can be, of his valiant accomplishment" (Green diary, 10 December 1971, PG-SHC).

1. Raymond Lowery, reporter for the *News and Observer* in Raleigh, was writing an article for *Pembroke Magazine* on Green's work as a screenwriter. On 3 September 1977 he interviewed Green, then wrote asking if Green liked any recent movies, particularly *One Flew Over the Cuckoo's Nest* (1975), based on Ken Kesey's novel. Lowery liked the

*Cuckoo's Nest* was worth while, and I still remember *A Man for All Seasons* with pleasure[2]—though I have always found selfish, ego-mad Henry the Eighth offensive to my better nature, whatever that is. True, he wrote good music and loved the arts, but his murderous career is abhorrent or ought to be. And yet he continues to pop up ever and anon as subject matter for a movie, play or biography. I guess dynamic action in a human being—lurid, evil, benign or what not, accompanied by enough fanfare, commands man's attention, even enjoyment, as witness the to-do about Elvis Presley,[3] the front page spread on Berkowitz,[4] etc., etc. Isn't this to say that we human beings maybe first of all have in us a deep (and dangerous) yearning, maybe a psychic inheritance, that is apart from our ethical and humanely developed imperative? We must be eternally vigilant, mustn't we?, as to cruelty, darkness, barbarism.

I knew Louise Fletcher slightly when she was a student here. Good voyage for her!

And good luck on your stories.[5]

Best greetings, Paul G.

---

movie and wondered if Green knew its star, Louise Fletcher, when she was a student at UNC and involved with Carolina Playmakers productions (1955–57) (6 September 1977, PG-SHC).

2. Motion picture (1966) based on Robert Bolt's play about the last years of Thomas More, when he refused to sanction Henry VIII's divorce and was executed.

3. The singer and teen idol died 16 August 1977. The night before his funeral on 18 August, several thousand people gathered outside Graceland, his home in Memphis, Tennessee, and lined the five-mile route from the mansion to Forest Hill Cemetery, while vendors sold Elvis Presley T-shirts and postcards. Until early September the *New York Times* and other papers regularly printed letters from people attempting to explain what Presley meant to them, and sales of his records skyrocketed.

4. On 11 August 1977 serial killer David Berkowitz was arrested in New York City. For five months, during which time he shot the last three of his six victims and was stalked by New York City police, the case of the "Son of Sam" killer received extensive coverage in New York City papers ("Notes and Comments," *New Yorker*, 15 August 1977, pp. 21–22). And following his arrest papers ran articles almost daily into September about Berkowitz's background, his sanity, and pretrial legal maneuvers. On some days papers that presented sensational coverage doubled their circulation (" 'Son of Sam' Case Poses Thorny Issues for Press," *New York Times*, 22 August 1977, sec. A, p. 1, cols. 1–3; p. 38, cols. 3–6).

5. Lowery's "Paul Green as Screenwriter" appeared in *Pembroke Magazine* 10 (1978): 50–53, an issue devoted to Green.

## 321. To Robert Aldridge[1]

[Windy Oaks, Old Lystra Road, Chapel Hill, N.C.]
18 April 1978

Dear Bob—

I've just got back from a play rehearsal and opening in Galveston, Texas, of *The Lone Star*—a revived symphonic drama I wrote last year. Very successful so far. We hope for a long 6-months run.[2]

Your chapter on my view of violence shows a lot of hard work, but, Bob, some of your conclusions don't seem entirely to jibe with mine. Maybe in my interviews I didn't express my ideas clearly.[3] The fact is I have been opposed to violence in any form all my life, except when as in the case of, say, the spanking of a spoiled brat or the picking up of a gun to oppose a risen Hitler, being sure to make it clear as to the whys and wherefores that accounted for the actualizing of both examples. Of course it is a deep and complicated matter, and each such happening has its history. But I still say that when the entire history of each and all is known there must, often must, be stern (violent, if you will) action—and this is where the mystery of law comes in. Right action (violence) must be lawful. Then who makes the law? The body or bodies of lawful, knowledgeable men. Essential violence is, I guess, irrational—unrestrained cruelty, such as is widely loose in the world at this time. Take war. Is it ever justified? Only when an evil victory threatens and threatens horribly. Thus we come to the subject of evil. Evil is what wastes man's virtues, isn't it? Then who decides what is wasteful? Again knowledgeable, judicious men. To repeat, it is a vastly complicated matter, but I am sure it is not entirely eel-slippery as to our handling it. Why am I sure? Because men by nature (I'm speaking of normal men, and these are the vast majority and have the sanity of the world in their keeping mainly) prefer the better to the worse. Of course, again, sick souls often yearn for their own perdition and

1. Robert Aldridge (b. 1940), a doctoral student in the theater department at the University of Wisconsin, was writing his dissertation on Green and had sent him a chapter for review.

2. Green was in Galveston 9–15 April readying the play for its second season (Green diary, PG-SHC).

3. Aldridge had interviewed Green several times since 1973, and his chapter on violence ("War and Peace," chapter 4 in "Heraclitean Idealism in the Plays of Paul Green," Ph.D. dissertation, University of Wisconsin, 1979) stressed the inevitability of strife, force, and violence in Green's view of life.

get it. Too bad for the whole but only fatal to a part, and therefore we work and sing on our way. And how do we know we prefer the better to the worse? From innate knowing and certainty and from history itself.

Then when is violence excusable? To repeat with a difference—only when the cause defended (including the innocent ones) requires it. And then there is always the terrible danger that the manner of defense can become so powerfully impressive that the sensibilities of man are corrupted, infected if you will, and the "cause" is lost sight of in the drama of carnage. Take the pictured "Holocaust" on the TV screen now.[4] We've had so much mad violence in the world of late years—Hitler, Stalin, the U.S. in Vietnam, etc.—that humanity is developing a taste, an appetite for it. Woe! Woe![5]

Mrs. Wynn always helps me in criticizing my plays, and I have asked her to read your chapter and comment if she will. I hope she will drop you a note.[6]

We all send love, Paul

## 322. To Ellen Wright[1]

[Windy Oaks, Old Lystra Road, Chapel Hill, N.C.]
5 October 1978

Dear Ellen—

Your visit to Chapel Hill was a joy to all of us, and I send you a heartful of thanks for the help you gave all of us on the *Native Son* production. I am busy

4. Gerald Green's play based on Hitler's attempt to exterminate the Jews (broadcast as a nine-and-a-half-hour special on 16–19 April 1978 on NBC).

5. "Holocaust" starred Green's friend Rosemary Harris (wife of John Ehle), and on the day of the present letter the *News and Observer* ran three stories about the program, one a front-page interview with a Raleigh woman who survived the holocaust (" 'Holocaust' Reawakens Memories of Horror," p. 1, cols. 6–7), another a review (" 'Holocaust': Epic Warning of Man's Capacity for Evil," p. 16, cols. 1–4). The next night Green noted in his diary: "More and more violence on T. V. Now 'Holocaust'—all misguided stuff. Why do certain suffering ones continue to relish horror? Strange, but it is so, even if apparently rational reasons are given for naming it 'warning' " (19 April 1978, PG-SHC).

6. Aldridge quotes much of the present letter at the beginning of chapter 4 of his dissertation ("Heraclitean Idealism in the Plays of Paul Green," pp. 172–73).

---

1. In the fall of 1978 UNC inaugurated the Paul Green Theatre with a production of *Native Son*, and Green invited Ellen Wright, Richard Wright's widow, who flew from

getting the script in shape for publication and will send you a copy, as we agreed, for your good comments in a few weeks.[2] The play is a sell-out. No more tickets available. Maybe Housman[3] will hold it over for a bit—I can't say.[4] Rhoda will send you clippings, etc. right away. I guess you are now back in Paris and all snugly and safe at home. The production here has created a lot of interest among the blacks,[5] and to say nothing of the whites. (Why do we have to have adjectival nomenclatures like these? But being creatures of five senses only, we do.)

The bookstores here report increased interest in Richard's work, and I'm sure when we get the script published and widely available, some good theatre productions ought to result.[6]

We all send much love to you and your daughters. And please visit us again!

Ever, Paul

---

Paris on 24 September (Paul Green to Ellen Wright, 6 July 1978, and Wright to Green, 4 September 1978, PG-SHC). The play opened 29 September, and at a ceremony that afternoon Green, speaking from a text entitled "Proff Koch—A Word in Memory at the Dedication of the New Theatre," prayed that the theater would be home to "the creative spirit of man" exemplified by Koch (PG-SHC). Ellen Wright remained through the opening, then returned to Paris by way of New York City (Ellen Wright to Paul Green, 19 October 1978).

2. In 1970 Green upset Ellen Wright by publishing a revised version of *Native Son* without her consent (in William Brasmer and Dominick Consolo, eds., *Black Drama: An Anthology*). This time, therefore, he sent her a script shortly after inviting her to Chapel Hill (Paul Green to Ellen Wright, 27 July 1978, PG-SHC), then talked with her by phone about her suggestions for the last scene—she wanted Green to bring out "Bigger's groping awareness of himself within a social context, that is, the dawning of his concern for himself as inextricably linked up with the fate of others, who, victims of the same inequalities, might wind up like him" (Ellen Wright to Paul Green, 4 September 1978). She also participated in rehearsals during the four days before the opening.

3. Arthur Housman, chairman of the UNC drama department.

4. The production closed as scheduled on 7 October 1978.

5. "I know you rejoice that so large a number of black people came," Green wrote to Housman. On closing night "maybe as much as 25% or 30% of the audience was black. Maybe now that the ice is broken we will have an improvement in this sort of attendance at our plays. The lack of black attendance in the past has been discouraging. I know you want to reach out to people" (8 October 1978, PG-SHC).

6. Samuel French published the 1978 version in 1980.

## 323. To Clara Byrd[1]

[Windy Oaks, Old Lystra Road, Chapel Hill, N.C.]
15 April 1979

Dearest Clara—

Thanks for your beautiful letter and as always in your equally beautiful handwriting.

Golly, to think that all these years you have kept that little book of my boyish verses, *Trifles of Thought*!

I remember I got a local Greenville, S.C., printer to bring it out just before I sailed for France[2] as a volunteer to help make the world safe for democracy—a help it needs now more than ever. (Right here I am reminded of the wasted dead.) I had in mind the suggestion that in case I was killed in the war these few verses would show I wanted to be a writer—a want that after all these sixty-plus years has only partially been fulfilled. I was under the spell of the local Carolina poet, John Charles McNeill, at the time.[3] And oh how keenly I felt the beauty, the joy, the tragedy of the world! My feelings were richly poetic enough, but I didn't have the ability to bring them into fitting words.

Time does wondrous things, doesn't it? (And by time I mean to include men's actions and strivings.) It often turns once-evil into present good, and unimportant items into some importance.

1. Clara Byrd, Green's cousin, spent her career at the University of North Carolina at Greensboro, where she was secretary of the Alumnae Association and much involved in fund-raising and library development. Recently she had retired and moved to a Society of Friends retirement home. She wrote Green that "yesterday afternoon, I went over to the library at UNC-G and presented to the library a little book, entitled *Trifles of Thought*. By P. E. G. You sent it to me shortly before you left for France in 1917 [actually 1918], and I have treasured it all these years. . . . [The] director of the library was very much pleased to have it. . . . (Especially since this copy is most likely one of the very few in existence.) I am glad that the book is now where it will be kept safe and also greatly appreciated" (Clara Byrd to Paul Green, 12 April 1979, PG-SHC).

2. In May 1918.

3. John Charles McNeill, who died in 1907 at the age of thirty-three, grew up near Green's family home and was perhaps the first North Carolina writer to achieve regional recognition. He published widely in newspapers and magazines (including *Atlantic Monthly*), and in 1905 President Theodore Roosevelt came to Raleigh to present him the state's major literary award. Shortly before his death he published a selection of his poems entitled *Songs, Merry and Sad* (1906).

And so it is that your gift of the above little book to the library there bespeaks some bit of significance—but surely only a bit.

Elizabeth and I wish we could join you on the 18th[4] but we can't. You are ever kind and not only we two, but the State of N.C. owes you much for your creative life.

Ever with admiration and *love*!

## 324. To Jesse Helms[1]

[Windy Oaks, Old Lystra Road, Chapel Hill, N.C.]

3 July 1979

Dear Jesse:

I much appreciate the trouble you took amid your piling-up duties and commitments to answer so fully my letter about support for the SALT II.

I am acquainted with the Russian tyranny, just as you are. So are the Soviet

4. For the meeting of the Friends of the Library at which the director would announce the gift.

---

1. Jesse Helms (b. 1921), formerly political commentator for a Raleigh television station and sometime critic of Green (see letter 295), was elected to the U.S. Senate in 1972, then appointed to the Foreign Relations Committee early in 1979 as President Jimmy Carter began to make known provisions of the agreement under negotiation at the Strategic Arms Limitation Talks between the Soviet Union and United States in Geneva. When Carter met Soviet leader Leonid Brezhnev in Vienna on 15–19 June 1979 to sign the SALT II agreement, Green wrote several senators, among them Helms, saying that "the horror of possible nuclear destruction now hanging over the world demands a vision and action beyond the ordinary processes of politics" and urging support of the agreement when it came up for Senate ratification (Paul Green to Jesse Helms, 18 June 1979, PG-SHC). Helms's two-page reply was cordial but gave his reasons for thinking SALT II "a dangerous treaty." He was surprised by Green's "unqualified endorsement of a lengthy and complicated treaty which you could not possibly have studied, and perhaps have not even read. . . . If the choice were as simple as you implicitly contend that it is—peace versus nuclear destruction—a man would have to be demented if he hesitated in making up his mind. But that is not the choice. In fact, SALT II does not even diminish nuclear proliferation. It increases it substantially, both as to the U.S. and the Soviet Union." He concluded by cautioning Green that the Carter administration was already misrepresenting the agreement to the public (Jesse Helms to Paul Green, 25 June 1979).

people more and more. I am also acquainted with perfervid nationalisms that work to evil likewise. The time calls for statesmanship, not politics. (I hear the gaspings of democracy.) Suppose, instead of opposing SALT II, you as a statesman could speak for it, at least as a beginning toward peace. Your voice would carry great weight and thousands, even millions, would breathe easier and feel a new surge of hope.

You know, Jesse, that if this arms race continues, and ill-feeling with it, *someone is going to "pull the trigger,"* *and the world will be engulfed in* flames. Mankind's survival is at stake. This fact is enough to give you voice, speaking our voice—the people's voice.

We were the first to embark on this race toward total death (called total defense at the beginning). Our dedicated and creative technological genius found the way to produce this ultimate weapon, the atom bomb, the hydrogen bomb. And we were the first to use it—using it in the massacre of thousands of innocent human beings. (Recently in Moscow I read a statement from a Russian journalist that at the moment of the first atomic explosion a sense of world brotherhood, a need for world brotherhood, was born.)[2]

Even as modern technology has produced this means of universal death it has at the same time produced means for the making of a beautiful and happy world for living. The time has come for choosing, and the choice is clear. You can exert great leadership in the making of this choice.

May I go further even and say that you, Senator, at this hour have a challenge, a chance to speak around the world. The following suggested action may have already been weighed in your mind. It is this: that you take the bold step of proposing not only a limit on the arms competition between the United States and the USSR but that the two great powers lead the way in an effort toward total nuclear disarmament. Yes, clean the earth of this accumulating horror.

The future demands bold and just leadership. If we don't get it, there will be no future! The need is desperate, the call is clear.[3]

Best greetings,

2. On a trip from Moscow to Helsinki in 1977 Green reached Leningrad on 25 October and that night noted in his diary: "One Yuri Shkolenko has written in the 'Soviet Life' magazine of October that 'with the advent of the atomic age humankind perhaps for the first time in history felt a global unity' " (PG-SHC).

3. Helms replied: "I don't believe you read my response carefully. *I agree with you!* I favor *a* SALT II treaty. But this one isn't something that you want. . . . It is an arms

## 325. To Robert Aldridge

[Windy Oaks, Old Lystra Road, Chapel Hill, N.C.]
17 July 1979

Dear Bob:[1]

Thanks for your full and good letter of a few days ago reporting your progress on your manuscript. It all sounds good, and I know you are happy to approach the end of your long and fruitful endeavor.

I am sending by separate mail a little volume[2]—not much more than a pamphlet—of Negro radio plays, three one-acters which are dramatizations of short stories. They are not happy reading. You mentioned not having them.

As to my finding that the symphonic dramas spreading across the land and variously named historical dramas, outdoor dramas, festival dramas, etc.—as to my finding that this form has fulfilled my expectation, the answer is yes and no.[3] The form which makes use of all the constituents of theatre art—speech, pantomime, music, lighting, sound effects and so on—is thriving pretty well. What is not thriving, what is not improving, is the quality of the scripts. We have not been able to interest the best playwrights to work in this form of theatre. I do not for one moment say that this type of drama is better than other forms. What I claim for it is that it is a form of people's theatre that has a great future if properly developed. I could say the same thing for the movies, television and the Broadway theatre—"if properly developed." Take TV, for instance. The huge storehouse of historical material which is our heritage—our historical characters, events, hopes, struggles, dreams, etc., etc.—is perfectly fitted for both the movies and TV. The historical outdoor dramas—

---

*escalation* treaty, not an arms *limitation* treaty." At a recent Foreign Relations Committee hearing he had asked Secretary of State Cyrus Vance "why the U.S. did not demand an arms *reduction* treaty. [Vance's] answer was vague—something to the effect that the Soviets didn't want that. Big deal! Why did the U.S. not back off and appeal to world sanity. I am convinced that we could have made monkeys out of the Soviets, and created a worldwide demand for reduction" (12 July 1979, PG-SHC).

---

1. In a recent letter Aldridge said he was revising the last chapter of his dissertation on Green (see letter 321) and had only a brief conclusion left to write. The final hurdle toward his Ph.D., defense of the dissertation, was scheduled in September (4 July 1979, PG-SHC).

2. *Wings for to Fly*, which Aldridge requested.

3. Aldridge's main reason for writing was to solicit Green's evaluation of the symphonic drama movement, which he needed for the conclusion of his dissertation.

symphonic dramas—are one type of this theatre production and up to the present have been the main form through which the American people have had a chance to know their past, to feel its impact, its inspiration, its warnings.

I've done a lot of movie writing, and time after time I have urged the studios to draw on our storehouse, to repeat, of historical dramatic material as at least part of their offering on the screen. But violence, sex, cheapened human behavior continue to be our fare because they are easiest to sell and easiest with which to make money.

I am still hoping![4]

Maybe you've seen the enclosed bit.[5] It sounds awfully propagandic, but story, collision of wills, struggles are the essence of drama, of course, and I'm for them.

Your attaching me to Heraclitean idealism is interesting.[6] As you know, many historians of philosophy have written Heraclitus down as a pessimist. Again yes and no to this. His "everything flows, changes and always will change" sounds pessimistic enough. But his belief in man's reason which is able to so discern and describe and adjust to is not pessimistic. I subscribe to that. Einstein with his doctrine of the continuum follows, I think, Heraclitus' thinking.[7] Do you know that old poem—

4. Aldridge quotes this and much of the two previous paragraphs in his conclusion ("Heraclitean Idealism in the Plays of Paul Green," pp. 252–53).

5. "Of Heroes and the Making of Nations," which Green prepared for the souvenir program of *Drumbeats in Georgia* (revision of "Dramatizing Our Heritage," in Paul Green, *Dramatic Heritage* [New York: Samuel French, 1953], pp. 49–51). It urges American writers to emulate the ancient Greeks by interpreting and reinterpreting important figures from the American past.

6. As a model for explaining Green's thought Aldridge first took Hegel's scheme of thesis-antithesis-synthesis. He found it "a bit 'closed' in tone for a man of your expansive view," however, and switched to the ideas of Heraclitus (Robert Aldridge to Paul Green, 4 July 1979, PG-SHC). Heraclitus, a Greek philosopher who lived from the late sixth into the early fifth century B.C., is associated with the idea of flux, the idea that constant but regulated change is the unifying principle of life. His writings survive only in fragments, so his views are open to widely different interpretations.

7. Einstein thought of physical reality as a four-dimensional space-time continuum in which events have none of the randomness of quantum mechanics but are wholly determined by causal relationships.

They told me, Heraclitus
They told me you were dead.
They brought me bitter news to bear
And bitter tears to shed.

I learned this somewhere as a boy. There's more to it, of course. A man named Corley wrote it, I think.[8]

Best to you,

## 326. To Jesse Helms

[Windy Oaks] Old Lystra Road, Chapel Hill, N.C.
1 August 1980

Dear Jesse:[1]

You are kind and generous in taking time to write me your appreciation of the book of short stories, *Home to My Valley*. As to your inquiry about what

8. Actually, William Johnson Cory, in whose "Heracleitus" the speaker remembers long and happy talks with the philosopher, then concludes:

And now that thou art lying, my dear old Carian guest,
A handful of gray ashes, long, long ago at rest,
Still are thy pleasant voices, thy nightingales, awake;
For Death, he taketh all away, but them he cannot take.
(E. C. Stedman, ed., *A Victorian Anthology, 1837–1895* [Boston: Houghton, 1896], p. 232)

---

1. In November 1979 the Senate Foreign Relations Committee sent the SALT II treaty to the full Senate with a favorable recommendation on a 9 to 6 vote, Helms in the minority (see letter 324). Senate debate continued into the new year, then was suspended by President Carter when the Soviet Union invaded Afghanistan in January 1980. Meanwhile the Greens sent Helms a Christmas card, to which he responded warmly (Jesse Helms to Paul Green, 20 December 1979, PG-SHC), then on 10 May 1980 Helms visited Green at Windy Oaks. For much of the afternoon the two sat beneath the trees in Green's backyard and talked about their upbringing in rural North Carolina, Helms's work in the Senate, Green's writing, relations between the Soviet Union and the United States, and disarmament (Jesse Helms to Paul Green, 13 May 1980, and Green to Helms, 18 May 1980). Later Green sent Helms

happened to the girl in "The Corn Shucking," I have to report that the boy went away to the university at Chapel Hill, and in the separation that followed the budding romance between them faded and finally died. She married a plodding young farmer and bore her share of children, now grown and scattered up and down the Valley. The husband died years ago and she continued to live alone in the little run-down house there by the road that leads toward Dunn. The "boy" went to see her some years ago after a Guggenheim absence in Europe. She was sitting on her porch—a big spraddled-legged woman of some two hundred pounds, dressed in a red-flowered wrapper. She was dipping snuff, and her front teeth were gone. When he spoke to her and gave his name, no light of interest or remembrance showed in her dimmed eyes or flaccid face. And maybe in the healing creativity of time they shouldn't have. Still—alas, alas! She is dead now.

But the sorrow, even grief, I feel over the perished past is small indeed compared to what I feel as to the blighting present. The dark pall hanging over this man-tormented world makes the thought or remembrance of all other weals and woes of less concern indeed. The coming of the apocalypse of horror becomes more probable every day of the earth's turning. The lack of strong and cooperative statesmen leadership is hastening it on. The old dueling, field of honor, psycho-pathos between nations continues its hold over competing men and the rivaling governments. Say that Russia does have enough thermo-nuclear power (fission and fusion) to destroy us a hundred times, and we have only enough to destroy her fifty times, or vice versa. What of it! Why add more when one or two or three or four hydrogen bombs would be enough to destroy most of the human race and leave this once lovely habitat of man a wheeling mockery in an eyeless universe.

Take note that this Edward Teller[2] and all his concurring followers are of Machiavellian mind. They are evil and dangerous fellows, in that they are willing to consider a possible, even probable, use of their bomb for "national

---

inscribed copies of several of his books. Helms especially enjoyed *Home to My Valley* (1970), which he found "among the most poignant yet entertaining volumes I've ever experienced." He asked particularly about "The Corn Shucking," an autobiographical story about the first stirring of love between a boy and a girl on a neighboring farm. "The little girl at the cornshucking—whatever happened to her?," Helms wanted to know (28 July 1980).

2. Physicist who helped develop the hydrogen bomb and a frequent advocate of nuclear buildup as a deterrent to war.

defense." By its very nature it is an internationally offensive weapon and cannot be limited nationally in its use.

But thanks be, a majority of the world scientists feel their responsibility to mankind and stand in strong-voiced opposition to such crass cynicism.

But this is not enough.

As I wrote you once, my friend, the need to stop this mad arms race is direfully urgent. We know that, you know that. If continued, it can have only one result—the ultimate end of the human race, or so nearly the end that those who survive will shriek out their wishes that they were dead.

A strong voice is needed to sound the call back to common sense and reason. You with your persuasive powers and your pretty-much center stage position could make such a call to the world—all the while standing firm in your support of an adherence to our democracy and the principles of, yes, the American dream. 'Way back Jimmy Carter said the world should get rid of this nuclear arms madness.[3] And then his voice faded out. As I know you, yours would not fade. And your call, your summons, would be heard by all the world, and I mean all. You know when and just how to do it—and do it convincingly and dramatically!

It is always good to hear from you. I still remember the frank and pleasant interview we had here some weeks ago under the shade of the maple trees.

Best greetings, and warm regards to Mrs. Helms, Paul

## 327. To Tony Buttitta[1]

[Windy Oaks, Old Lystra Road, Chapel Hill, N.C.]
20 August 1980

Dear Tony—

When I was researching for *The Lost Colony* I happened to read in Shakespeare's *Merry Wives of Windsor* two references to the song "Greensleeves," Act

3. A campaign theme in the 1976 presidential race that led to the SALT II agreement.

---

1. Tony Buttitta (b. 1907) came to Chapel Hill from Texas in 1930 for graduate work in sociology and helped establish the lively magazine *Contempo* (1931–32). Then he operated a bookstore in Asheville, North Carolina, until joining the Federal Theatre Project as editor and press representative in 1936. In 1938 he began a two-season stint as press representative for *The Lost Colony*, which had received Federal Theatre

II, Scene 2,[2] Act V, Scene 5.[3] I looked it up and liked it so much that I used it in the play, hoping it might catch on and someday I'd hear it whistled on the streets of Manteo. I did. The tune was the milkmaids' dance in the drama.[4] It was first noticed in England in 1580[5] (seven years before Roanoke) and became tremendously popular. But then in time it passed from remembrance. I think the use of it in *The L. C.* maybe helped reestablish it in the world. I hope so.[6]

All good greetings, Paul

## 328. To Jesse Helms

[Windy Oaks] Old Lystra Road, Chapel Hill, N.C.
3 September 1980

Dear Jesse:

I have been traveling around the country a lot lately looking after dramas in Florida, Texas, Kentucky, Ohio and North Carolina and am late getting to my mail. Thank you, my friend, for your good letter of August 7.[1] The latter part of it, especially, lifts my spirits.[2]

---

support. At the time of the present letter he was writing a book about his experience with the Federal Theatre and recently asked Green about his use of the folk song "Greensleeves" in *The Lost Colony.* "Mrs. Green said that you researched the songs for the score," Buttitta wrote. "In that event would you know whether or not it came from the Shakespeare period—about its age—also the fact that *Lost Colony* is responsible for re-introducing it to our century and helping to make it the hit that it has become" (Tony Buttitta to Paul Green, 17 August 1980, PG-SHC).

2. Actually scene 1, where Mrs. Ford complains of Falstaff's hypocrisy by saying his words and his true feelings "do no more adhere and keep place together than the Hundredth Psalm to the tune of 'Green Sleeves.'"

3. Where Falstaff, thinking he is about to enjoy Mrs. Ford's favor, exclaims: "Let the sky rain potatoes; let it thunder to the tune of 'Greensleeves.'"

4. Act 1, scene 3, in the first edition (1937), scene 4 in later editions, just before Raleigh's talk with William Shakespeare.

5. In the Register of the Stationers' Company that year, which describes the song as "a newe northern Dittye" (*A Transcript of the Registers of the Company of Stationers of London; 1554–1640 A.D.*, ed. Edward Arber [London: Privately printed, 1875], 2:171b).

6. In *Uncle Sam Presents: A Memoir of the Federal Theatre, 1935–1939* (Philadelphia: University of Pennsylvania Press, 1982) Buttitta uses information from this letter in a discussion of *The Lost Colony* (p. 160).

---

1. Actually 5 August.

2. Helms said that in a Foreign Relations Committee hearing he asked an admin-

I have been twice to Russia, trying to appraise and understand a bit of what is actually going on there. I first went in the 1960's and a second time in 1977. My stays were short but intensely active. As a playwright (and therefore harmless) I was given many courtesies and saw much, especially behind what you might call the cultural scene. Both visits convinced me beyond any doubt that the people—*the people*—instead of getting the good things of life as promised by Marx, Engels and Lenin in the dictatorship of the proletariat—have got belt-tightening and deprivation of goods and freedom from an entrenched *dictatorship of bureaucracy.* Long lines of waiting, waiting in markets, etc., etc. year after year. Mrs. Green, for instance, needed a comb to replace the one she broke.[3] If I told you the difficulty we had in buying a single comb, you'd hardly believe it. Leaving solemn Leningrad, in forty minutes we were in Helsinki where I had a play running.[4] Shops overflowing with goods a-plenty, people moving, chatting, buying and selling—not a single line of long waiting, waiting.

After sixty-three years of promised freedom and plenty, the action-stopped people, the mouth-hushed people of Russia still suffer under this tyranny—power determined to keep power.

But (and there is a "but") I found in that country—in the magazines, in the constitution, in Brezhnev's speeches, etc.—an outspoken cry as to the horror of a possible atomic war. Even a day or so ago this leader was quoted here as calling for such arms reduction. Say it is a blind—which I don't believe to be the case—still he and other Russians are sounding the call. Let us do the same, loudly, loudly, challenging these Russians to mutual cooperative action on this humankind-extermination threat.

---

istration official "if our government had ever considered launching an all-out drive for true arms *reduction* instead of engaging in a veiled agreement which can only *escalate* the arms race." The official replied "that such a suggestion was naive, that the Soviets wouldn't buy it. That begged the question, I thought. Why not at least attempt it, and see where and how the world stands? I do not mean a unilateral disarmament, and I wouldn't have you think that I do. But I feel it would be interesting to attempt a world psychological and political campaign, and thus determine the posture of our adversaries and allies alike. Who knows? It might just work." He concluded: "After the first of the year, I'm going to try to promote the idea" (Jesse Helms to Paul Green, 5 August 1980, PG-SHC). In his diary Green summarized this passage from Helms's letter and added, "Bravo! Will wonders never cease!" (10 August 1980, PG-SHC).

3. During the visit in October 1977.

4. The antiwar musical, *Johnny Johnson.*

Your voice sending forth the challenge would be heard. It could prove a summoning. I believe so.

Best to you and Mrs. Helms,

## 329. To John Ehle

[Windy Oaks] Old Lystra Road, Chapel Hill, N.C.
7 March 1981

Dear John—[1]

*The Winter People* script arrived all okay, and I've just finished reading it. Thanks for sending it and thanks too for the lovely photo of you three.[2] Jennifer is already a beautiful young lady. Think of that! Well, naturally she would be with such parents.

When I think of the amount of work you have put into this novel and others[3]—as well as all the multitude of creative things you bring to pass outside and beyond your writing—I berate myself for my laziness.[4]

1. Ehle, who wrote his first novel (*Move Over, Mountain* [1957]) under Green's close guidance, frequently asked Green to read drafts of his novels and on 2 March called from his home in Winston-Salem to see if Green could make suggestions about his latest, *The Winter People*. Green "had begun to wonder what had happened to John's writing," he recorded in his diary, and thought it "great news" that Ehle was back at the typewriter. "Now if it can only be a good novel! I pray for that" (2 March 1981, PG-SHC).

2. Ehle, his wife (the actress Rosemary Harris), and their daughter, Jennifer, who was twelve. "Elizabeth always asks for evidence of Jennifer's growth and health," Ehle wrote, "so I'm sending [the snapshot] along to her as proof" (John Ehle to Paul Green, 3 March 1981, PG-SHC).

3. *The Winter People* was Ehle's ninth novel and thirteenth book.

4. Ehle came to prominence in state affairs during Terry Sanford's term as governor (1961–65), when he was the driving force behind several educational projects, among them the North Carolina School of the Arts in Winston-Salem, established by the state legislature in 1963 as a residential high school and college concentrating on the arts (the first such public school in the country). More recently he led the way in establishing the North Carolina School of Science and Mathematics, a residential high school in Durham that enrolled its first class in the fall of 1980. When he received the present letter, Ehle was preparing for a conference in Fort Worth, Texas, at the end of the month where he would discuss the founding of these schools and others such as the North Carolina Governor's School, a summer program for gifted students in

You have certainly in this latest work described—brought to life a whole neighborhood of people and kept the sense of winter present all through. The reader "experiences" most of the experiences of the characters, and that's the purpose of a novel, isn't it? A mighty part of its purpose certainly. Then there is—always for me—the matter of the story-line[5] and the creating of expectancy and the fulfilling of the expectancy. There is such an upswelling of rich material here, John, that maybe at your convenience we could get together and talk about it. Do you mind if Rhoda and Earl[6] read your script? They say they would like to.

Congratulations once more on the new school in Durham! What a great thing it is for us all![7]

Love, Paul

---

various areas of the arts or academic subjects (John Ehle to Laurence Avery, 4 July 1989).

5. Which Green thought weak in the present draft of the novel (Green diary, 5–10 March 1981, PG-SHC).

6. Wynn, Rhoda's husband.

7. On 11 March, following a meeting in Durham about the School of Science and Mathematics, Ehle and his wife drove to Windy Oaks, where he and Green "talked for a couple of hours about his novel" and arrived at a "good understanding." Then the Ehles took the Greens out to dinner, where the talk turned to Green's folklore collection, or wordbook, in which Ehle had a long-standing interest (Green diary, 11 March 1981, PG-SHC). On 21 and 23 April, during Green's final illness, Ehle visited him in the hospital and promised to try to find a publisher for the wordbook (John Ehle to Laurence Avery, 4 July 1989). *The Winter People* was published in 1982, *Paul Green's Wordbook: An Alphabet of Reminiscence* (with an introduction by Ehle) in 1990.

# Works by Paul Green

Works are listed chronologically within categories: first productions of plays, produced film scripts for which Green had sole or major responsibility, and book publications.

## FIRST PRODUCTIONS

"Old Wash Lucas" and "The Old Man of Edenton," produced by the Carolina Playmakers, University of North Carolina, Chapel Hill, 11 February 1920.

"The Last of the Lowries," produced by the Carolina Playmakers, University of North Carolina, Chapel Hill, 30 April 1920.

"Wrack P'int," produced by the Carolina Playmakers, University of North Carolina, Chapel Hill, 26 January 1922.

"The Lord's Will" and (in collaboration with Elizabeth Lay) "Blackbeard," produced by the Carolina Playmakers, University of North Carolina, Chapel Hill, 10 March 1922.

"White Dresses," produced by the Studio Theatre, Buffalo, New York, 1923.

"Fixin's" (in collaboration with Erma Green), produced by the Carolina Playmakers, University of North Carolina, Chapel Hill, 8 February 1924.

"The No 'Count Boy," produced by the Little Theatre, Chicago, Illinois, 6 December 1924.

"Quare Medicine," produced by the Carolina Playmakers, University of North Carolina, Chapel Hill, 23 November 1925.

"In Aunt Mahaly's Cabin," produced by the Vagabond Players, Baltimore, Maryland, fall 1925.

"The Man Who Died at Twelve O'Clock," produced by the Western Players, Thermopolis, Wyoming, fall 1925.

*In Abraham's Bosom*, produced by the Provincetown Players at the Provincetown Playhouse in New York City, opened 30 December 1926 for 200 performances.

*The Field God*, produced by the Provincetown Players at the Greenwich Village Theatre in New York City, opened 21 April 1927 for forty-five performances.

*The House of Connelly*, produced by the Group Theatre at the Martin Beck Theatre in New York City, opened 28 September 1931 for seventy-two performances.

*Tread the Green Grass*, produced by the University of Iowa Theater, Iowa City, July 1932. No professional production.

*Potter's Field*, produced by Margaret Hewes at the Plymouth Theatre in Boston, opened 16 April 1934 for eight performances.

*Roll Sweet Chariot* (revision of *Potter's Field*), produced by Margaret Hewes at the Cort Theatre in New York City, opened 2 October 1934 for seven performances.

*Shroud My Body Down*, produced by the Carolina Playmakers, University of North Carolina, Chapel Hill, opened 7 December 1934 for five performances. No professional production.

*The Enchanted Maze*, produced by the Carolina Playmakers, University of North Carolina, Chapel Hill, opened 6 December 1935 for three performances. No professional production.

"Hymn to the Rising Sun" and "Unto Such Glory," produced by the Federal Theatre Project at the Civic Repertory Theatre in New York City, opened 12 January 1936.

*Johnny Johnson* (music by Kurt Weill), produced by the Group Theatre at the Forty-fourth Street Theatre in New York City, opened 19 November 1936 for sixty-eight performances.

*The Lost Colony*, produced by the Roanoke Island Historical Association at the Waterside Amphitheatre in Manteo, North Carolina, opened 4 July 1937 and continues each summer.

*The Highland Call*, produced by the Fayetteville Historical Celebration at the LaFayette Opera House in Fayetteville, North Carolina, opened 20 November 1939 for five performances and repeated the next year.

*Native Son*, from the novel by Richard Wright, produced by Orson Welles and John Houseman as a Mercury Production at the Saint James Theatre in New York City, opened 24 March 1941 for 114 performances.

*The Common Glory*, produced by the Jamestown Corporation at Lake Matoaka Amphitheatre, Williamsburg, Virginia, opened 17 July 1947 and continued summers (with interruptions) through 1974.

*Faith of Our Fathers*, produced by the National Capital Sesquicentennial Commission at Rock Creek Park in Washington, D.C., opened 5 August 1950 and repeated the next summer.

*Peer Gynt*, from the play by Henrik Ibsen, produced by Cheryl Crawford at the American National Theatre and Academy Playhouse in New York City, opened 28 January 1951 for thirty-two performances.

*Carmen*, from the libretto by Henri Meilhac and Ludovic Halévy for Georges Bizet's opera, produced by the Opera Festival in Central City, Colorado, 27 June 1953.

*Serenata* (with Josephina Niggli), produced by Santa Barbara, California, 8 August 1953.

*The Seventeenth Star*, produced by the Ohio Sesquicentennial Committee at the State Fairgrounds in Columbus, Ohio, 27 August 1953.

*Wilderness Road*, produced by Berea College at Indian Fort Amphitheatre in Berea, Kentucky, opened 29 June 1955 and continued summers (with interruptions) through 1974.

*The Founders*, produced by the Jamestown Corporation at the Cove Amphitheatre in Jamestown, Virginia, opened 13 May 1957 and repeated the next summer.

*The Confederacy*, produced by the Tidewater Historic Drama Association at the Robert E. Lee Amphitheatre in Virginia Beach, Virginia, opened 1 July 1958 and repeated the next summer.

*The Stephen Foster Story*, produced by the Stephen Foster Drama Association at the J. Dan Talbott Amphitheatre in Bardstown, Kentucky, opened 26 June 1959 and continues each summer.

*Cross and Sword*, produced by St. Augustine 400th Anniversary, Incorporated, at the Anastasia Island Amphitheatre near St. Augustine, Florida, opened 27 June 1965 and continues each summer.

*Texas*, produced by the Texas Panhandle Heritage Foundation at the Pioneer Amphitheater in Palo Duro Canyon, opened 1 July 1966 and continues each summer.

*Sing All a Green Willow* (revision of *Tread the Green Grass*), produced by the Carolina Playmakers to commemorate their fiftieth anniversary, University of North Carolina, Chapel Hill, 28 March 1969.

*Trumpet in the Land*, produced by the Ohio Outdoor Historical Drama Association at the Tuscarawas Valley Amphitheatre in New Philadelphia, Ohio, opened 3 July 1970 and continues each summer.

*Drumbeats in Georgia*, produced by the Jekyll Island Authority on Jekyll Island, Georgia, opened 30 June 1973 and repeated the next summer.

*Louisiana Cavalier*, produced by the Louisiana Outdoor Drama Association at the Grand Ecore Amphitheatre in Natchitoches, Louisiana, opened 19 June 1976 and continued summers through 1979.

*We the People*, produced by the Maryland Bicentennial Committee at the Merriweather Post Pavilion in Columbia, Maryland, opened 6 August 1976.

*The Lone Star*, produced by the Lone Star Historical Drama Association at the Mary Moody Northen Amphitheatre in Galveston, Texas, opened 29 June 1977 and continued summers through 1989.

## PRODUCED FILM SCRIPTS

*Cabin in the Cotton*, from the novel by H. H. Kroll, starring Richard Barthelmess and Bette Davis, produced by Warner Brothers, released in 1932.

*State Fair*, from the novel by Phil Strong, starring Will Rogers and Janet Gaynor, produced by Fox Film Corporation, released in 1933.

*Voltaire*, starring George Arliss, produced by Warner Brothers, released in 1933.

*Dr. Bull*, from *The Last Adam* by James Gould Cozzens, starring Will Rogers, produced by Fox Film Corporation, released in 1933.

*David Harum*, from the novel by E. N. Westcott, starring Will Rogers, produced by Twentieth Century–Fox, released in 1934.

*Work of Art*, from the novel by Sinclair Lewis, produced by Twentieth Century–Fox, released in 1934.

*Green Light*, from the novel by Lloyd C. Douglas, starring Errol Flynn and Anita Louise, produced by Warner Brothers, released in 1937.

*Captain Eddie*, based on the life of Eddie Rickenbacker, starring Fred MacMurray and Lynn Bari, produced by Twentieth Century–Fox, released in 1945.

*The Green Years*, from the novel by A. J. Cronin, starring Charles Coburn and Dean Stockwell, produced by Metro-Goldwyn-Mayer, released in 1946.

*Time Out of Mind*, from the novel by Rachel Field, starring Phyllis Calvert and Robert Hutton, produced by Universal Pictures, released in 1947.

*Roseanna McCoy*, from the novel by Alberta Hannum, starring Charles Beckford and Raymond Massey, produced by Samuel Goldwyn, released in 1949.

*Black Like Me*, from the autobiography of John Howard Griffin, starring James Whitmore and Clifton James, produced by Julius Tannenbaum, released in 1964.

## BOOK PUBLICATIONS

*Trifles of Thought*, by P. E. G. (poems). Greenville, S.C.: Privately printed, May 1918.

*The Lord's Will and Other Carolina Plays.* New York: Holt, October 1925. Includes: "The Lord's Will," "Blackbeard," "Old Wash Lucas," "The No 'Count Boy," "The Old Man of Edenton," and "The Last of the Lowries."

*Lonesome Road: Six Plays for the Negro Theatre.* New York: McBride, May 1926. Includes: "In Abraham's Bosom," "White Dresses," "The Hot Iron," "The Prayer-Meeting," "The End of the Row," and "Your Fiery Furnace."

*The Field God and In Abraham's Bosom.* New York: McBride, March 1927. Includes: *In Abraham's Bosom: The Biography of a Negro* (original heavy dialect version) and *The Field God* (comic ending).

*In the Valley and Other Carolina Plays.* New York: Samuel French, January 1928. Includes: "In the Valley," "Quare Medicine," "Supper for the Dead," "Saturday Night," "The Man Who Died at Twelve O'Clock," "In Aunt Mahaly's Cabin," "The No 'Count Boy," "The Man on the House," "The Picnic," "Unto Such Glory," and "The Goodbye."

*Wide Fields* (short stories). New York: McBride, April 1928.

*The House of Connelly and Other Plays.* New York: Samuel French, October 1931. Includes: *The House of Connelly* (comic ending), *Potter's Field*, and *Tread the Green Grass.*

*The Laughing Pioneer* (novel). New York: McBride, September 1932.

*Roll Sweet Chariot: A Symphonic Play of the Negro People* (revision of *Potter's Field*). New York: Samuel French, February 1935.

*Shroud My Body Down.* Iowa City: Clio Press, October 1935.

*This Body the Earth* (novel). New York: Harper and Brothers, October 1935.

*Johnny Johnson: The Biography of a Common Man.* New York: Samuel French, April 1937. 2d ed., rev. New York: Samuel French, September 1971.

*The Lost Colony: An Outdoor Play in Two Acts.* Chapel Hill: University of North Carolina Press, August 1937. Revised editions: Memorial Edition, June 1946; Roanoke Island Edition, 1954; Four Hundredth Anniversary Edition, privately printed, December 1980.

*The Lost Colony Song-Book.* New York: Fischer, July 1938.

*Out of the South: The Life of a People in Dramatic Form.* New York: Harper and Brothers, April 1939. Includes: *The House of Connelly* (comic ending), "The No 'Count Boy" (revised), "Saturday Night," *The Field God* (tragic ending), "Quare Medicine," "The Hot Iron," *In Abraham's Bosom* (revised), "Unto Such Glory," "Supper for the Dead," *Potter's Field*, "The Man Who Died at Twelve O'Clock," "White Dresses," *Johnny Johnson*, "Hymn to the Rising Sun," and *The Lost Colony.*

*The Enchanted Maze: The Story of a Modern Student in Dramatic Form.* New York: Samuel French, November 1940.

*Native Son: The Biography of a Young American* (with Richard Wright, from Wright's novel). New York: Harper and Brothers, April 1941. Revised edition. New York: Samuel French, fall 1980.

*The Highland Call.* Chapel Hill: University of North Carolina Press, summer 1941.

*The Highland Call Song-Book.* Chapel Hill: University of North Carolina, summer 1941.

*The Hawthorn Tree: Some Papers and Letters on Life and the Theatre* (essays). Chapel Hill: University of North Carolina Press, December 1943.

*Forever Growing: Some Notes on a Credo for Teachers* (essays). Chapel Hill: University of North Carolina Press, fall 1945.

*Salvation on a String and Other Tales of the South.* New York: Harper and Brothers, September 1946.

*Song in the Wilderness: Cantata for Chorus and Orchestra, with Baritone Solo* (with composer Charles Vardell). Chapel Hill: University of North Carolina Press, summer 1947.

*The Common Glory: A Symphonic Drama of American History.* Chapel Hill: University of North Carolina Press, spring 1948.

*Dog on the Sun* (short stories). Chapel Hill: University of North Carolina Press, November 1949.

*Ibsen's Peer Gynt: American Version.* New York: Samuel French, May 1951.

*The Common Glory Song-Book.* New York: Fischer, 1951.

*Dramatic Heritage* (essays). New York: Samuel French, spring 1953.

*Wilderness Road: A Parable for Modern Times.* New York: Samuel French, June 1956.

*The Founders: A Symphonic Outdoor Drama.* New York: Samuel French, summer 1957.

*Drama and the Weather: Some Notes and Papers on Life and the Theatre* (essays). New York: Samuel French, June 1958.

*The Confederacy: A Symphonic Outdoor Drama Based on the Life of General Robert E. Lee.* New York: Samuel French, summer 1959.

*Wings for to Fly: Three Plays of Negro Life.* New York: Samuel French, summer 1959. Includes: "Fine Wagon," "Lay This Body Down," and "The Thirsting Heart."

*The Stephen Foster Story: A Symphonic Drama Based on the Life and Music of the Composer.* New York: Samuel French, summer 1960.

*Five Plays of the South*, ed. John Gassner. New York: Hill and Wang, March 1963. Includes: *Johnny Johnson, The House of Connelly* (tragic ending), *In*

*Abraham's Bosom* (revised), "Hymn to the Rising Sun" (revised), "White Dresses" (revised).

*Plough and Furrow: Some Essays and Papers on Life and the Theatre.* New York: Samuel French, October 1963.

*Cross and Sword: A Symphonic Drama of the Spanish Settlement of Florida.* New York: Samuel French, summer 1966.

*Texas: A Symphonic Outdoor Drama of American Life.* New York: Samuel French, spring 1967.

*Texas Song-Book.* New York: Samuel French, spring 1967.

*Words and Ways: Stories and Incidents from My Cape Fear Valley Folklore Collection.* Special issue of *North Carolina Folklore* 16 (December 1968).

*Home to My Valley* (short stories). Chapel Hill: University of North Carolina Press, December 1970.

*The Honeycomb* (revision of *Shroud My Body Down*). New York: Samuel French, 1972.

*Trumpet in the Land: A Symphonic Drama of Peace and Brotherhood.* New York: Samuel French, spring 1972.

*The Land of Nod and Other Stories.* Chapel Hill: University of North Carolina Press, fall 1976.

*The Lone Star: A Symphonic Drama of the Texas Struggle for Independence.* New York: Samuel French, spring 1986.

*Paul Green's Wordbook: An Alphabet of Reminiscence* (folklore). Chapel Hill: Paul Green Foundation with Appalachian Consortium Press, December 1990.

# Index

Asterisks mark principle identifications of Green's correspondents.

www.ingramcontent.com/pod-product-compliance
Lightning Source LLC
Chambersburg PA
CBHW050606110726
47899CB00001B/2

*9781469613734*